At Work

BRIAN DOBEN

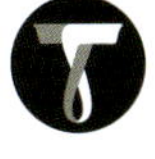

TROPE
PUBLISHING
Co.

LCCN: 2024946698
ISBN: 978-1-951963-30-9

Printed and bound in China
First printing, 2025

Trope Publishing Co.
WWW.TROPE.COM

+ INFORMATION:
For additional information,
visit TROPE.COM

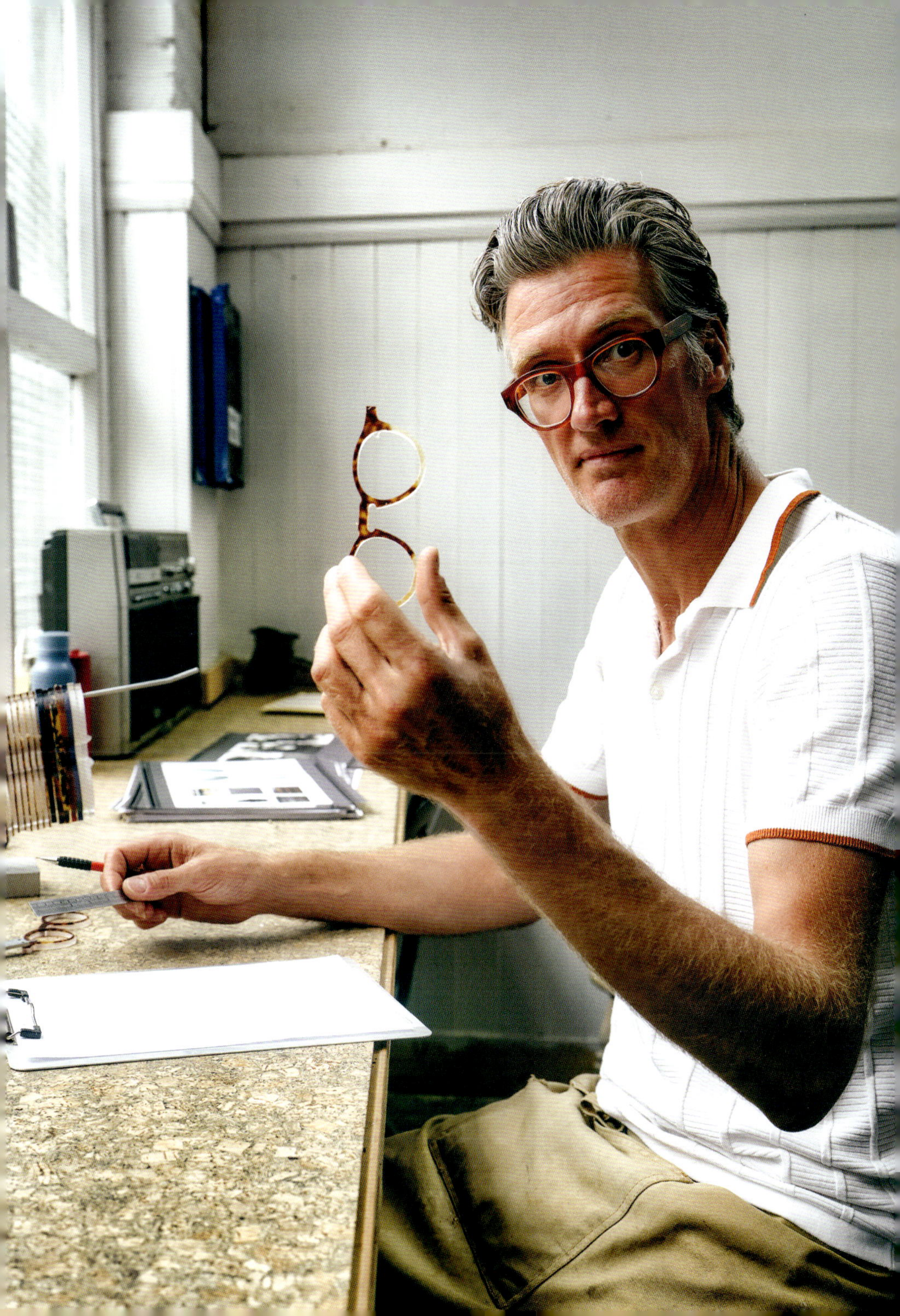

This journey is dedicated to
my daughter Genevieve.

I hope these stories inspire you
to live the life you dream of.
Fly, my love, fly.

At Work is my endeavor to explore photography,
to celebrate the dignity of work. To remember
what it's like to love what we do. To have a conversation,
capture a moment, relay a message, create an image
you won't soon forget.

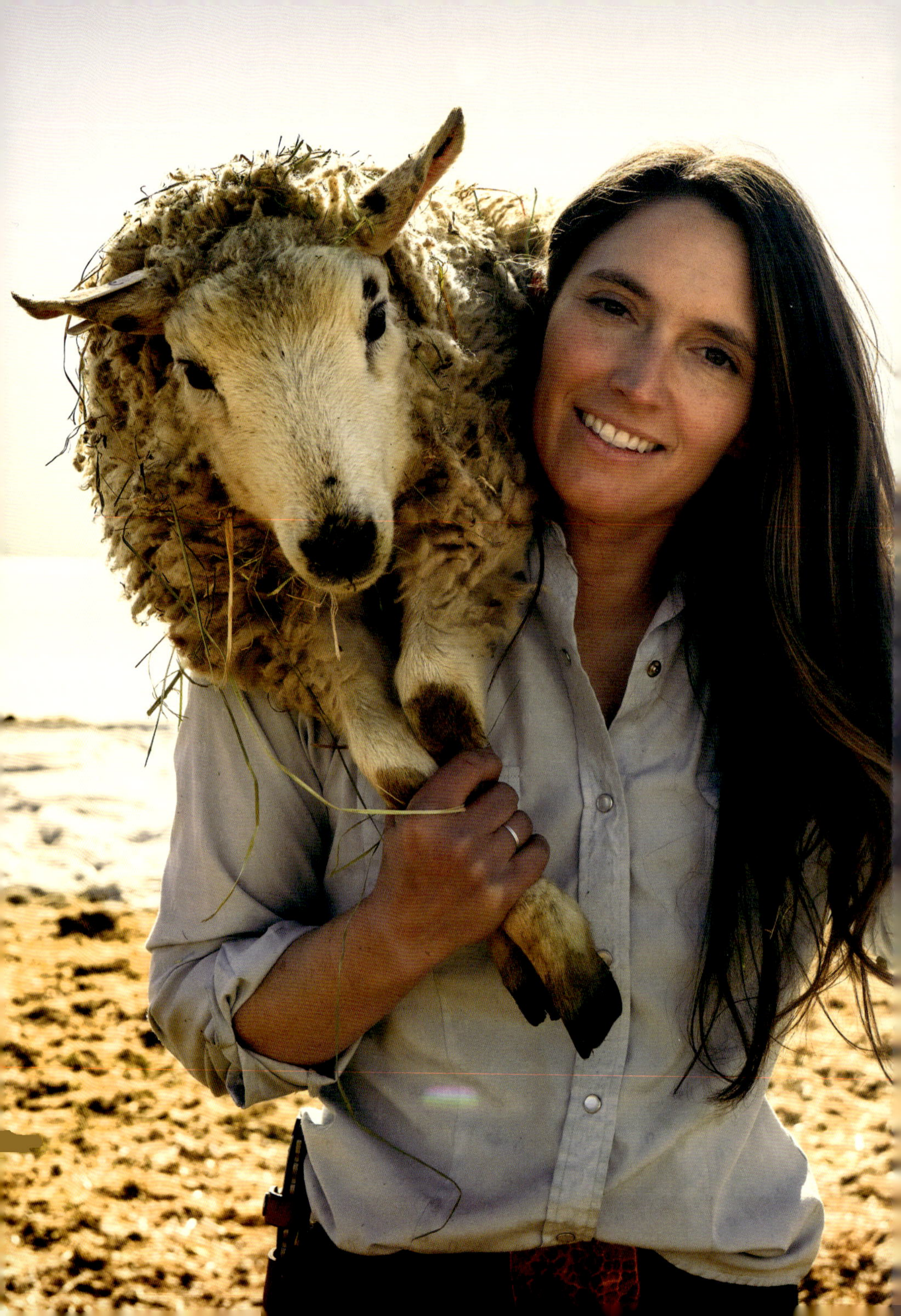

At Work

"If you're not having fun, it's not worth doing."

It was something that my mom always said. I hadn't thought much about it, but it came back to me, years later, in a hotel room in Nashville. I had spent the day photographing a country music artist. The shoot went well, as these things go. But I didn't feel anything.

I called my wife, Nancy. Ever since college, she's been my anchor. She understands me like nobody else. "I'm done," I told her over the phone. "I don't want to do this anymore."

I could hear confusion in her response. And concern. By a lot of measures, I was successful. I had a great career. But I was feeling more and more like a one-hit wonder. As if my voice as a photographer were missing. Maybe I lost it? Or maybe I'd never really found it.

Nancy encouraged me to go right back out there. I went into the streets of Nashville, camera in hand. Not with a goal of taking pictures, but of connecting. I wanted to listen to others just as much as I wanted to speak.

The more strangers I talked to, the clearer it was. Something about being with people who loved what they did for a living was bringing me back — to myself, to what I loved, to feeling truly alive.

I found that when I spoke my truth, the truth was coming back.

Soon after I got home from Tennessee, I survived a horrific, life-threatening bicycle accident. I lost the use of my hands, and many of my teeth. I had countless stitches on my face and neck. Worst of all, I struggled with a brain injury that tested my resilience beyond anything I could have imagined.

I fought hard for my family. And once I got back on my feet, this project was waiting for me.

Now, over a decade later, I am excited to share the journey with you. This is a scrapbook of the experience. Of going around the world, meeting people, sharing stories, and capturing evidence of the time we spent together. It has filled my soul in a way that I didn't think was possible.

Welcome to *At Work.*

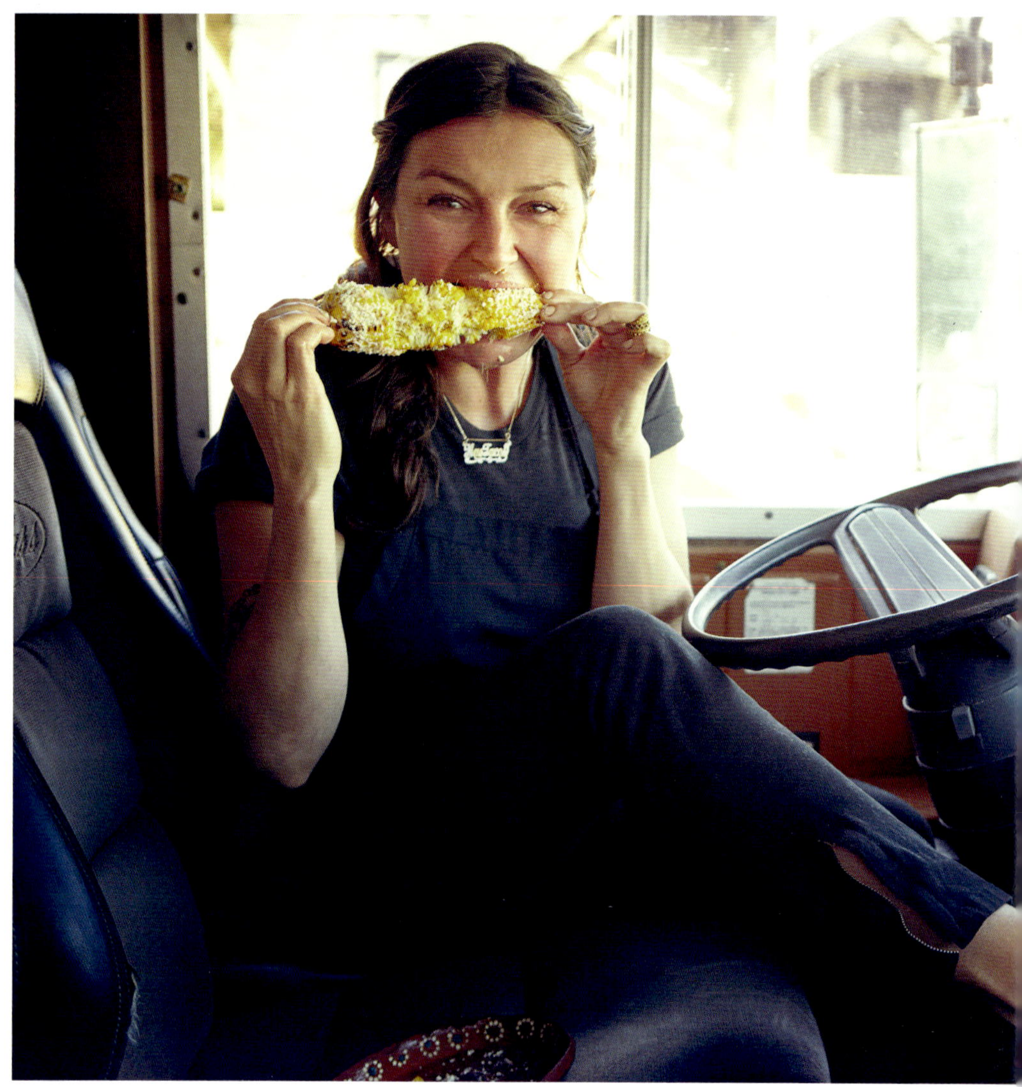

Teresa was the first person I photographed for what became *At Work*. At the time,
I didn't know that it would turn out to be anything, let alone a book. I had simply
shown up, bright-eyed and open-armed, hoping to find my way back to something
I'd lost: a sense of real connection in my work.

Teresa was just getting started with her taco truck. Her warmth was disarming.
Her laugh was infectious. She made me feel as if it was okay to be me. She had a
way of making all of her customers feel that way.

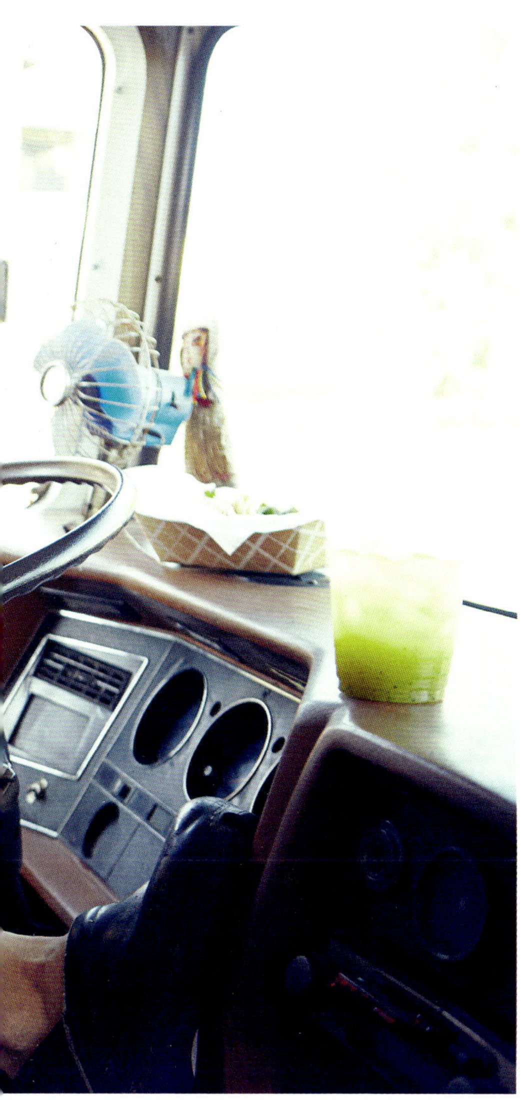

She was focused on making great food. And it was delicious. But it was more than that. Something greater emerges when you put all of yourself—your love—into what you're doing.

I walked away nourished. More alive. And clear on how to go forward. I wanted to find more people with that kind of energy, and to put my own love into capturing images of the connections between us.

Teresa Mason Mas Tacos Food Truck > Nashville, Tennessee

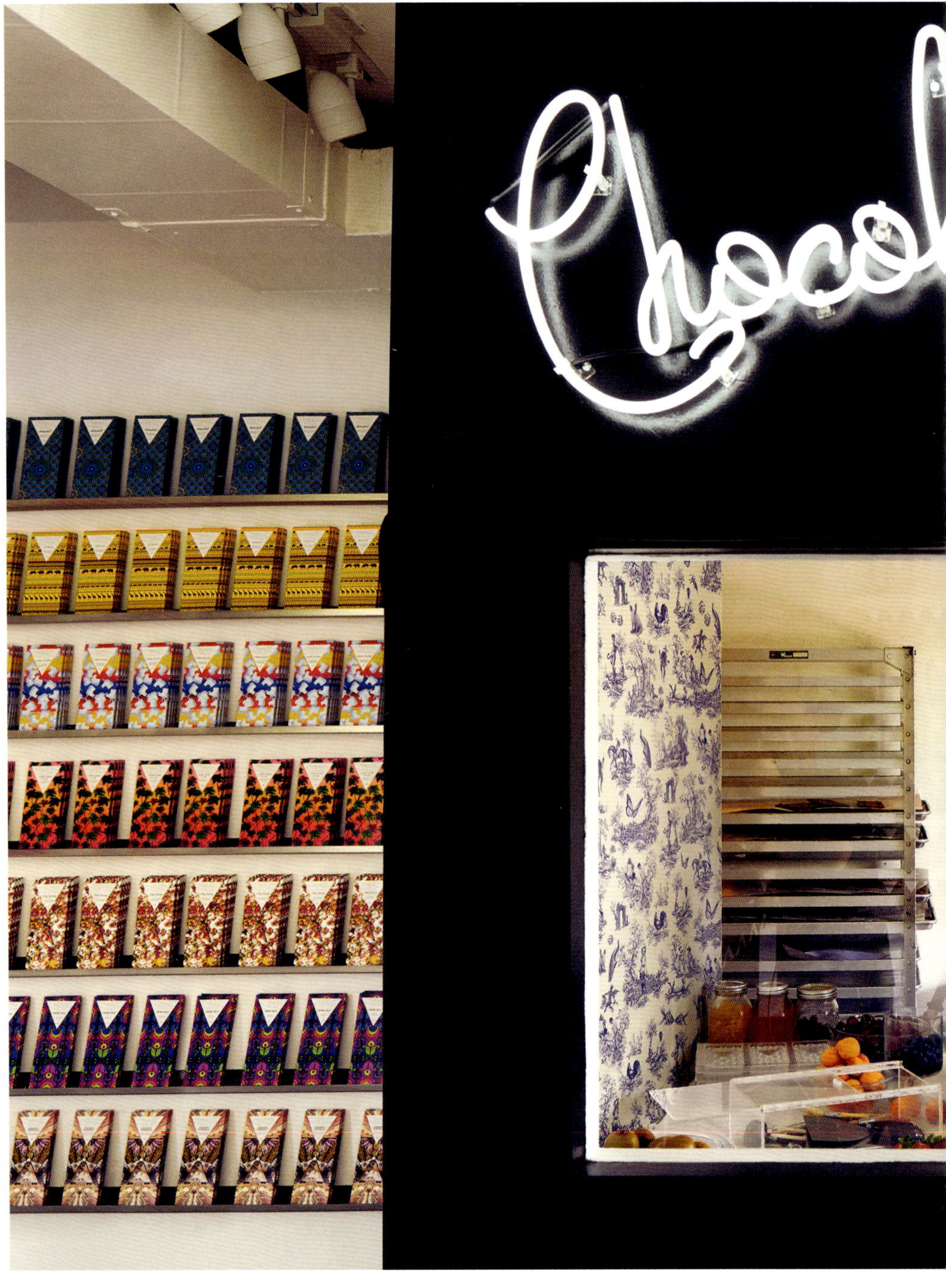

Jonathan Grahm Owner and Chocolatier, Compartés Chocolates > Los Angeles, California

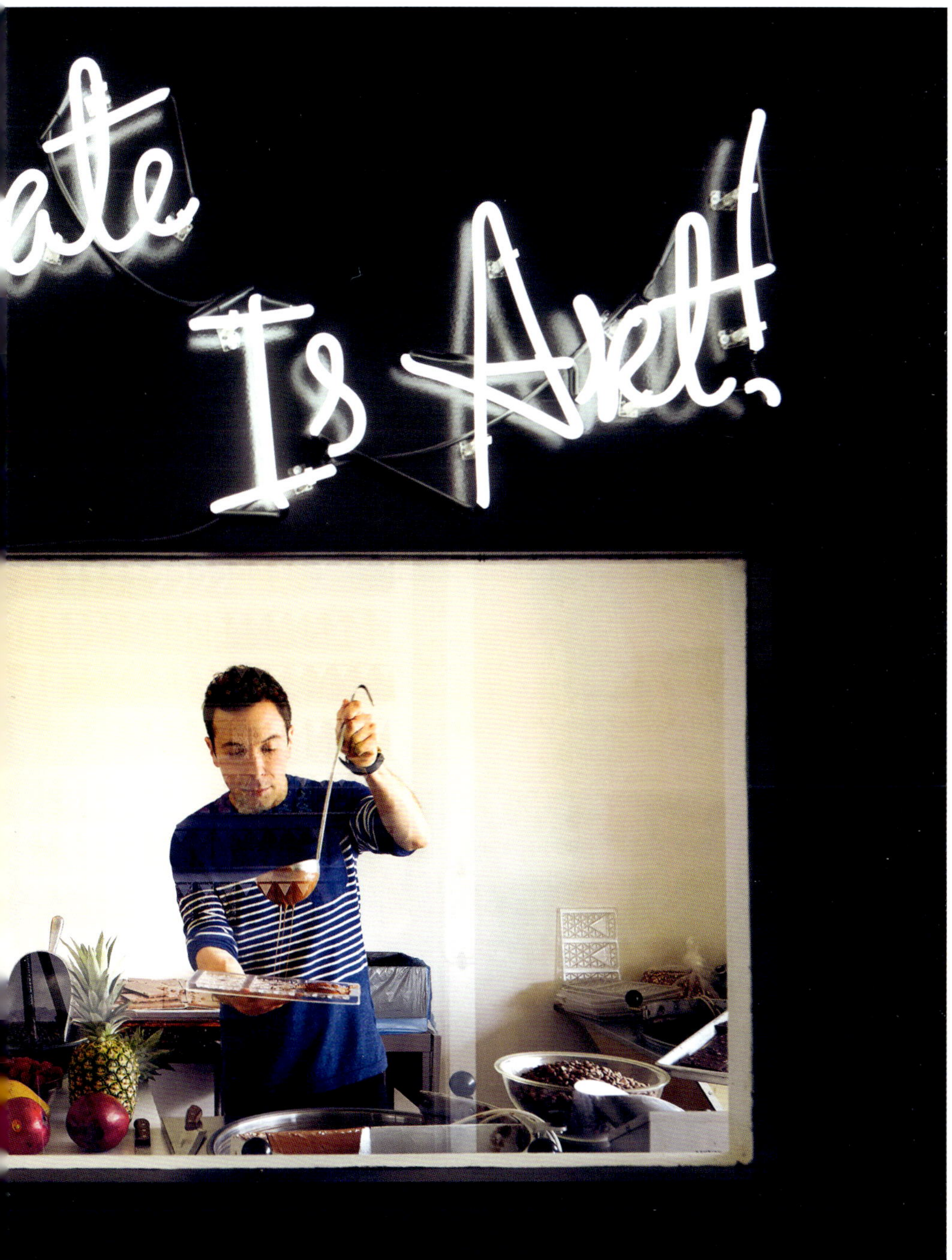
ate Is Art!

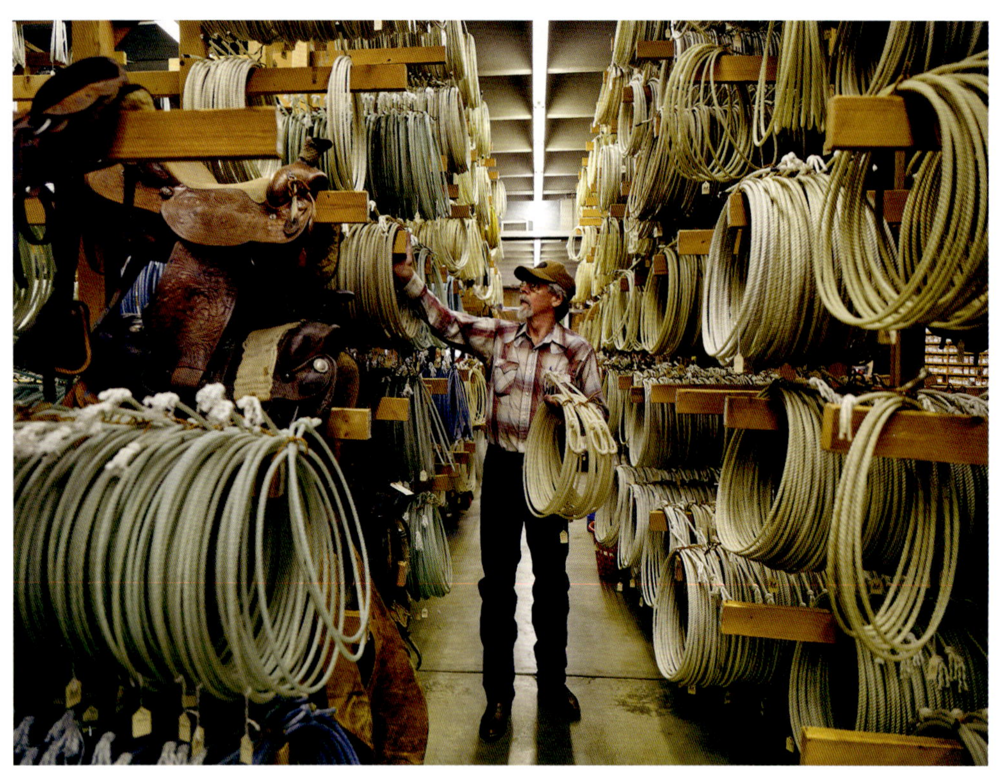

Gary Mefford King Ropes > Sheridan, Wyoming

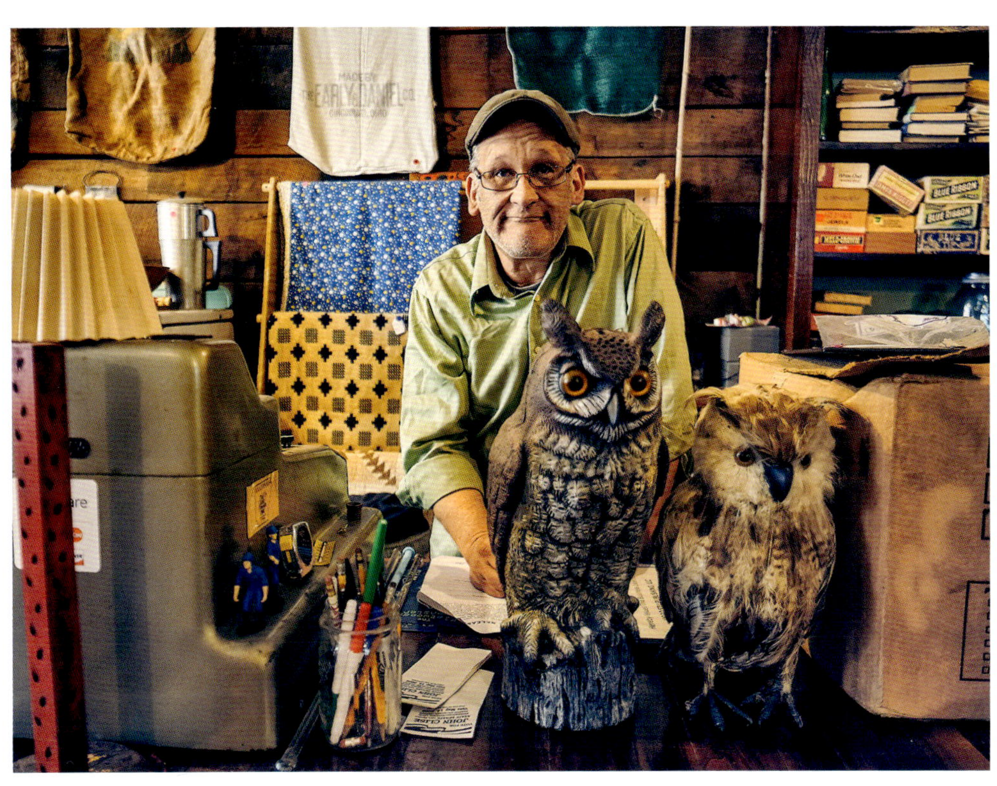

John Clise Grandpa's Antique > Flatwoods, Kentucky

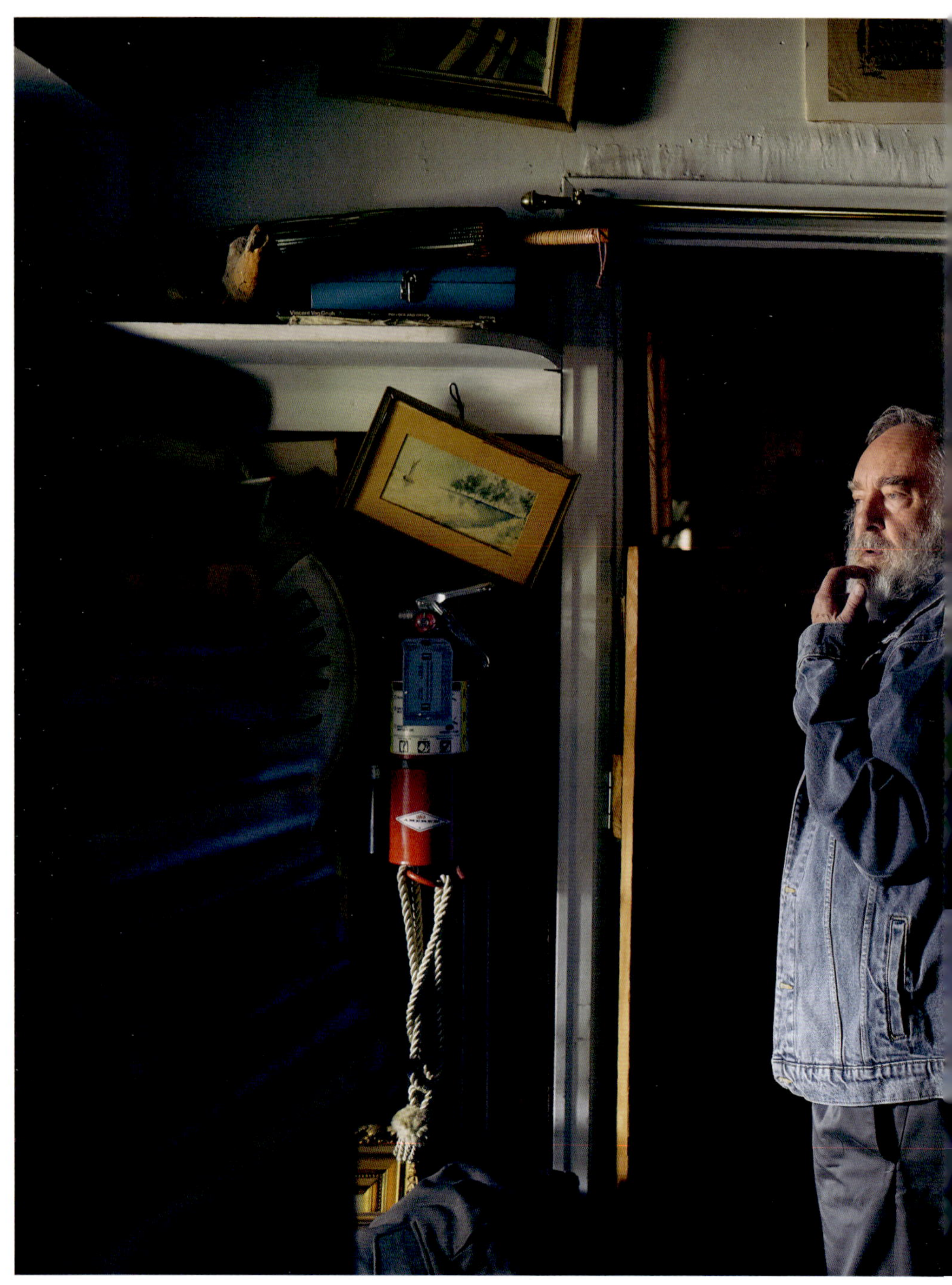

Jon Quarterman Q Man Music & Antiques > Sheridan, Wyoming

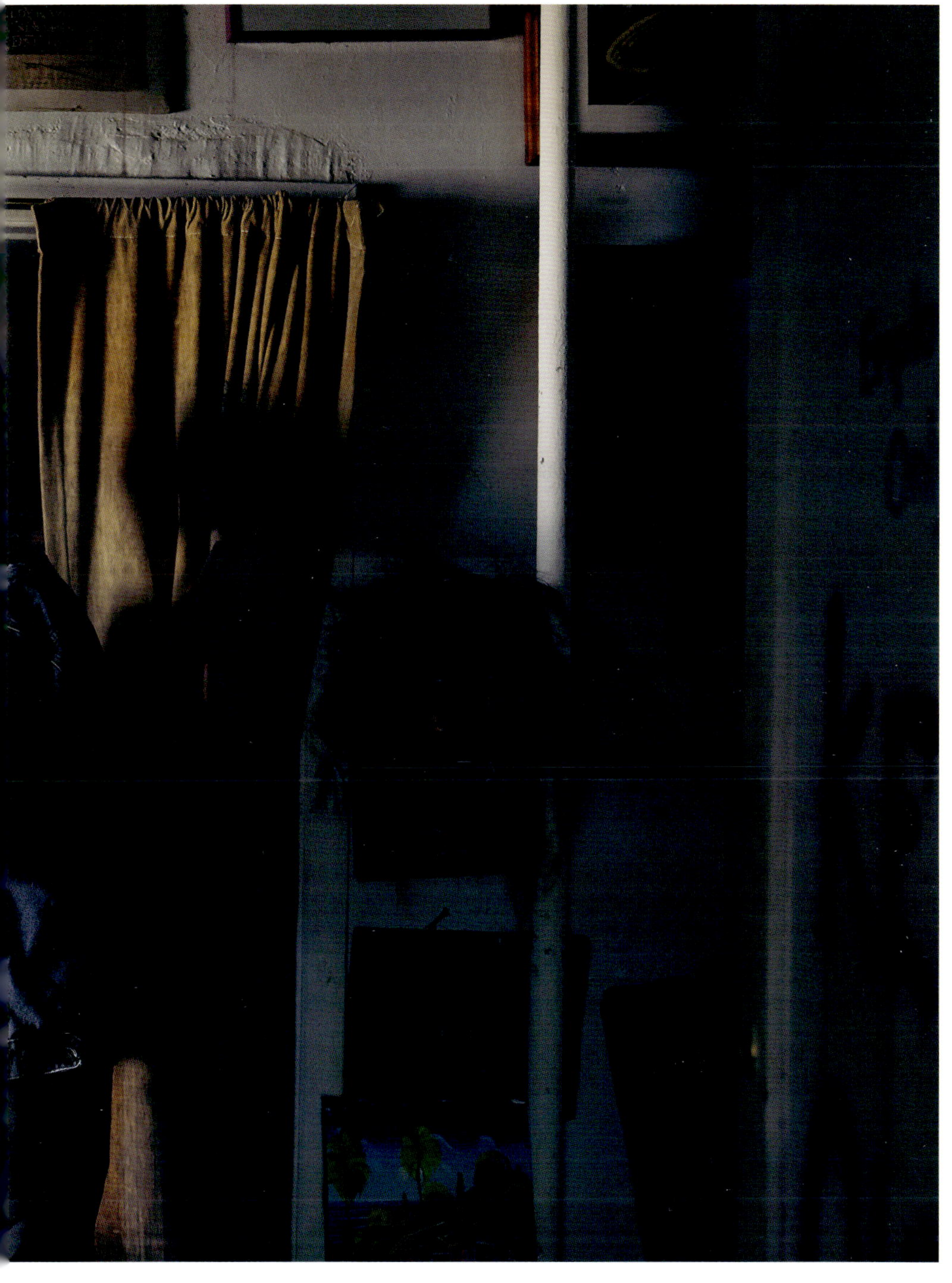

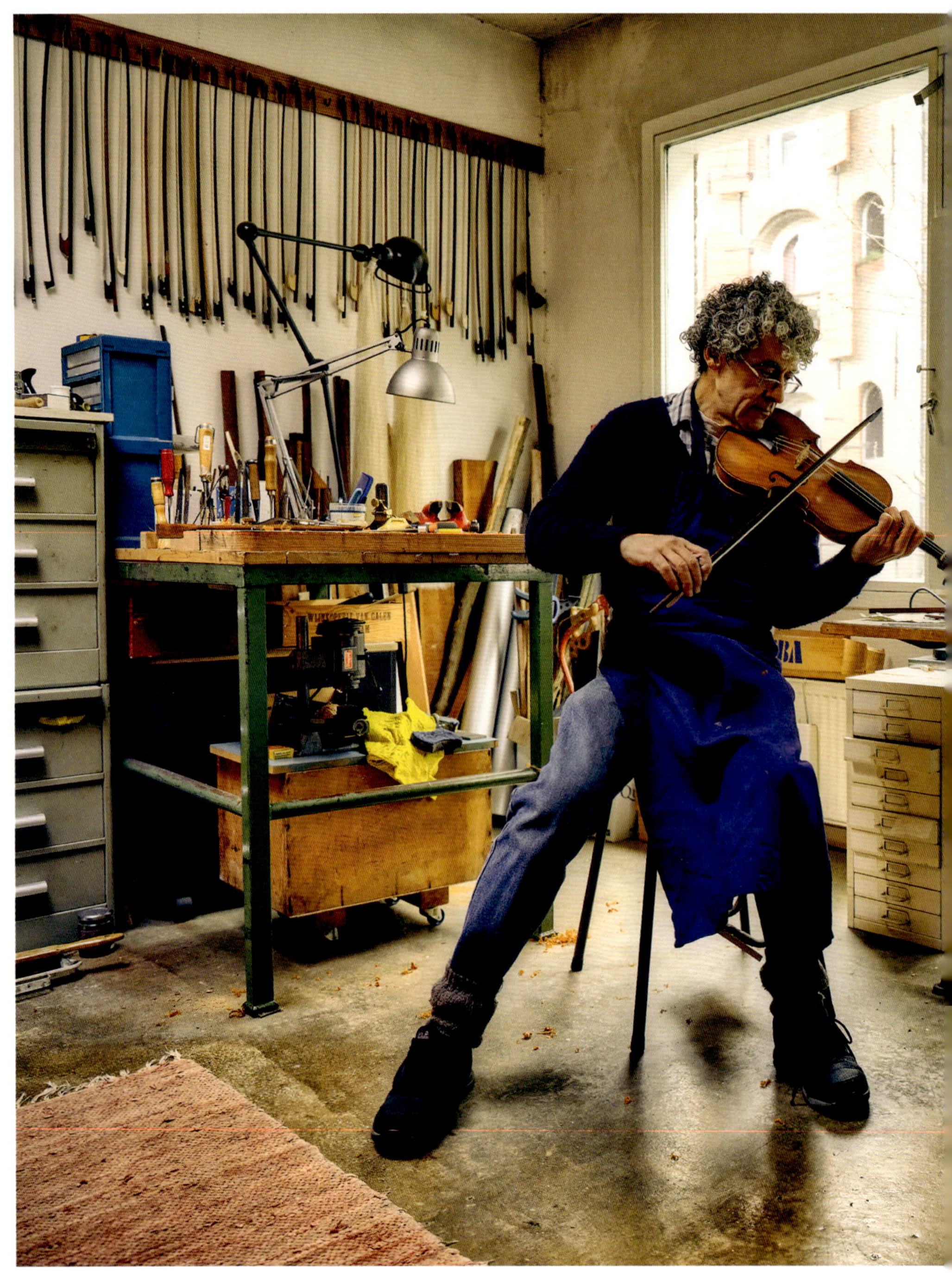

Elio de Miranda Bow Maker > Amsterdam, Netherlands

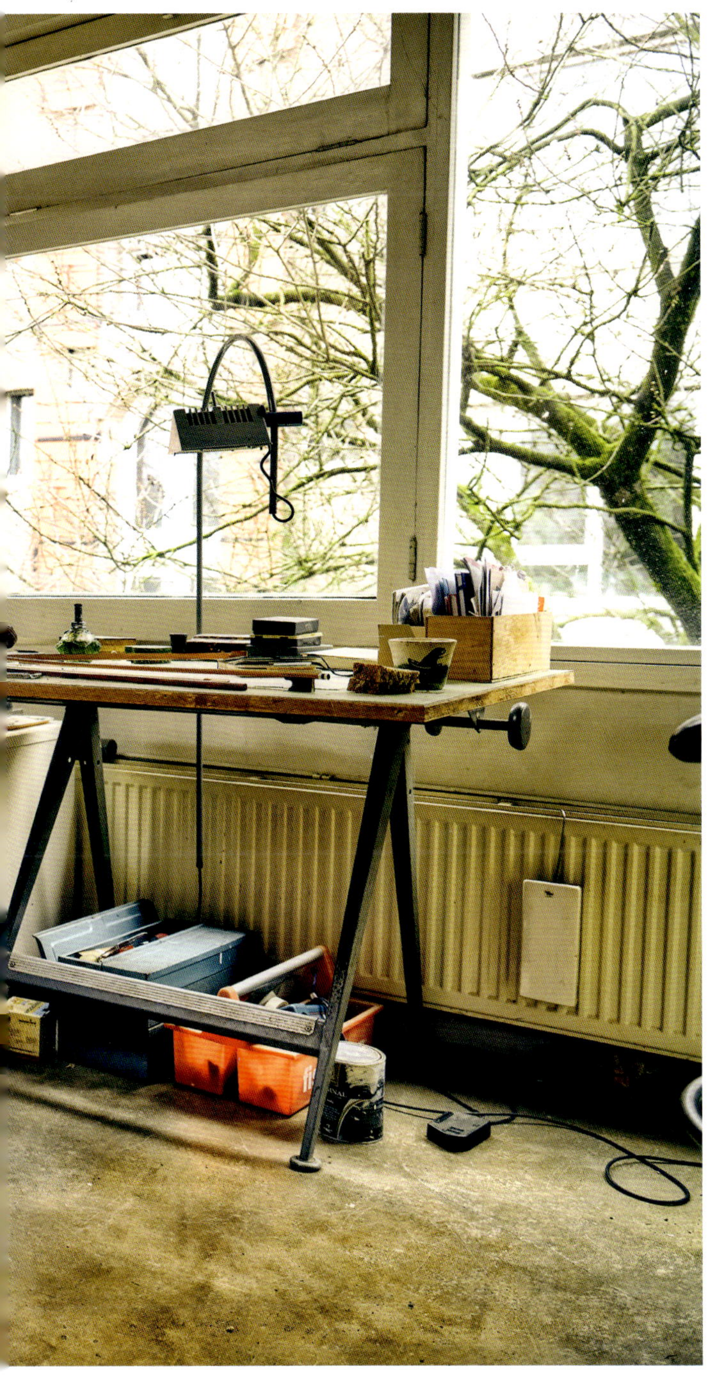

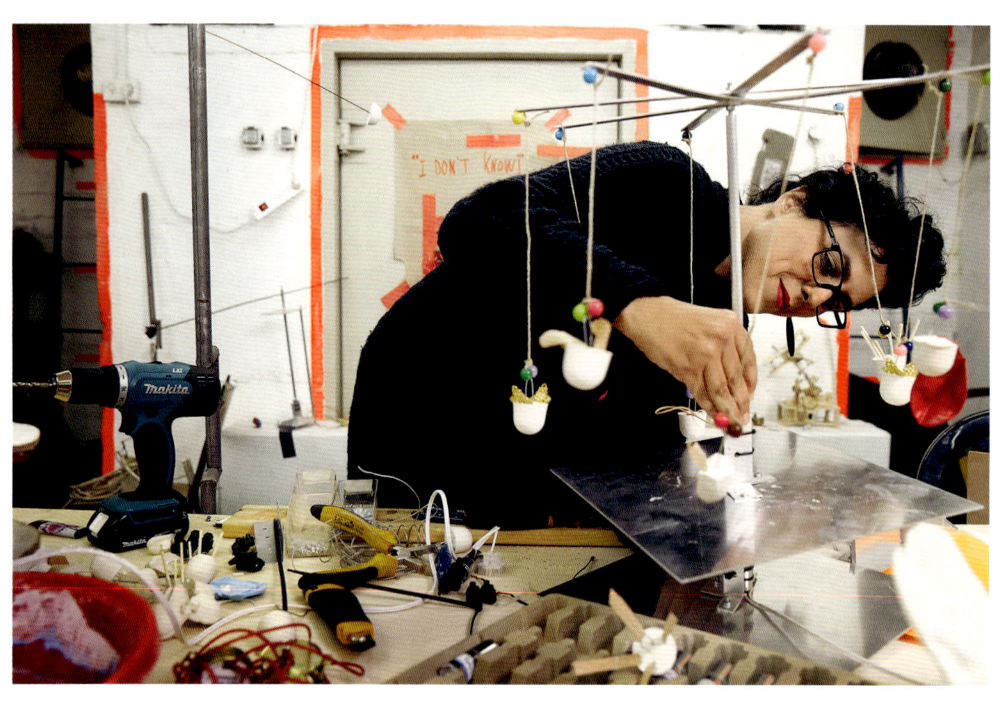

Eili Levy Kinetic Artist, Tzzazit (Art in Motion) > Holon, Israel

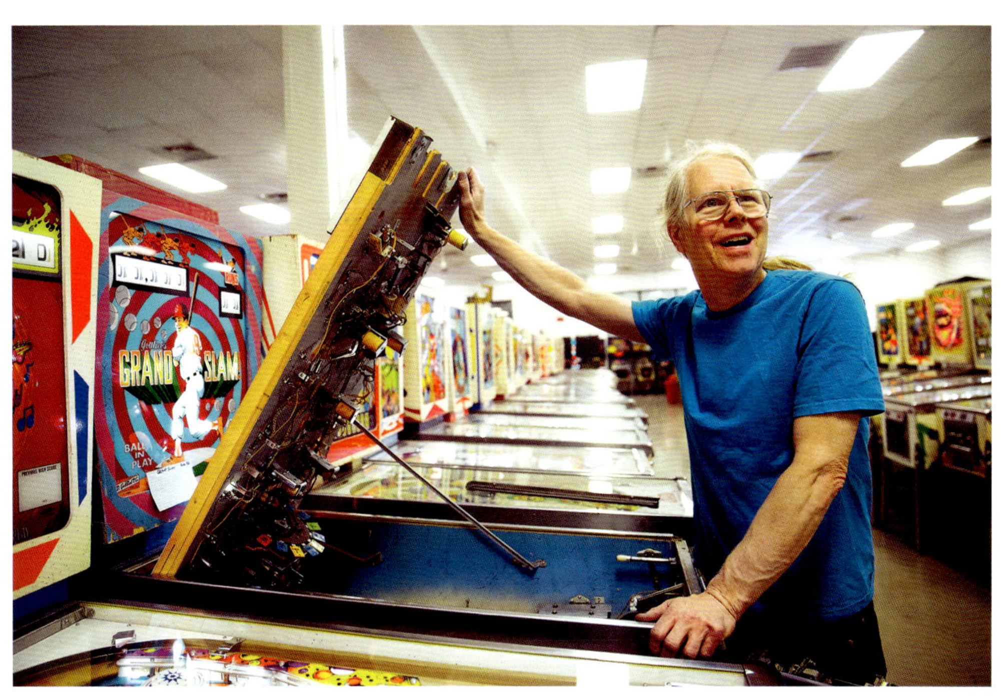

Tim Arnold Owner, Pin Ball Hall of Fame > Las Vegas, Nevada

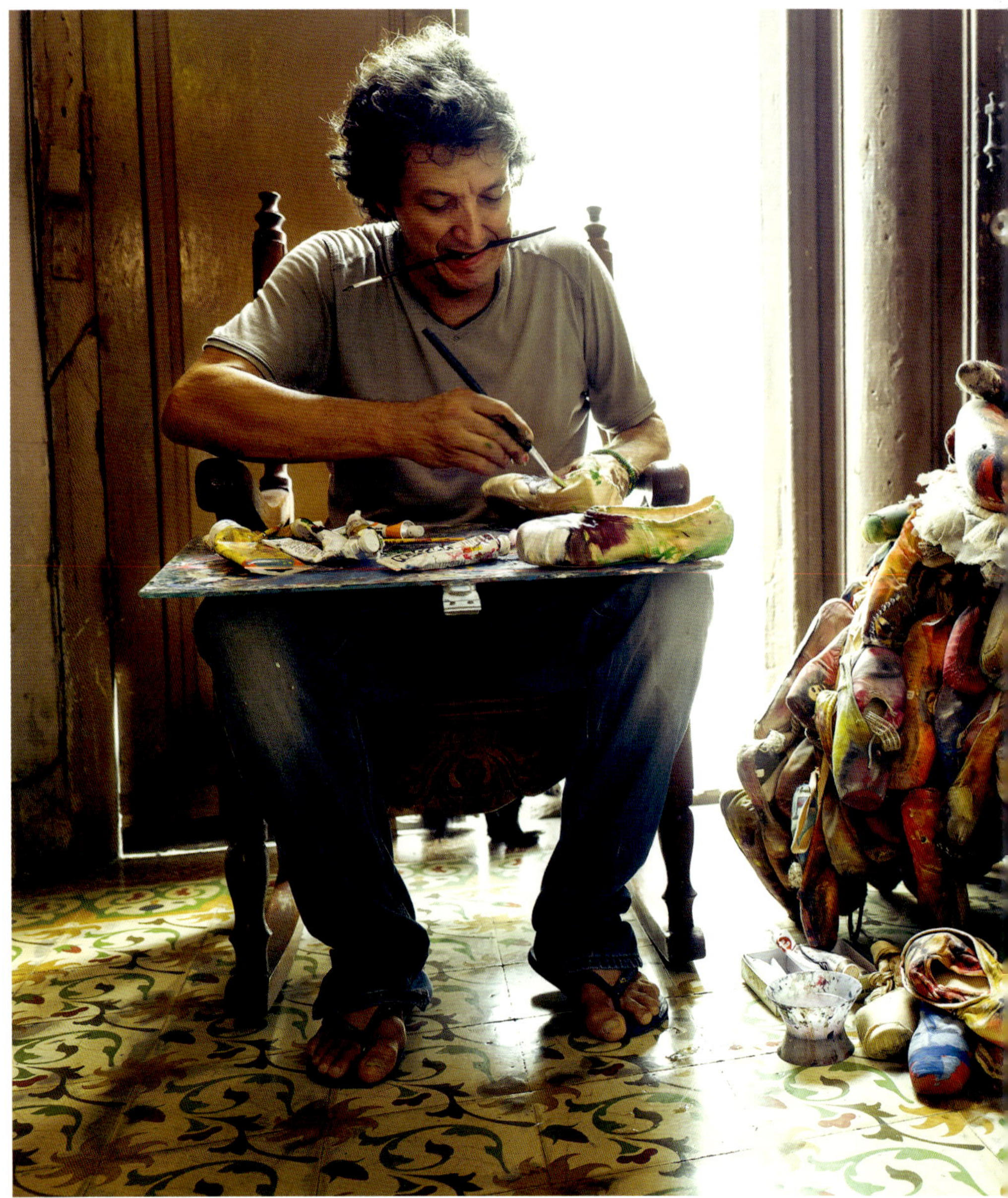

I met Félix at his home in Havana. For years, he had been a ballet master with the Ballet Nacional de Cuba. But time is hard on dancers. Eventually, he could no longer do the thing he loved.

He told me how this had led to a period of deep depression. But his mother encouraged him, saying that it was important to find a new way to connect with ballet, even if he couldn't dance.

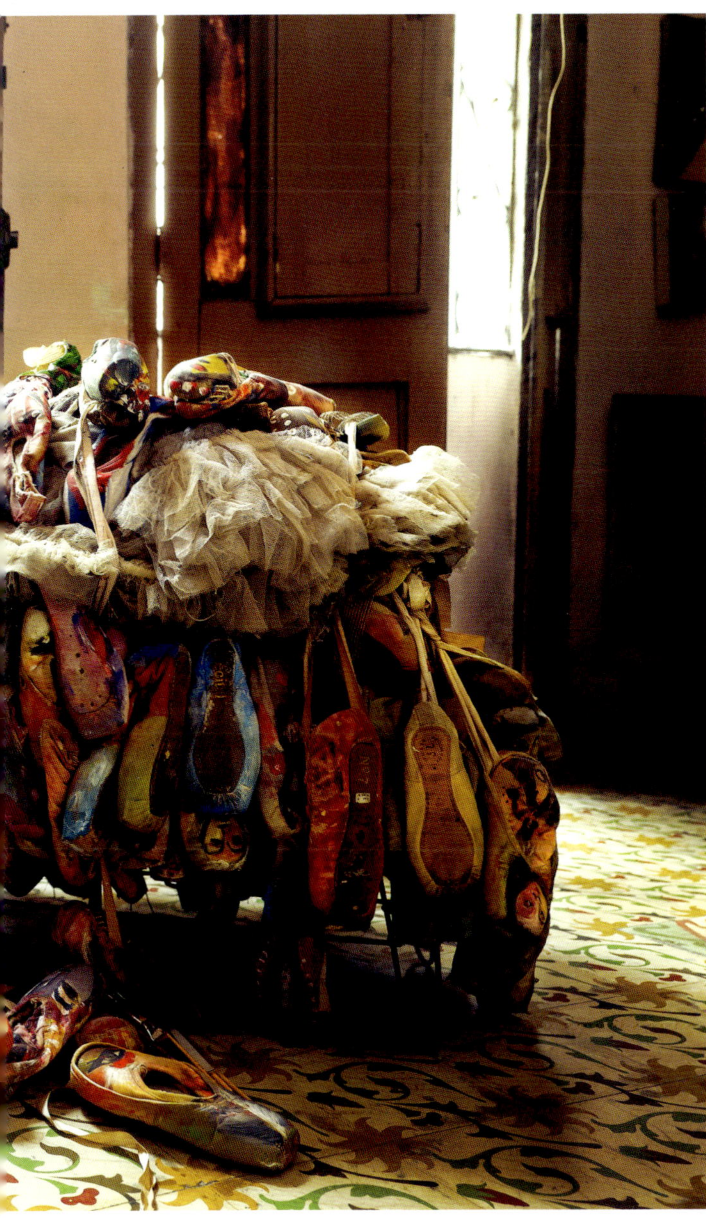

Time is hard on pointe shoes, too. So Félix found a way to transform the old, broken ones, creating beauty from the things that had once enabled dancers to create beauty. When one door closes, another opens.

Félix Rodriguez Brocetaz Ballet Shoe Painter > Havana, Cuba

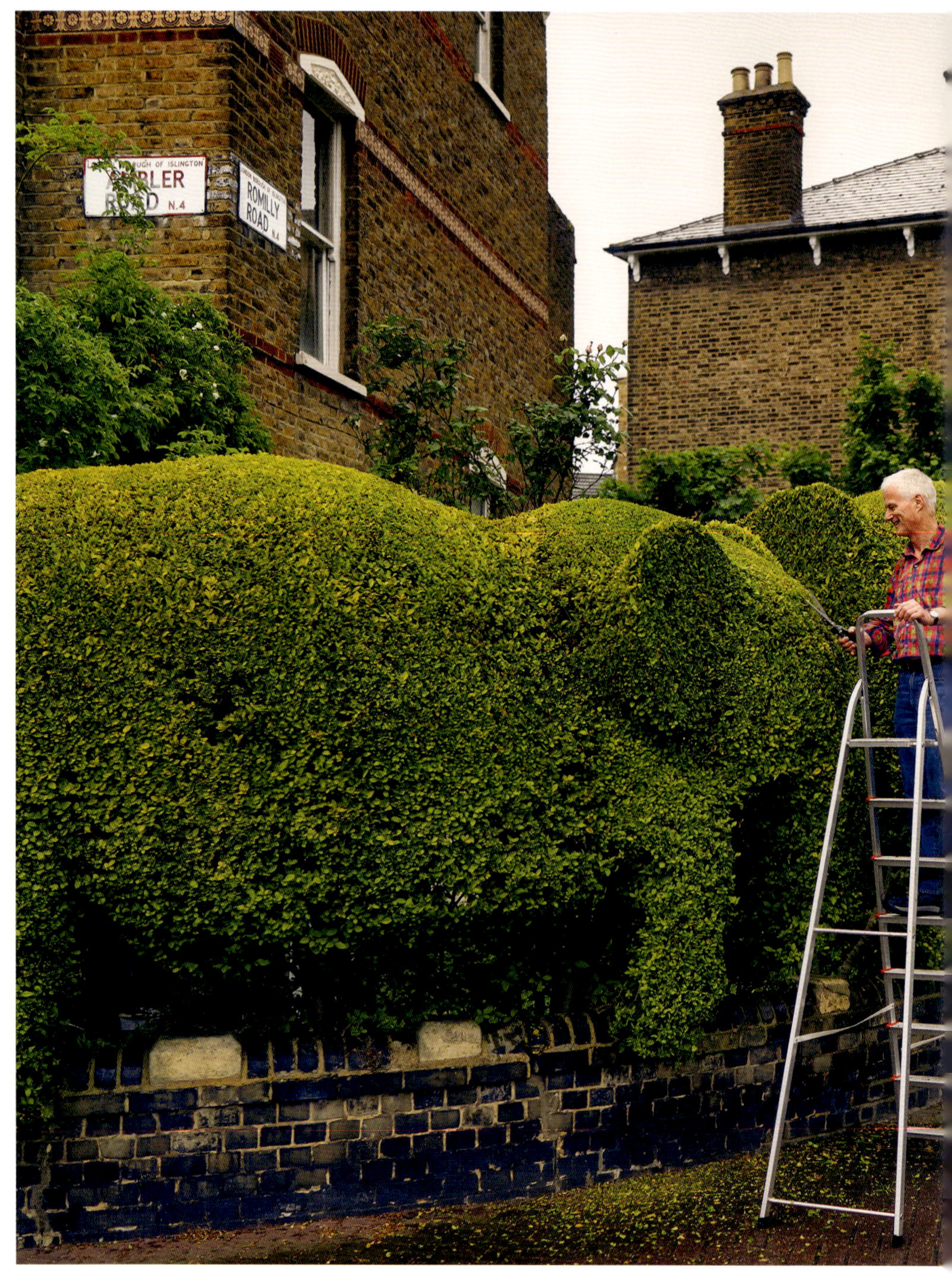

Tim Bushe Urban Topiarist > London, England

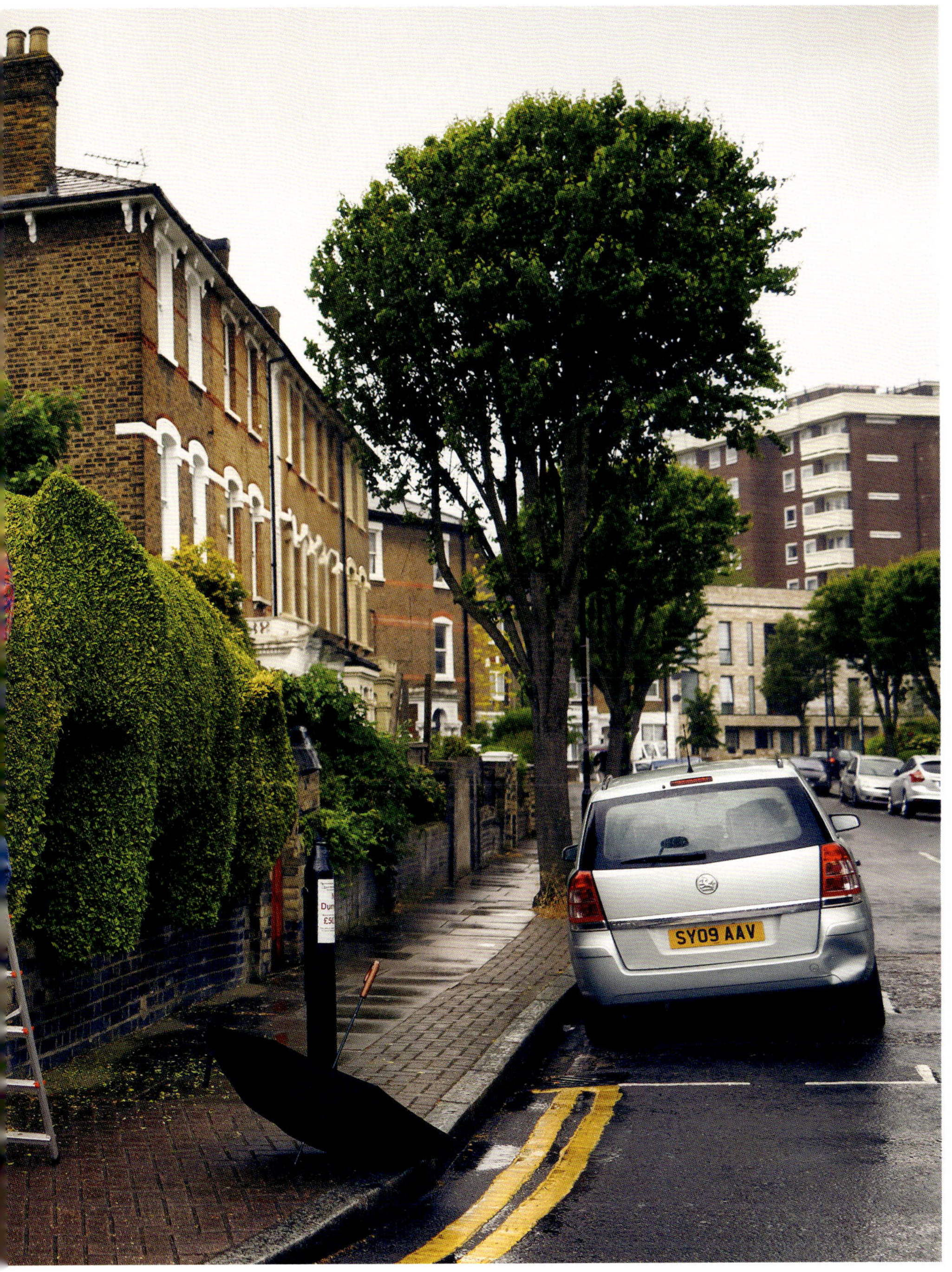

SY09 AAV

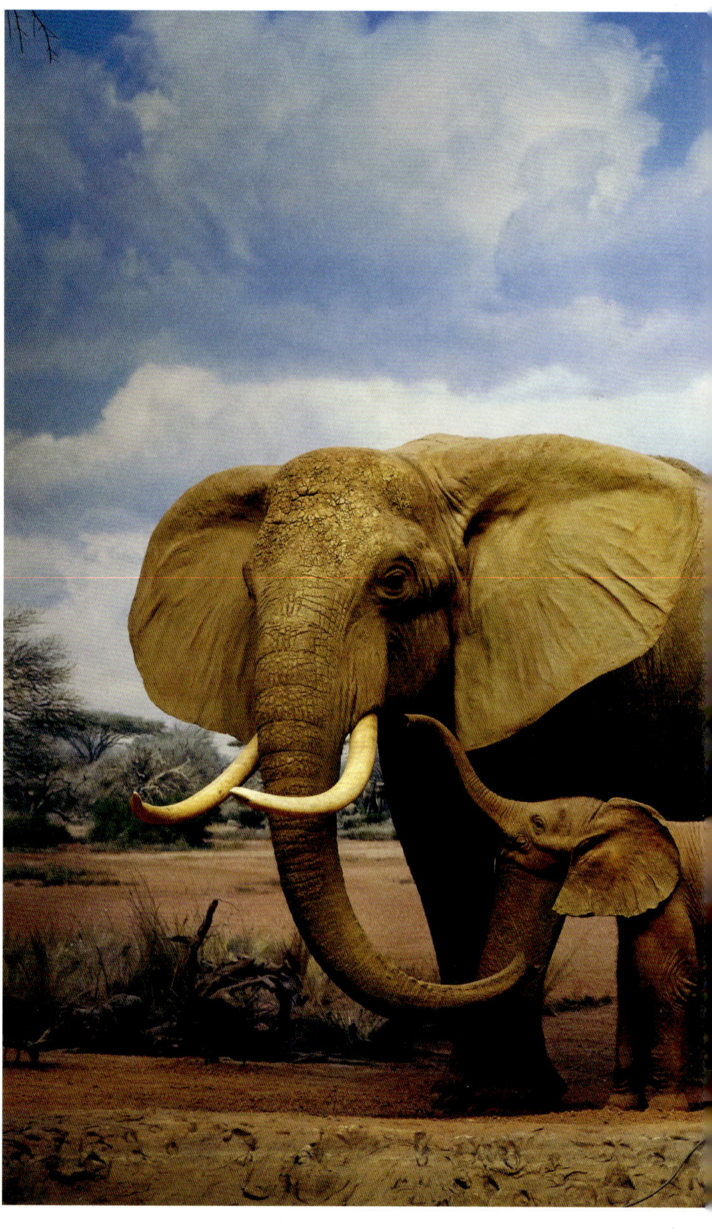

I brought my wife and daughter with me to spend the day at the Natural History Museum. We got such a kick out of being behind the scenes.

Tim invited us to come along while he cleaned up the exhibits. I couldn't help but laugh as he led us to this particular diorama.

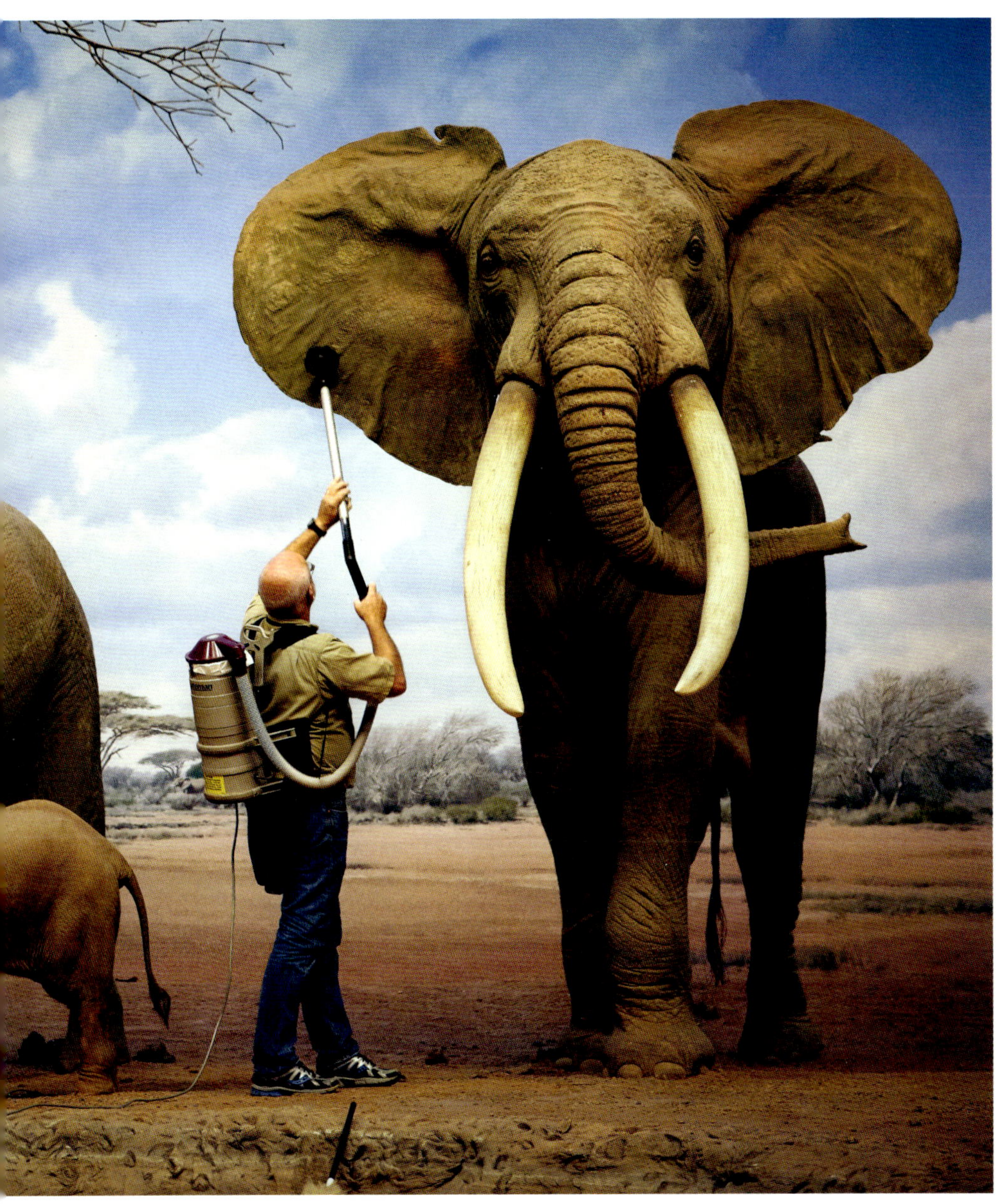

He could have never guessed what tremendous significance it had for me.

The three elephants — papa, mama, and baby — were exactly like those I'd had tattooed on my upper arm to symbolize my commitment to my wife and daughter.

May we always walk the same path.

Tim Bovard Taxidermist, Natural History Museum > Los Angeles, California

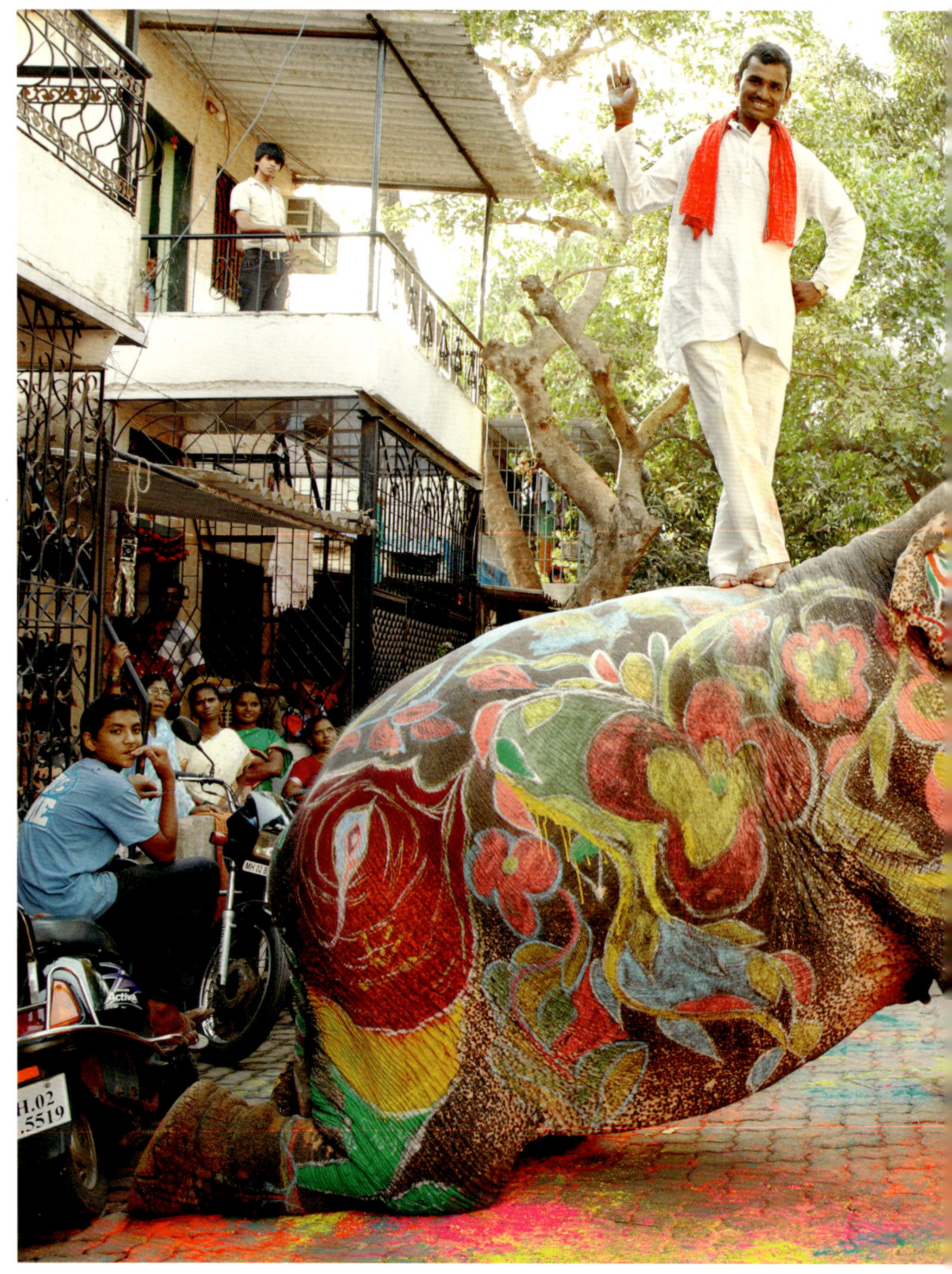

Deepak Elephant Painter > Mumbai, India

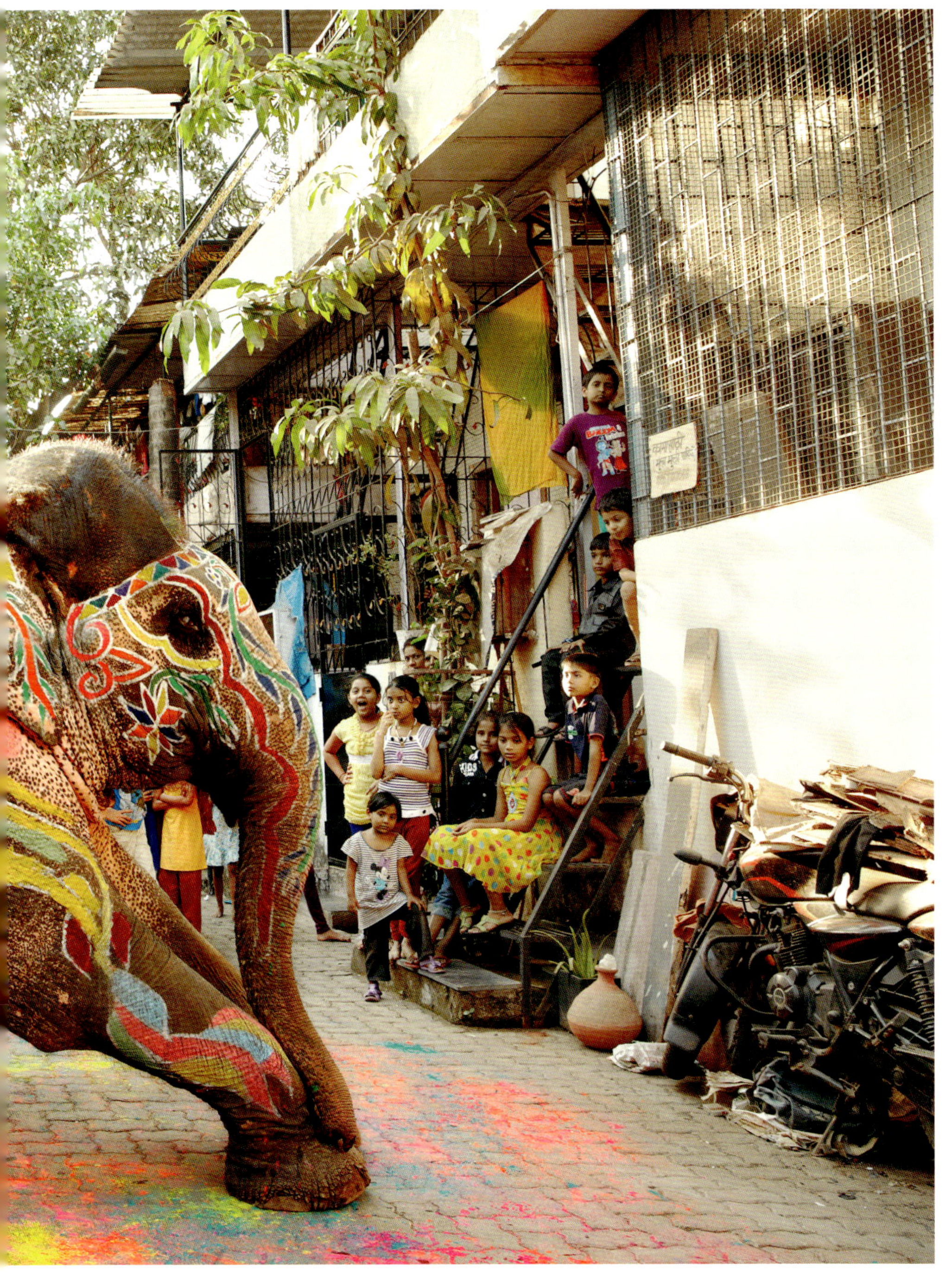

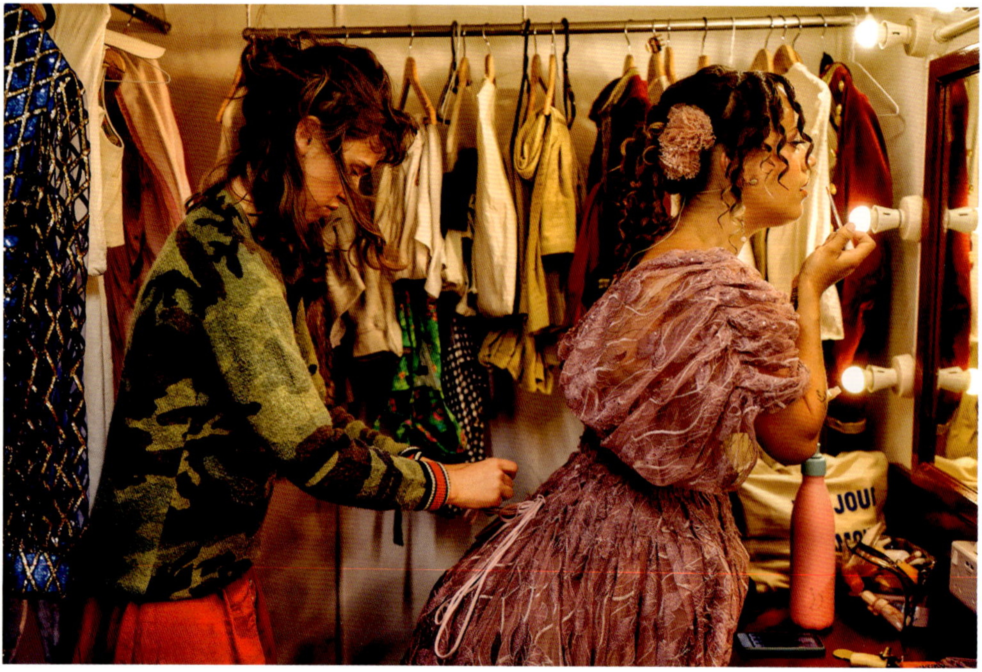

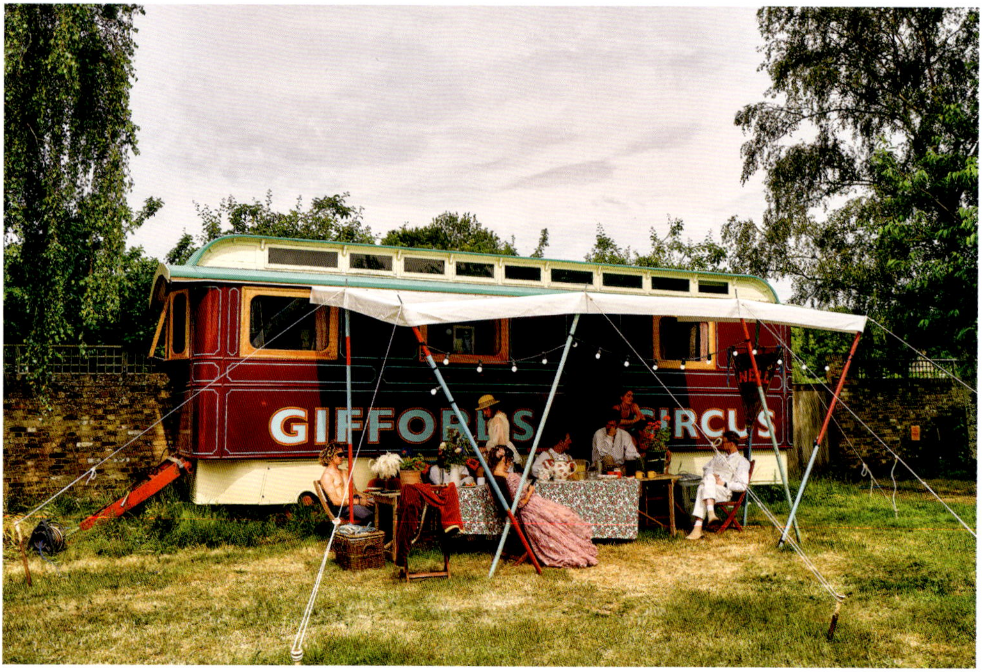

Giffords Circus Performers > London, England

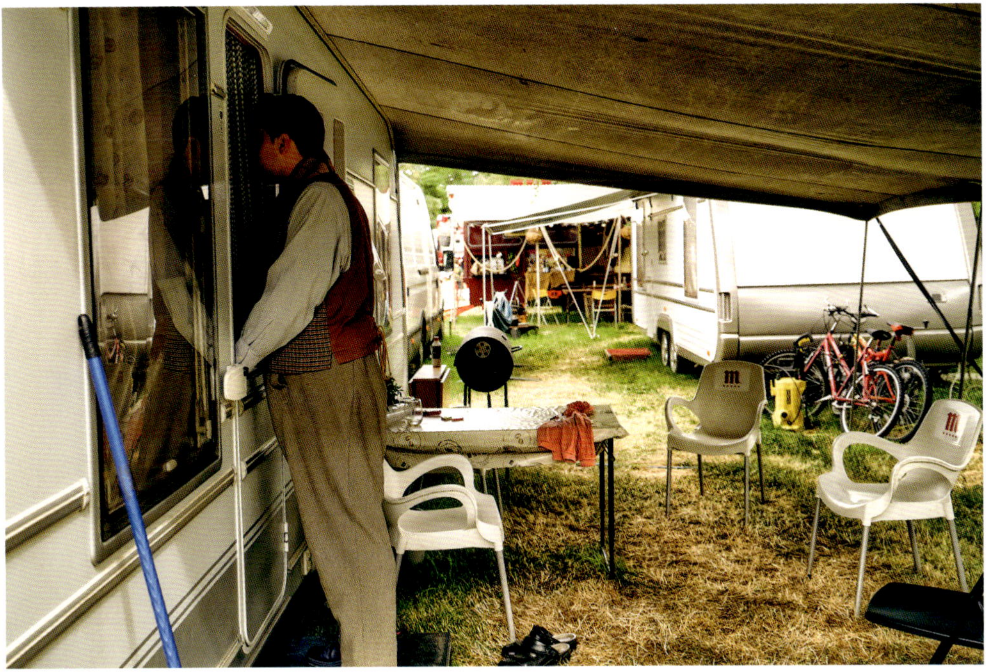

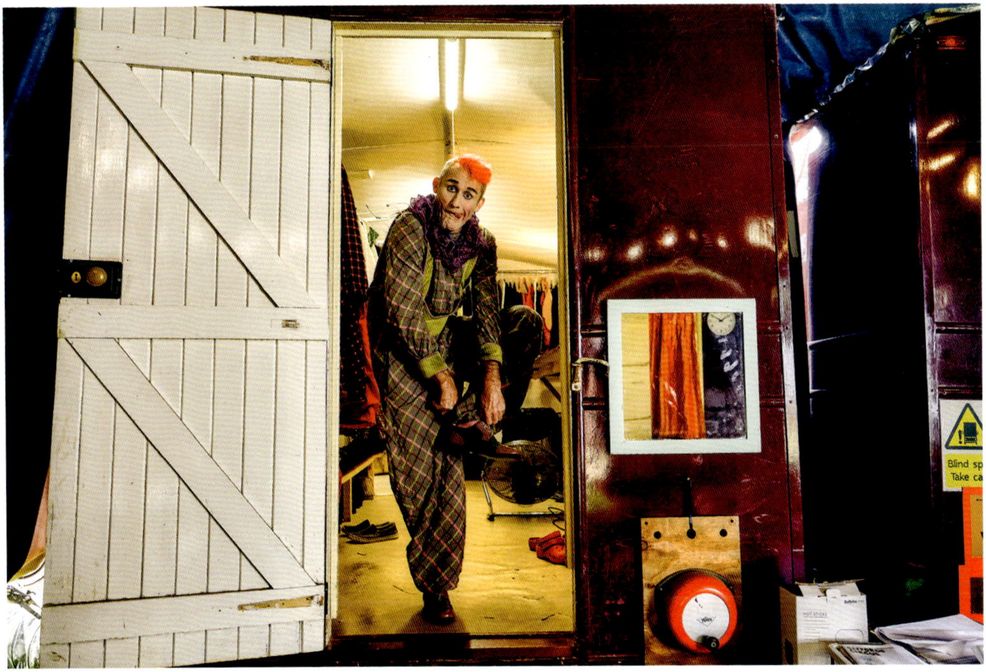

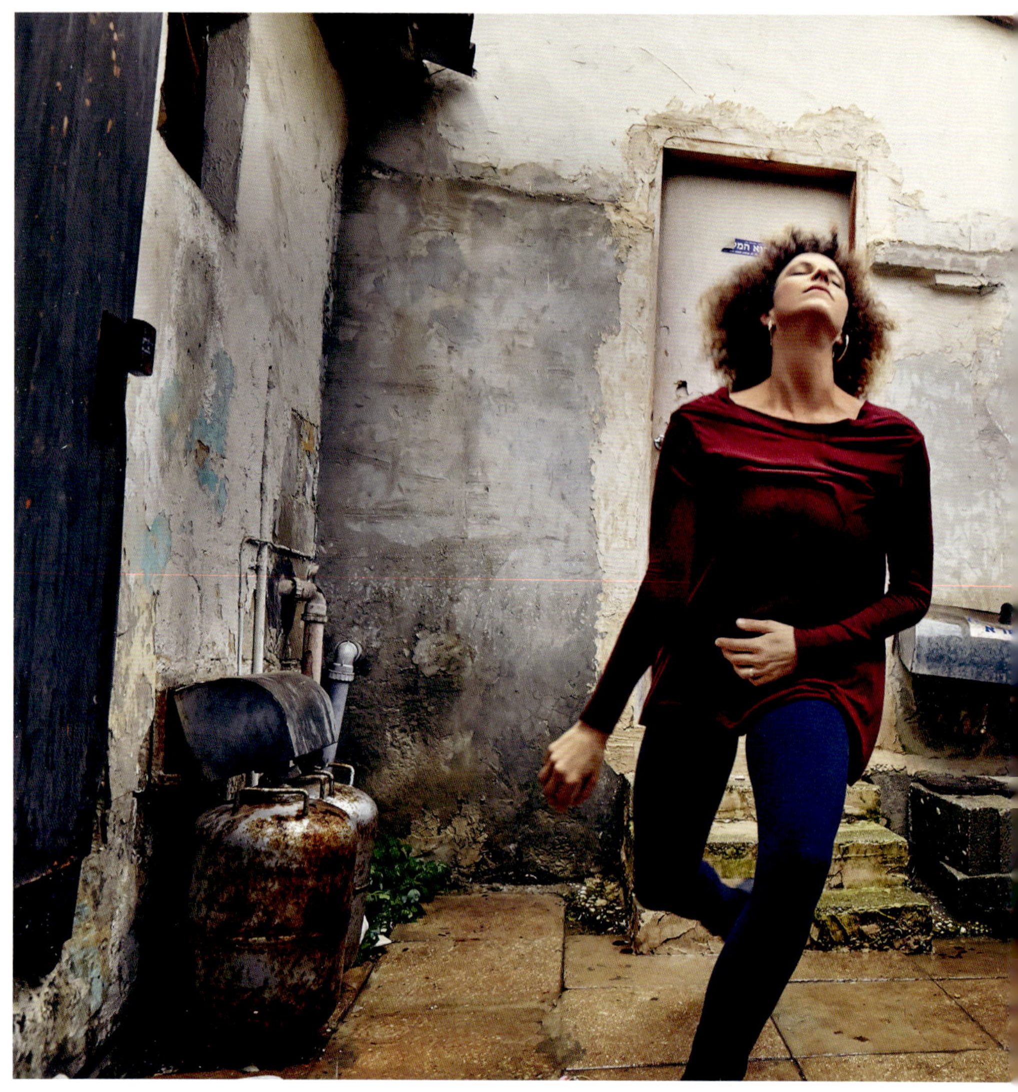

Ruth told me that she knew from the moment she could walk that she had to dance—
not wanted to; *had to.*

It had been pouring rain all day. I was trying to capture her dancing on the building's
rooftop. Even though it was striking, with the skyline of Tel Aviv, it wasn't coming
together. It didn't feel right. It didn't feel real.

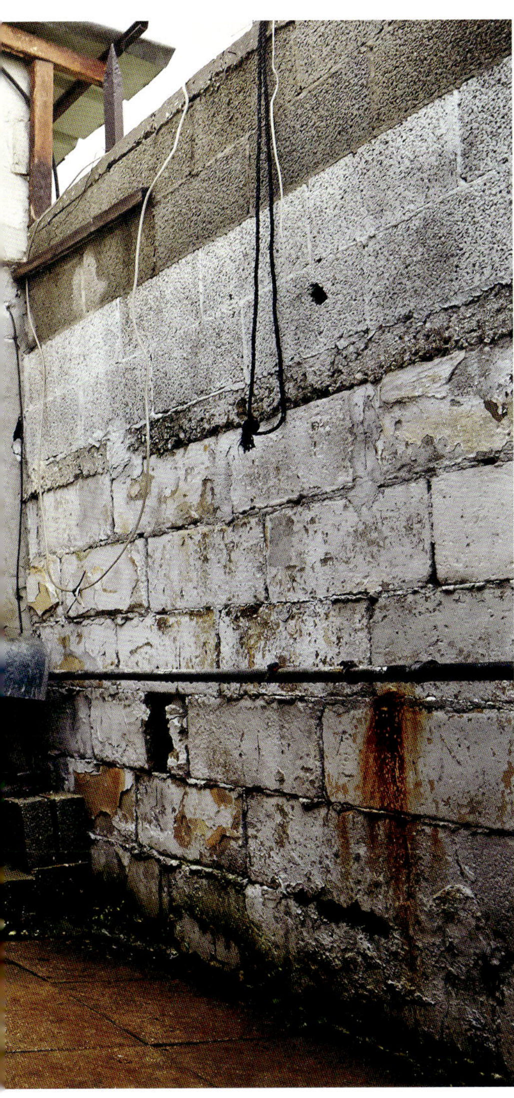

  I suggested that we head down into the alley I'd seen on my way into the building. I could see right away as she moved in this tight space that it was about far more than a change in backdrop. The rooftop had been too much of a stage.

  The alley freed her, somehow. She wasn't performing — for me, or anyone. It was as if she had become a little girl again. Unencumbered. No choreography. Just doing it for herself. She wept as she danced.

Ruth Aharoni Dancer > Tel Aviv, Israel

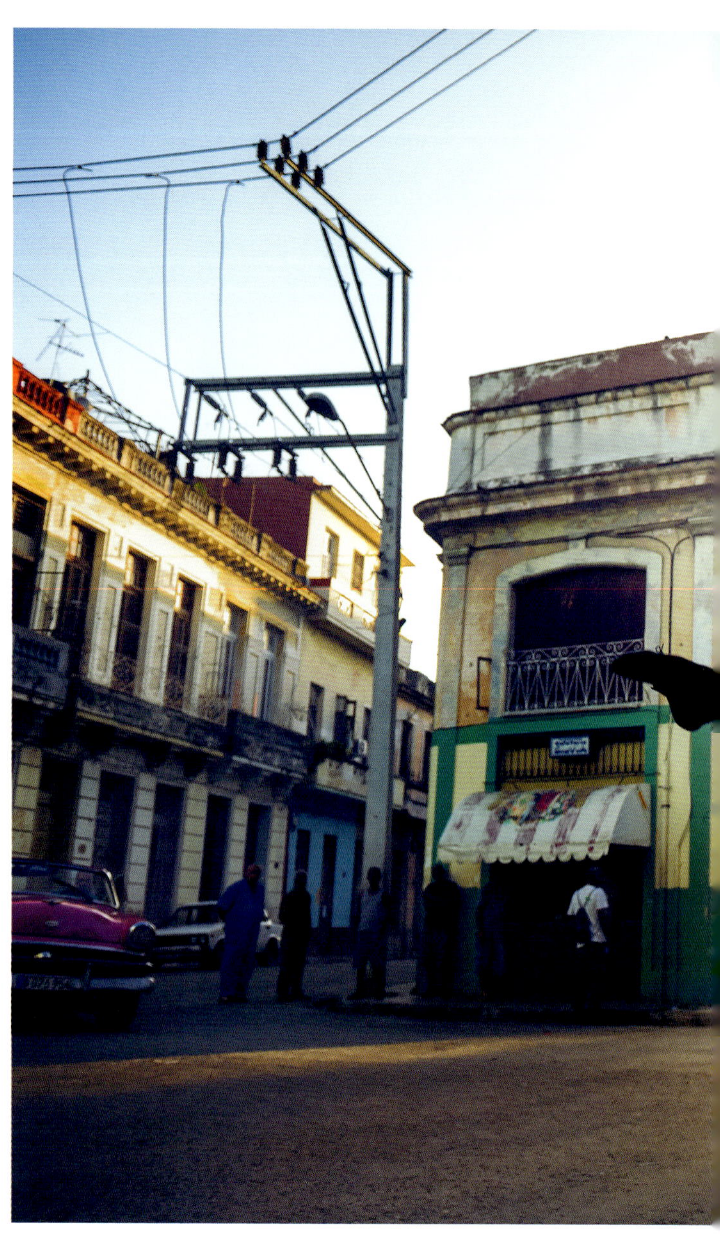

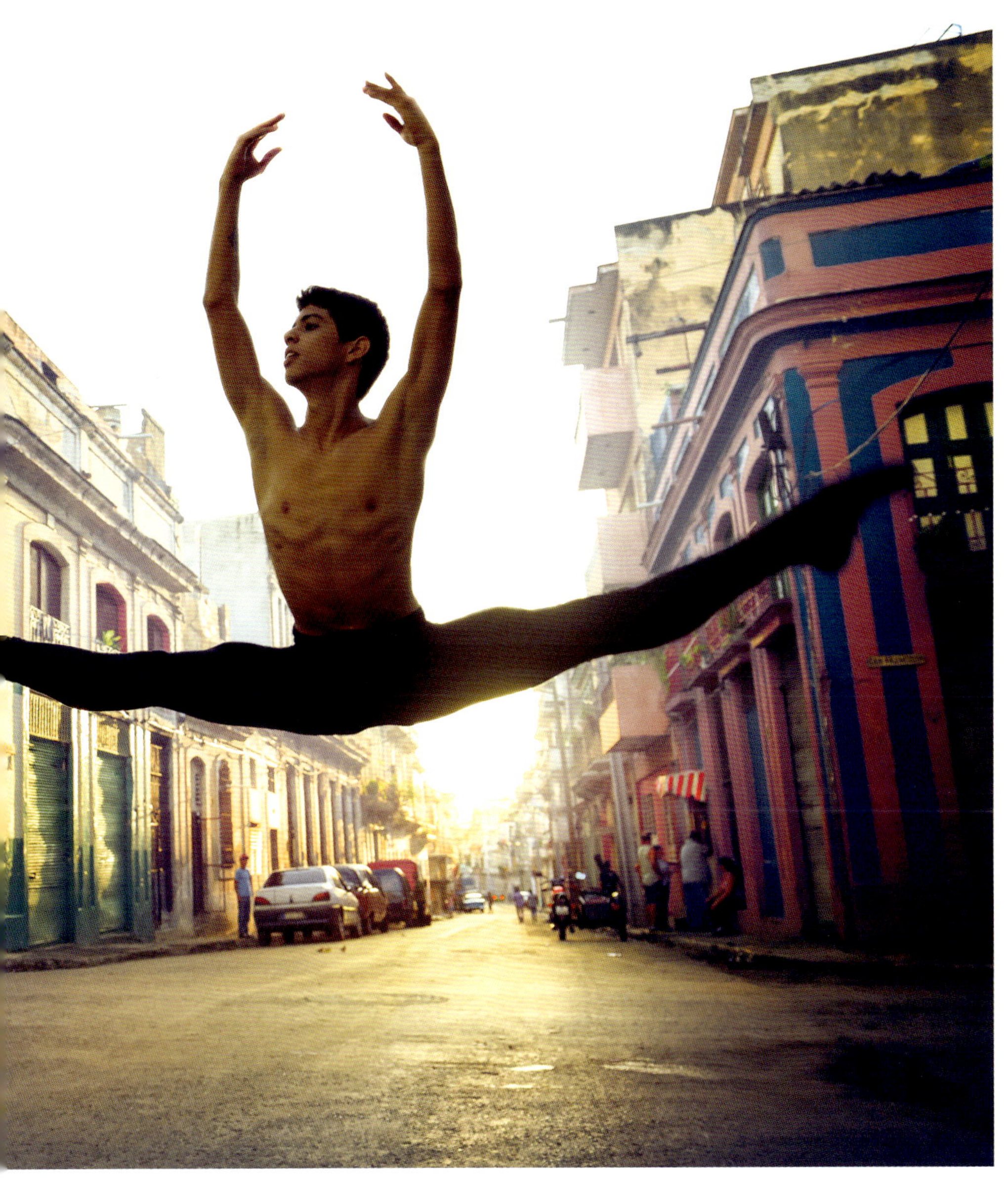

I asked Francois to do "something impressive."
Hats off to you, my friend.

Francois Llorente Ballet Dancer, Ballet Nacional de Cuba > Havana, Cuba

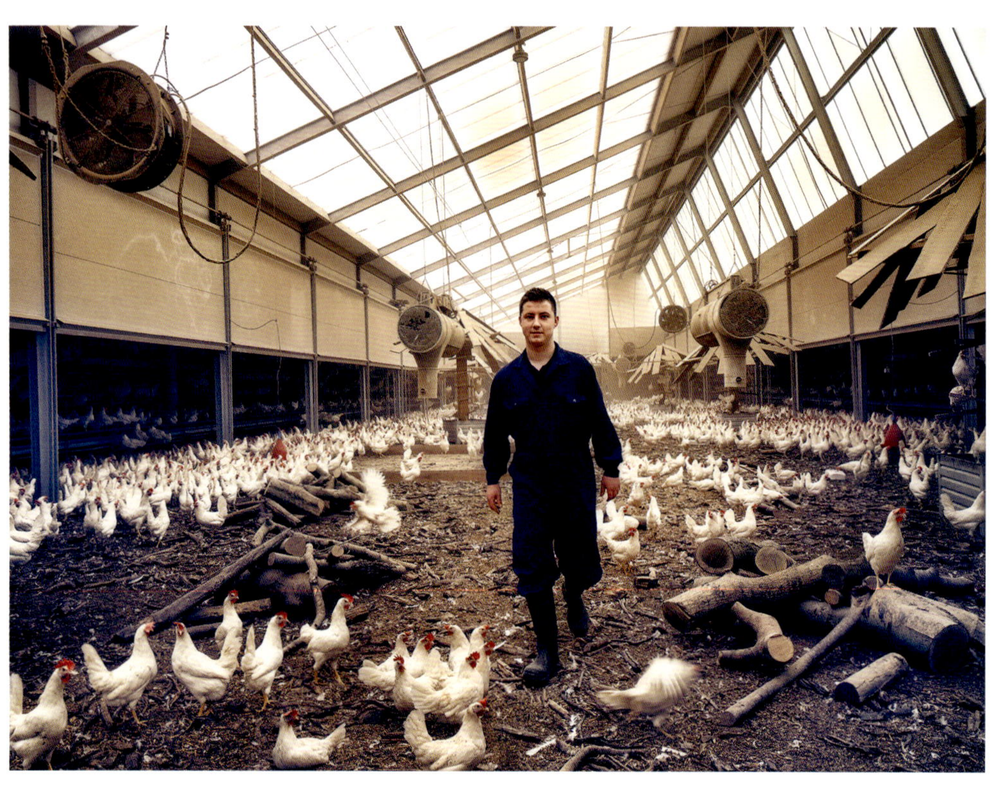

Twan Baltussen Chicken Farmer, Kipster > Hoogriebroek, Netherlands

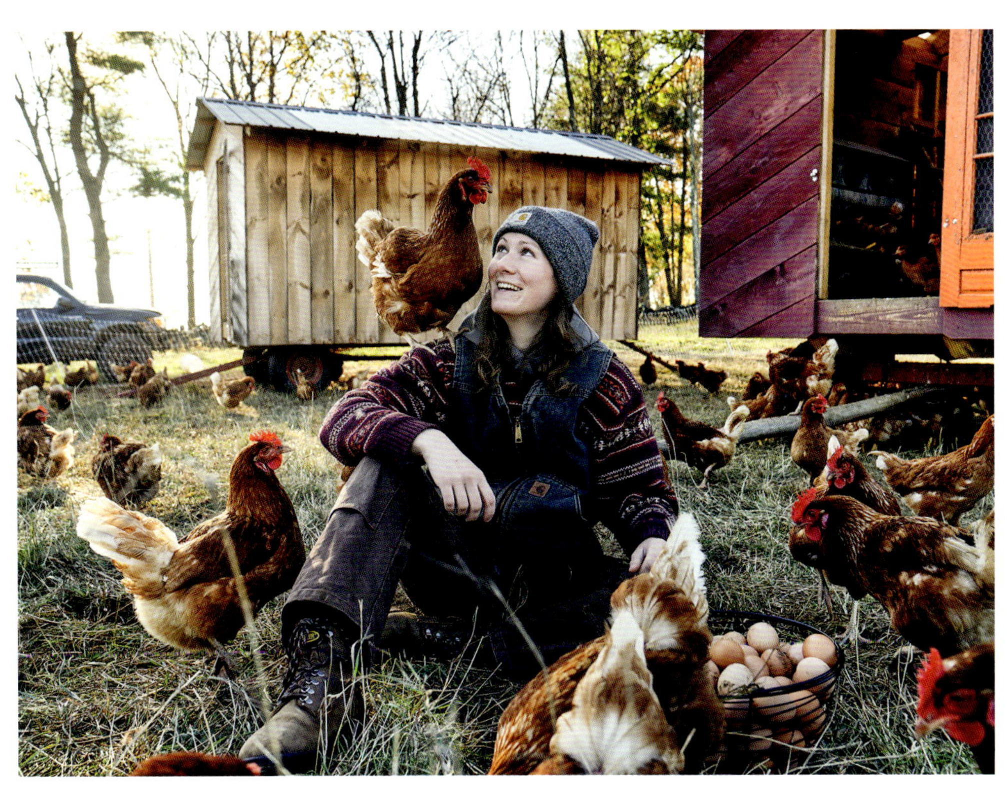

Hannah Miller Chicken Farmer, Maplebrook Farmstead > Sterling, Massachusetts

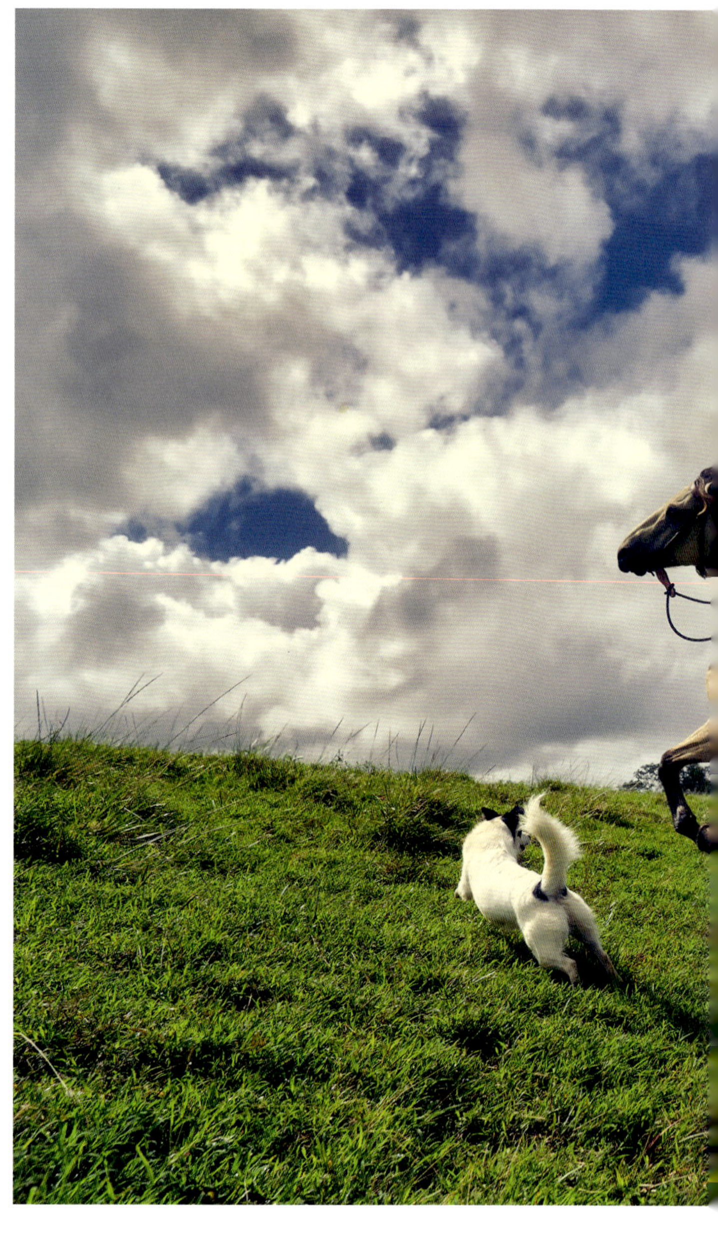

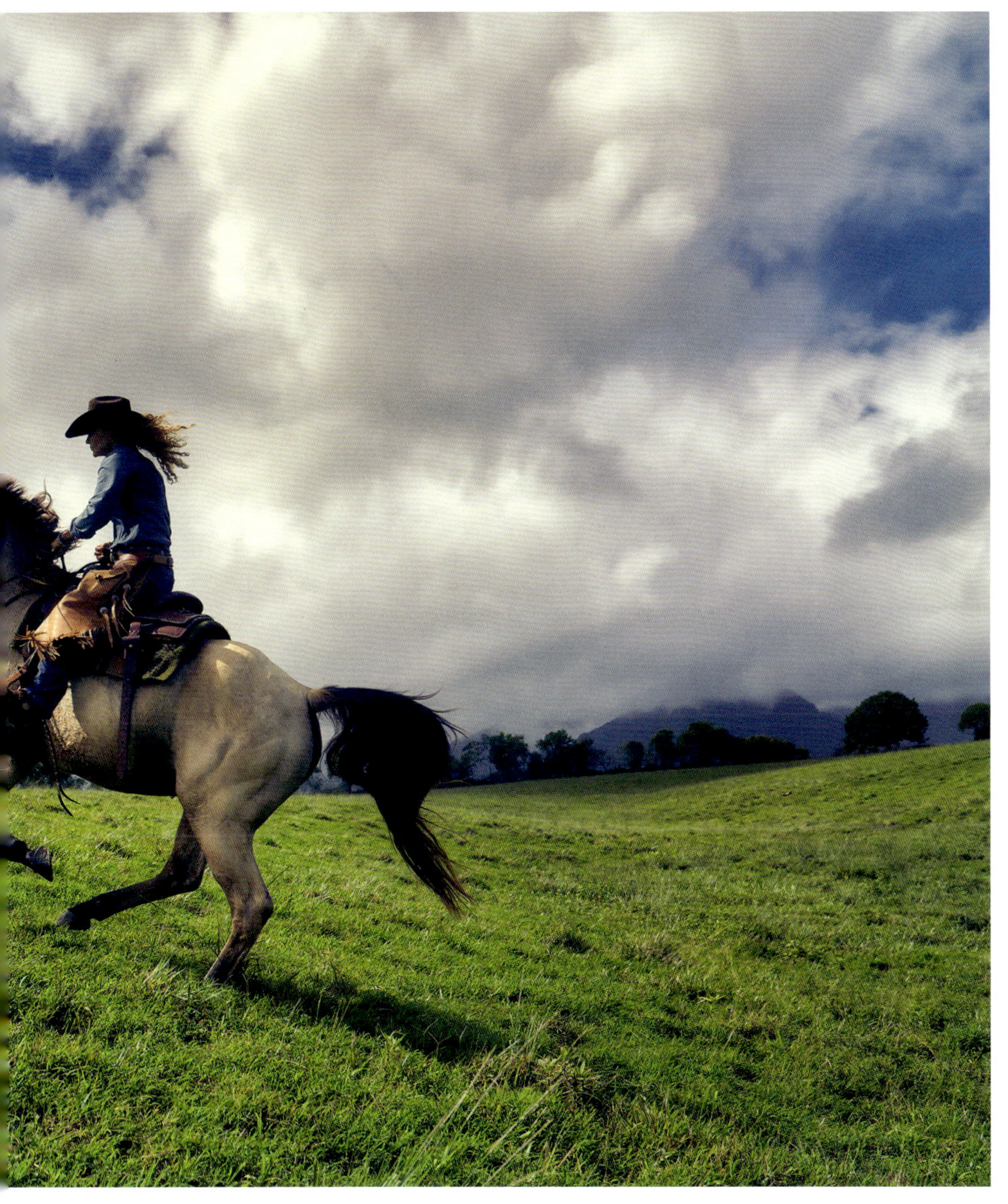

Karin Carswell Guest Paniolo, Princeville Ranch > Kaua'i, Hawaii

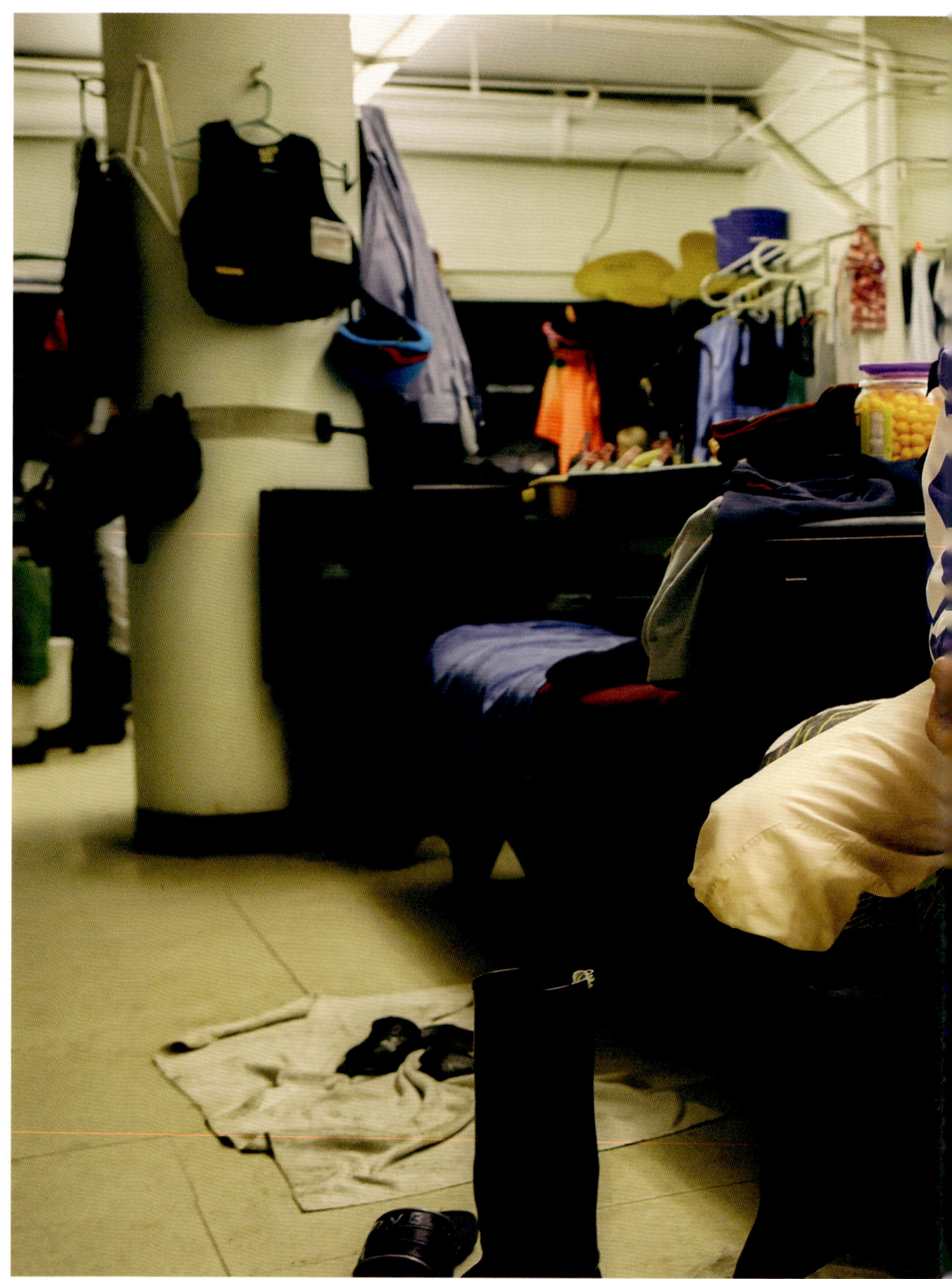

Jockey Suffolk Downs > Boston, Massachusetts

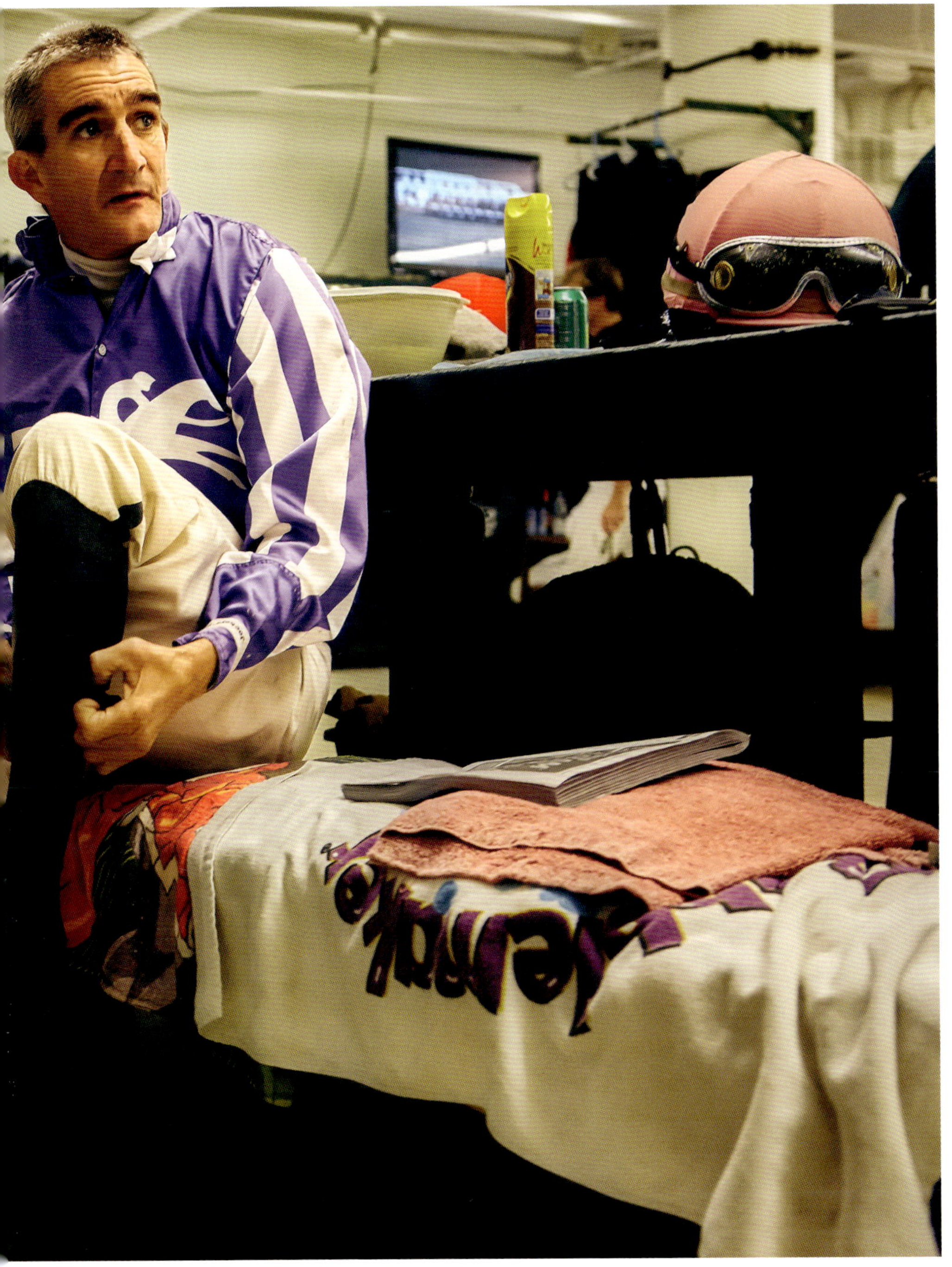

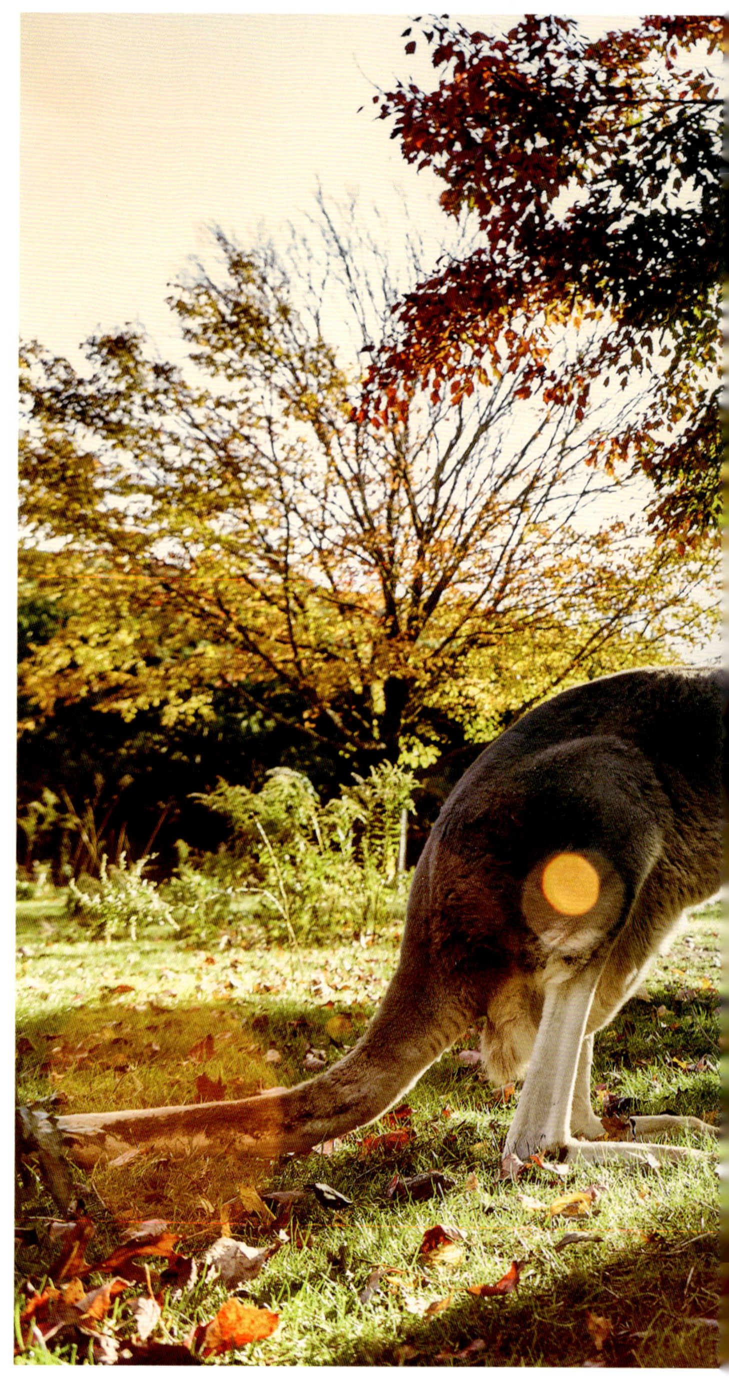

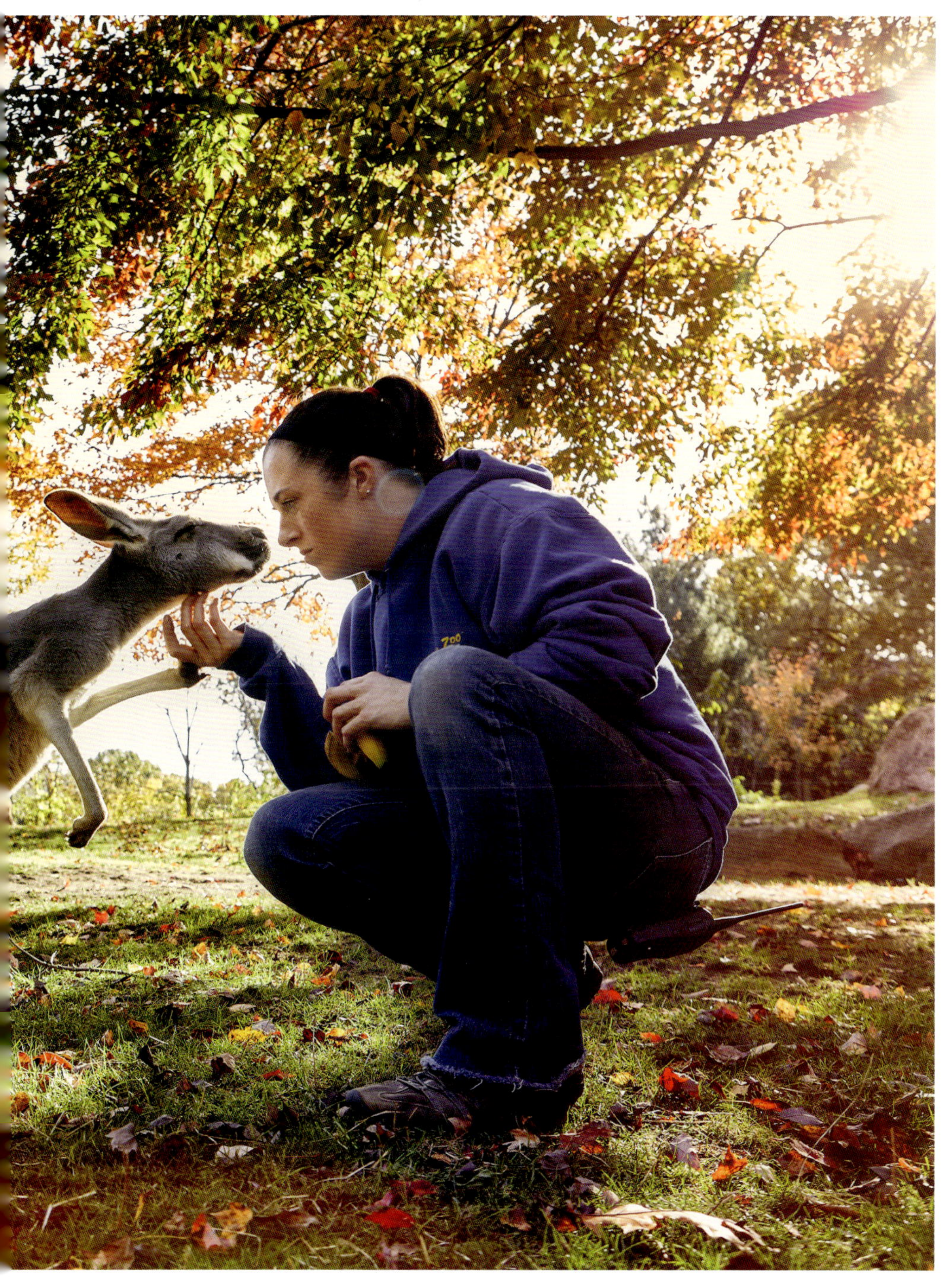

Michelle Breen Lead Primate Keeper, Southwick's Zoo > Mendon, Massachusetts

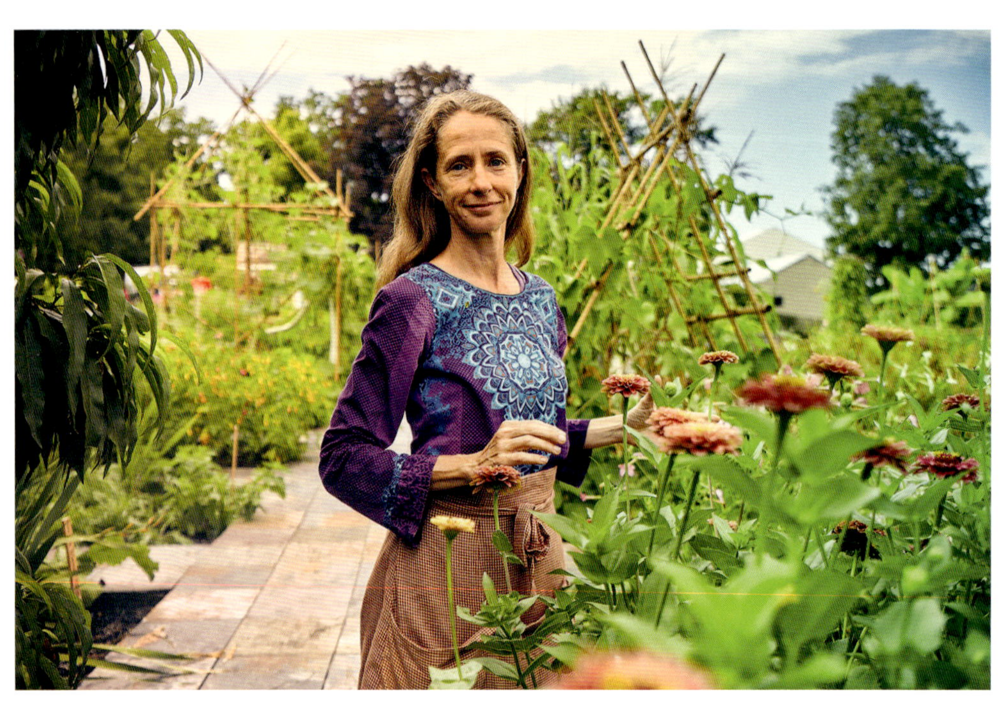

Jamie Jackson Proprietor, Baker Creek Heirloom Seeds > Mansfield, Missouri

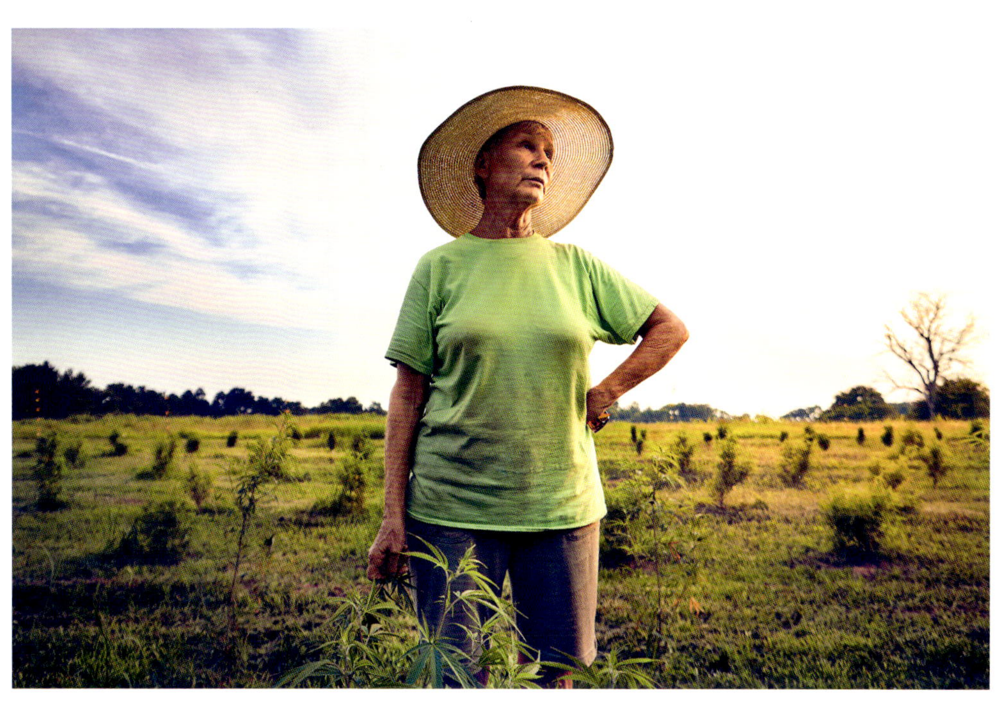

Jane Harrod Hemp Farmer, Early Bird CBD > Fayette, Kentucky

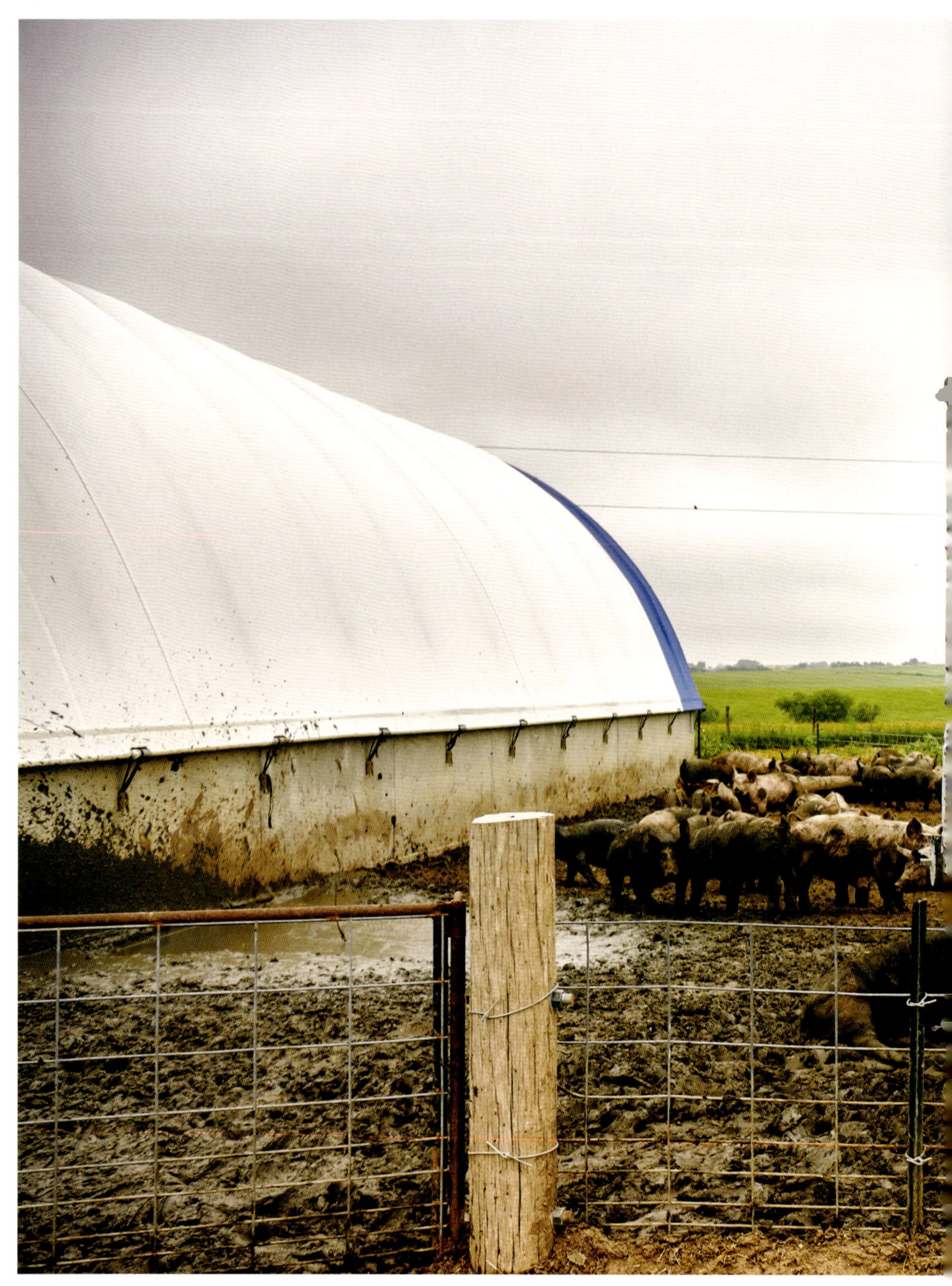

Kaden Rousch Pig Farmer, R Family Farms > Lebanon, Kansas

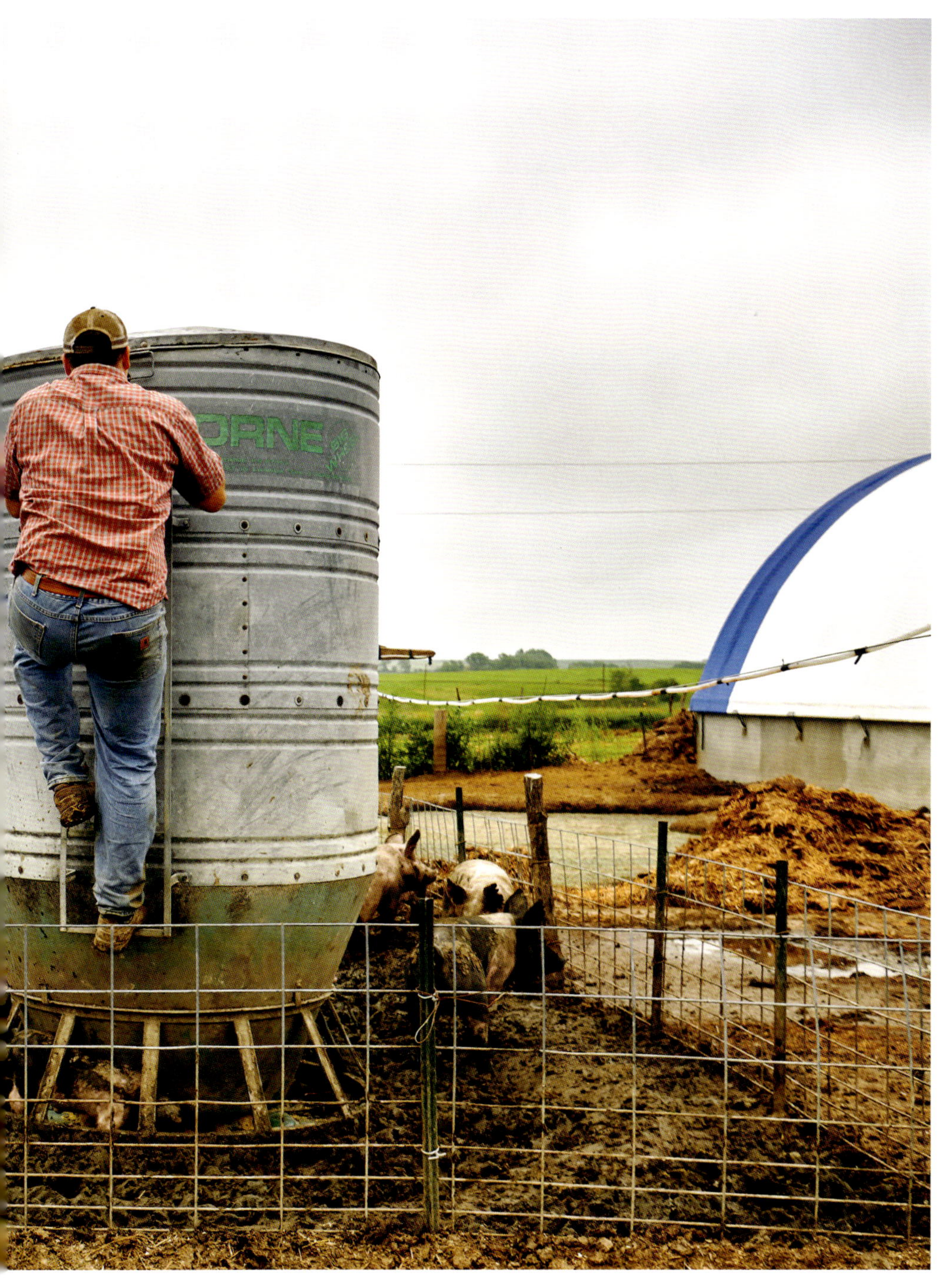

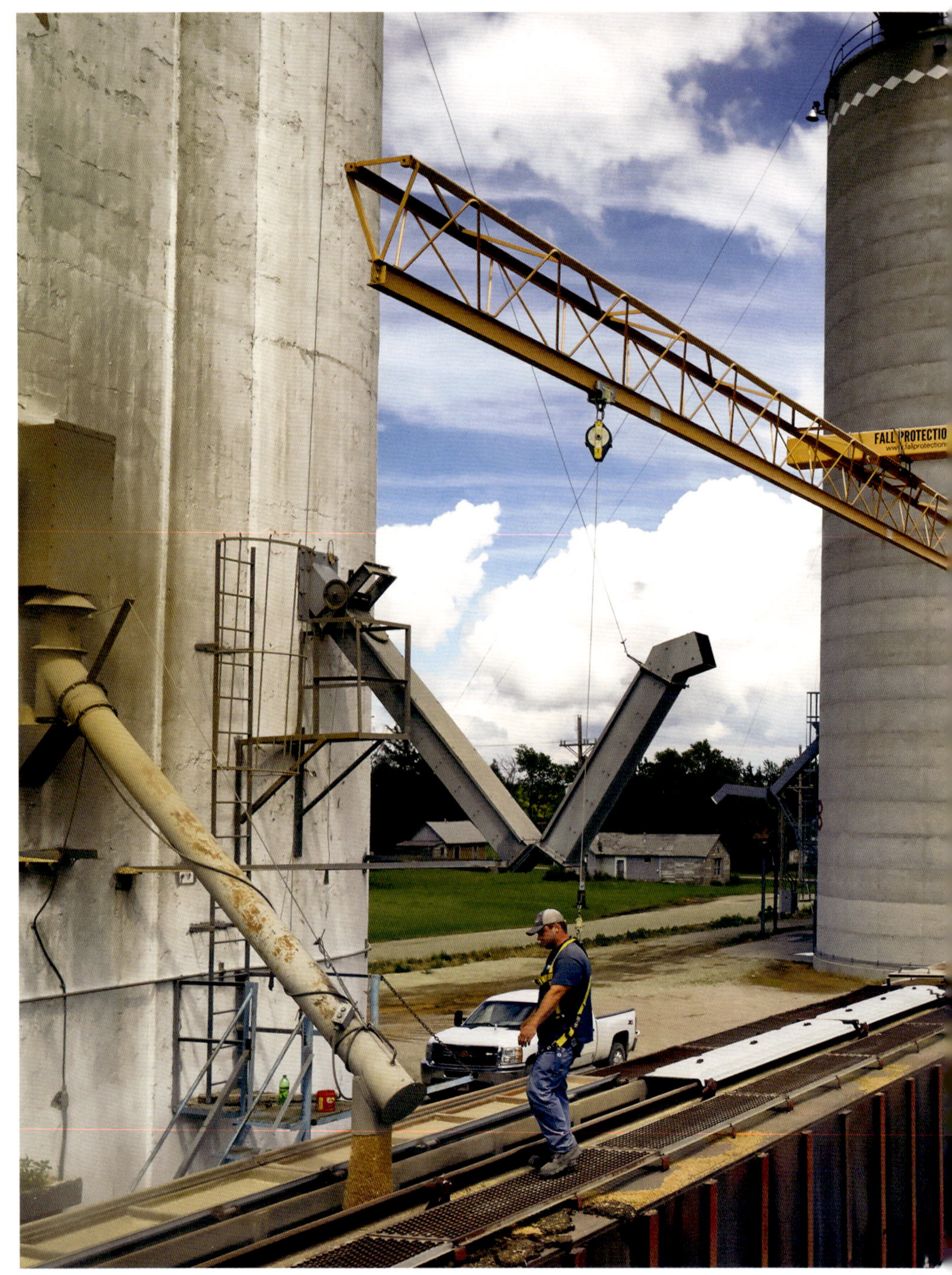

Jed Toynton Mill Worker > Lebanon, Kansas

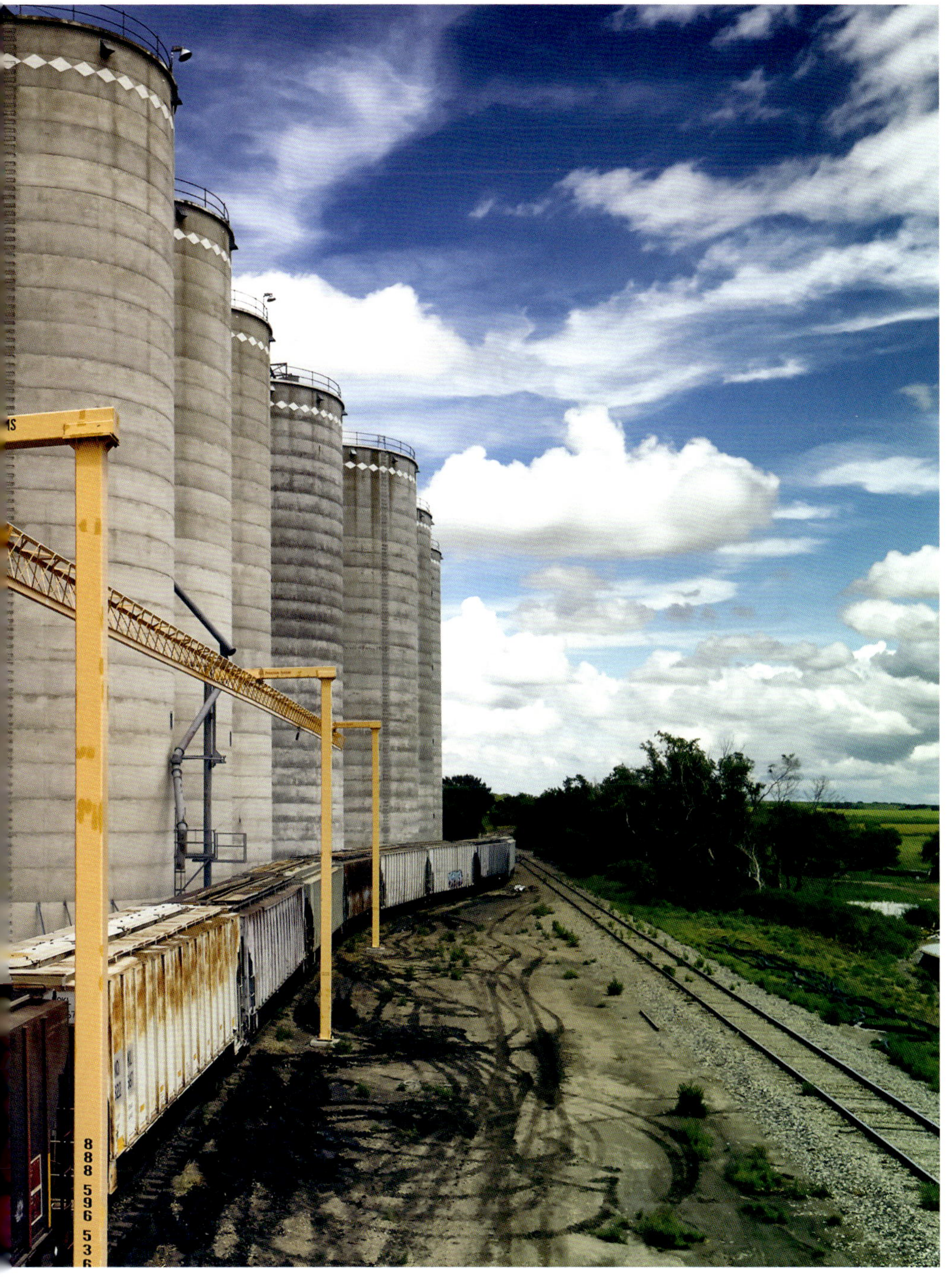

888
596
536

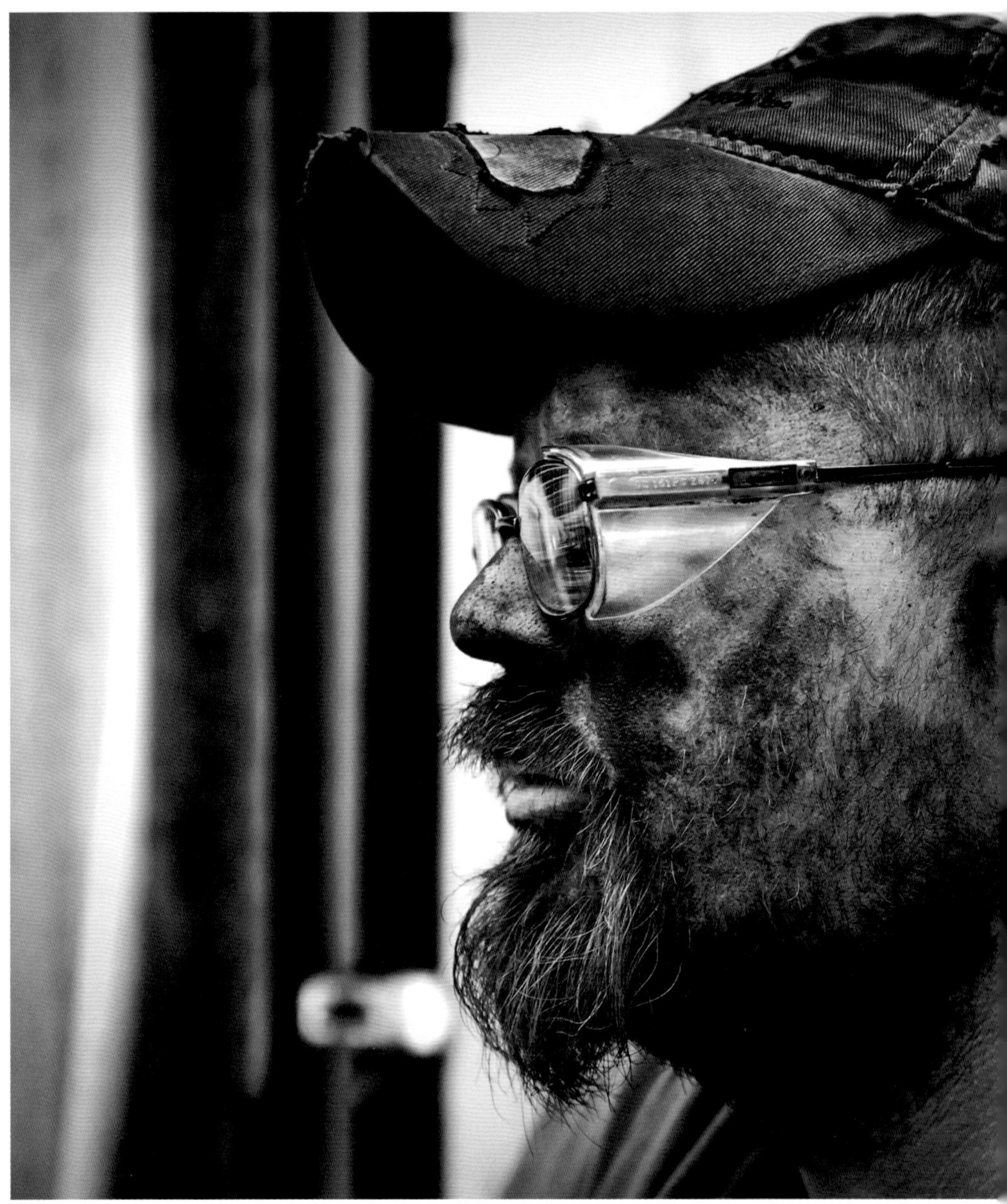

I was grateful that Brian was willing to talk to me. When stories about coal mining
are told, the experiences of the miners themselves can get overlooked.
    We met at his house after his night shift. As he cleaned his glasses, I could see
up-close just how gritty the work was, how physically uncomfortable.

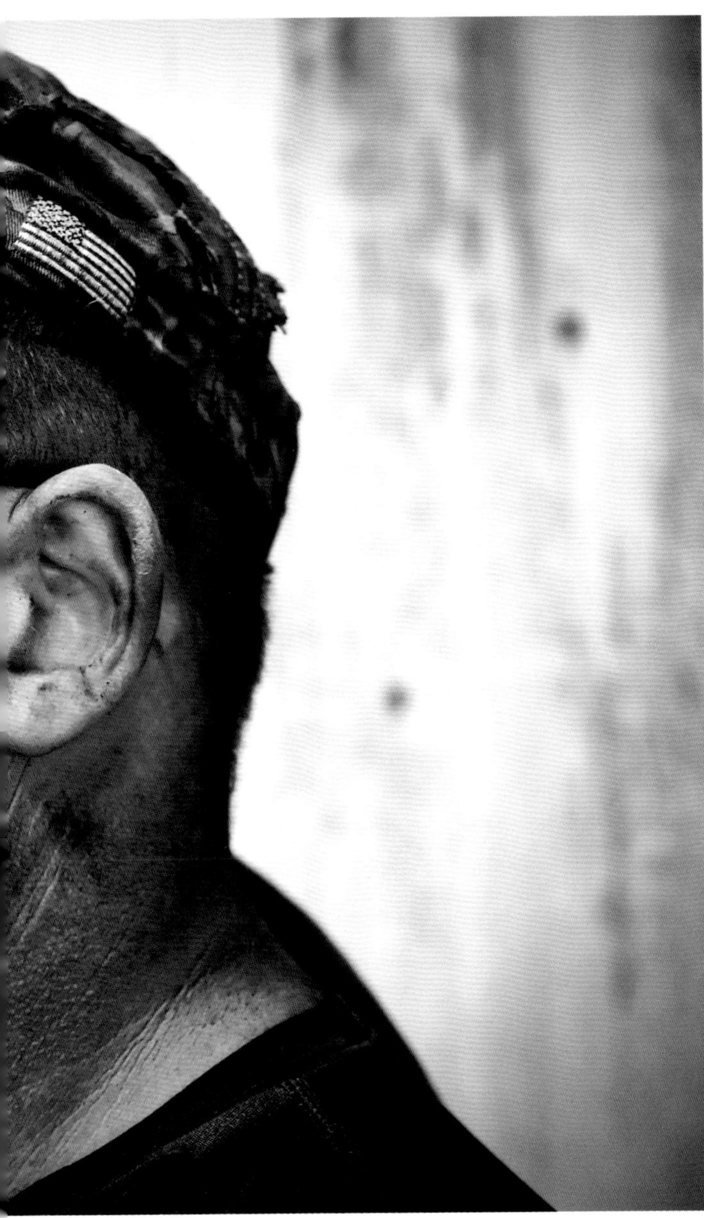

"This is the only way I have to feed my family," he said.
For me, that is the story.

Brian Blanecksky Coal Miner > Lester, West Virginia

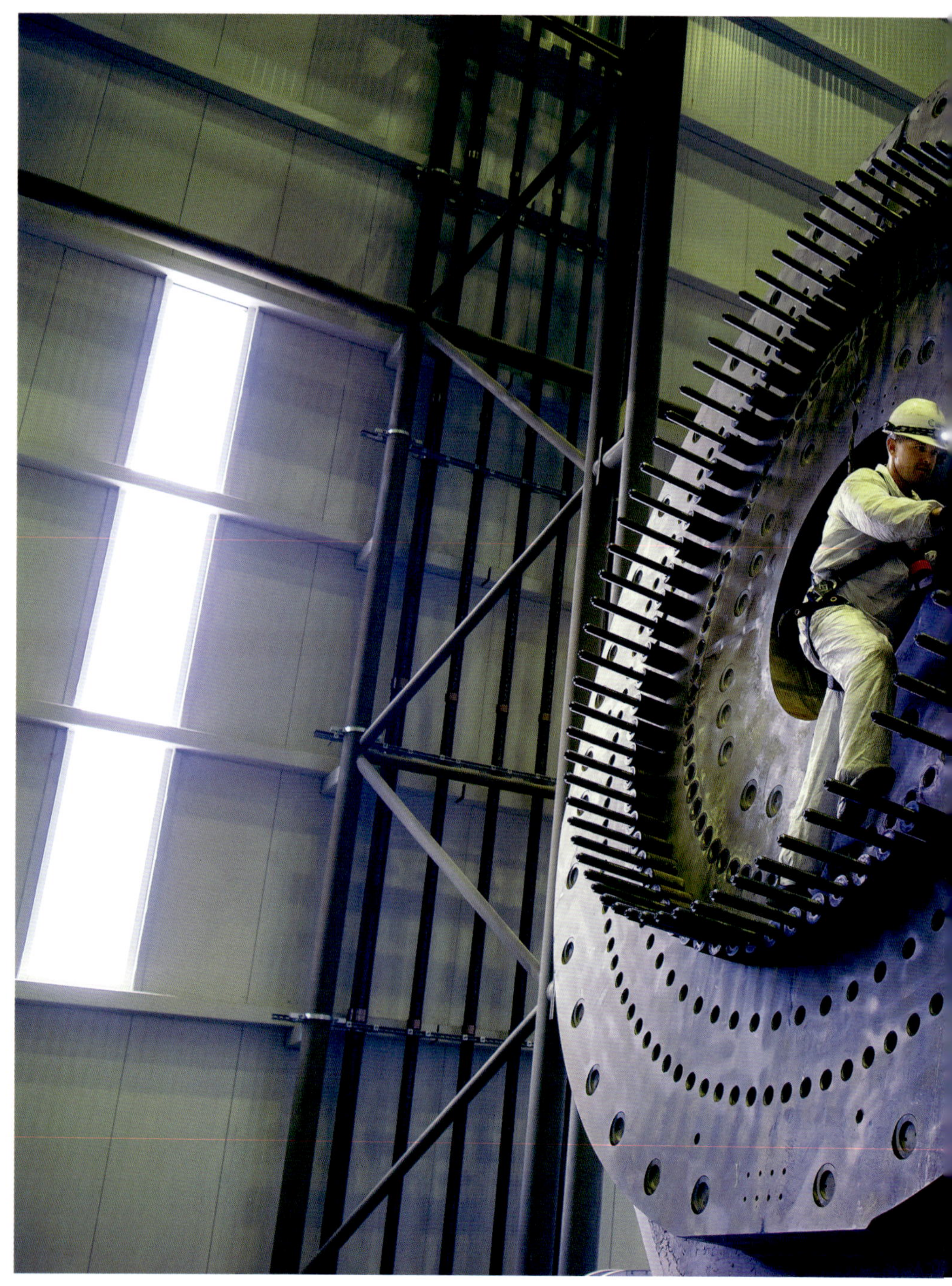

Lornie Thomas Wind Testing Technology Center > Boston, Massachusetts

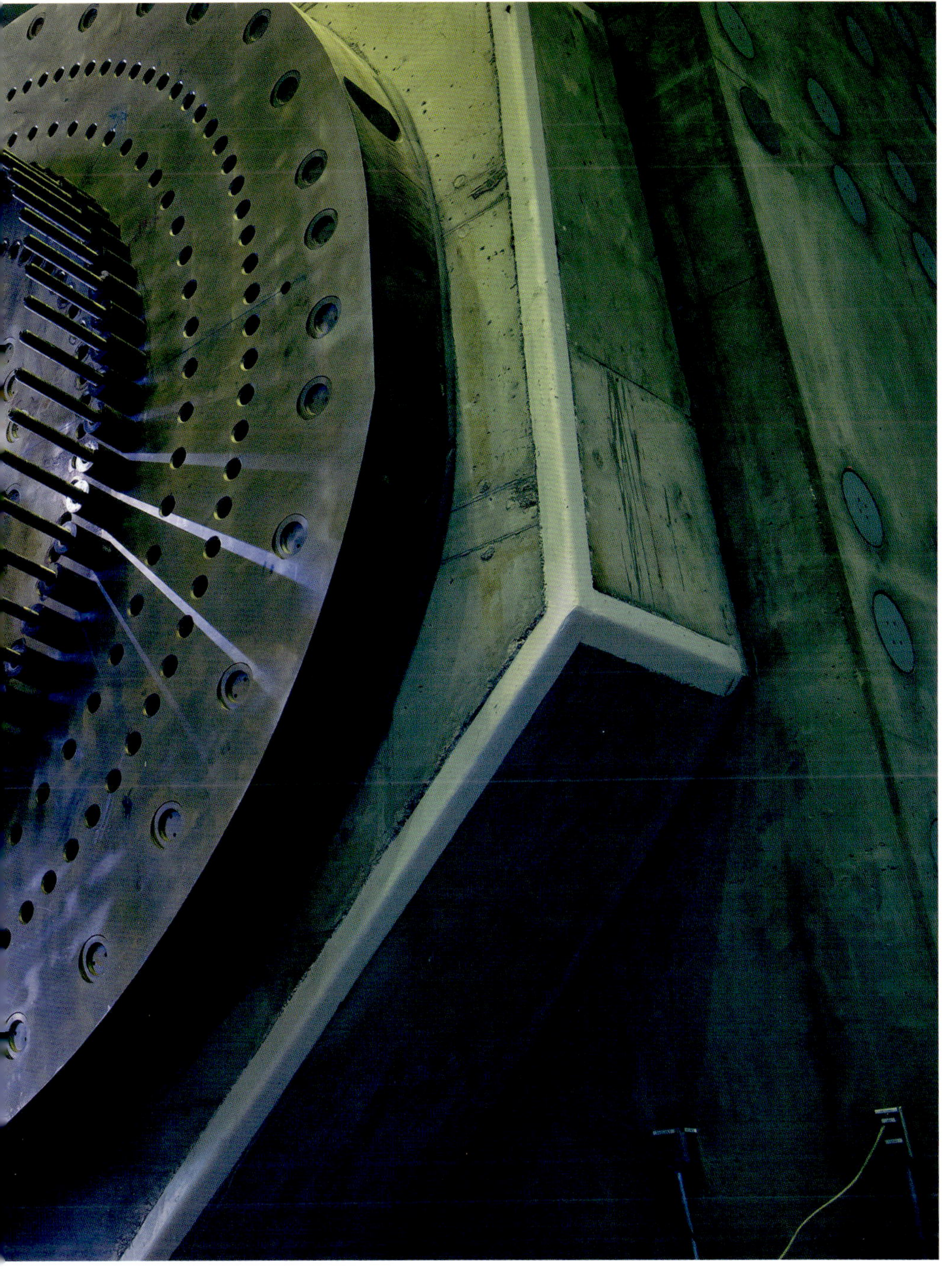

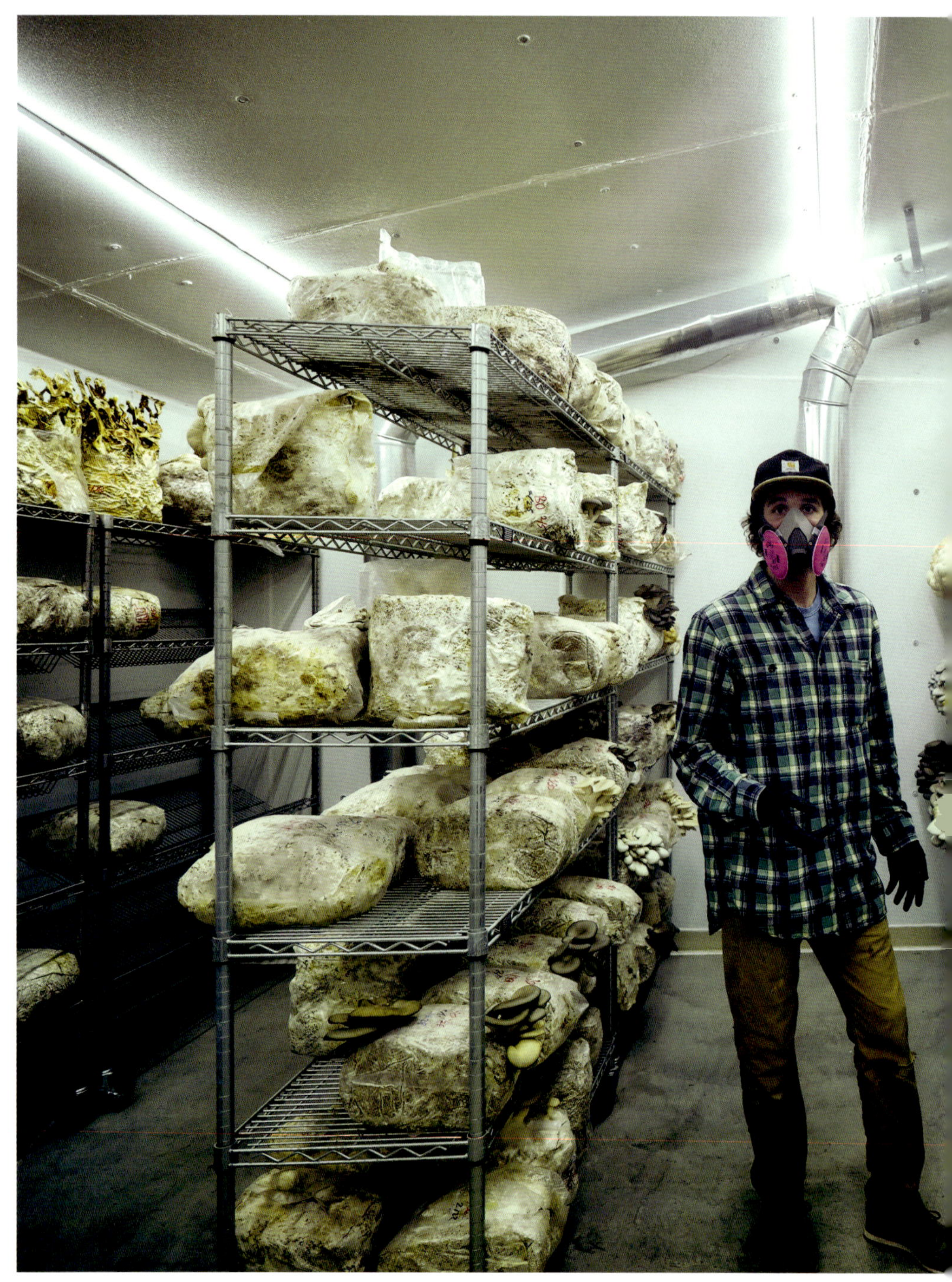

Benjamin Deuling Mushroom Farmer, Spore Attic > Bozeman, Montana

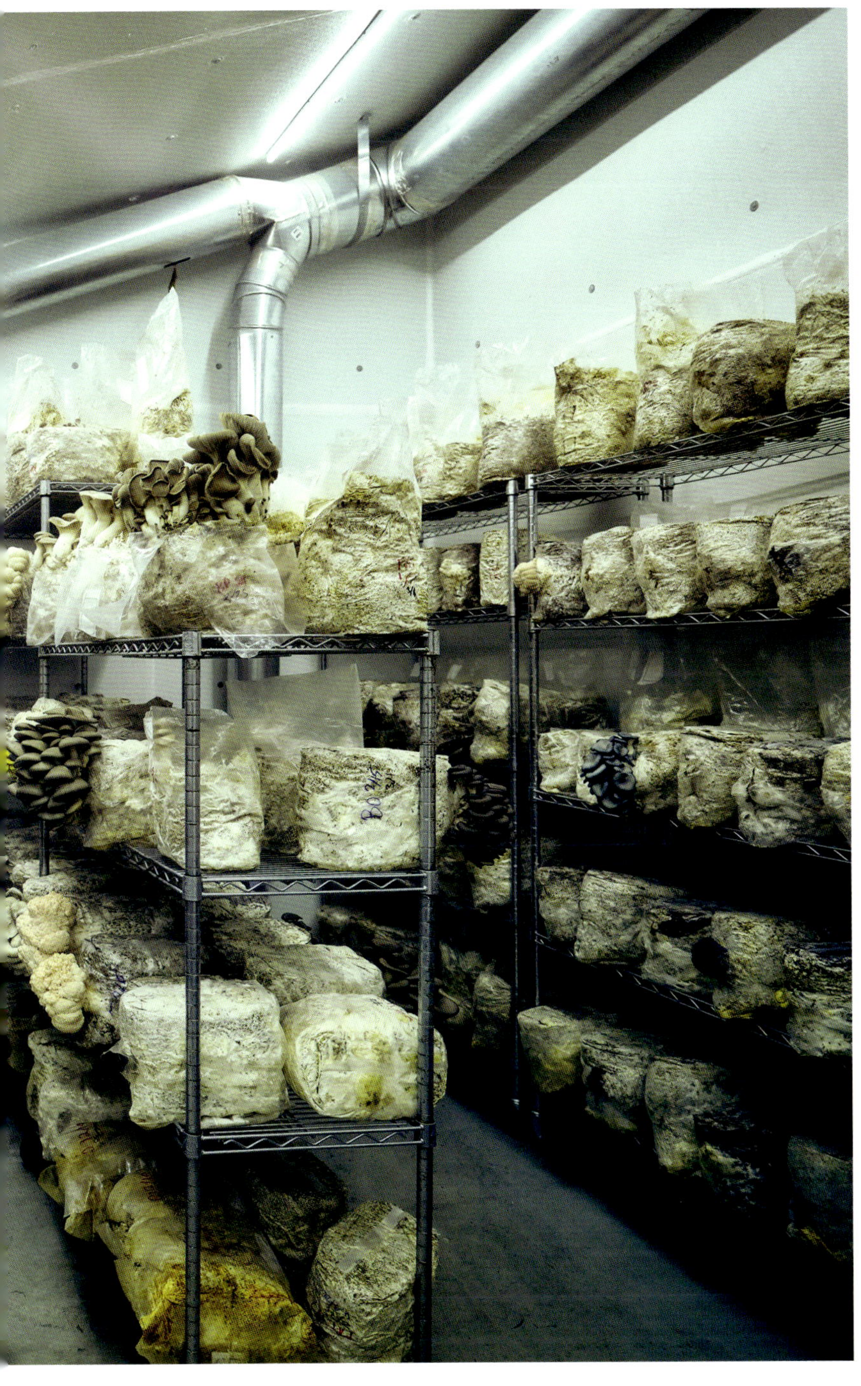

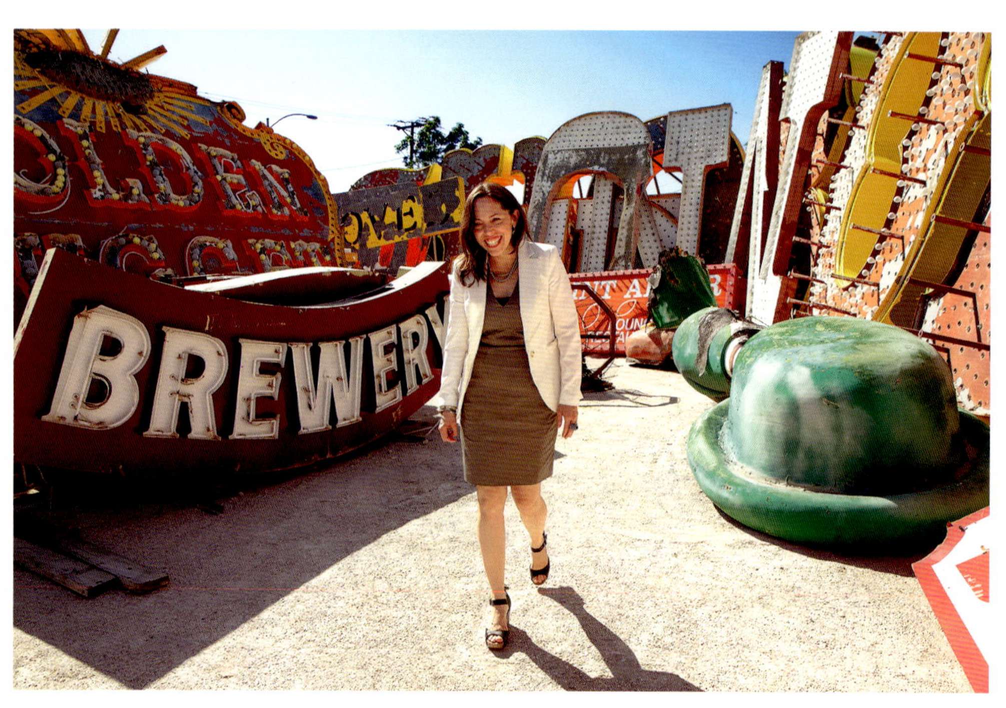

Danielle Kelly Director, Neon Museum > Las Vegas, Nevada

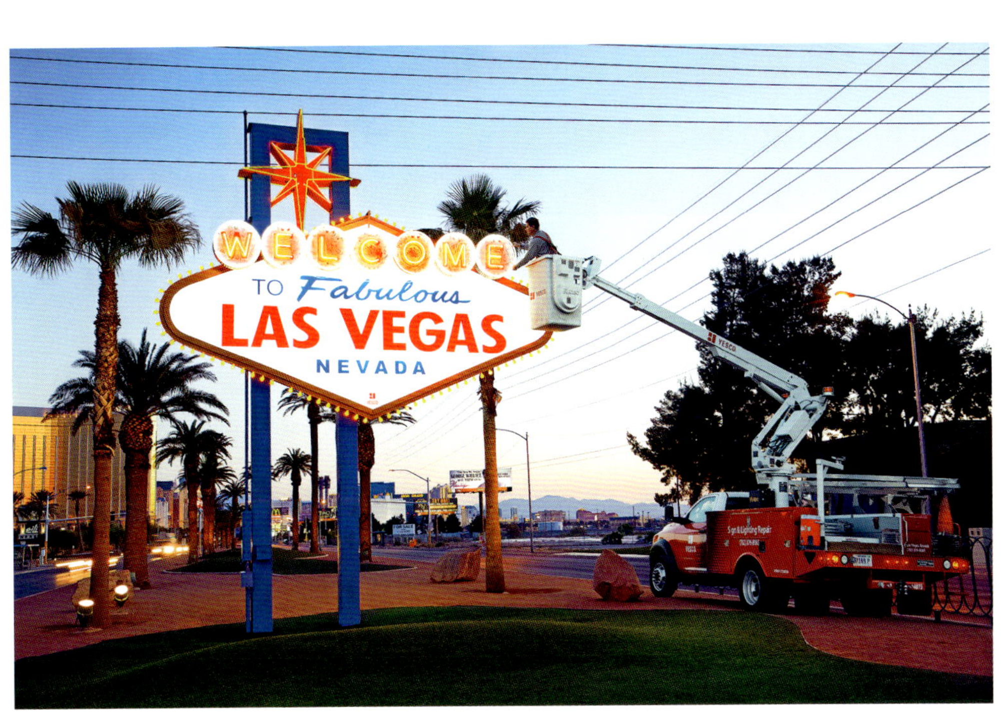

Kenny West Sign Maintenance, Welcome to Las Vegas > Las Vegas, Nevada

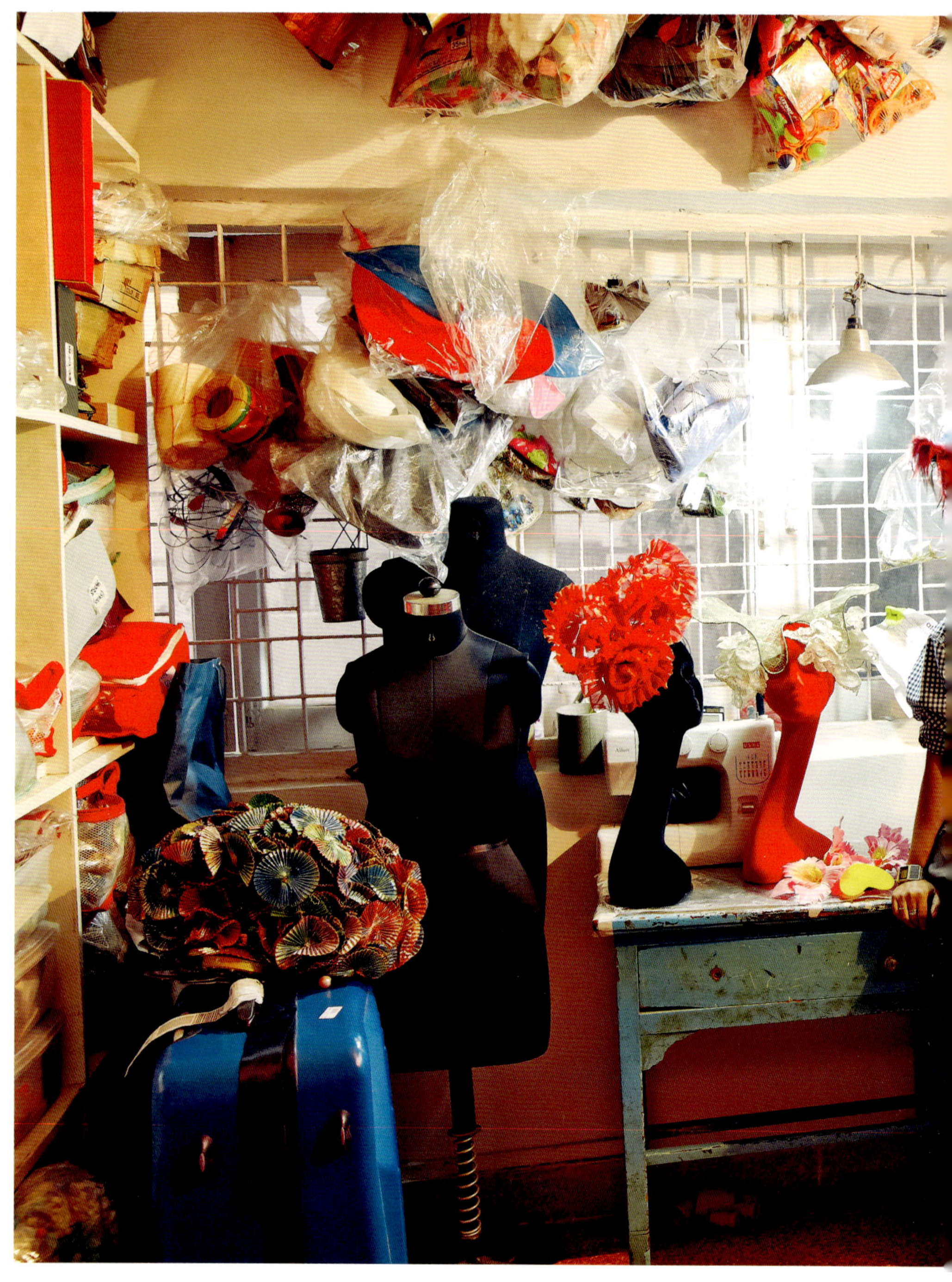

Shilpa Chavan aka Little Shilpa Hat Designer > Mumbai, India

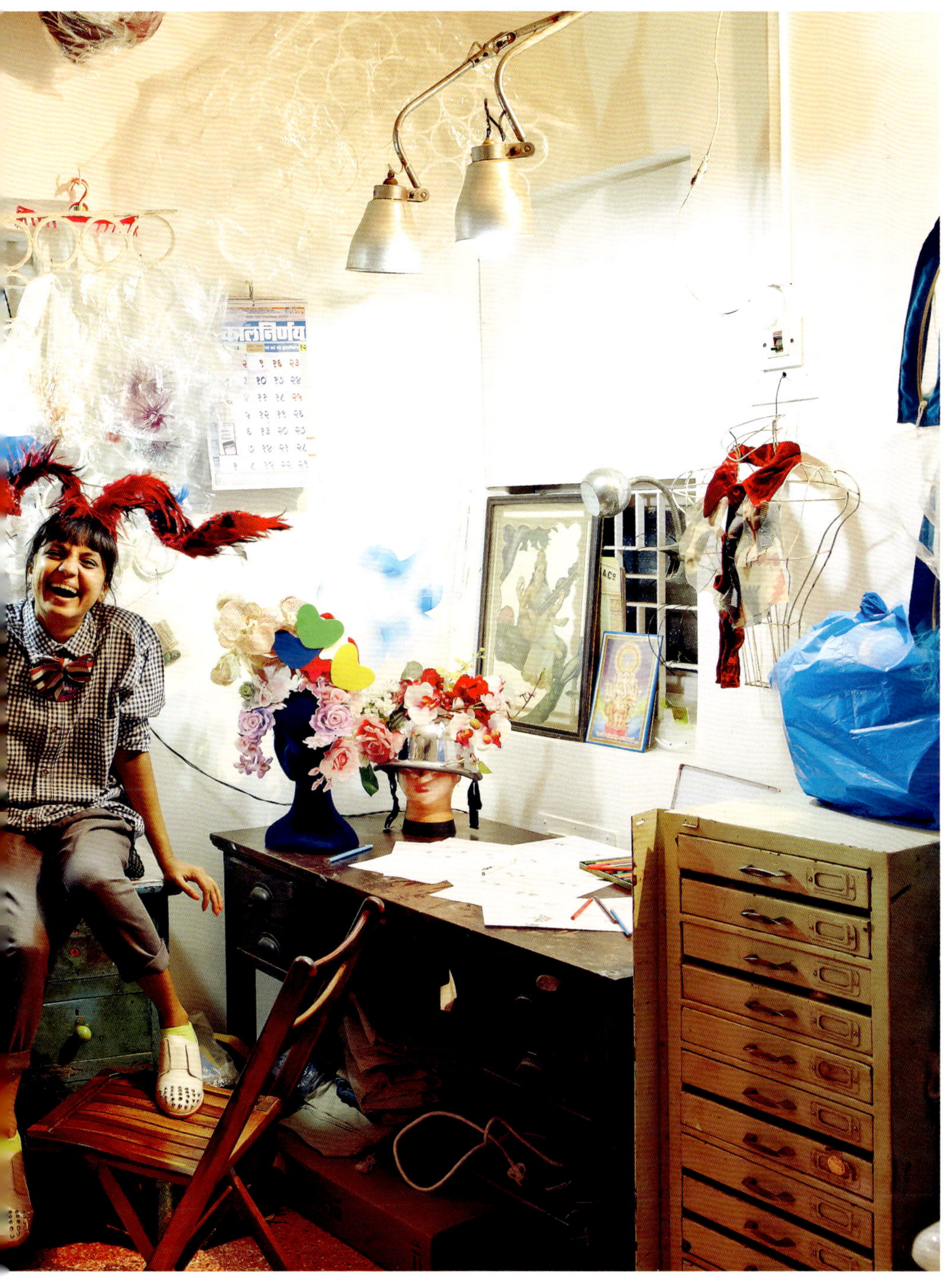

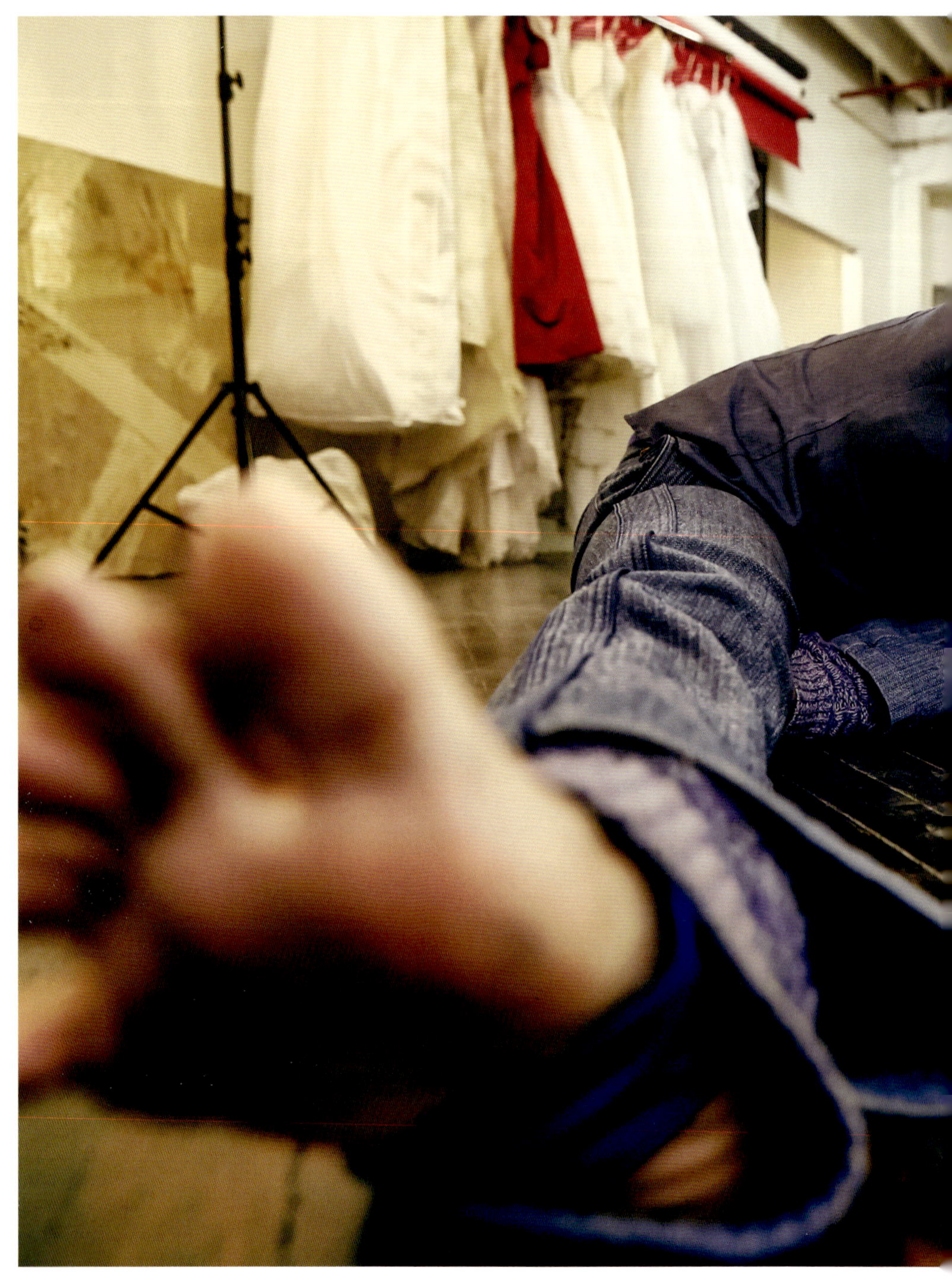

Stacy Patrice Photographer > Chicago, Illinois

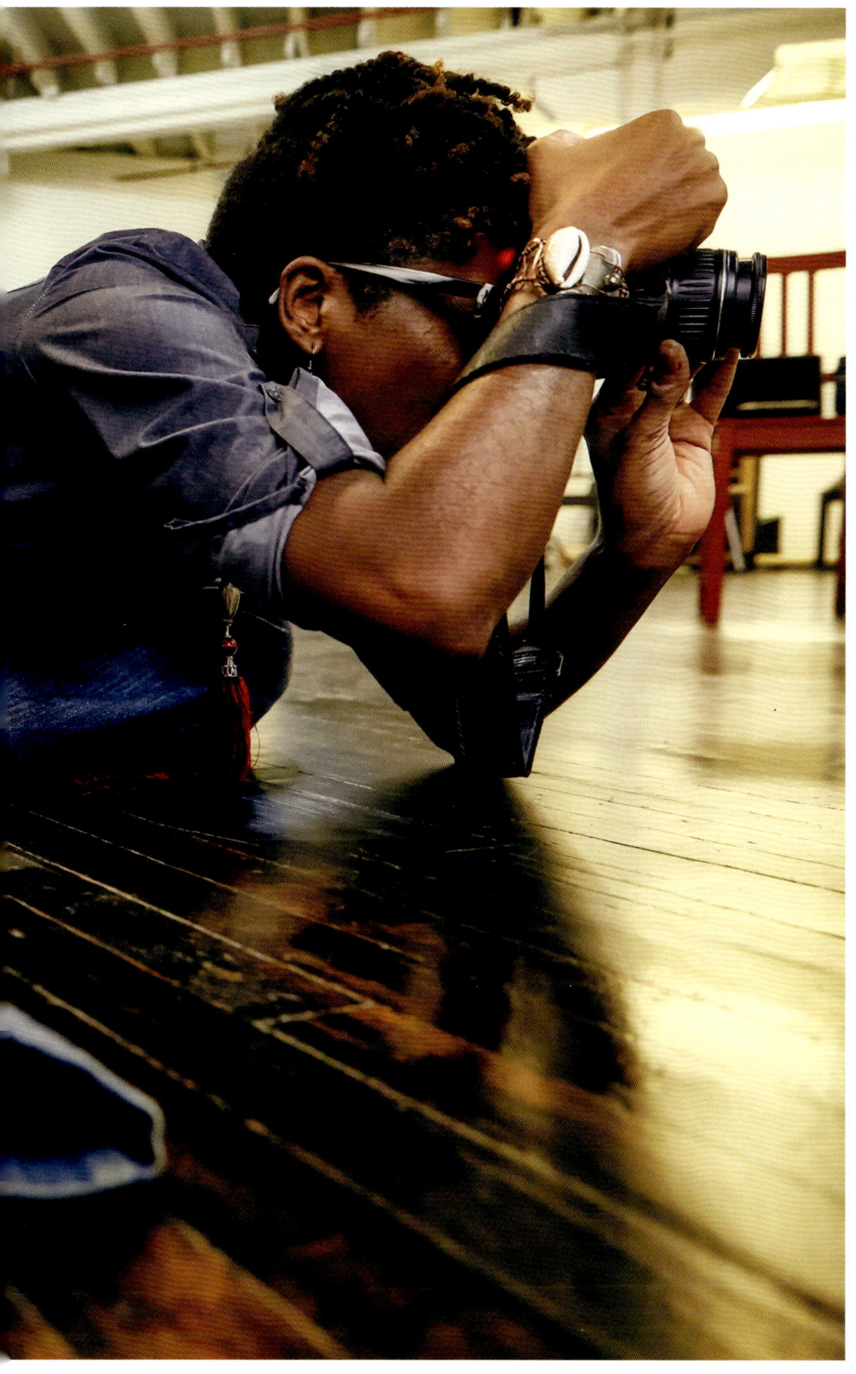

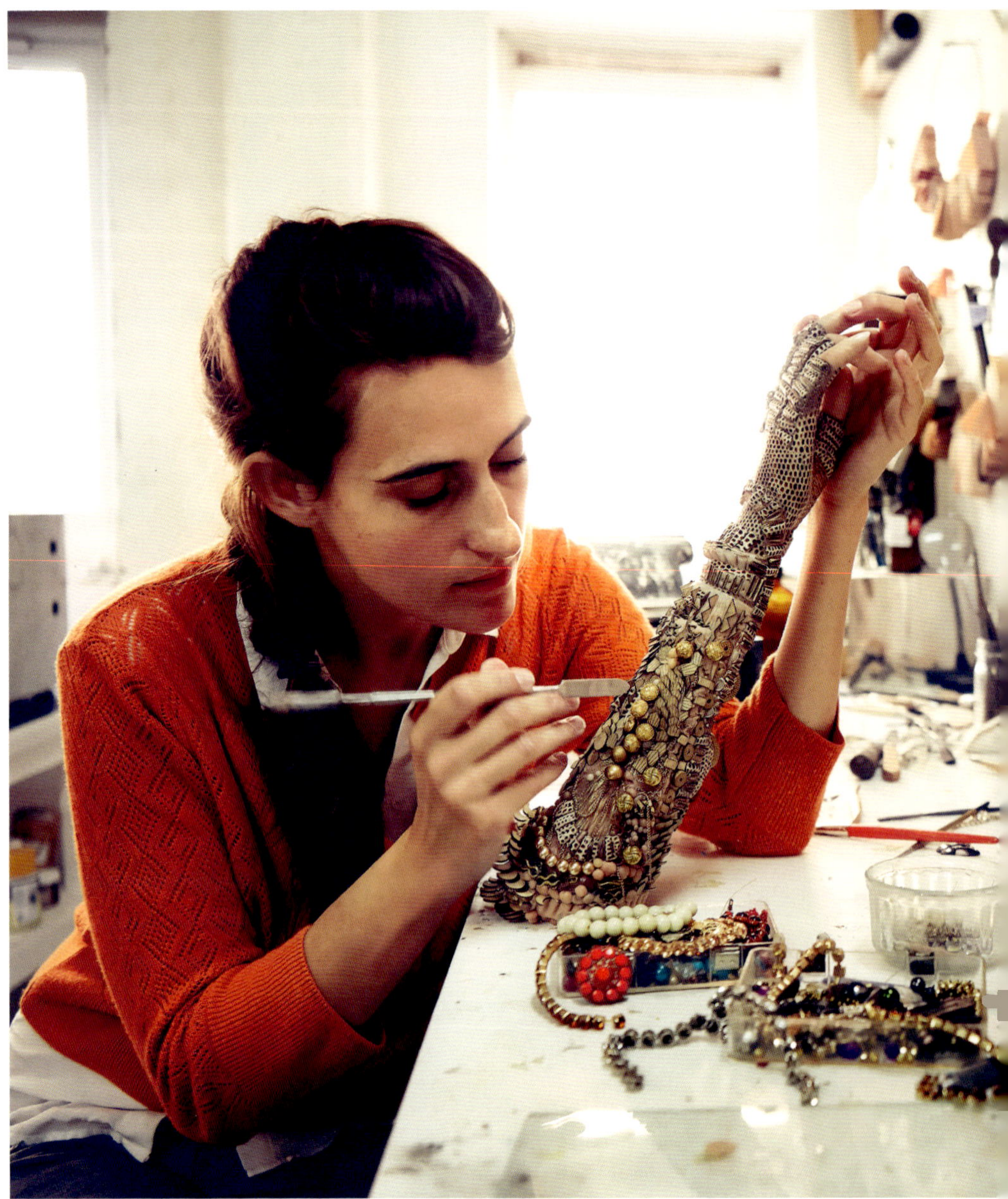

Sophie loves collaborating with her clients. She understands that for amputees, it's about the psyche, and identity; not just the body.

One client, trying on her robotic-looking leg with a skirt for the first time, dug how hot she looked. Another found that a realistic leg gave her the breathing space she needed to process her experience on her own time. And for some clients, a fantastic, alternative

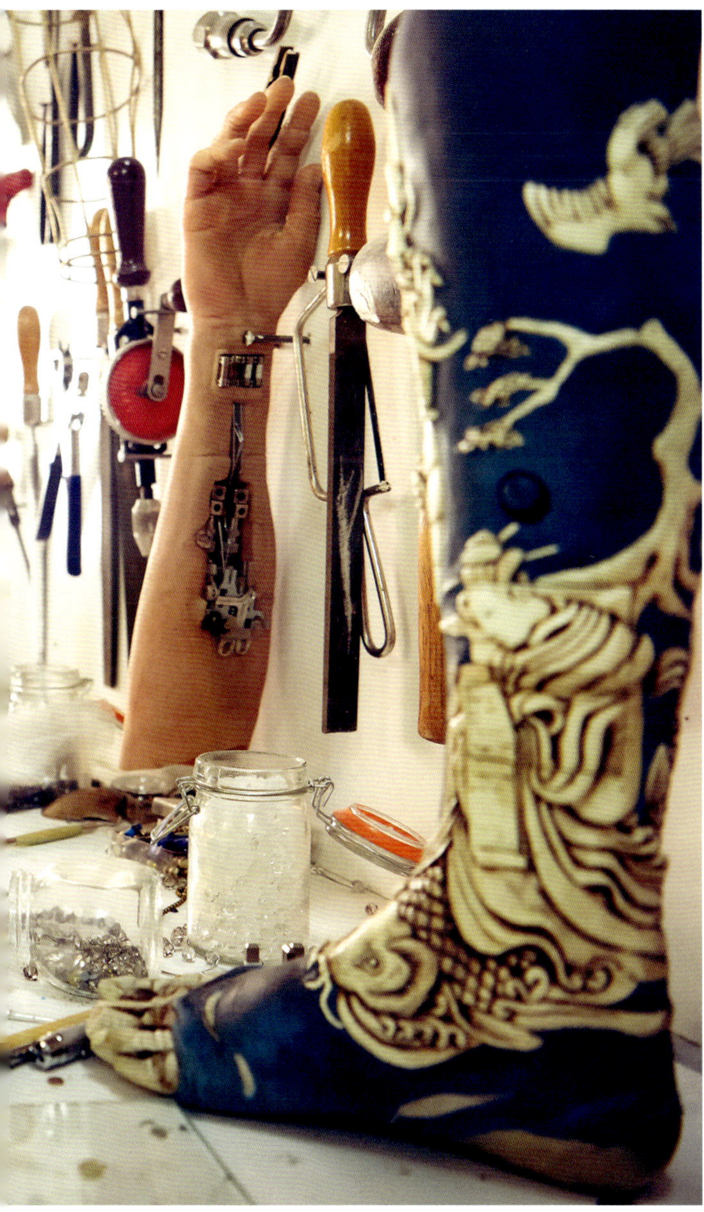

limb can be an act of defiance, a way of saying, "You want something to look at? Here it is."

Sophie's art protects their right to be seen for who they are, not for what they have lost.

Sophie de Oliveira Barata Prosthetic Limb Designer, Alternative Limb Project > London, England

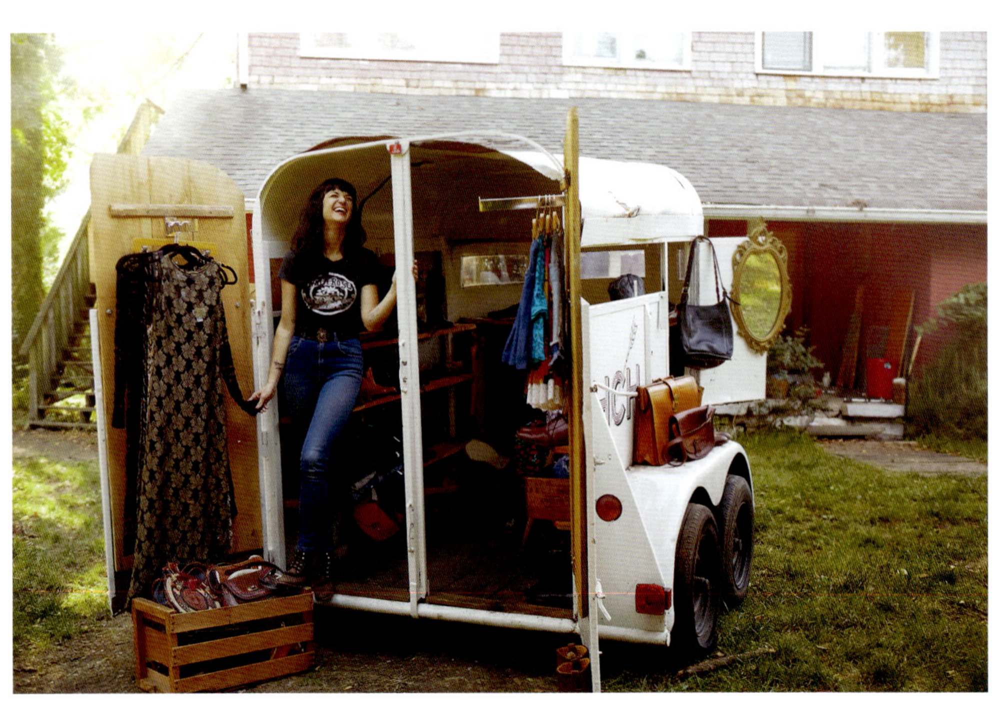

Nikki Lane High Class Hillbilly Vintage > Nashville, Tennessee

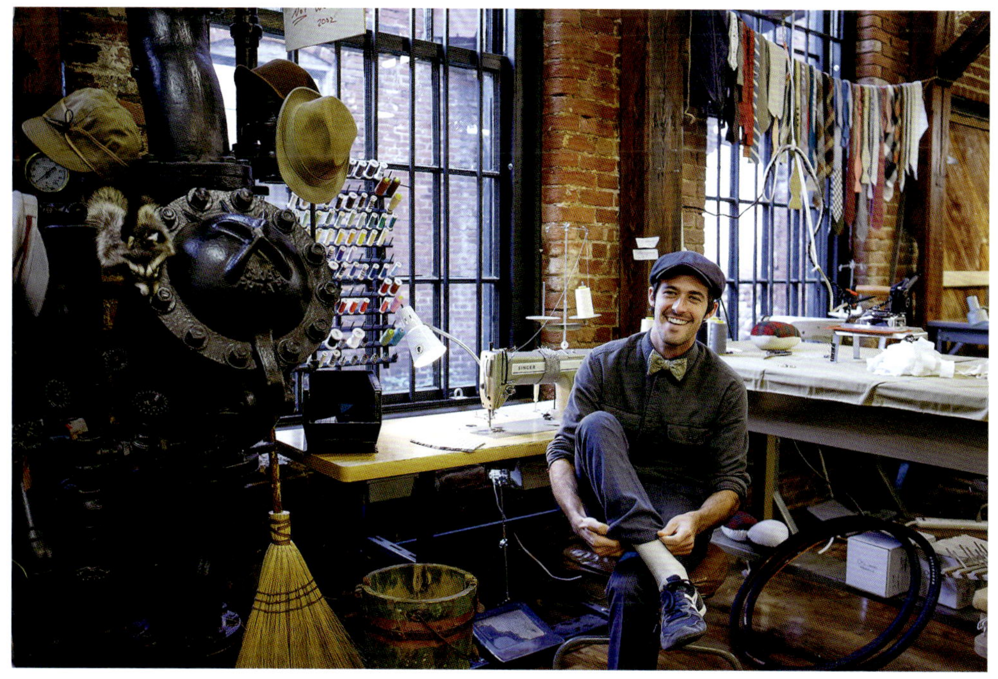

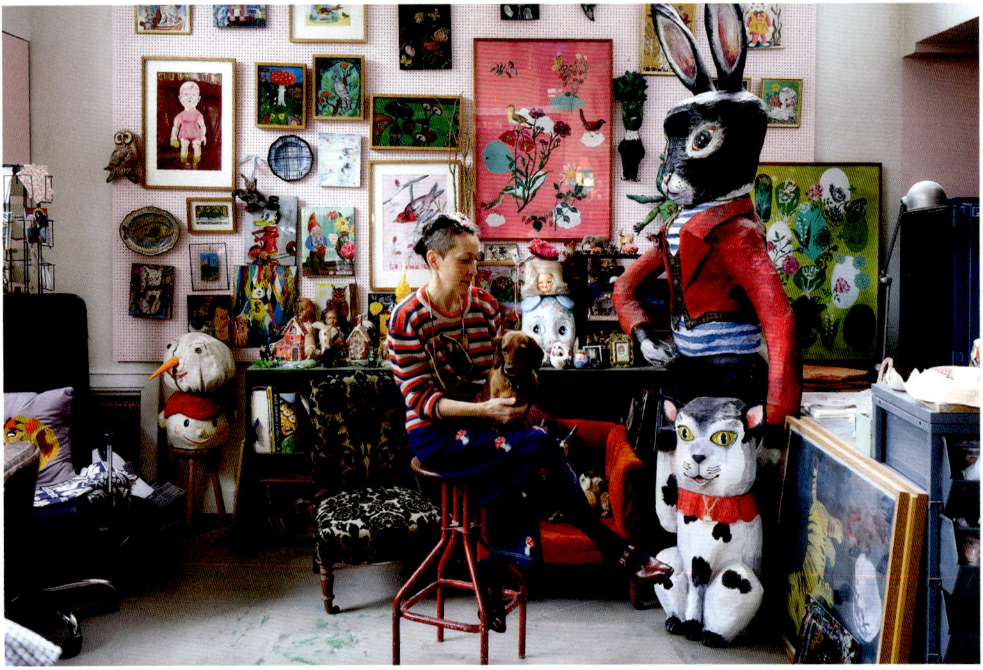

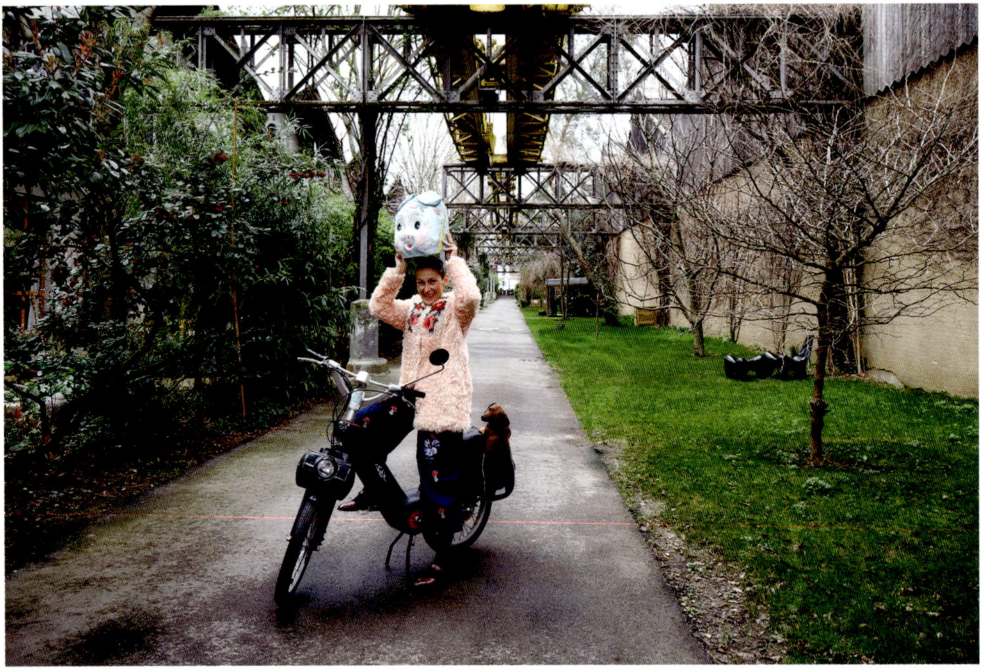

Nathalie Lété Artist and Designer > Paris, France

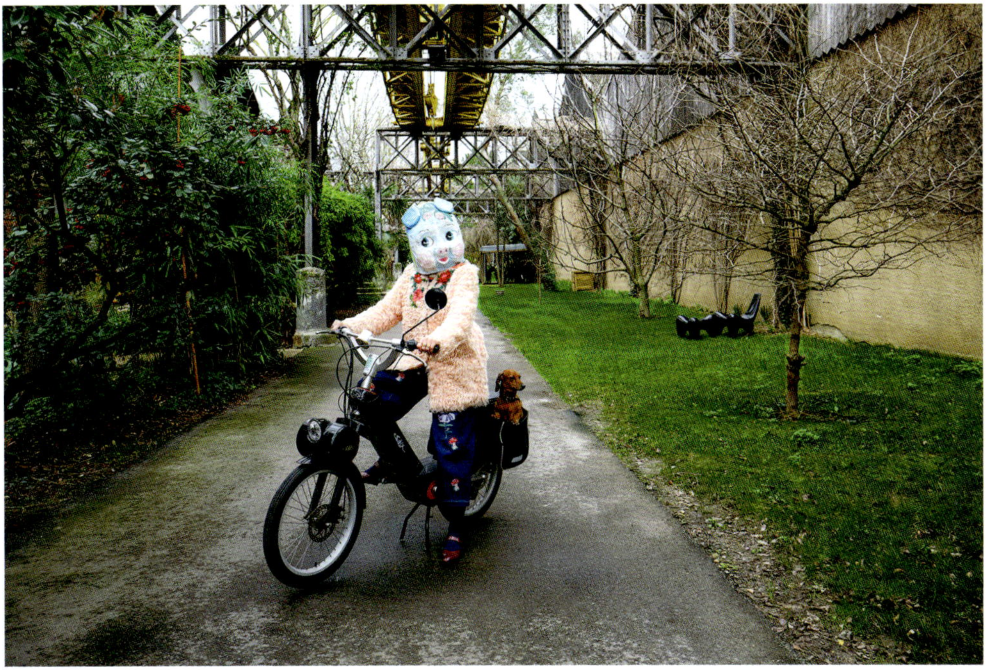

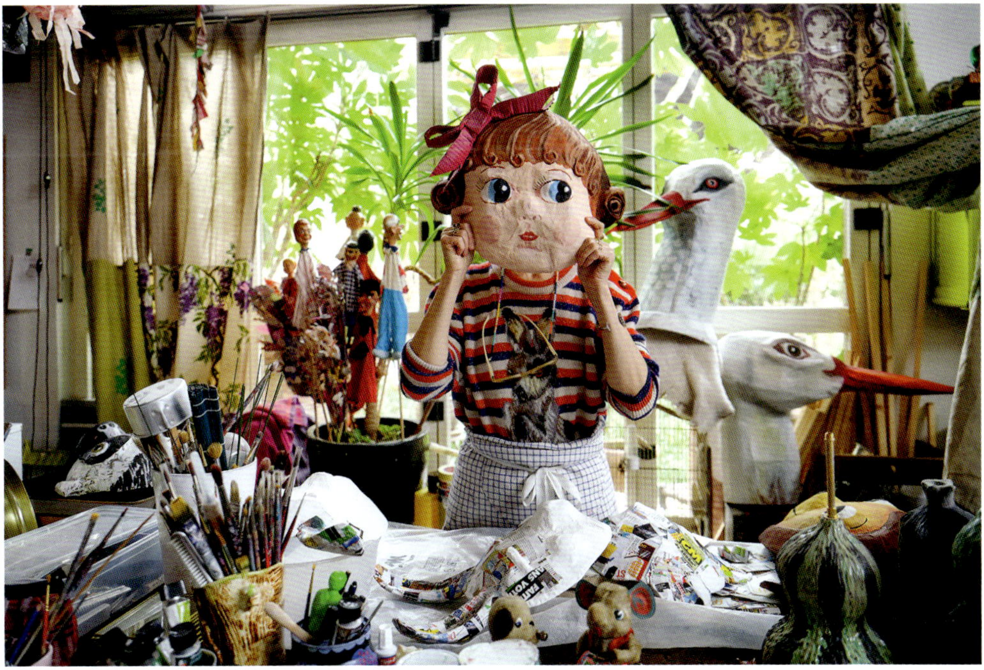

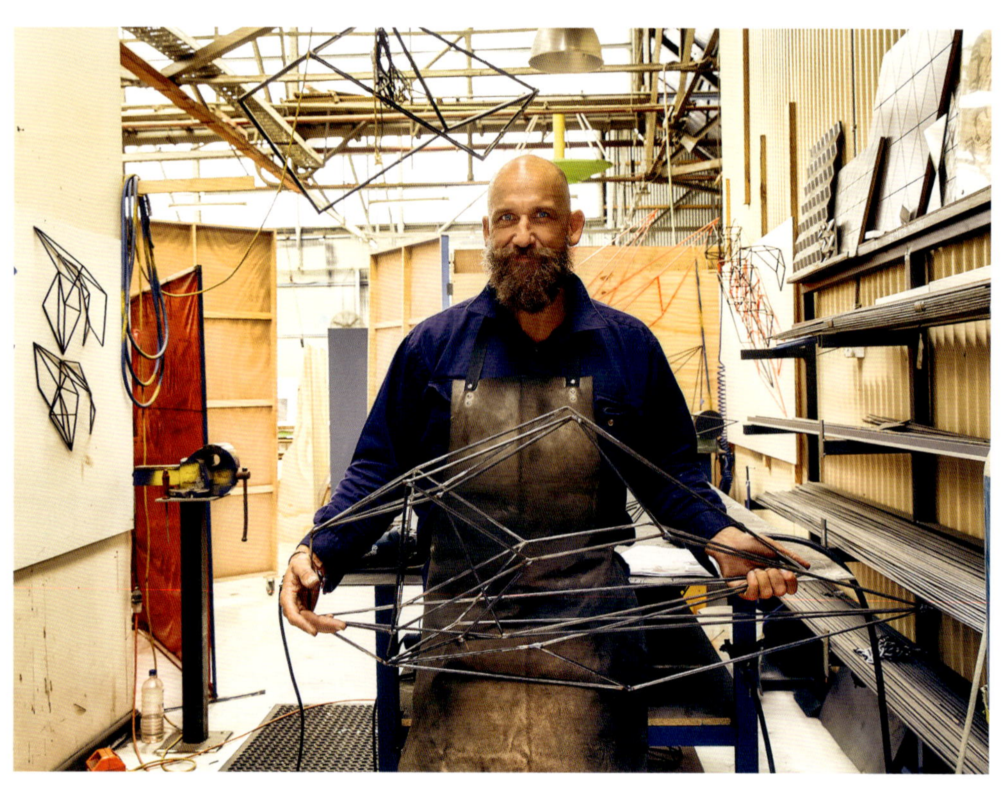

Dion Hortsmans Artist > Sydney, Australia

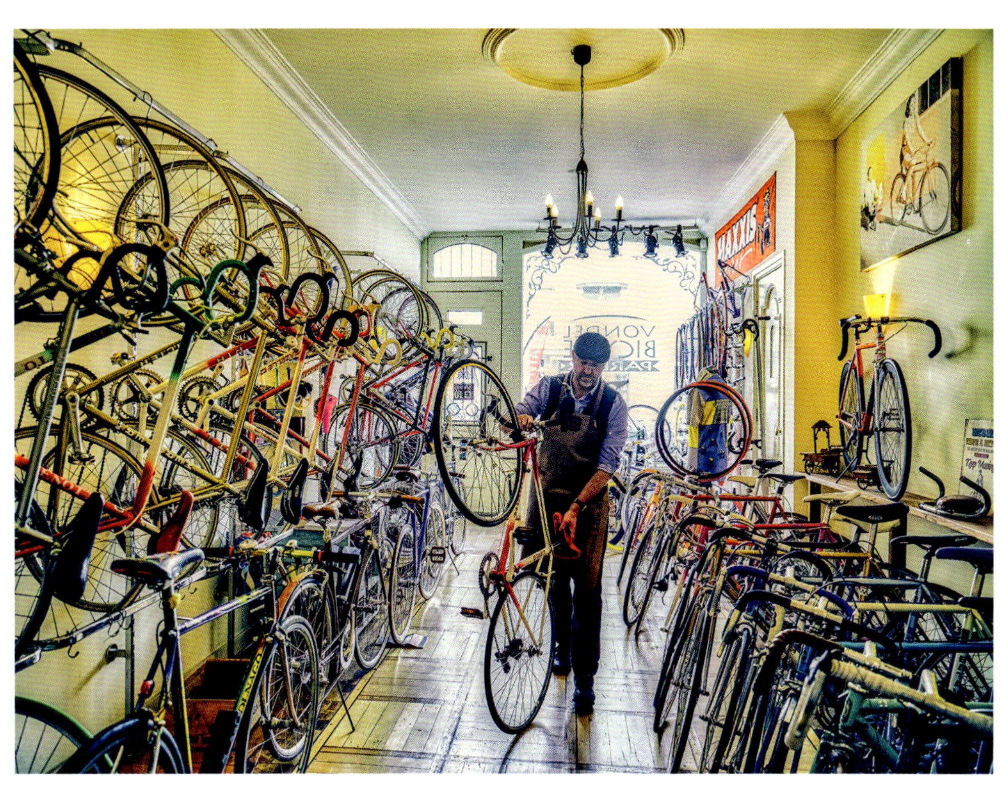

Alex Ciocanel Bike Tailor, Vondel Bicycle Parlor > Amsterdam, Netherlands

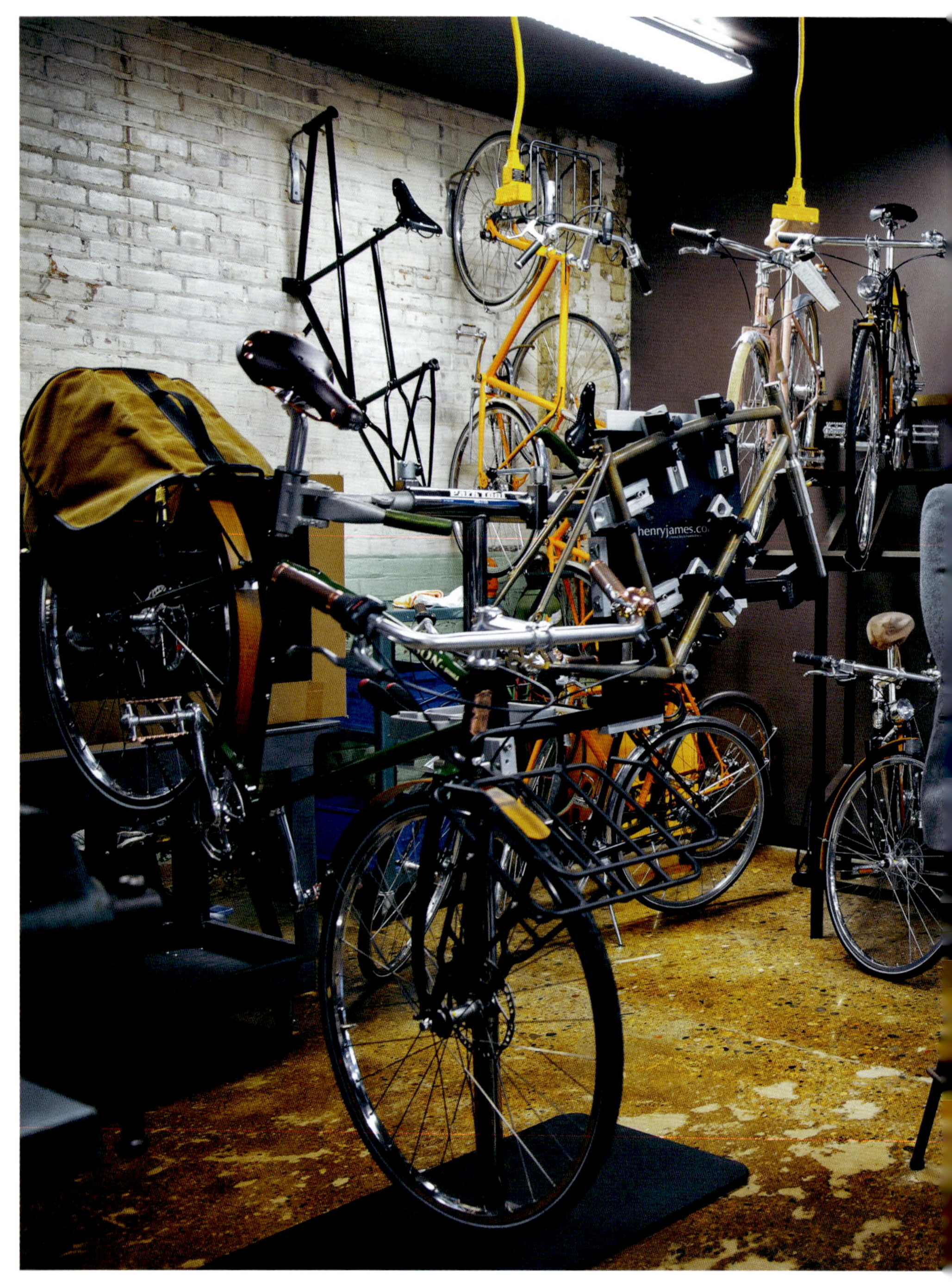

Daniel Caudill Creative Director, Shinola > Detroit, Michigan

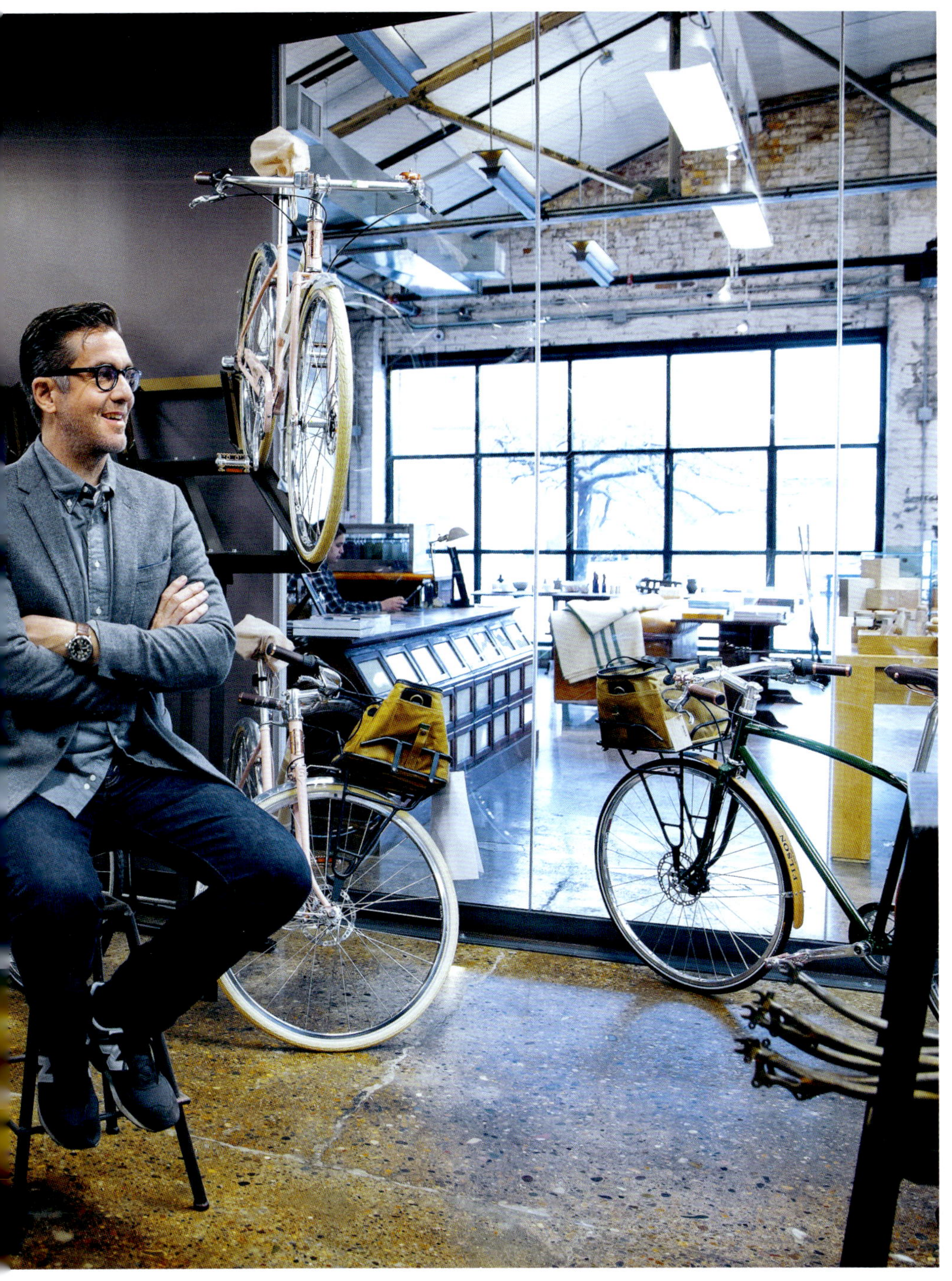

FILSON

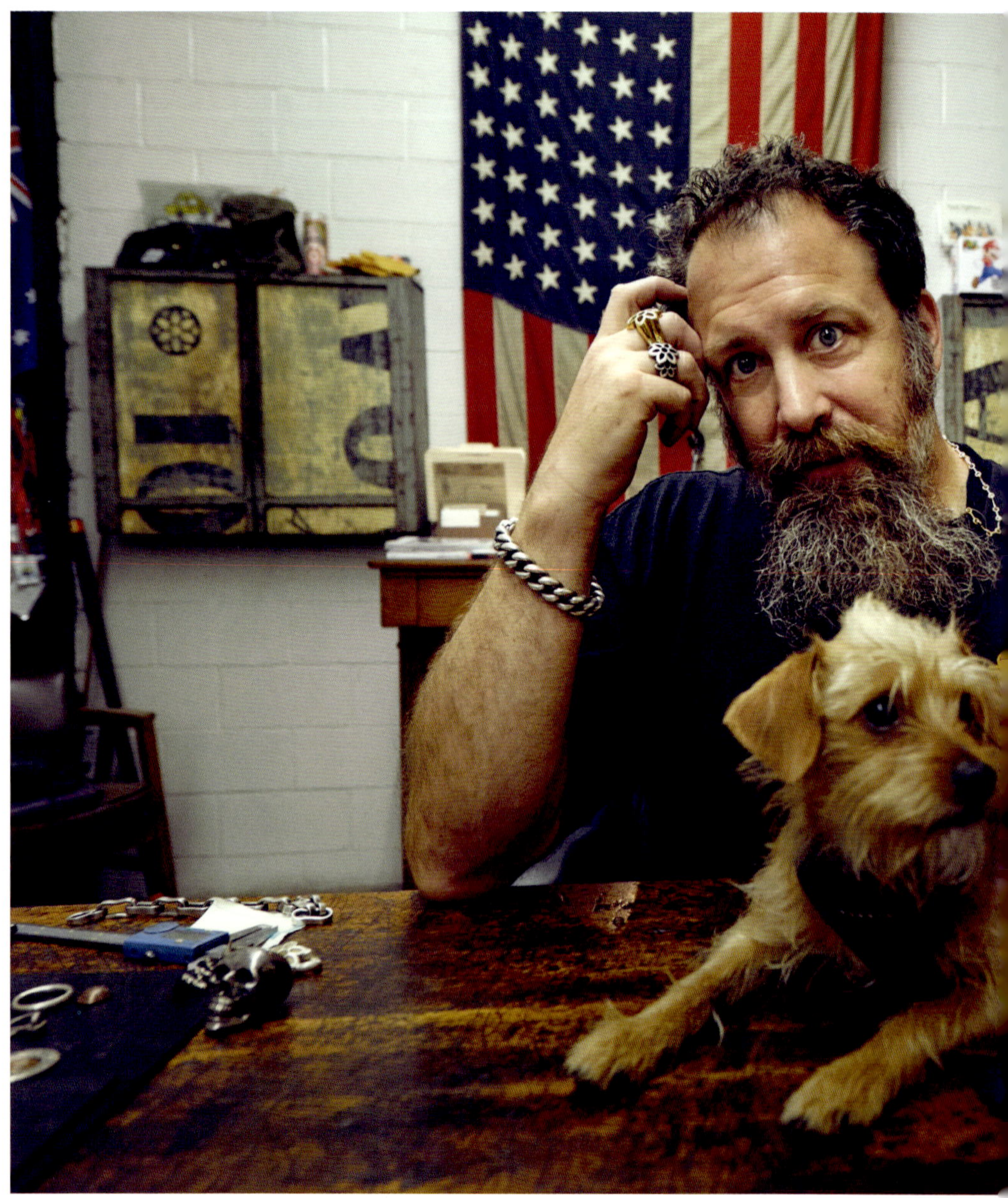

"Come on by, brother," Josh said to me the day that I called him out of the blue.

Meeting him was not part of my "official" *At Work* journey. I had wanted to have a piece of jewelry made to celebrate surviving my bike crash. But the way he said "brother" went straight to my heart. For me, it's not affectation. The word says to me, "If you need me, I'm here. I've got you."

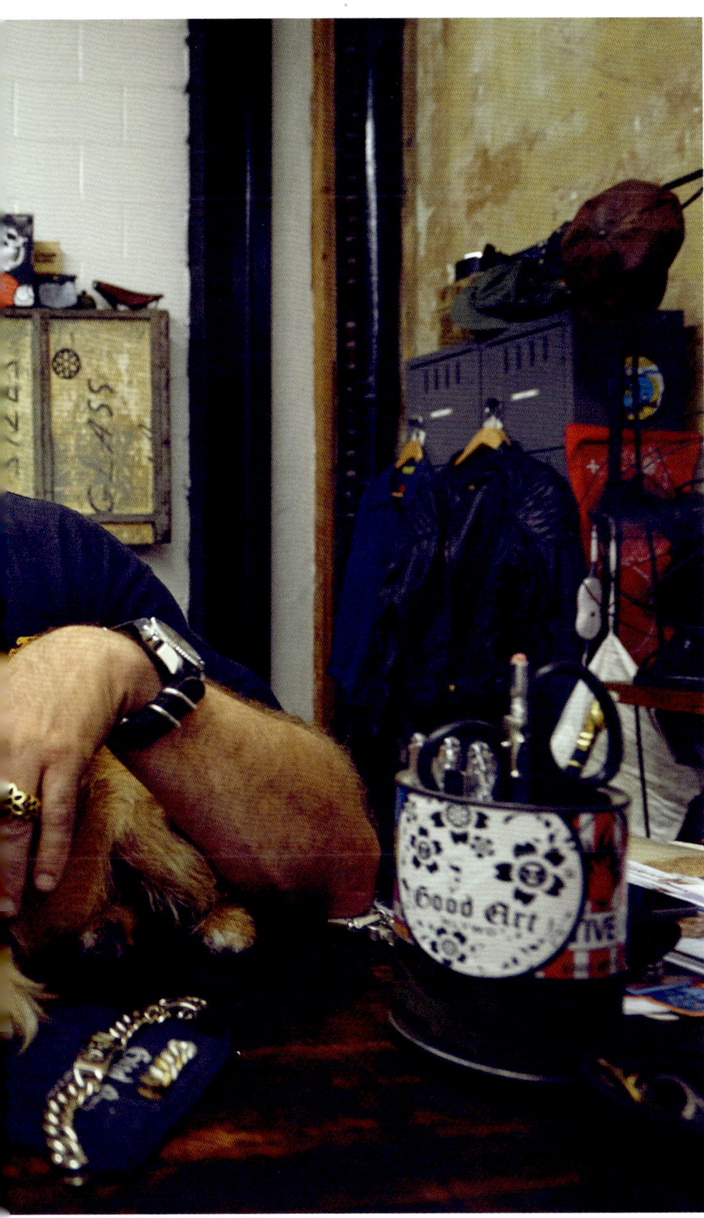

And that's how he made me feel. We talked for what felt like ages. About the skull
I wanted made to express the beauty of life and death, and plenty of other things.
We haven't spoken in a while. Life happens. But I know that when I do turn
up, it will feel like a reunion of brothers.

Josh Warner Owner and Jewelry Designer, Good Art Hollywood > Hollywood, California

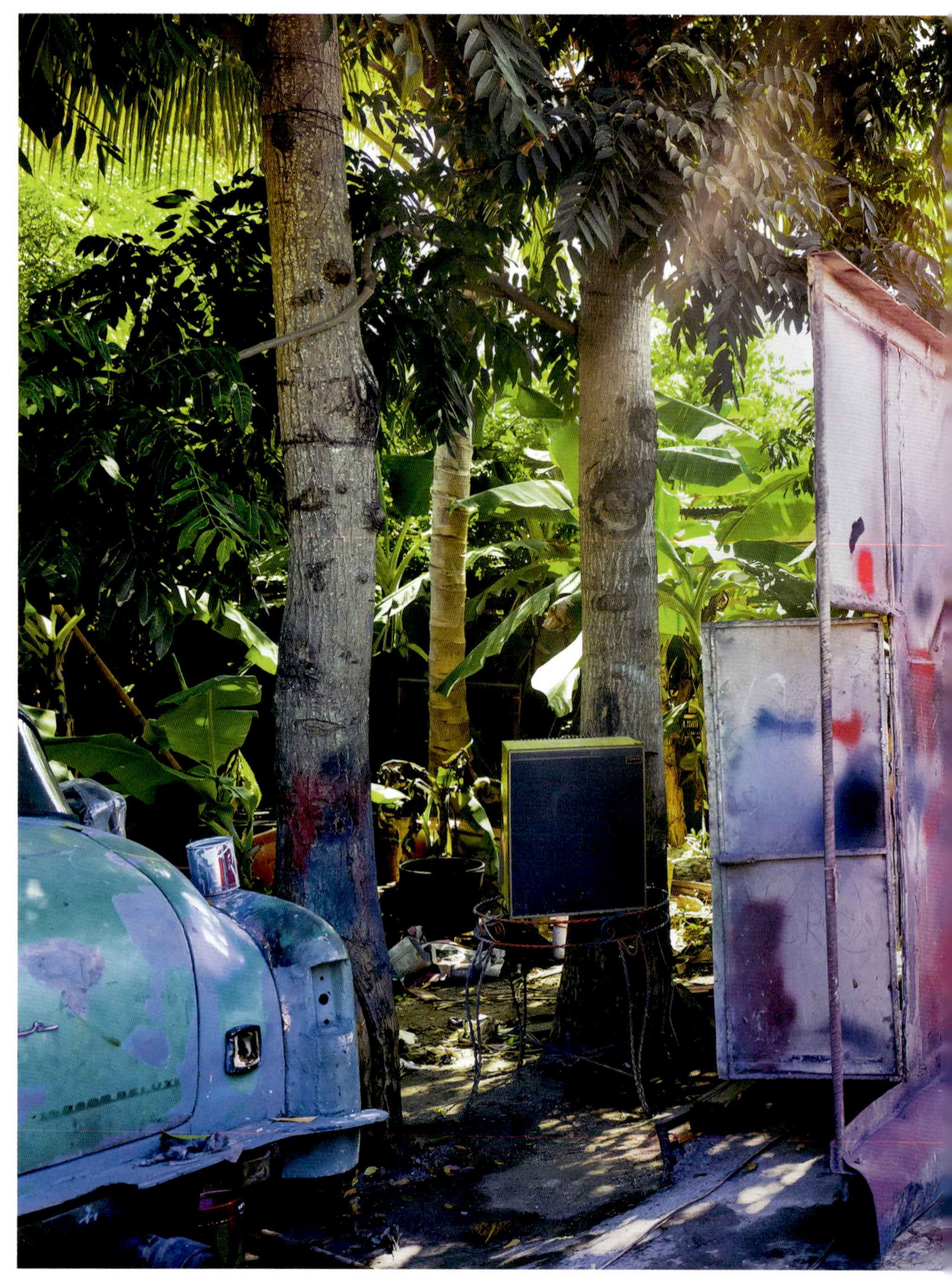

Armando Xique Antique Car Restoration > Havana, Cuba

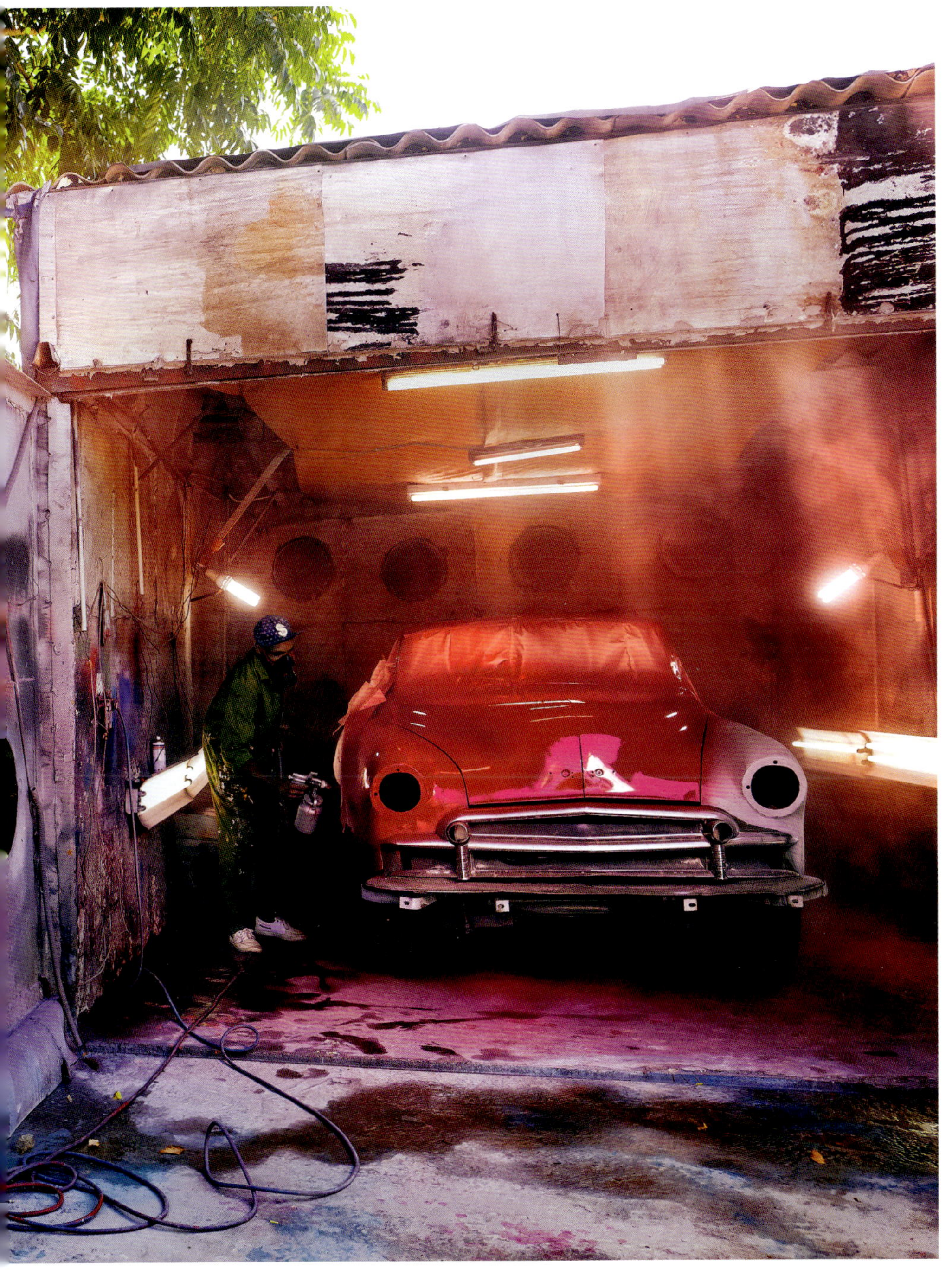

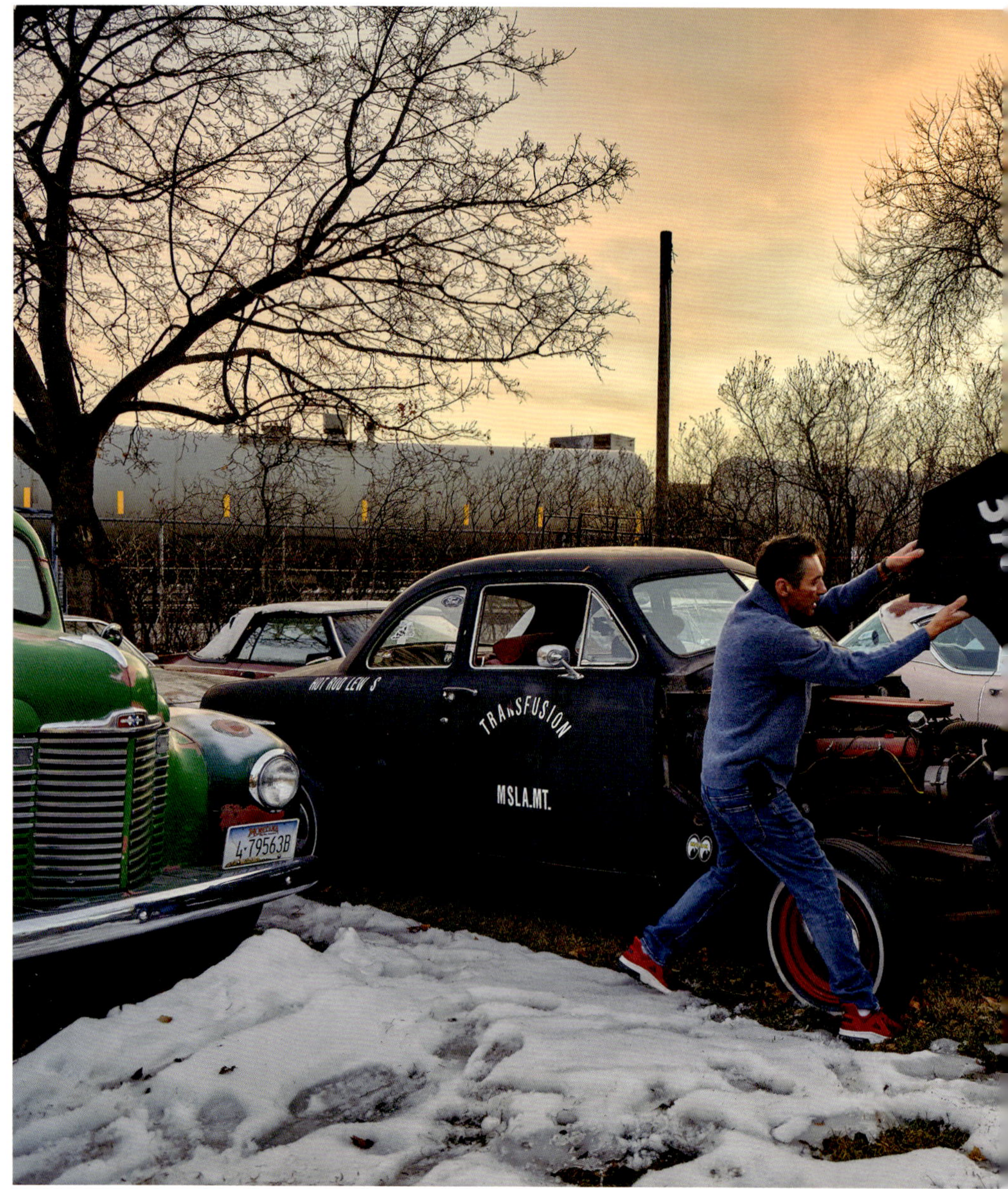

Tide had so many stories about cars to share. The ones he had loved as a child.
The ones that he had worked on as a younger man. The one he was in the process
of building for his daughter.

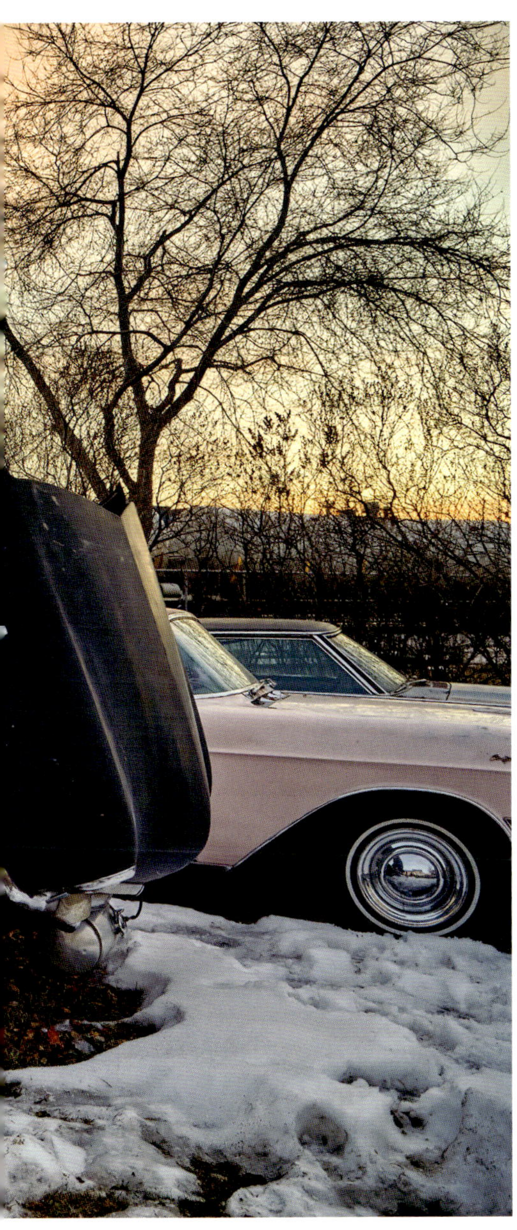

His passion was about so much more than restoring old vehicles. He was maintaining the throughline of a whole life. It stretched — like a road — back into the past, and ahead to the future.

Tide A. Aster Hot Rod Lewie > Missoula, Montana

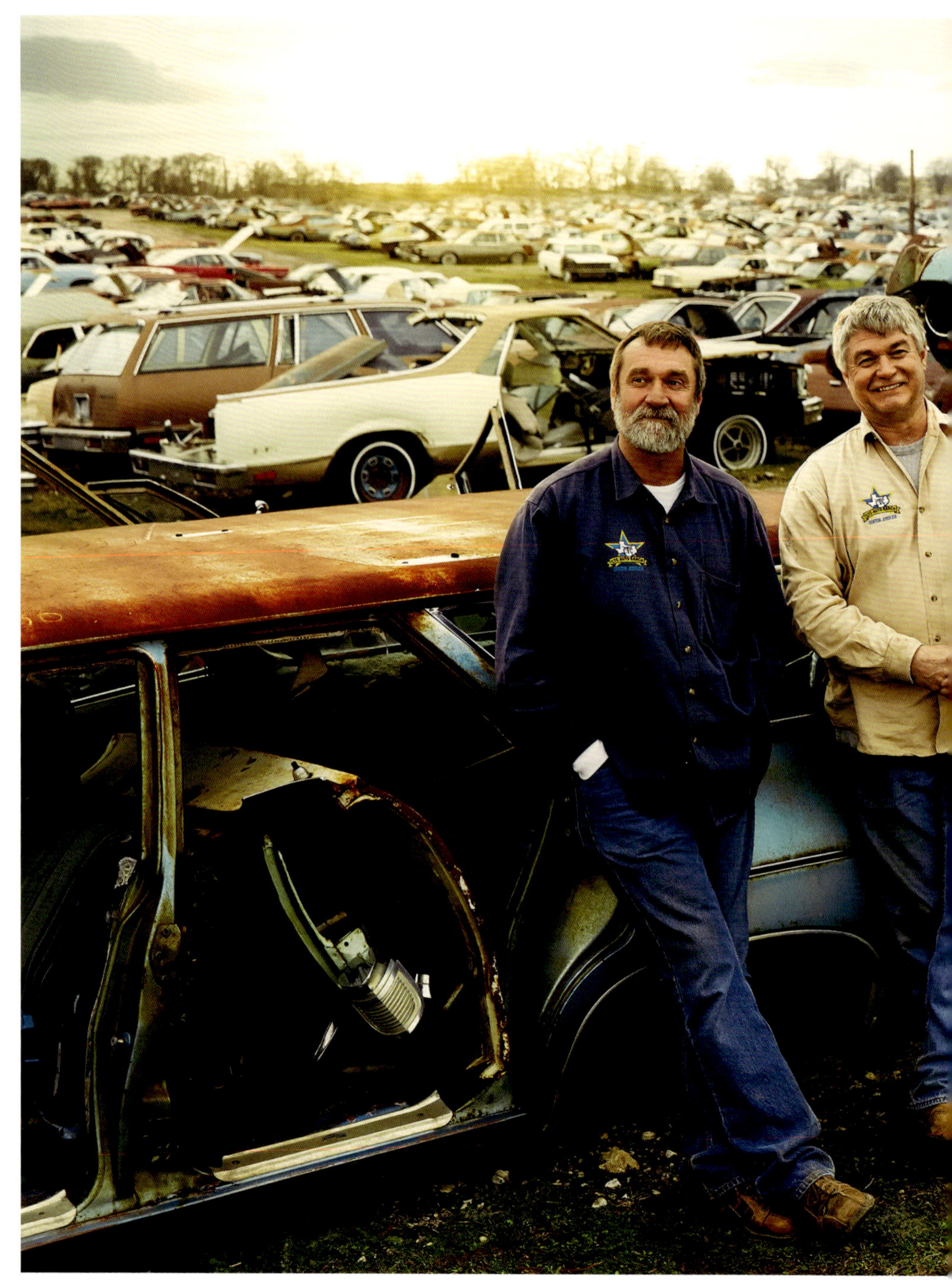

David & Allen Williamson CTC Auto Ranch > Denton County, Texas

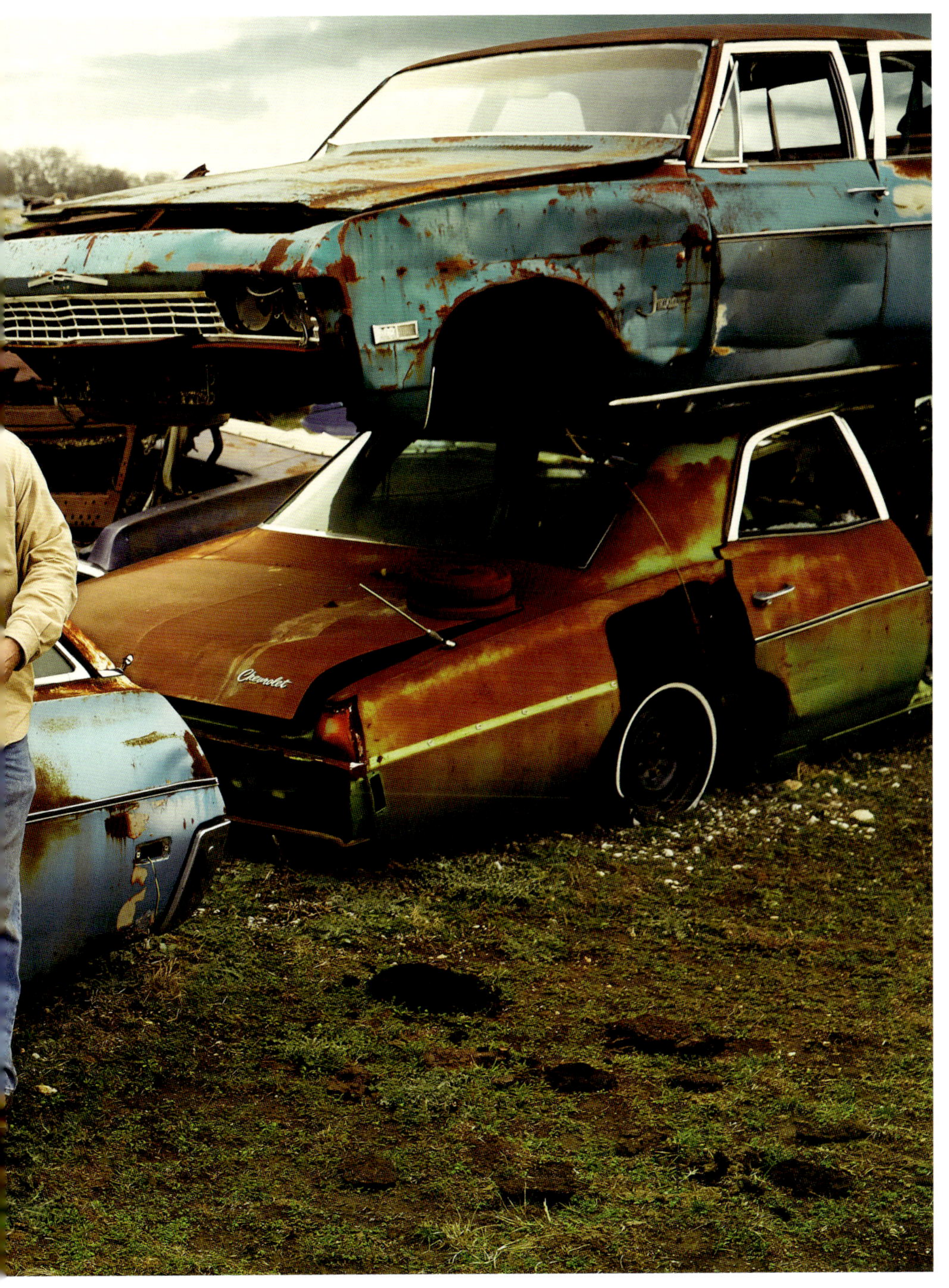

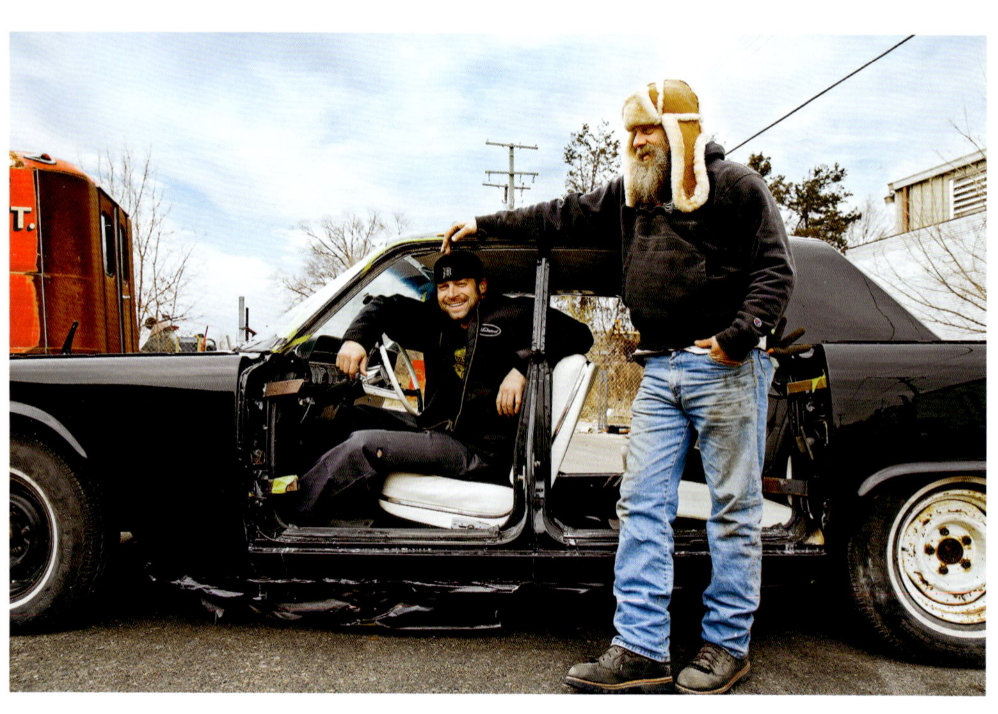

Adam Genei & Ron Coan Mob Steel Car Restoration > Detroit, Michigan

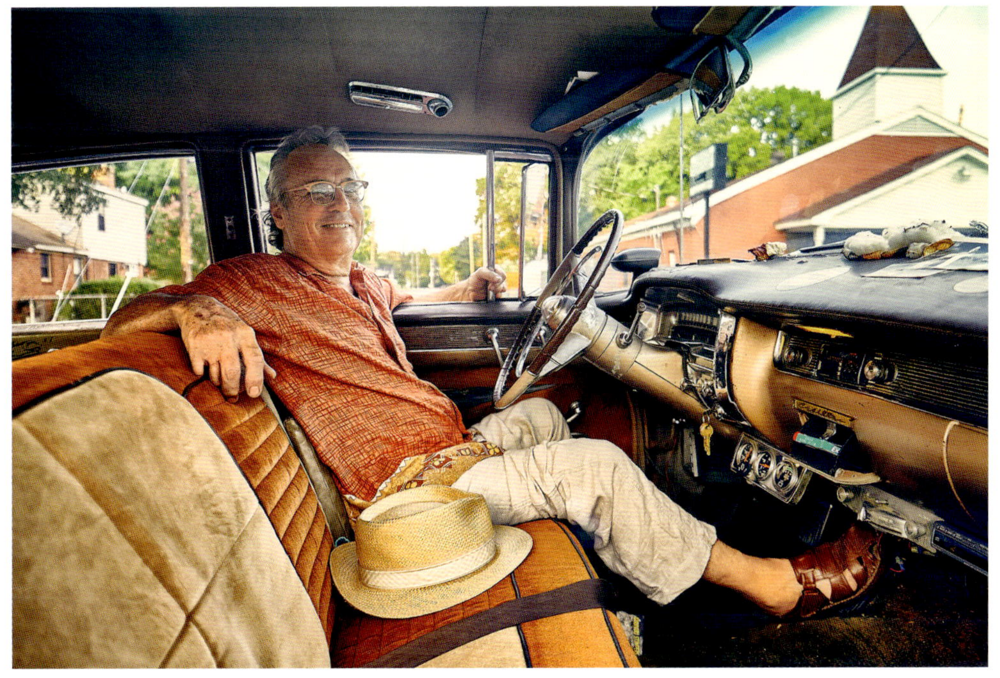

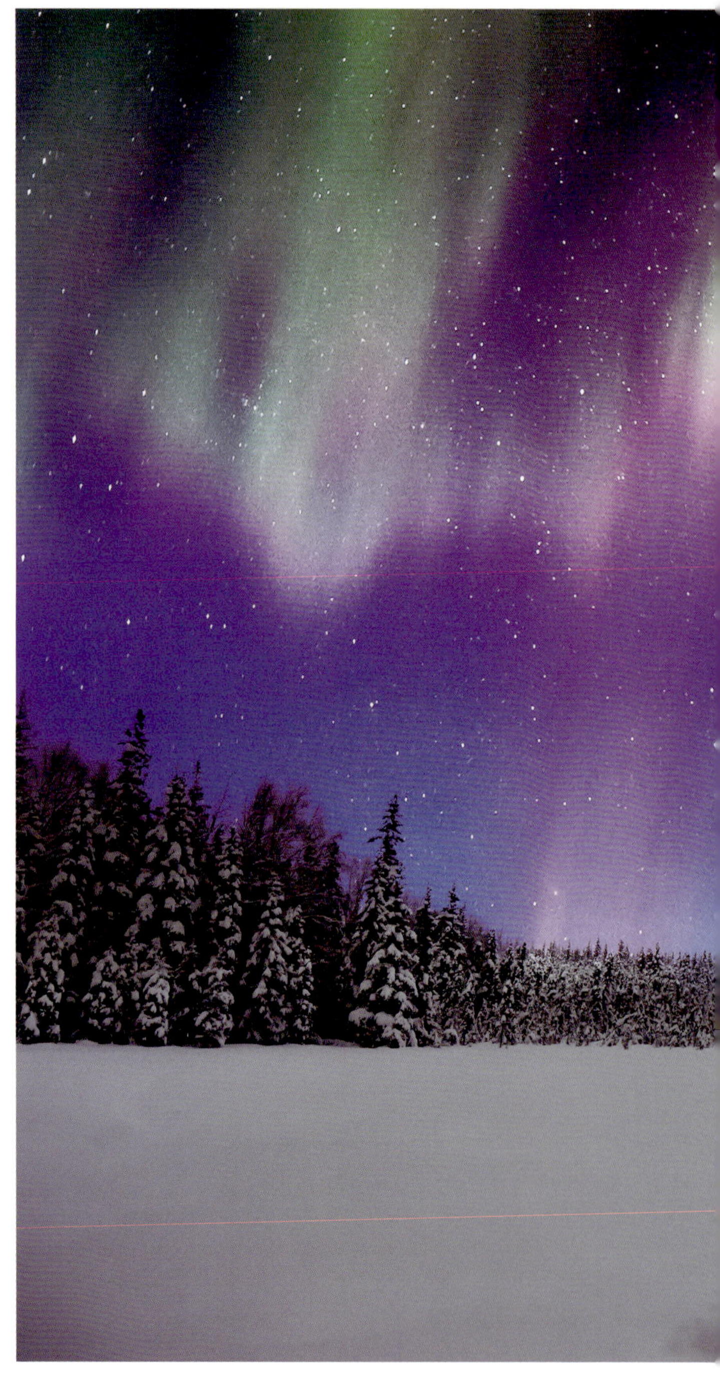

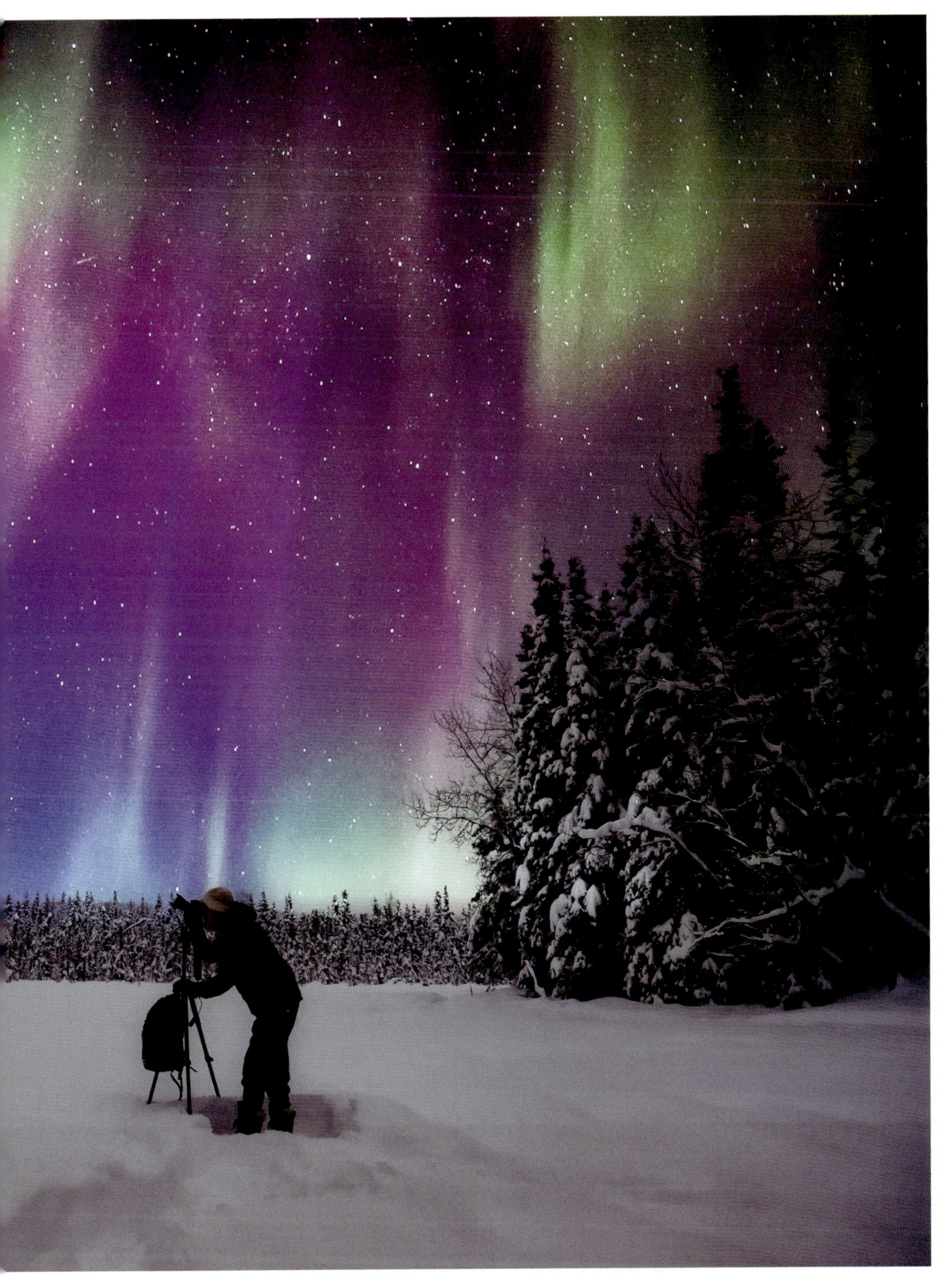

Dave Park Hurst Northern Lights Photographer > Alaska

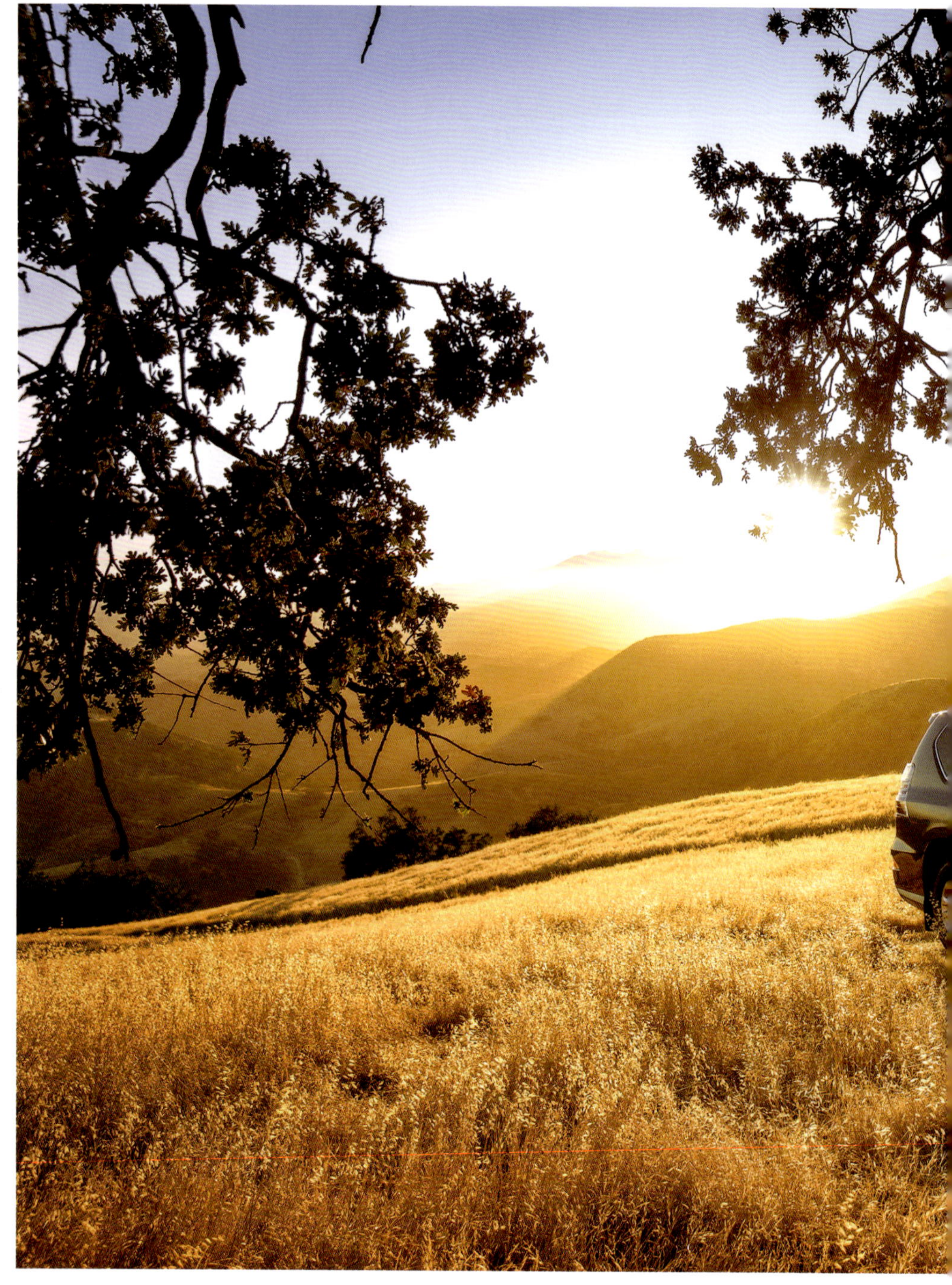

Gal Harpaz Lighting Director > Los Angeles, California

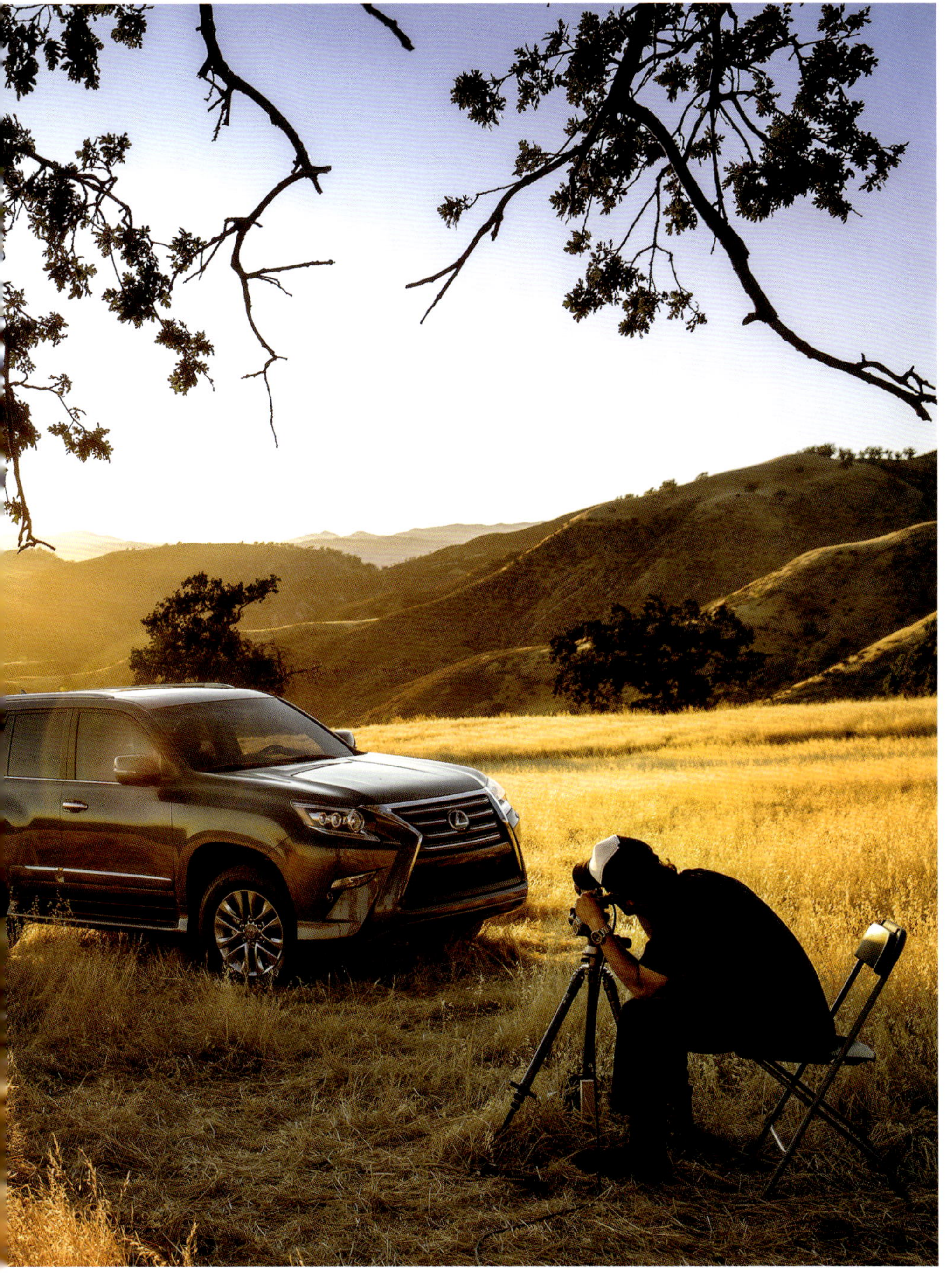

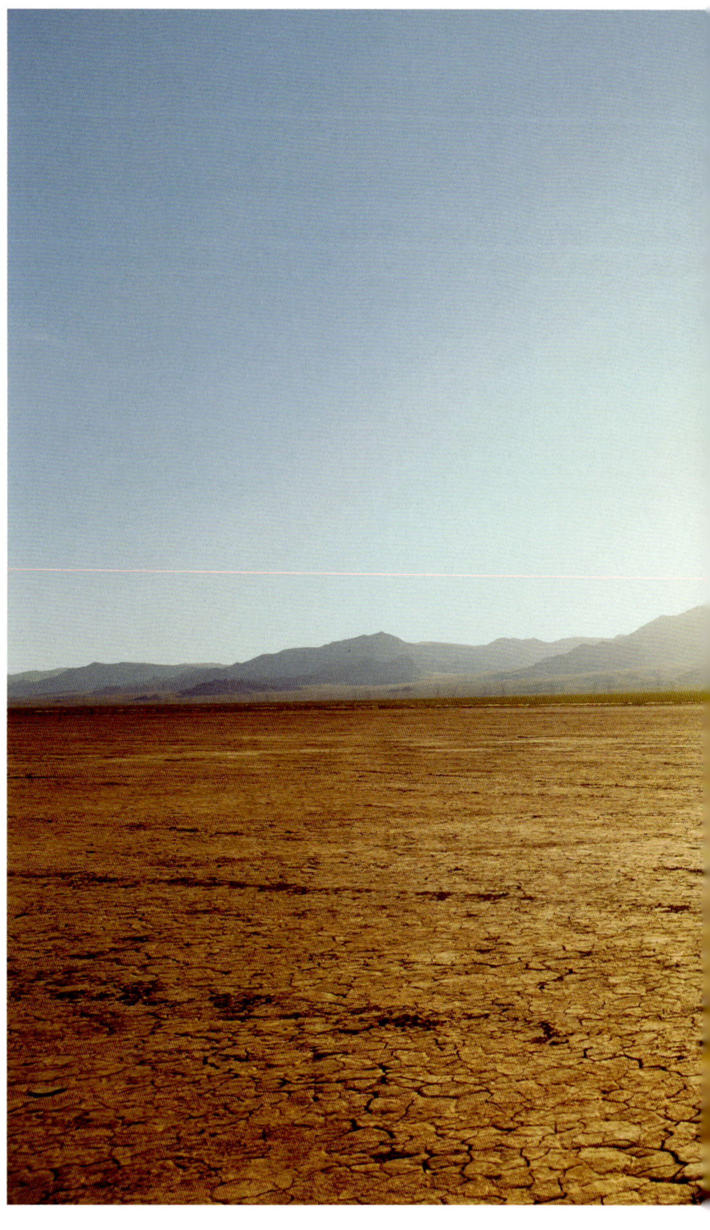

I was excited when Robin Leach — the host of TV's "Lifestyles of the Rich and Famous" back in the day — told me that he knew someone I should meet for *At Work*. But given his signature sign-off — "champagne wishes and caviar dreams" — I did not expect it to be someone new to Las Vegas. Let alone a juggler.

It felt like a Vegas cliché to shoot him on stage. I wanted to offer him something else.

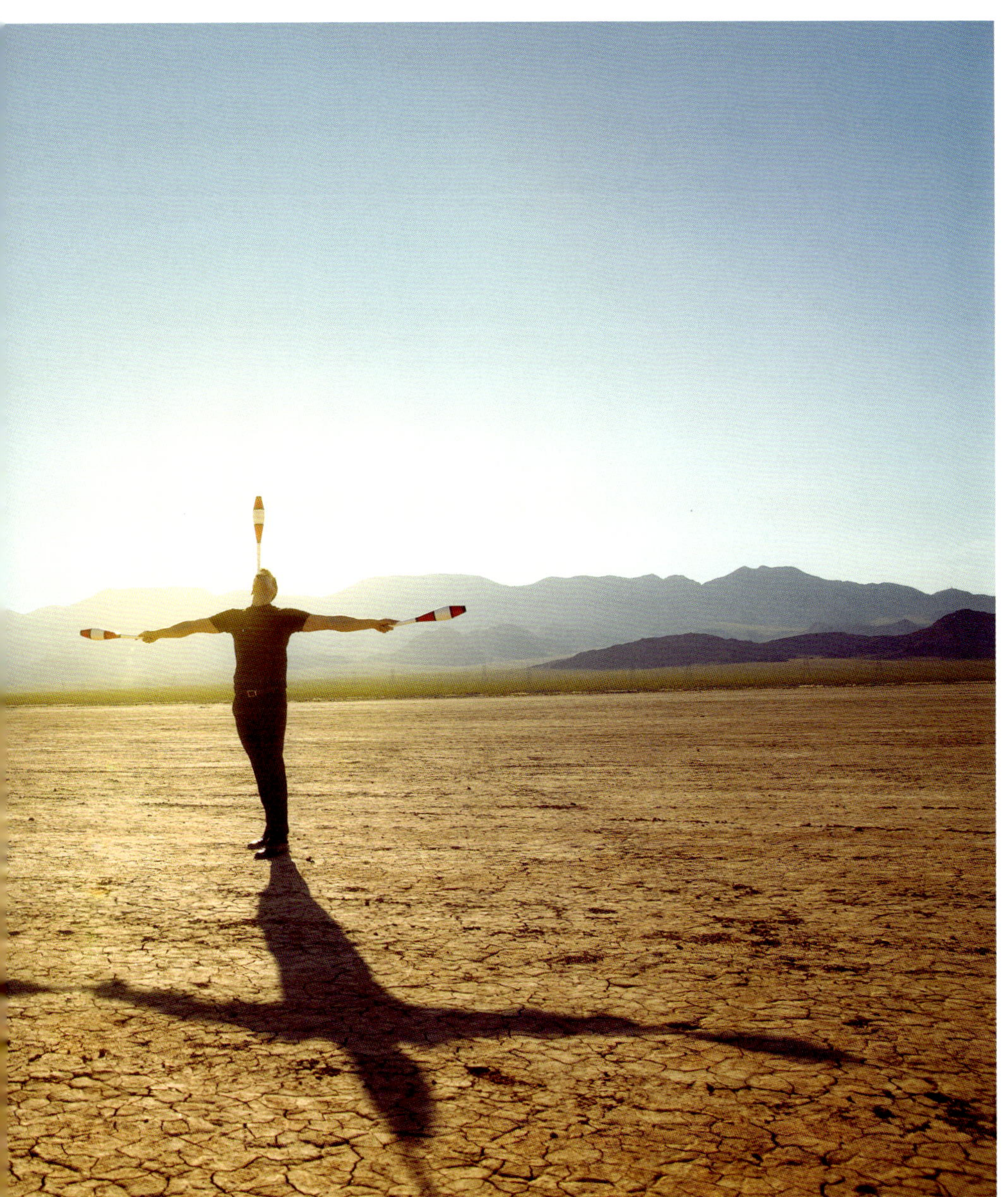

We drove to the salt beds 30 minutes outside the city. As he started warming up, I noticed how happy and relaxed he was. Like a kid playing with his toys.

I cannot take credit for this moment. I simply turned to look at him over my shoulder. There it was.

Jeff Civillico Juggler > Las Vegas, Nevada

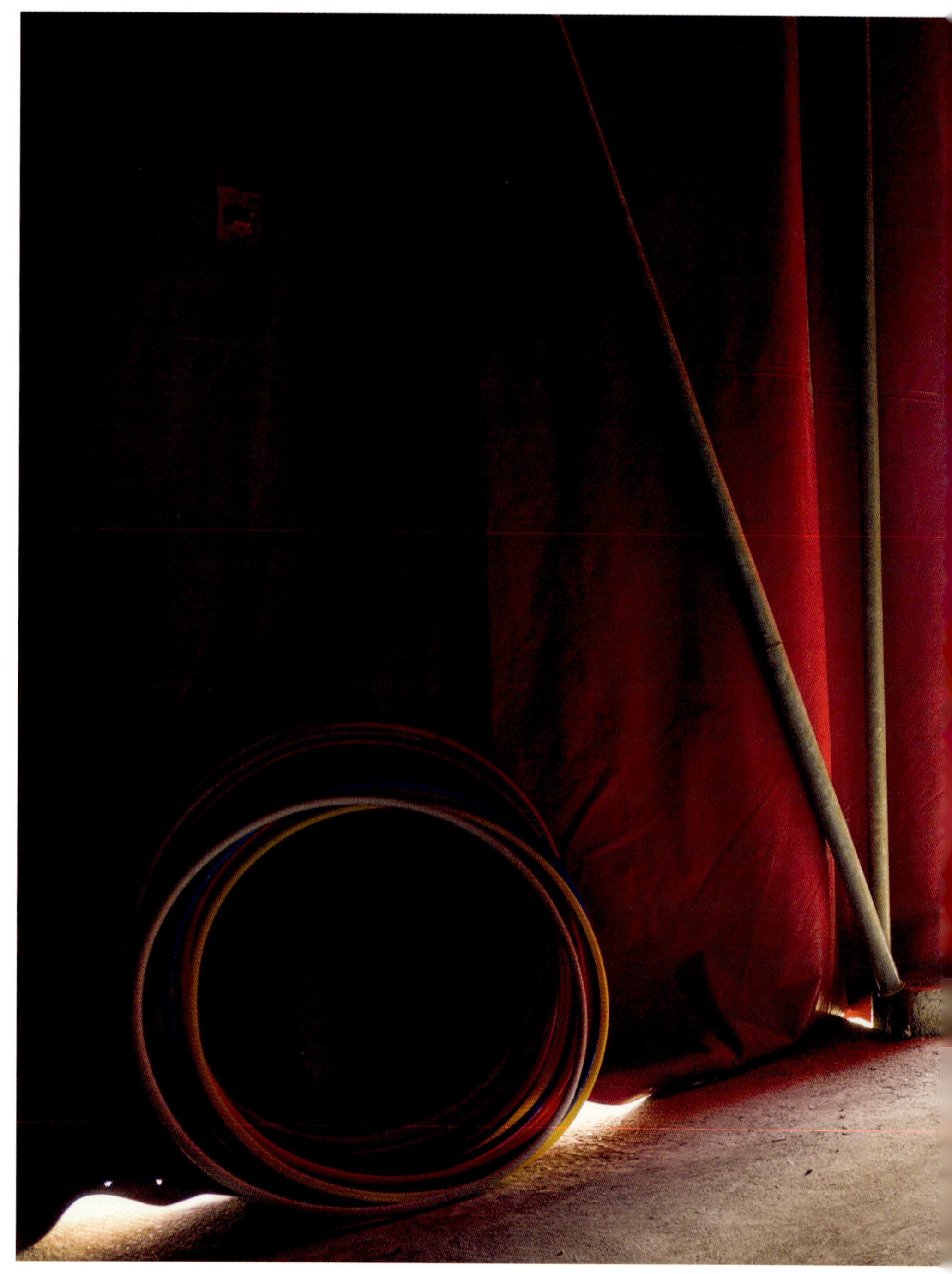

Yiset Ojeda Contortionist > Havana, Cuba

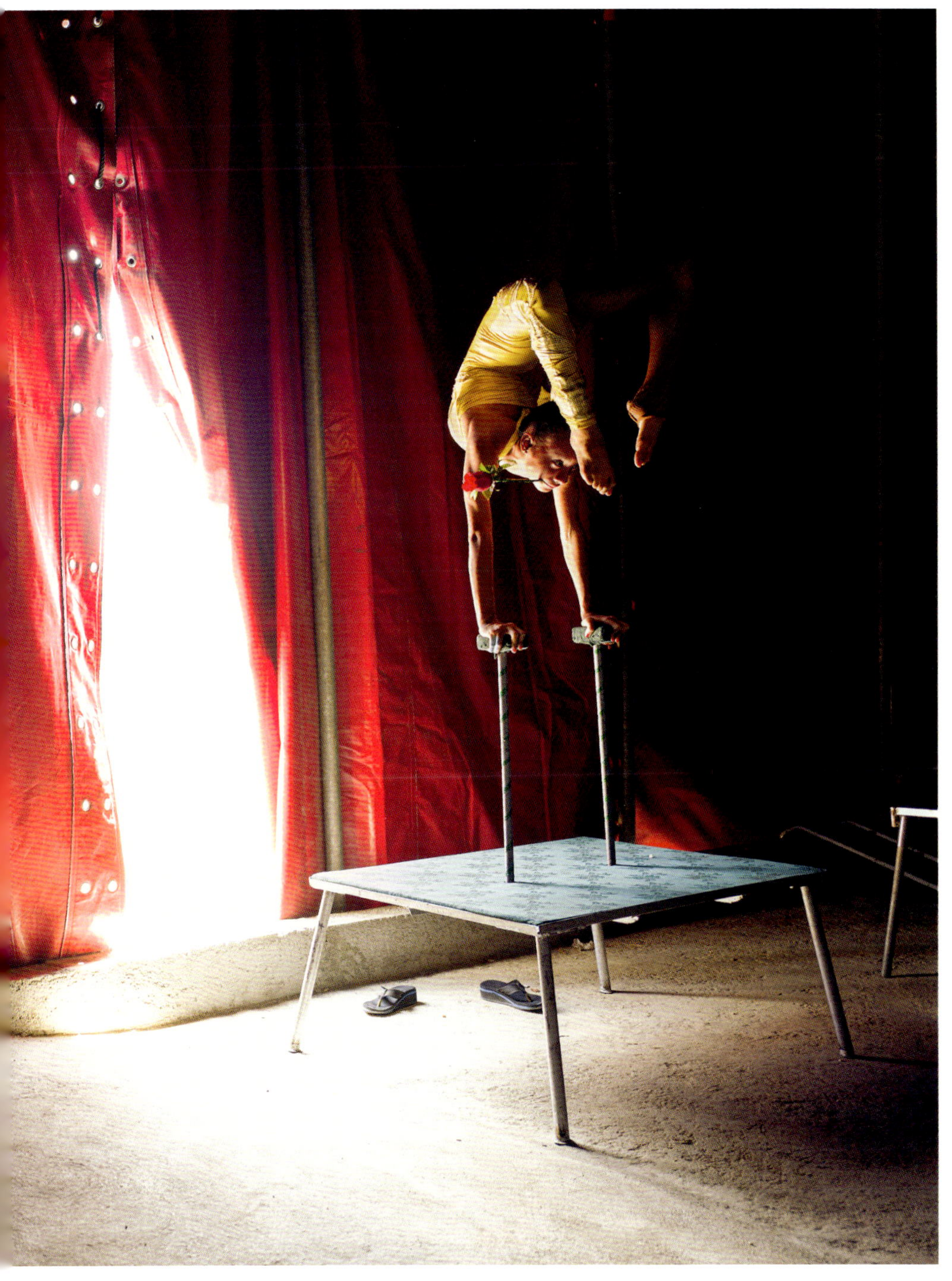

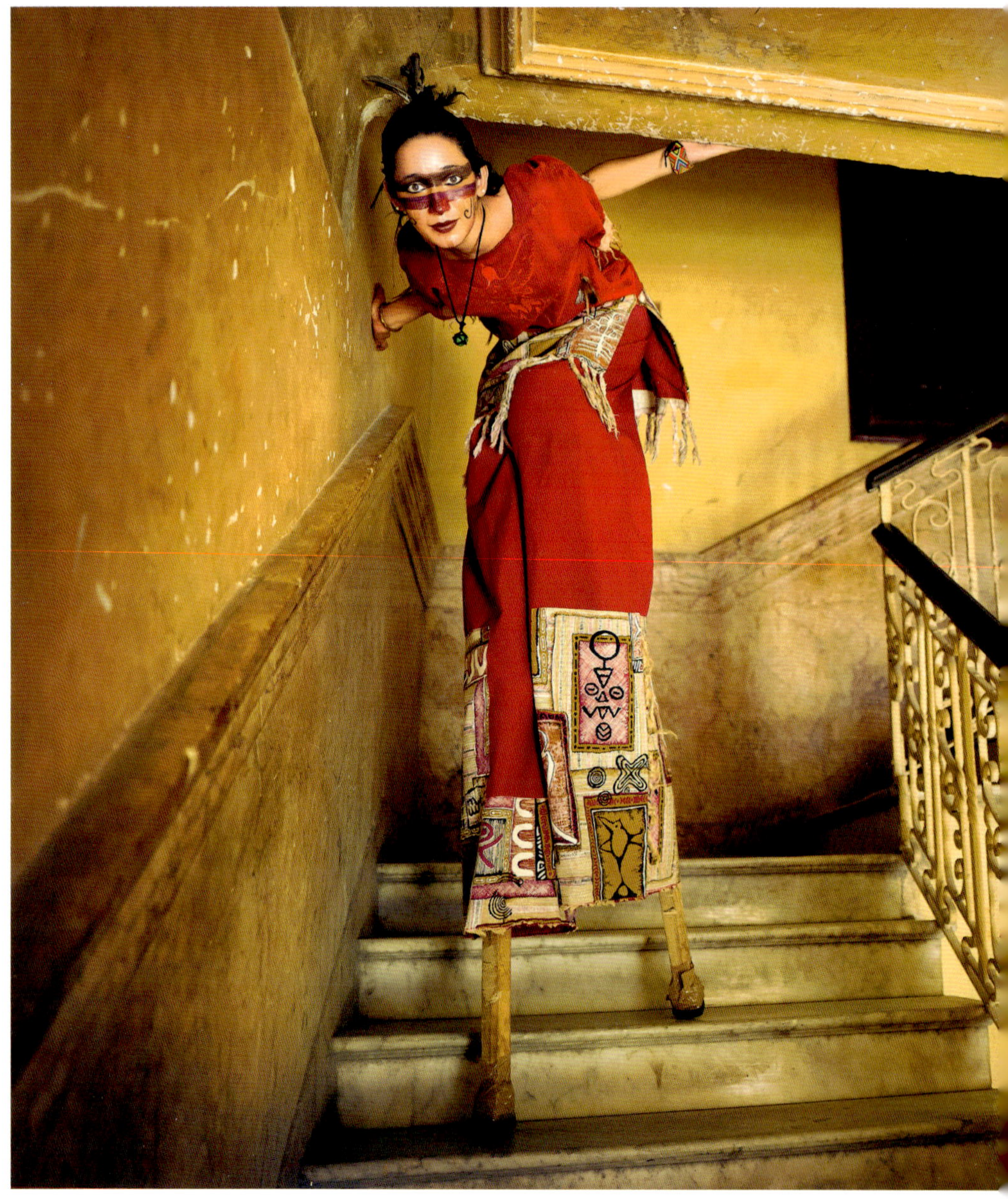

The night before, I'd had a dream that I met a giraffe.
Funny how things work out.

Eder Flores Giganteria Street Performers > Havana, Cuba

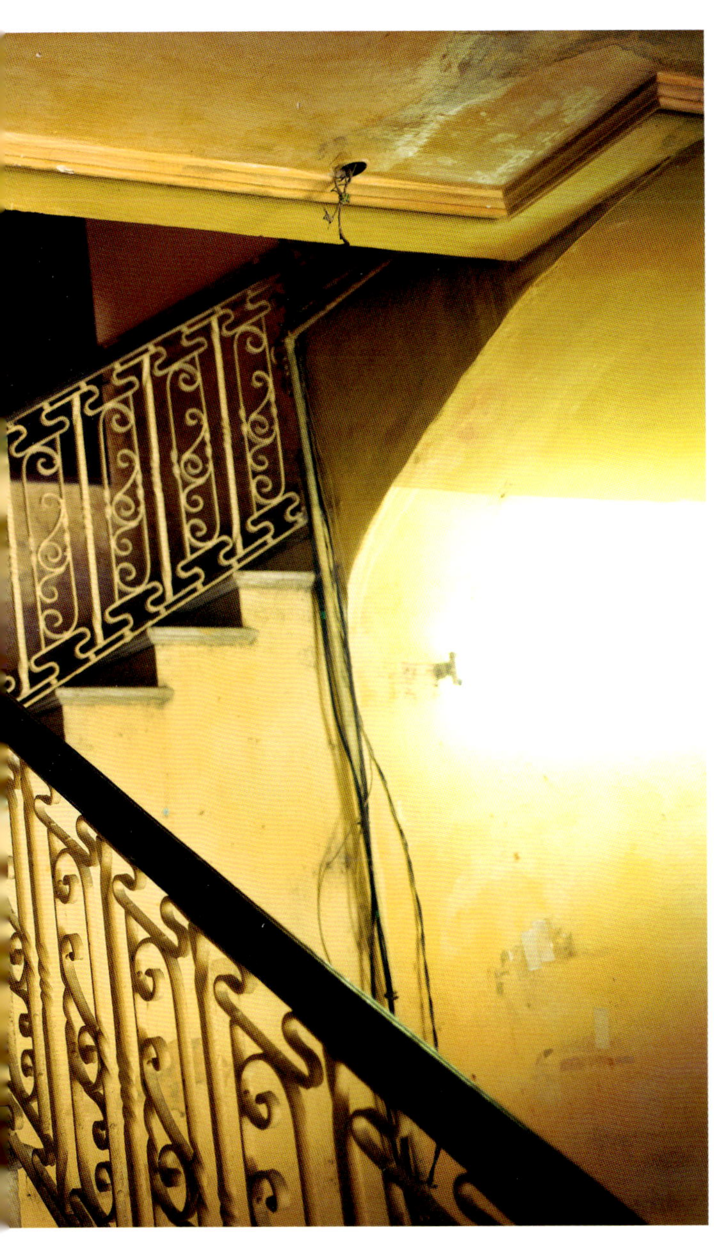

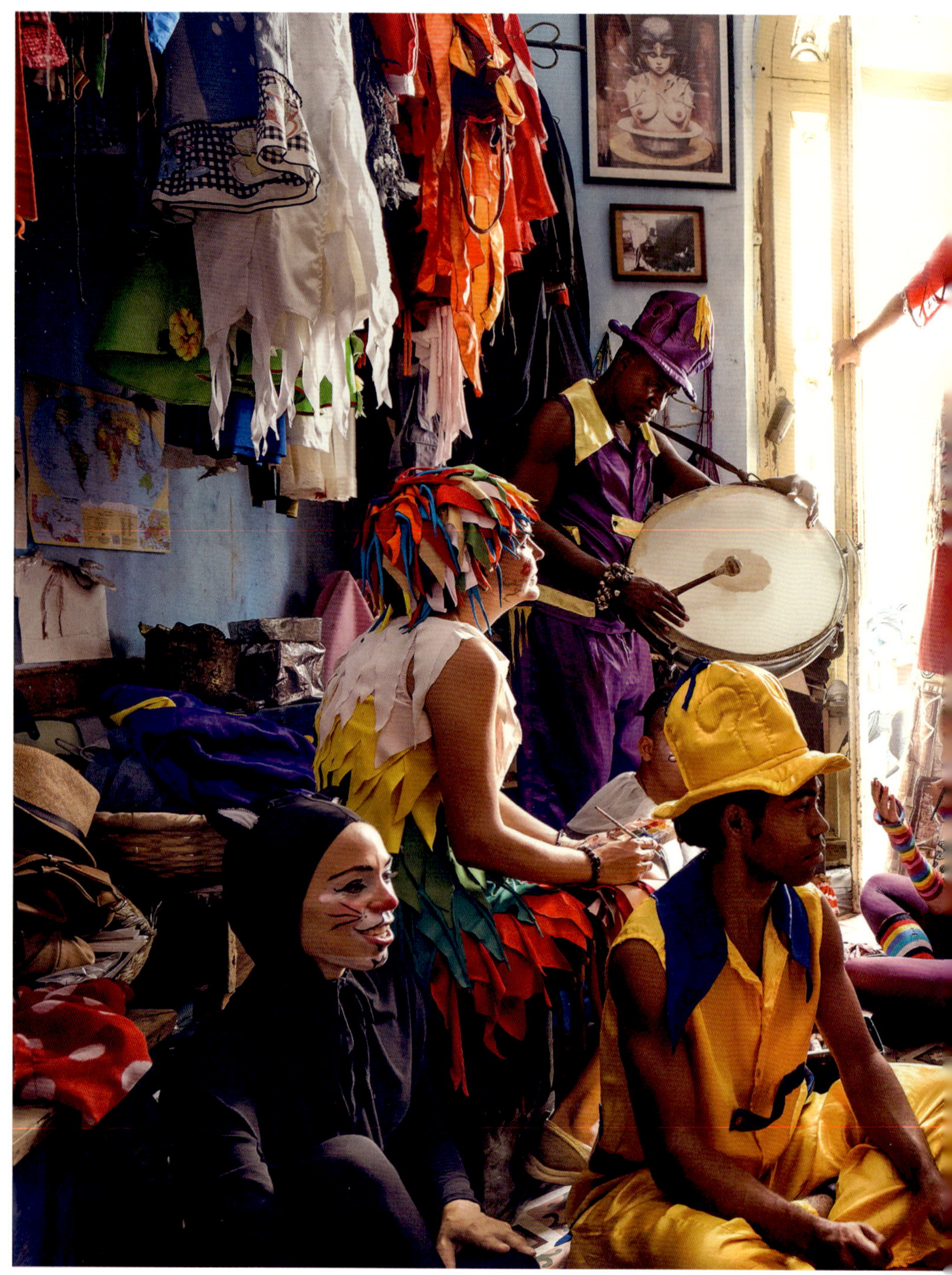

Giganteria Street Performers > Havana, Cuba

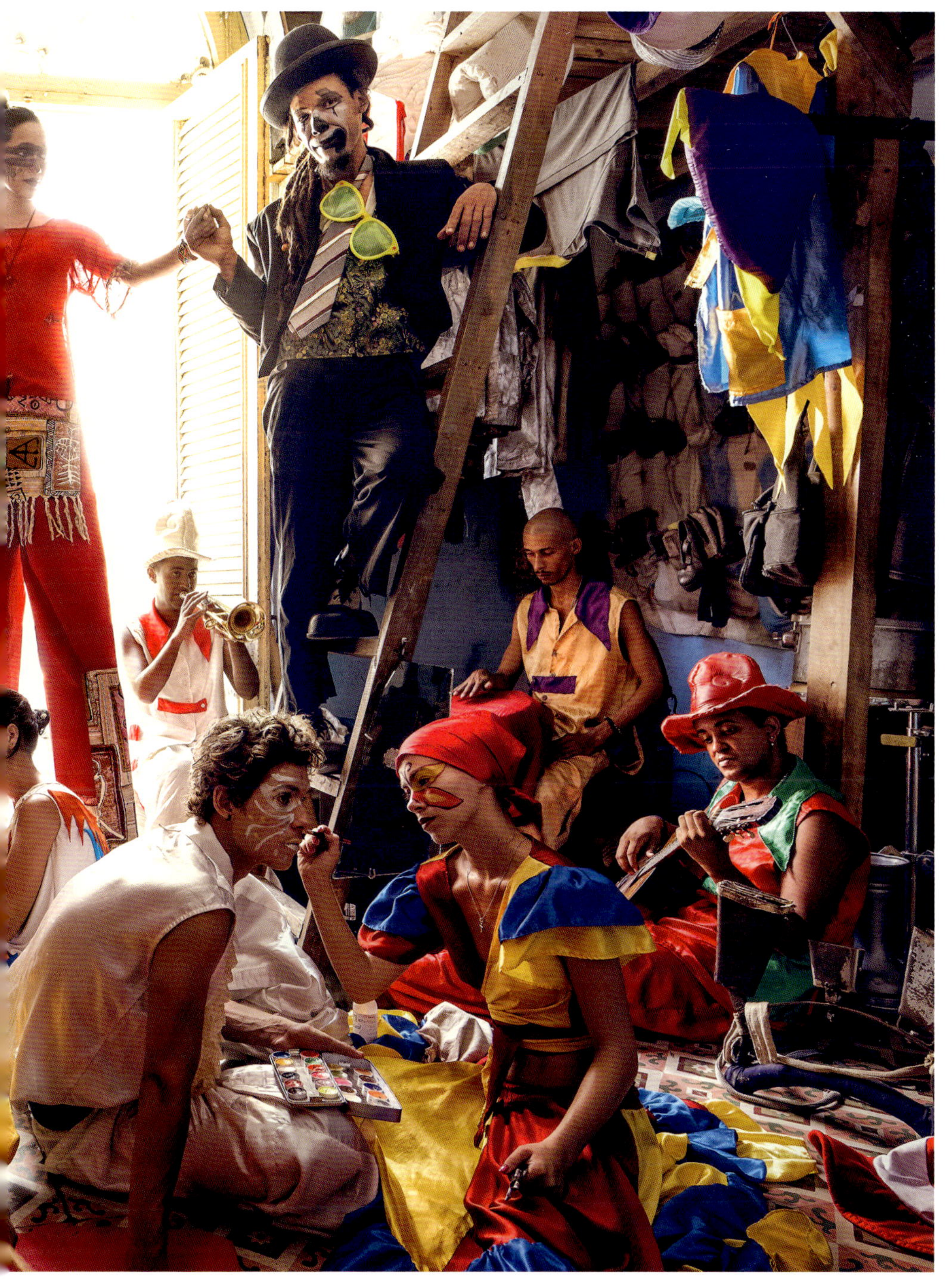

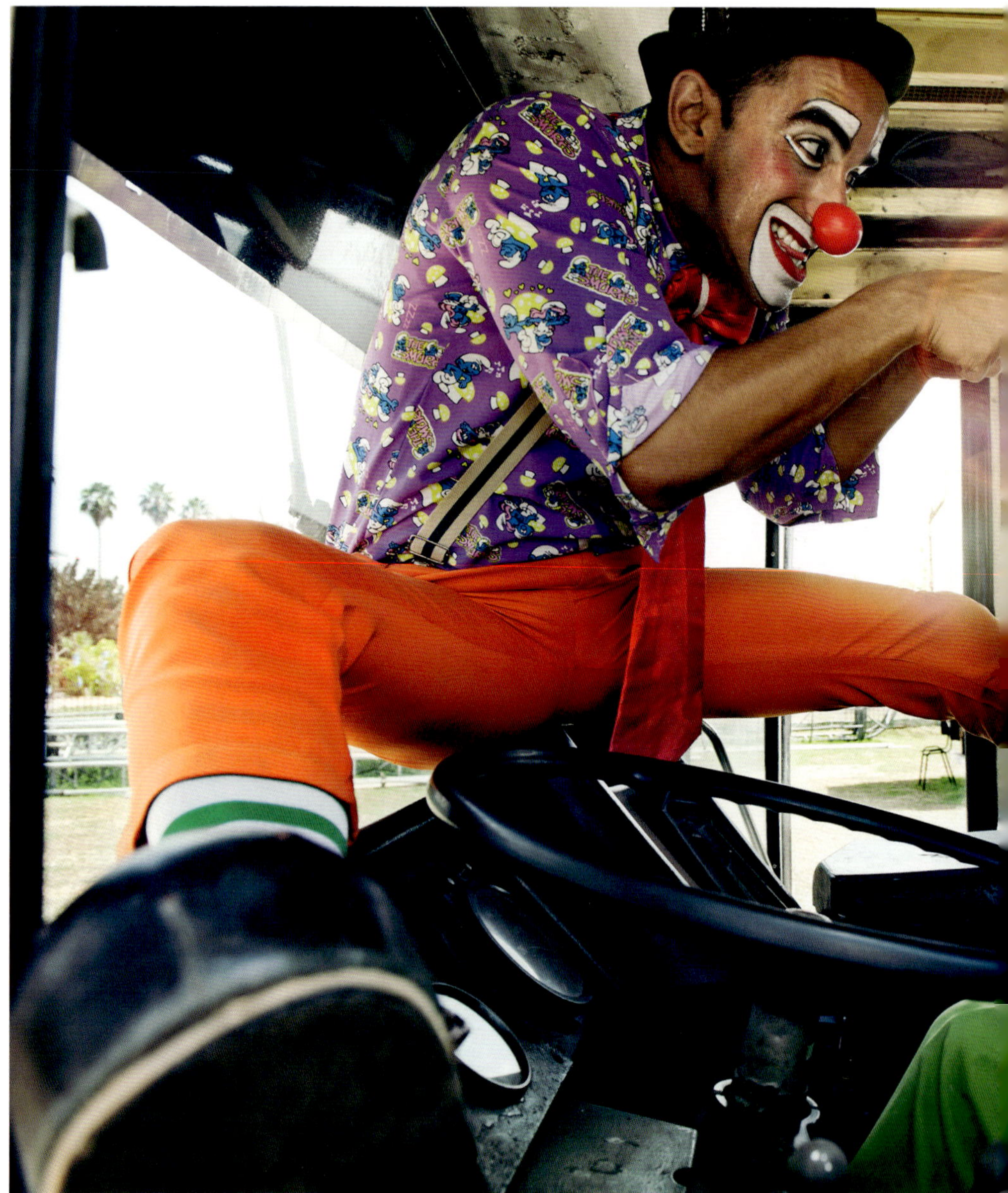

I spotted Eduardo and Luis practicing their routine next to a bus parked alongside the circus tent. Suddenly inspired, I asked if they would be willing to play along with me.

We climbed up into the bus and I walked them through my idea. Things were going well. We were all having a great time. But then Eduardo and Luis moved to the front of the bus — taking my idea, as well, in a new direction.

As I watched them, I realized my mistake. Creative magic cannot be commanded.

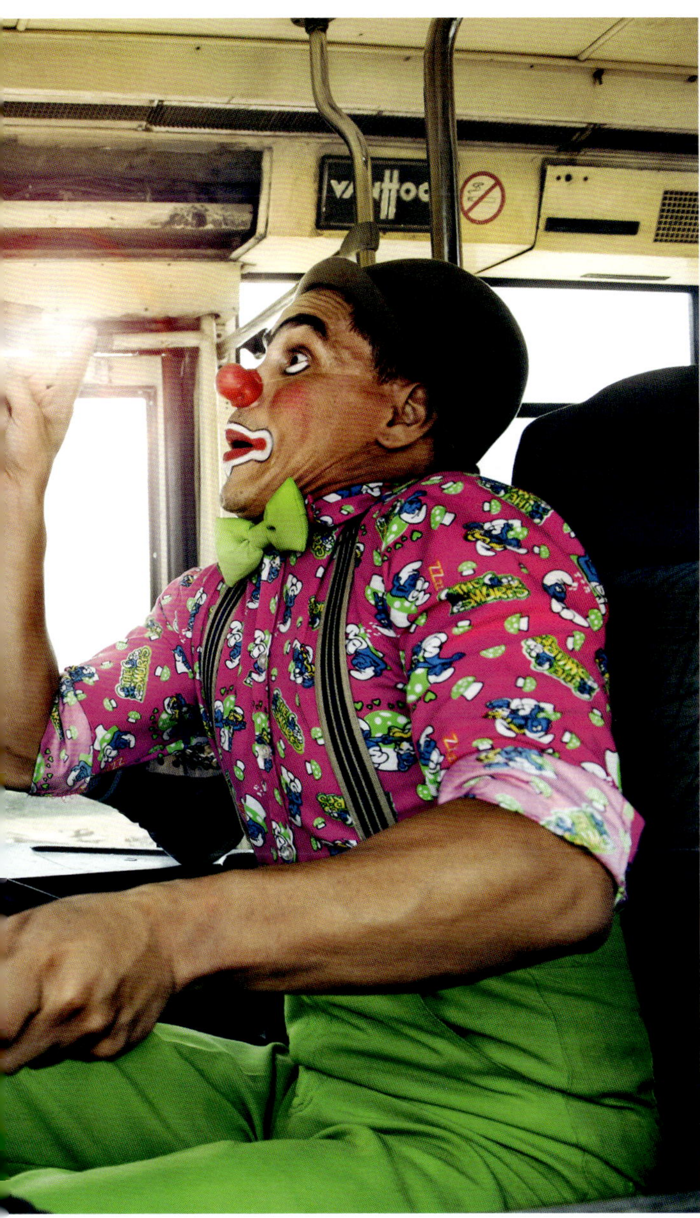

You need to make room for it. It only happens when you let people in — to a collaboration, or a conversation. It's not a one-way valve. It's worth loosening your grip, letting things unfold.

When we do, it can lead to extraordinary outcomes.

Eduardo Ceballos Pérez & Luis Manuel San Juan Diaz Clowns > Havana, Cuba

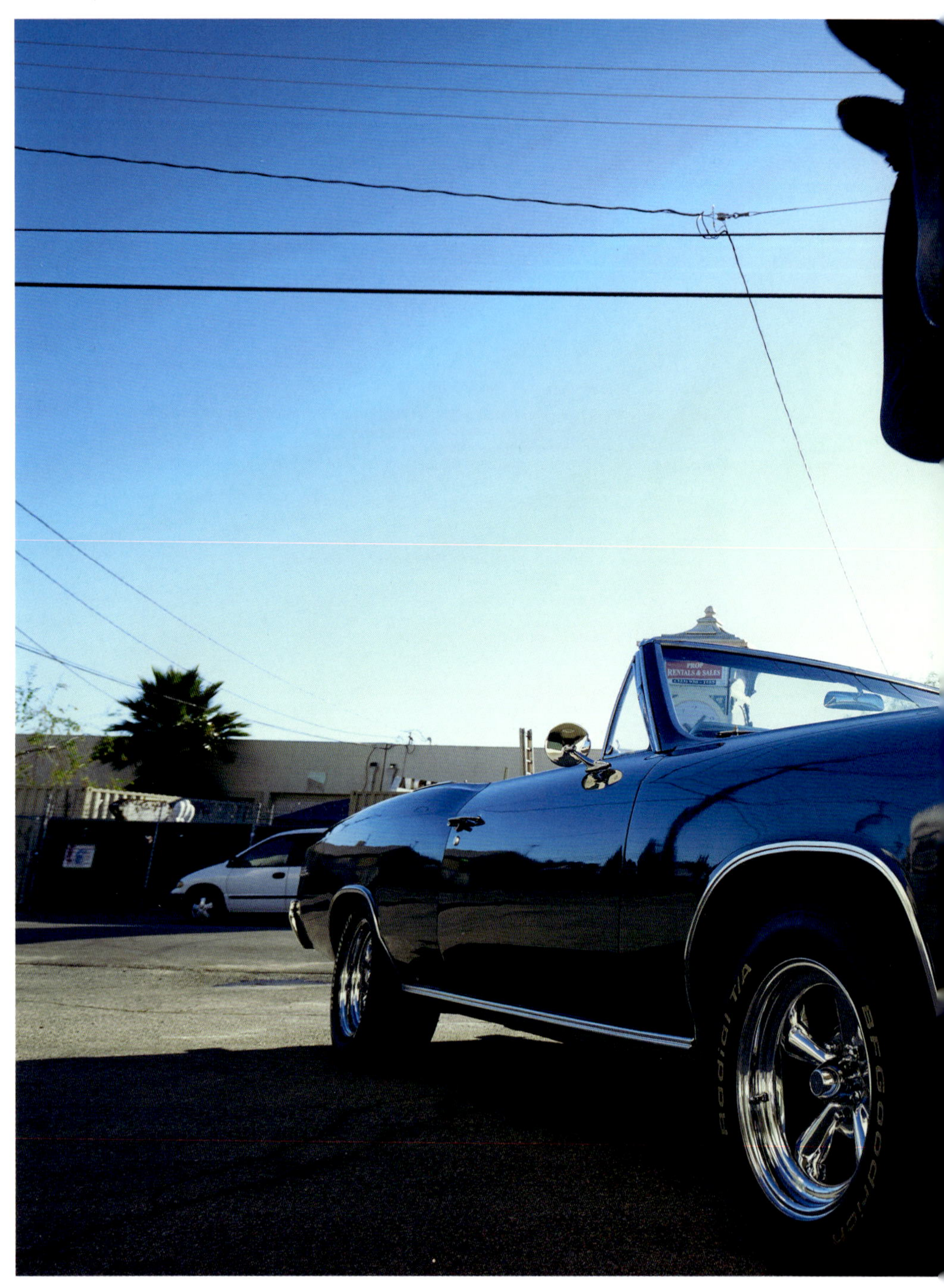

Caine Sinclair Stuntman > Los Angeles, California

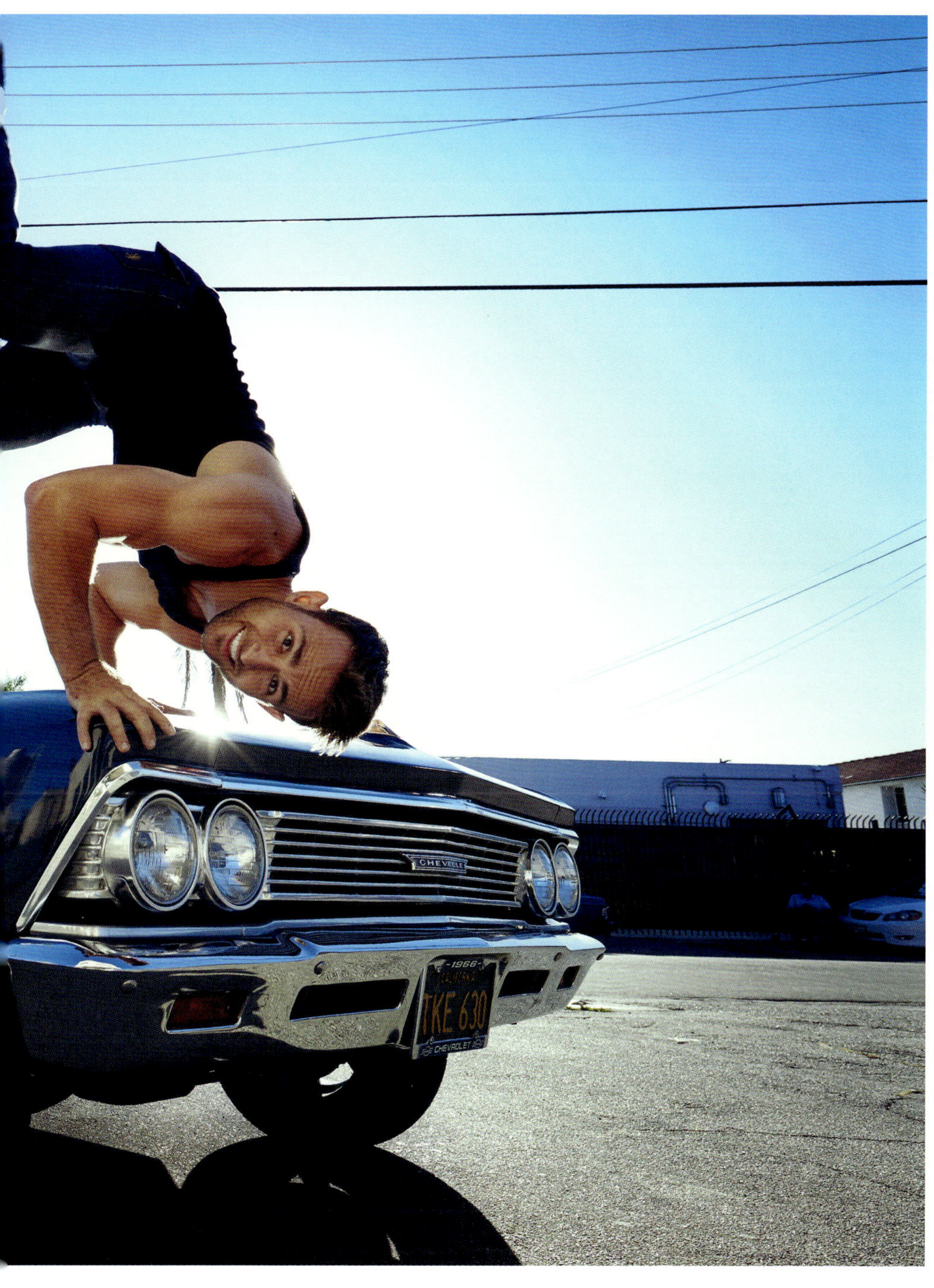

1966
CALIFORNIA
TKE 630
CHEVROLET
CHEVELLE

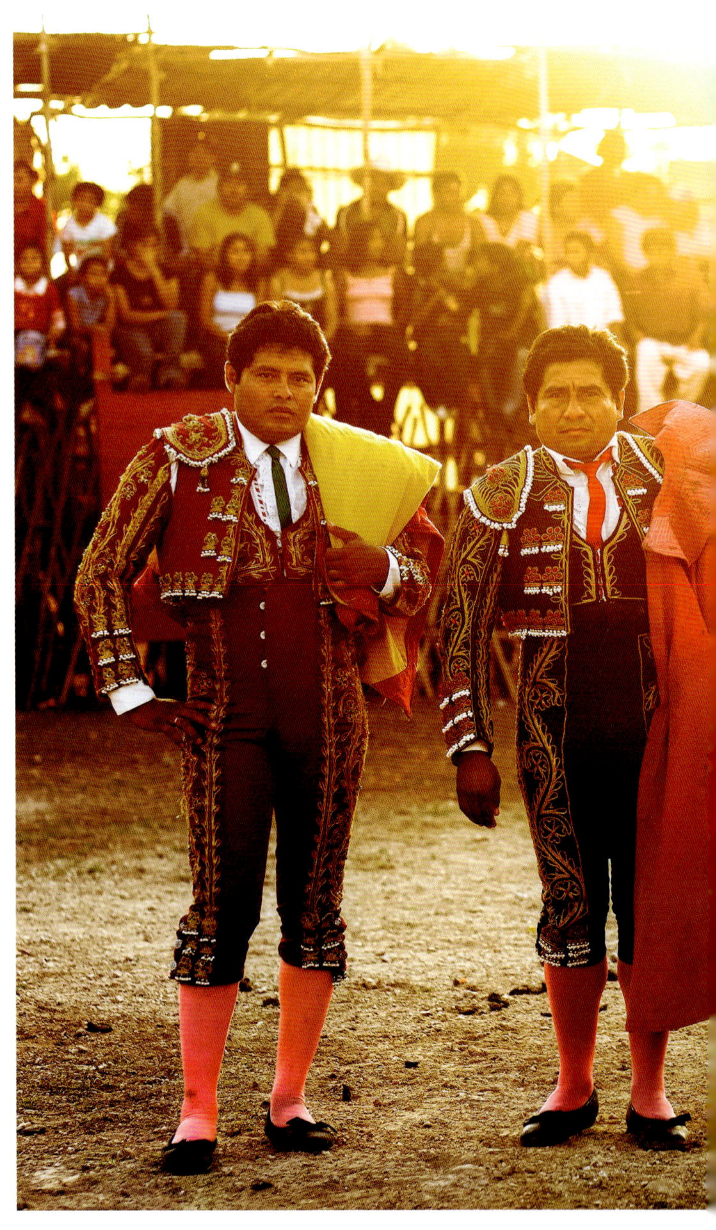

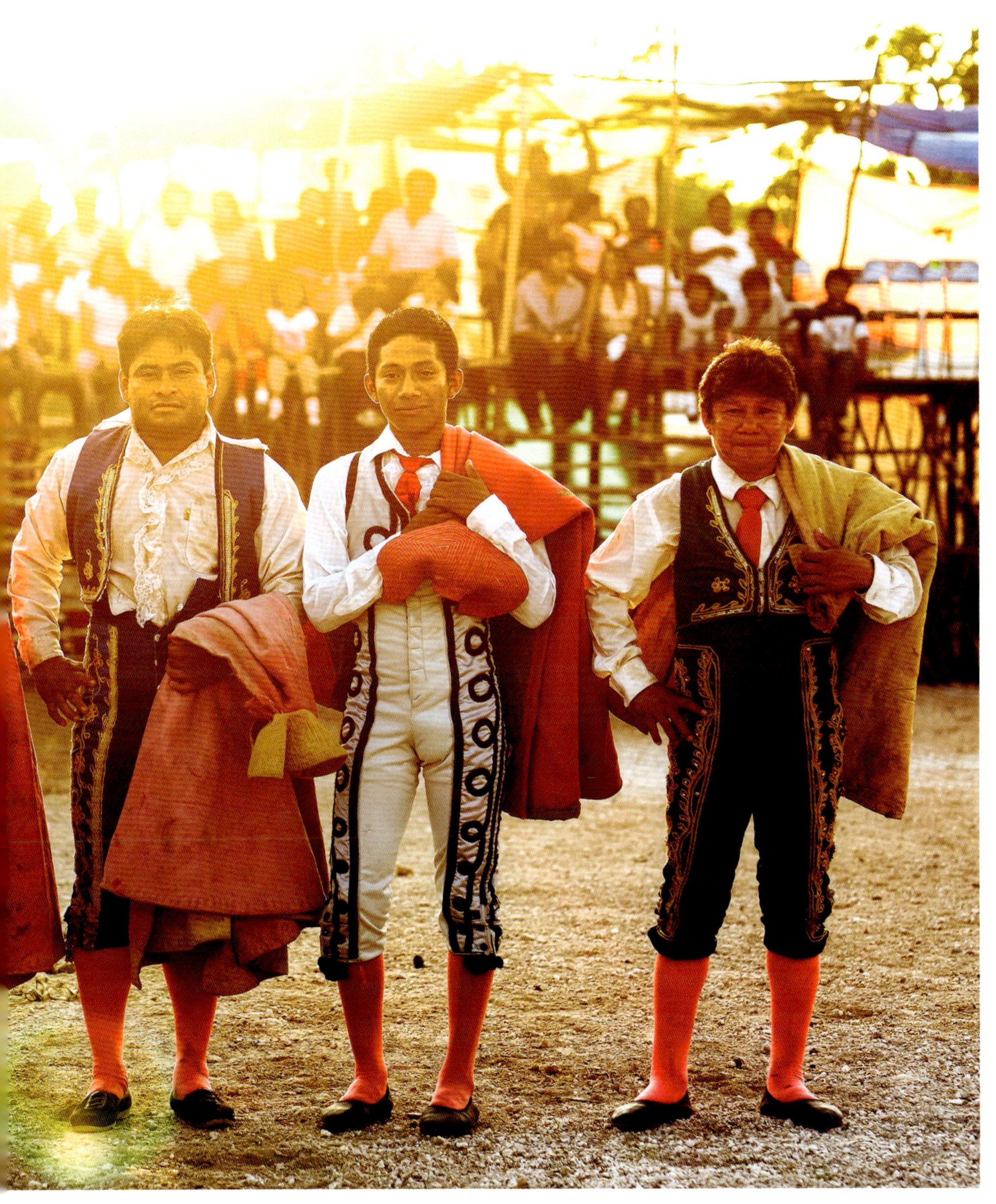

Toreros Bullfighters > San José Tzal, Yucatán, Mexico

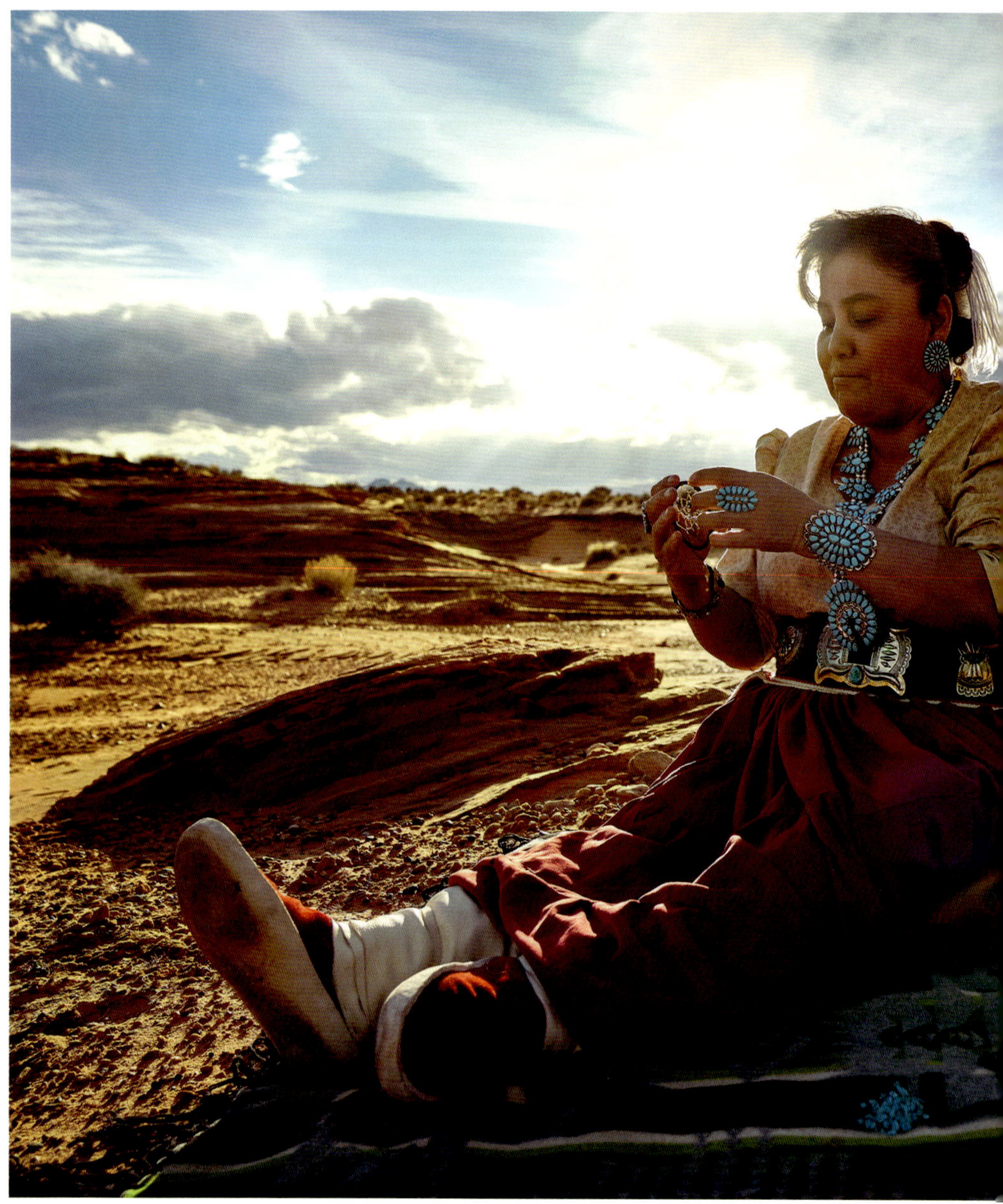

Pearl apologized for the weather when I arrived. It was storming. I told her what I've always thought: nature gives just what you need.

We'd met a few days prior, and I made a special trip cross-country to see her again. I'd had a remarkable experience here, on this land. I hoped that she might be

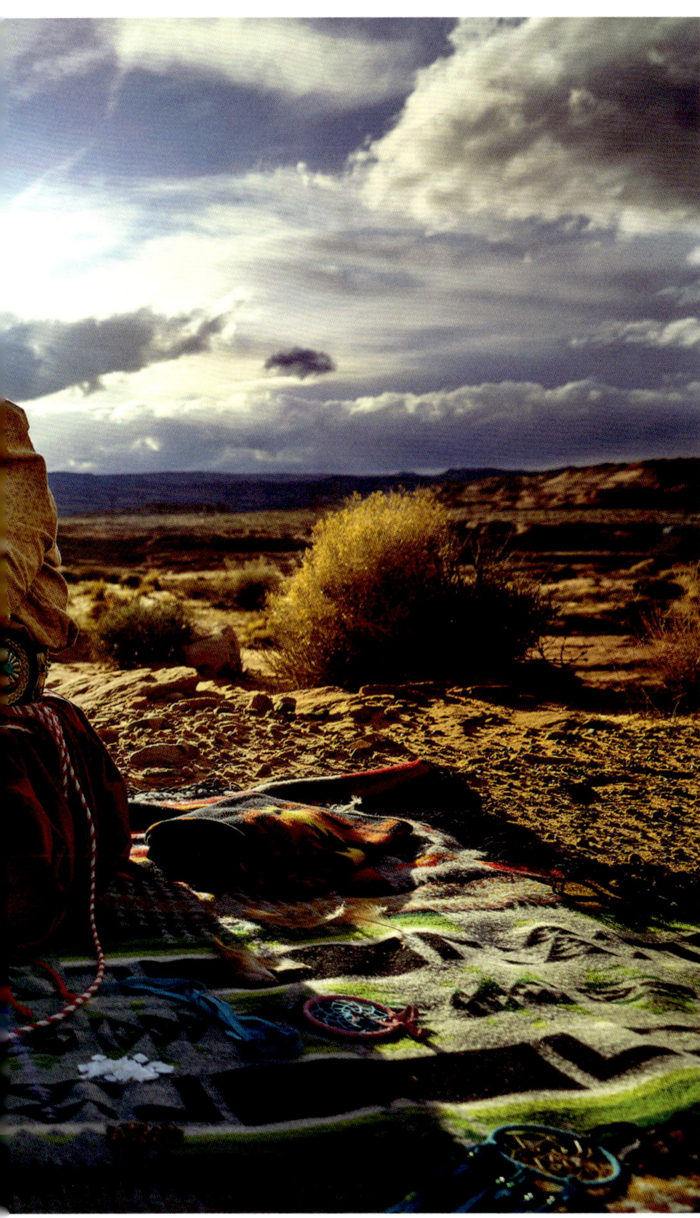

able — as someone who was of it, who had an ancestral relationship to it that I never would — to help me understand it better.

Our conversation ran deep. She helped me to see something differently. And as if on cue, the sun broke through the clouds.

Pearl A. Seaton Dream Catcher > Page, Arizona

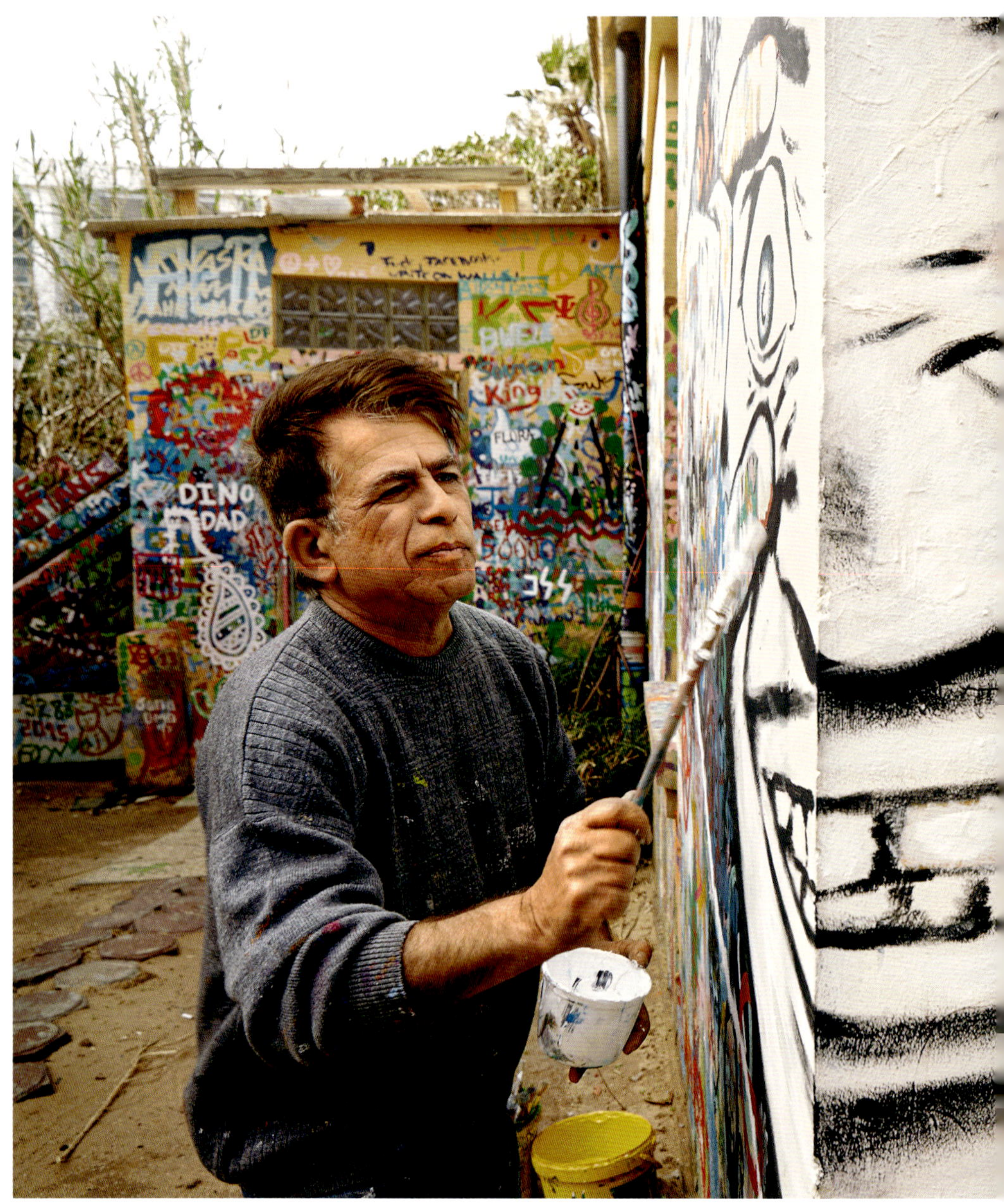

I asked Rami why he makes his street art.
"I create conversations for the people of Tel Aviv," he replied.

Rami Meiri Street Artist > Tel Aviv, Israel

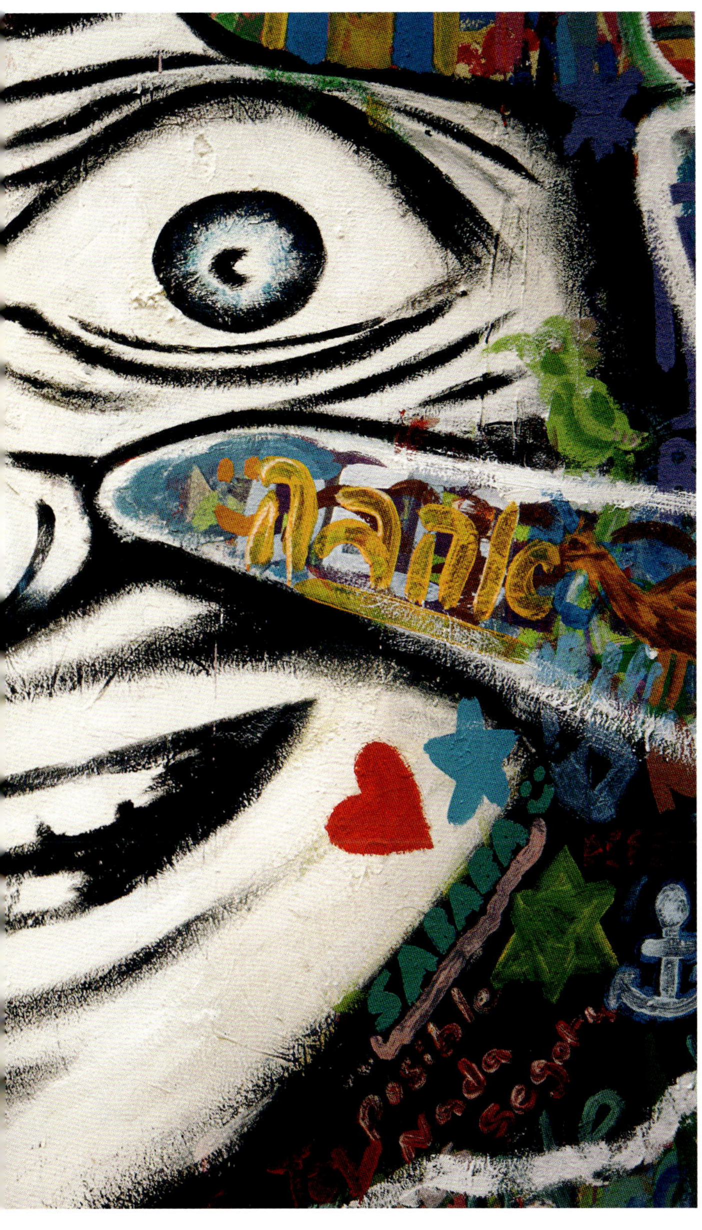

nanic
samba
posible
nada segura

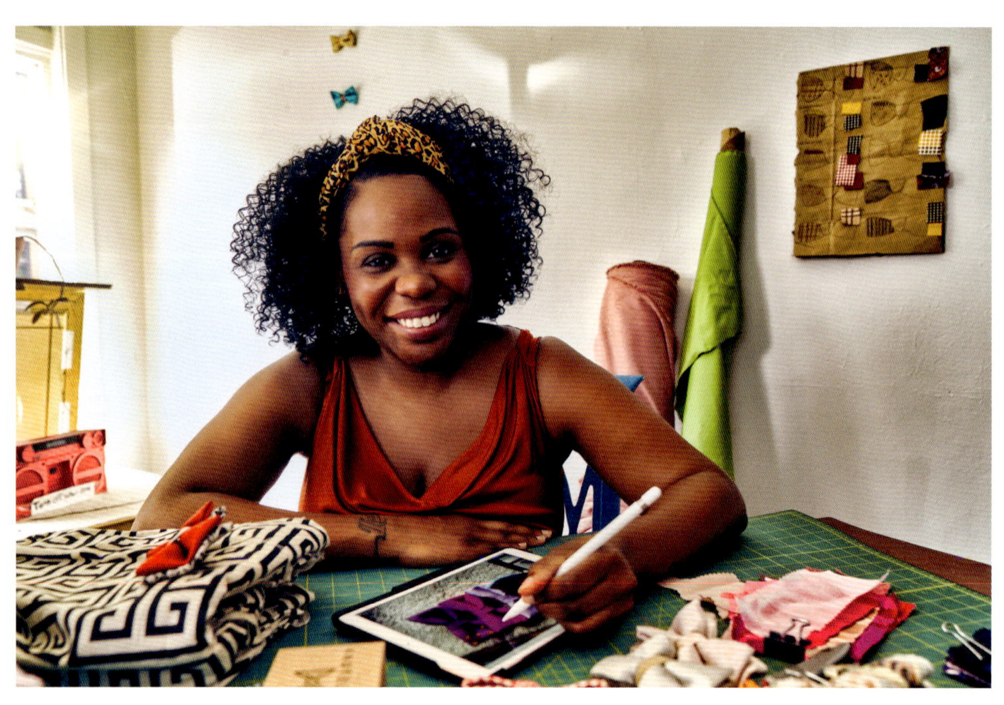

Nisha Blackwell Accessory Designer, Knotzland > Pittsburgh, Pennsylvania

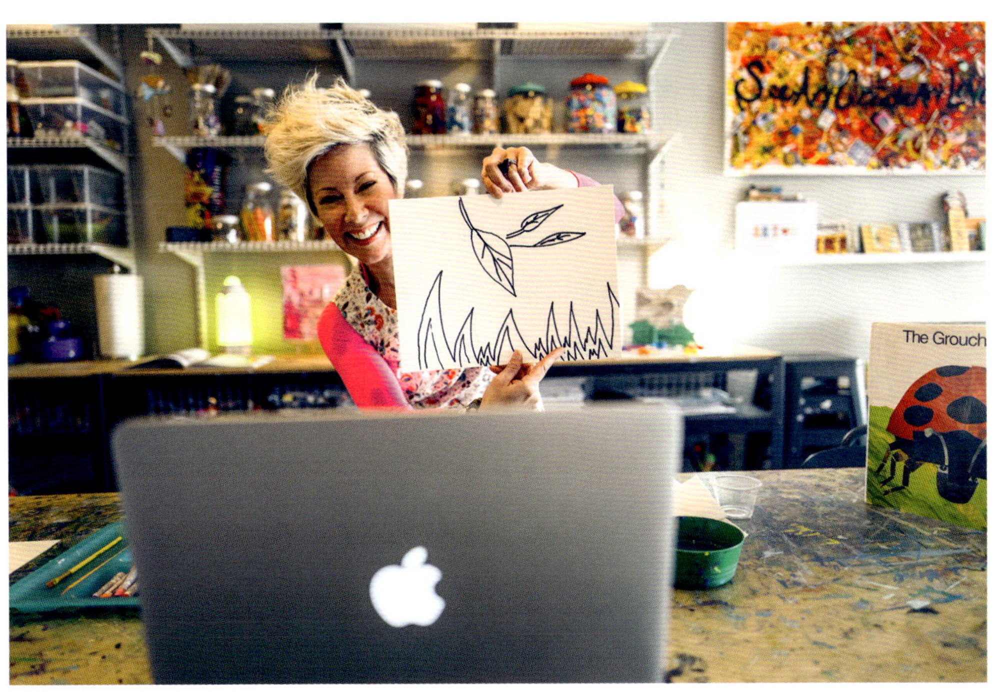

Laura-Marie Small Founder, Kidcasso Art Studio > Wakefield, Massachusetts

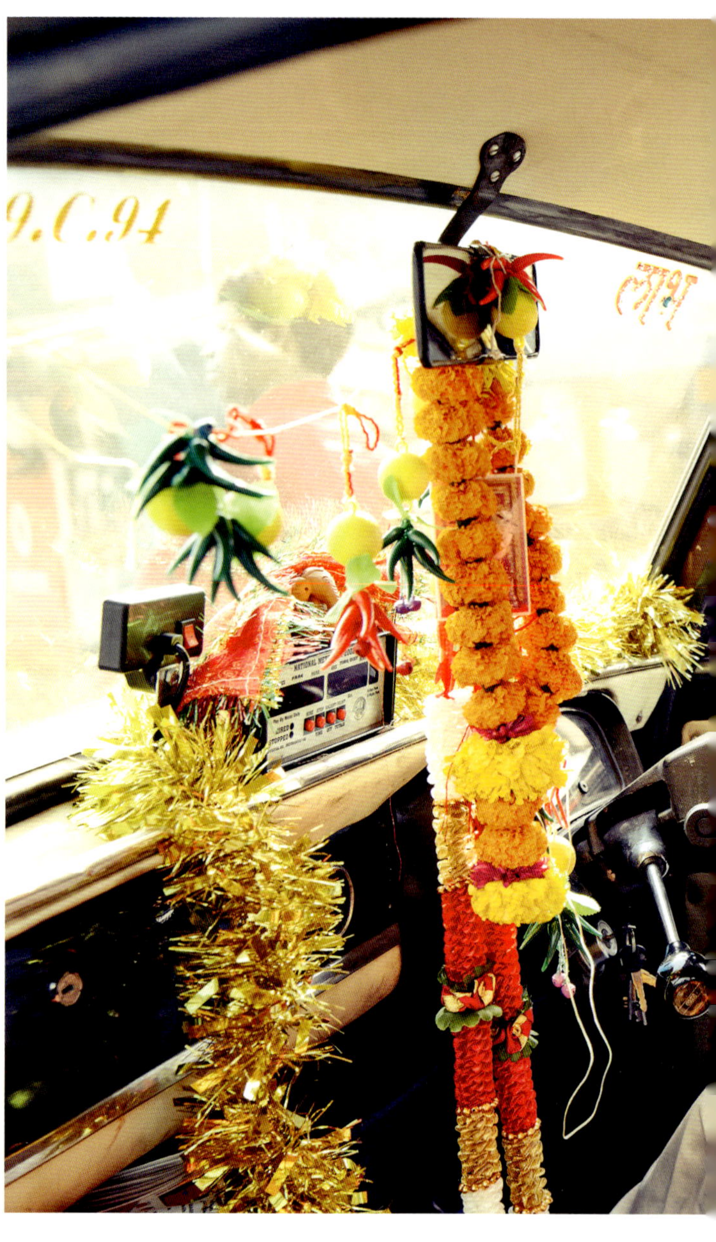

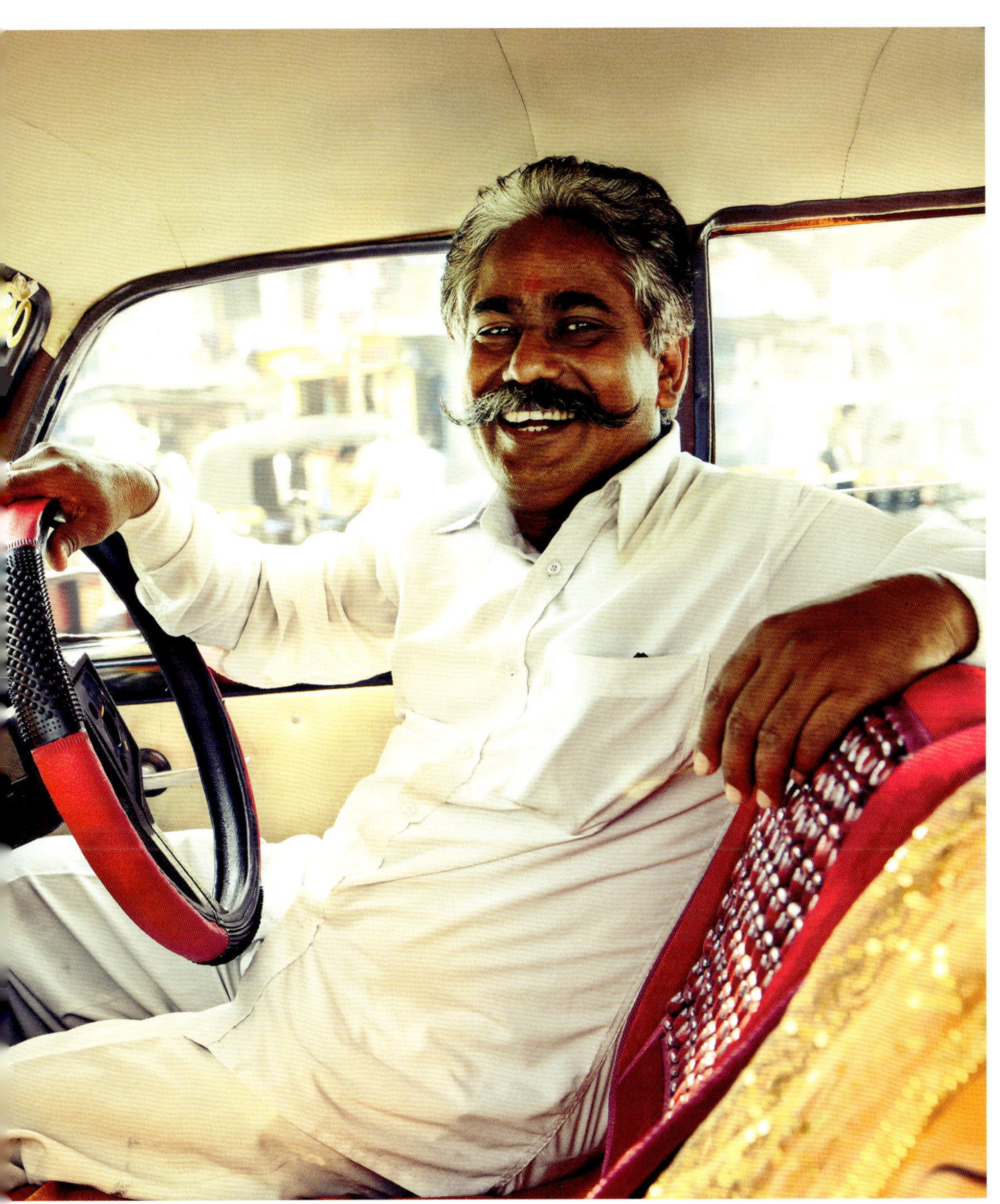

Ganga Prasad Yadav Taxi Driver > Mumbai, India

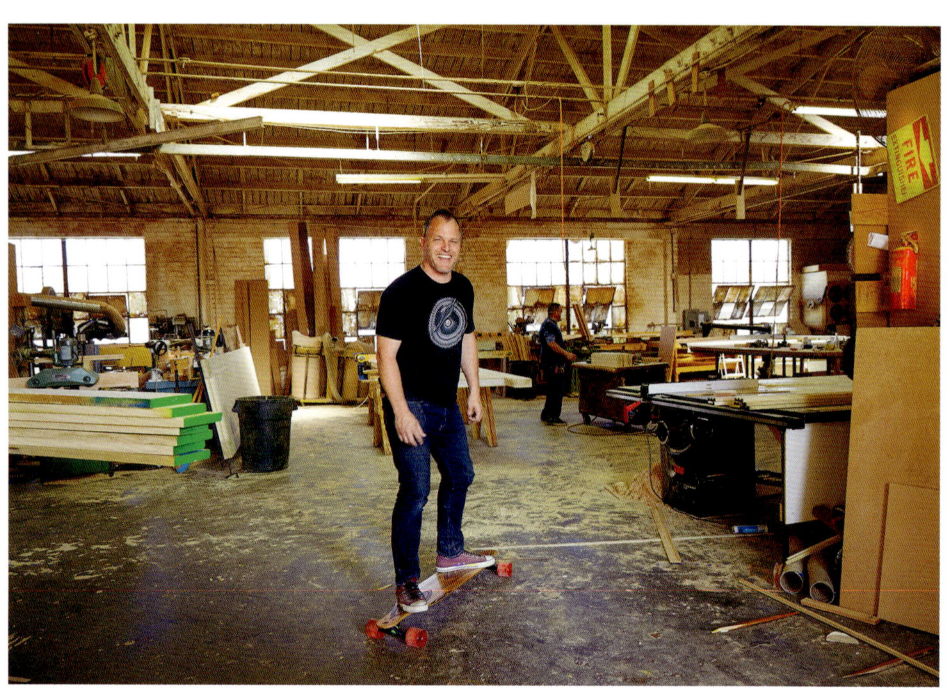

Dino Pierone Owner and Craftsman, Dean Longboards > Los Angeles, California

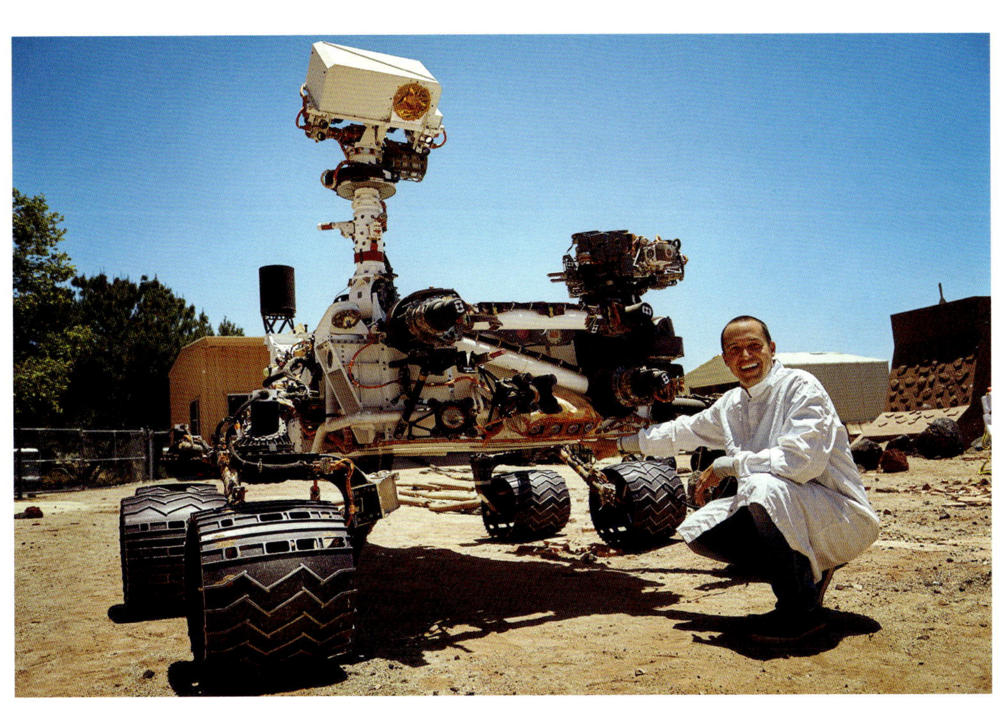

Matt Heverly Rover Driver, Jet Propulsion Labs > Los Angeles, California

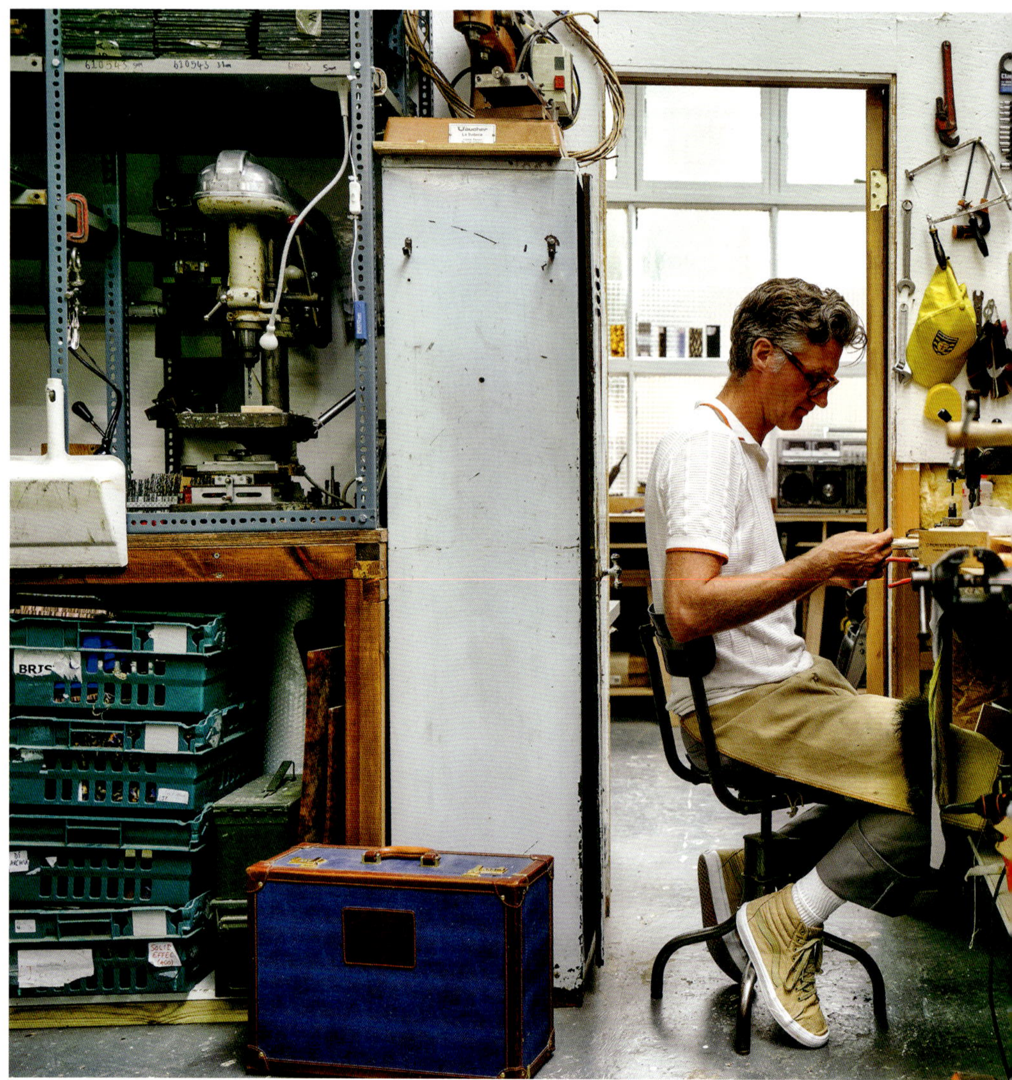

I was excited for Brian. He was setting out to produce hand-crafted eyewear under his own name after years of working for others. I was all encouragement. His work was so exacting. Amazing. Each component required its own specialized machine.

"So when is your book coming out?" Brian asked.

I'd told him about *At Work*. But I'd left out a crucial detail. I'd been hedging. I wasn't sure that anyone would want to pick up the book and look at it, let alone publish it.

"It's time," he said. "People will love it. They need to see it."

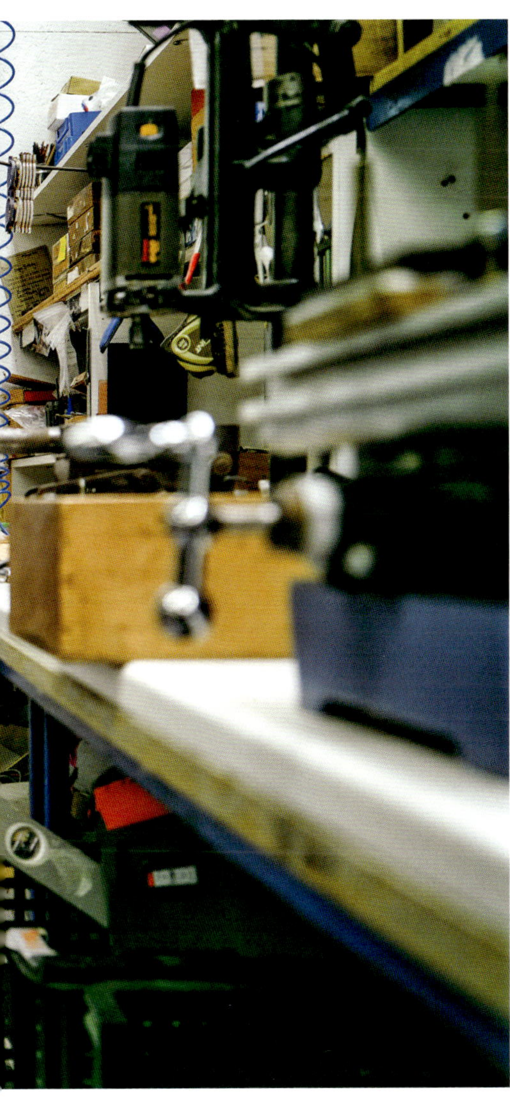

My family and friends have always been so supportive of me. But it was different to have a stranger—a fellow making a big leap of his own—tell me to go for it. It just landed differently. I knew he was right: it was time.

And as if helping me to believe in myself wasn't enough, he also made a pair of beautiful, custom eyeglasses, just for me.

Thank you, Brian.

Brian McGinn Eyewear Designer and Maker, Bonafide McGinn > London, England

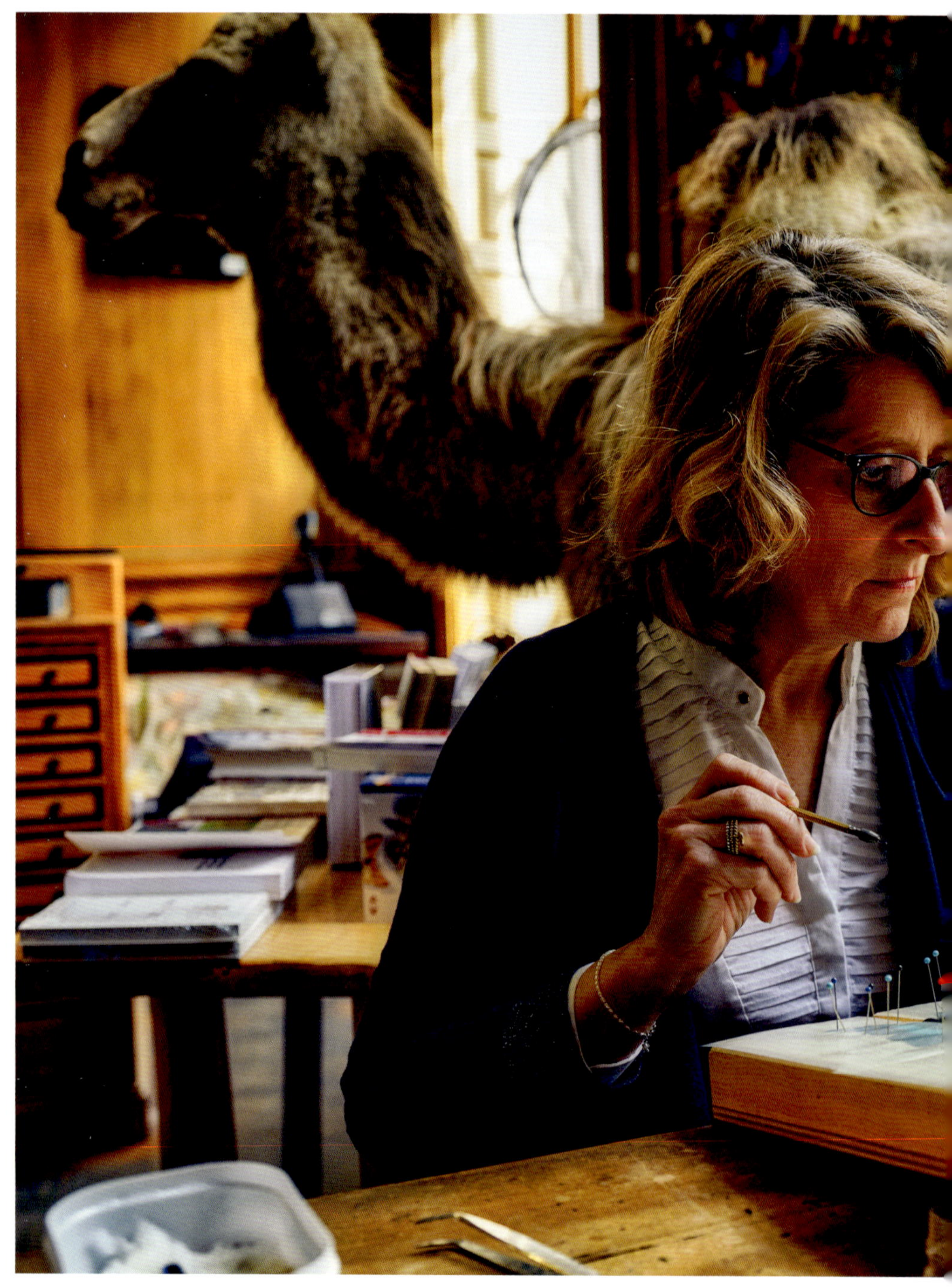

Valérie Breillat Entomologist, Deyrolle > Paris, France

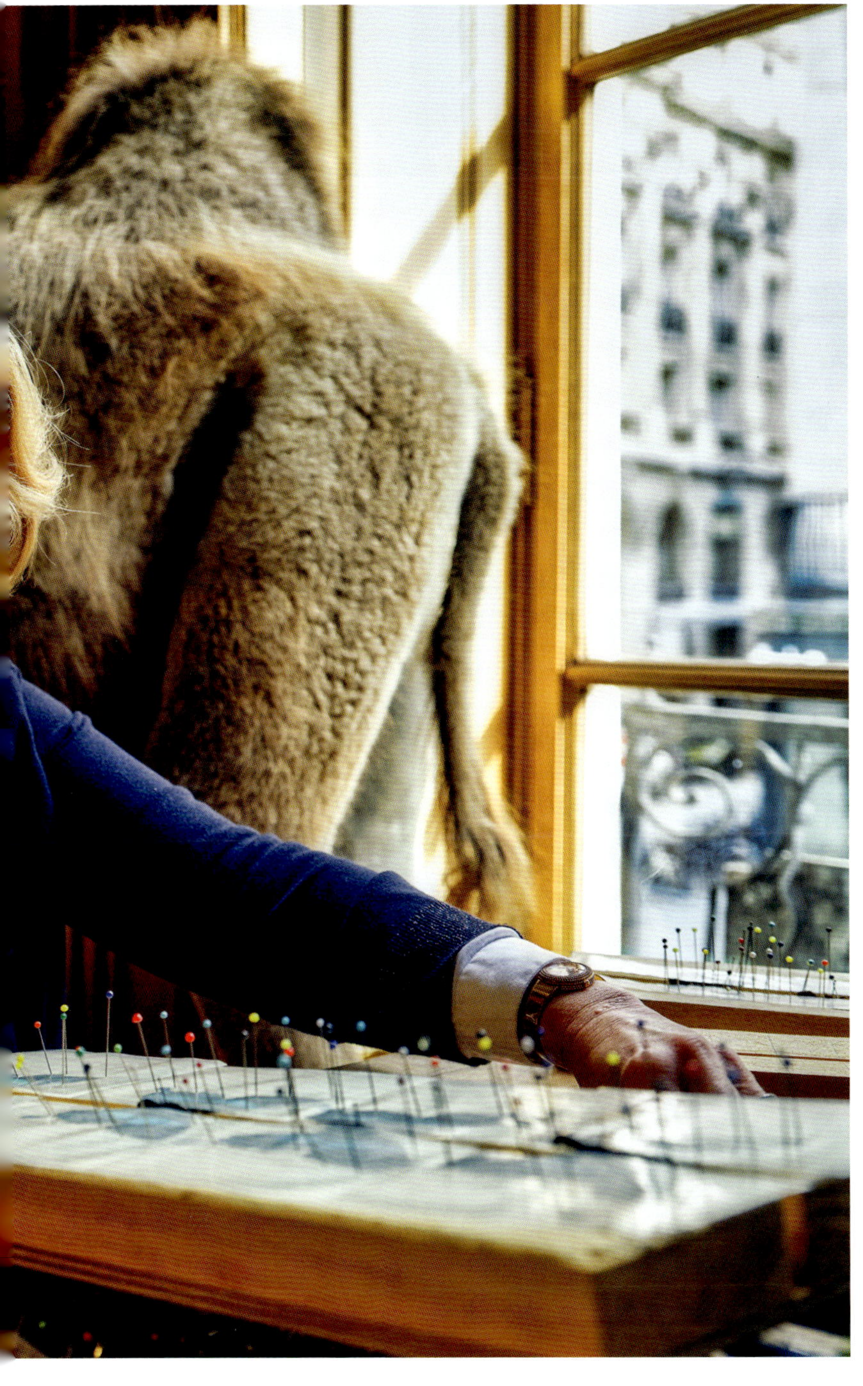

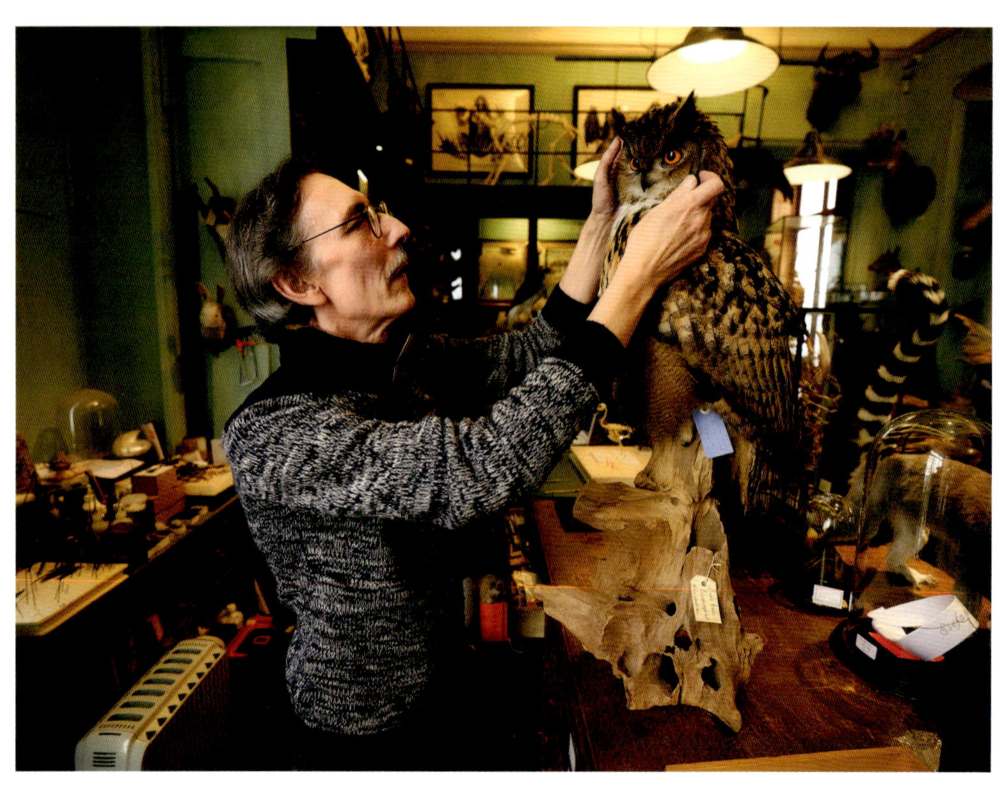

Yves Ceretti Taxidermist, Deyrolle > Paris, France

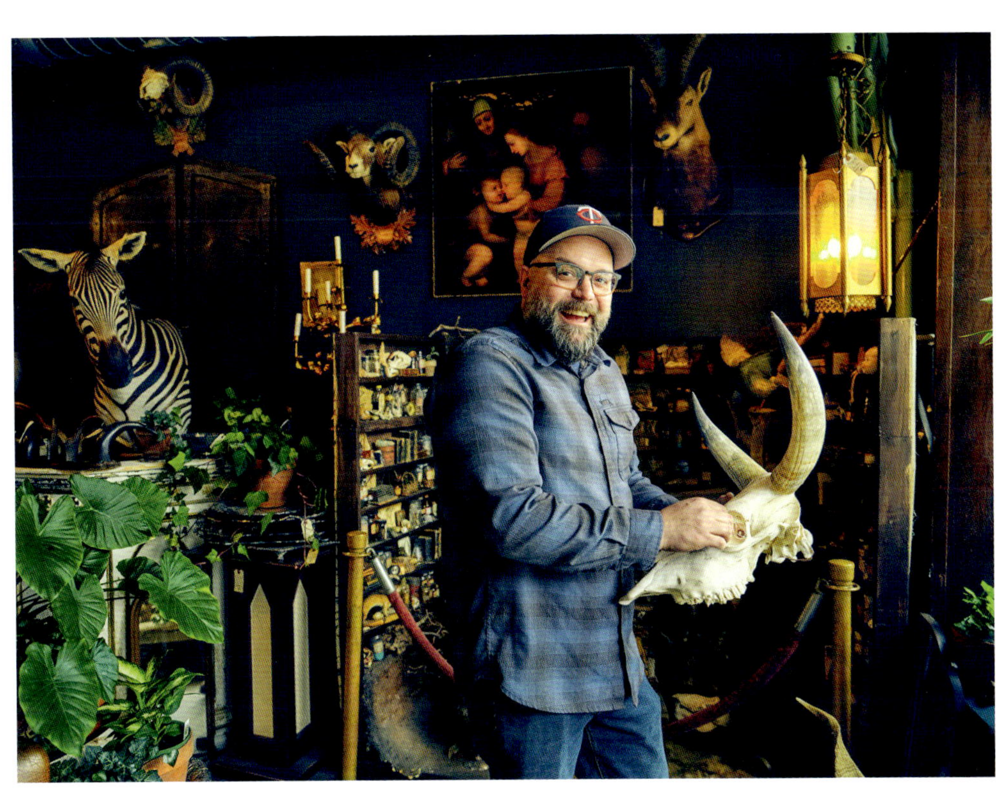

Adam DeJarlais Curator, Twelve Vultures Oddities > Minneapolis, Minnesota

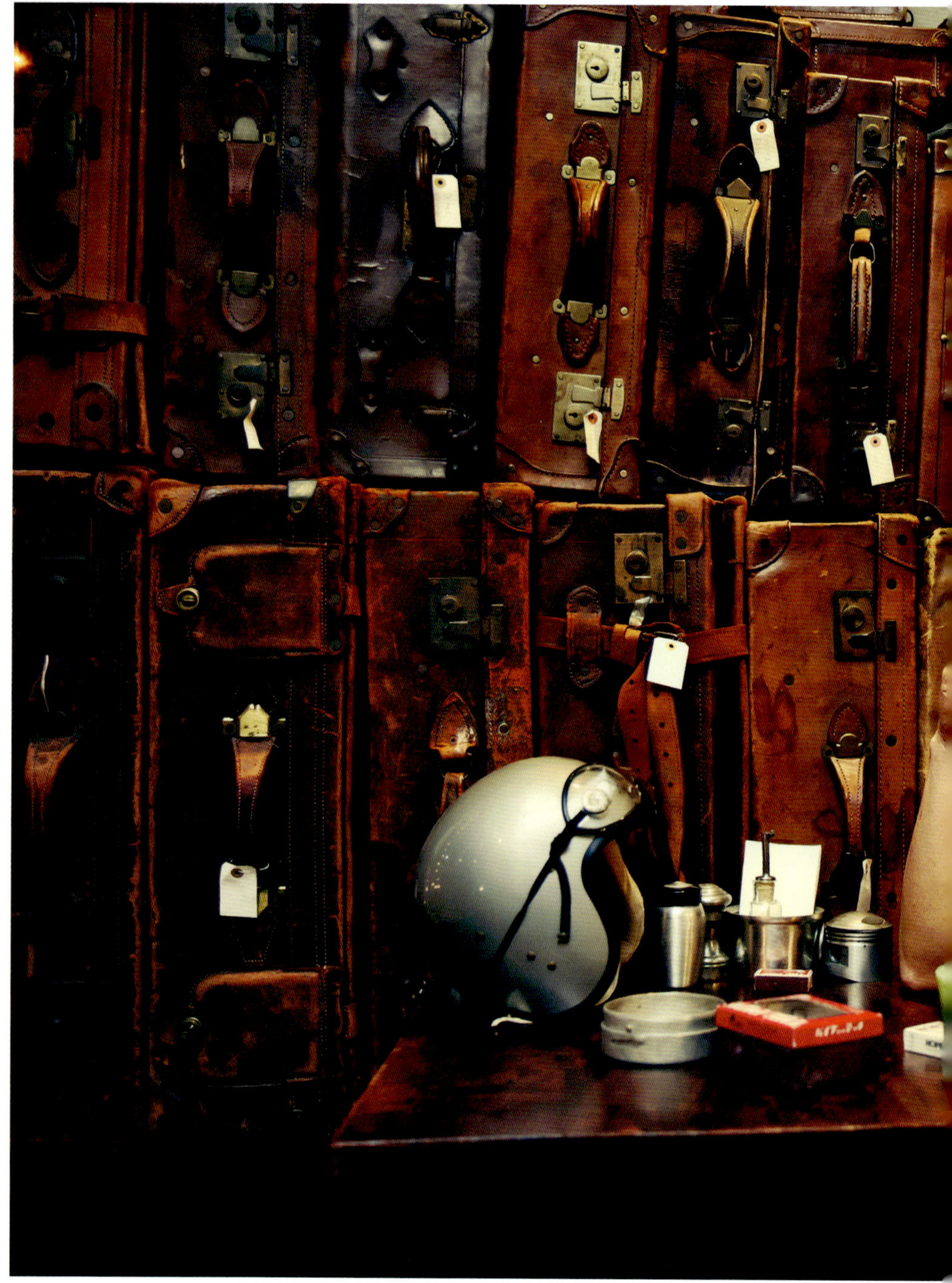

Ryuji Nakagawa Antiques Café > Tokyo, Japan

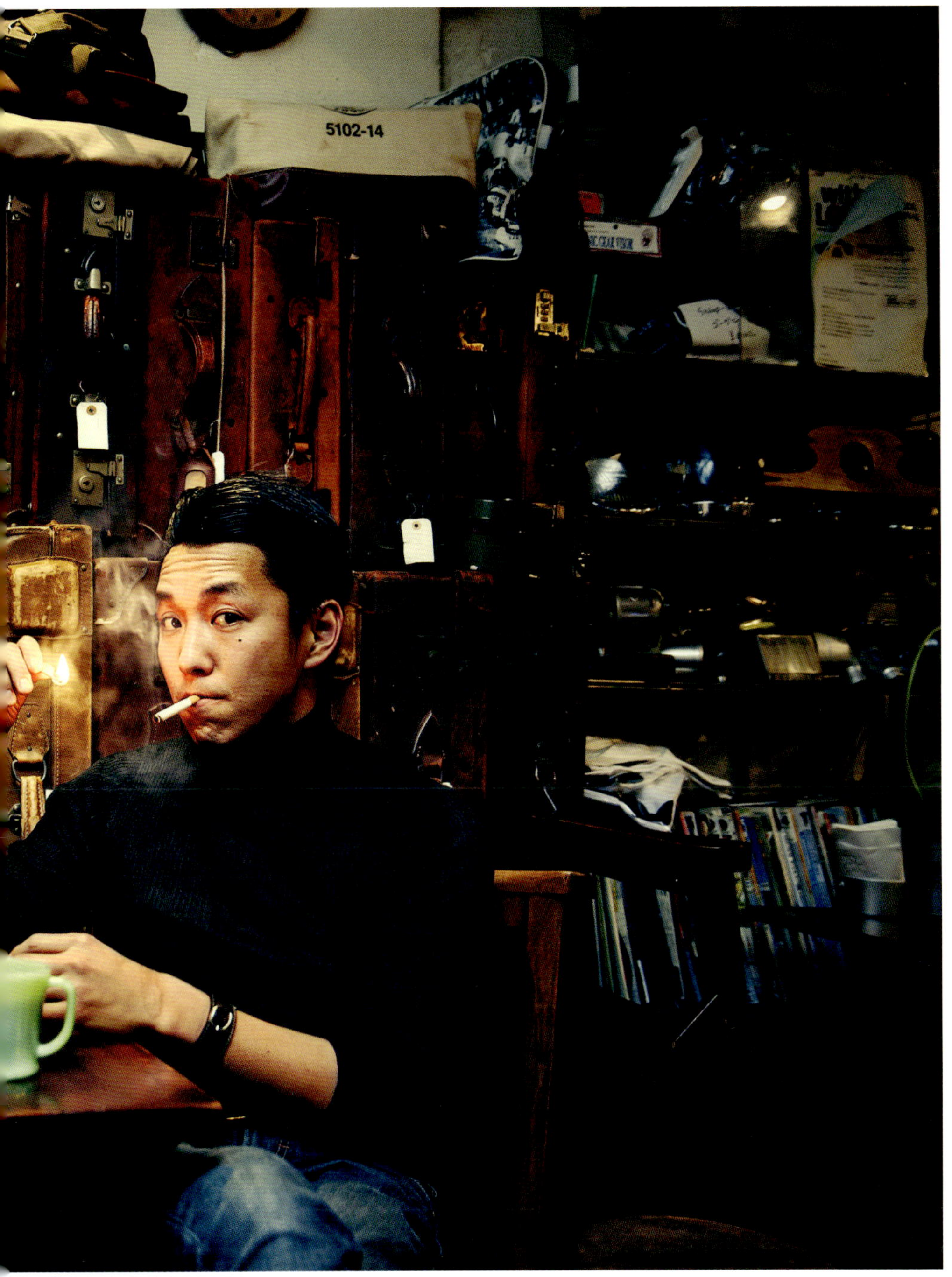
5102-14

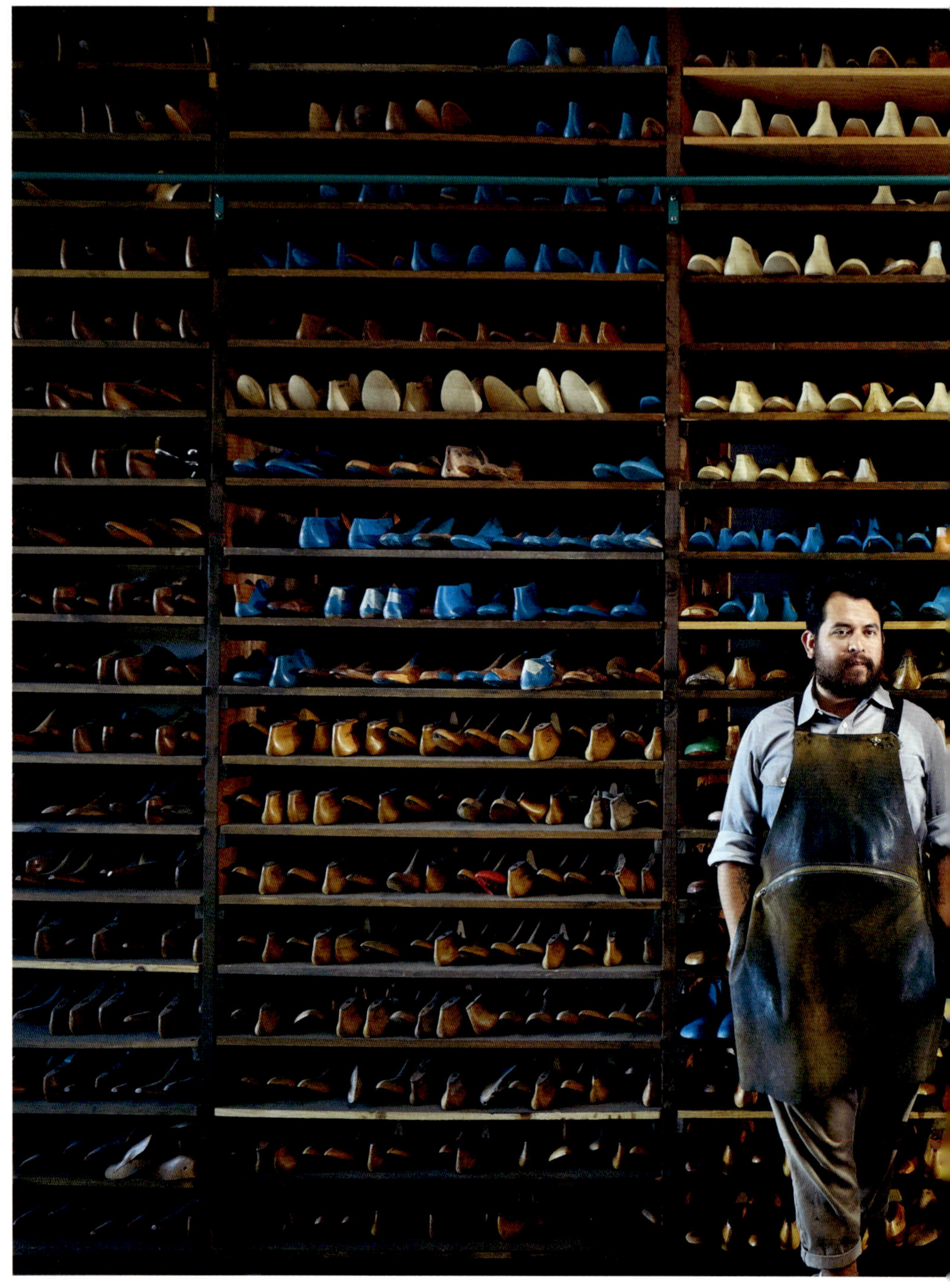

Raul Ojeda Shoemaker, Willie's Shoe Service > Los Angeles, California

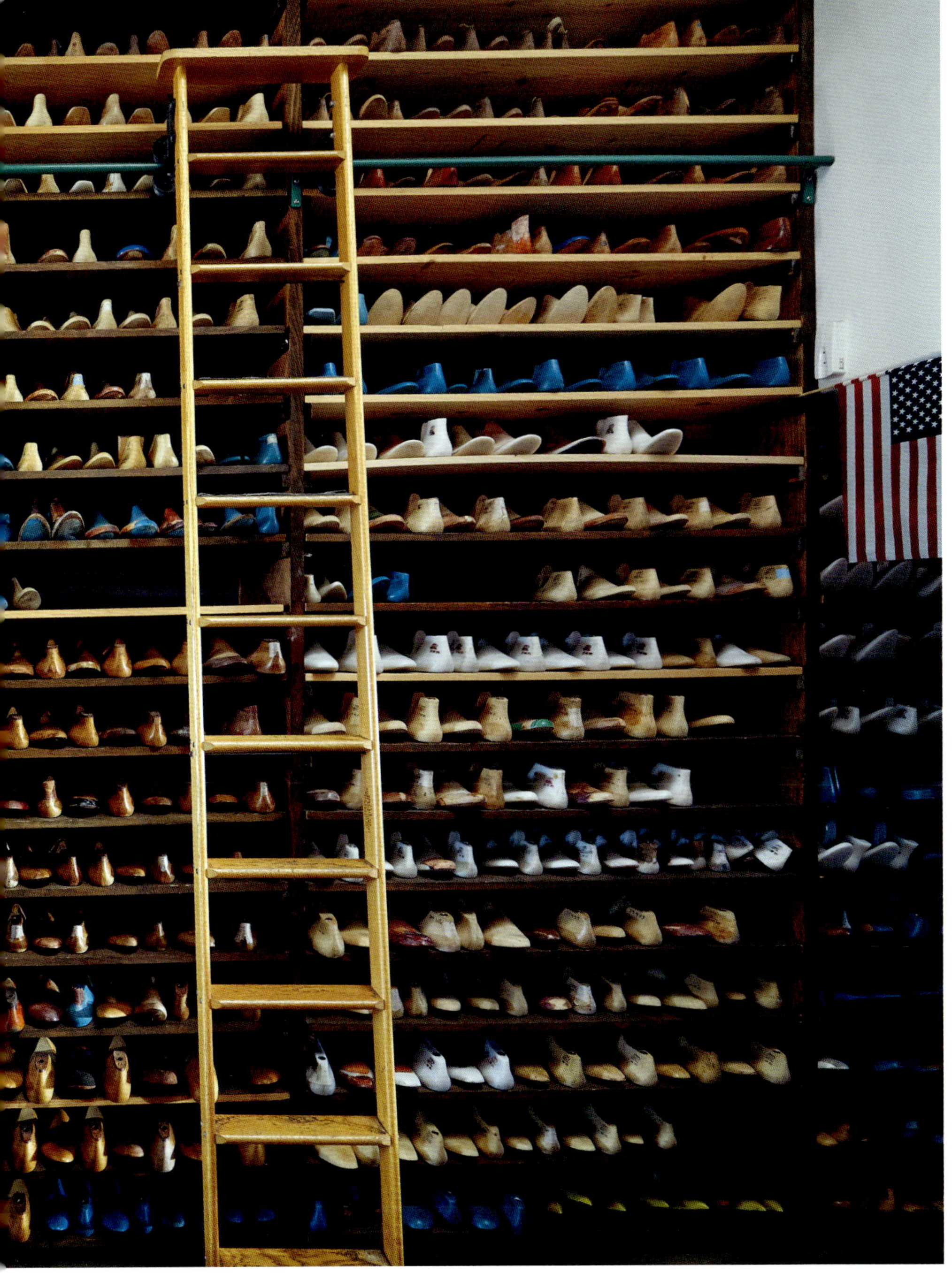

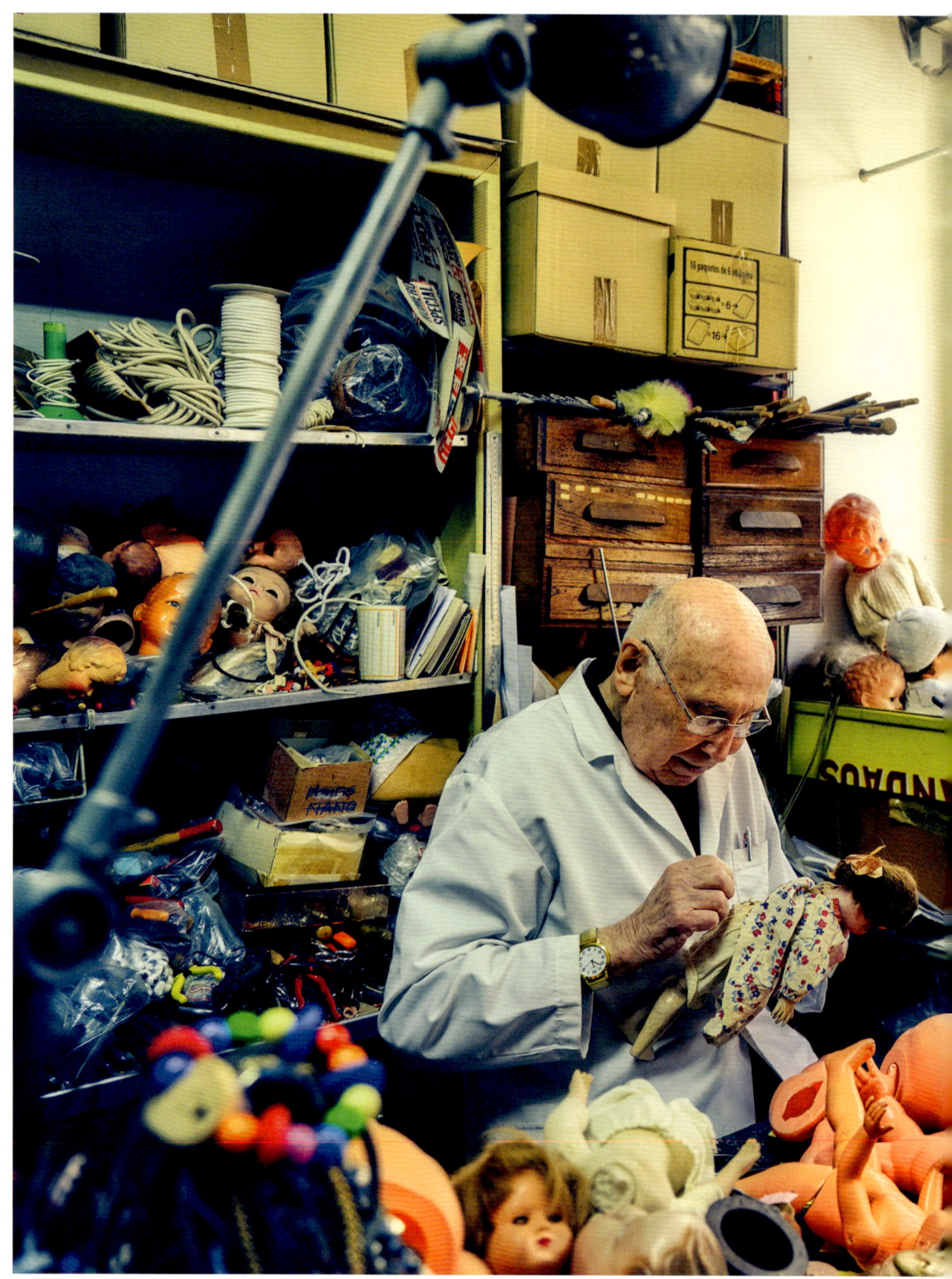

Doll Doctor > Paris, France

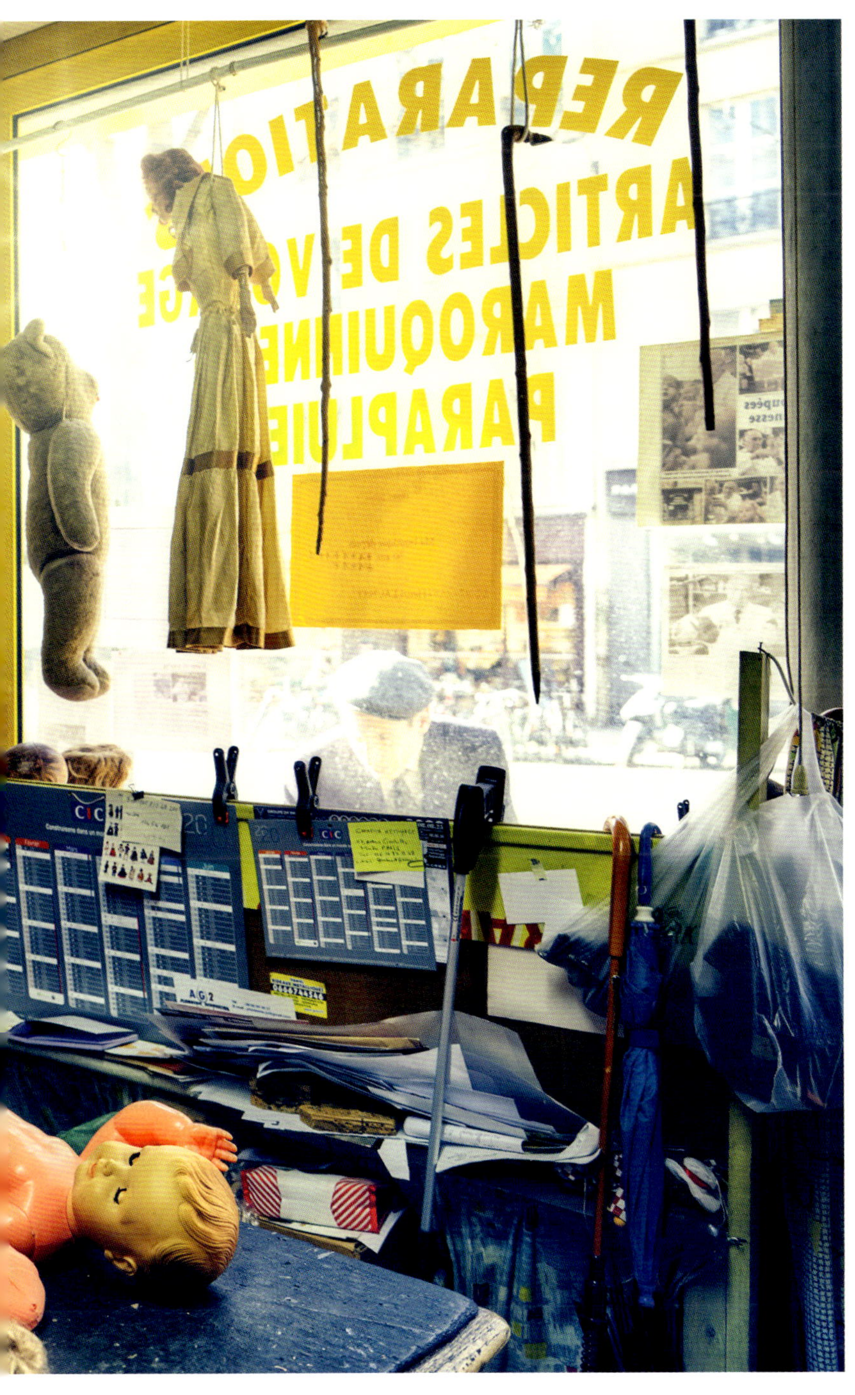
RÉPARATIONS
ARTICLES DE VOYAGE
MAROQUINERIE
PARAPLUIE

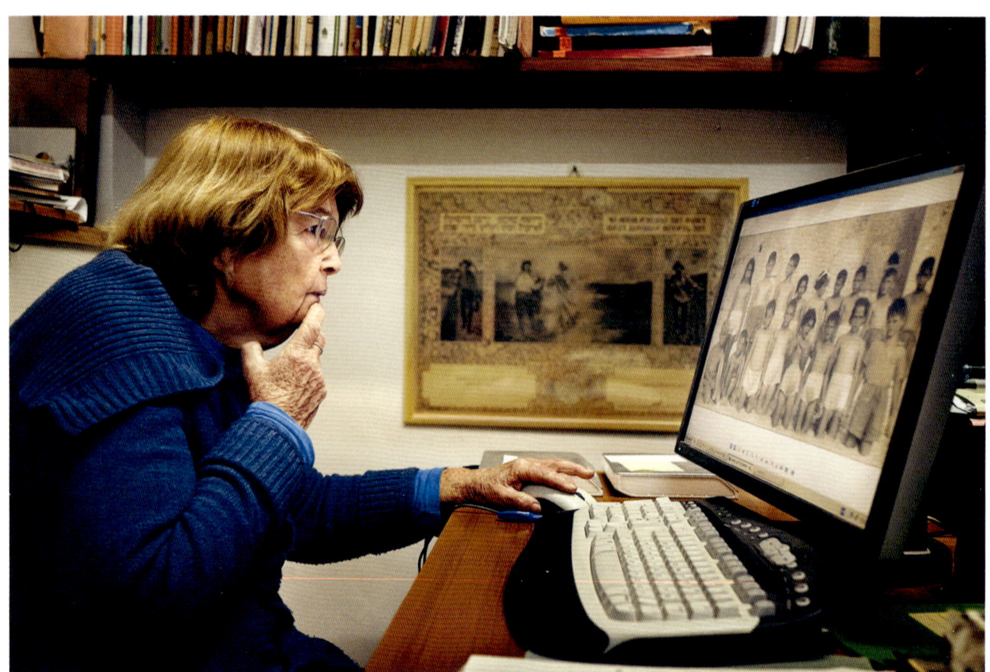

My mother and her family were Holocaust survivors from Holland. They had managed to escape to Israel after the war, eventually moving to the United States. Years later, I met Lena at the Kibbutz where they had lived.

She asked for my mother's maiden name. Within minutes, she pulled up a photograph of my uncle as a young boy. She knew him well; she'd even had a crush on him when they were kids.

Reverberations of the past continue to hum in all of us. A historian is there to protect the truth of those who are lost. I think of her as a guardian of my family's story.

Lena Krasnovski Archivist, Kibbutz Beit Hashita > Jezreel Valley, Israel

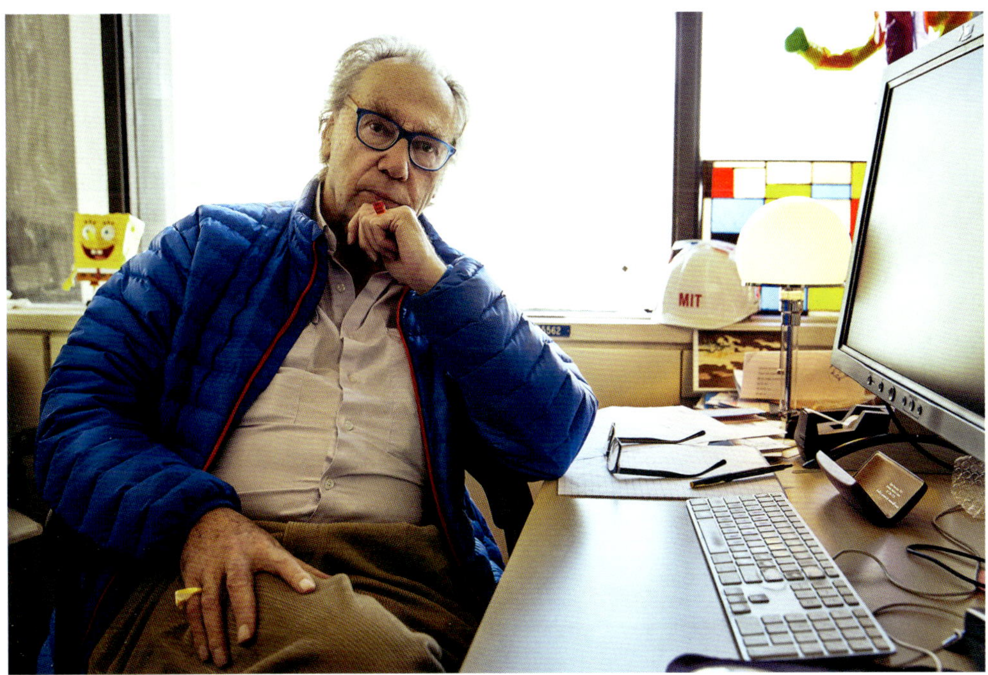

Right off the bat, Walter insisted these weren't going to be "true photographs" because they weren't shot in black and white.

I'm a professional. I've been on hundreds of shoots. But still, being challenged like that rattled me. It's not a great place to start with anybody.

I thought of how my sister-in-law says, "In business, it's never personal."

I wasn't there to debate. I didn't need to take it personally. I just needed to believe in myself. Was I up to it?

As SpongeBob would say, "I'm ready."

Walter Lewin Professor of Physics, MIT > Cambridge, Massachusetts

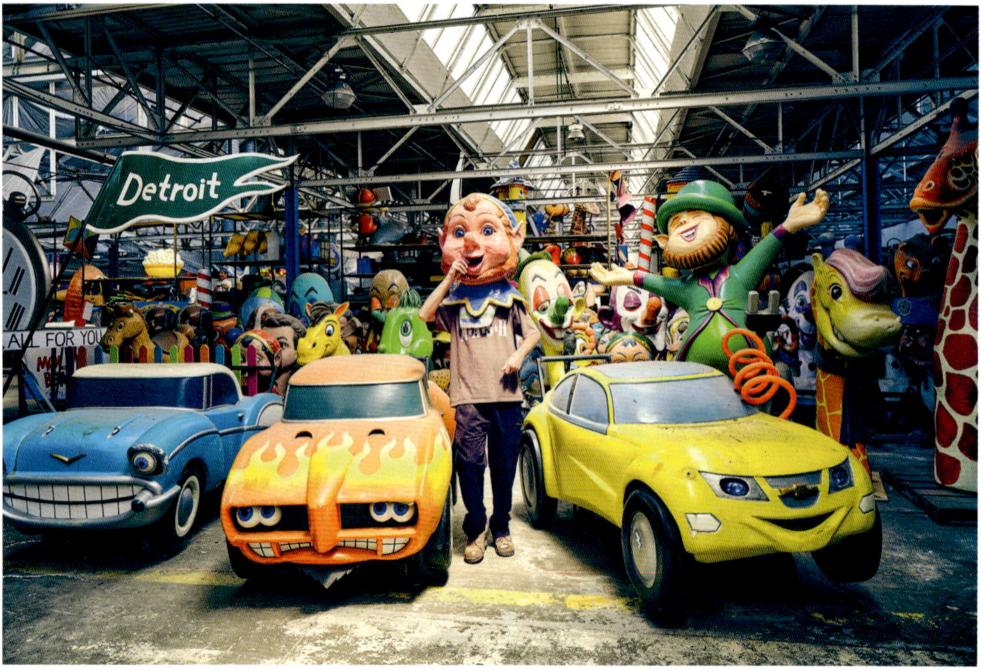

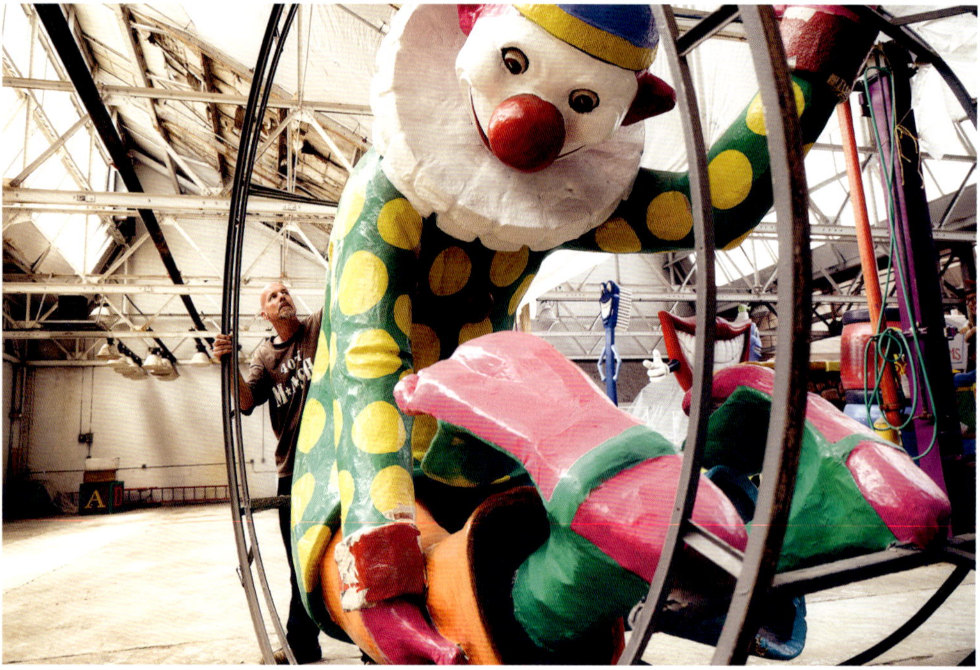

Parade Prop Makers The Parade Company > Detroit, Michigan

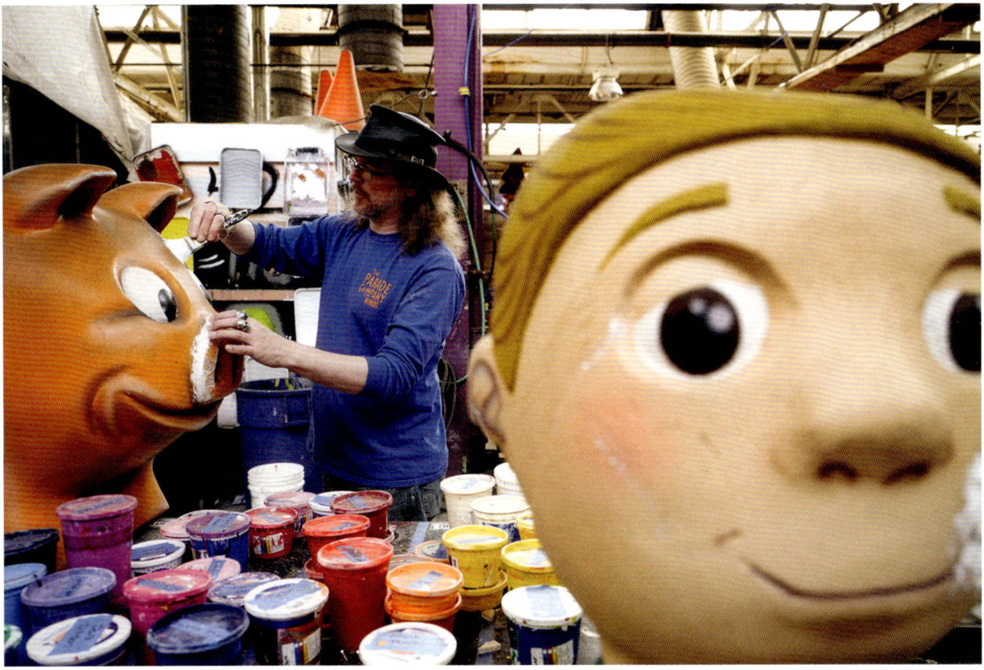

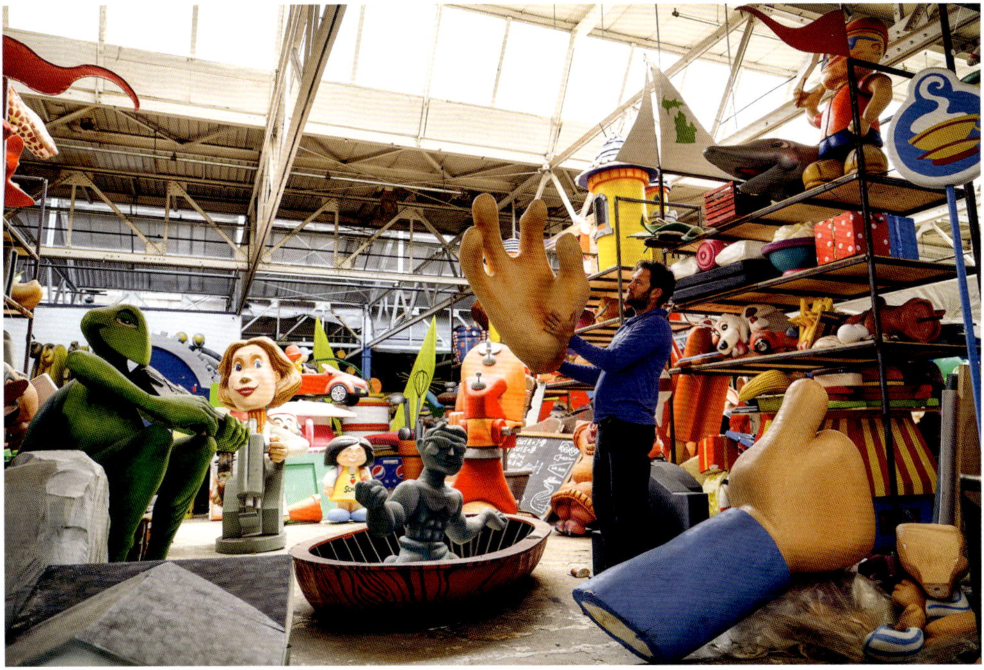

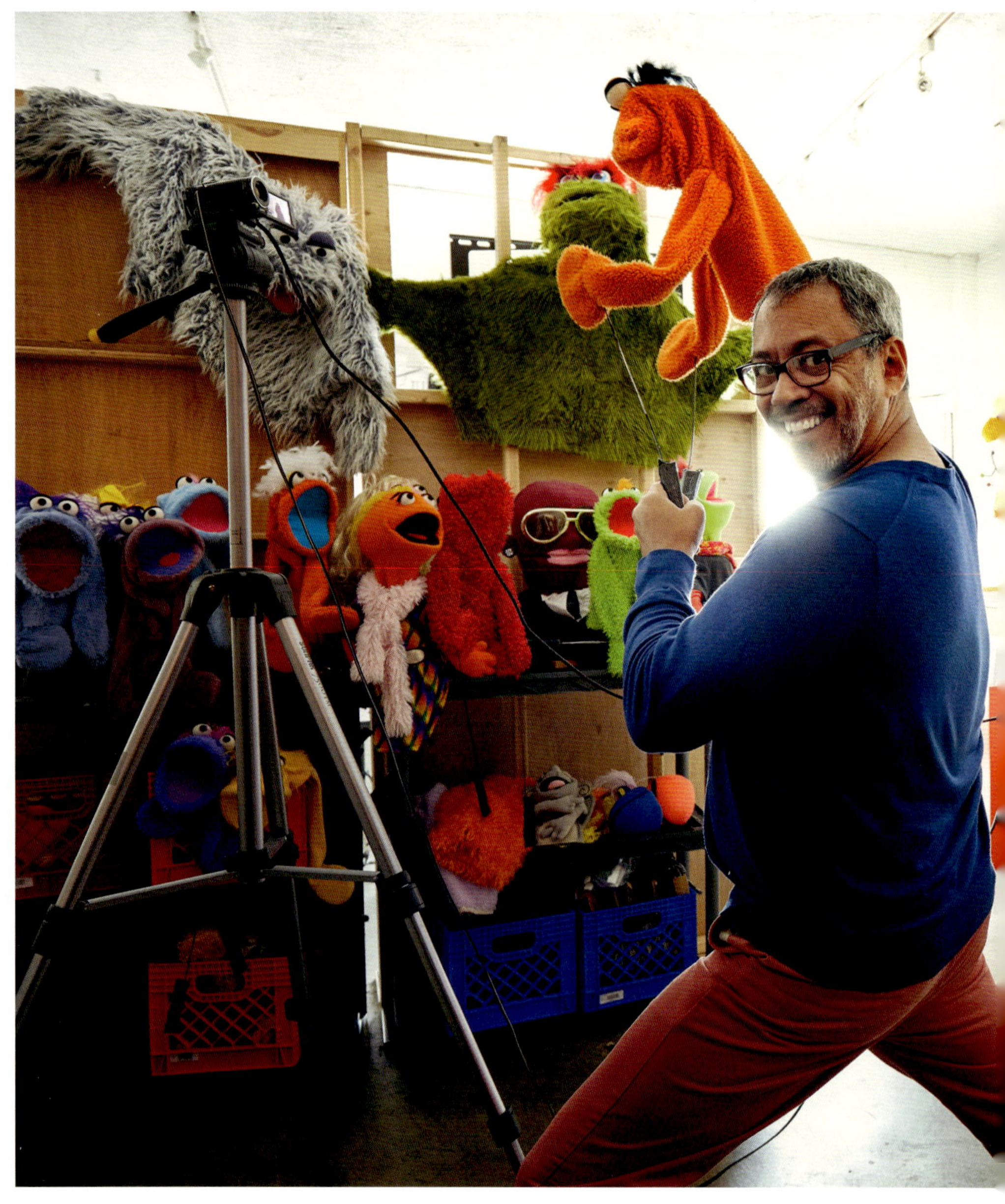

Roberto Ferreira Puppeteer, The Puppet School > Los Angeles, California

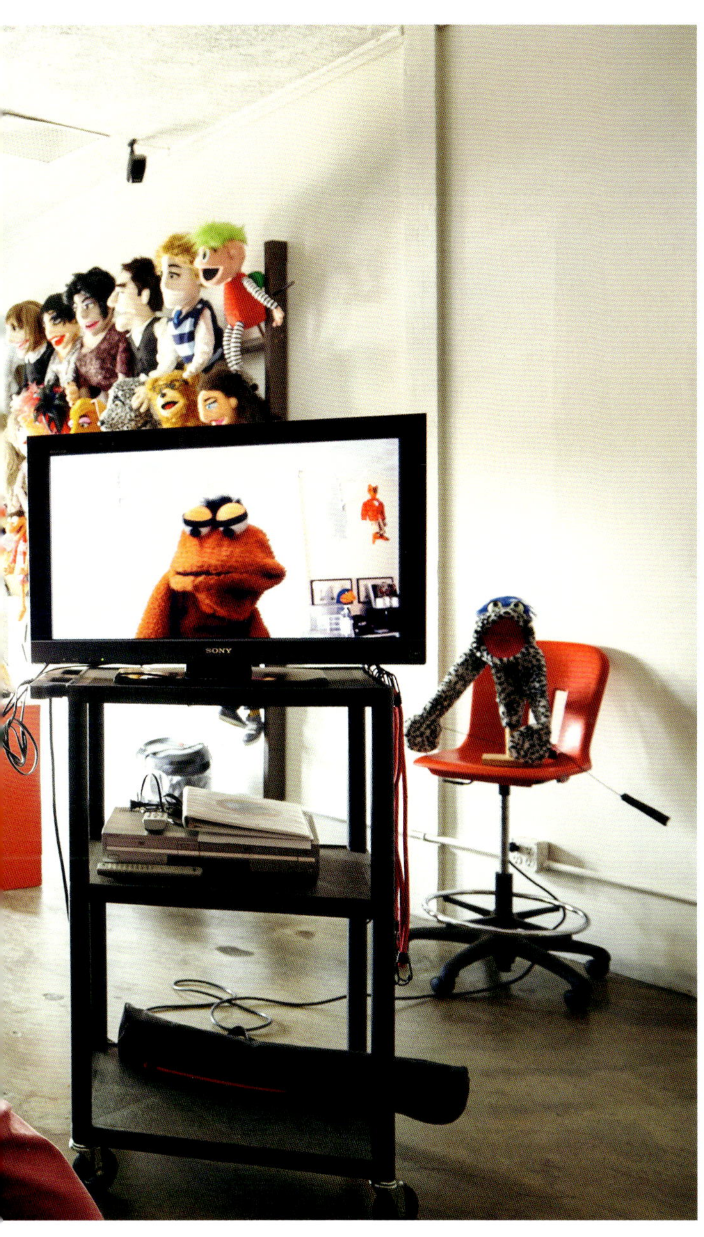

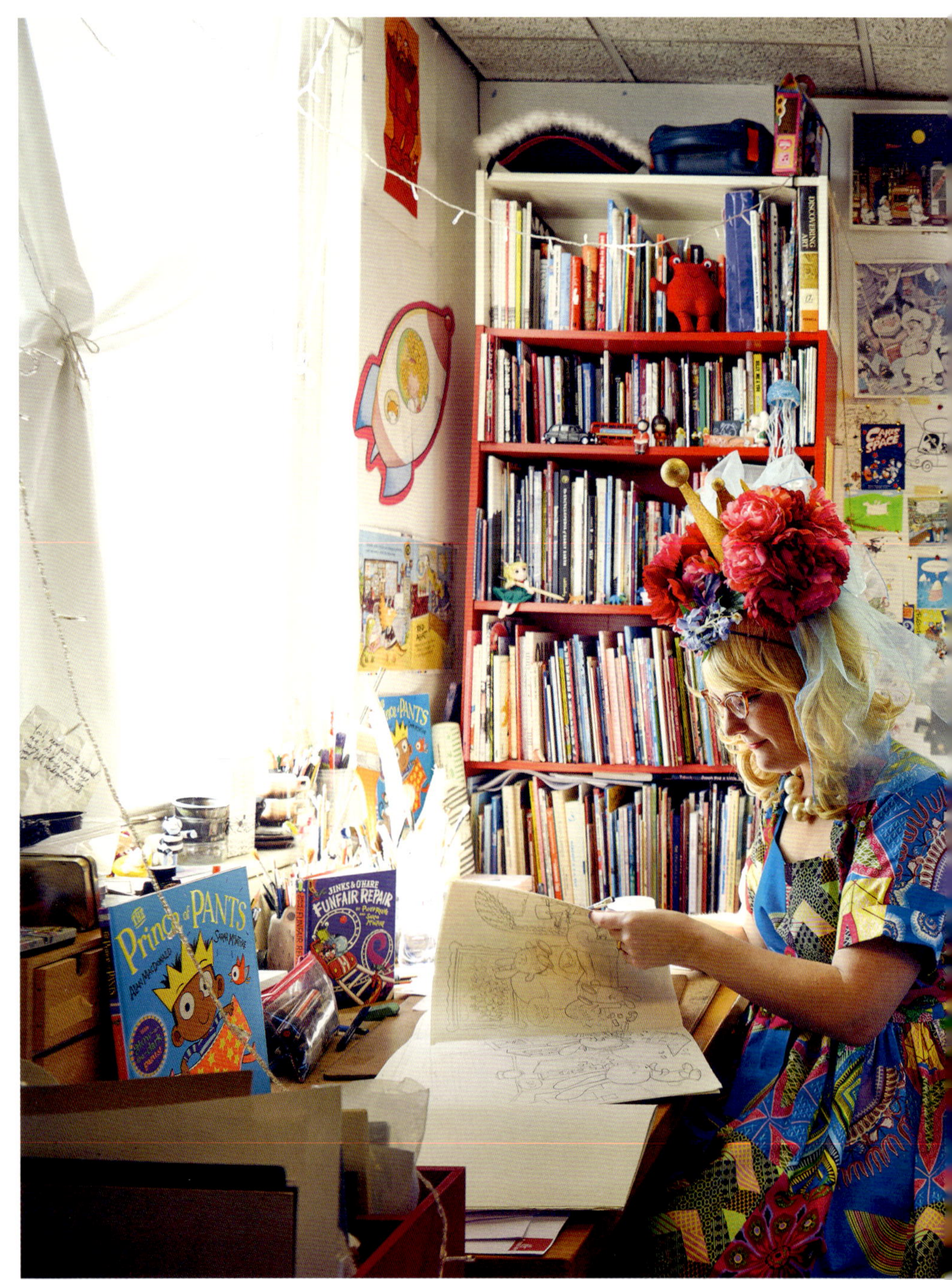

Sarah McIntyre Illustrator > London, England

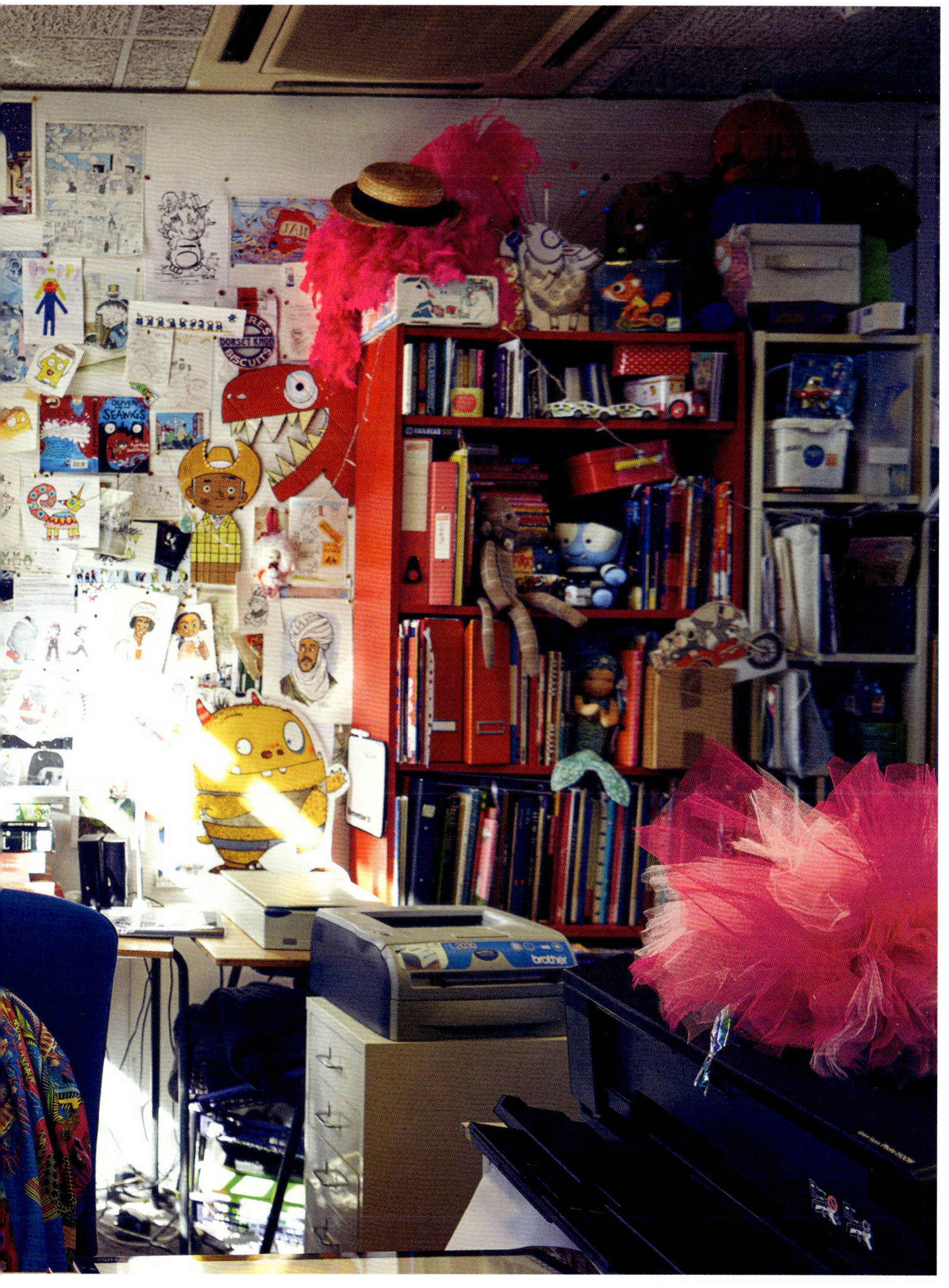

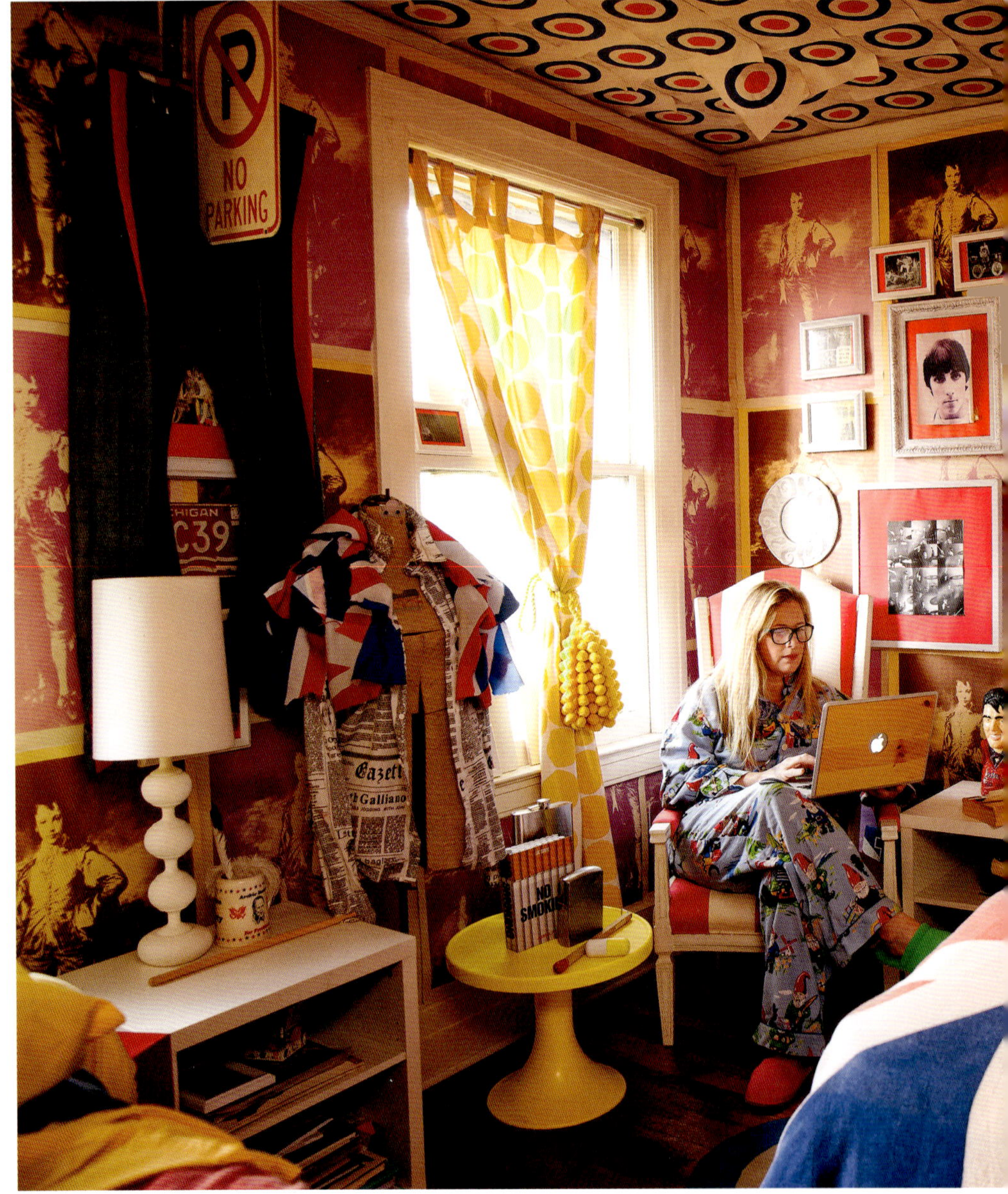

"I had a few friends from the UK stay at my house. I thought it would be nice to make them feel at home," she said.

Muffy Kroha Visual Manager, Neiman Marcus > Detroit, Michigan

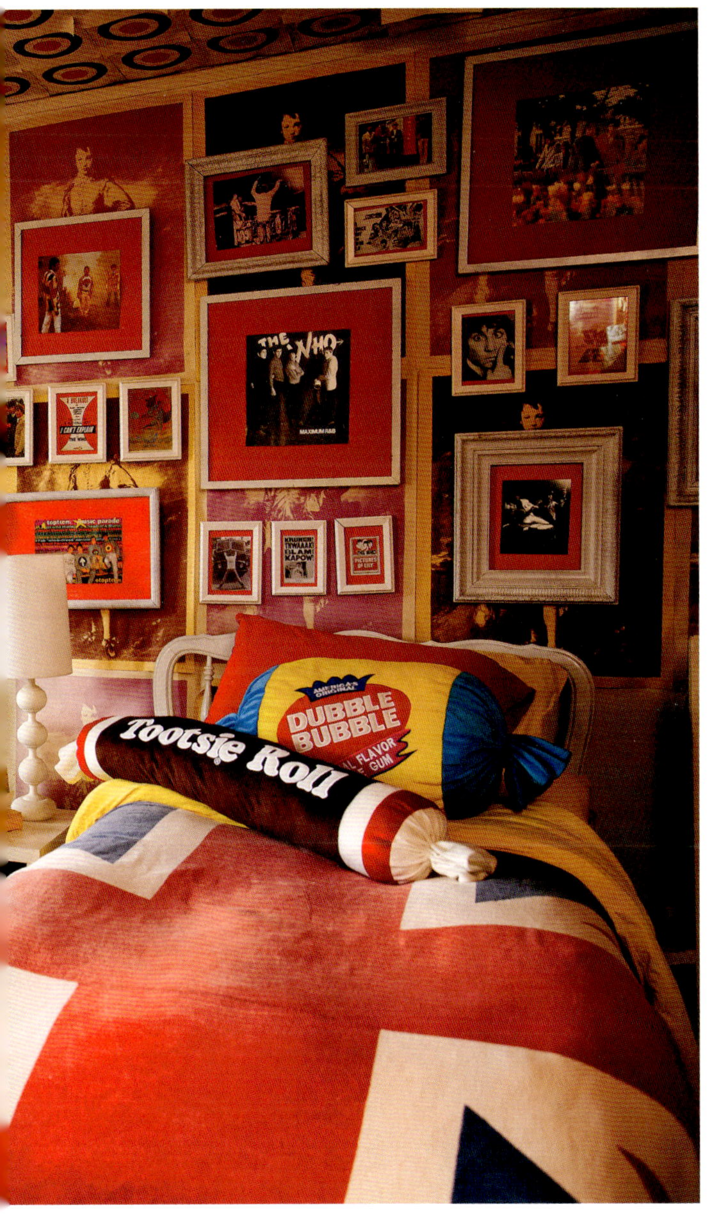

THE WHO
MAXIMUM R&B
DUBBLE BUBBLE
AMERICA'S ORIGINAL
REAL FLAVOR GUM
Tootsie Roll

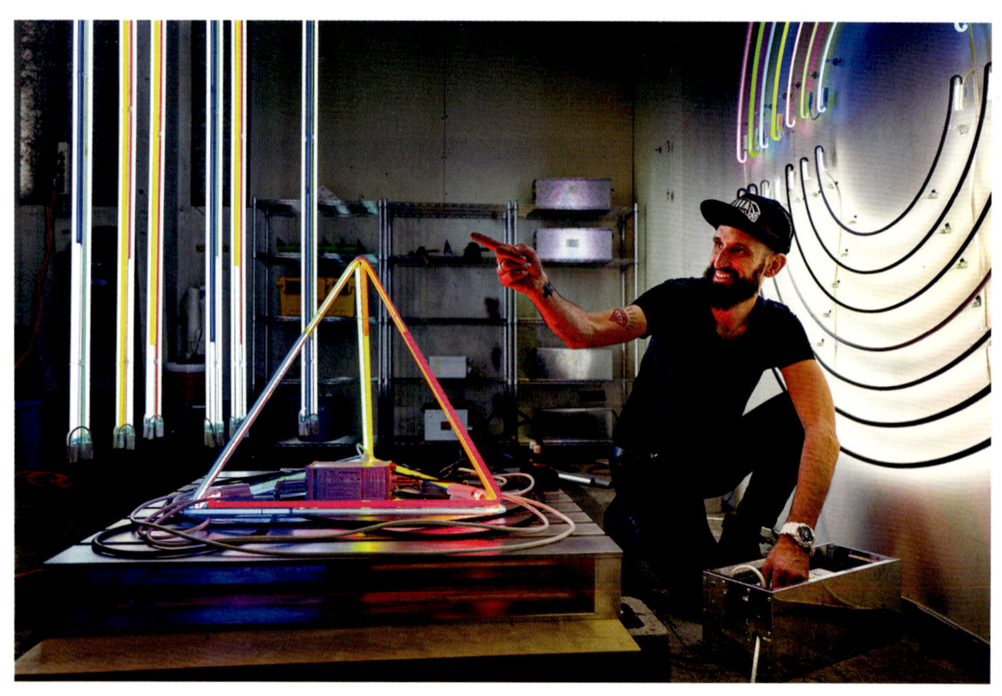

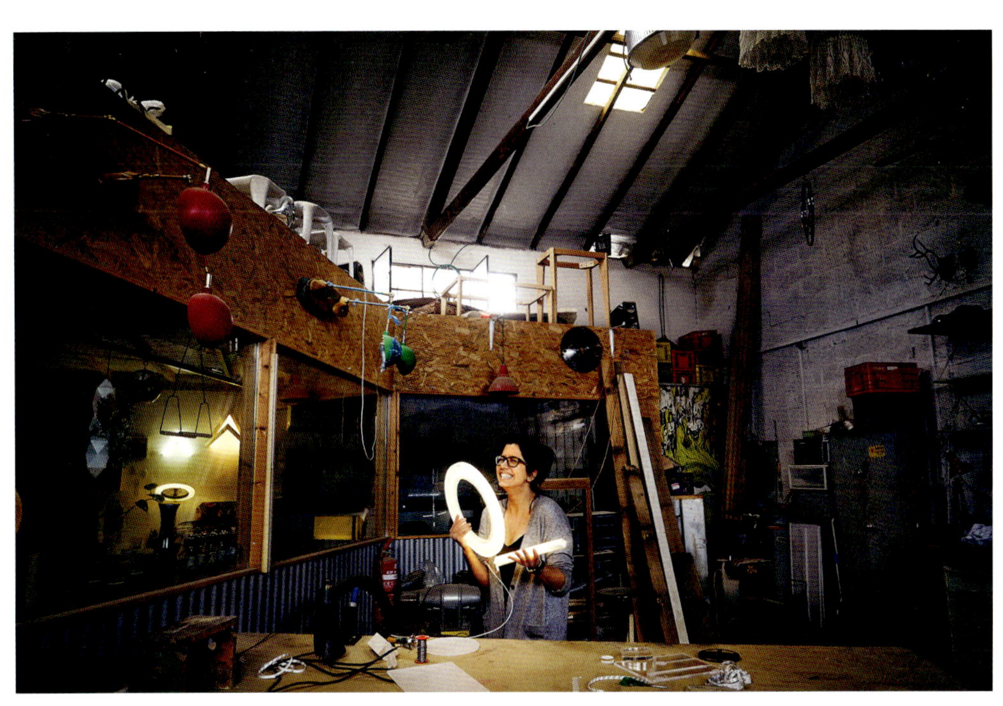

Talia Janover Industrial Designer, Ushki Design Studio > Tel Aviv, Israel

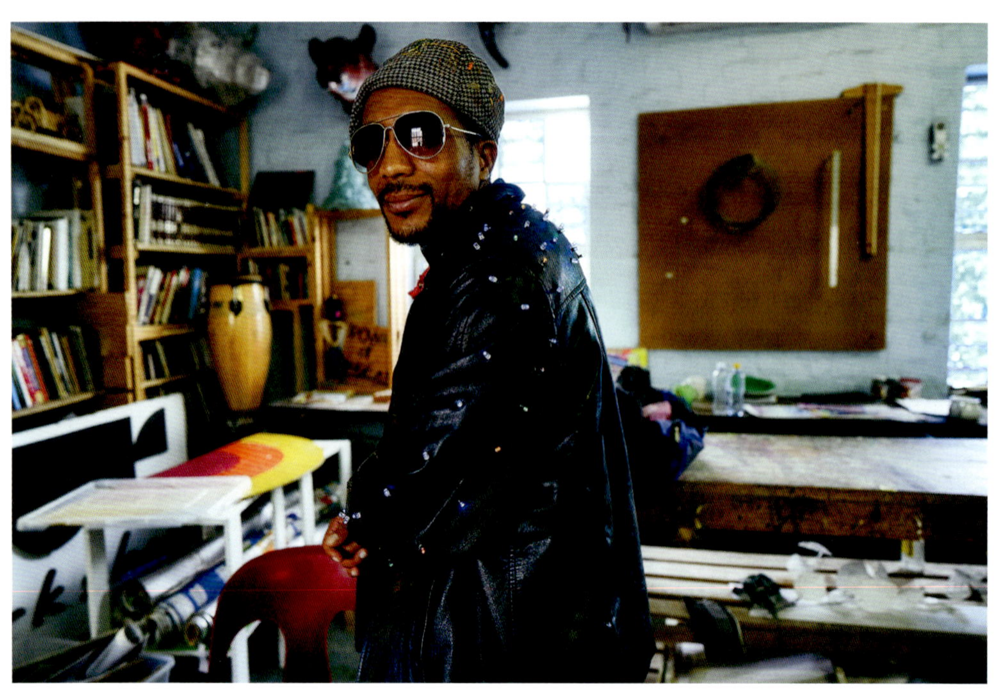

Sizwe Shumane Jacket Designer, Skhalo Roots > Langa Township, Cape Town, South Africa

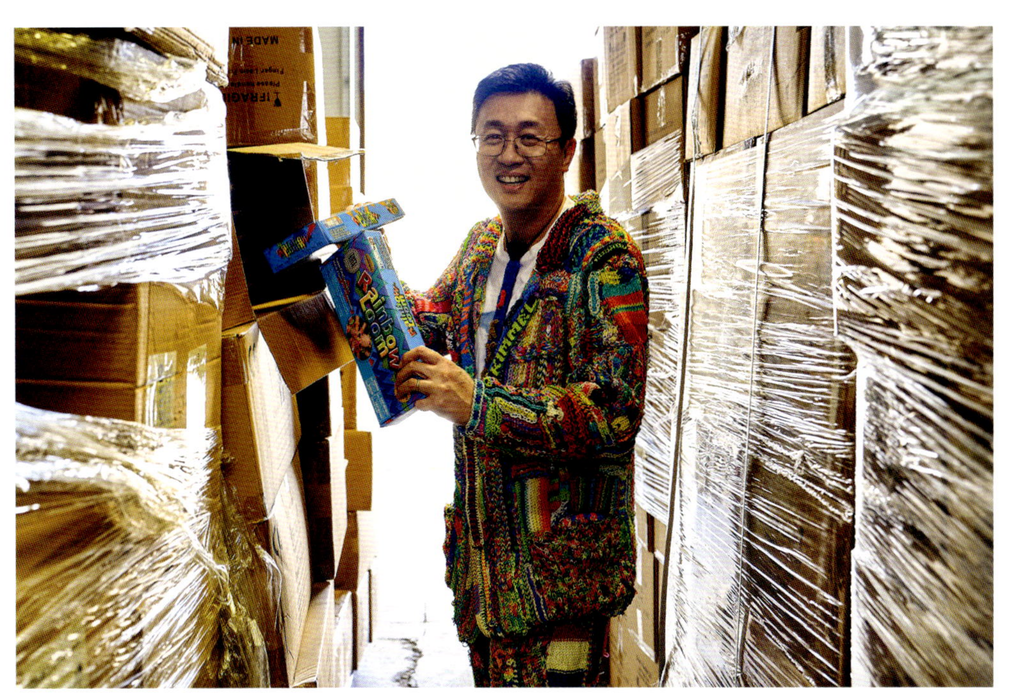

Choon Ng Creator, Rainbow Loom > Farmington Hills, Michigan

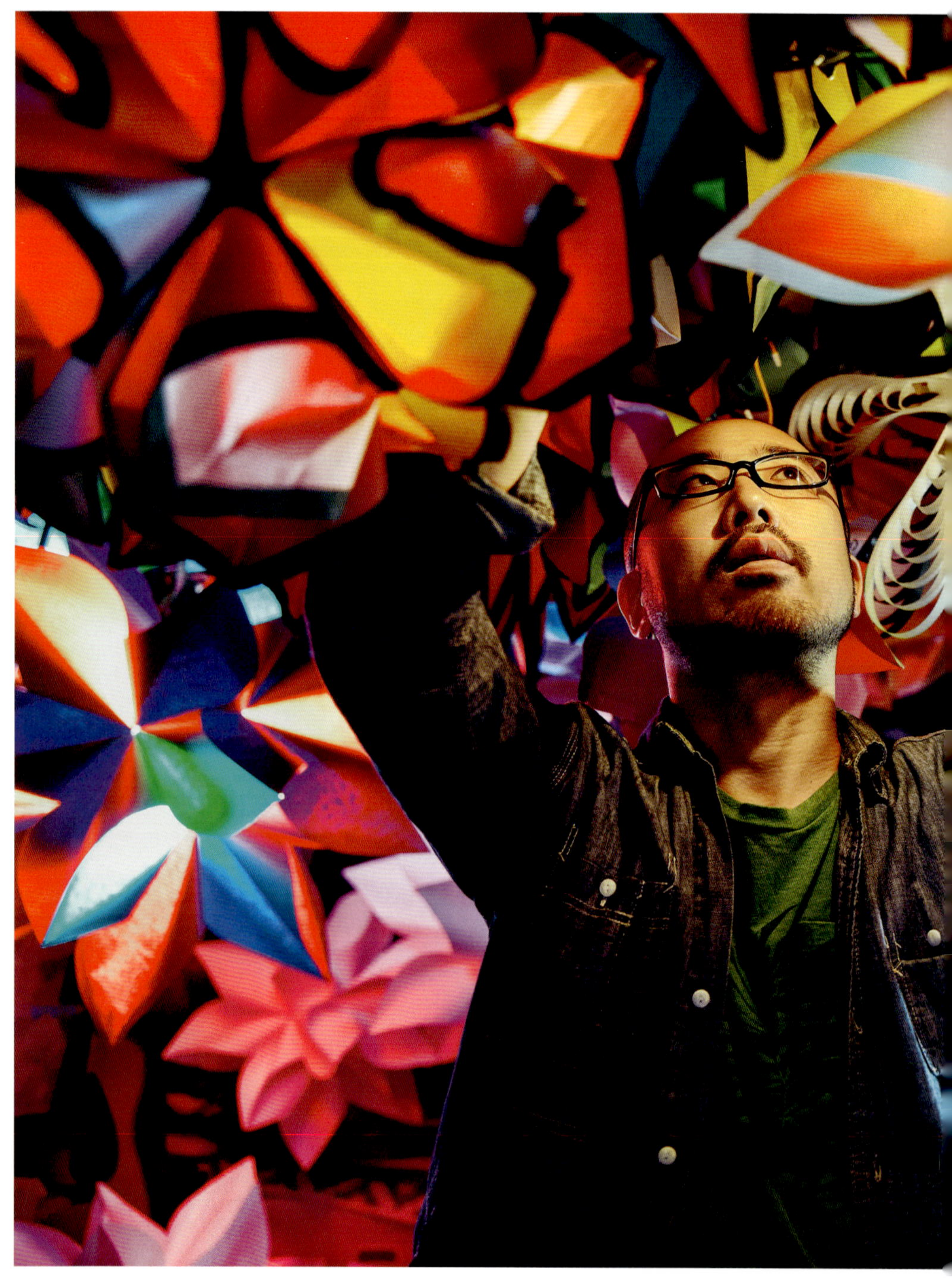

Nozomu Oshima Lighting Specialist, Oshima Electric > Tokyo, Japan

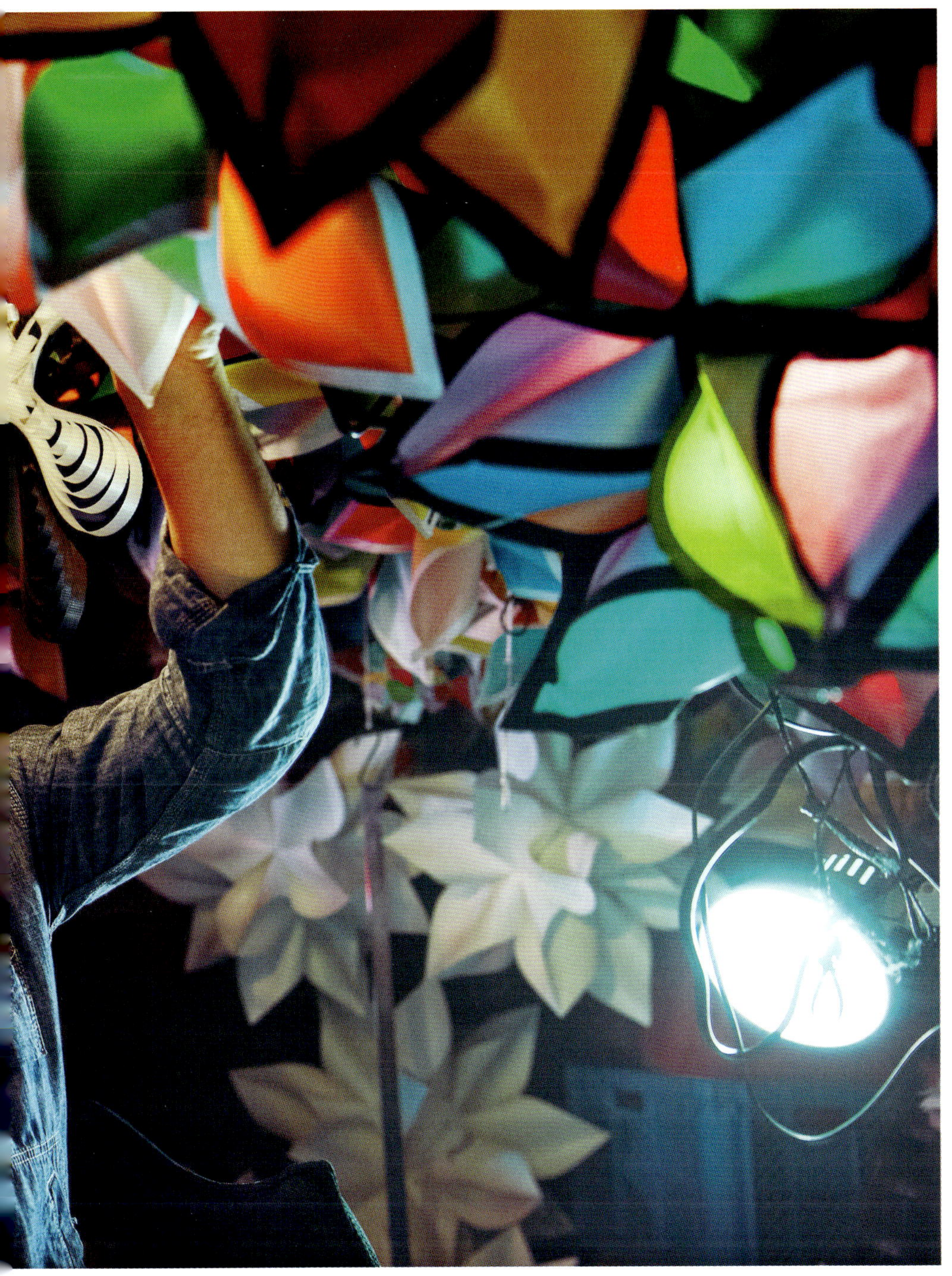

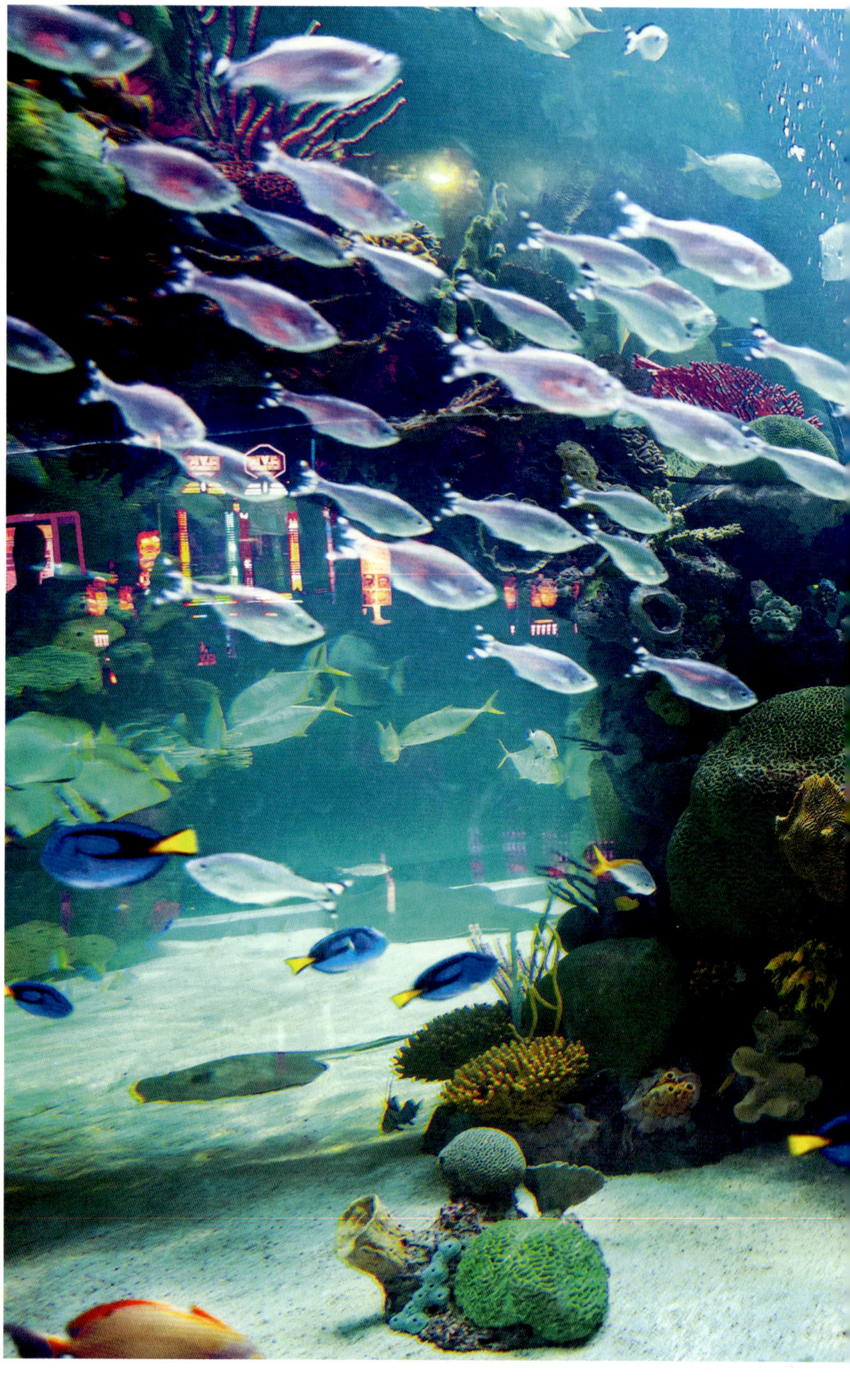

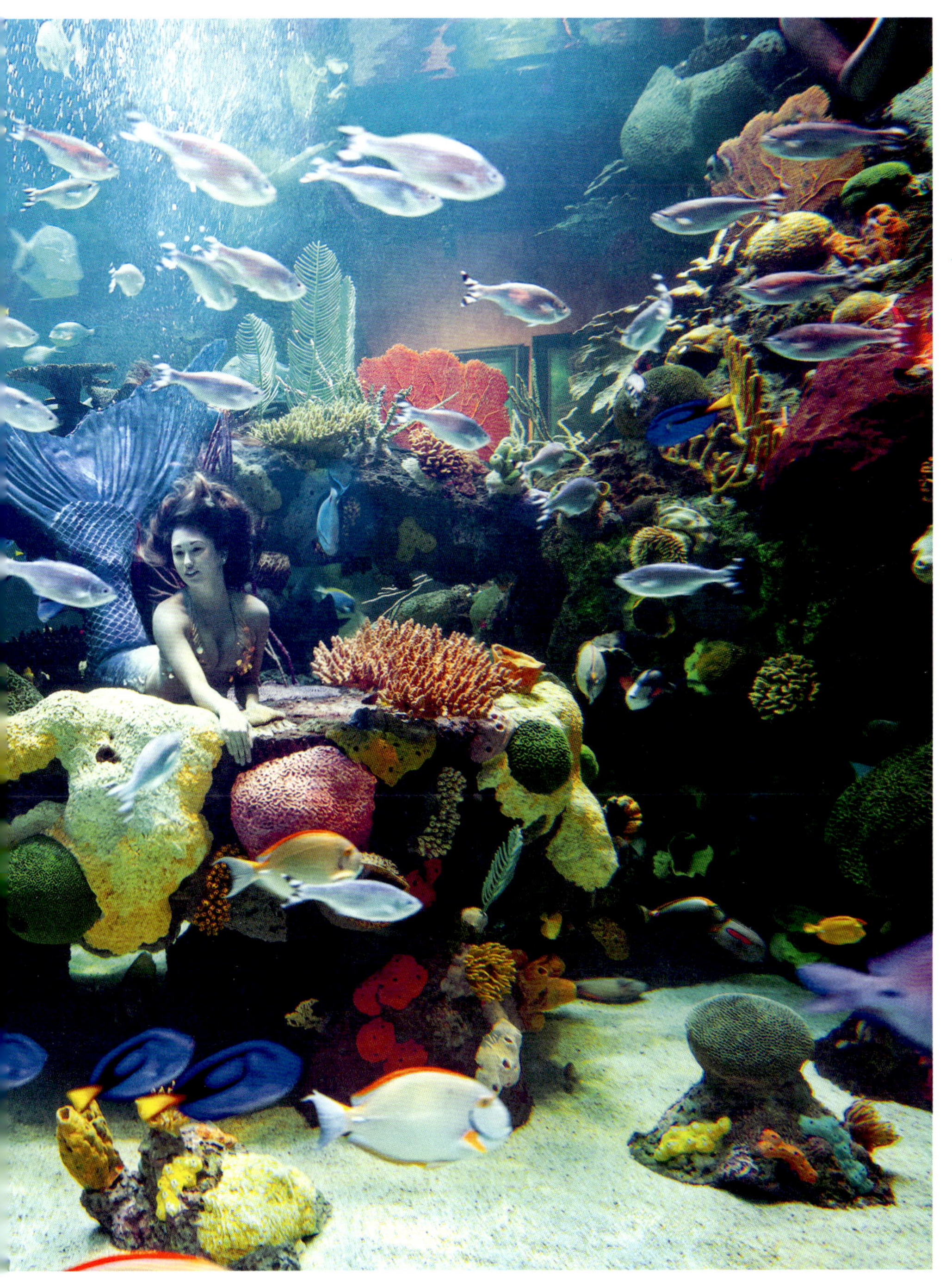

Ariana Liuzzi Mermaid > Las Vegas, Nevada

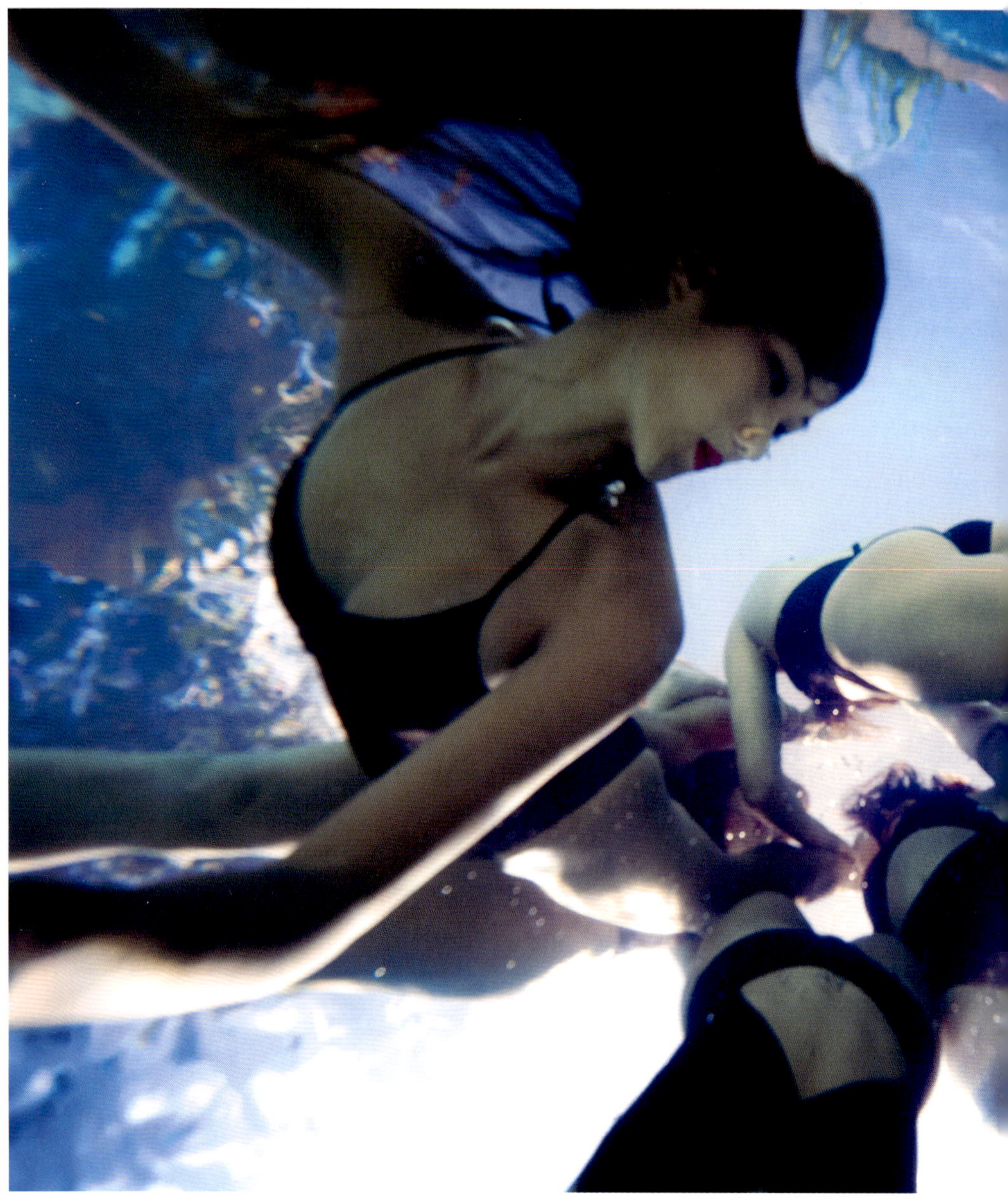

First off, I am not a strong swimmer. My assistant had to do most of the deep diving, securing the camera under the heavy shot bags.

The sun was relentless. I was on the pool deck, exhausted. At the end of a full day of shooting, the professional in me knew that I had nothing at all. Nothing.

There was one frame left on my camera. What could I do? I had to either

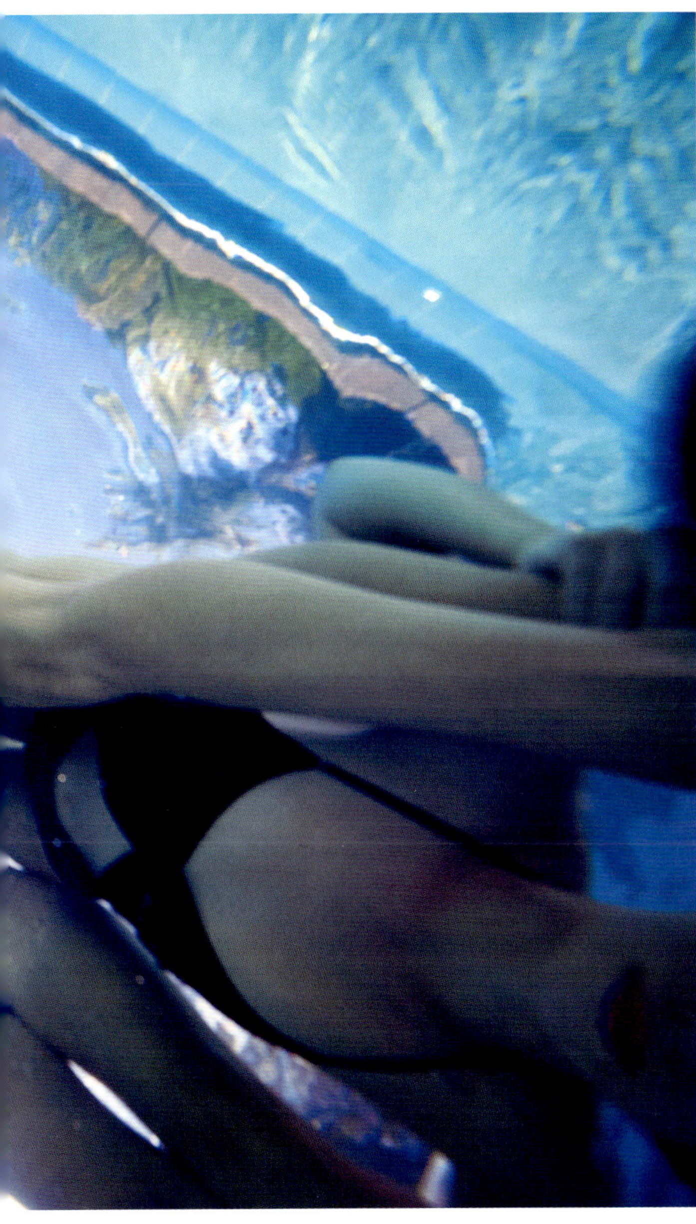

throw in the towel, or throw a Hail Mary.

I framed the image in my mind. I gave the women direction on how I wanted them to move. But I couldn't see what it was going to look like.

I fired the shot.

Aqualillies Synchronized Swimmers, Artistic Swimming Company > Los Angeles, California

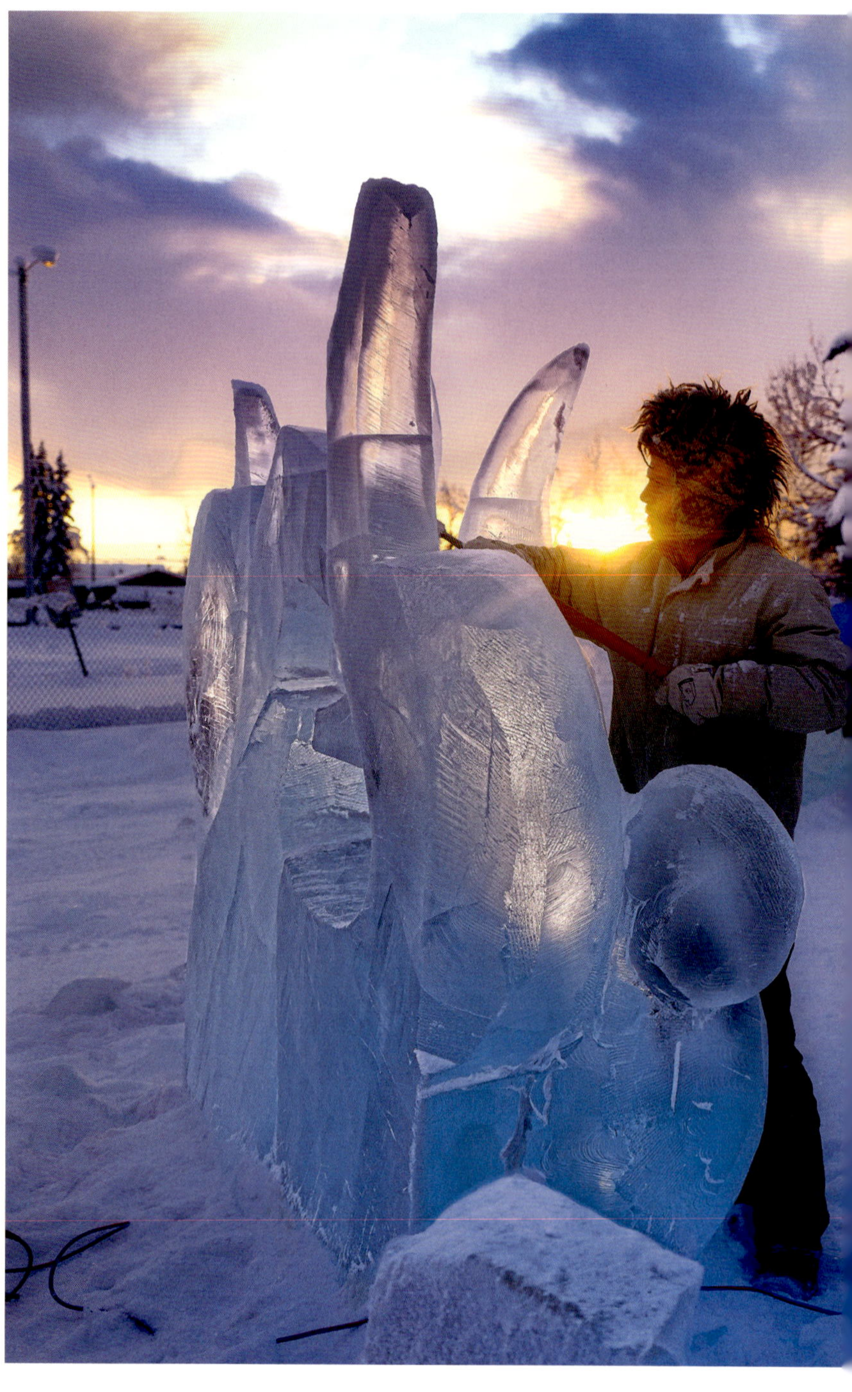

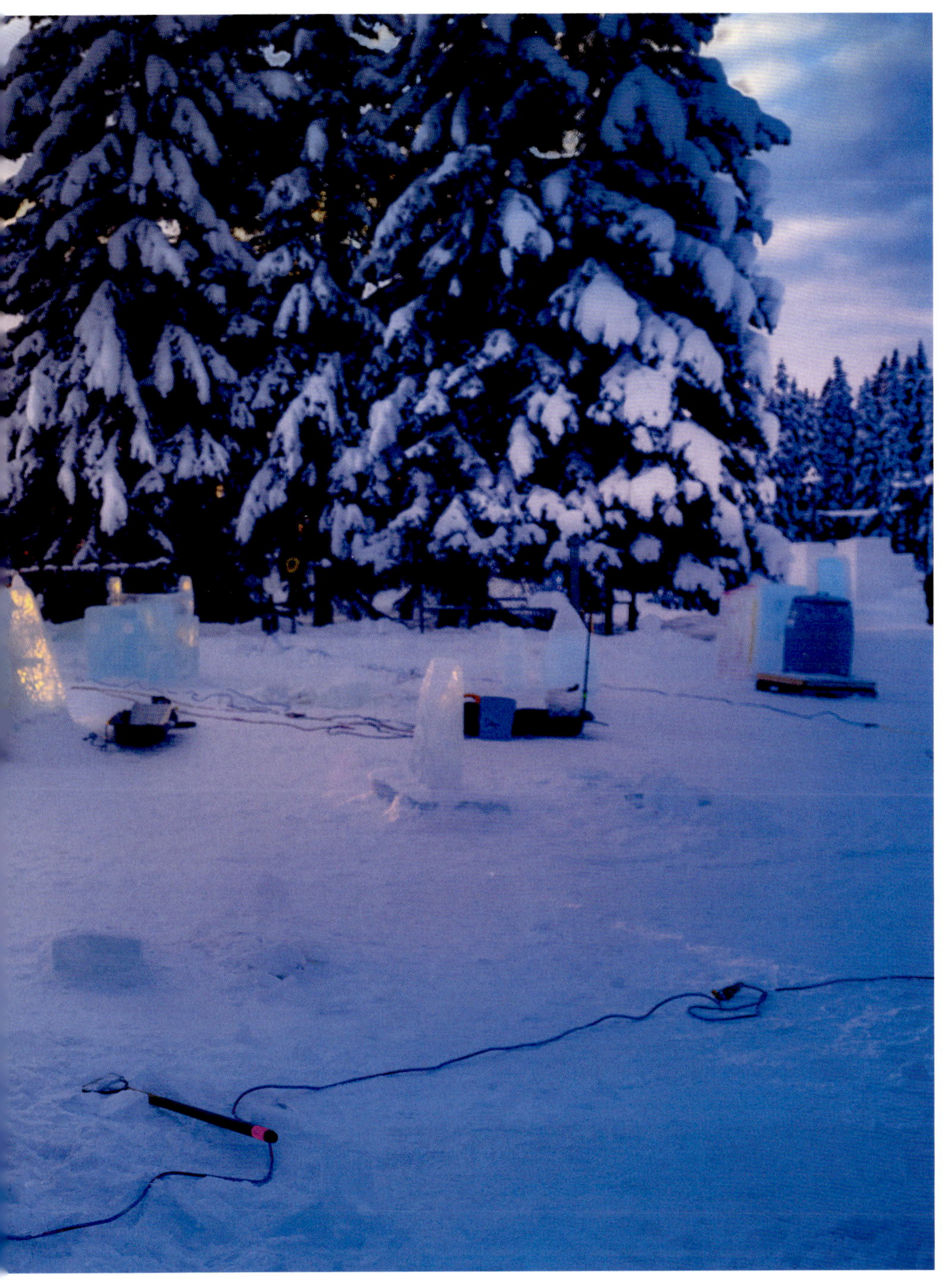

Abram Waterman Ice Sculptor > Fairbanks, Alaska

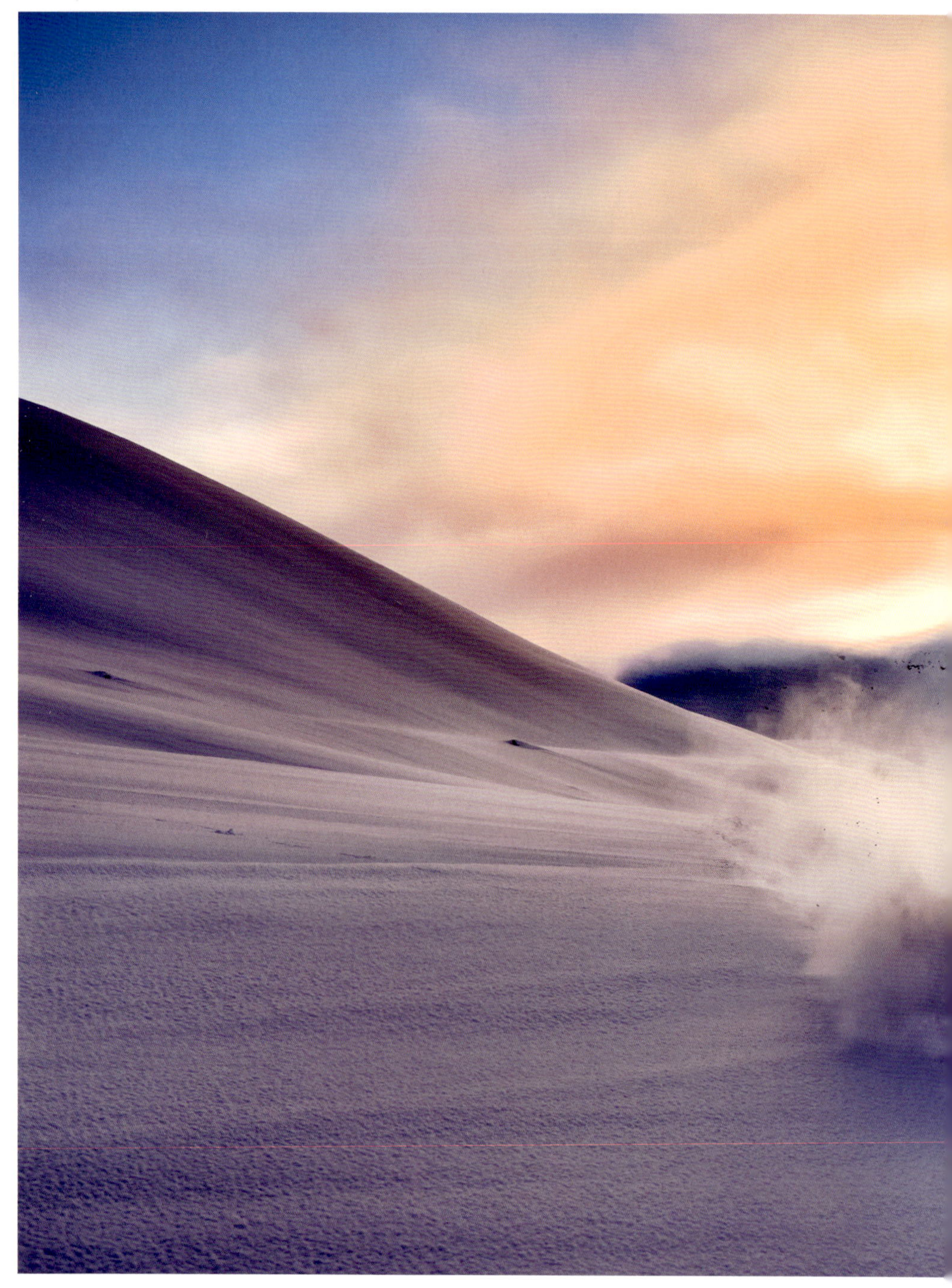

Trooper Austin McDaniel Alaska Wildlife Trooper > Hatcher Pass, Alaska

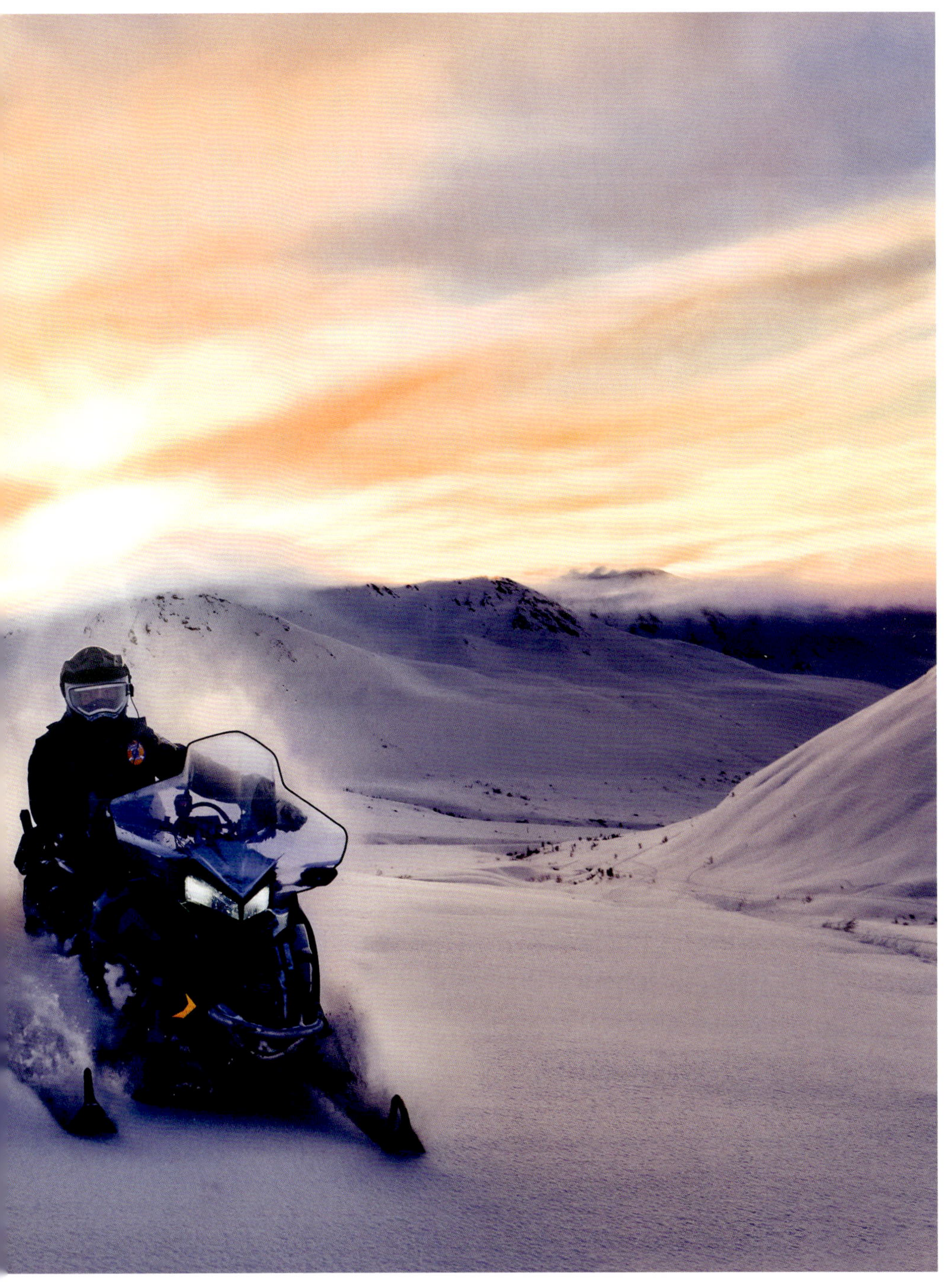

The Mount Washington Observatory is a national weather lab located on the summit of this New Hampshire mountain. It gets so windy up there (the record is 231 miles per hour), that the building itself is chained down in the winter.

This was not an easy shoot. Then again, Rebecca does not have an easy job. In some of the outtakes, that wind is literally lifting her off the ground. But every day, she and her

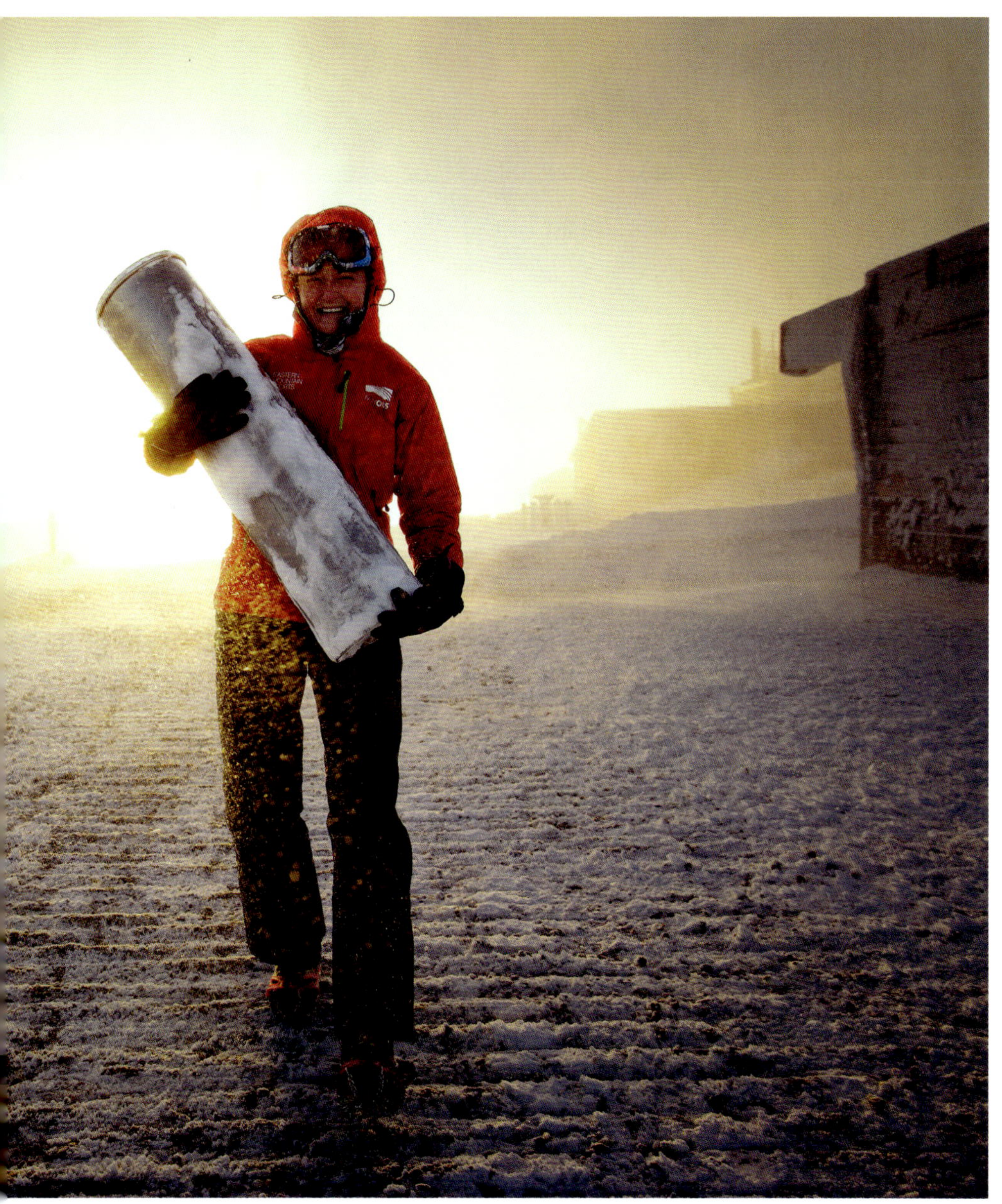

colleagues go out to collect water to analyze weather patterns all around the world.

This photograph reminds me that understanding nature is a commitment. The only way is to be in it. To feel it, taste it, experience it. And somehow, to keep smiling while surviving it.

Rebecca Scholand Weather Observer > Mt. Washington, New Hampshire

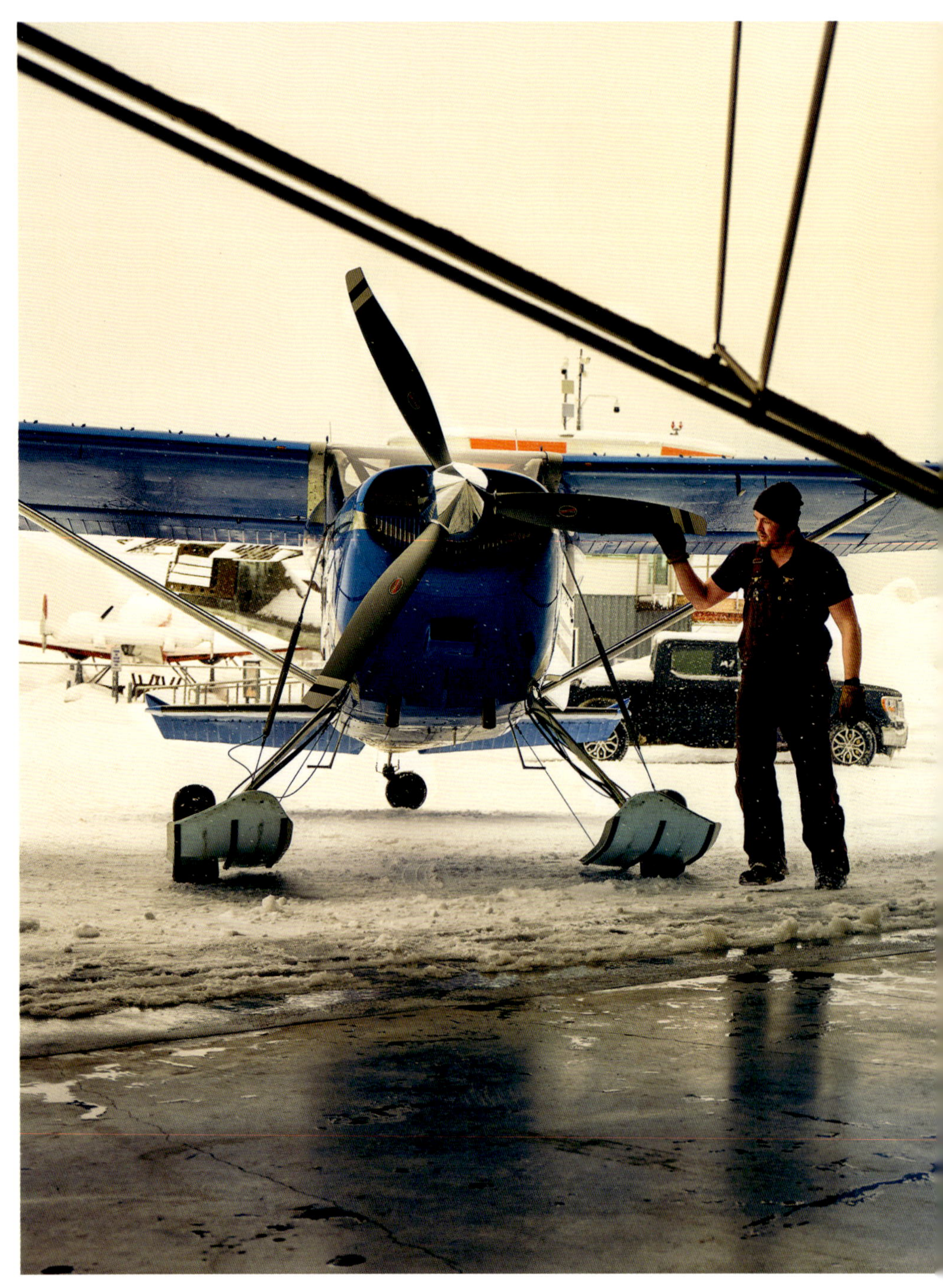

William "Billy" Bredin Back Country Pilot > Anchorage, Alaska

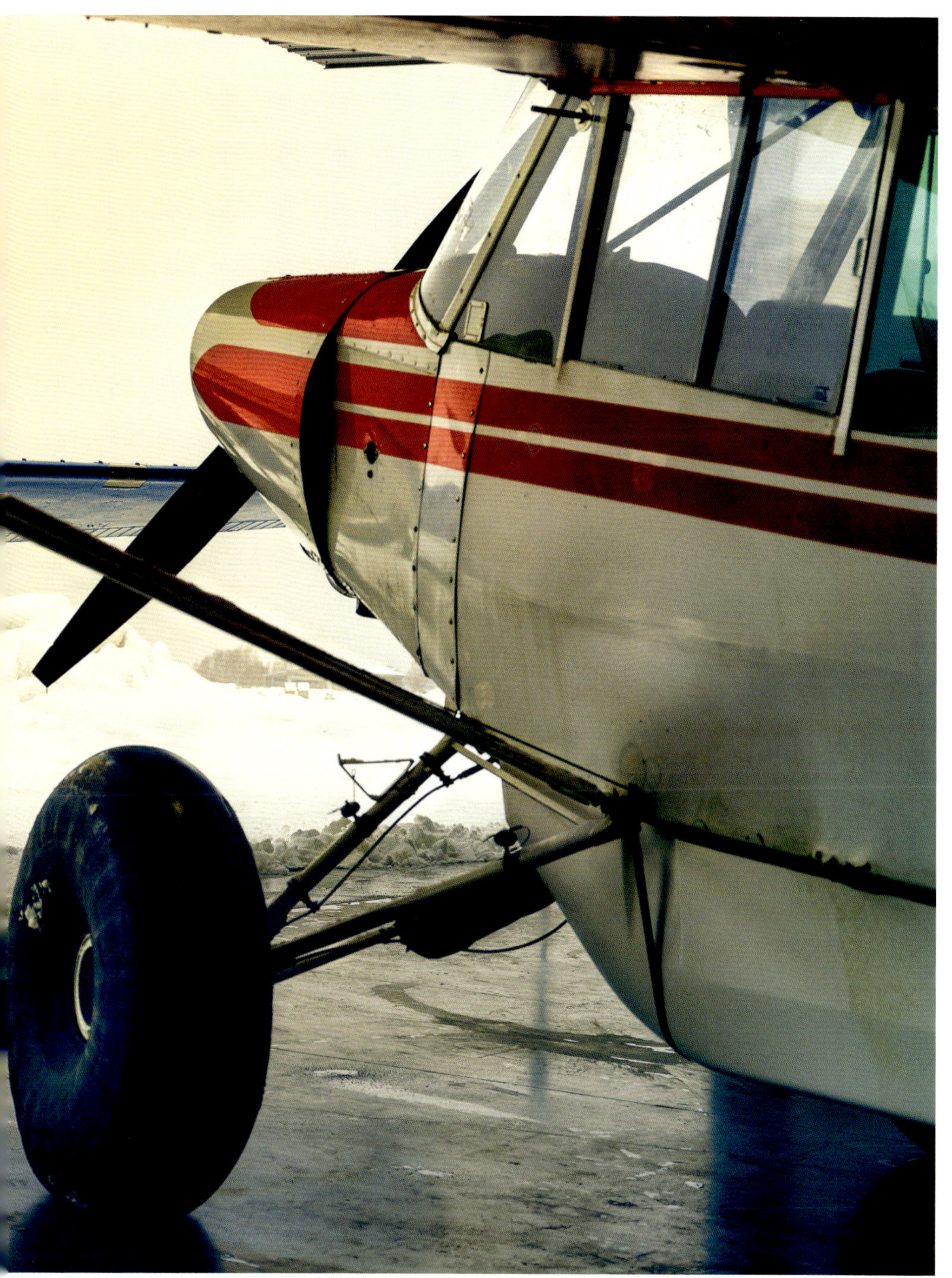

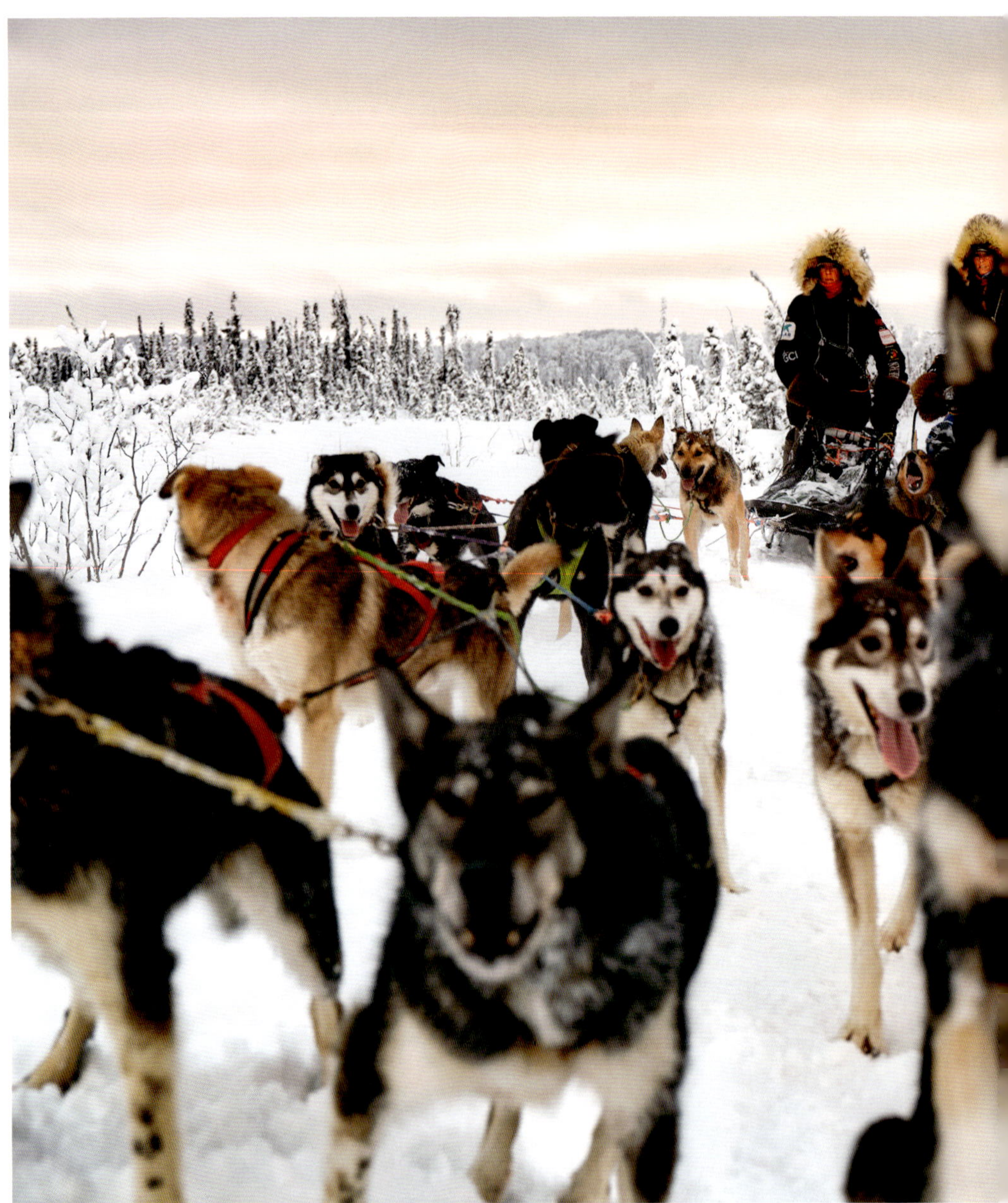

I've photographed world-class athletes as they train. Staying out in front of them, and out of their way, is a full-time job. But simply staying upright in the face of 18 sled dogs is another thing entirely.

I kept falling into snow three-feet deep.

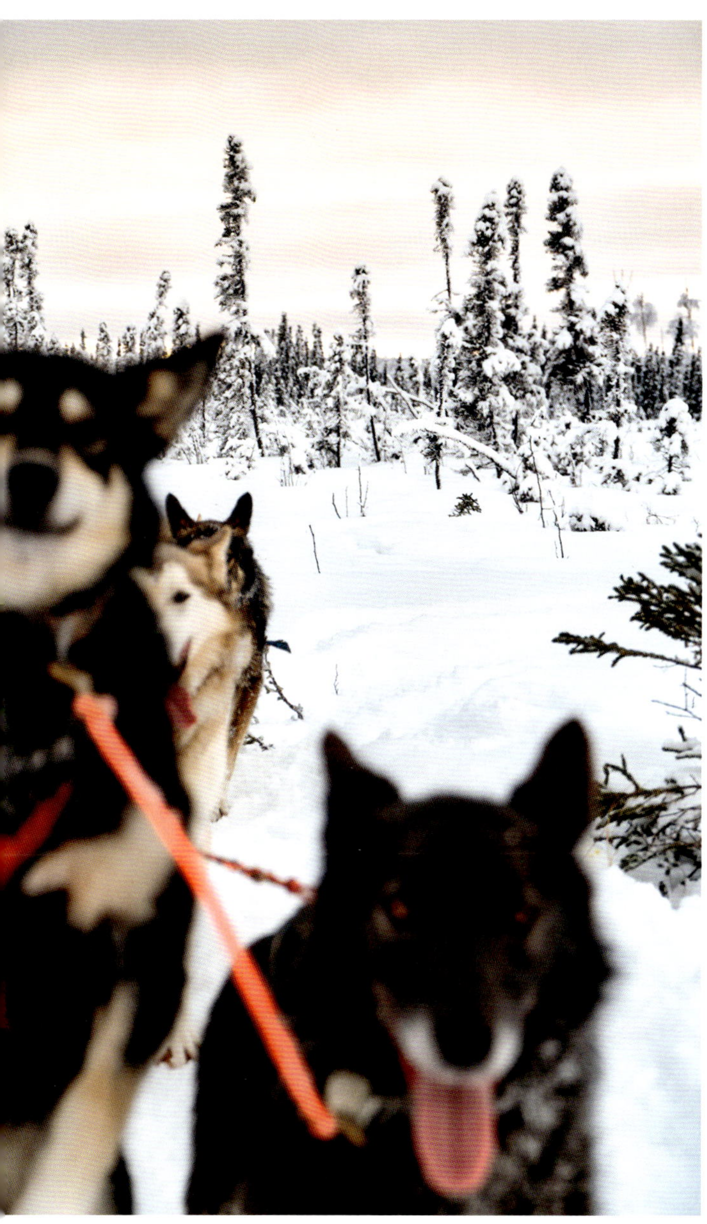

Every time I got back up, it became clearer. I wasn't simply shooting a heroic pair of racers, driving their team. They were working as one — women and dogs, all together — knocking themselves out to move forward.

Andrea & Kristy Berington Mushers, Seeing Double Sled Dog Racing > Wasilla, Alaska

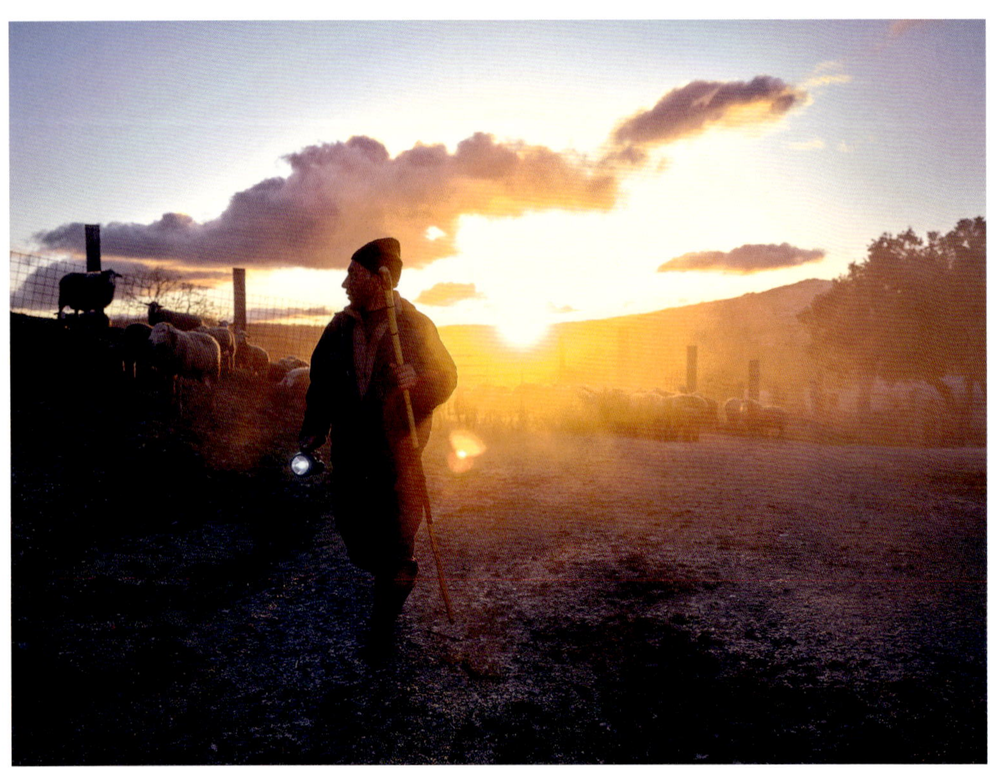

As a photographer, I believe that gratitude is essential in capturing the moment. I am thankful to have experienced this moment and even more grateful to share it with you, the reader.

Sheep Herder > Spain

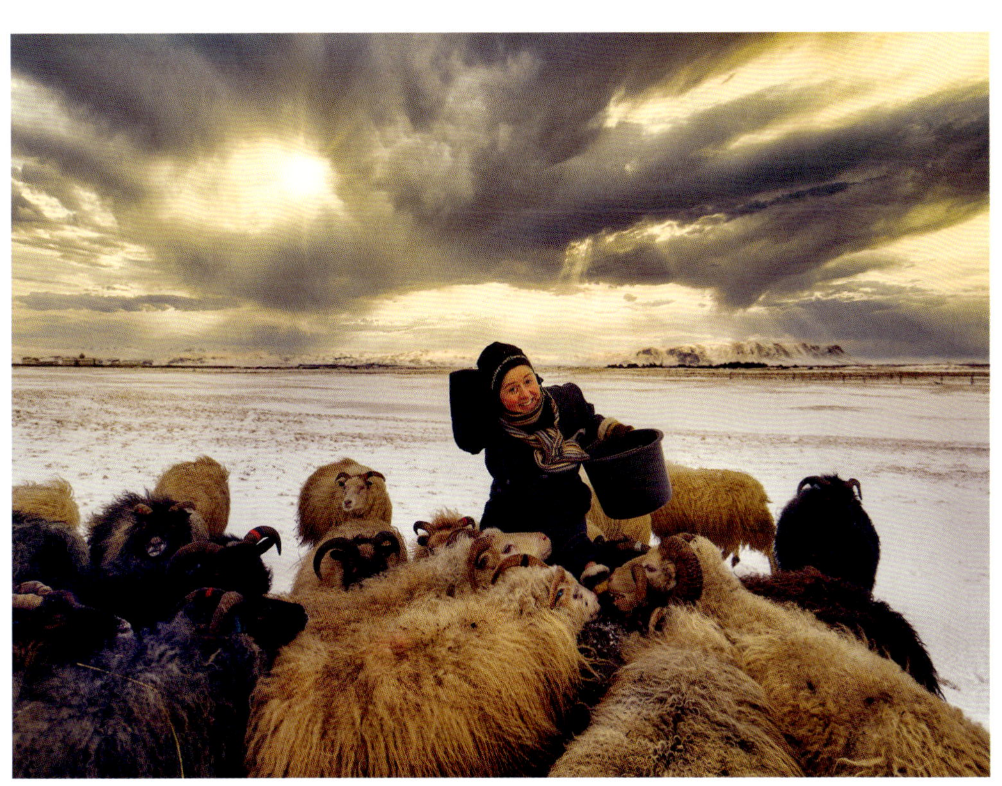

Jóhanna Sveinsdóttir Sheep Farmer > Eyrarbakki, Iceland

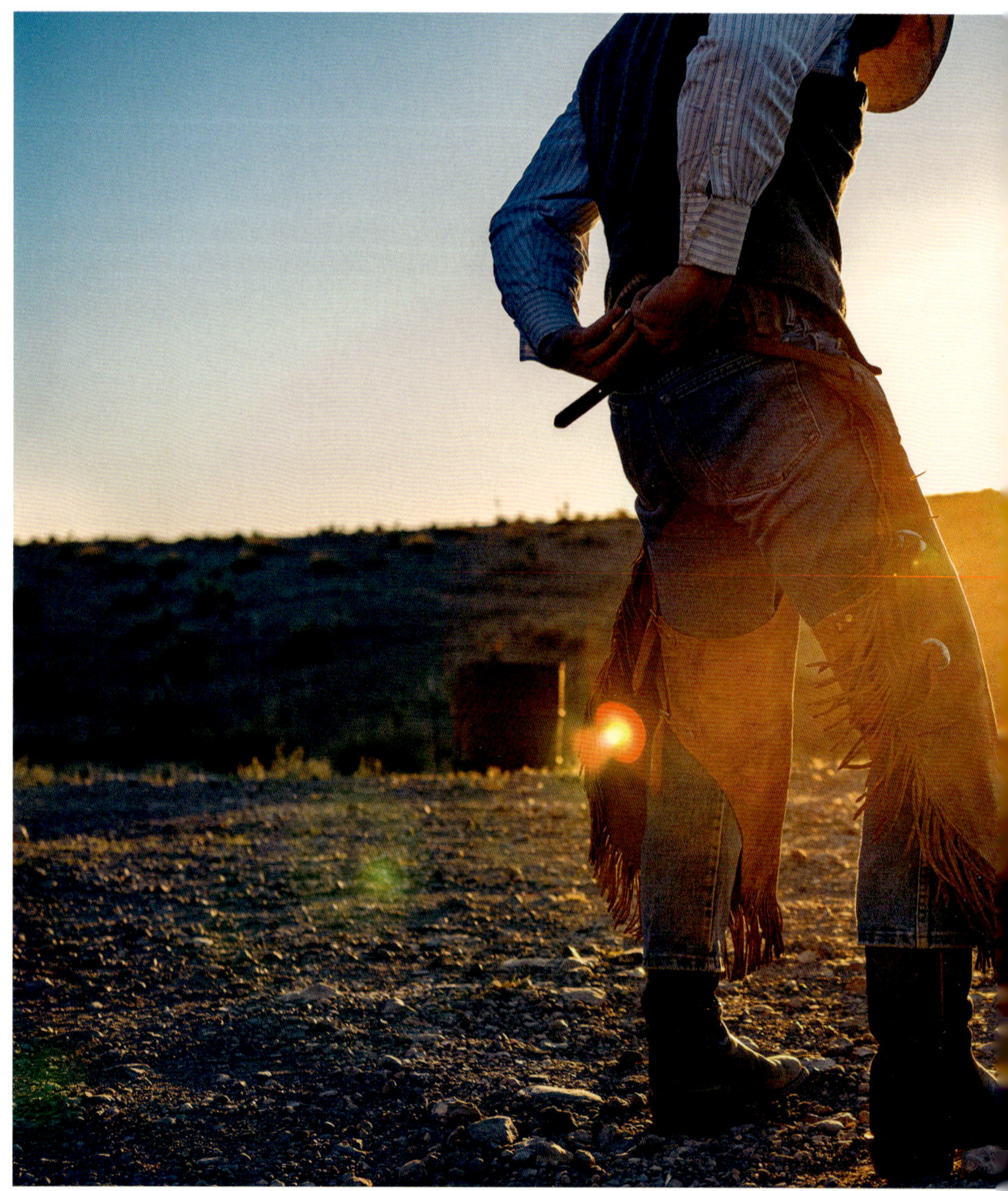

There was one pig that followed us around all day at Fletcher Ranch. The dogs seemed annoyed with it, but the guys took no notice.

I mustered a joke. "What did you name him? Breakfast?"

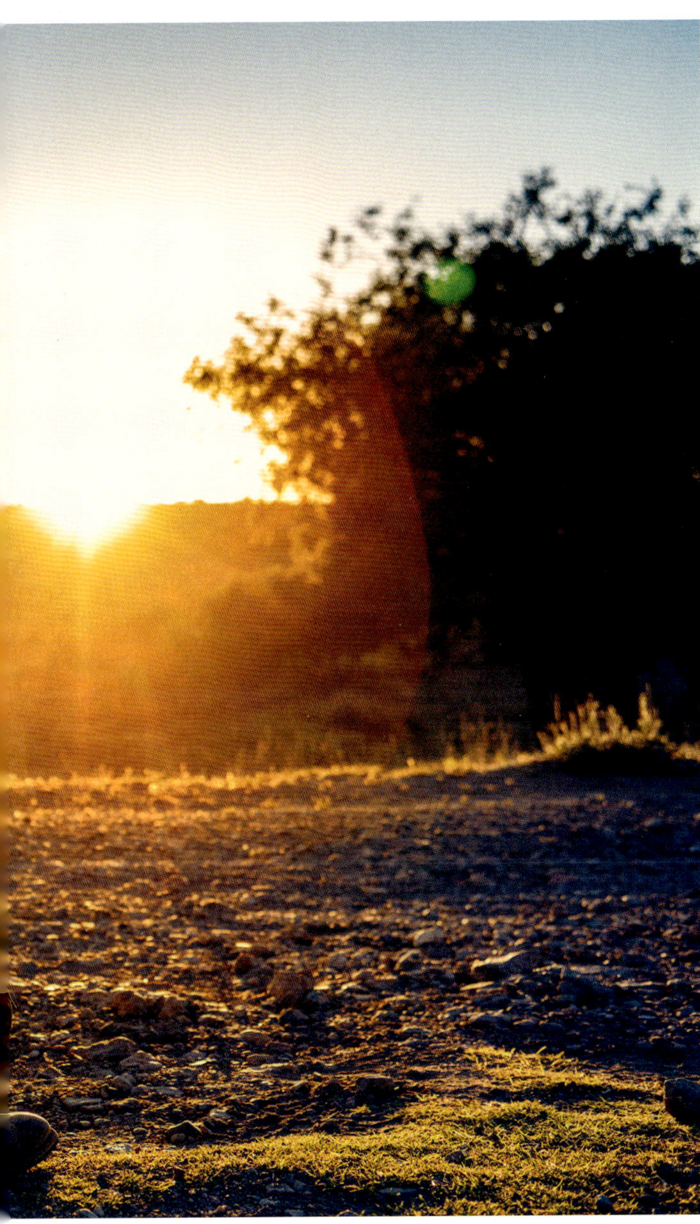

The way they looked at me made me feel every inch the city boy that I am.
   "No. This is our pig."

Aufdengarten Family Fletcher Ranch > Marfa, Texas

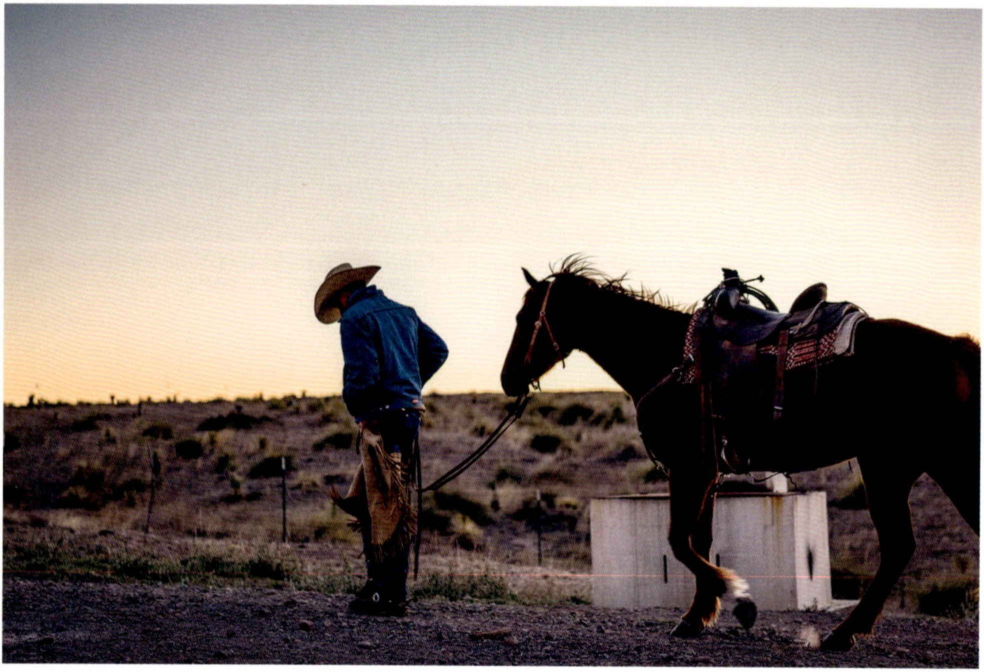

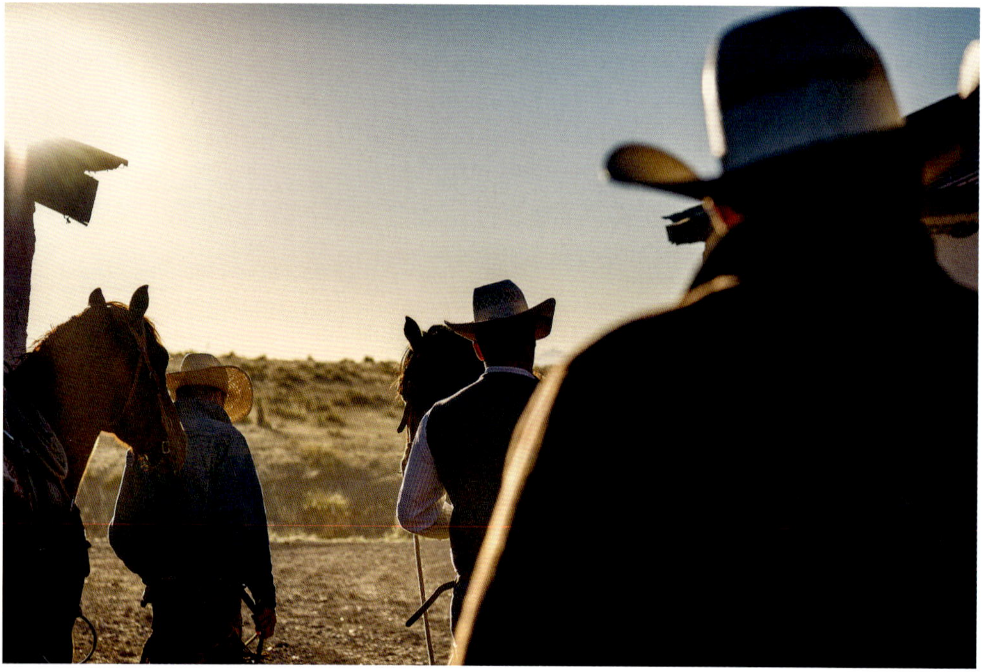

Aufdengarten Family Fletcher Ranch > Marfa, Texas

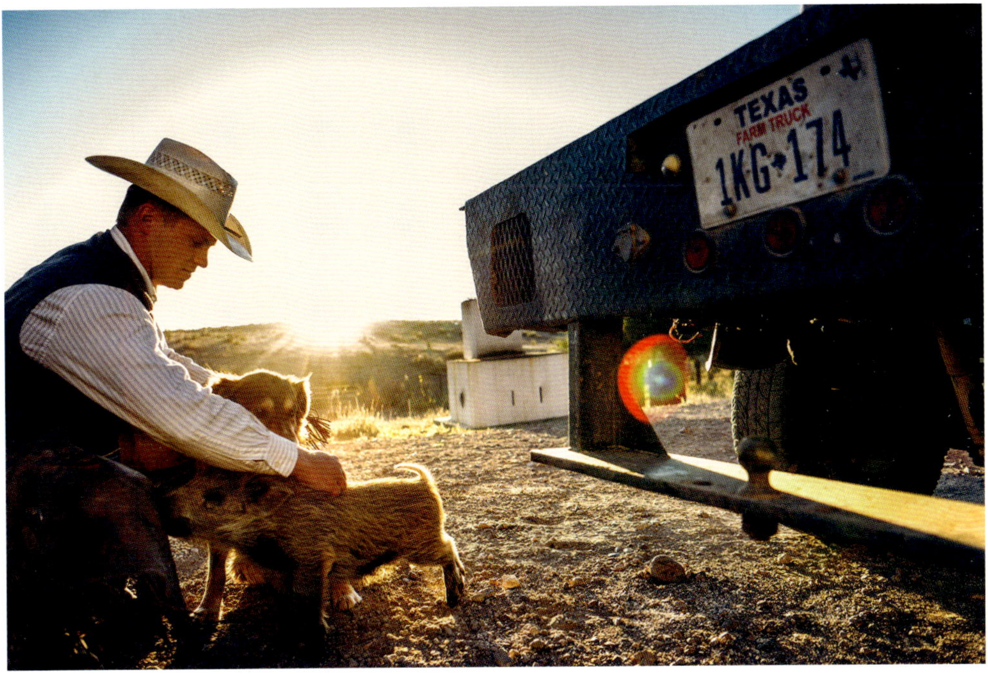
TEXAS
FARM TRUCK
1KG 174

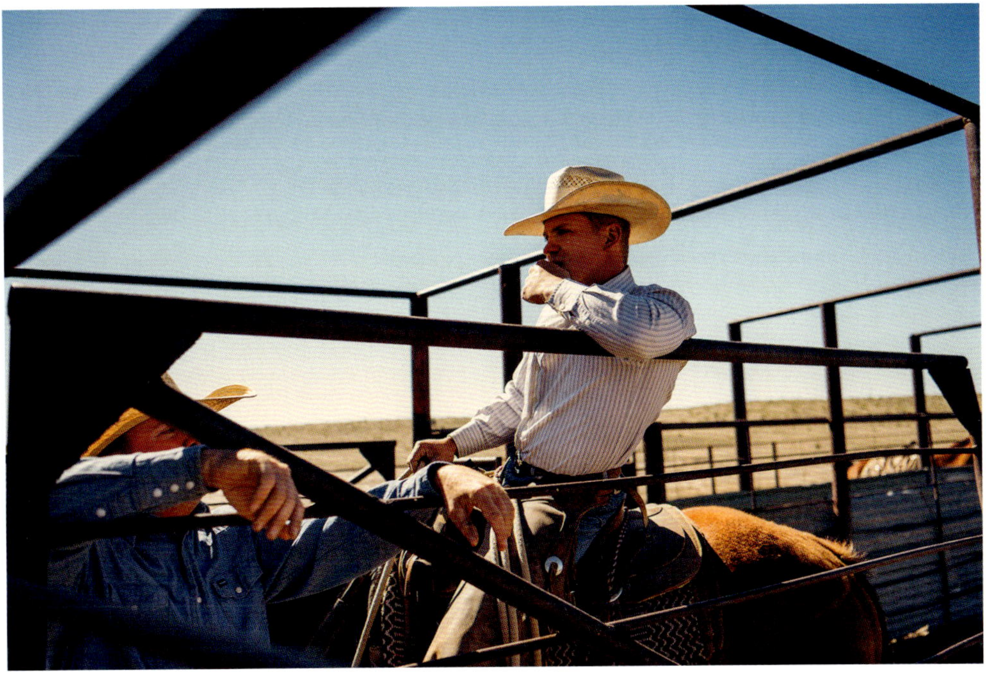

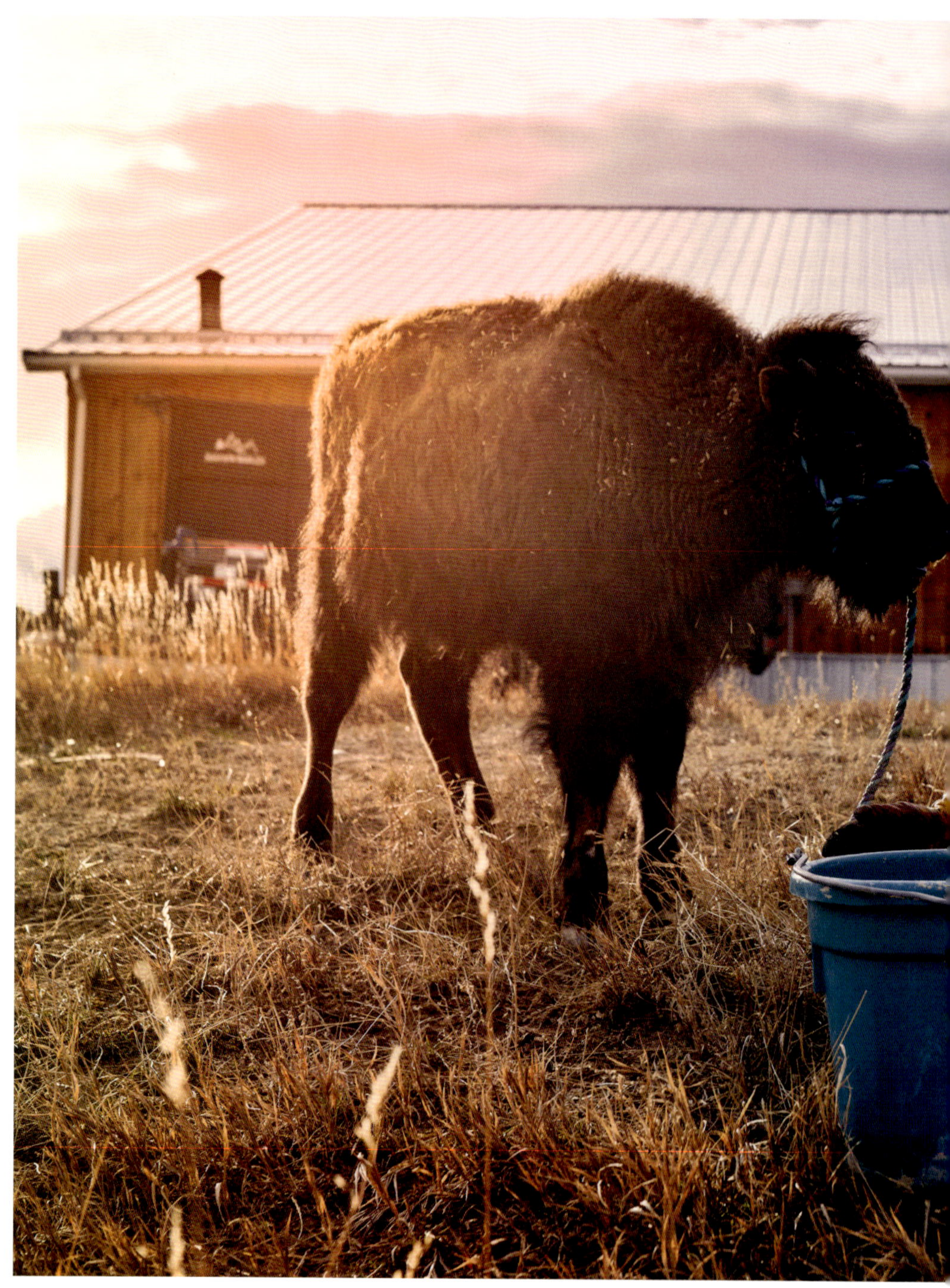

Jon Sepp Bison Rancher, Roam Free Ranch > Hot Springs, Montana

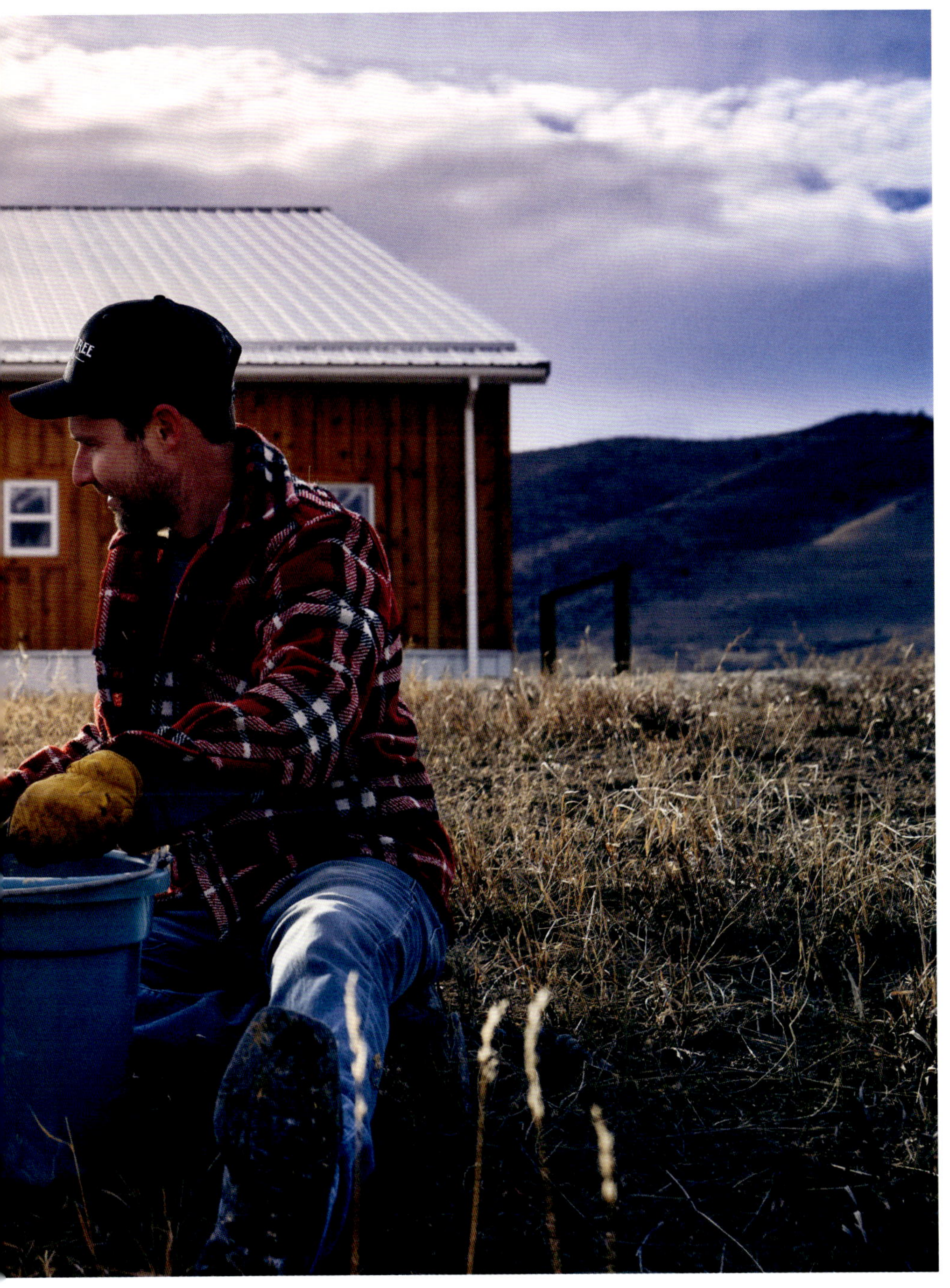

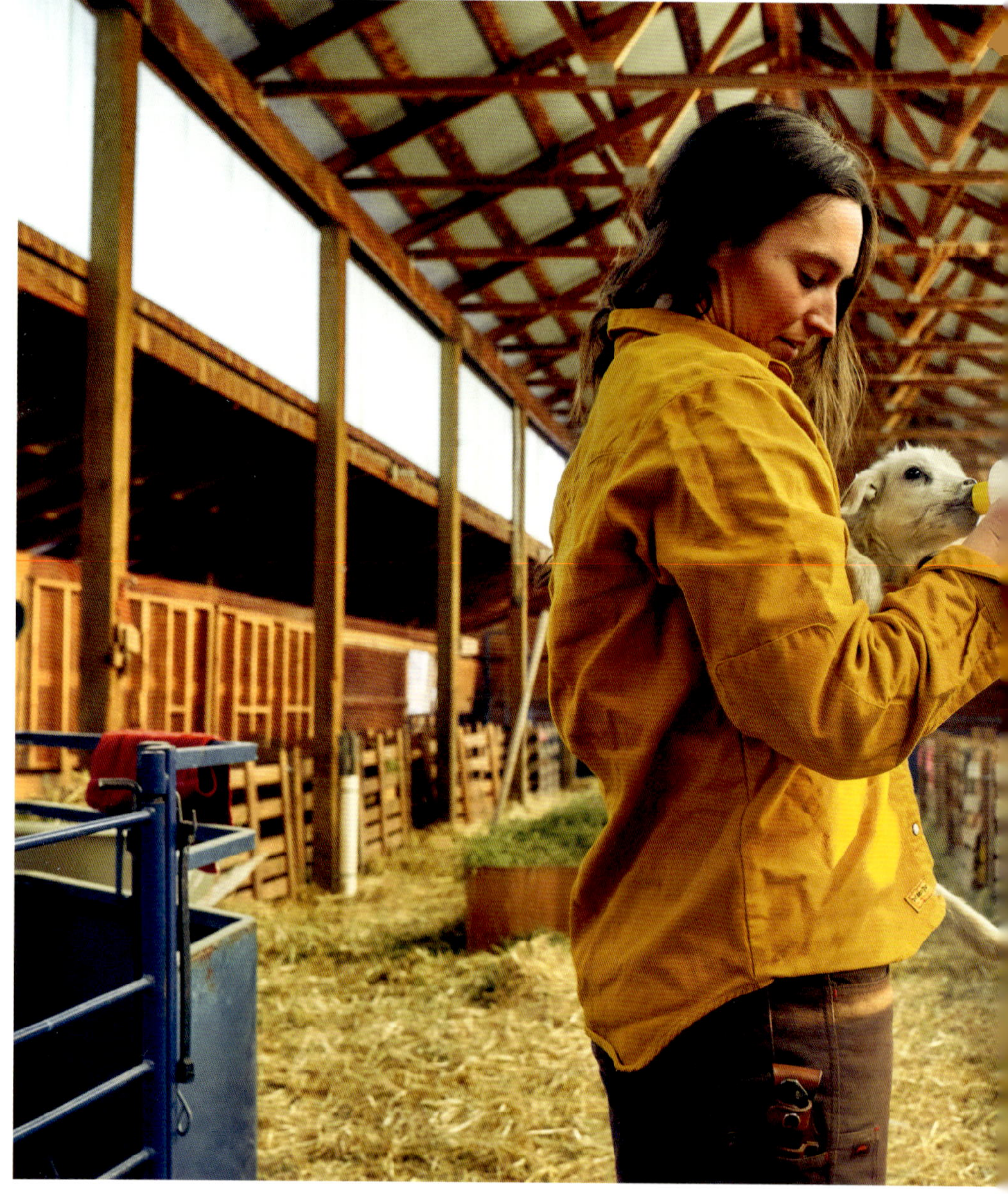

Alyssa Henry Lamb Rancher, Solana Mountain Ranch > Bozeman, Montana

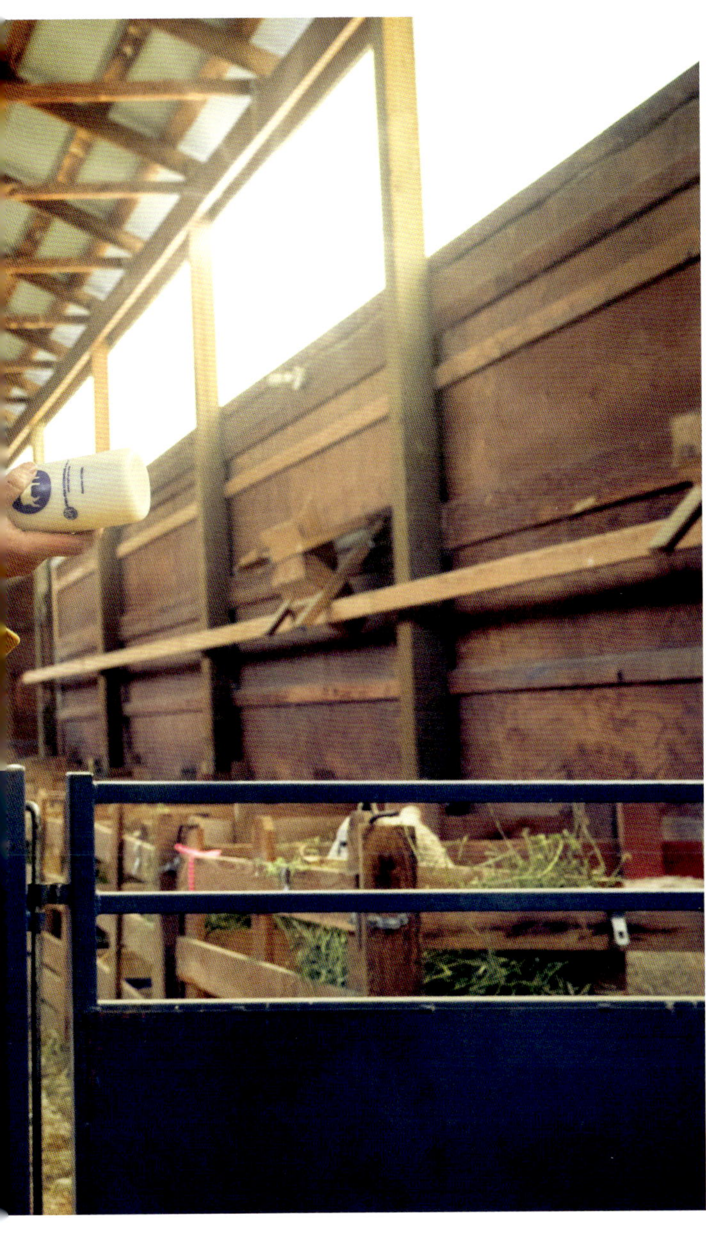

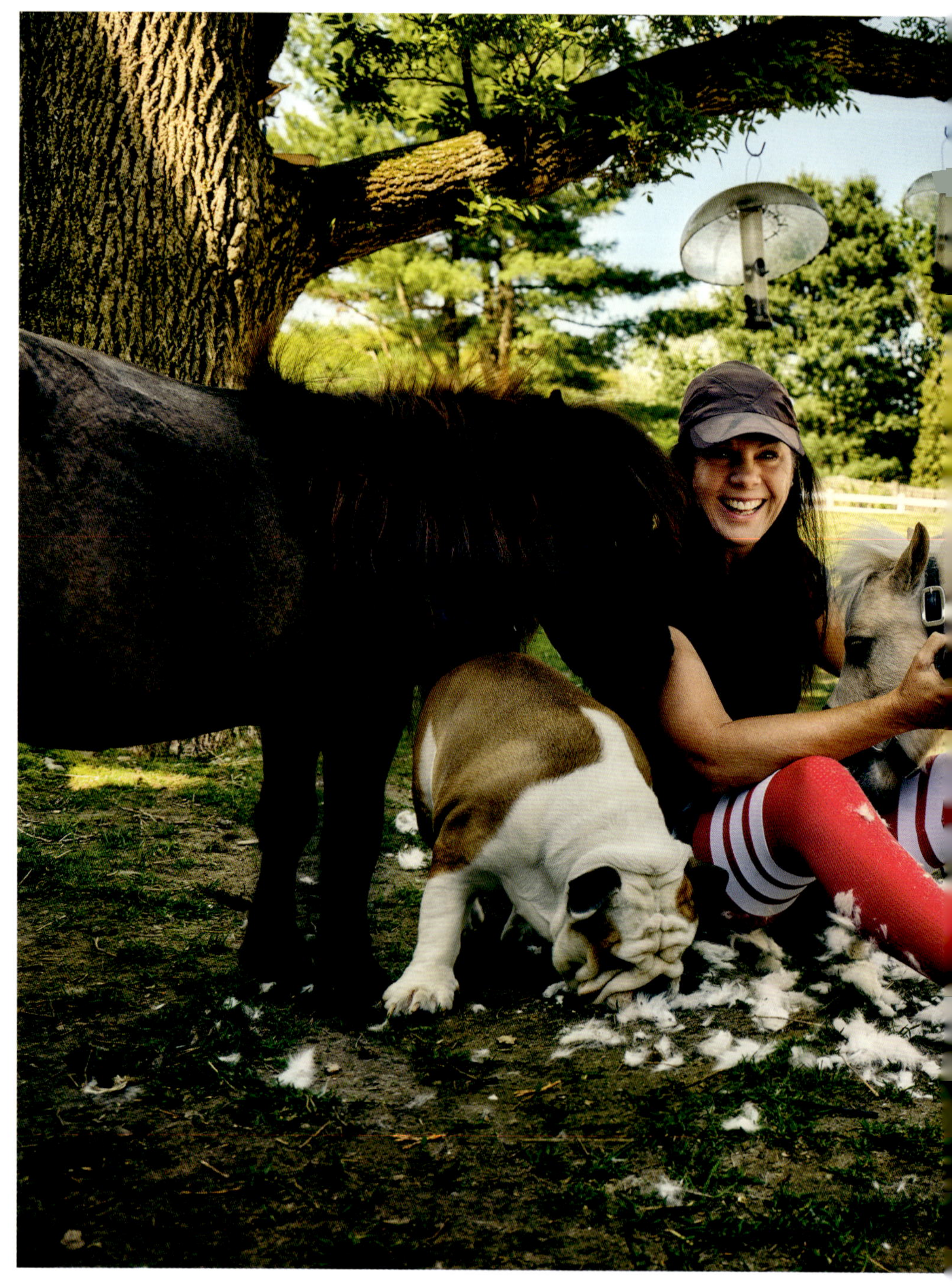

Toni Hadad Lifting Spirits Miniature Therapy Horses > Andover, Massachusetts

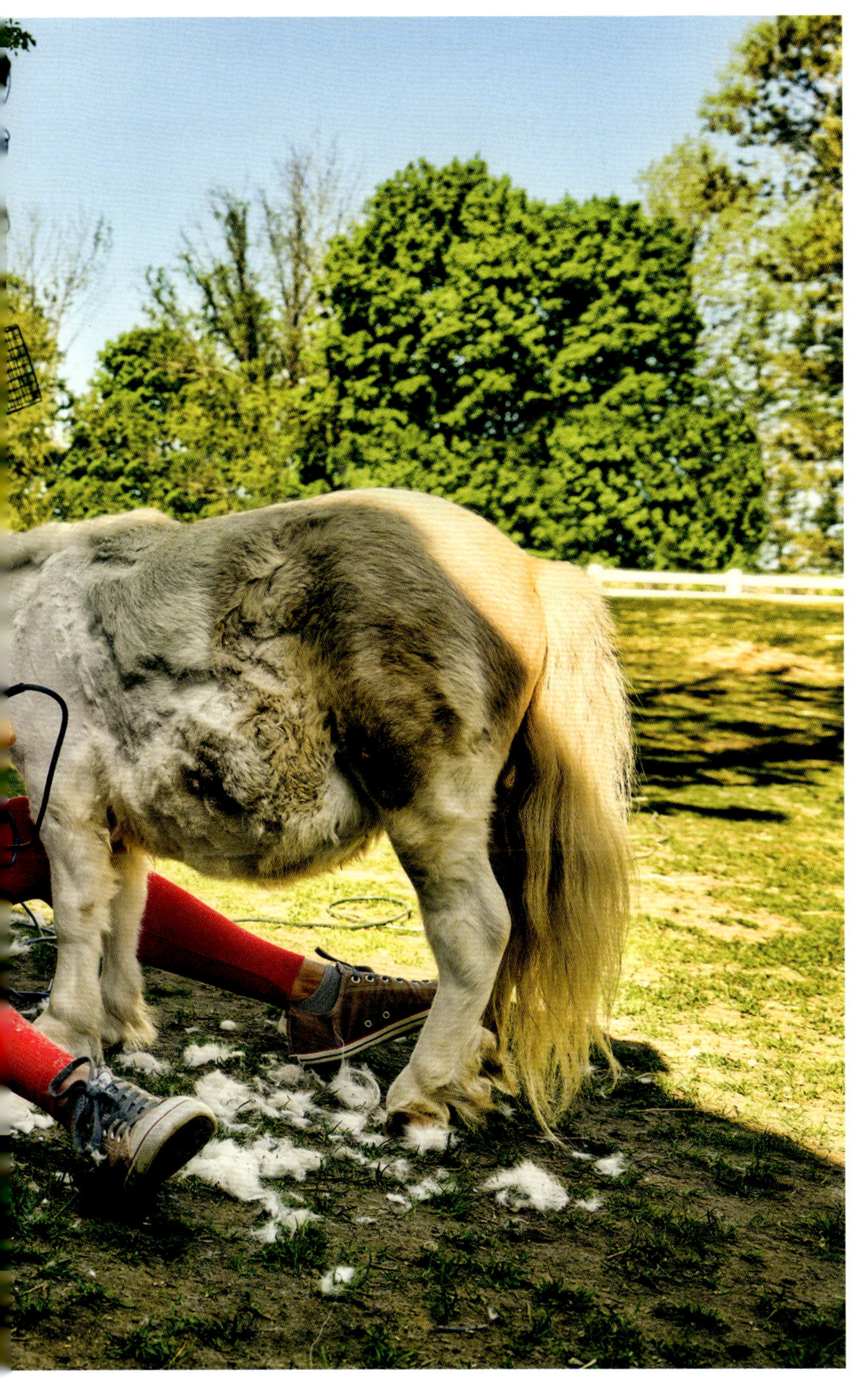

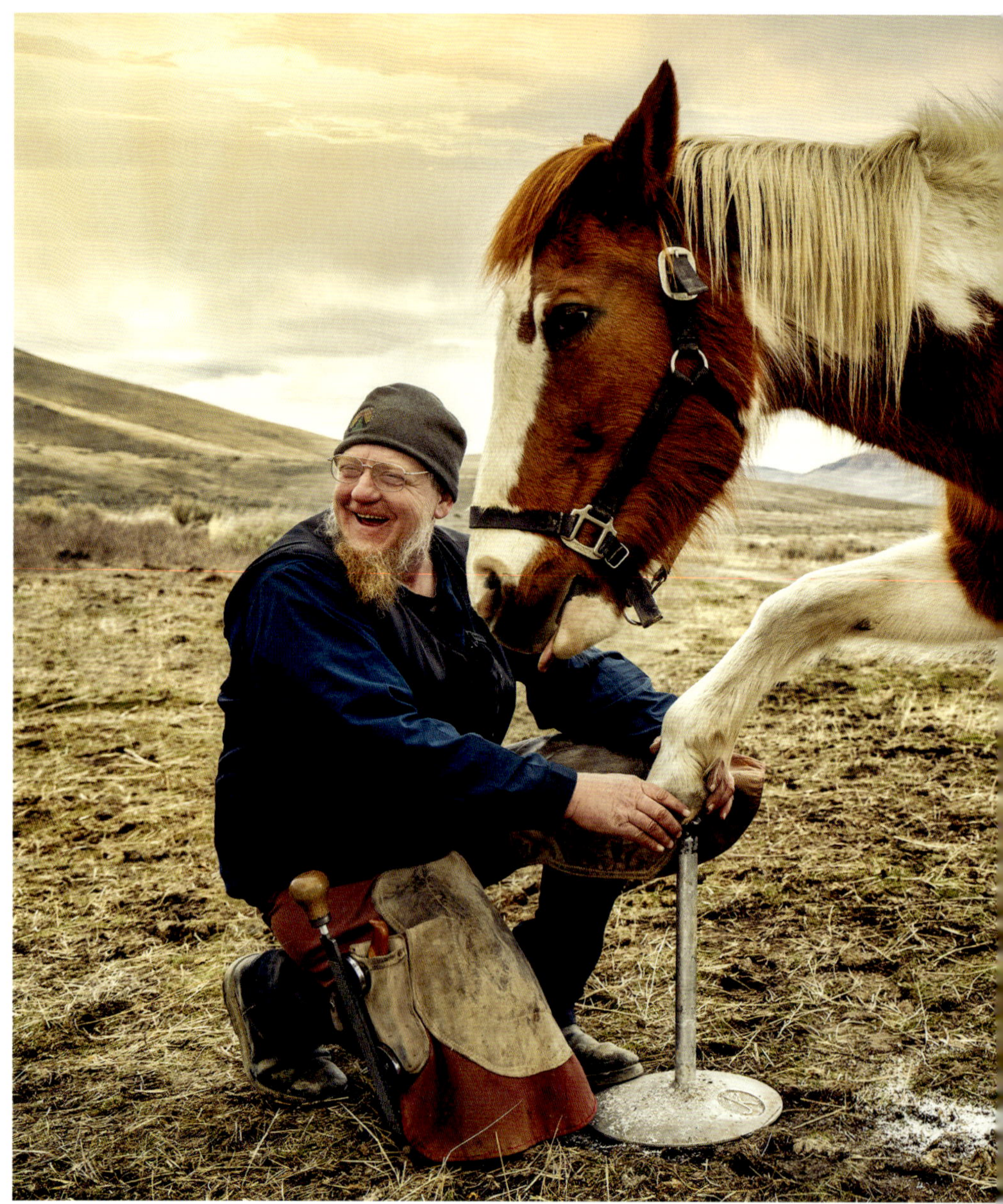

I'm here to witness moments, not to create them. Except for when I have driven
three and a half hours across Montana to photograph a farrier on the job.

    "I ain't shoeing no horse in this wind," he said.

    "You're shoeing in this wind," I replied.

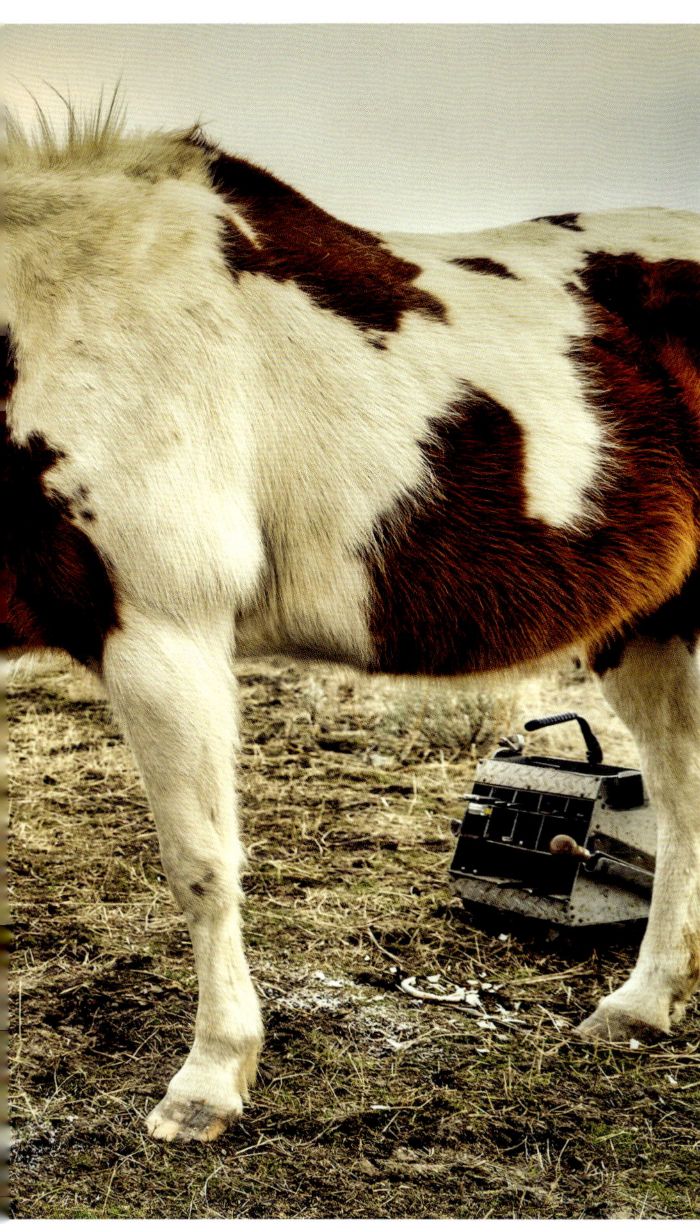

Just out of frame is my camper van, strategically positioned to block the wind, keep the horses calm, and prevent EM from getting injured in the process of my getting the shot.

EM J Slabaugh Farrier > Hotsprings, Montana

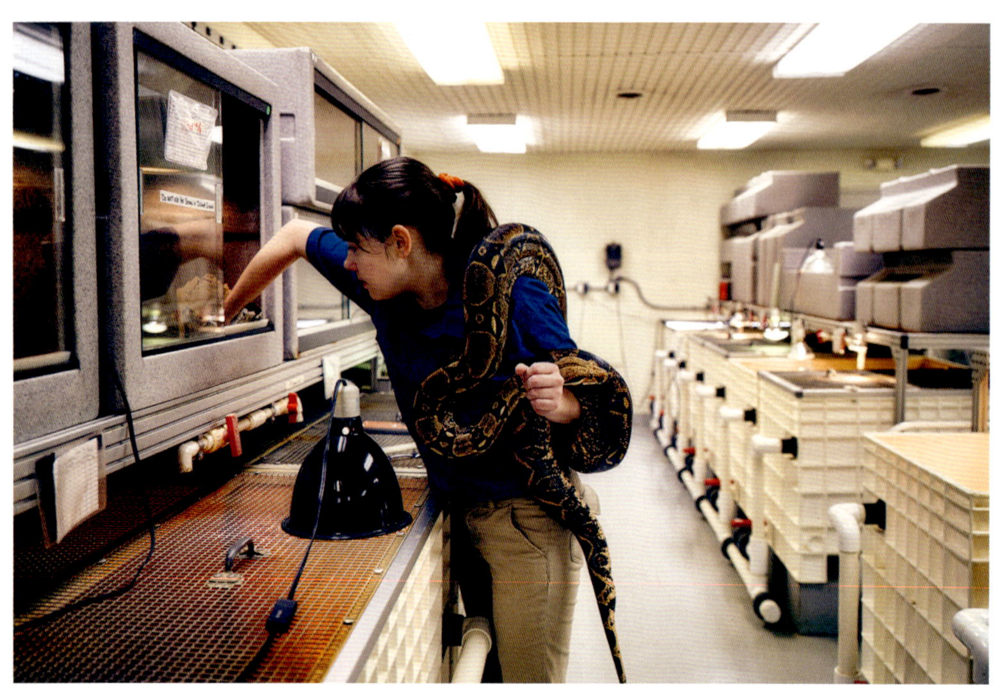

Tiffany Faull Senior Keeper, Clyde Peeling's Reptiland > Allenwood, Pennsylvania

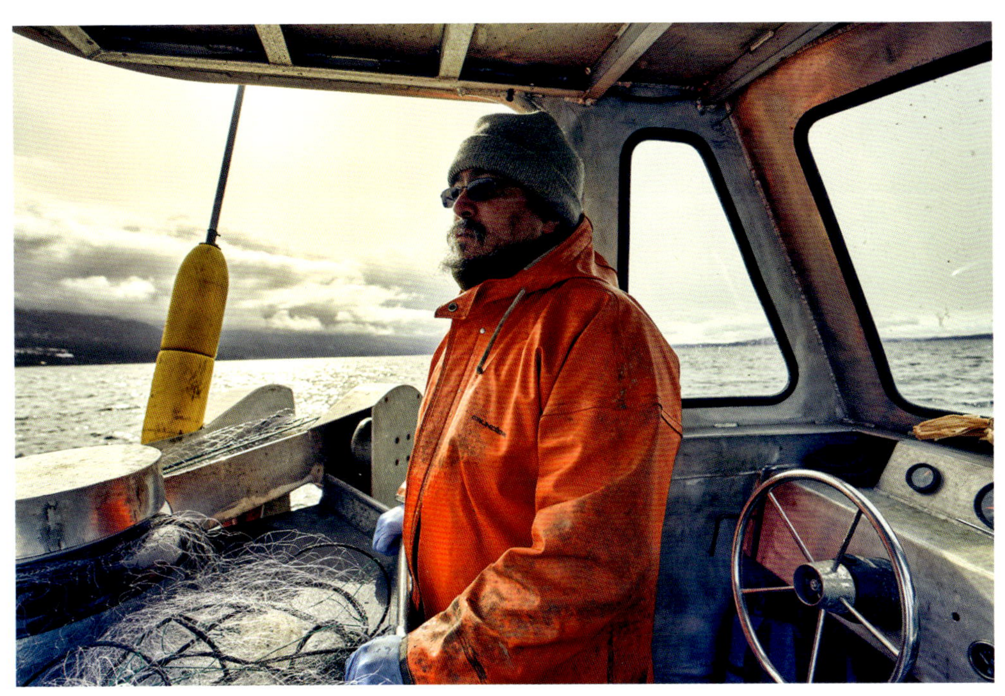

Mountain Wahl Captain, Native Fishkeepers > Flathead Lake, Montana

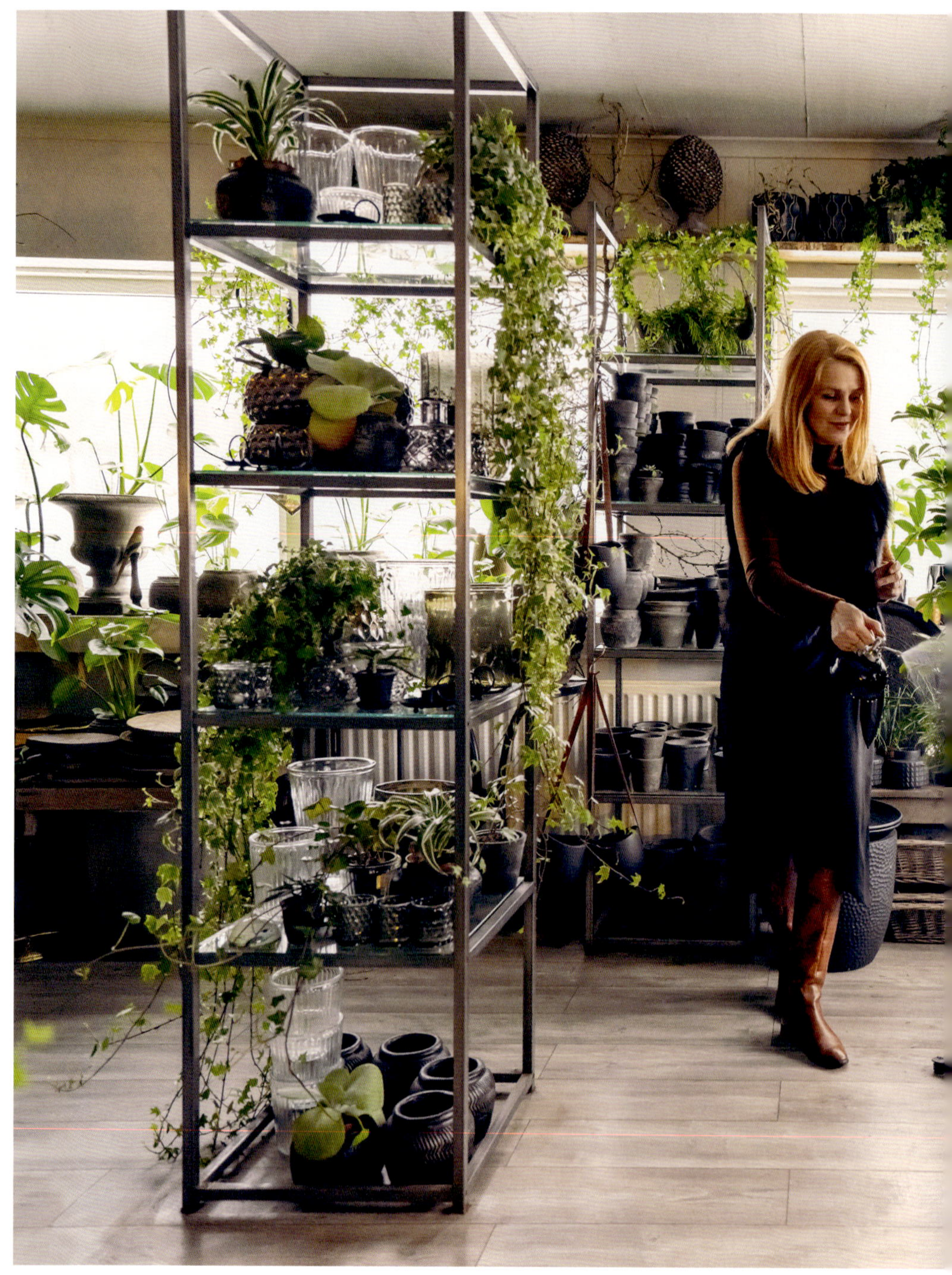

Elisa Guomundsdottir Florist > Reykjavik, Iceland

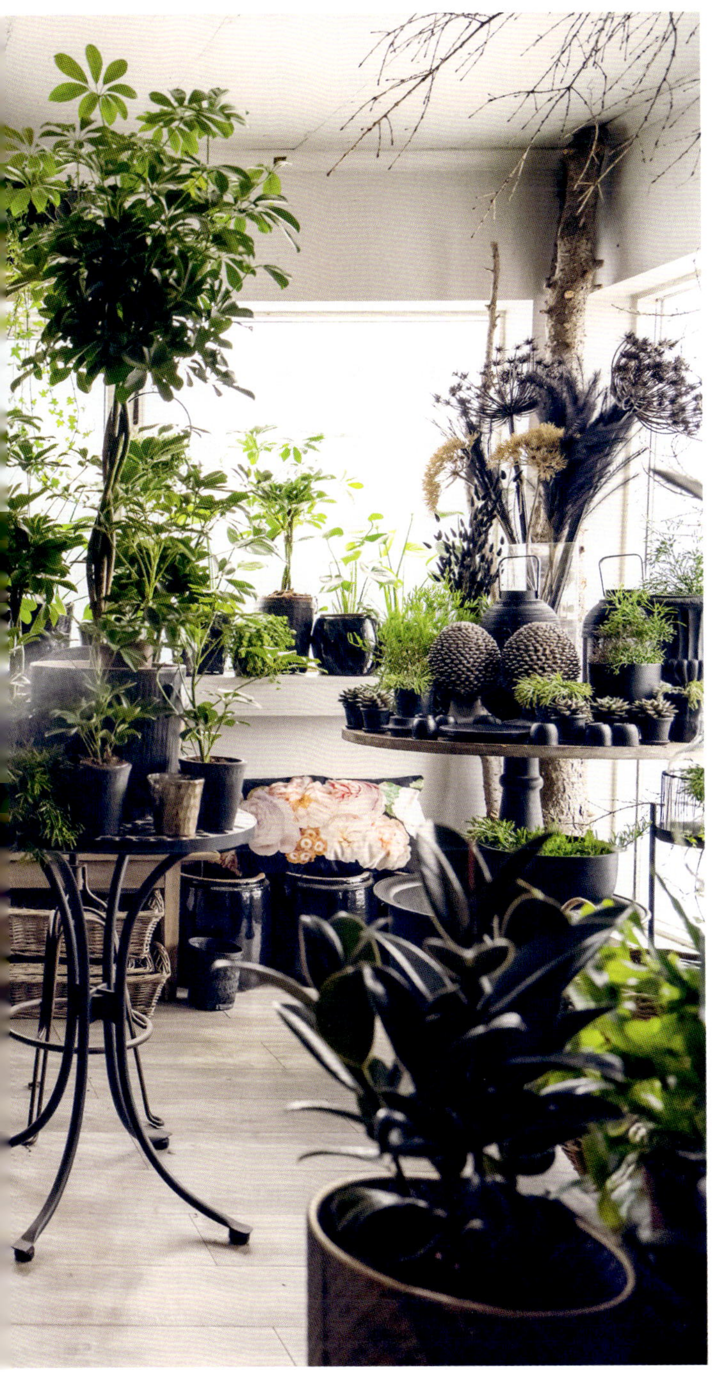

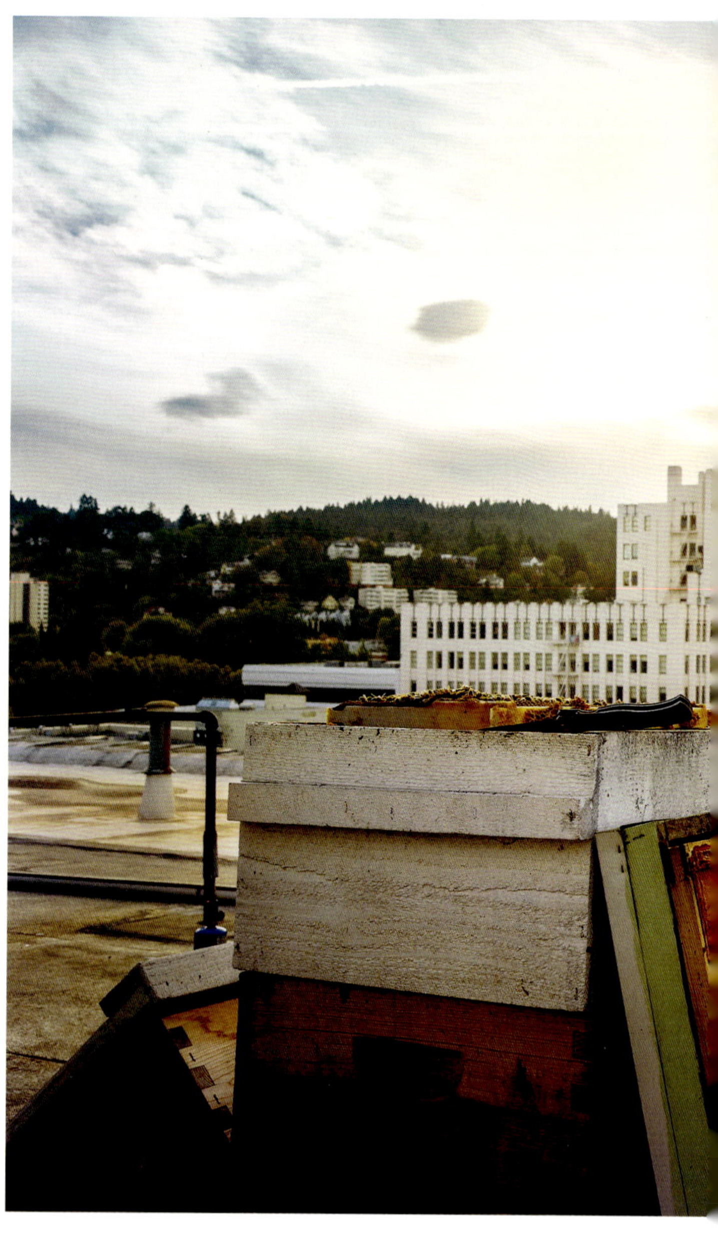

This peaceful moment quickly turned chaotic. Out of nowhere, Damian's bees attacked
him. Within seconds it was over, and his eye was swollen shut.

I felt terrible. It wasn't my fault, but it had — in a way — happened on my watch.

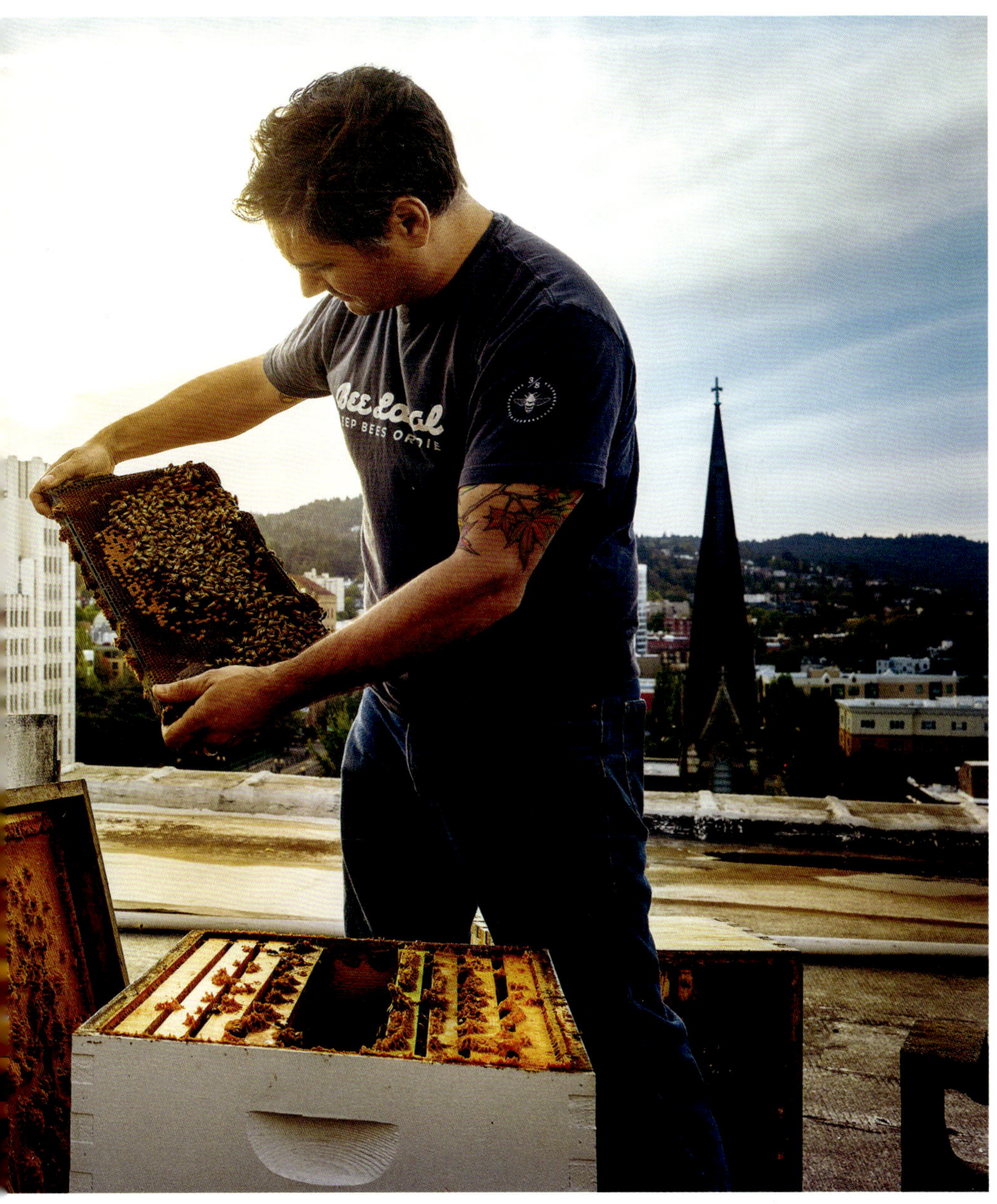

"Don't worry about it," Damian said later as we sat in a bar with our beers.
    "I used to be an MMA fighter. I've had worse days."

Damian Magista Urban Bee Keeper, Bee Local > Portland, Oregon

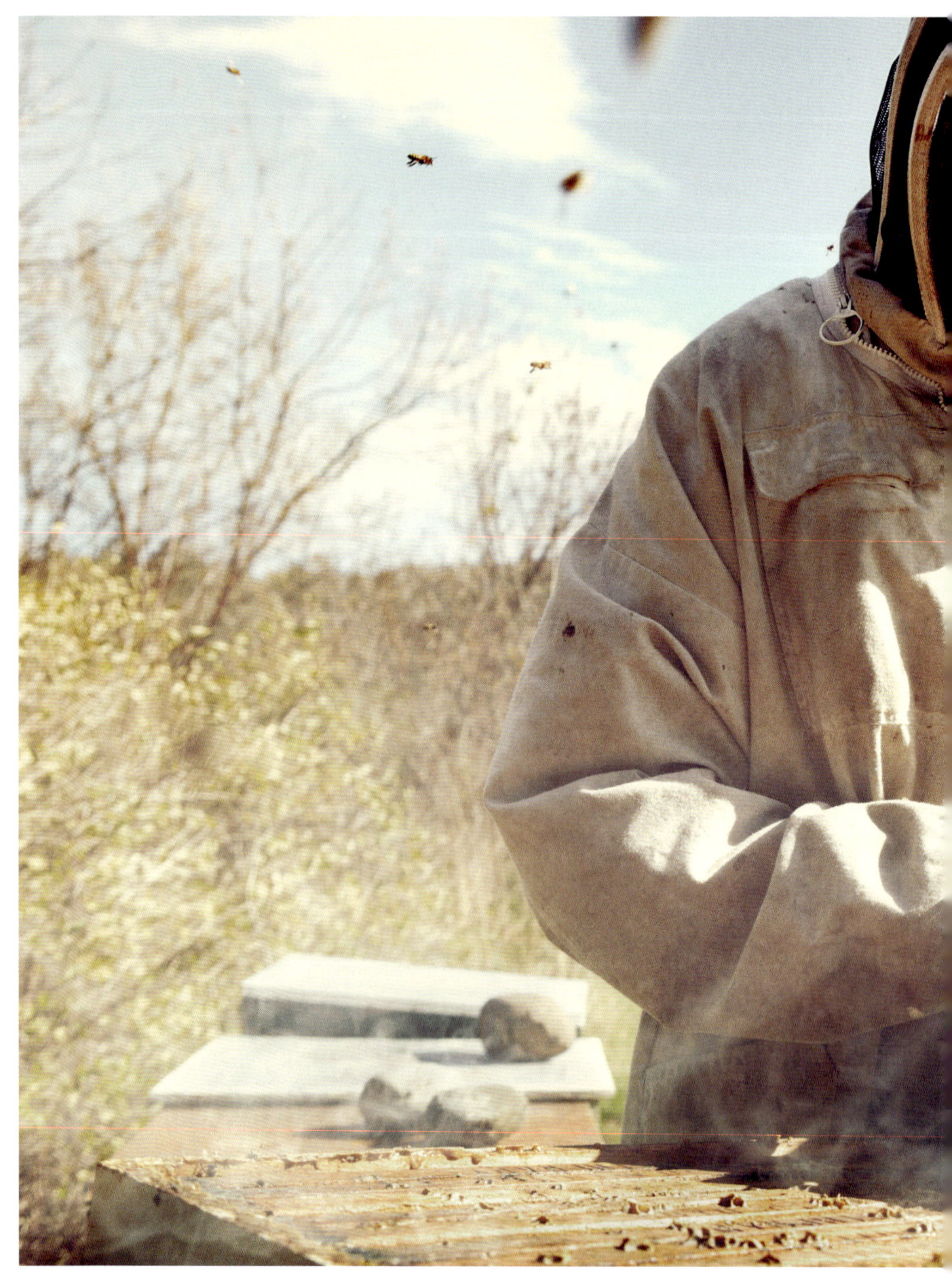

Todd Hardie Bee Keeper and Owner, Caledonia Spirits > Montpelier, Vermont

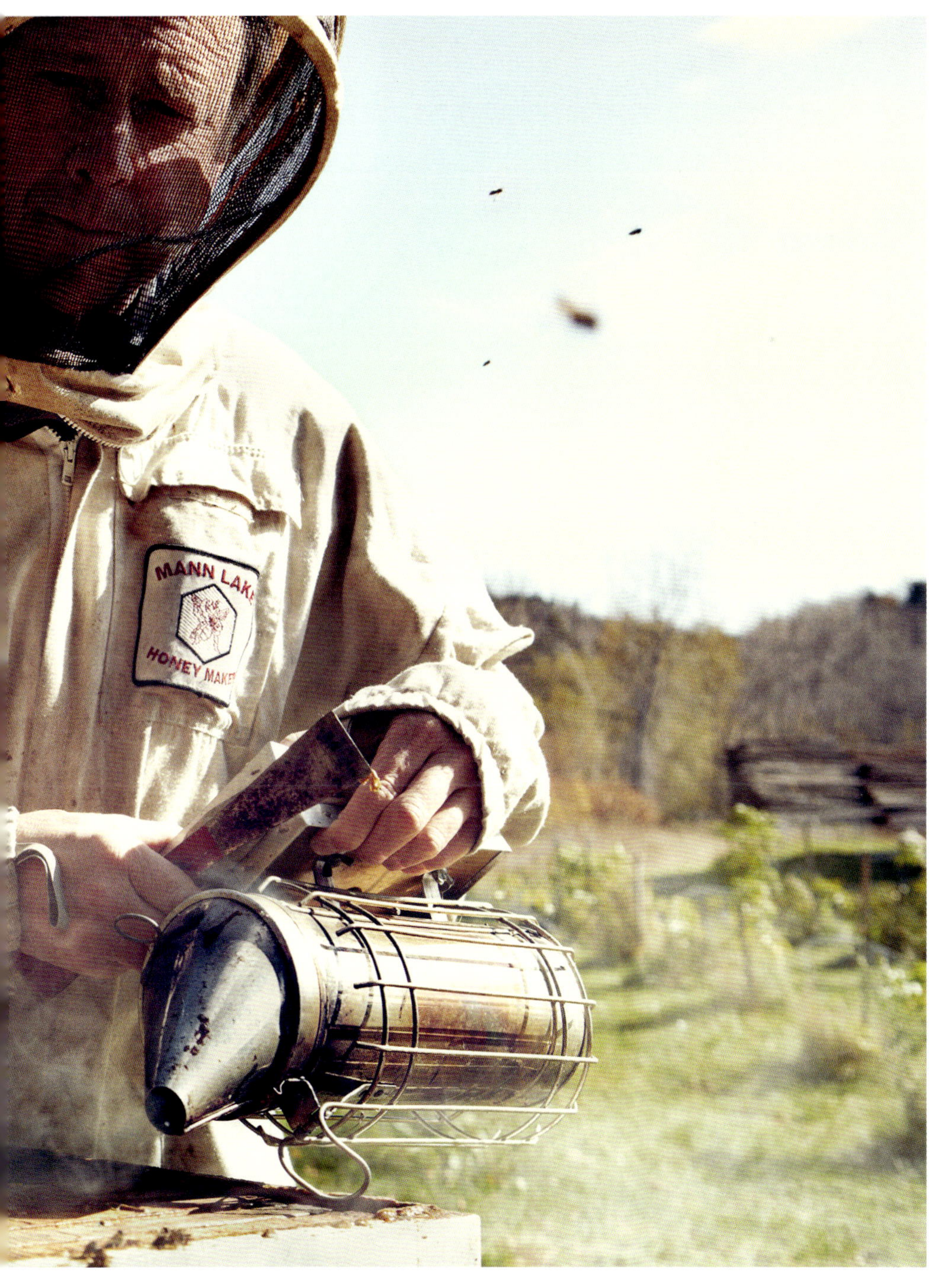
MANN LAKE
HONEY MAKER

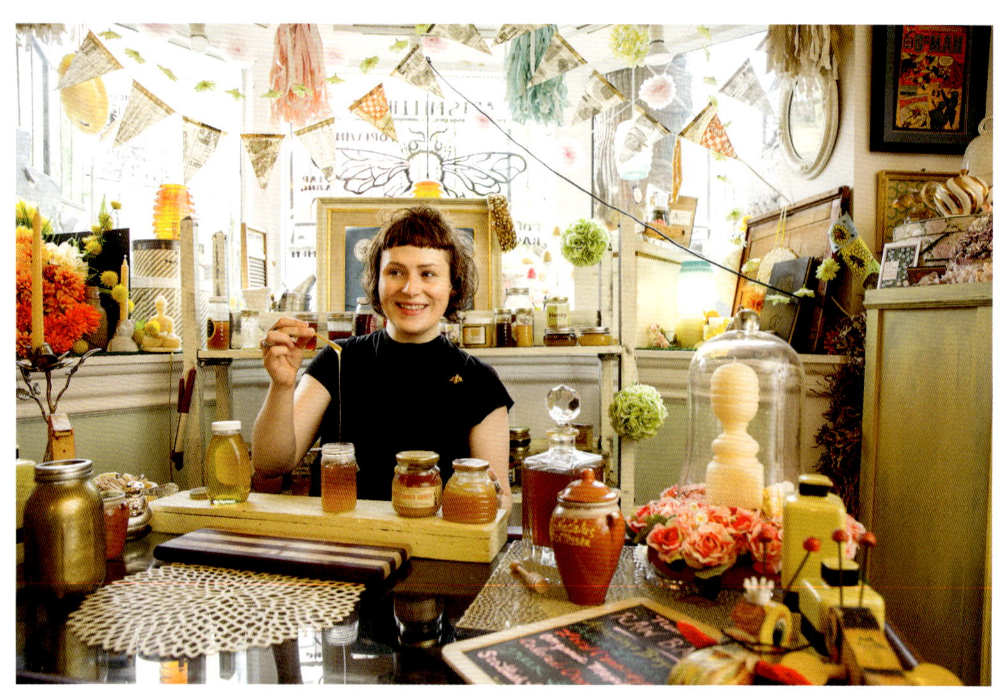

Caneen Canning Follow the Honey Shop > Cambridge, Massachusetts

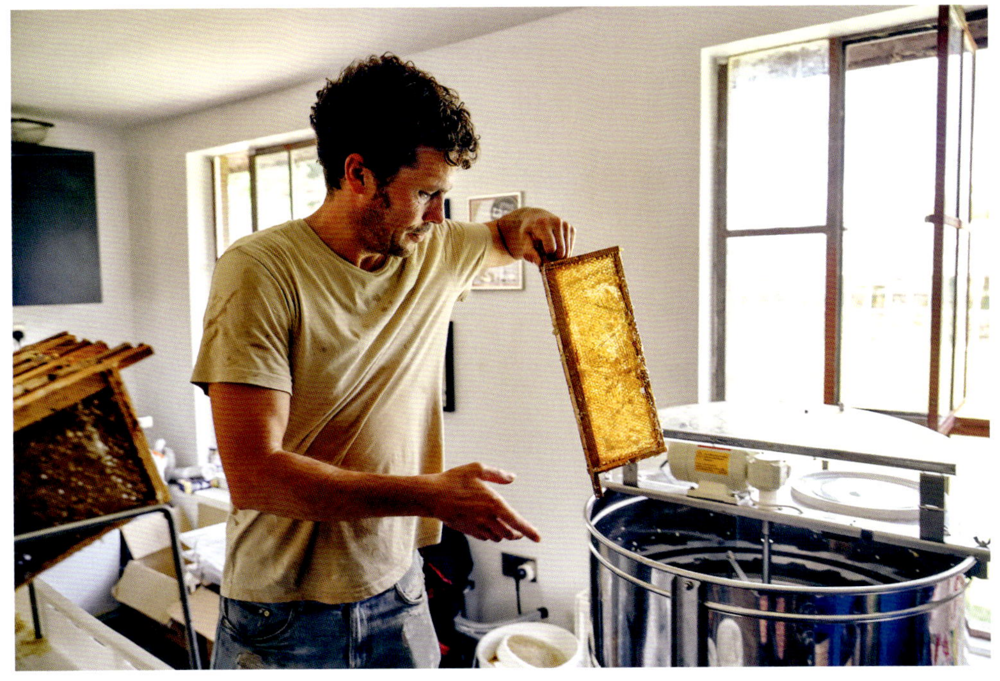

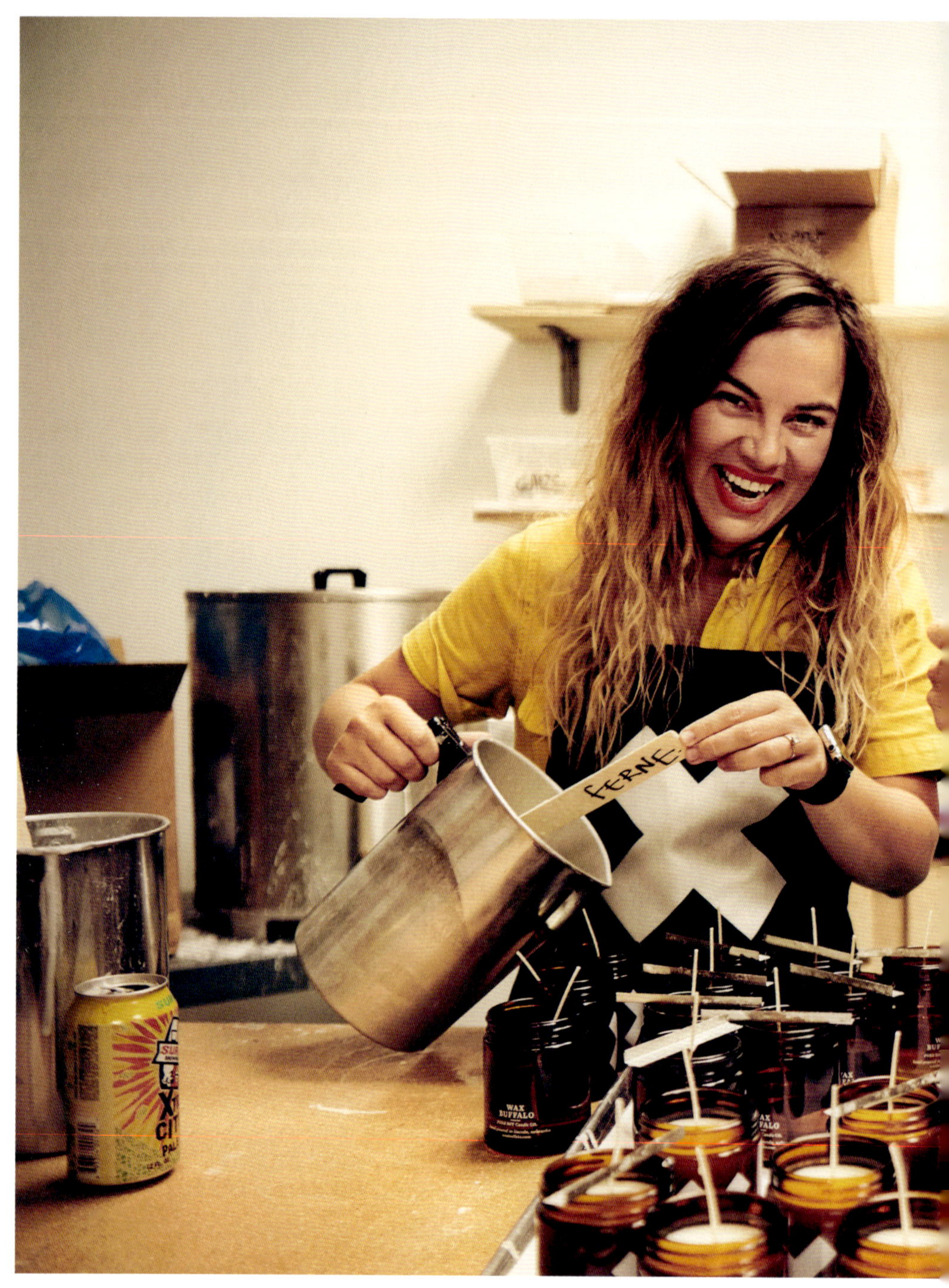

Alicia Reisinger & Nicole Norris Candlemakers, Wax Buffalo > Lincoln, Nebraska

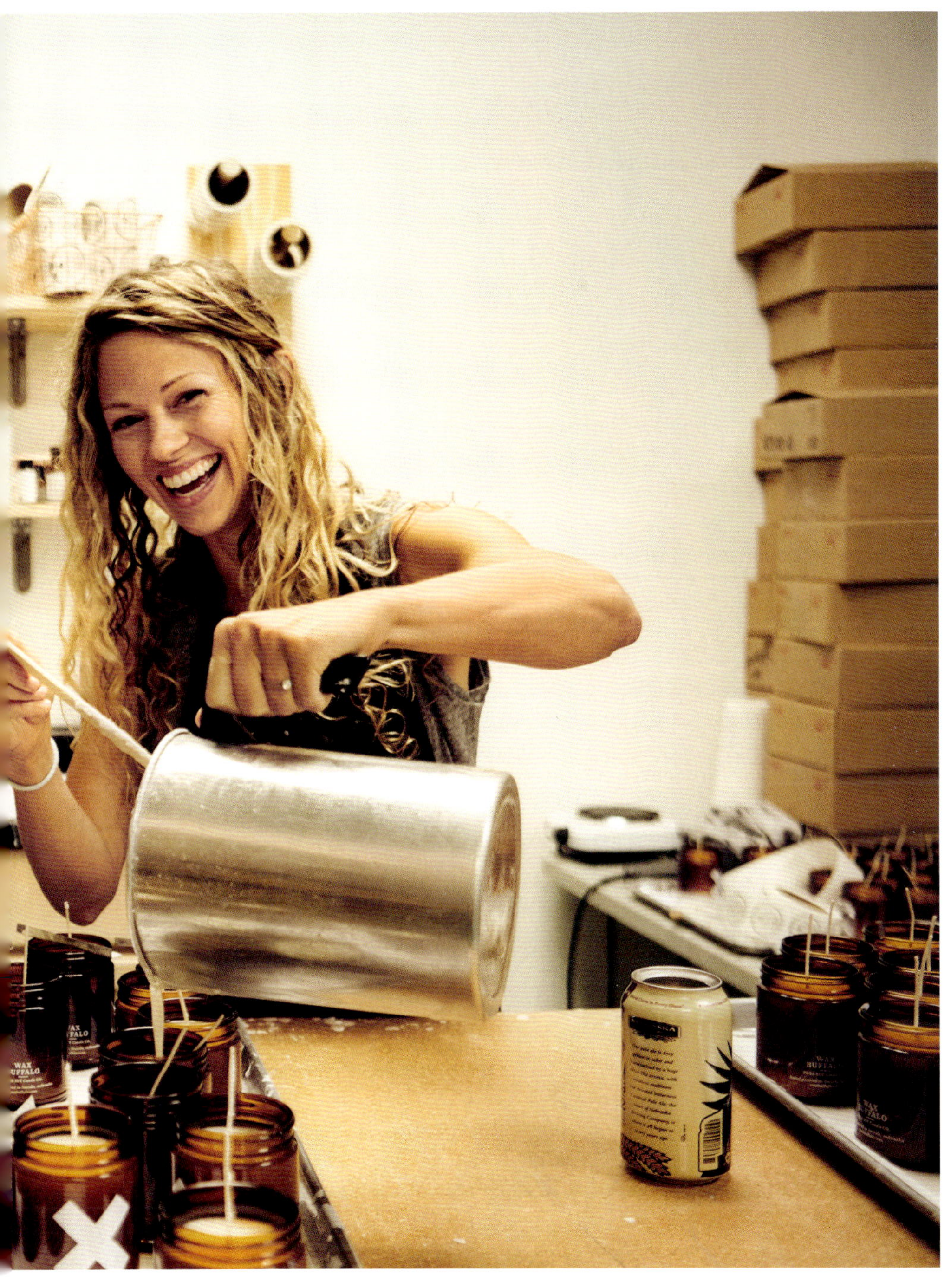

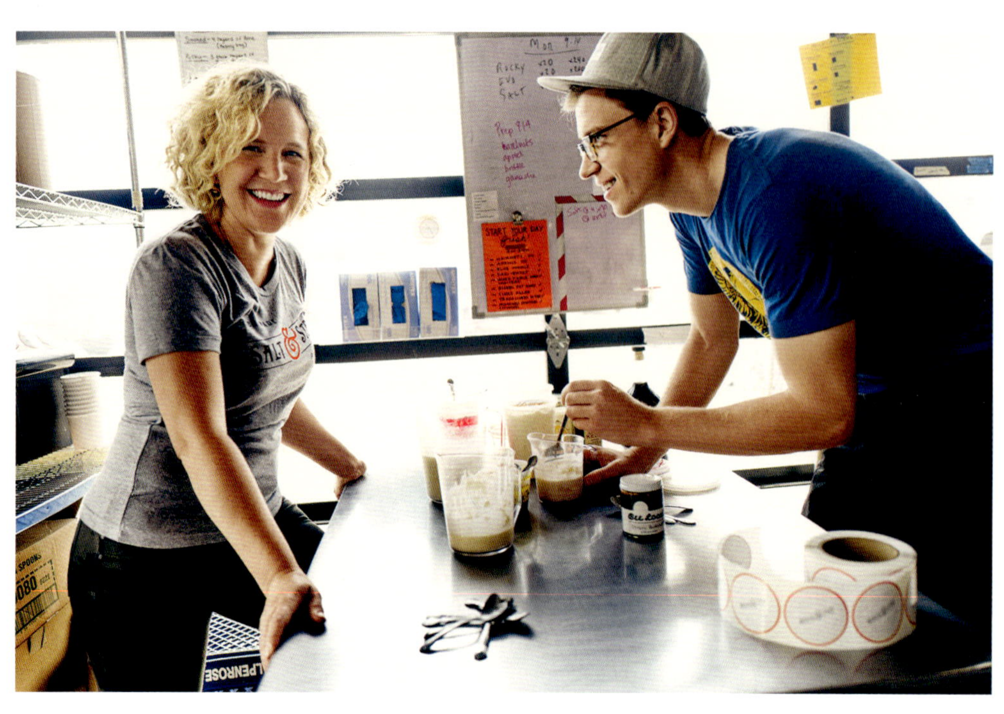

Kim & Tyler Malek Owners, Salt & Straw Ice Cream > Portland, Oregon

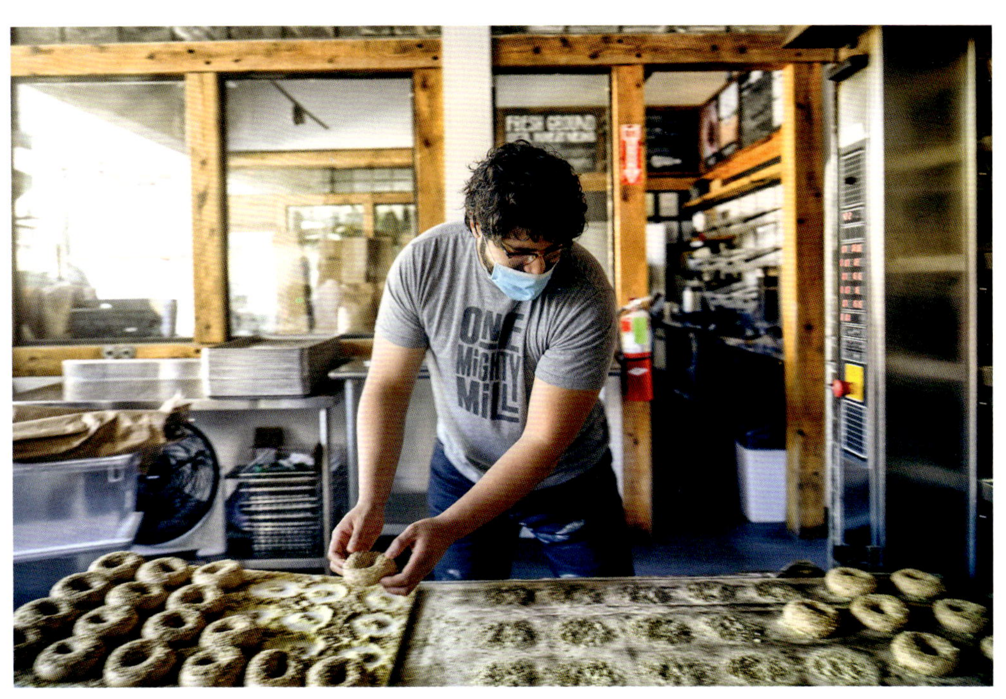

Mateo Velez Grain Miller, One Mighty Mill Bakery > Lynn, Massachusetts

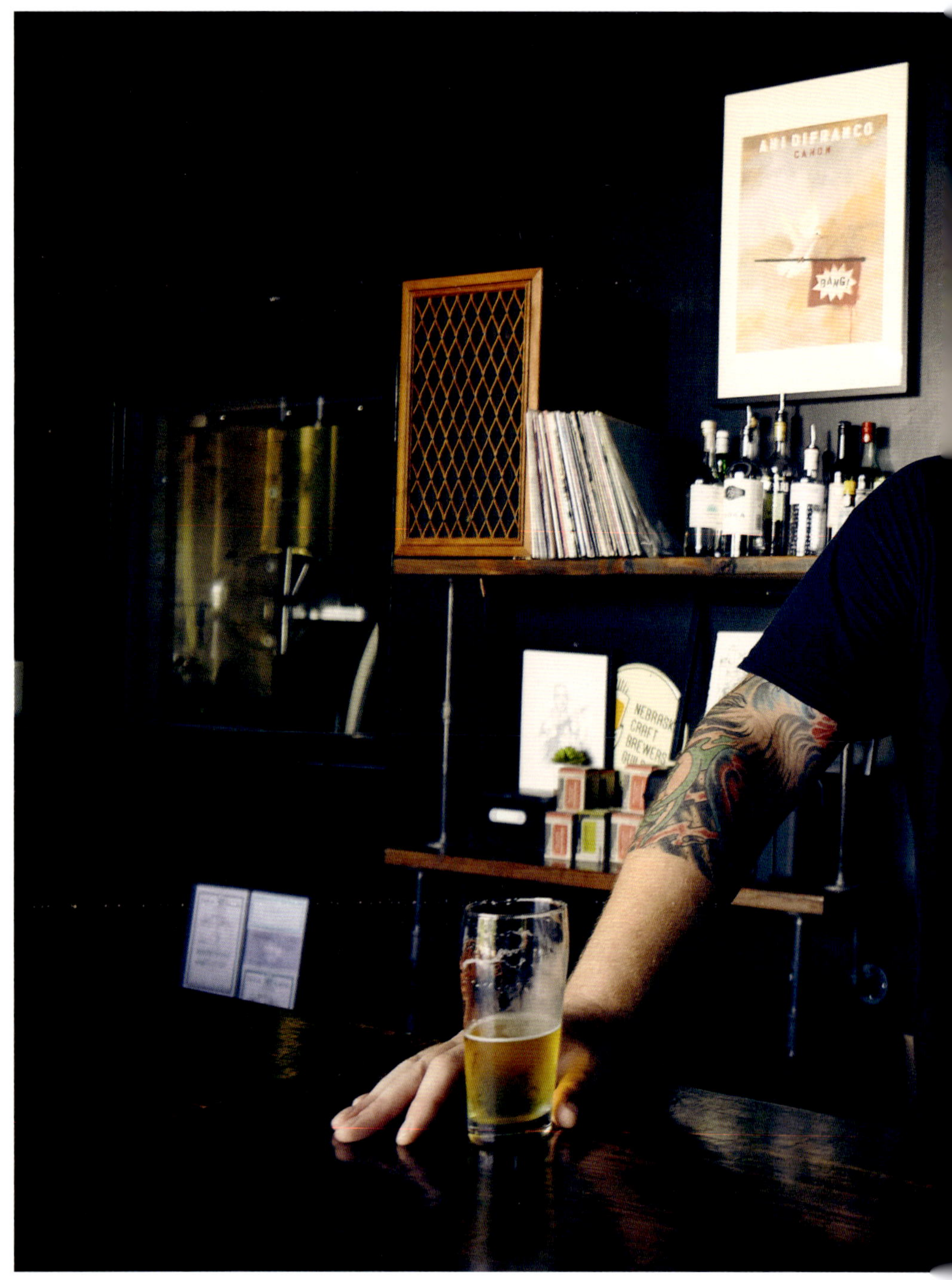

Kolby Wood Brewer, White Elm Brewing > Lincoln, Nebraska

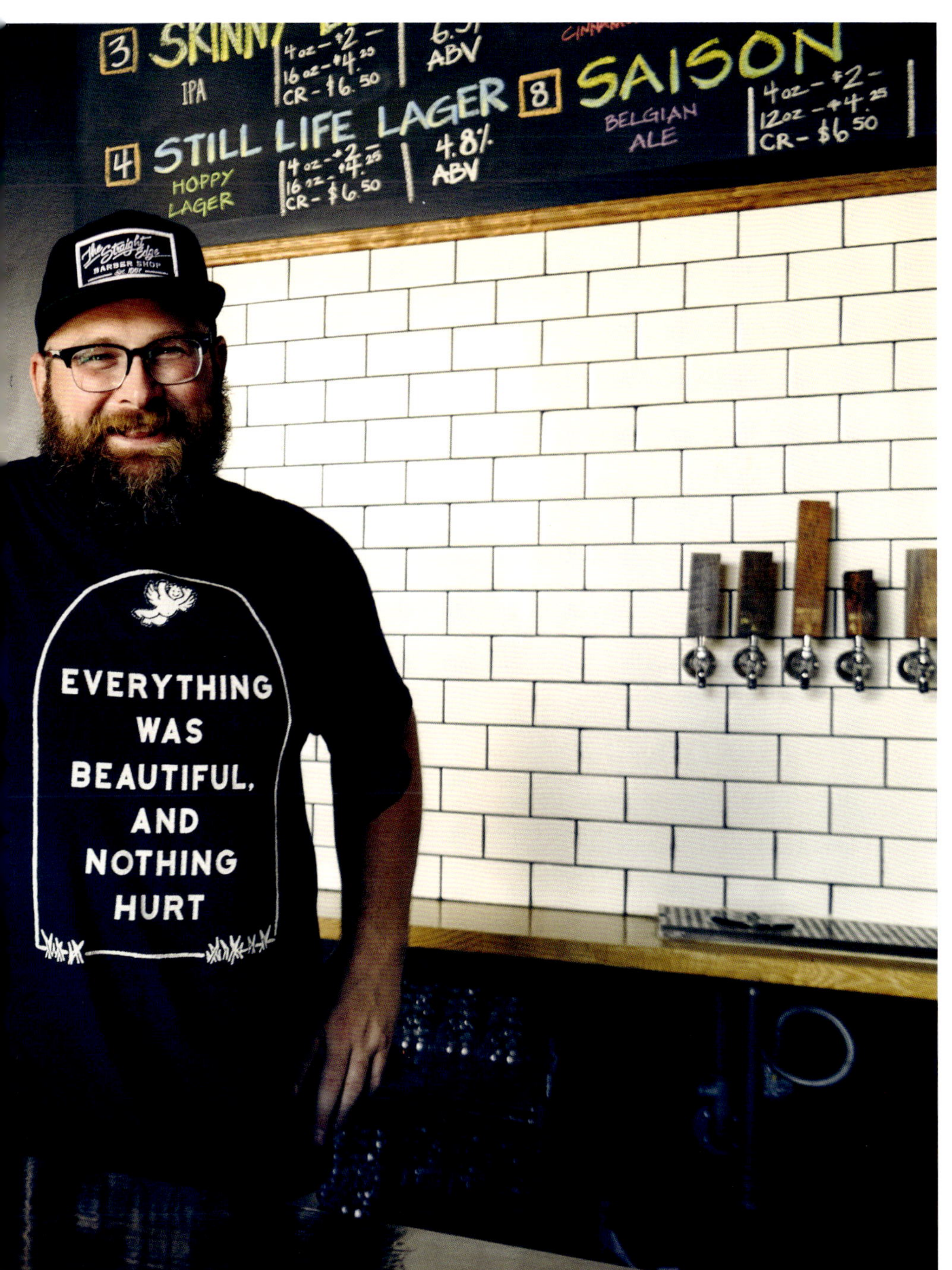
3 SKINNY
IPA
4 oz - $2 -
16 oz - $4.20
CR - $6.50
6.5
ABV
CINNAMON
8 SAISON
BELGIAN
ALE
4 oz - $2 -
12 oz - $4.25
CR - $6 50
4 STILL LIFE LAGER
HOPPY
LAGER
4 oz - $2 -
16 oz - $4.25
CR - $6.50
4.8%
ABV
The Straight Edge
BARBER SHOP
Est 1991
EVERYTHING
WAS
BEAUTIFUL,
AND
NOTHING
HURT

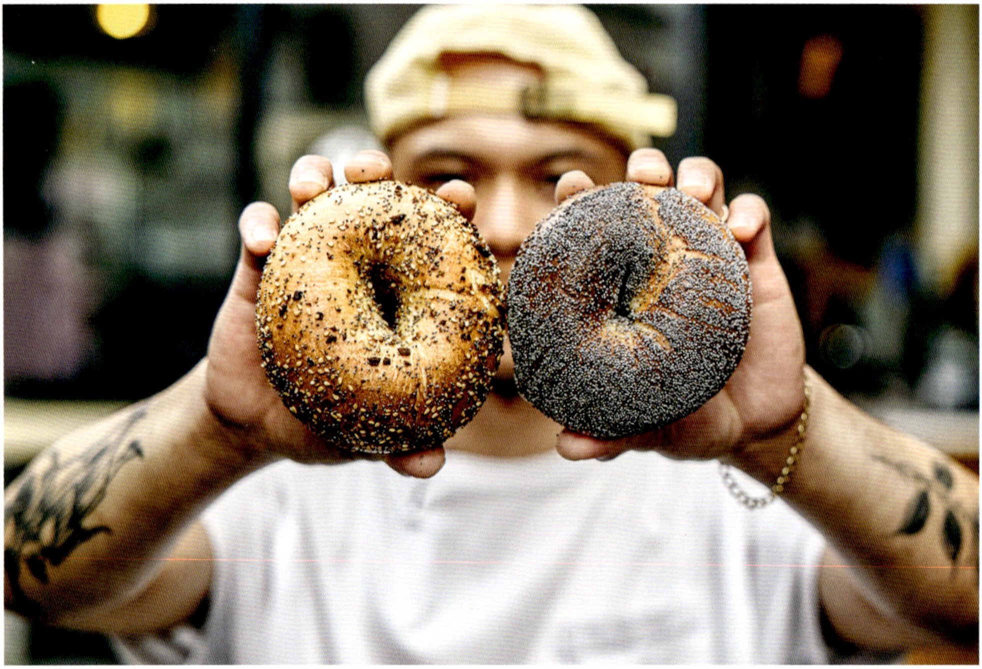

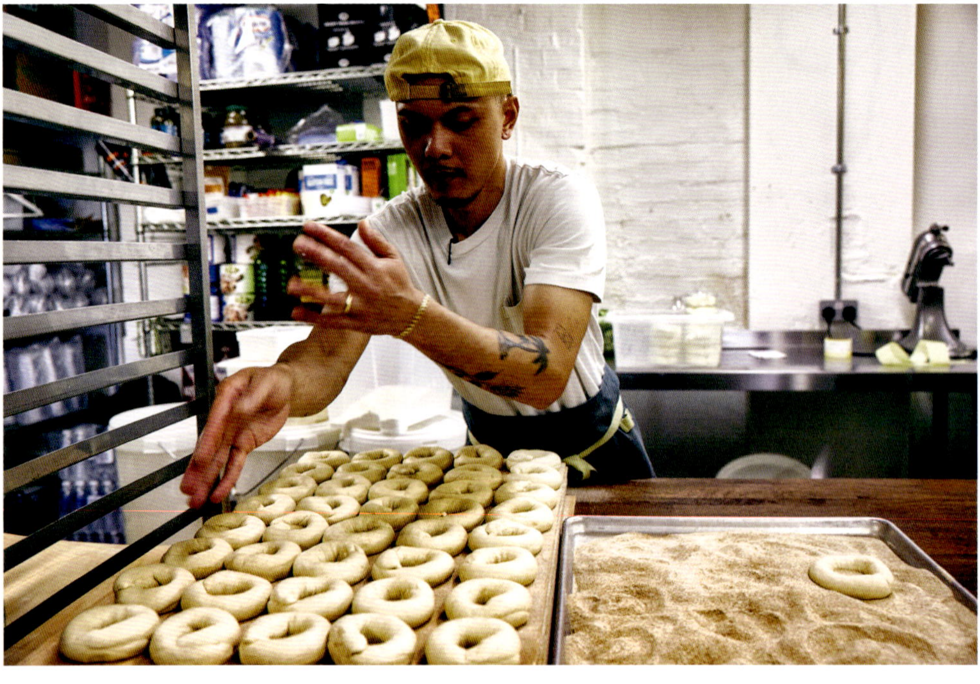

Gabriel Gomez Owner and Baker, Papo's Bagels > London, England

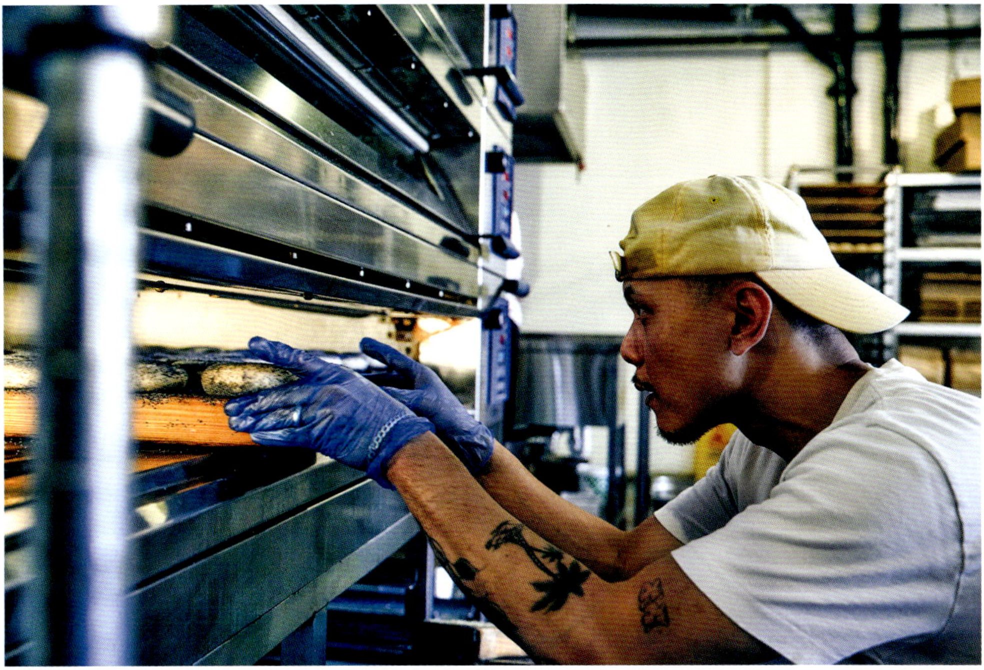

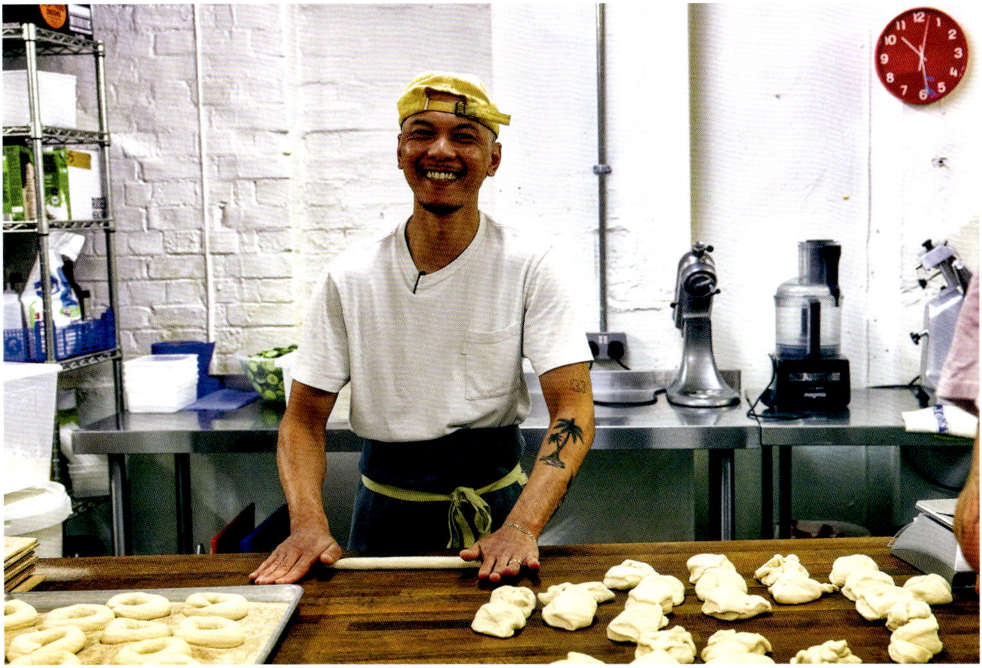

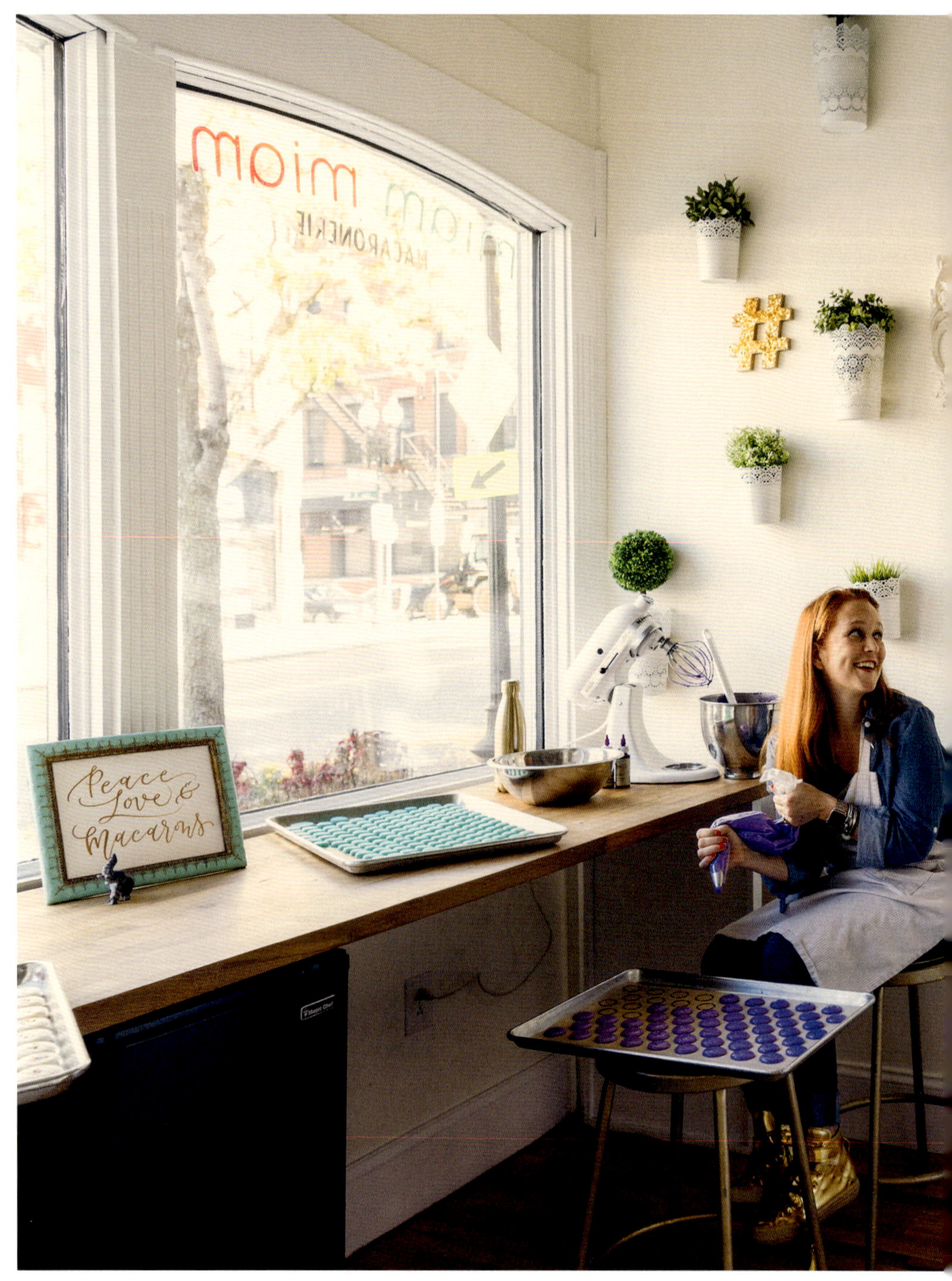

Jennifer Turner & Nicole Raukohl Miam Miam Macaronerie > South Boston, Massachusetts

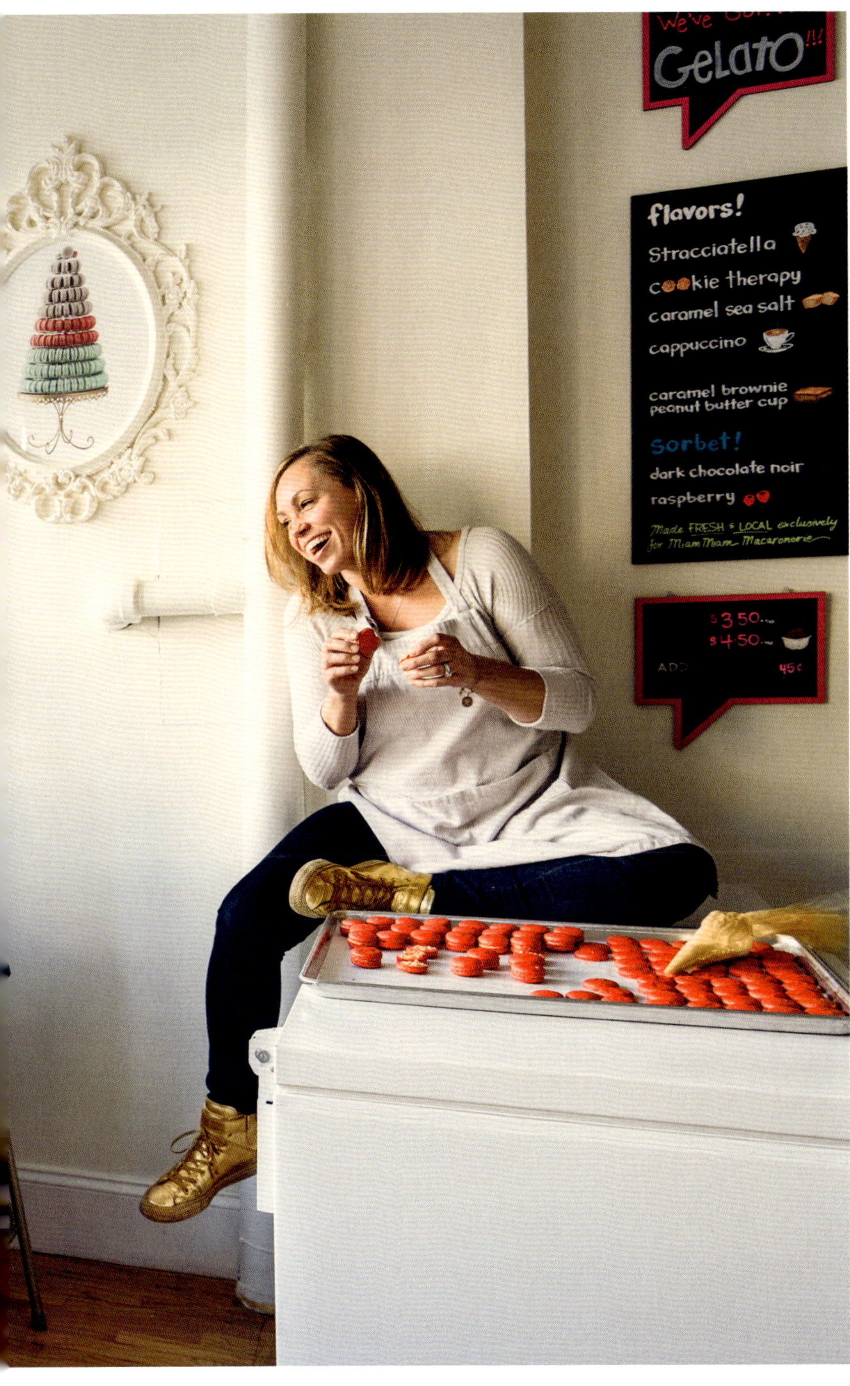
We've Got
Gelato!!!
flavors!
Stracciatella
cookie therapy
caramel sea salt
cappuccino
caramel brownie
peanut butter cup
sorbet!
dark chocolate noir
raspberry
Made FRESH & LOCAL exclusively
for Miam Miam Macaronerie
$3.50
$4.50
ADD   45¢

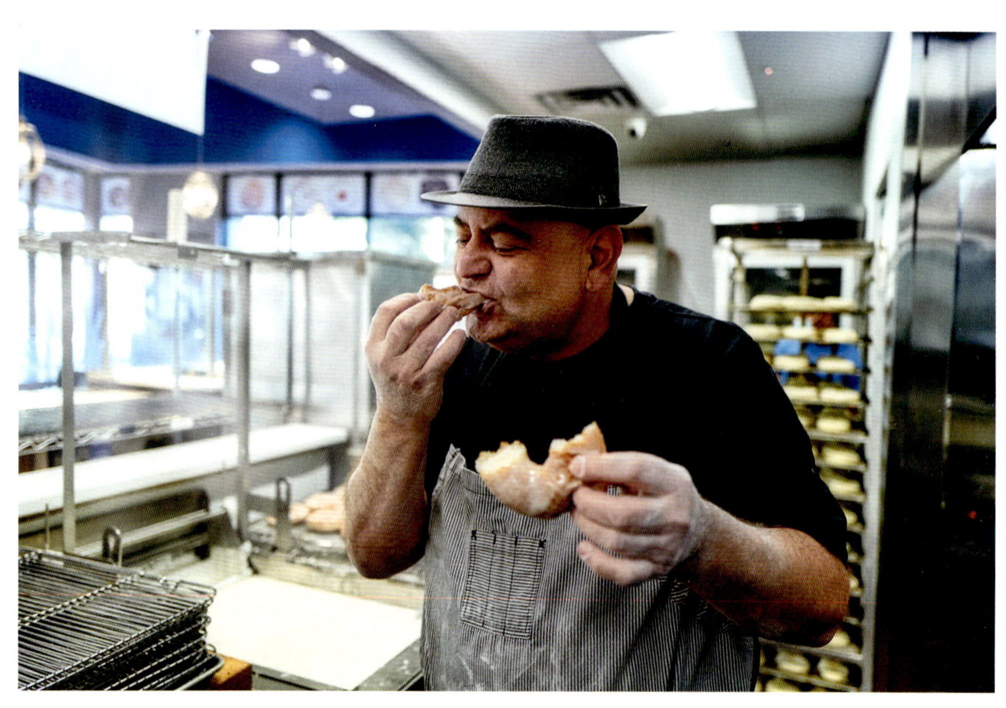

Paul Delios Owner and Donut Meister, Kane's Donuts > Saugus, Massachusetts

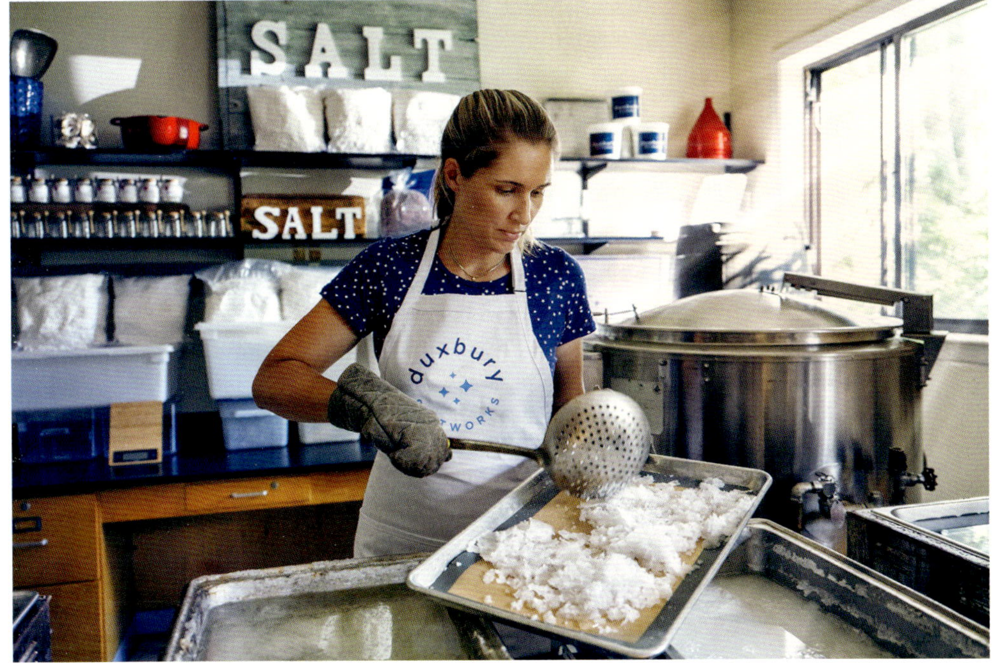
SALT
SALT
duxbury
SALTWORKS

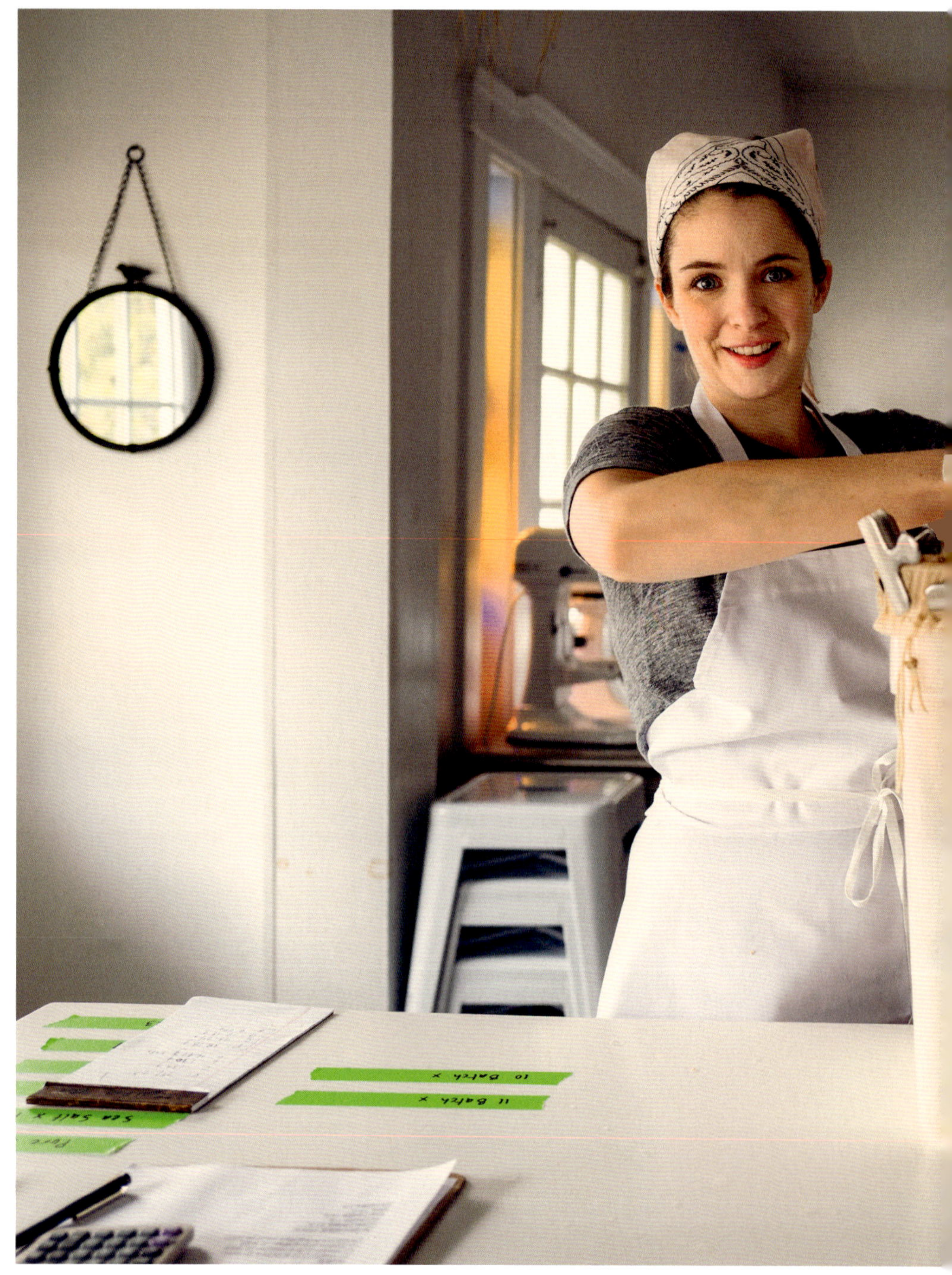

Laurel McConville Almond Milk Maker, Nectar & Green > Rockport, Massachusetts

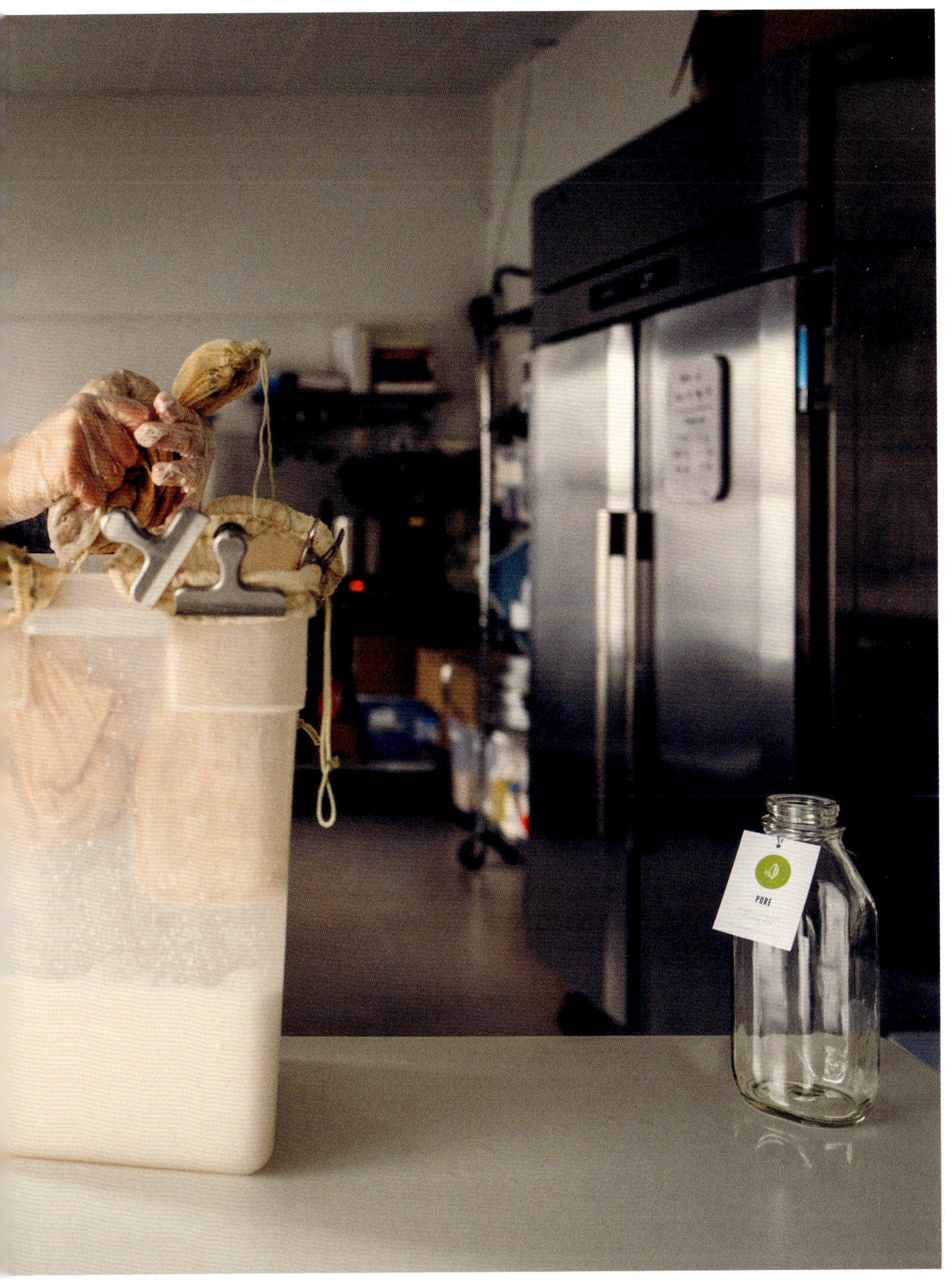
PURE

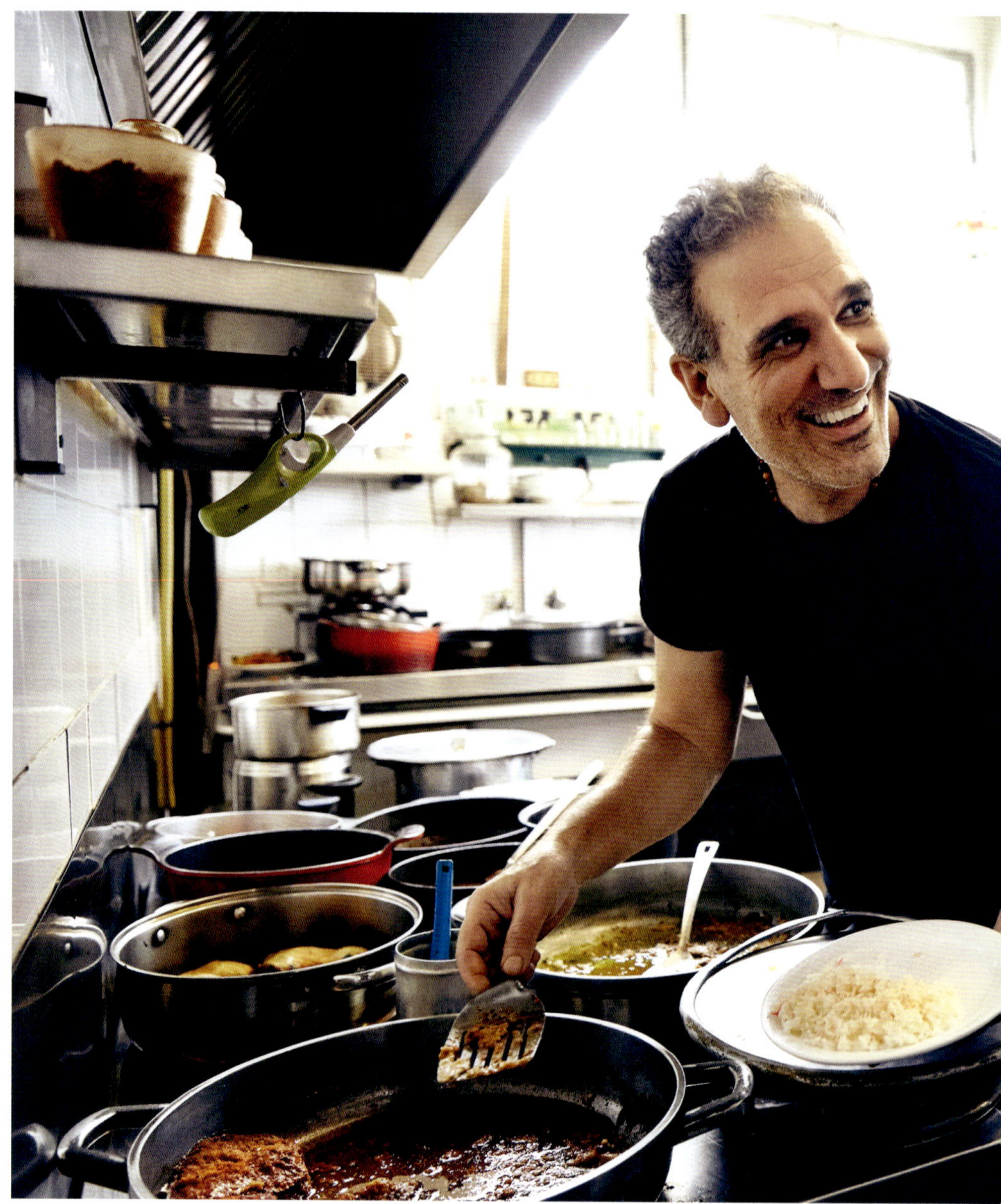

Spending a lunch shift with Shmaya shook up my image of a chaotic kitchen with a chef yelling at a team of cooks, pushing them to go faster.

Far from it. The kitchen was busy; everyone was hustling to keep pace. But it was

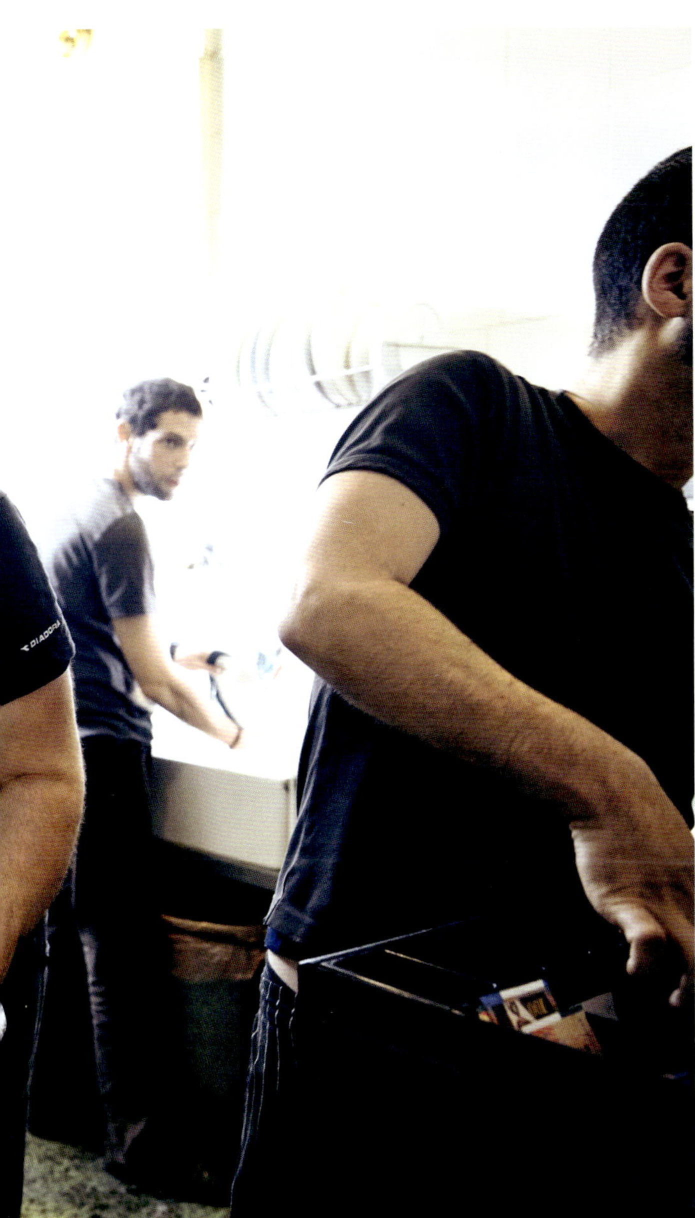

joyful and energetic, not tense. Shmaya set the tone, smiling, laughing, joking. He put so much of himself into making everyone — staff, diners, and the guy in the corner with the camera — feel welcome, and part of the family.

Shmaya Cohen Chef > Tel Aviv, Israel

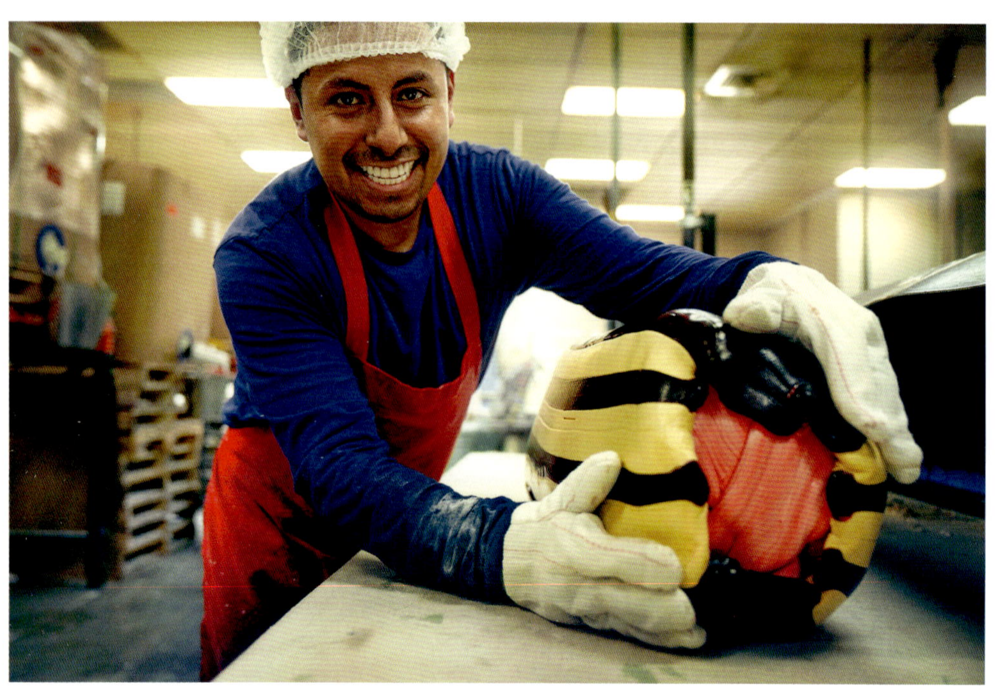

Victor Ortiz Torres Candymaker, Hammond's Candies > Denver, Colorado

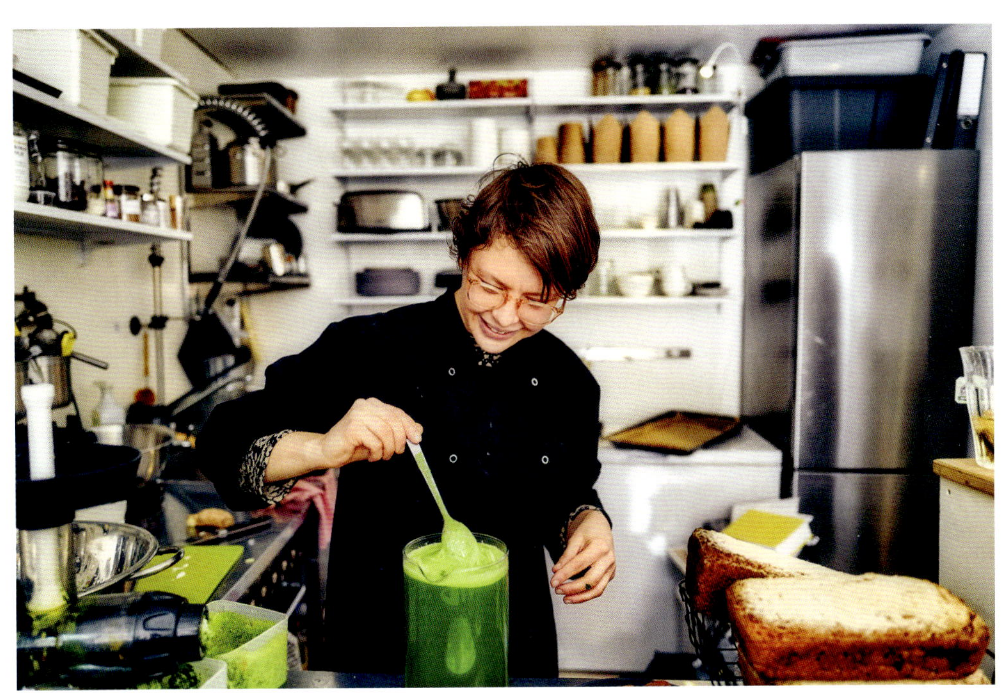

Emma-Lisa Forstorp Amazeball Maker, Oh My Raw Balls > Amsterdam, Netherlands

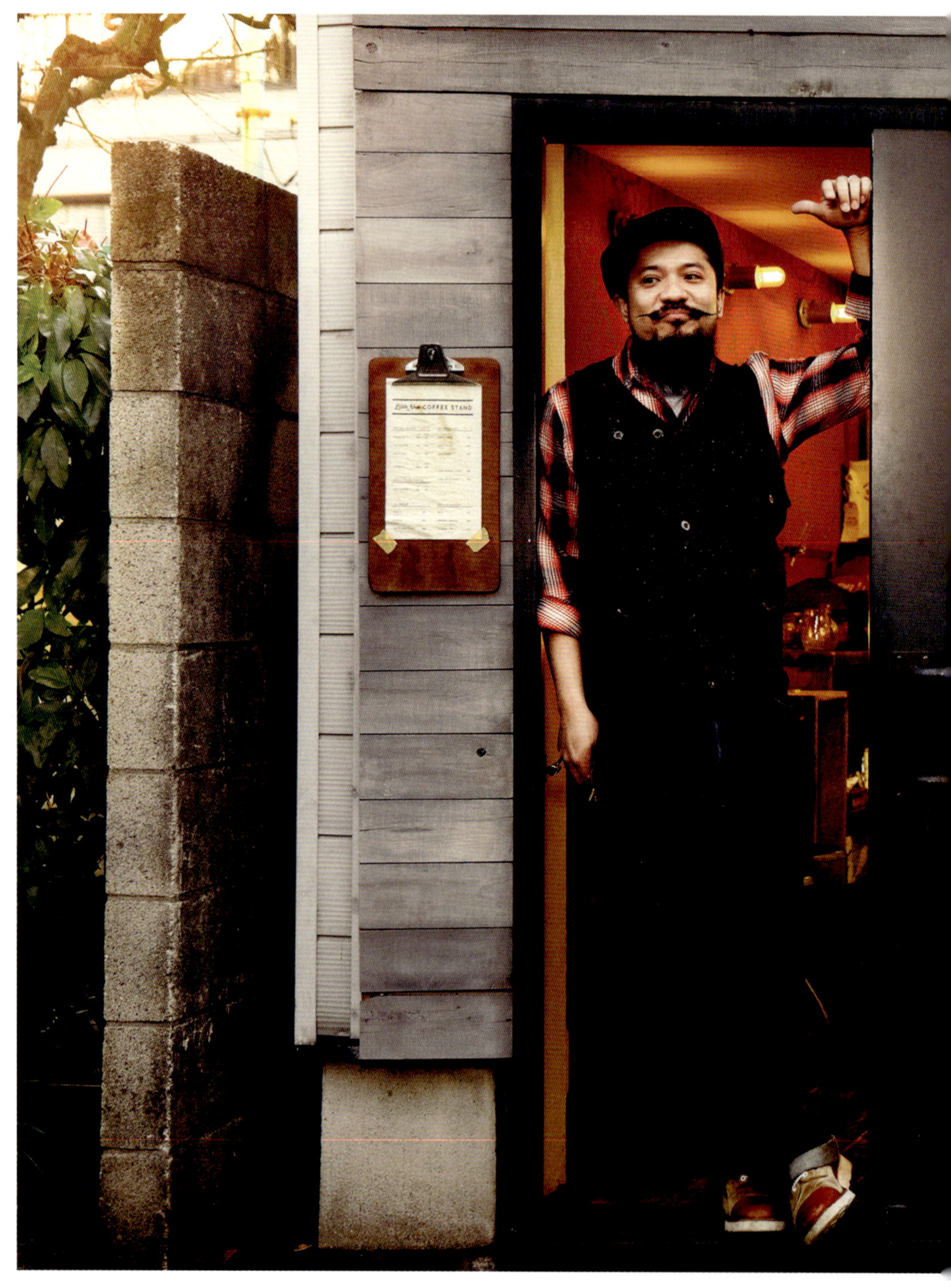

Daisuke Hamada Barista, Little Nap Coffee > Tokyo, Japan

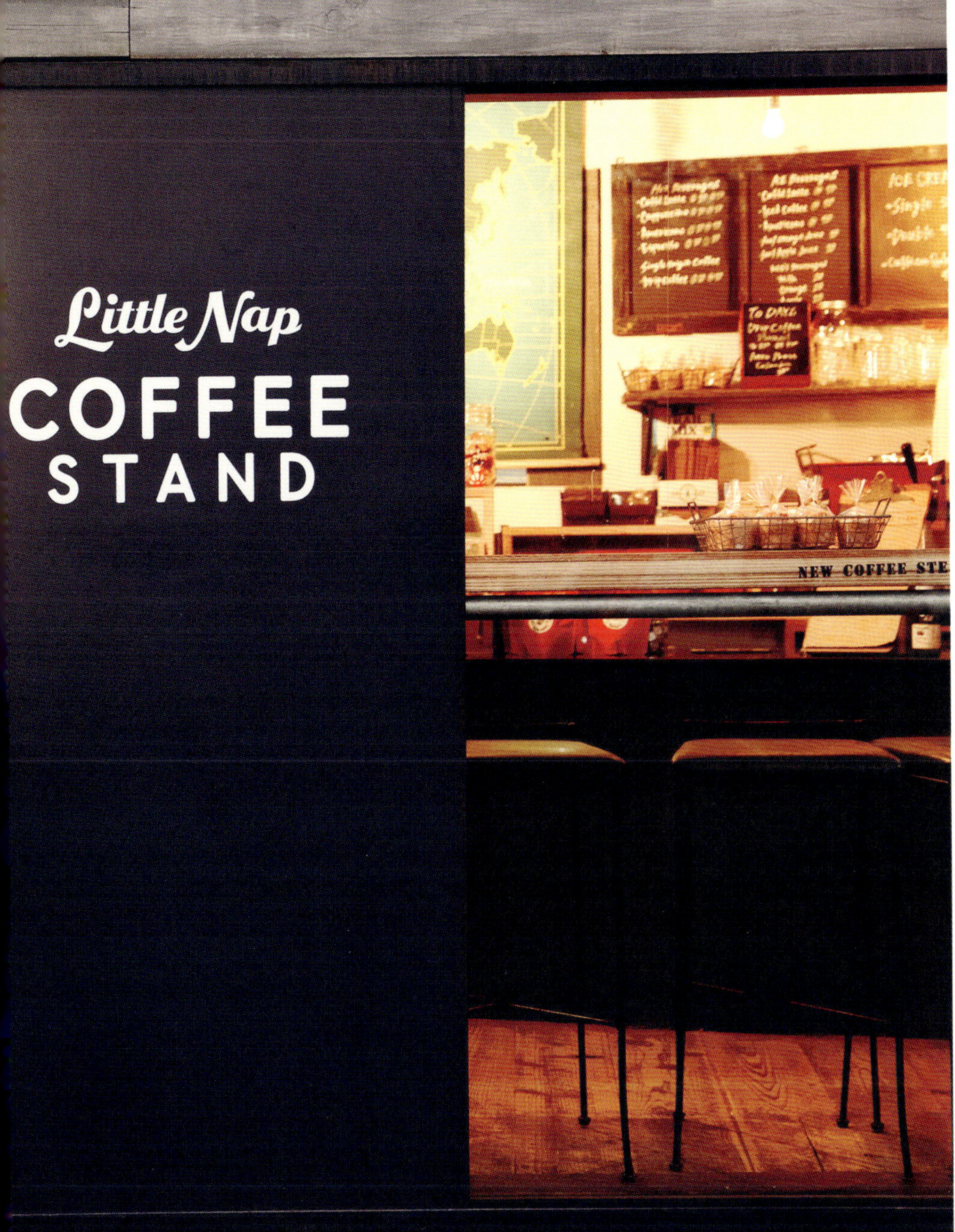

Little Nap
COFFEE
STAND
NEW COFFEE STE

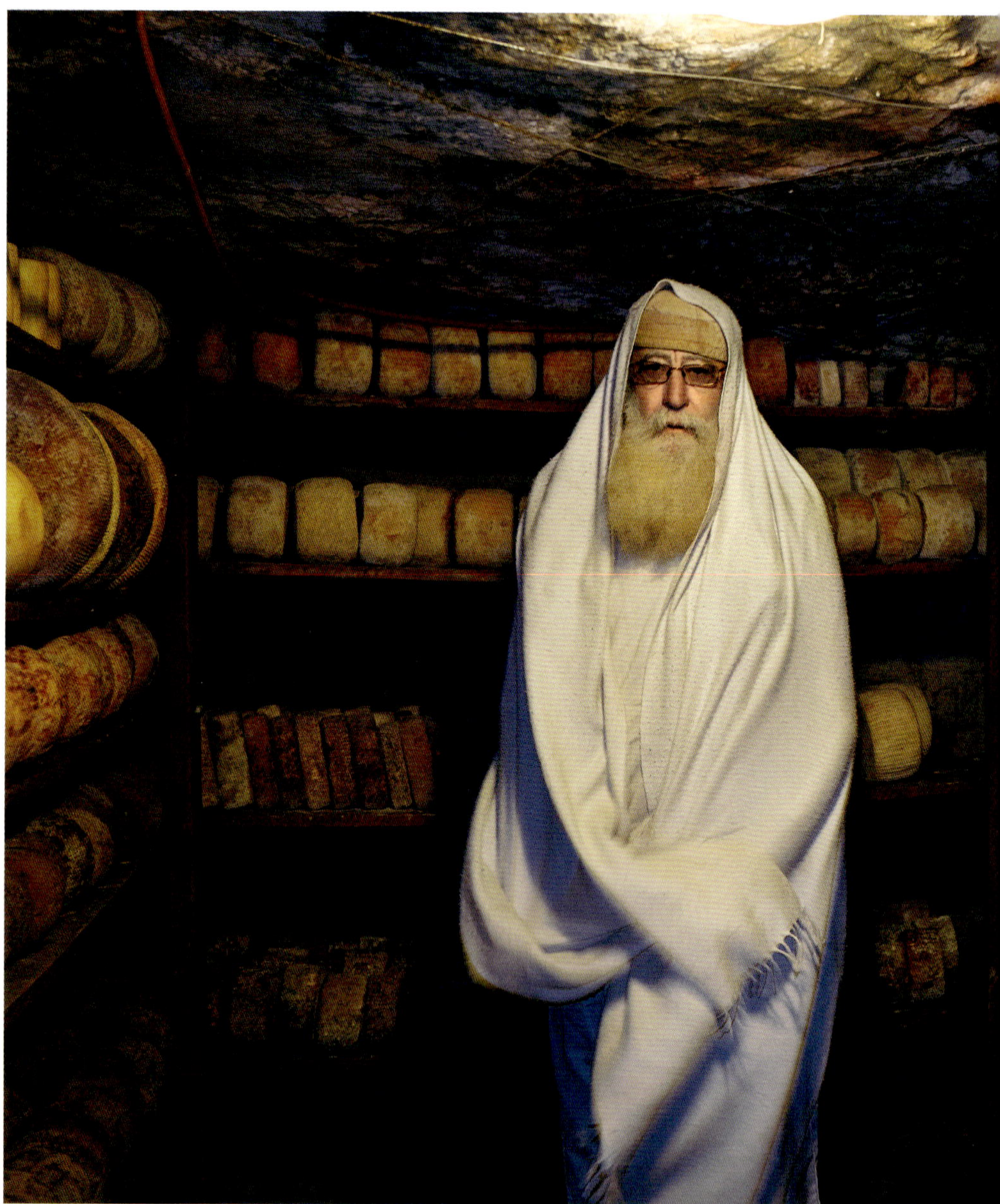

We drove for over an hour on rugged roads more suited for animals than vehicles. When we arrived, I met the cheesemaker. He'd forgotten that I was coming, and in fact looked a bit confused about why I was there.

After a brief chat, it seemed clear that he didn't want to be photographed, which was disappointing. I thanked him for his time, and though I was ready to leave, I sensed that he wanted me to follow him. Without a word, he headed towards what appeared to be a cave. I followed.

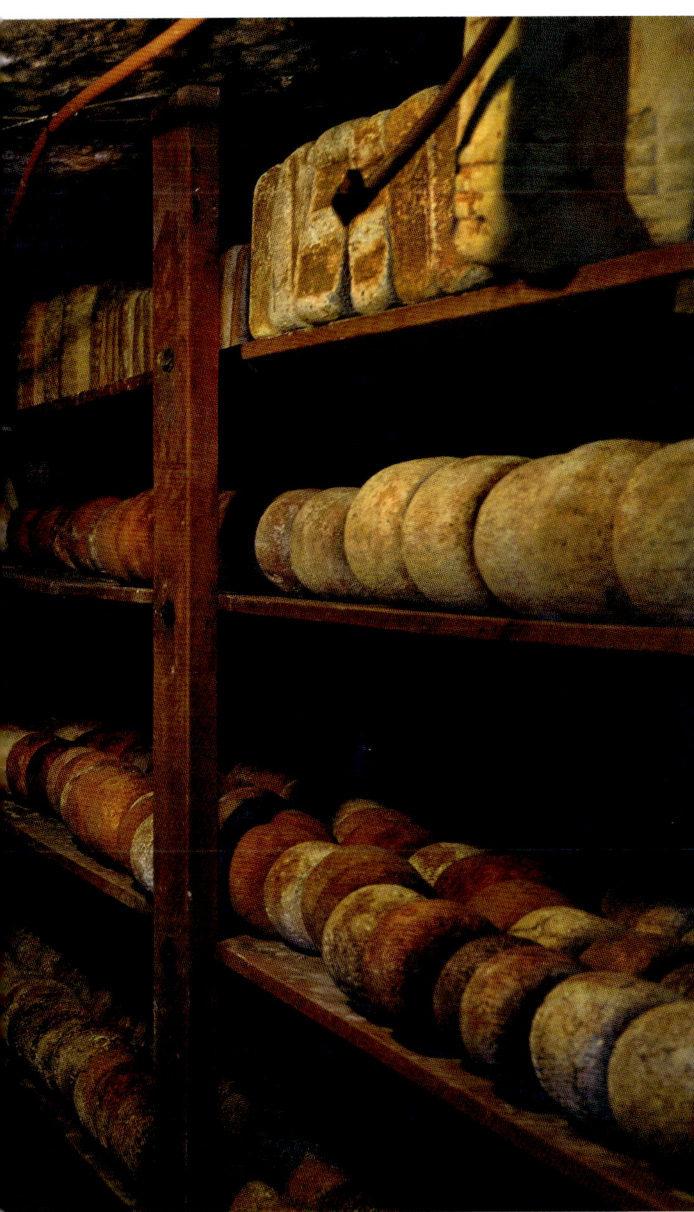

We entered a room filled with cheeses. He turned toward me, and—with just a glance—invited me to photograph him. I did. Out of respect for his silence, I said nothing as I left.

I was readying to get into my car when he walked up, and gently placed his hand on my shoulder. And with this silent goodbye, he moved on.

Cheesemaker > Judea Mountains, Israel

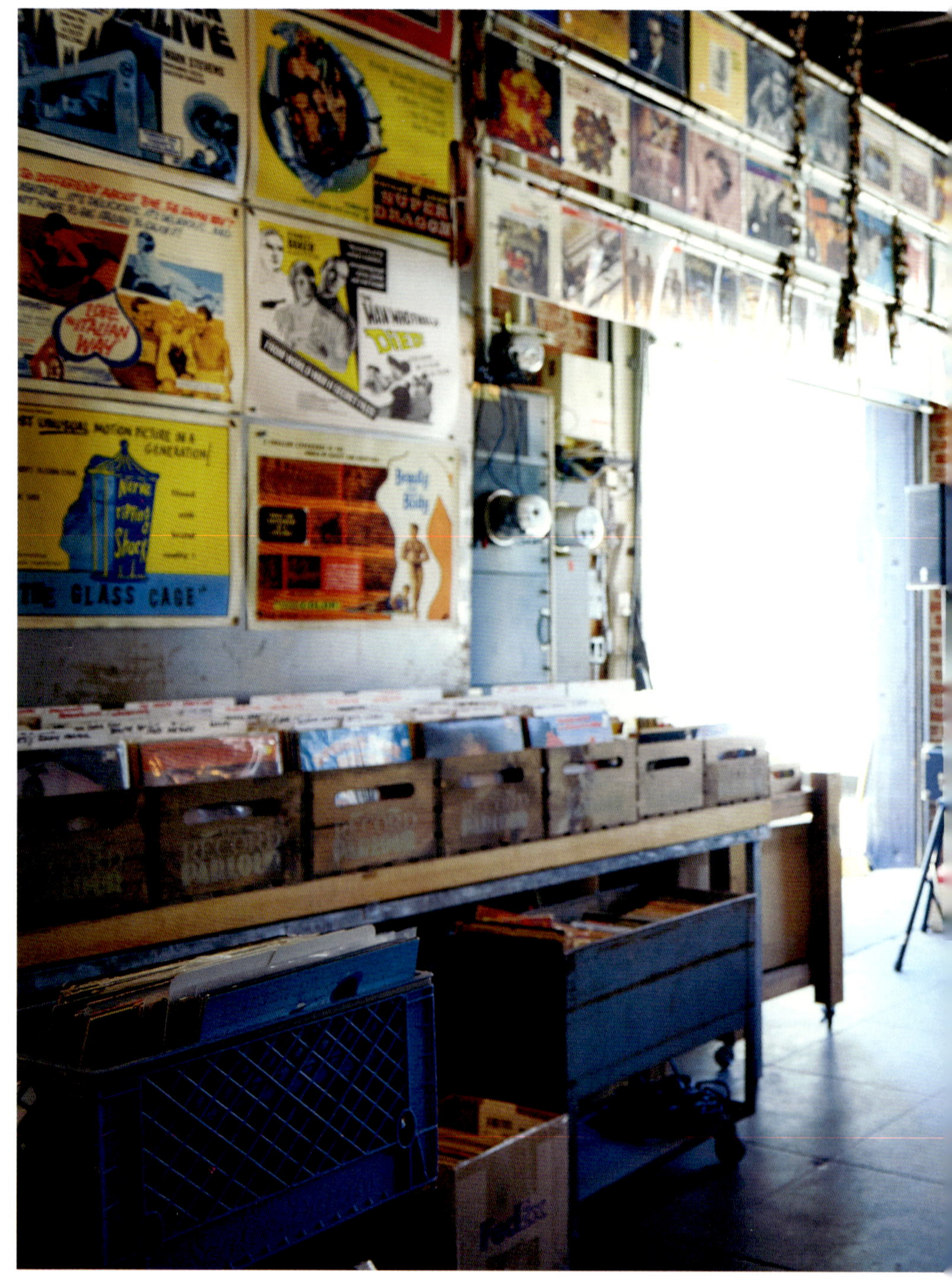

Chris Honetschlaeger Founder, The Record Parlour > Los Angeles, California

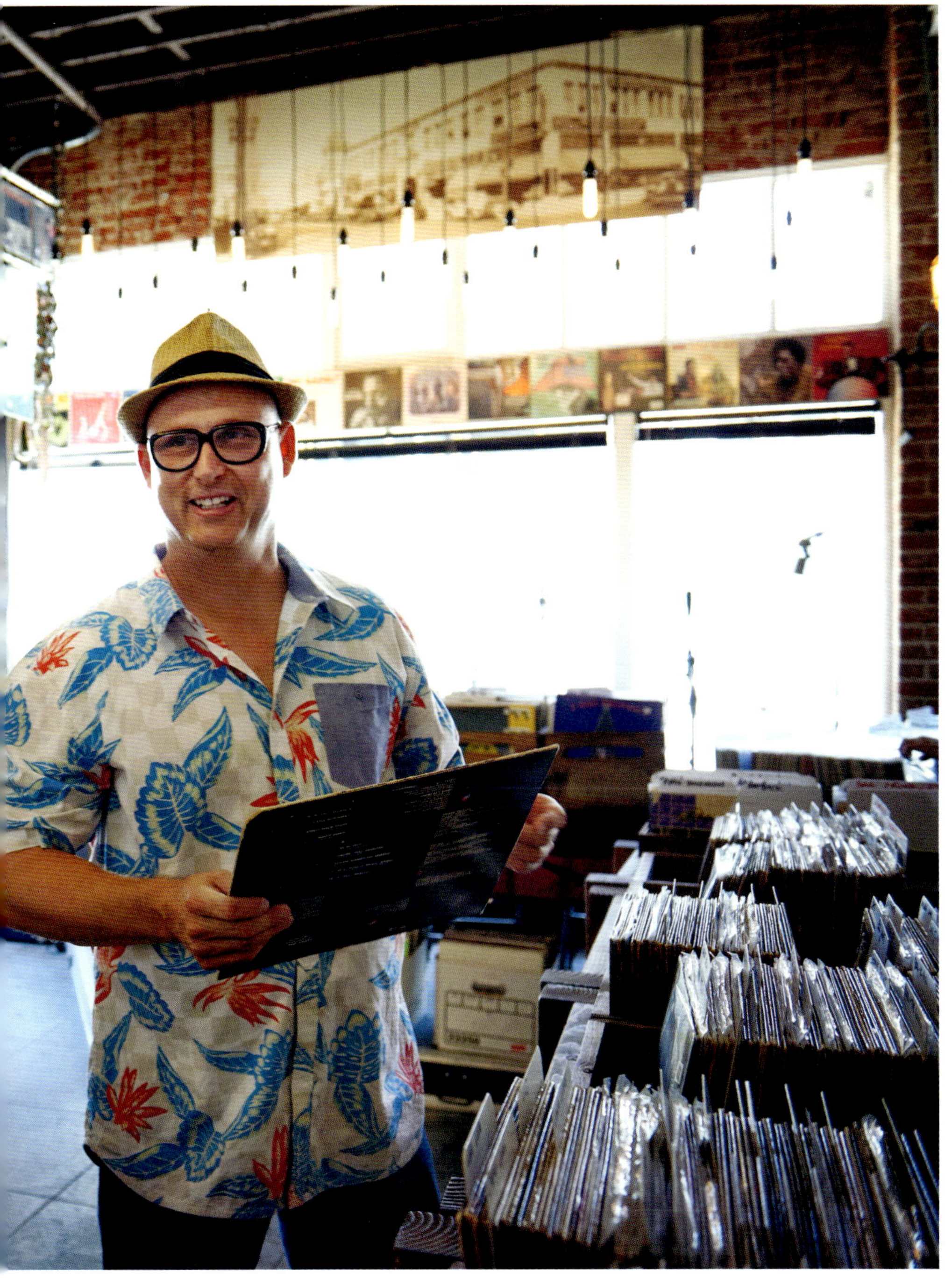

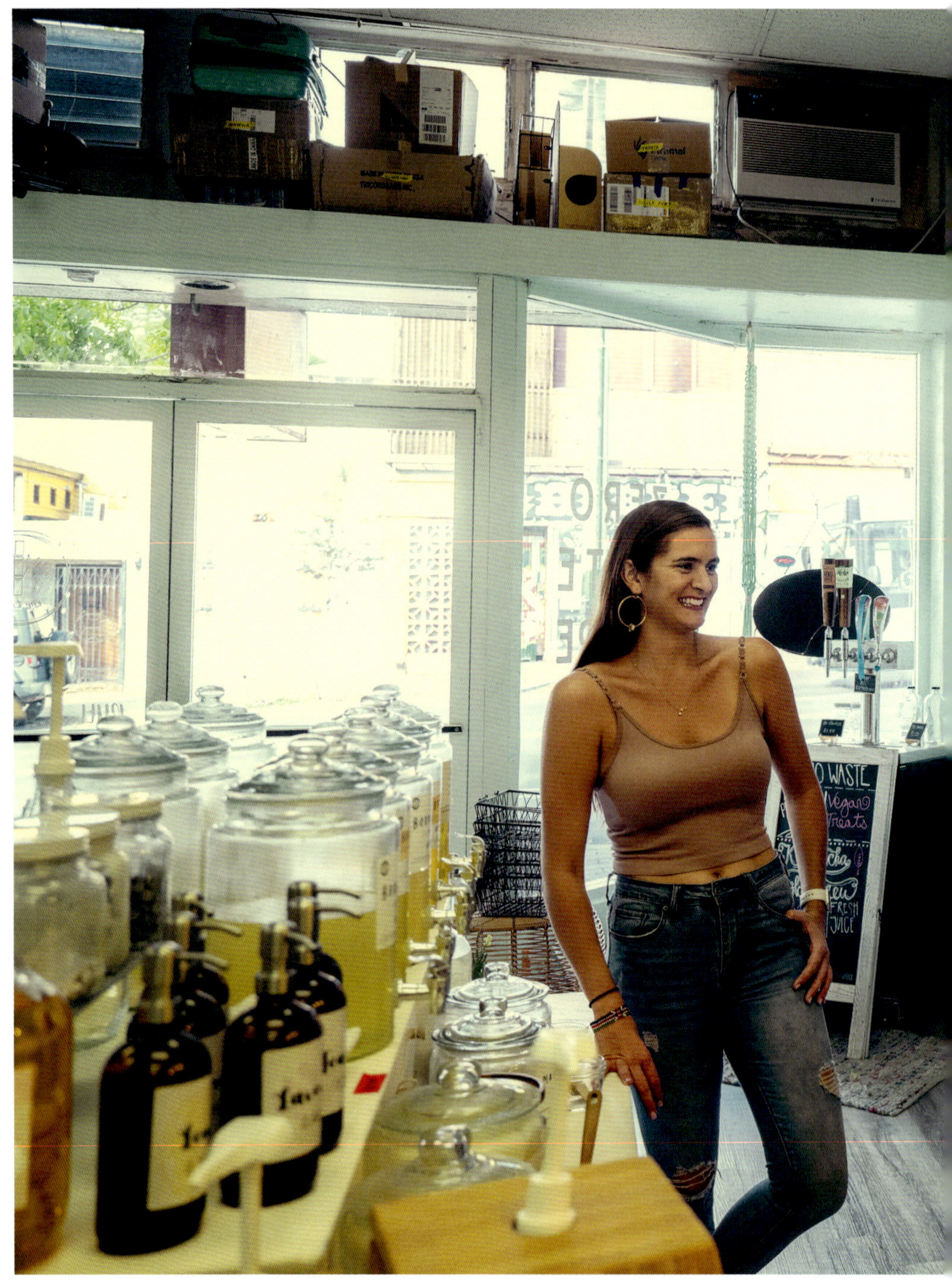

Hunter Long & Jillian Corn Keep It Simple Shop > Honolulu, Hawaii

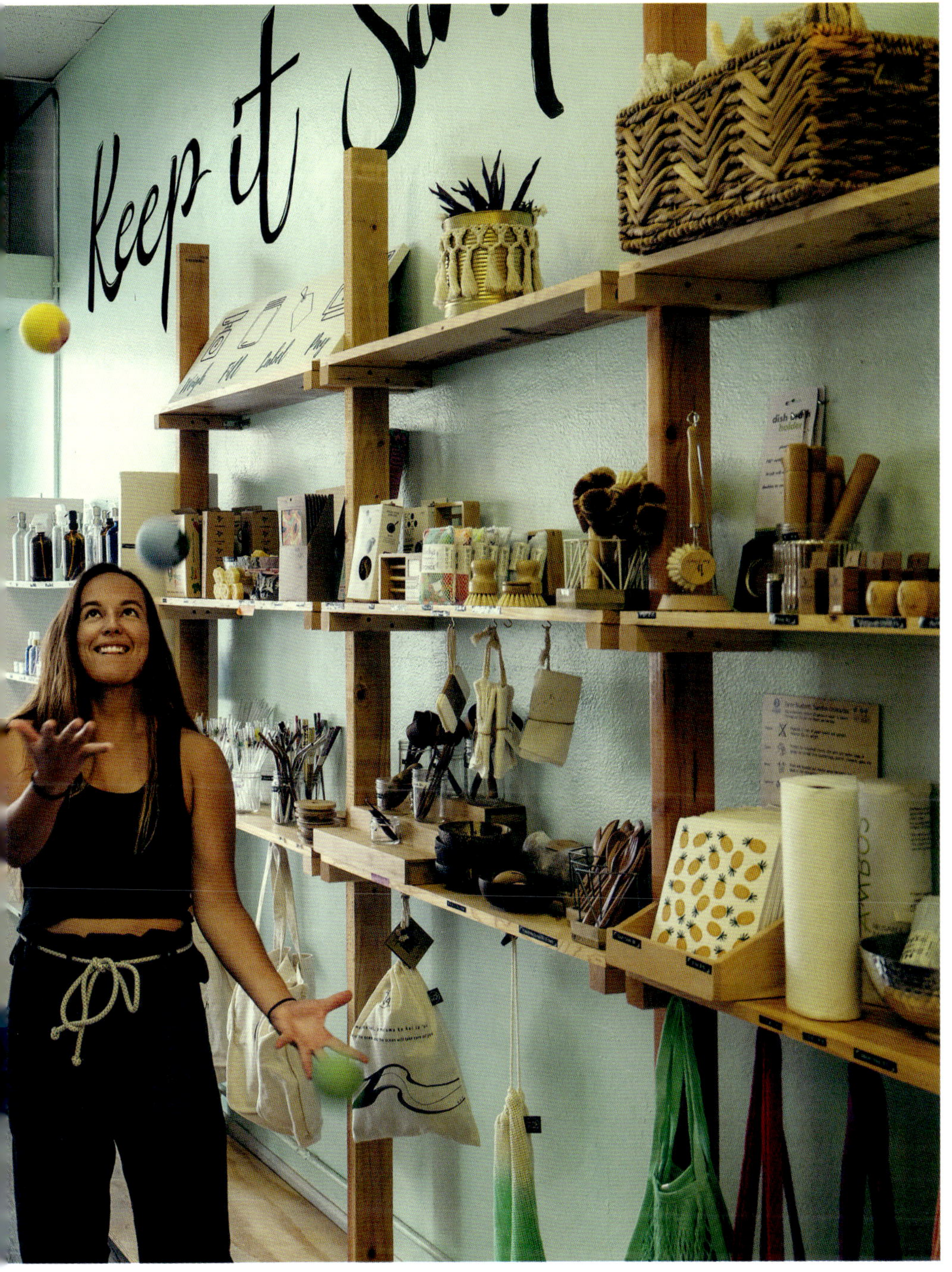
Keep it

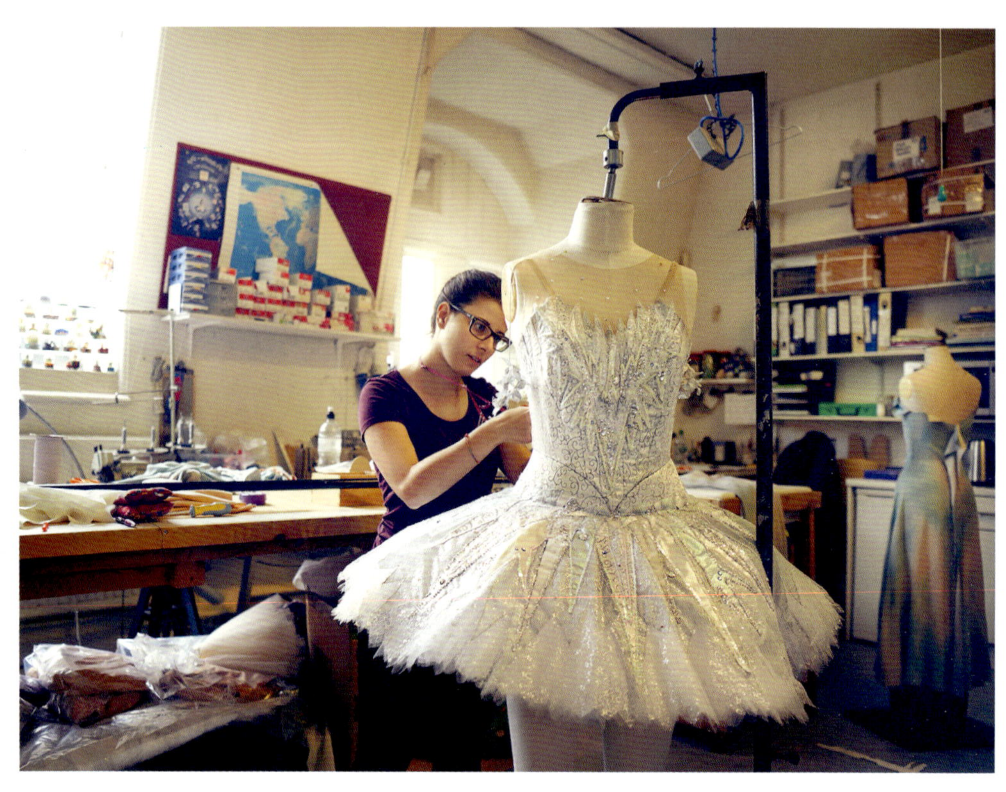

Serena Fusai Costumier, English National Ballet > London, England

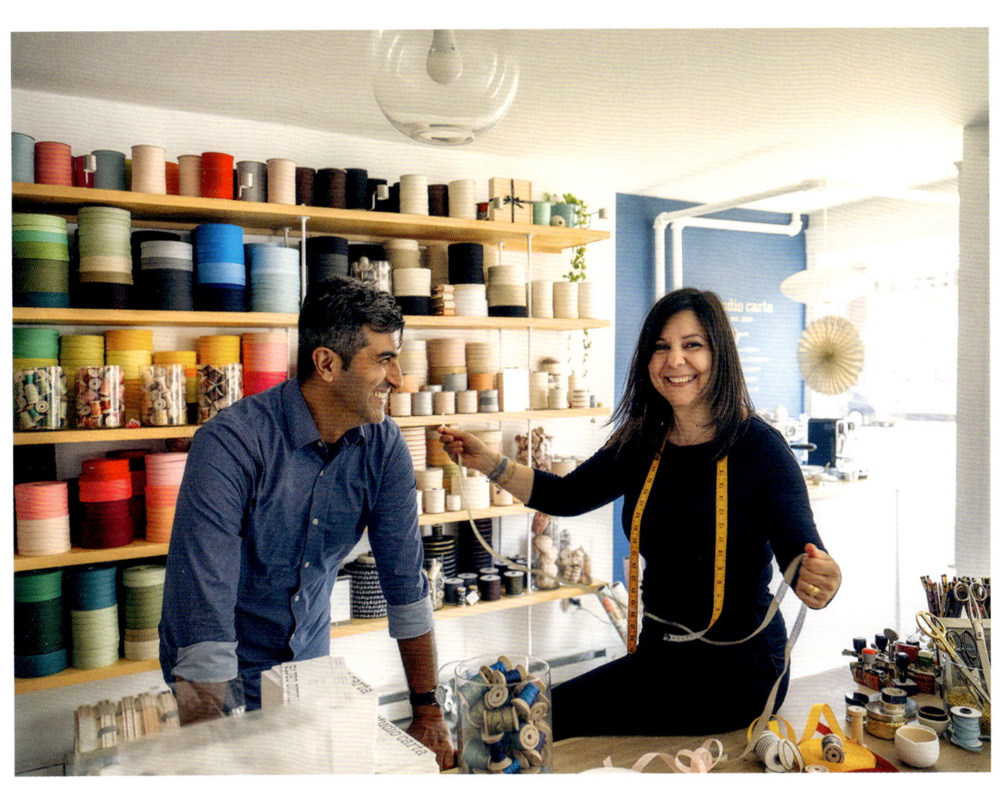

Angela Liguori & Mohamed Alaeddin Owners, Studio Carta Ribbon Shop > Boston, Massachusetts

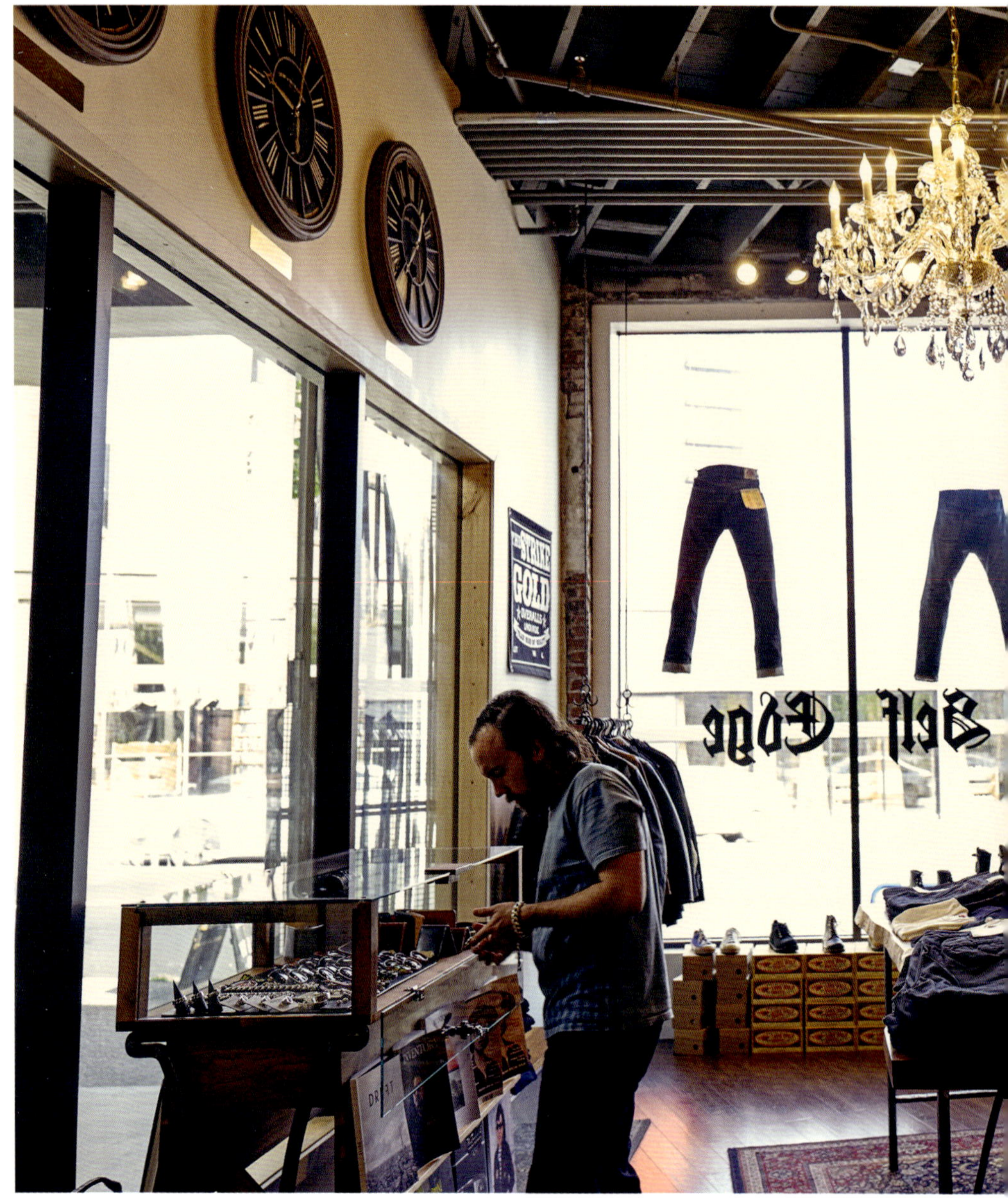

Given how cool the Self Edge denim brand is, I wanted to see how these two would respond in a totally mundane situation. Because we all put our pants on one leg at a time—even if they're the hippest jeans on the market.

And besides, those lightbulbs weren't going to change themselves.

Tyler Madden & Jonathan Guerrero Self Edge Denim > Portland, Oregon

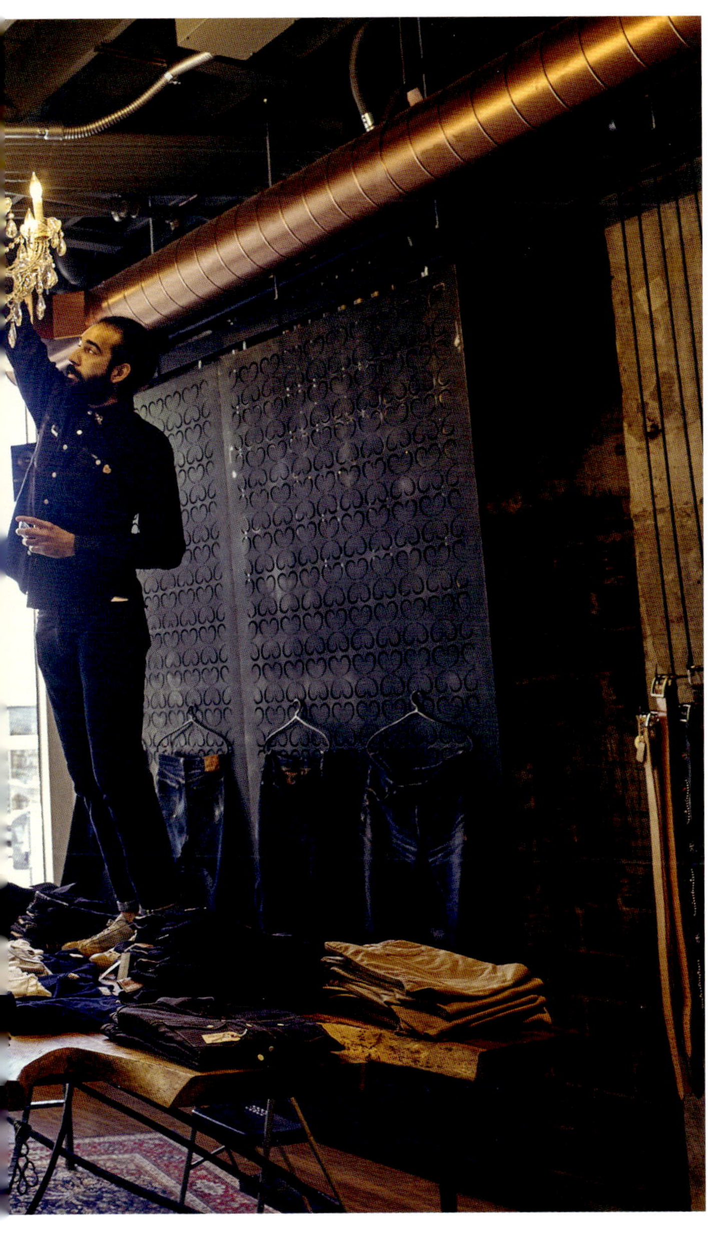

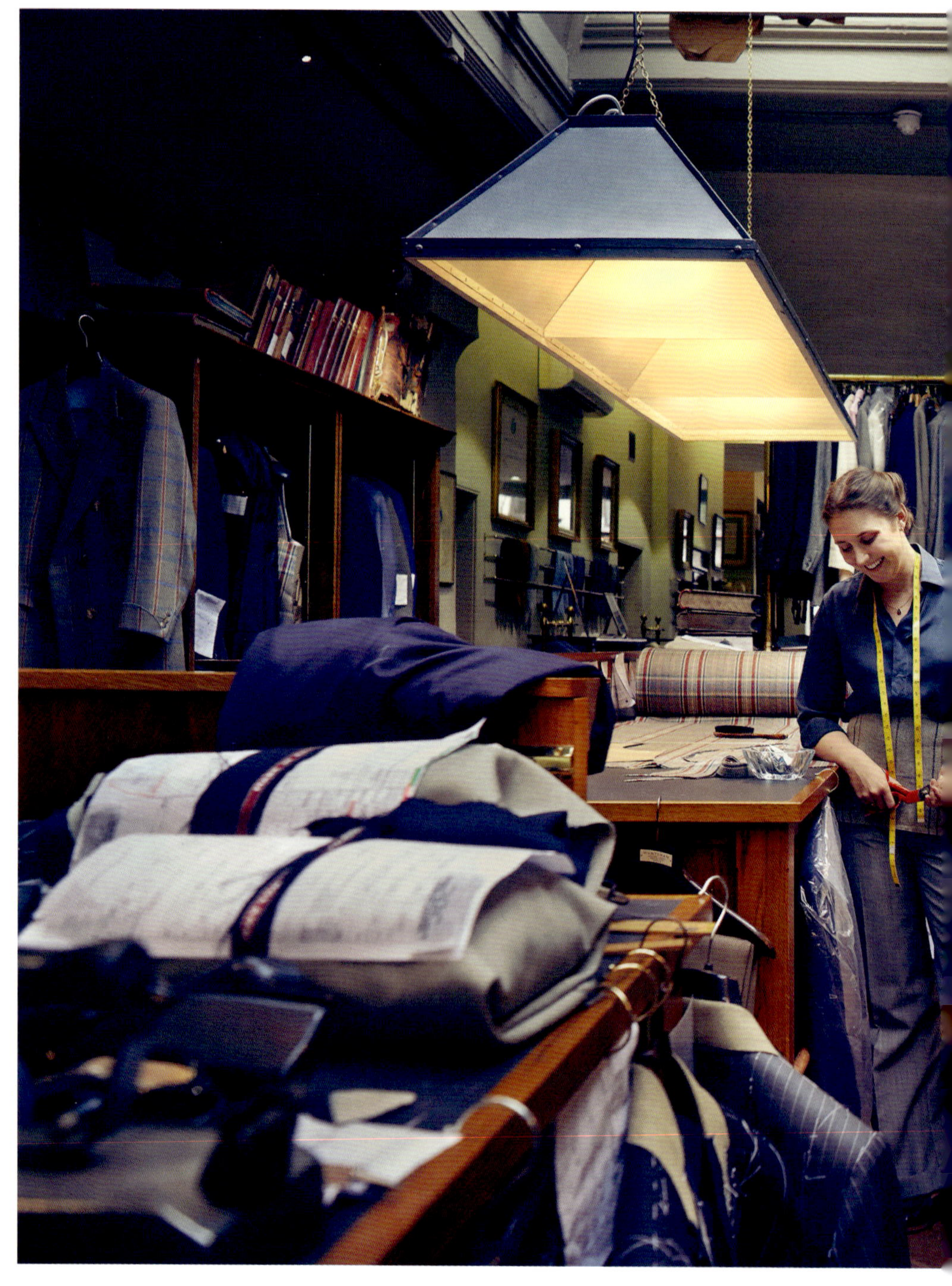

Antonia Ede Bespoke Menswear Cutter, Huntsman Savile Row > London, England

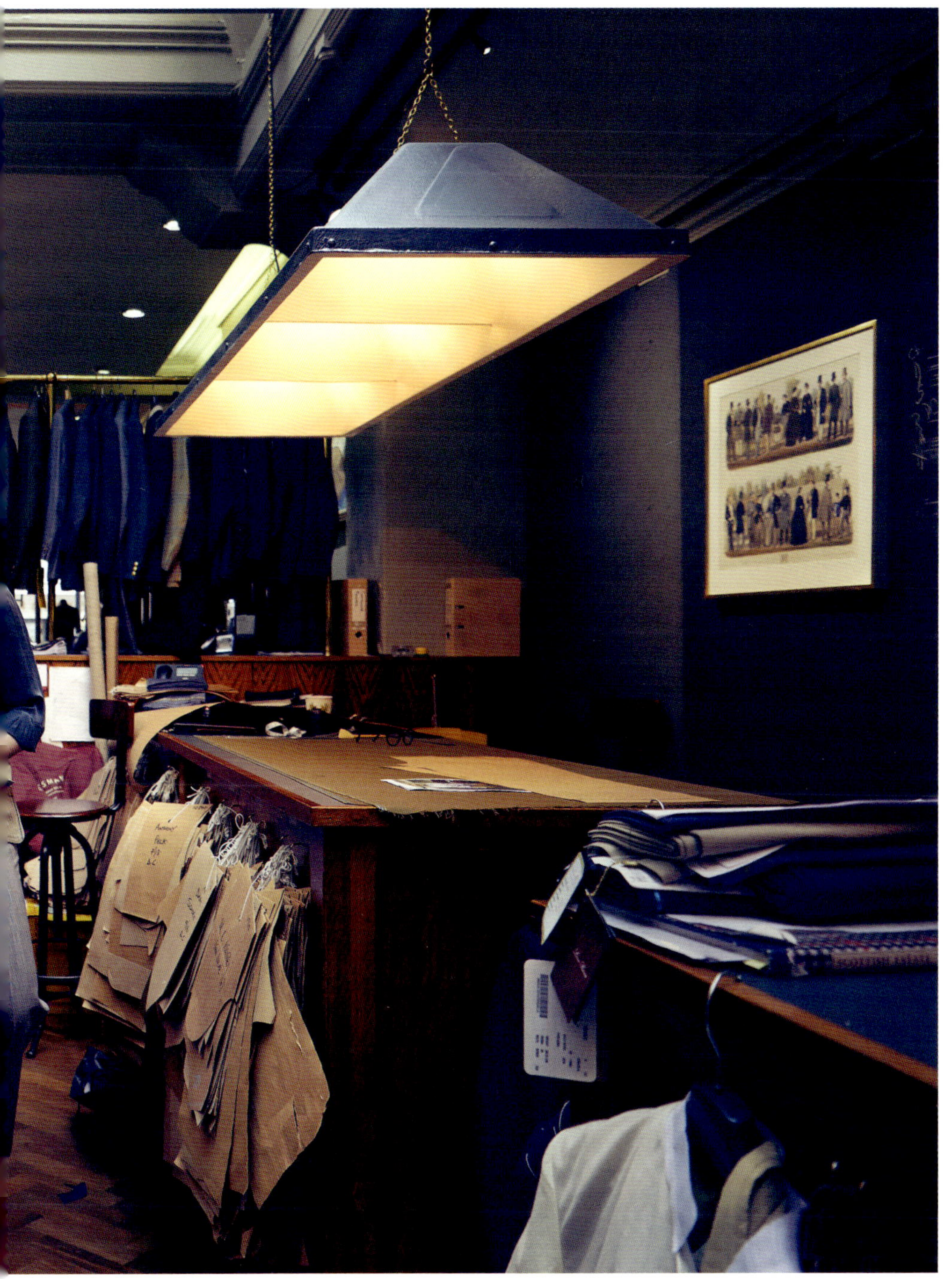

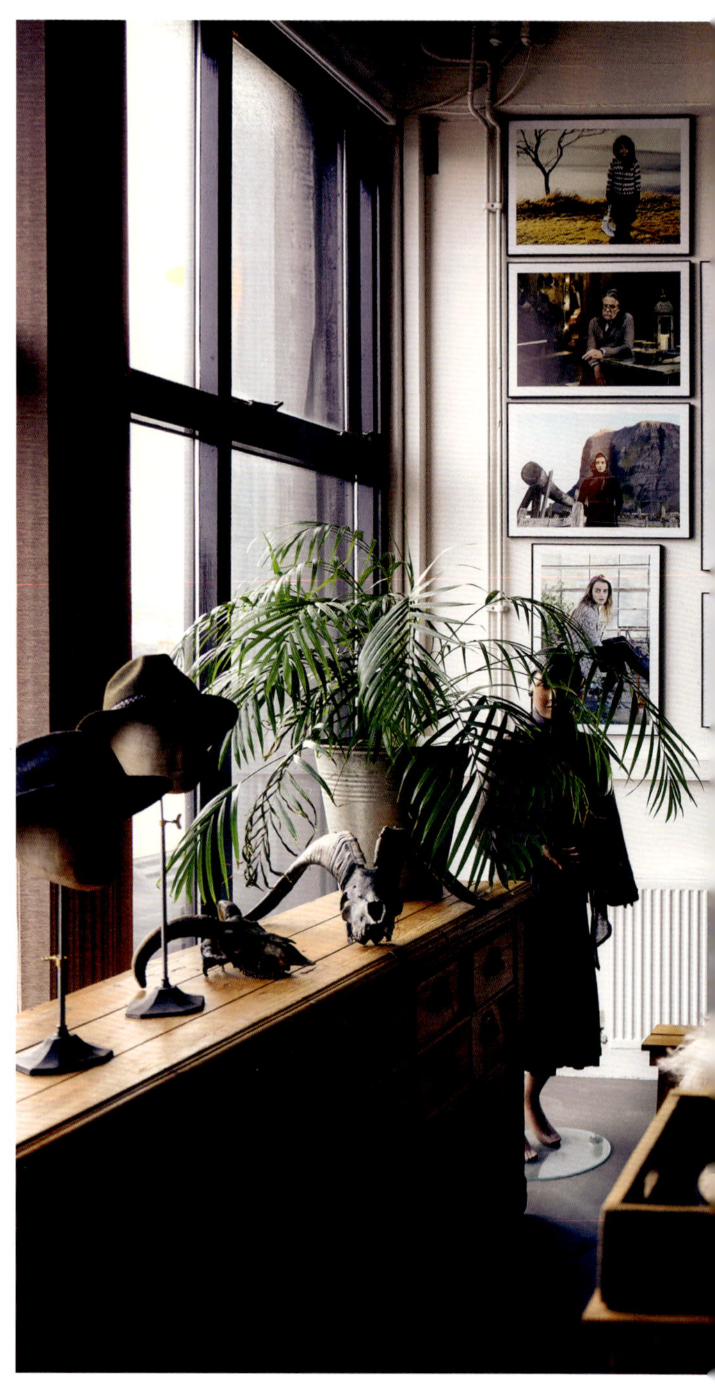

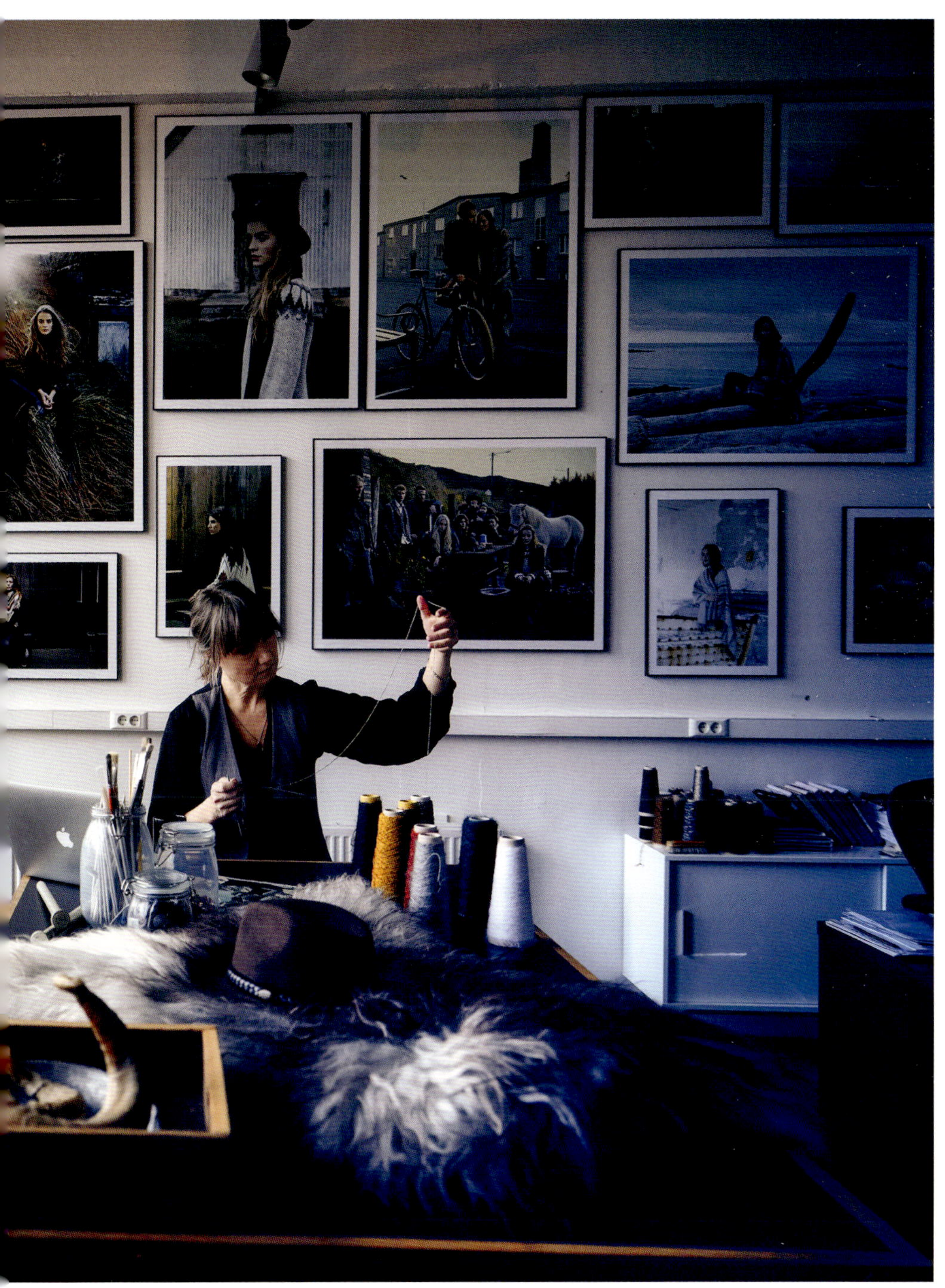

Bergthora Gudnadottir Founder, Farmers Market Design Co. & Clothing Brand > Reykjavik, Iceland

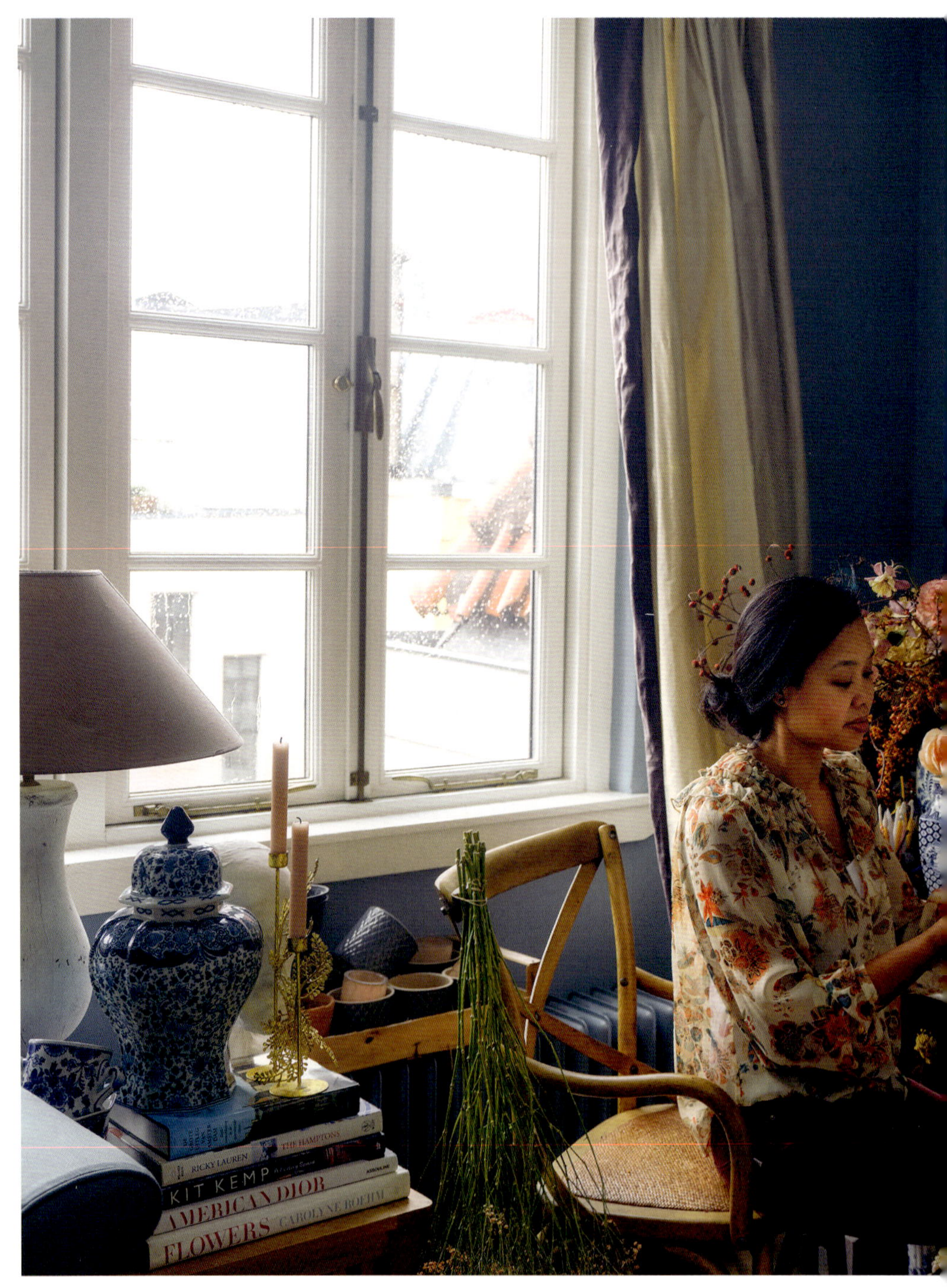

Natasja Sadi Sugar Floral Artist > Amsterdam, Netherlands

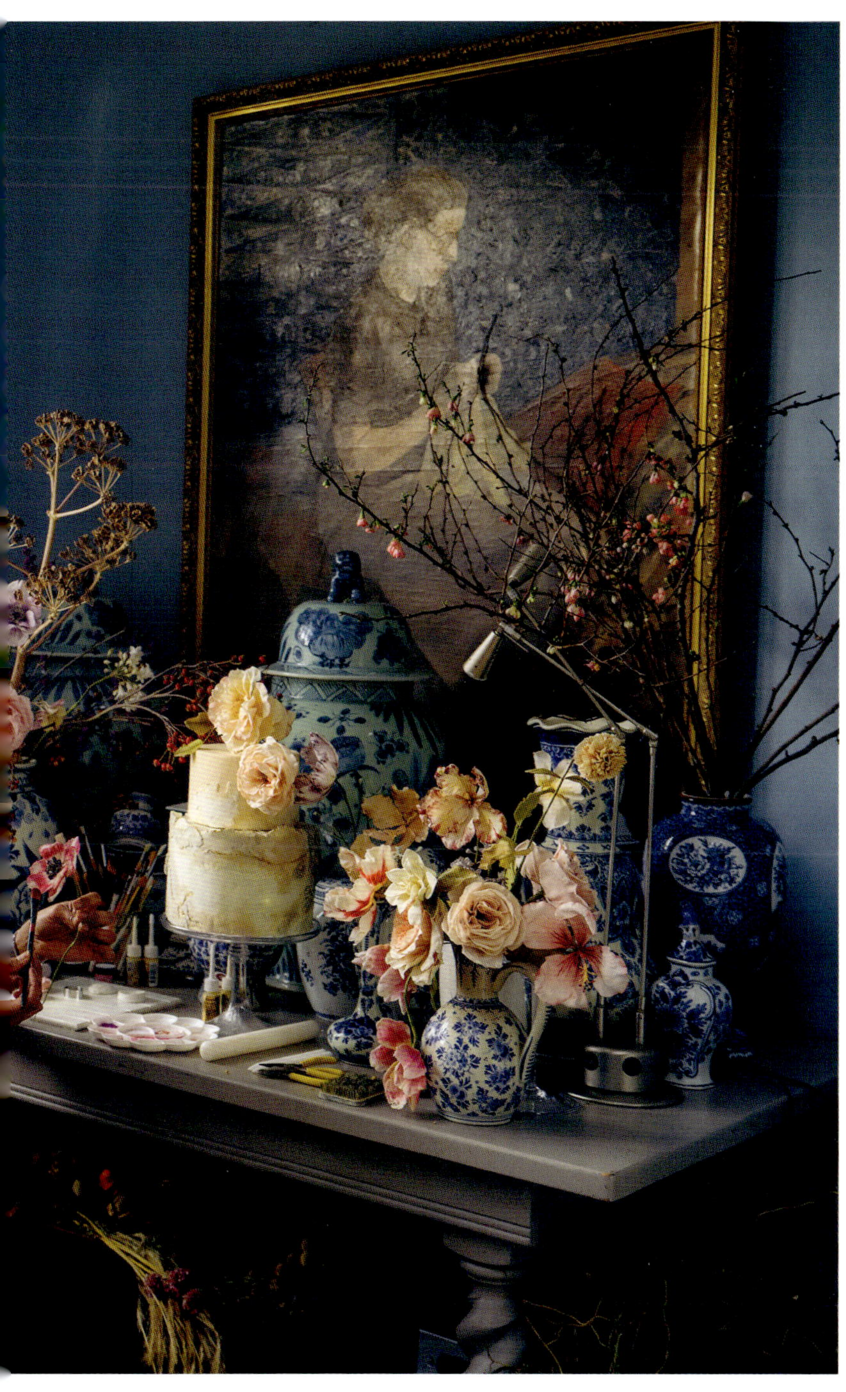

Twee said that she wanted to take me somewhere special. She brought her daughter with us, and together we hiked up the mountain.

Her daughter tripped, and I instinctively said, "Be careful."

Twee said that she and her husband didn't say that to their children. They didn't want to instill fear in them. "We say 'watch your edges.'"

After we captured this image—of Twee watching her edge so masterfully she could

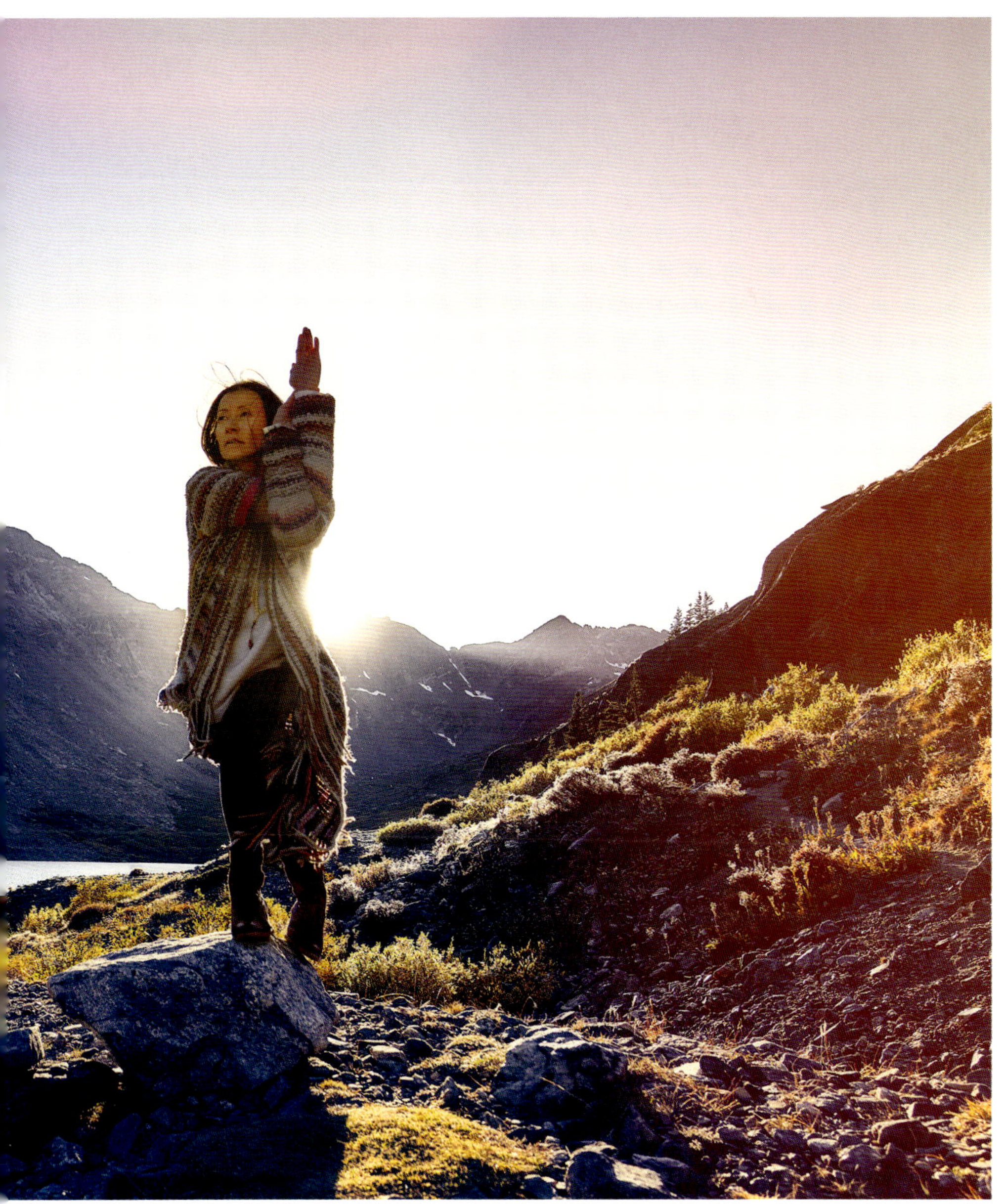

balance on it—she suggested I take some time up there on my own.

Sitting there, I realized that this "special" place she had chosen wasn't for the benefit of a photograph. It was for me. She'd recognized in me a man needing to find some balance of his own.

Twee Merrigan Founder and Yoga Teacher, Holy Spirit Yoga > Breckenridge, Colorado

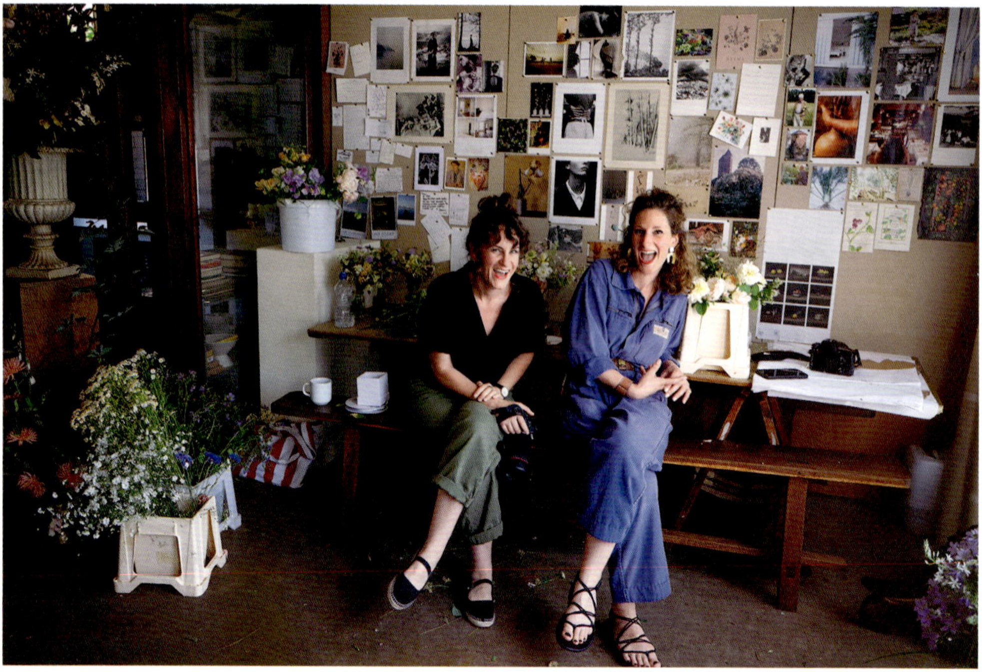

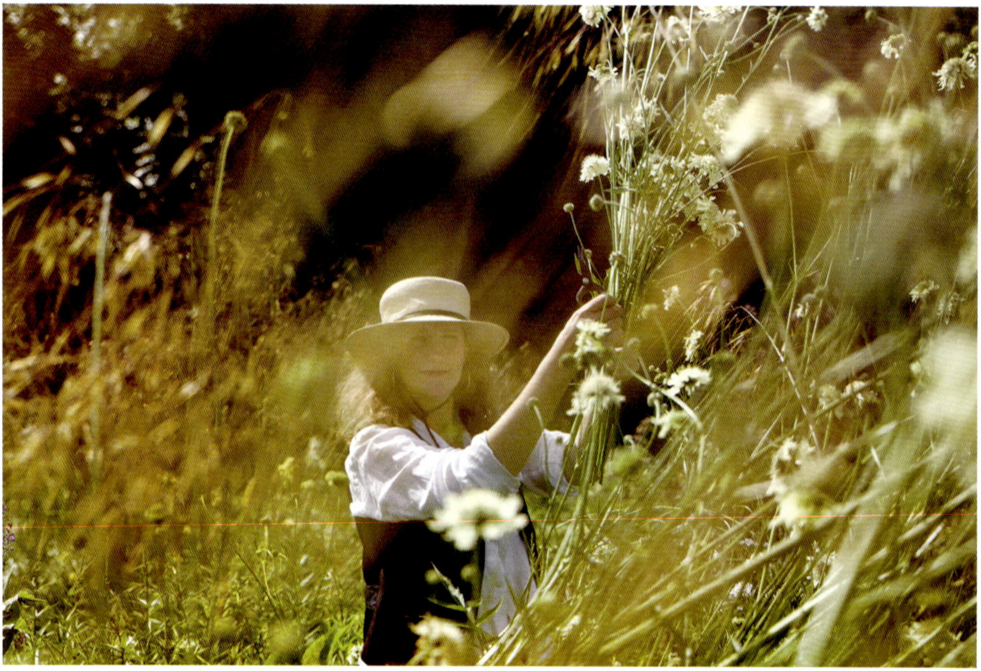

Alexandra Nuttine & Jessica Lister Florist and Gardner, Aesme Studio > Hampshire, England

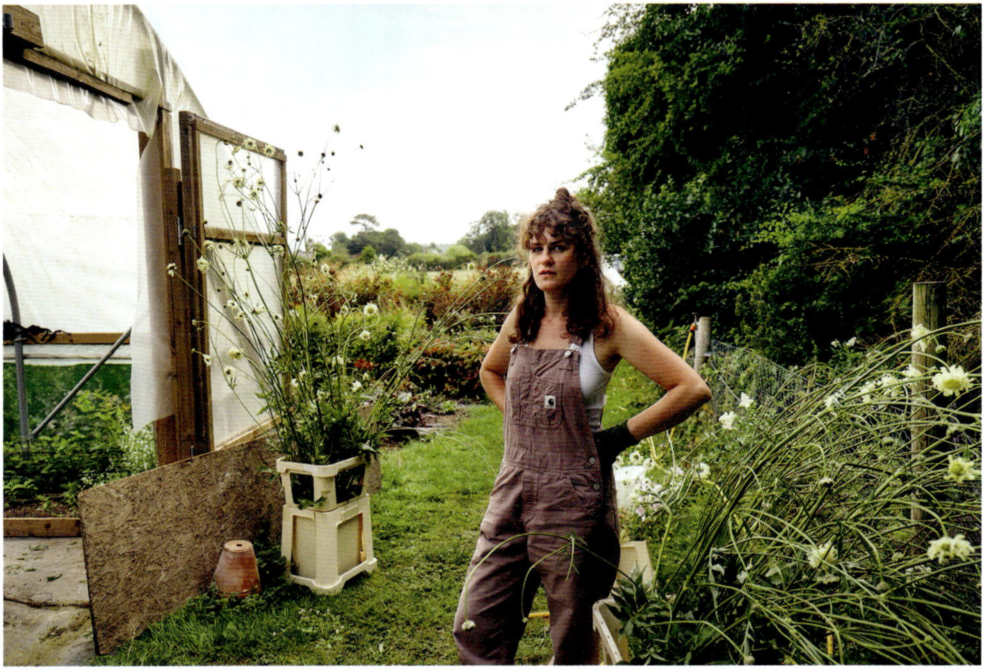

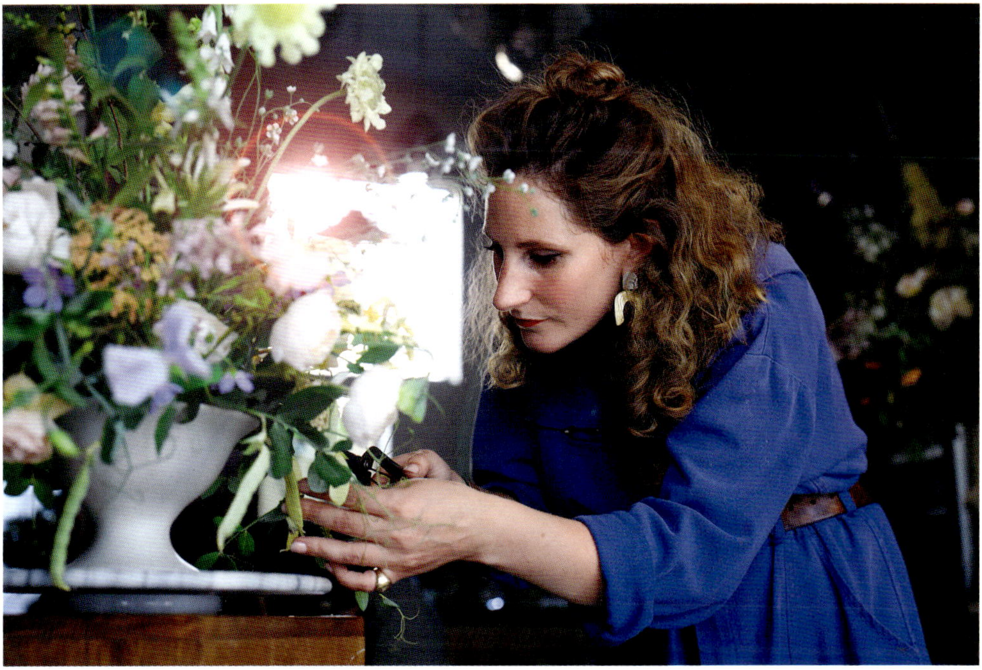

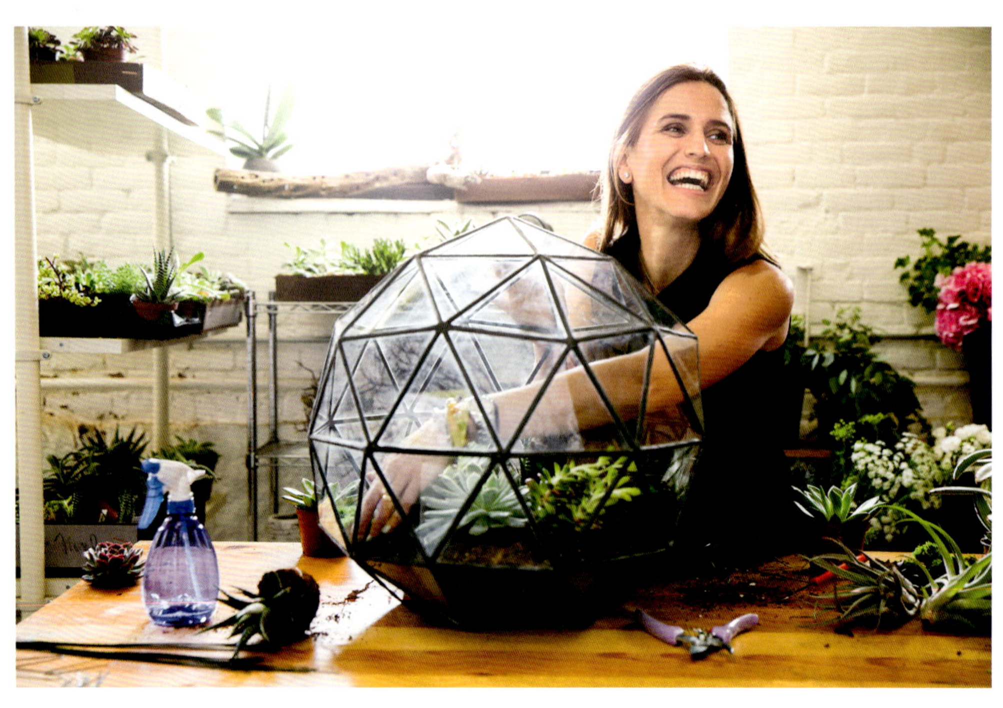

Orly Khon Floral Designer, Orly Khon Floral > Boston, Massachusetts

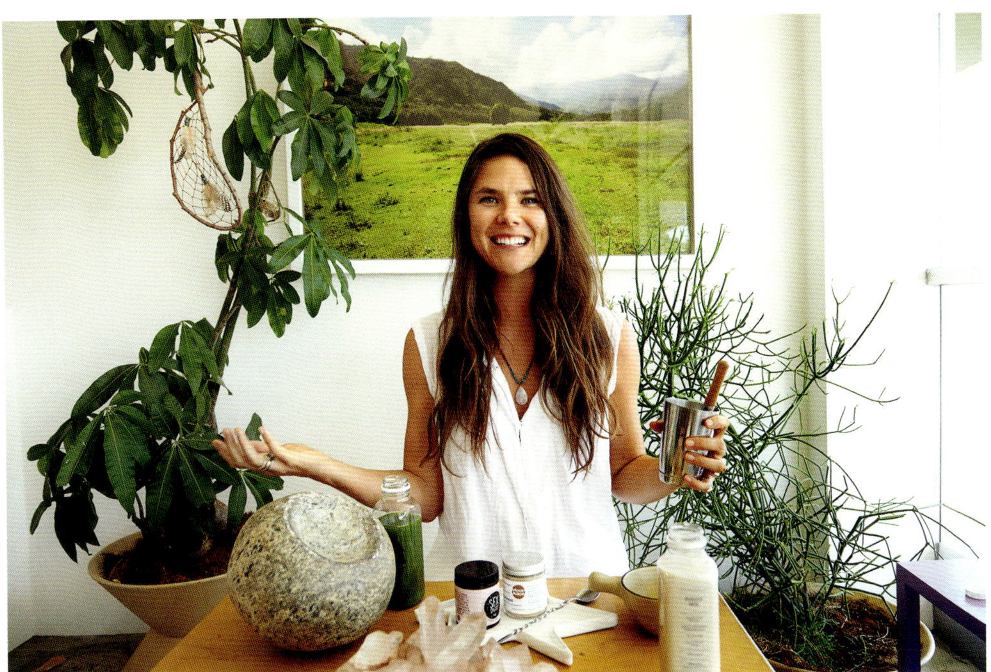

Amanda was actually being photographed by someone else when I showed up. And then the electricity in her building went out.

I felt up against a wall. Definitely not in the moment, I was pushing and insisting that we go ahead. Which is not how I like to work at all. But post-accident, anxiety sometimes gets the better of me.

She made space for me to sit down. "Breathe," she said.

And as she prepared a drink for me, she told me how she had used nutrition to take charge of her own health. She started her business to help others do the same for themselves.

Me, for one.

Amanda Bacon Founder, Moon Juice > Los Angeles, California

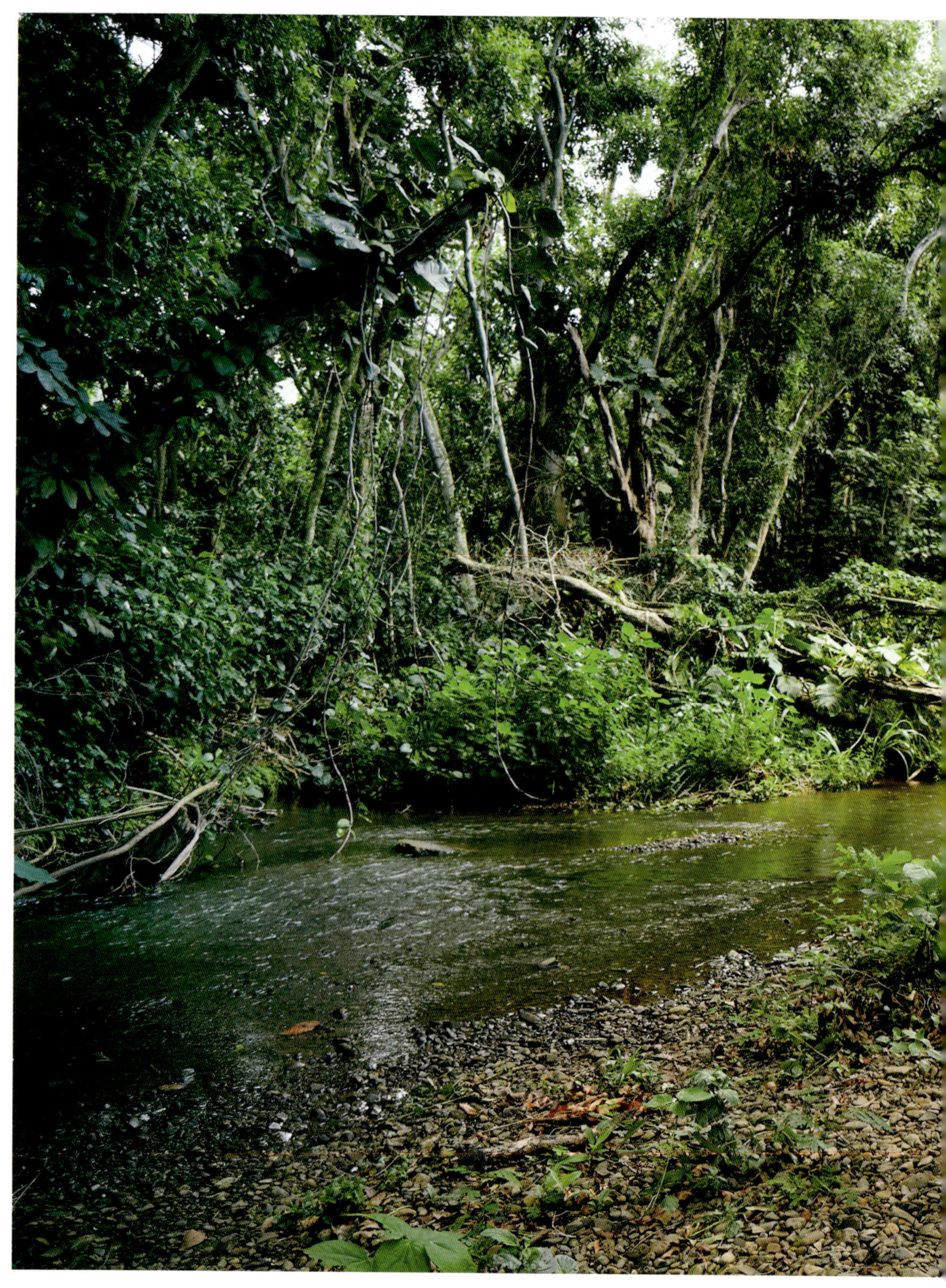

Pamakane Pico Lei Maker > Kailua, Hawaii

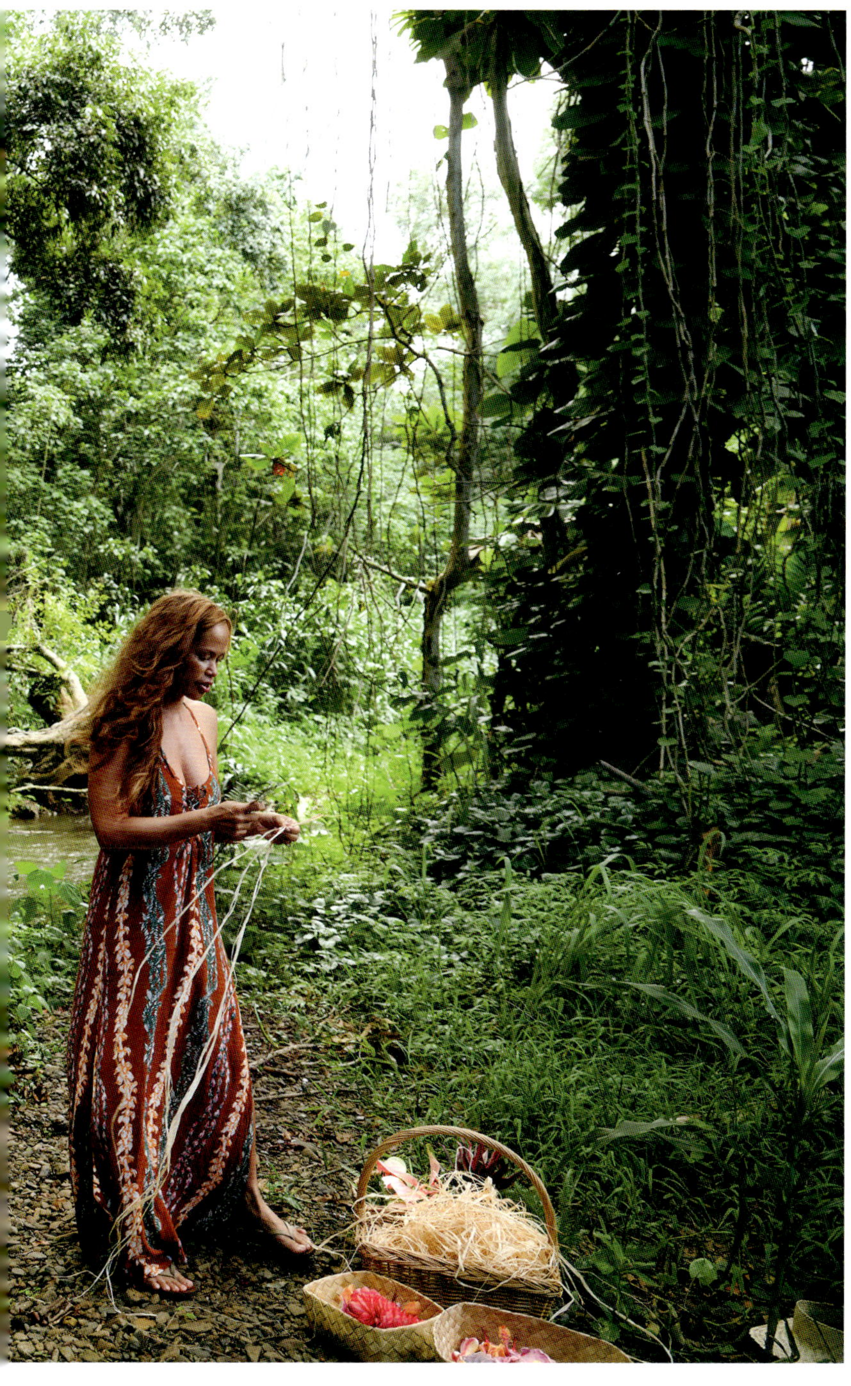

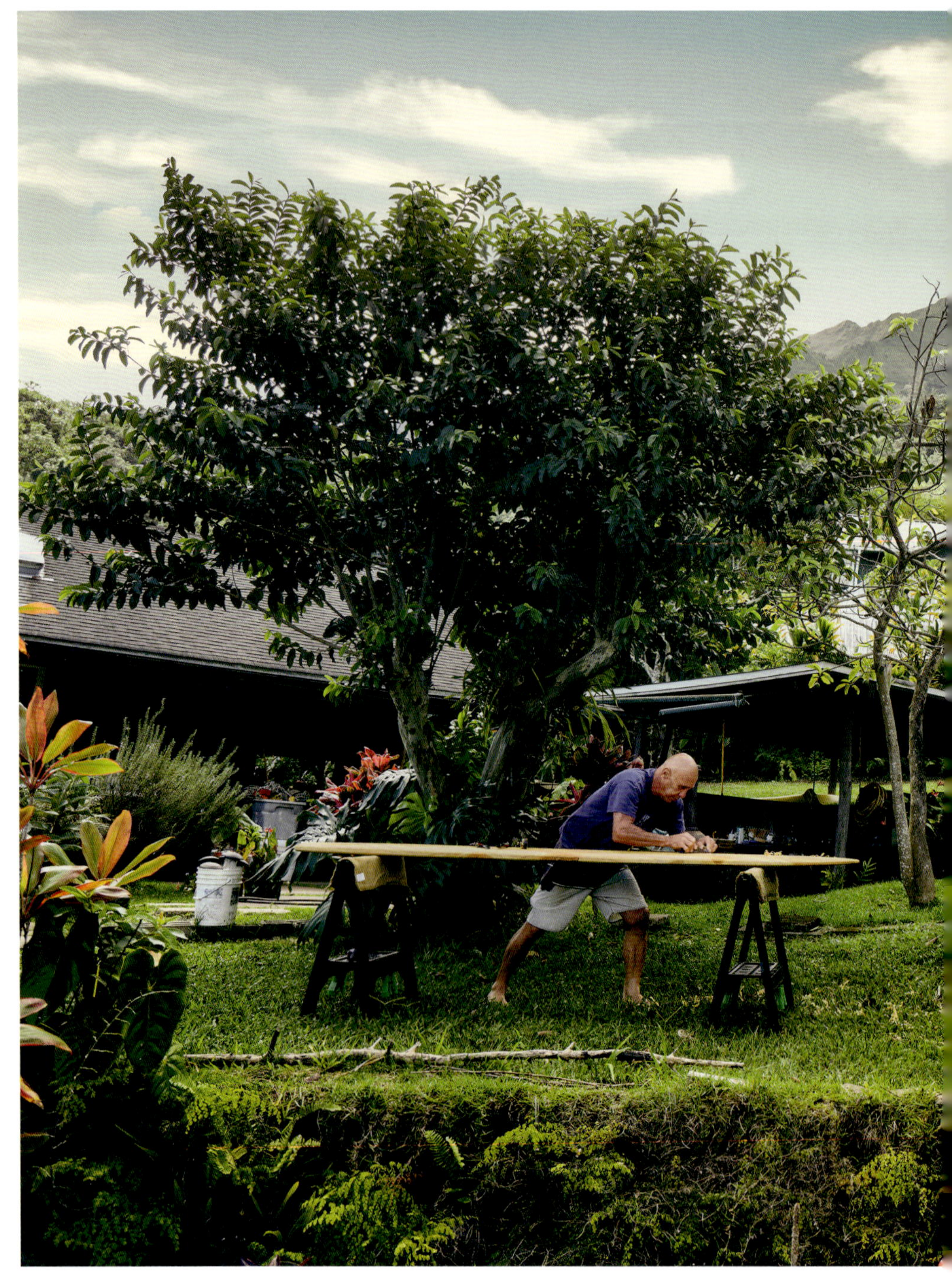

Tom Pohaku Stone Board Carver > Kanéohe, Hawaii

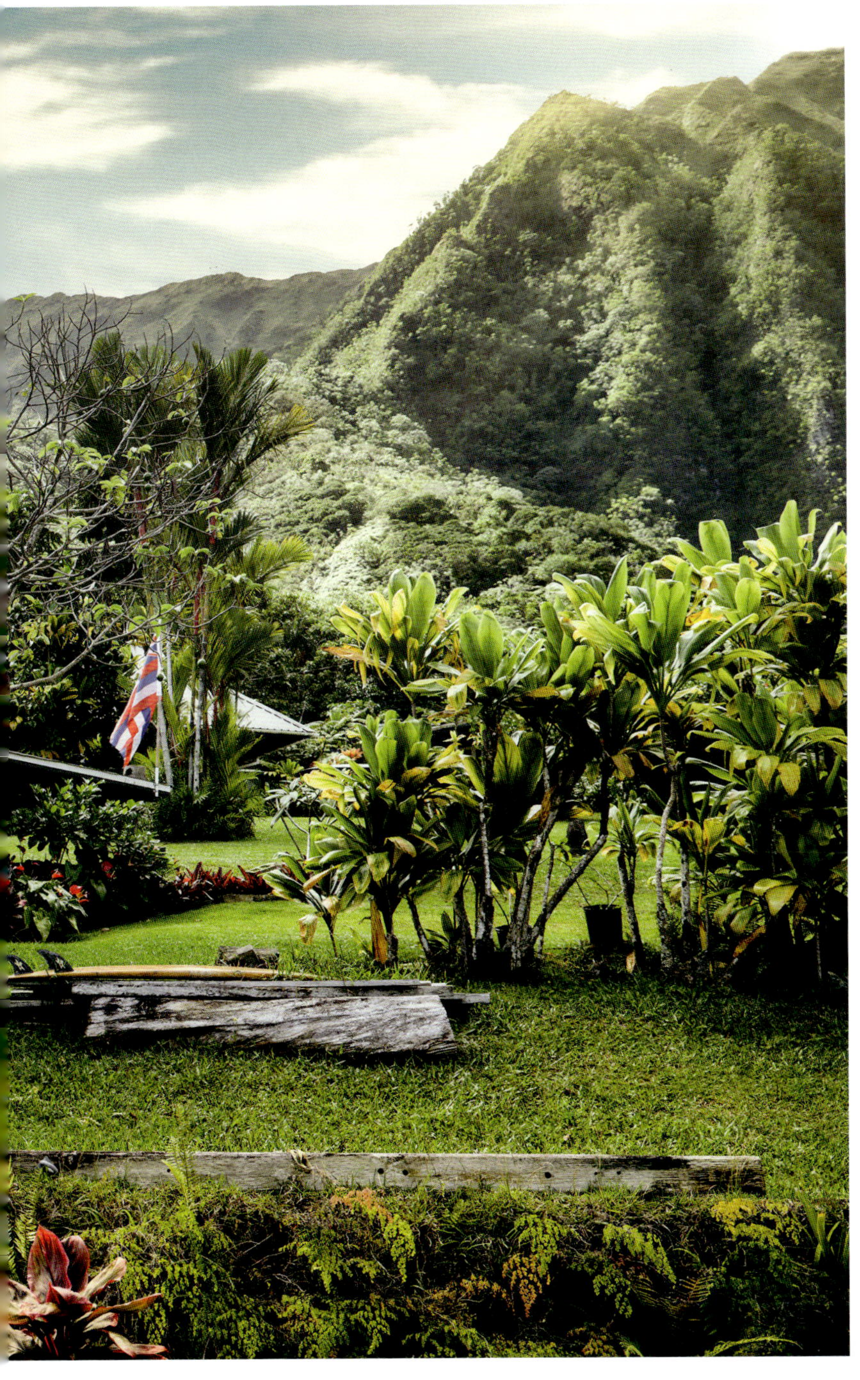

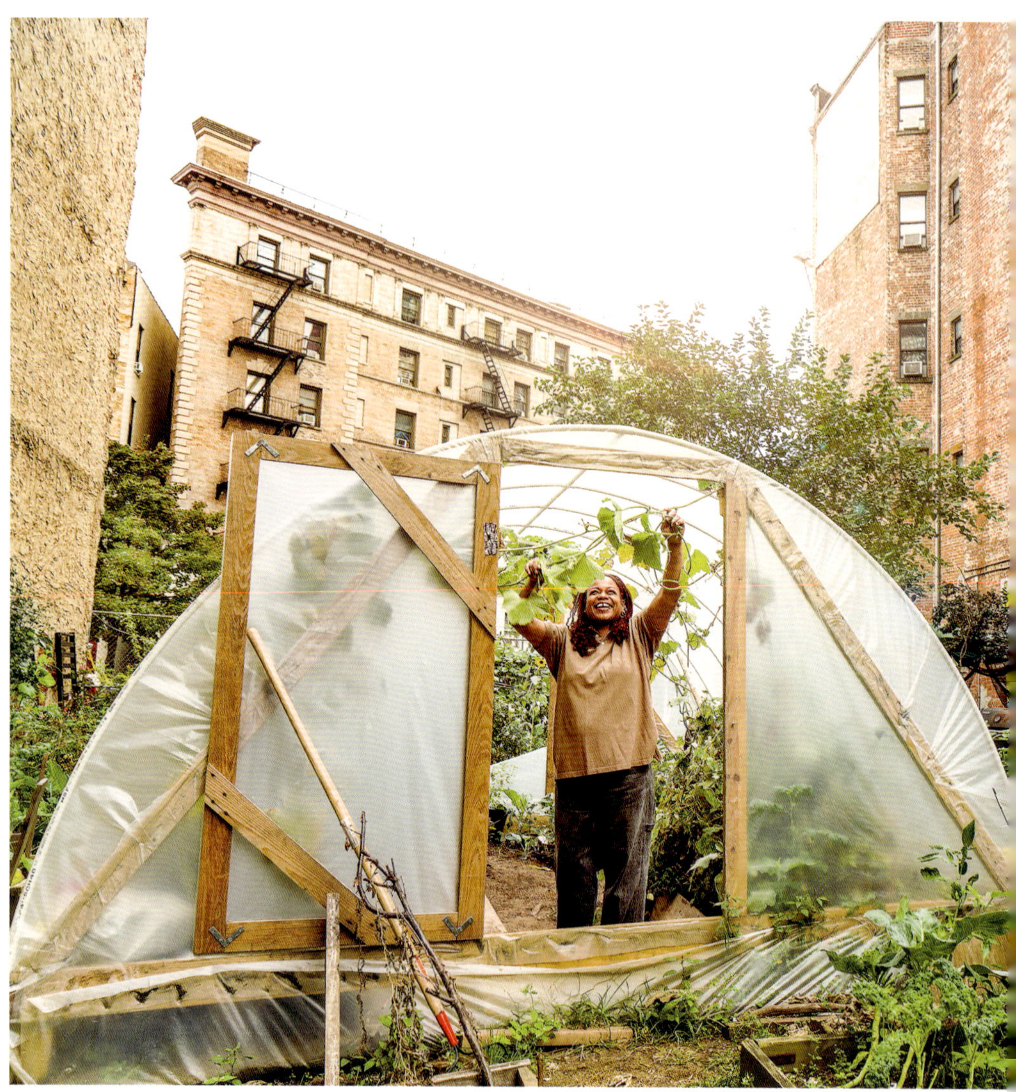

This was one of the first photographs I took for *At Work* after my near-fatal bike accident. I hadn't yet regained the full use of both of my hands, but I wanted to get back to work.

My idea was to photograph a person who used their hands to restore something to what it once had been.

It was a lovely spring day. Gamilah led me through the garden, showing me her plants and flowers. Her presence calmed me. We spoke of our childhoods: mine in Brooklyn; hers in Vermont. We didn't get too deep into the circumstances, but we did talk about how we don't get to pick the families we're born into.

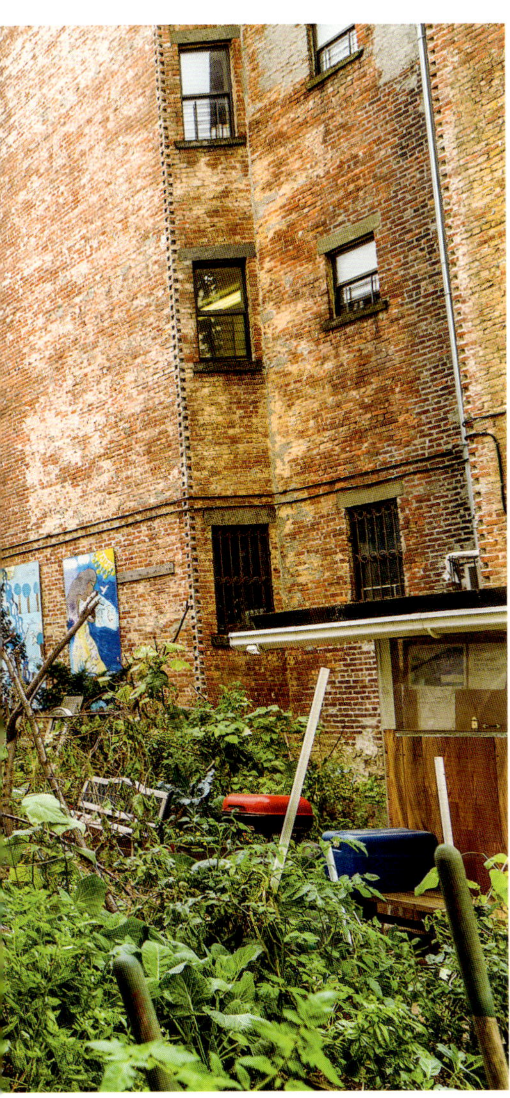

Gamilah said, "I spent my whole life running from something that doesn't matter. Your past doesn't make you who you are."

And my biking accident didn't need to define me, either.

Gamilah gave me such a gift. One I never knew to ask for. It wasn't until later that I read her signature on the release: *Gamilah Lumumba Shabazz*.

This beautiful woman who knew something about not being defined by the past was Malcolm X's daughter.

Gamilah Lumumba Shabazz Truce Garden > Harlem, New York

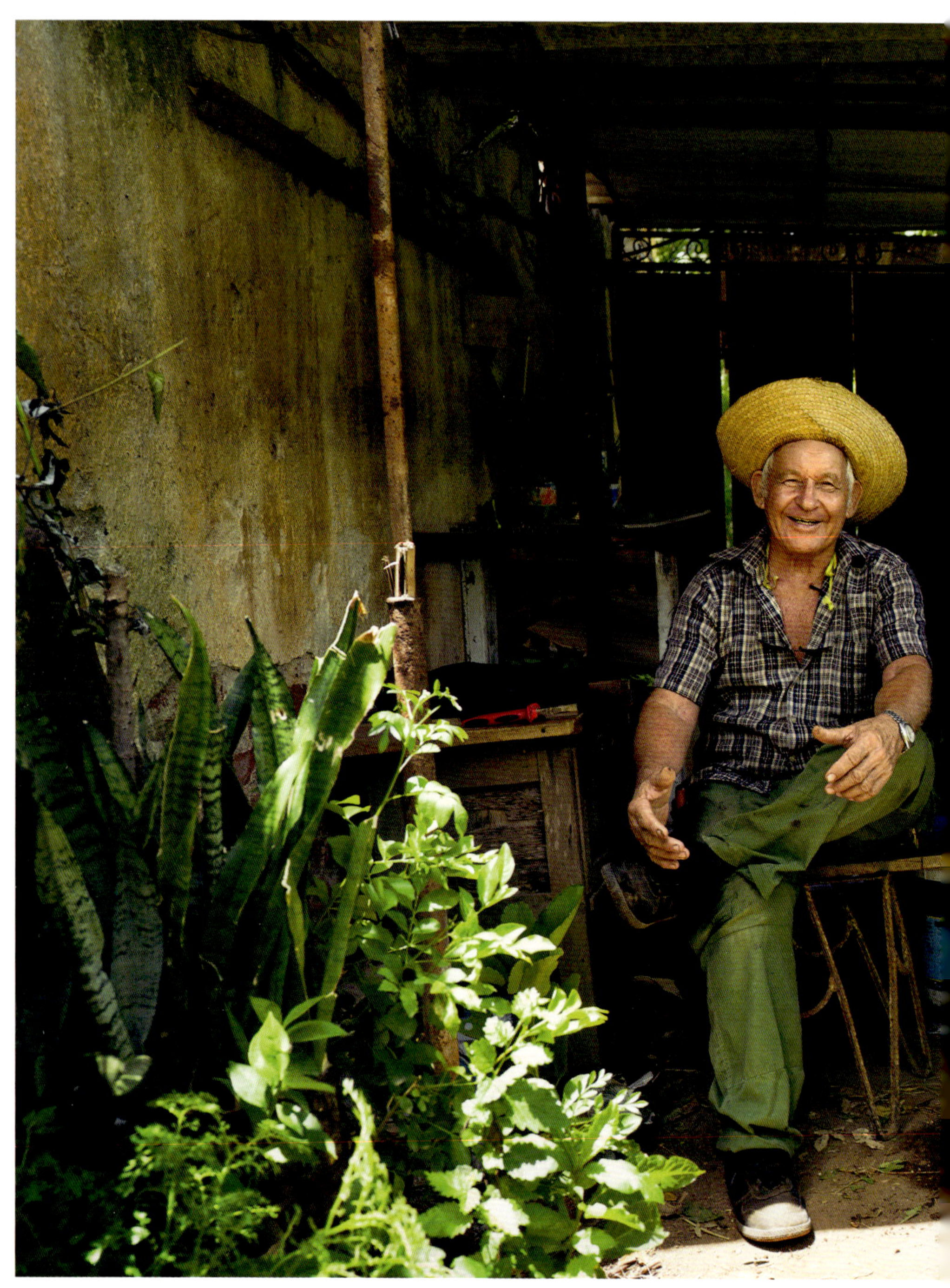

Oswaldo Falcón Nuñez Botanist > Havana, Cuba

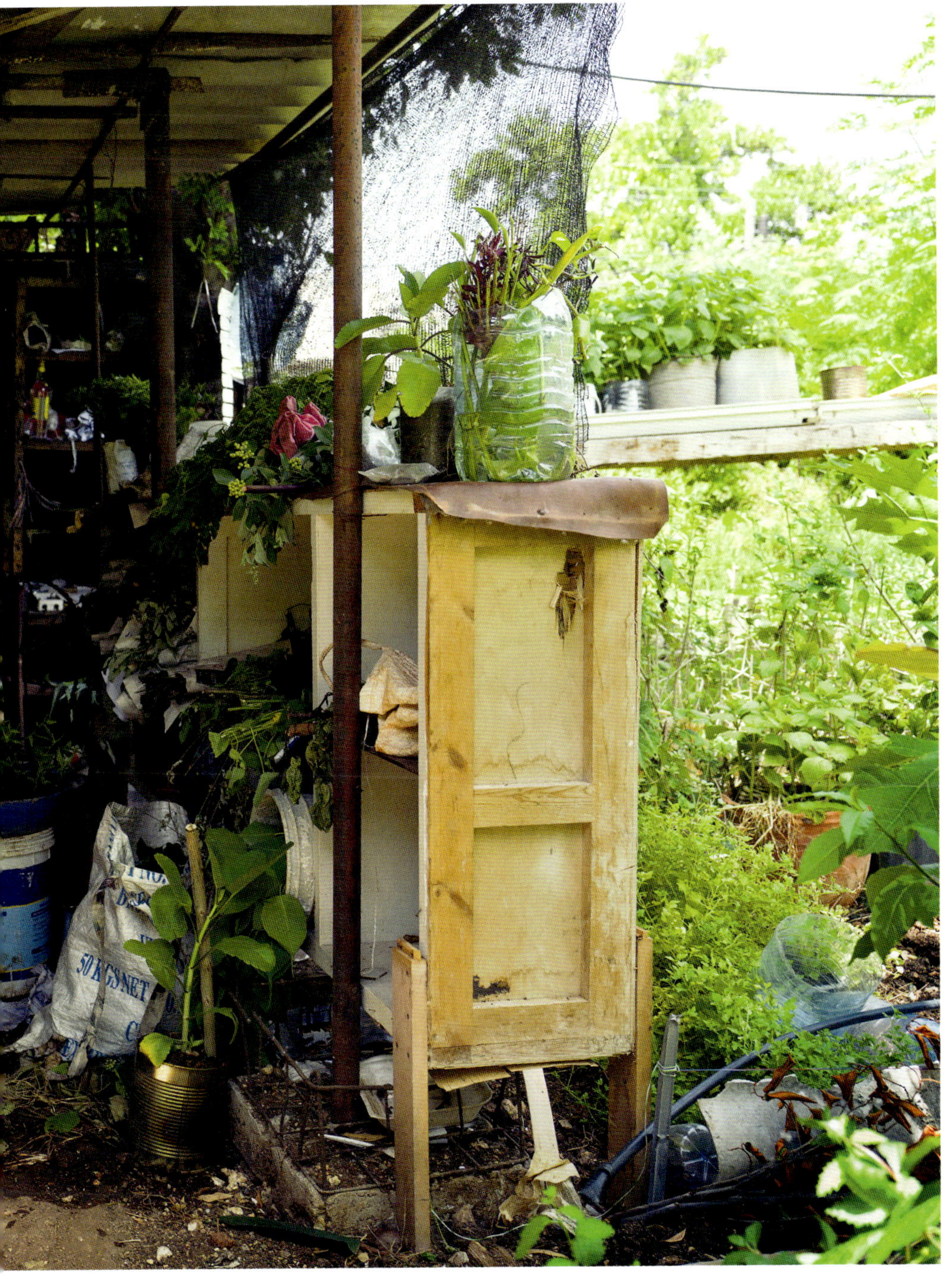

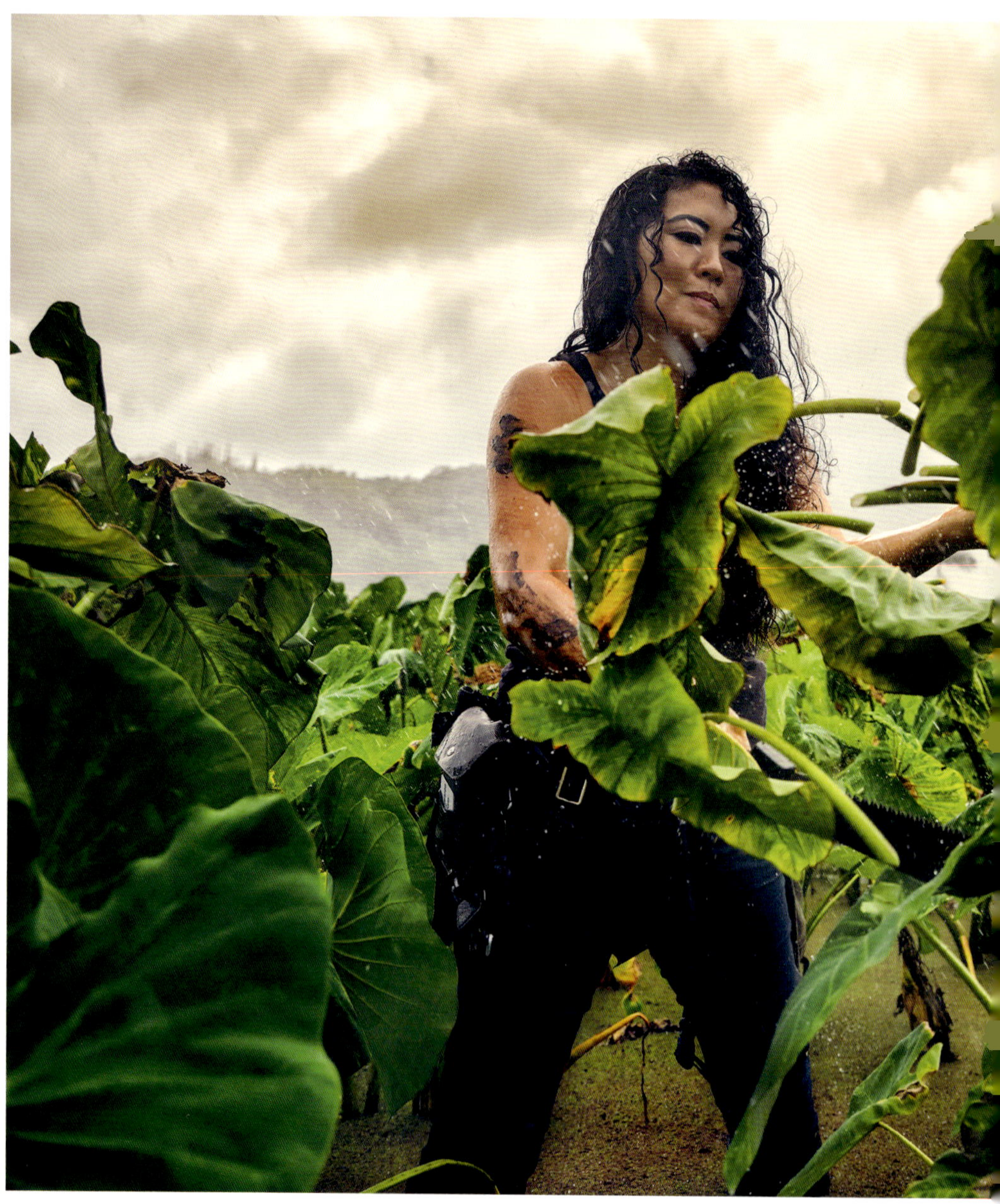

Lyndsey is a fifth-generation taro farmer. She's in the fields, every day. The work is intense, and it's done as it's always been: by hand.

She is keeping her farm and multiple generations of her family going, facing whatever nature throws at her. Armed with a machete, and unreal determination.

Lyndsey M. Alohalani Haraguchi-Nakayama Taro Farmer > Kaua'i, Hawaii

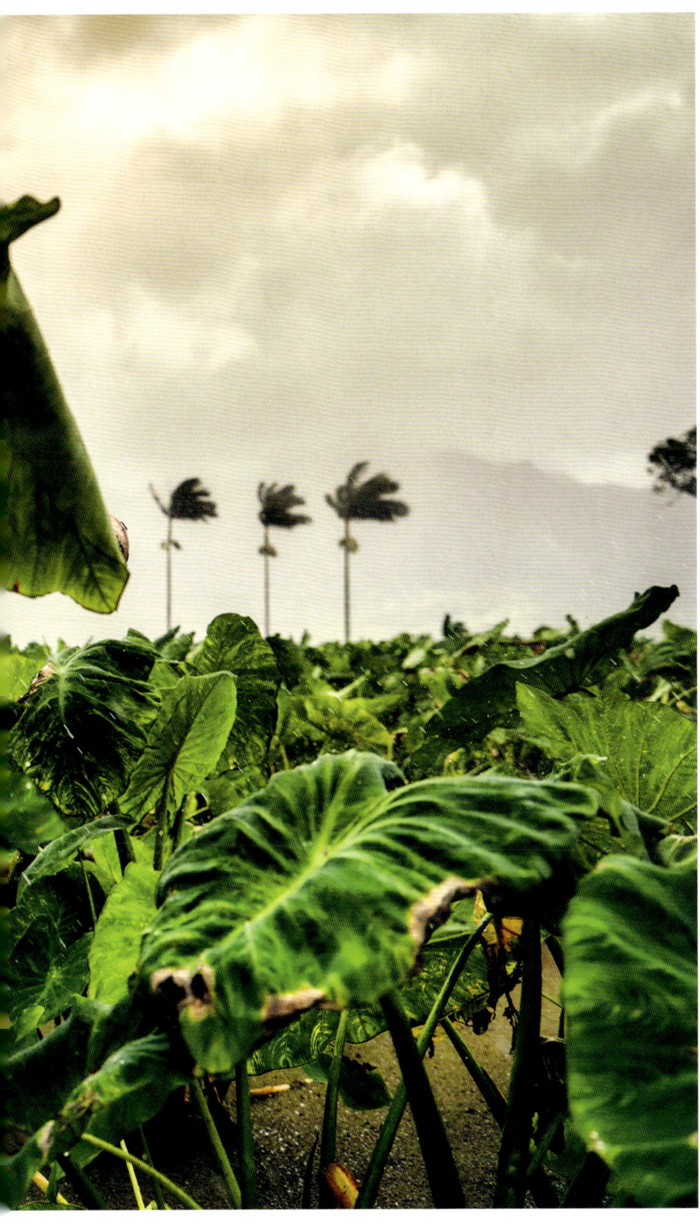

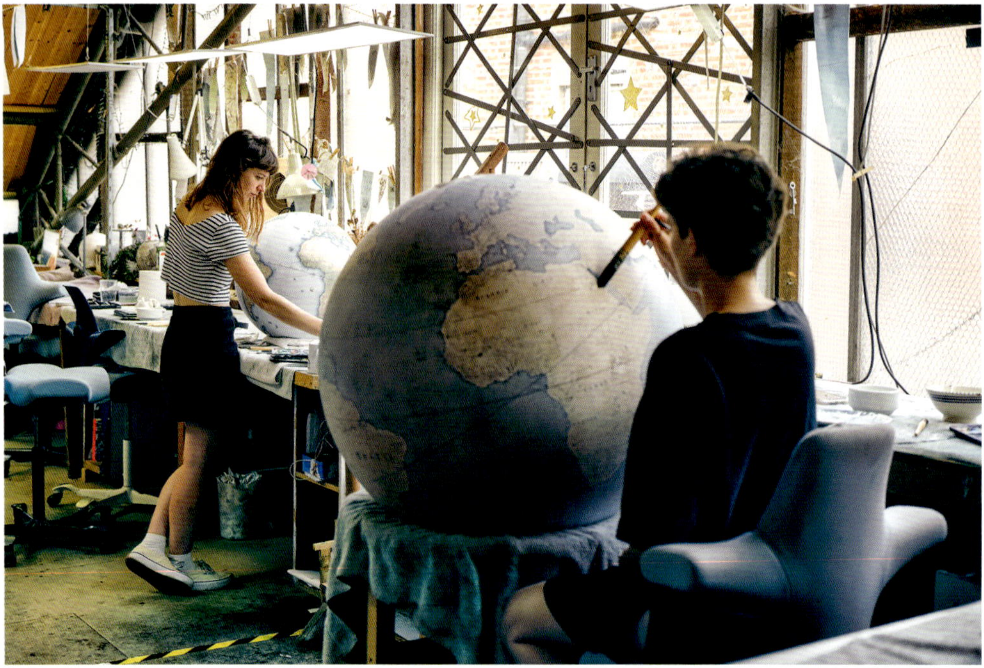

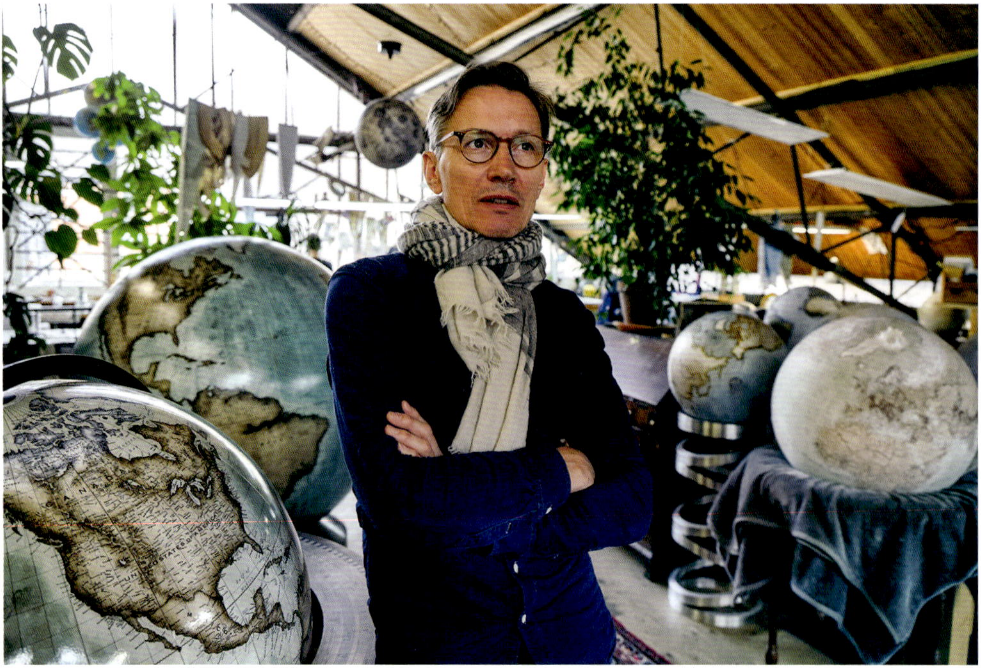

Bellerby & Co. Globemakers > London, England

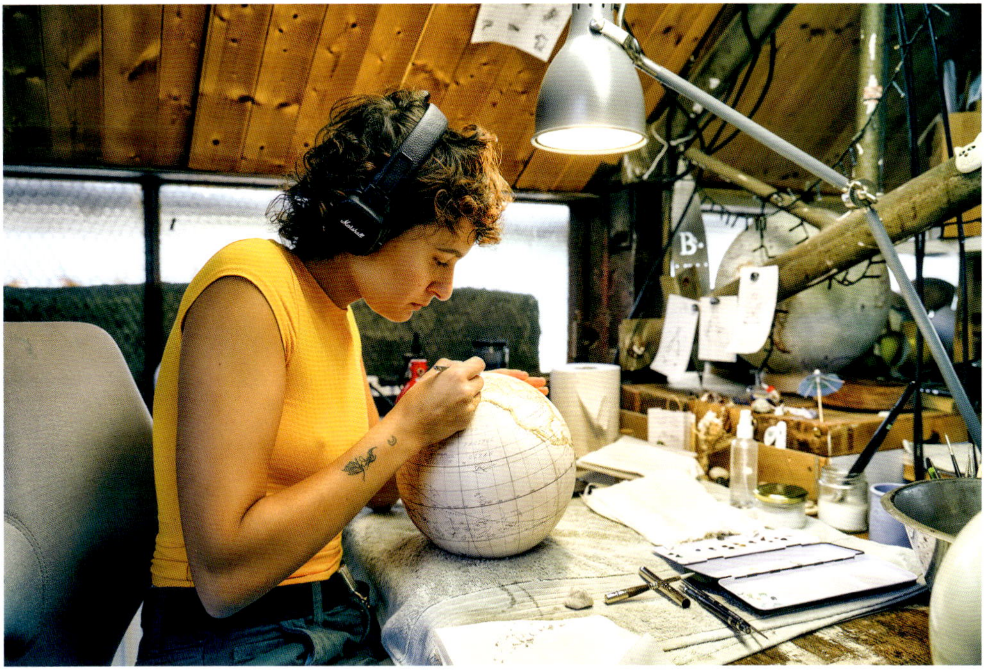

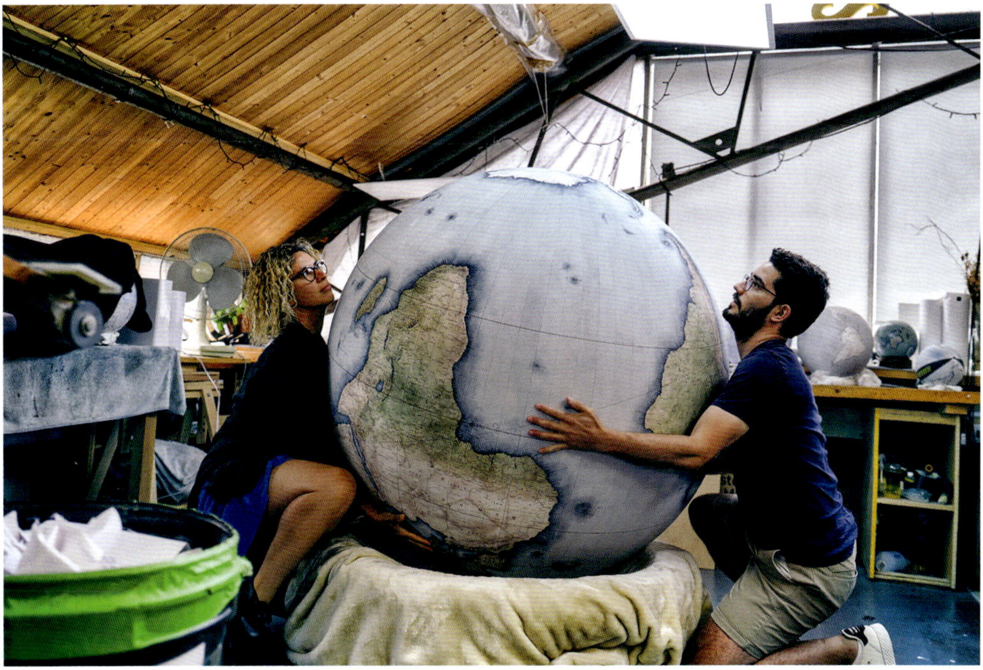

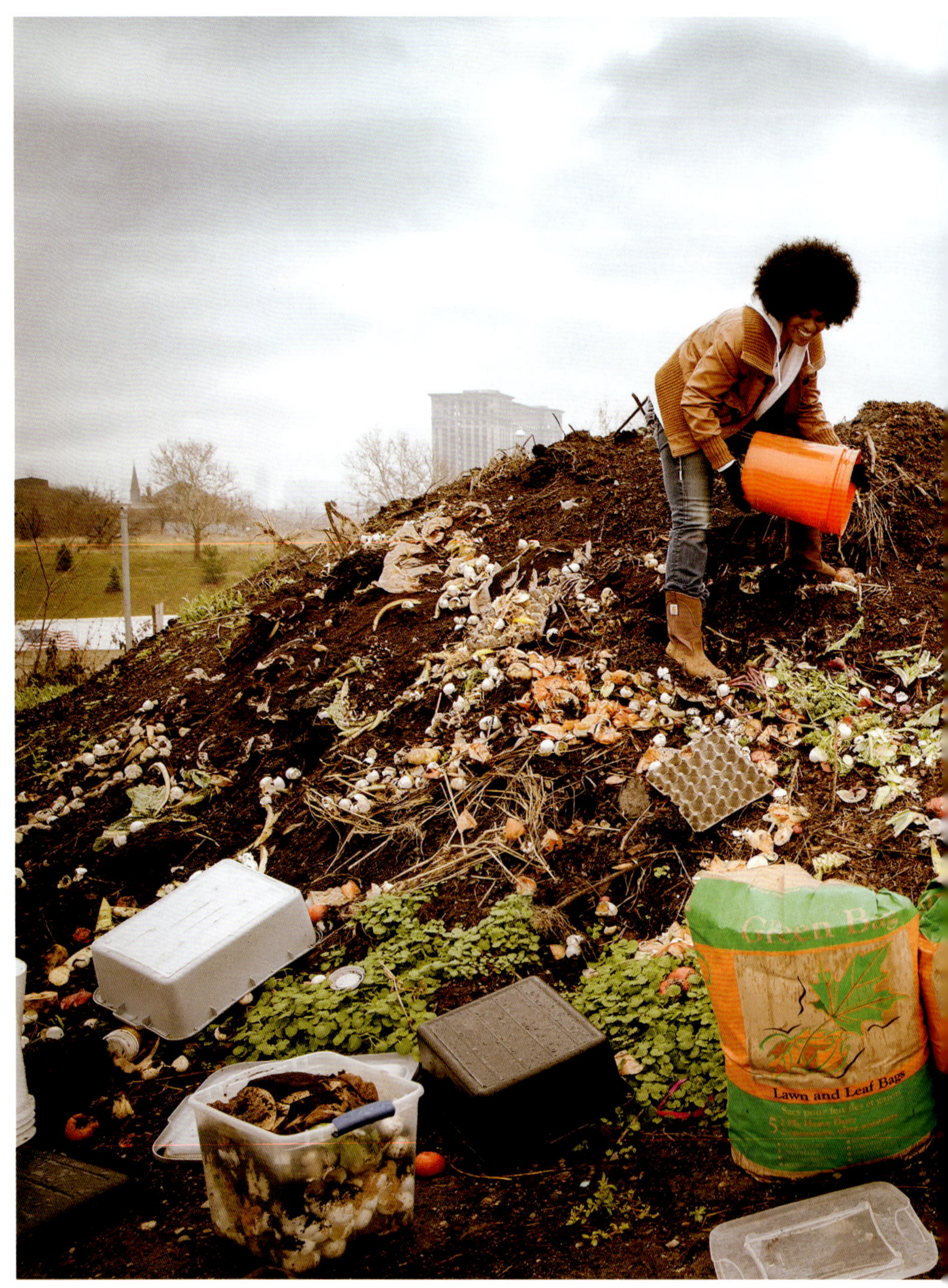

Pashon Murray Dirt Pioneer of Sustainable Culture, Detroit Dirt > Detroit, Michigan

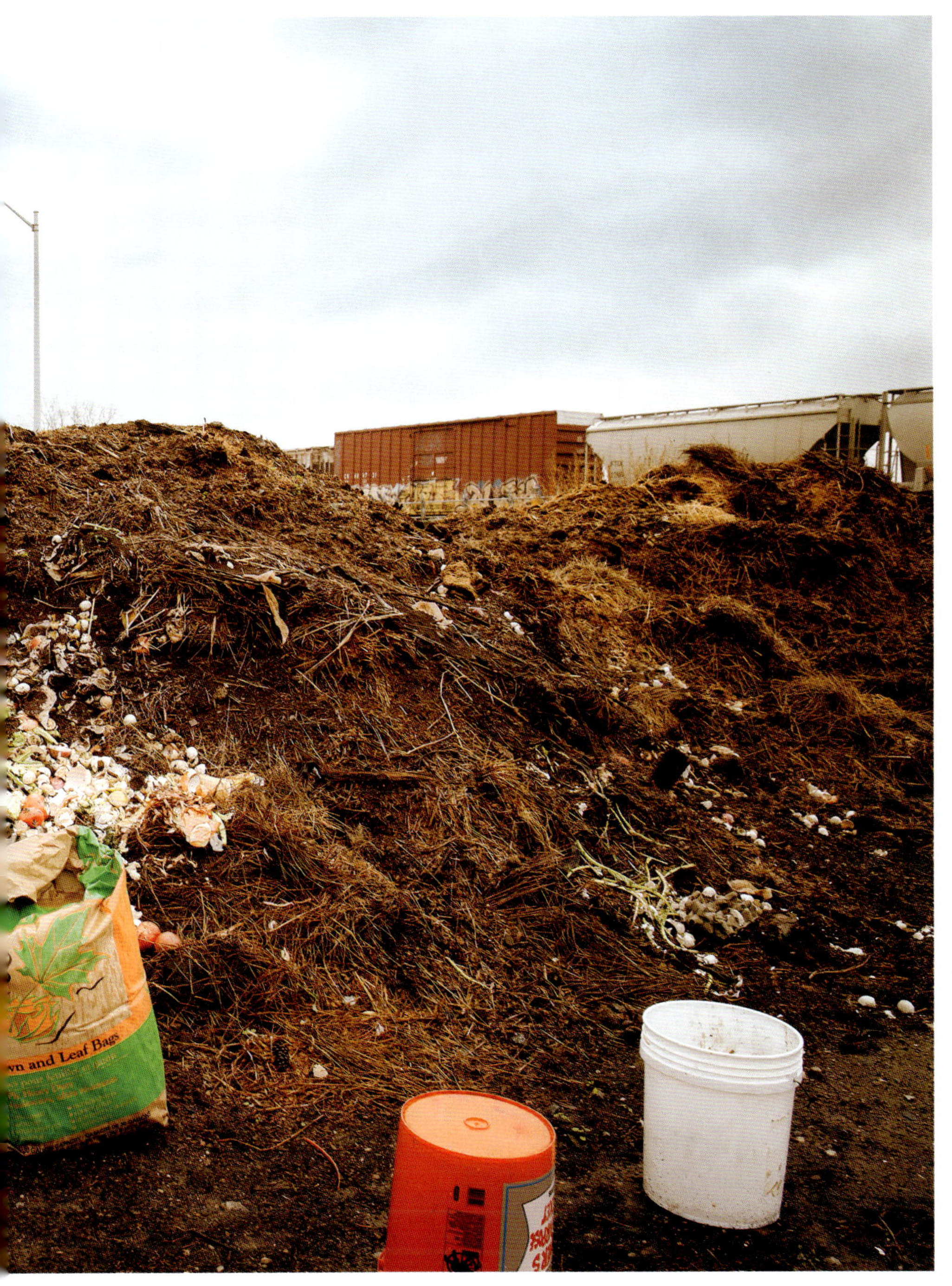

wn and Leaf Bags

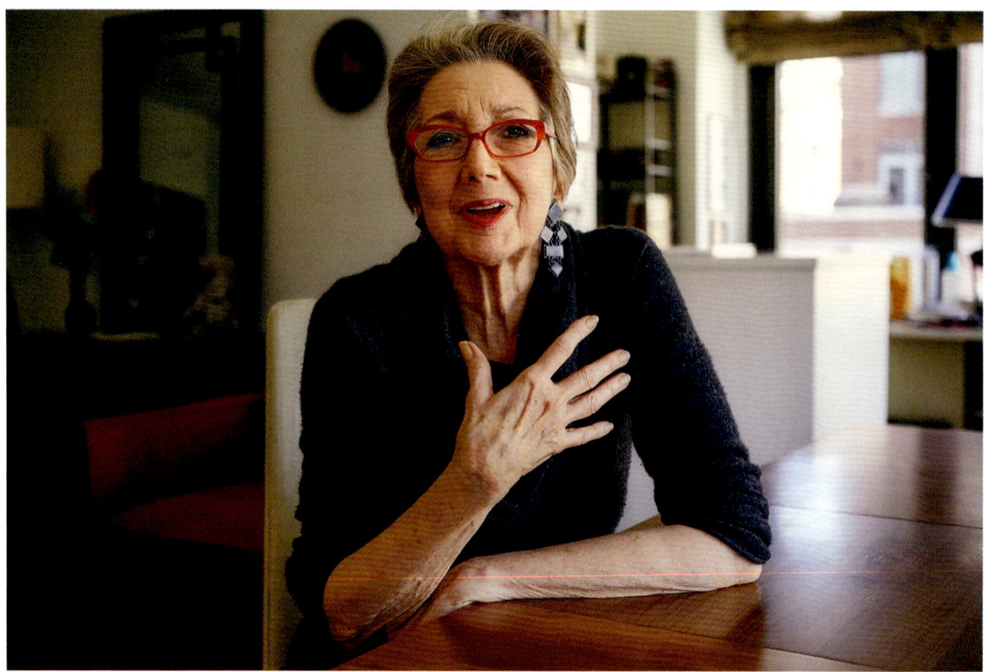

Margo came to corporate consulting and coaching via the worlds of theater, advertising, and art. I had come to her as a highly visual person wanting to build confidence in my words.

She is the epitome of a New Yorker: brash, unapologetic, direct. She coached me like a drill sergeant. She didn't hold back. Every time I started a sentence with "I think—" she'd stop me. "They want to hear what you know, not what you think."

I am better in so many ways for her expertise, her commitment, and her kindness. She modeled the importance of having a strong point of view by having one of her own. And she showed me what it is to be a creative partner by offering real partnership to me.

Margo Krasne Communications Consultant > New York, New York

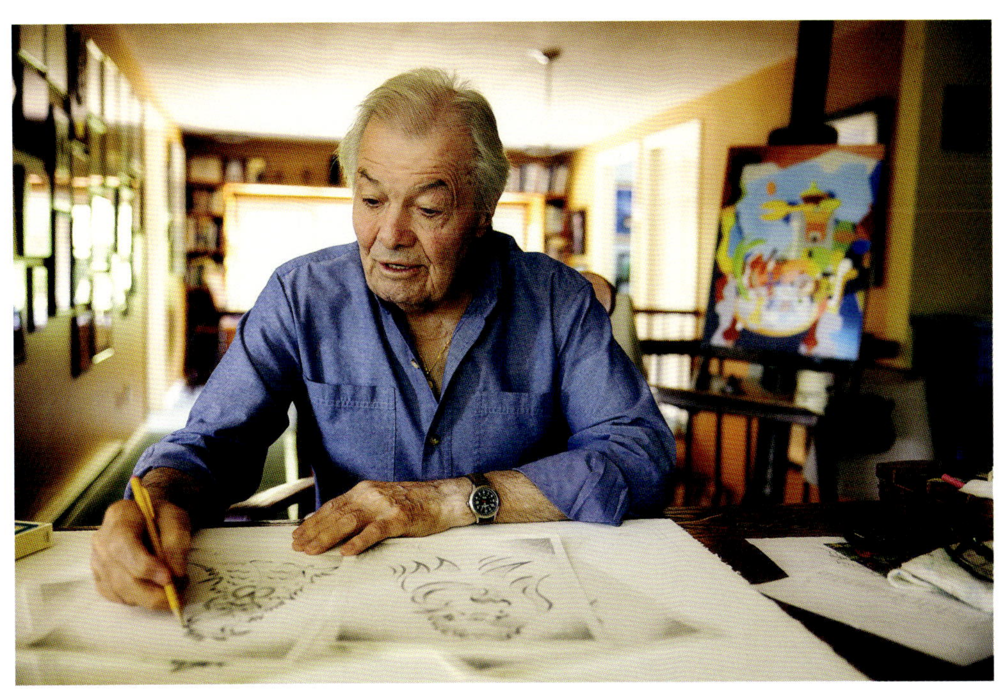

Jacques Pepin TV Personality, Chef, and Author > Cambridge, Massachusetts

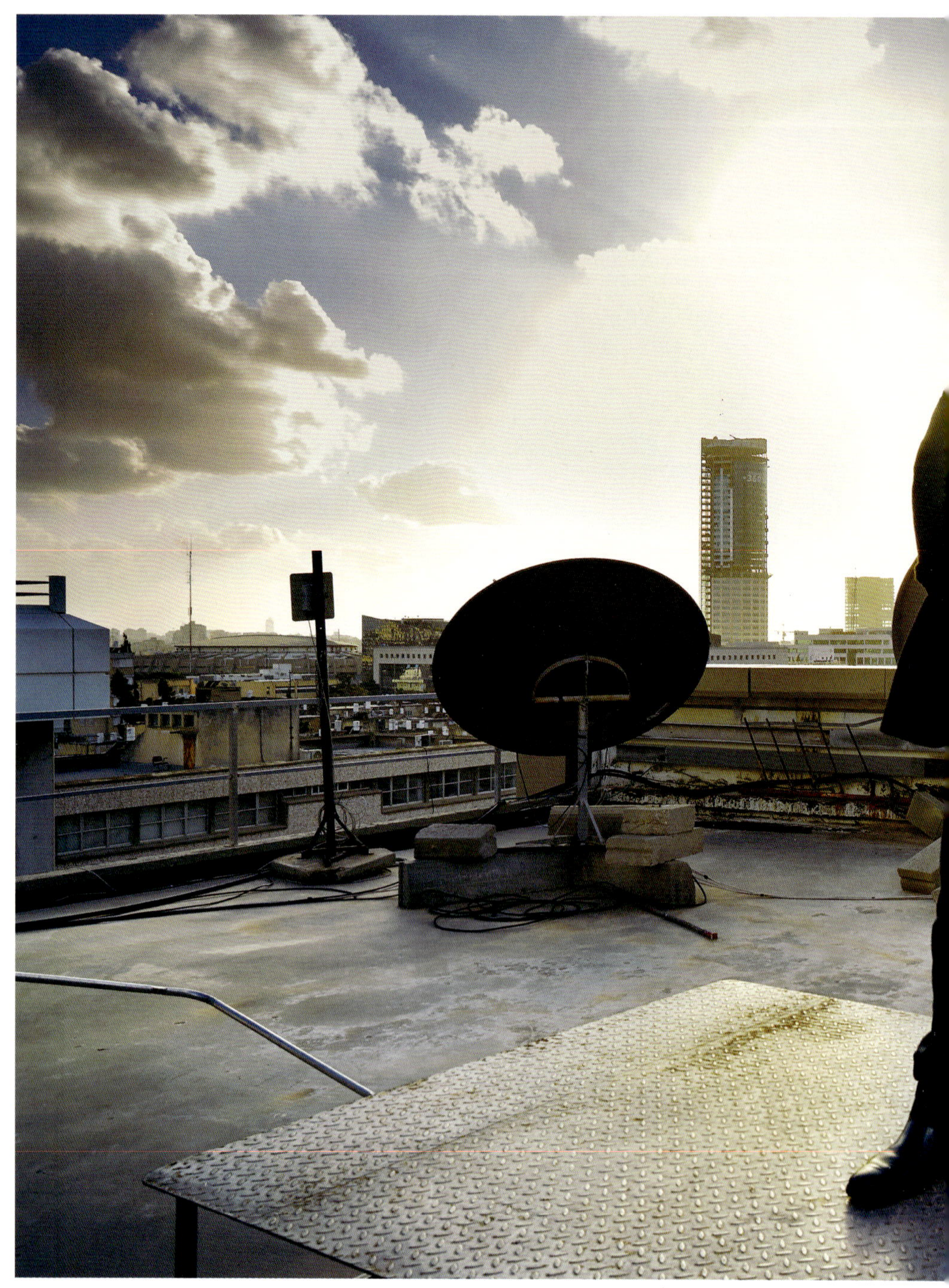

Henrique Cymerman International Journalist > Tel Aviv, Israel

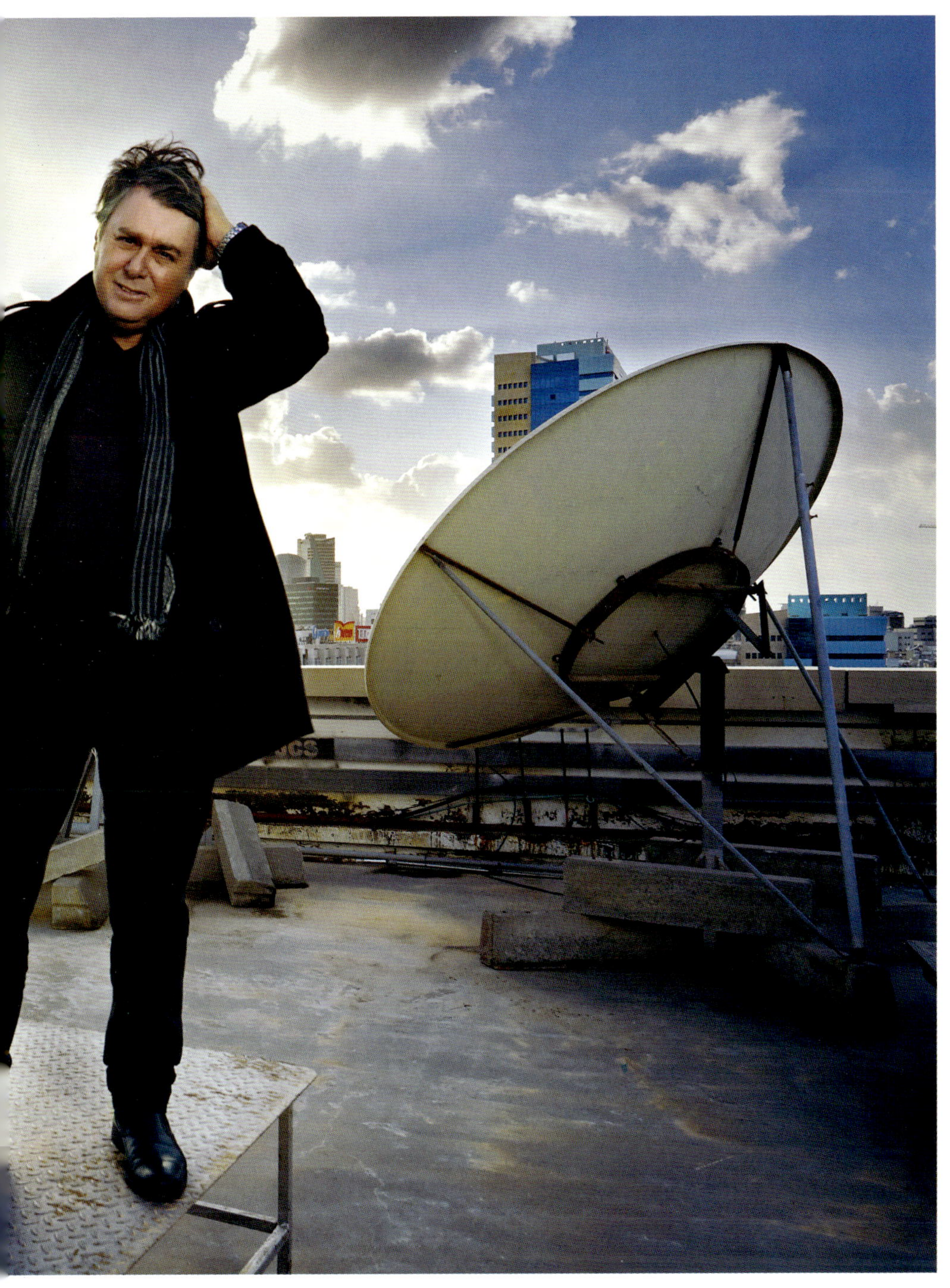

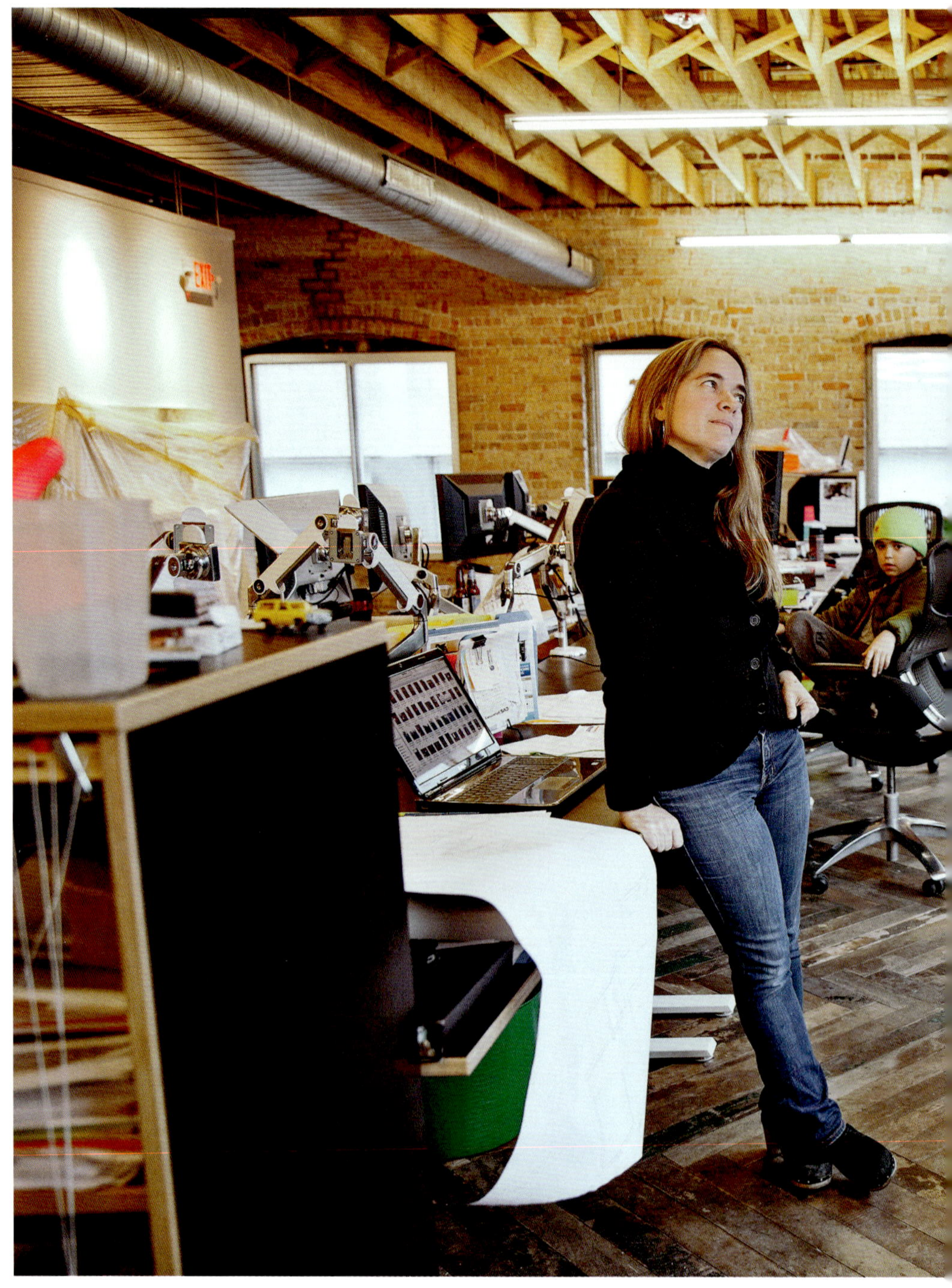

Gail & Thomas Von Staden Von Staden Architects > Detroit, Michigan

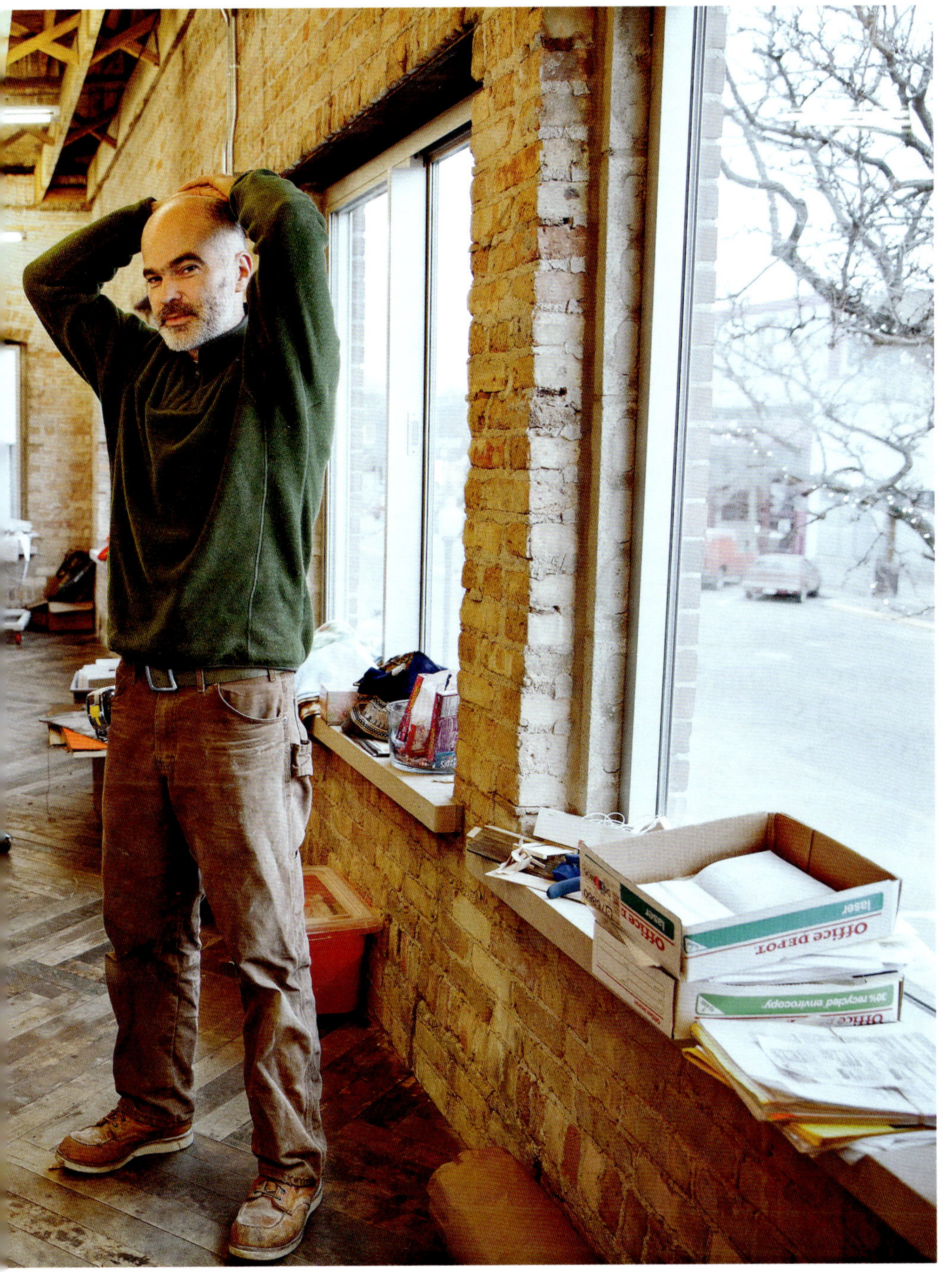

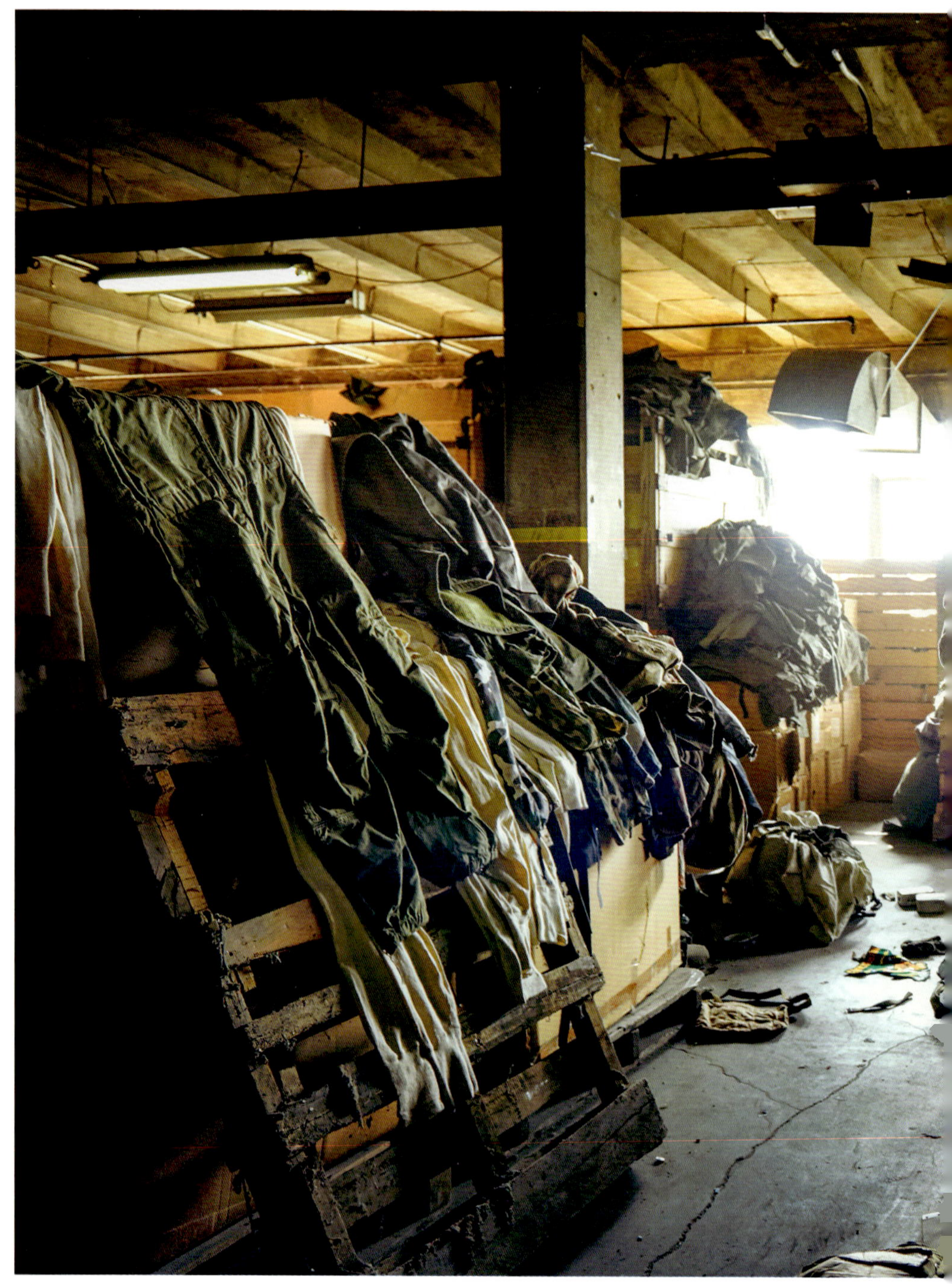

Mike Kalayjian Owner, Camo Surplus > Los Angeles, California

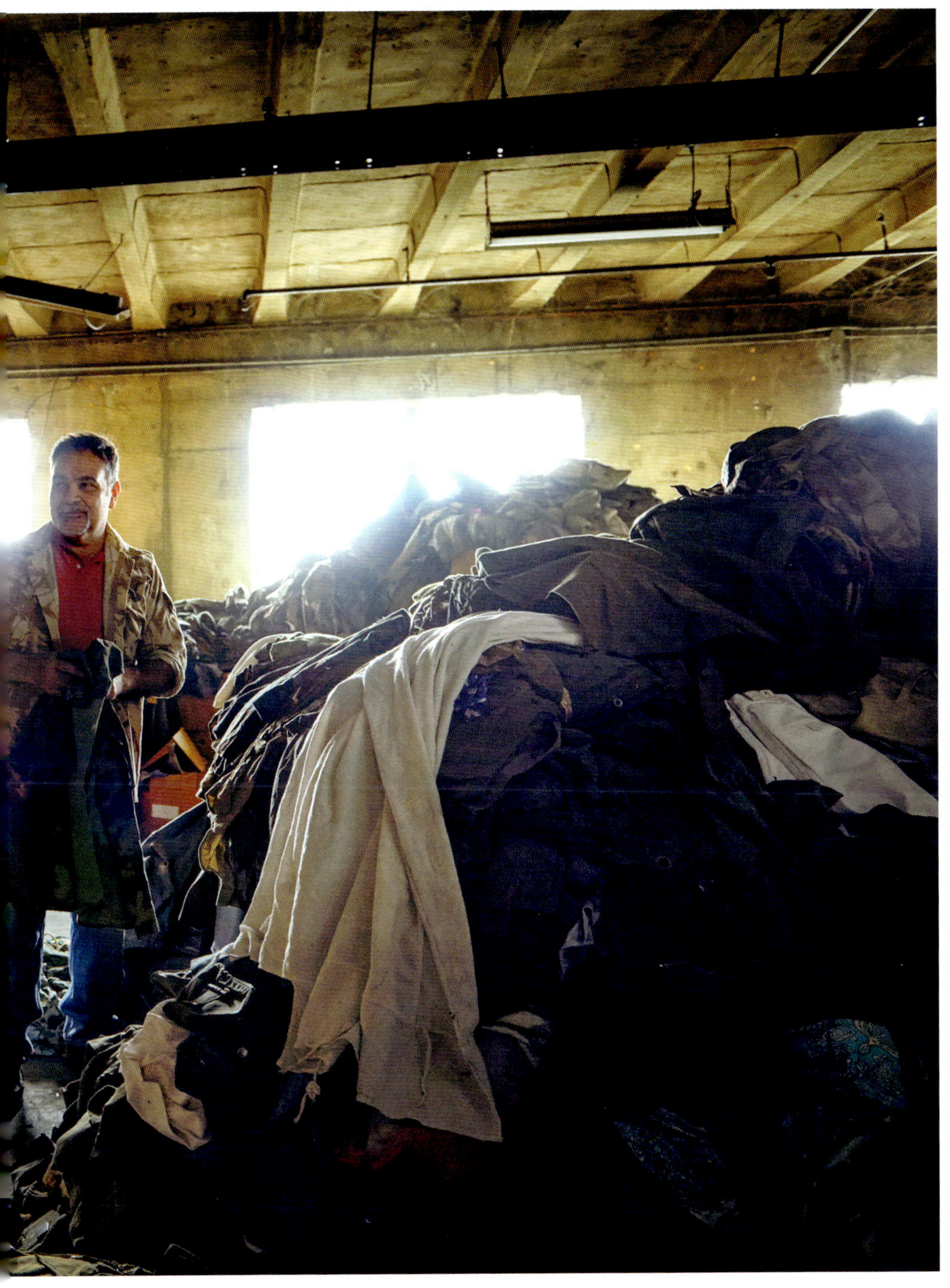

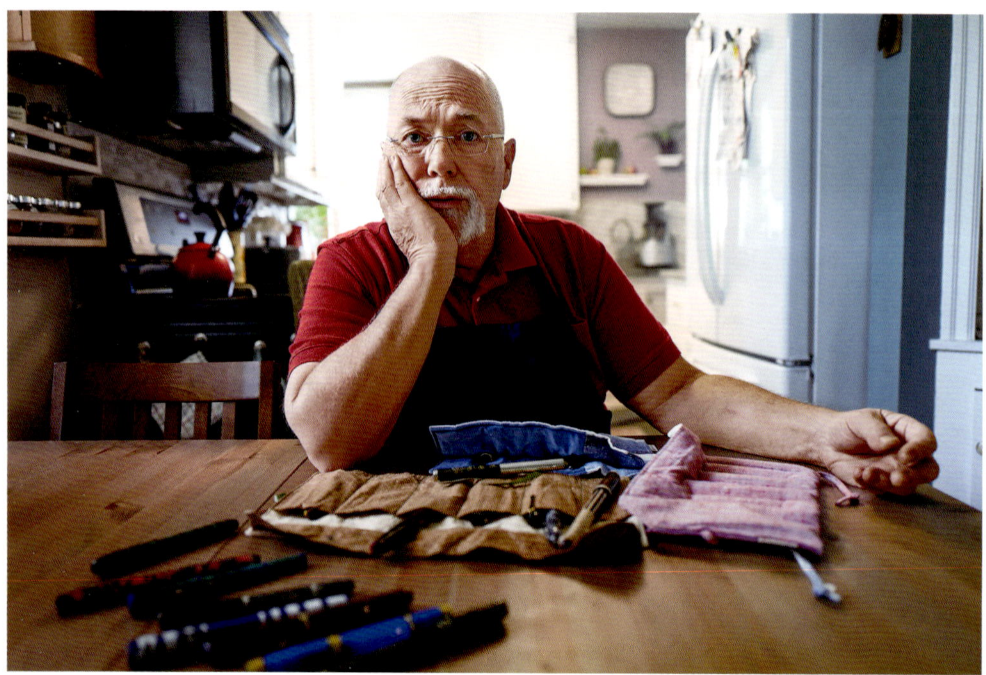

The pens were so beautiful. I knew as soon as I saw them in a shop that I needed to meet the person who made them.

Doug had been a psychiatrist by profession, and he began practicing EMDR when he found that medications were not working for many of his patients. I shared a bit with him about my accident. I'd healed in so many ways, but struggled still with anxiety. Airports were really challenging. I felt like I had to be there hours and hours in advance.

Which was frustrating, given how often I travel for work.

I did not hesitate when Doug offered me an EMDR session. I would be flying home to Massachusetts soon, anyway. I felt the most beautiful breeze come in through the open door as the session ended. I thanked him.

Arriving at the airport, I was startled to realize that it was only 90 minutes until flight-time.

Dr. Douglas Scott CEO and Master Craftsman, Kairos Pens > Portland, Oregon

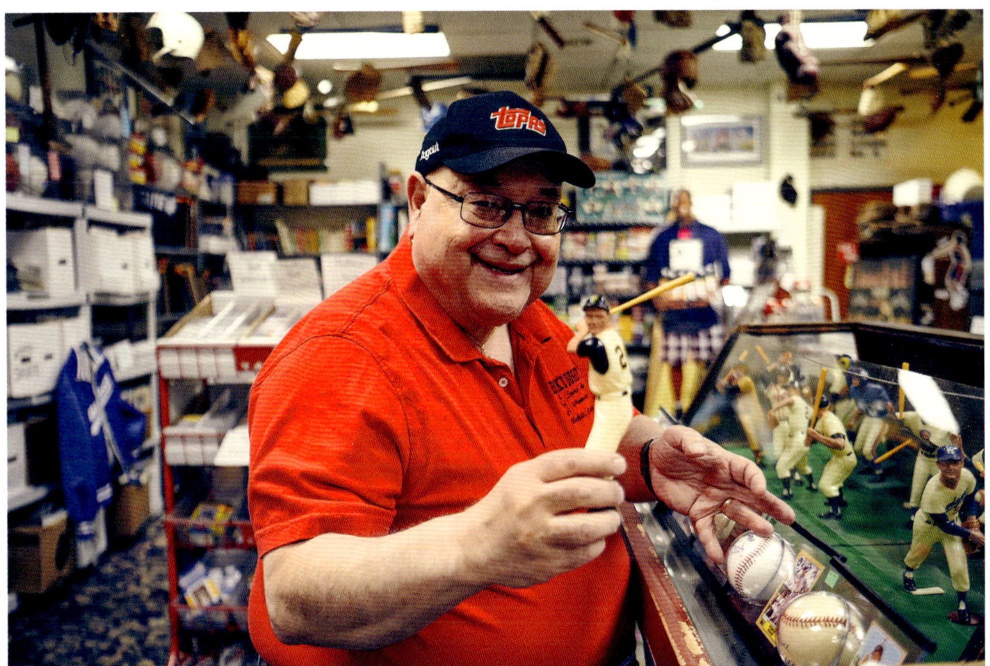

Joseph, a fellow New Yorker, is from the Bronx. He moved to Wichita for college and stayed, working as a teacher there for 30 years.

Despite the years between us, we had parallel reminiscences about growing up in the city. "When it was the real NYC," as he put it.

When he retired, he told himself, "Now it's time to get back to my real love: baseball cards." He had started collecting baseball cards as a kid, loving the stories they told as much as the game itself.

Over two million cards later, Joseph is selling his treasured collection out of a bowling alley in Wichita.

Joseph Ruocoo Sportscard Dealer > Wichita, Kansas

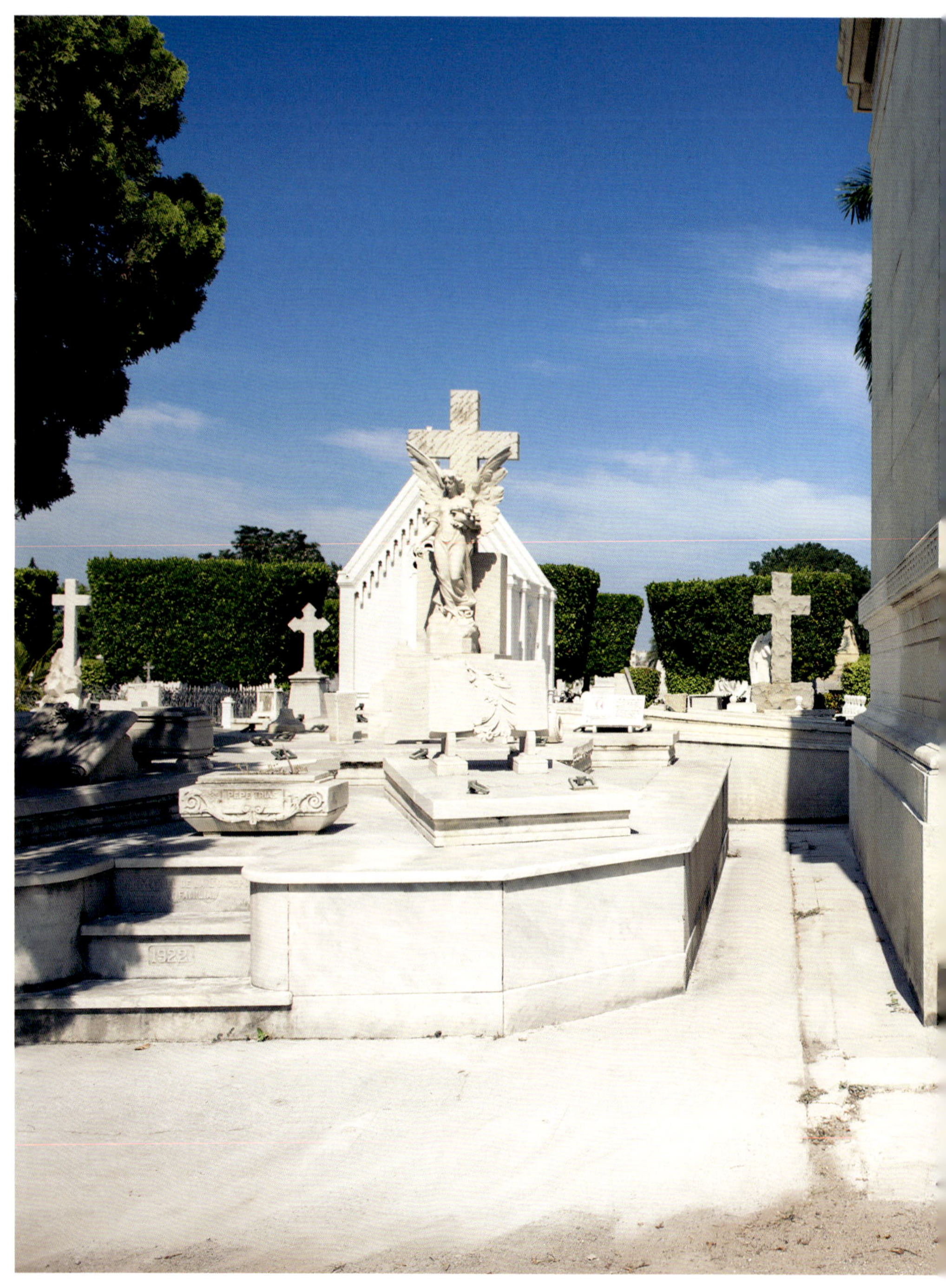

Juan Carlos Cremata Malberti Director > Havana, Cuba

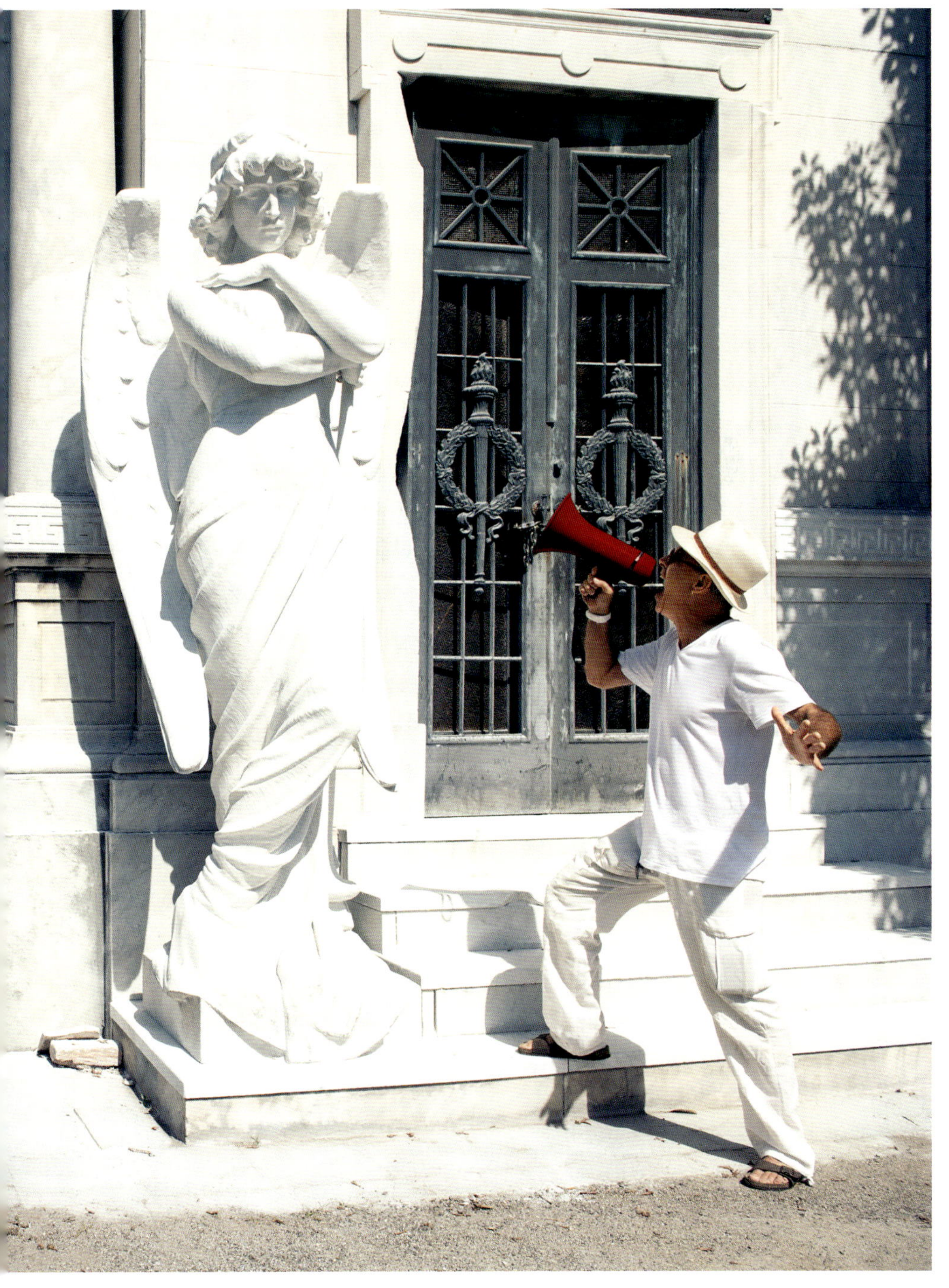

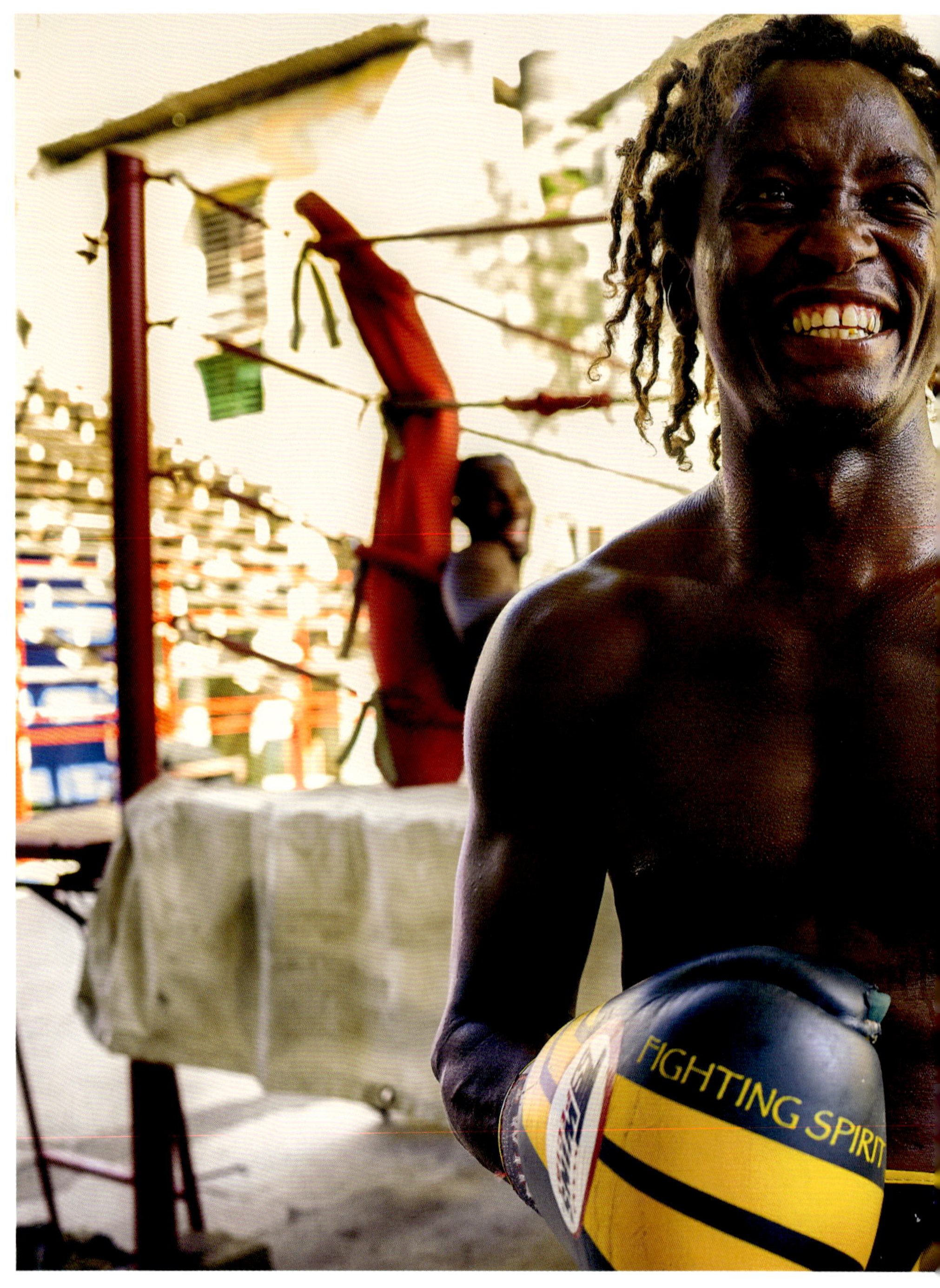

Maikel Gonzalez Boxer > Havana, Cuba

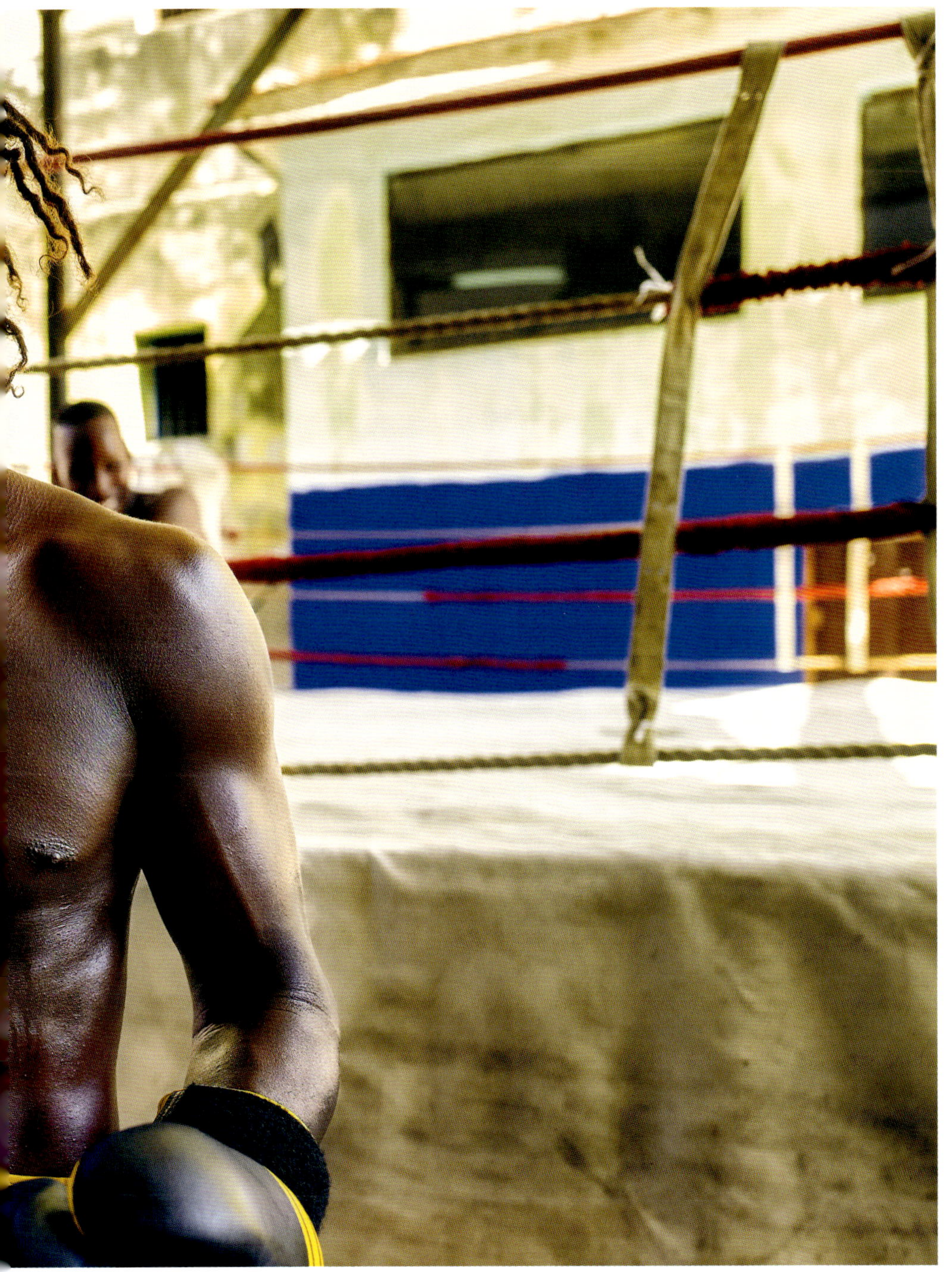

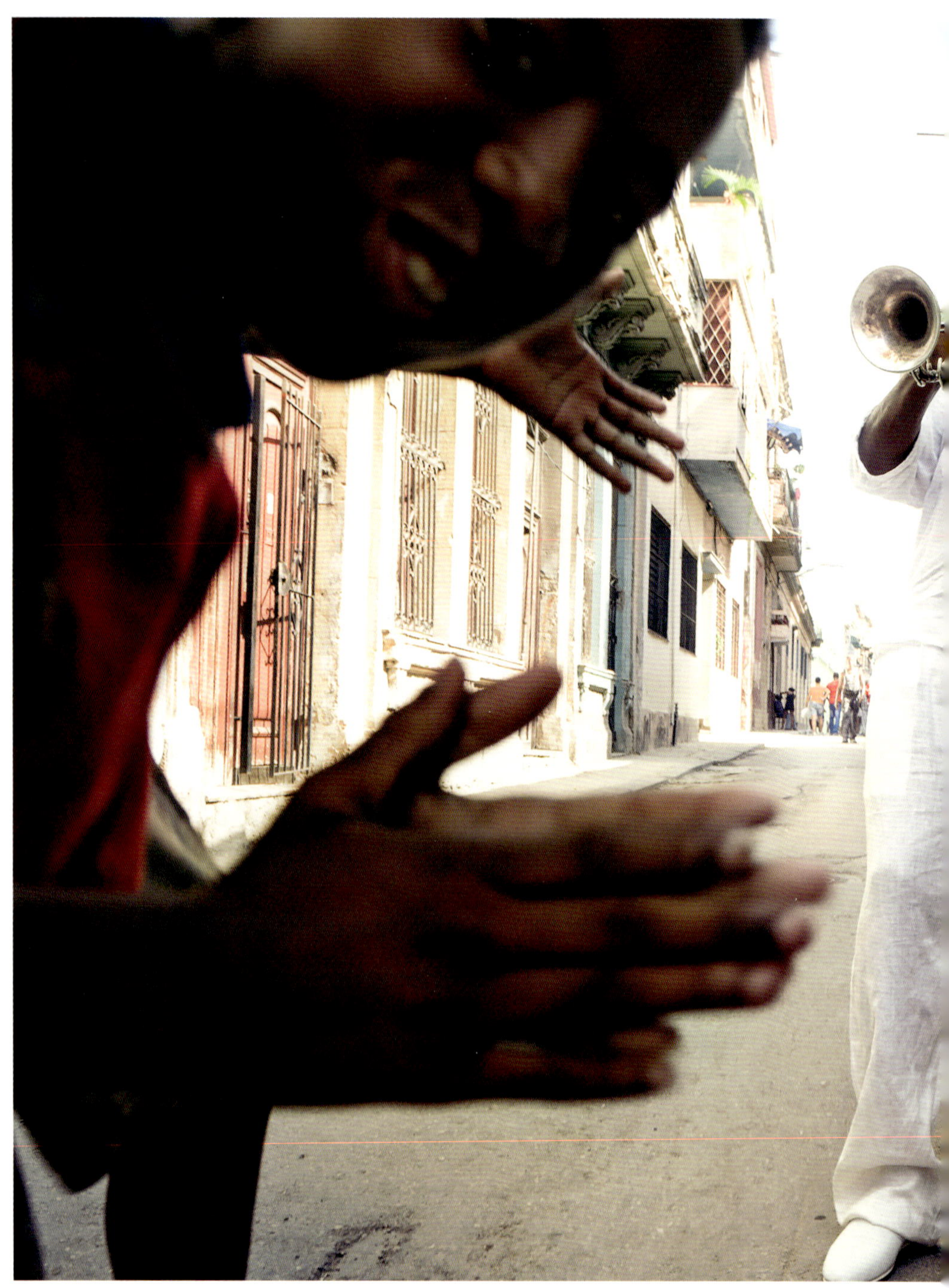

Julito Padrón Trumpeter > Havana, Cuba

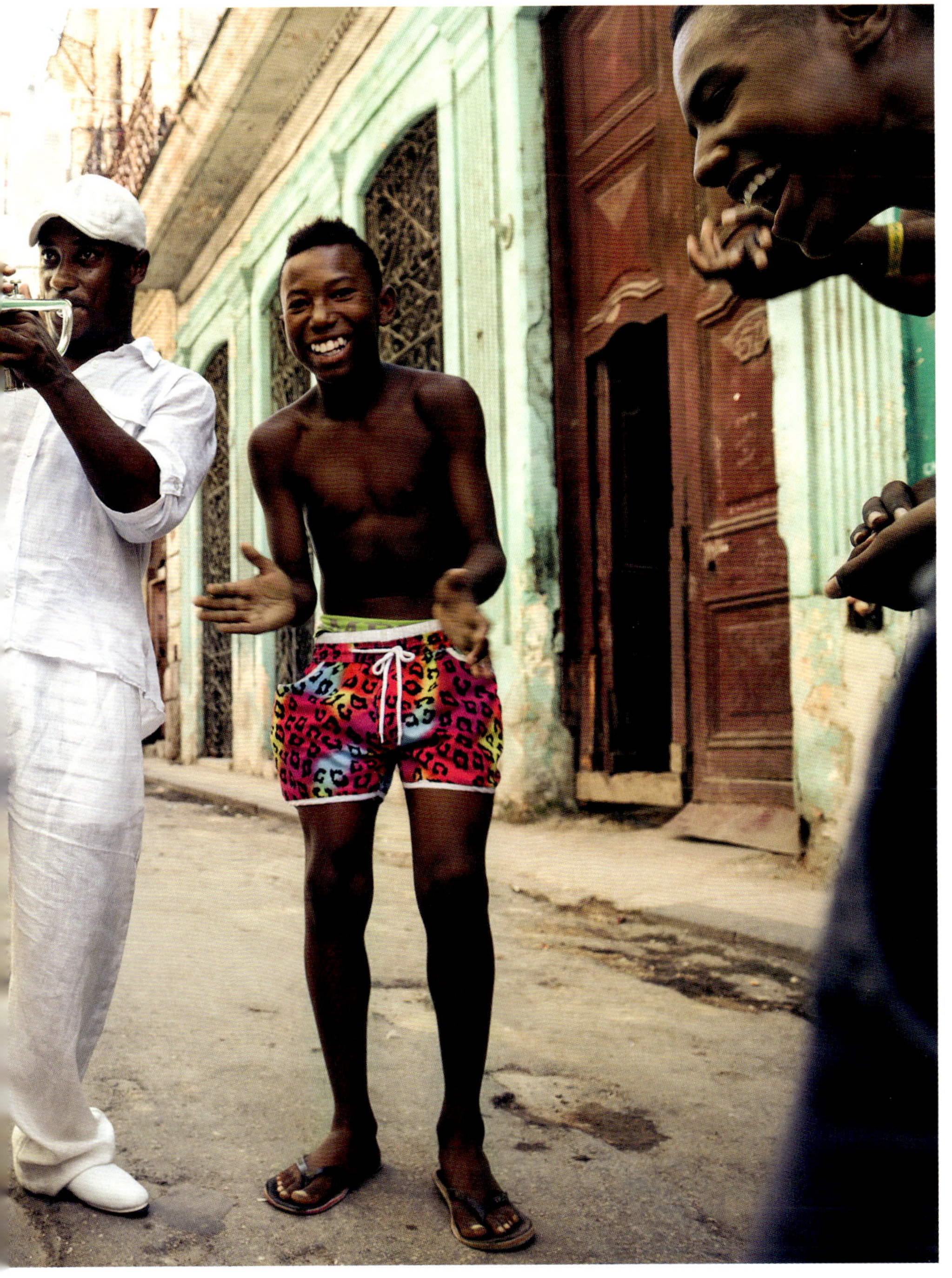

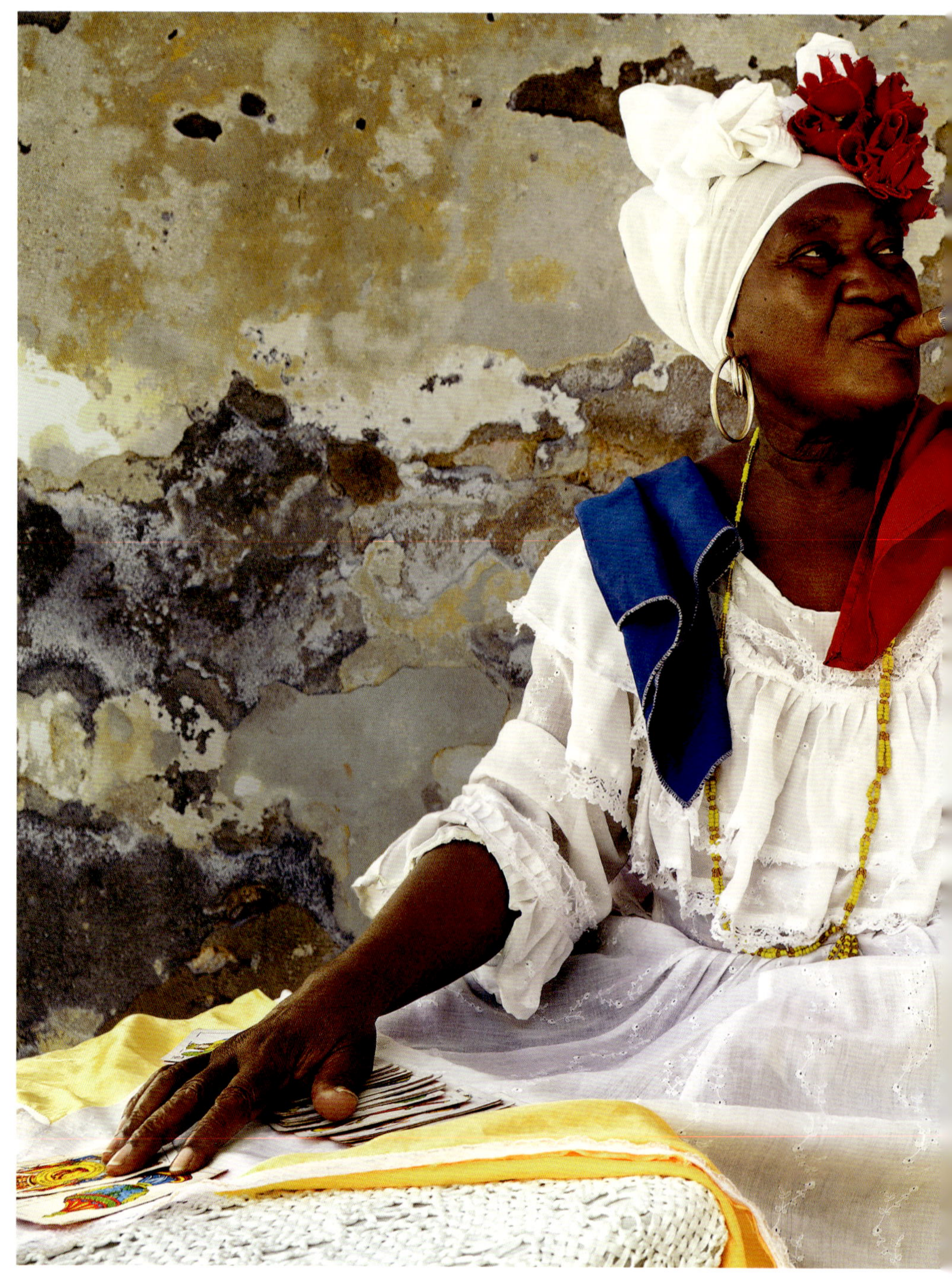

Juana La Cubana Tarot Card Reader > Havana, Cuba

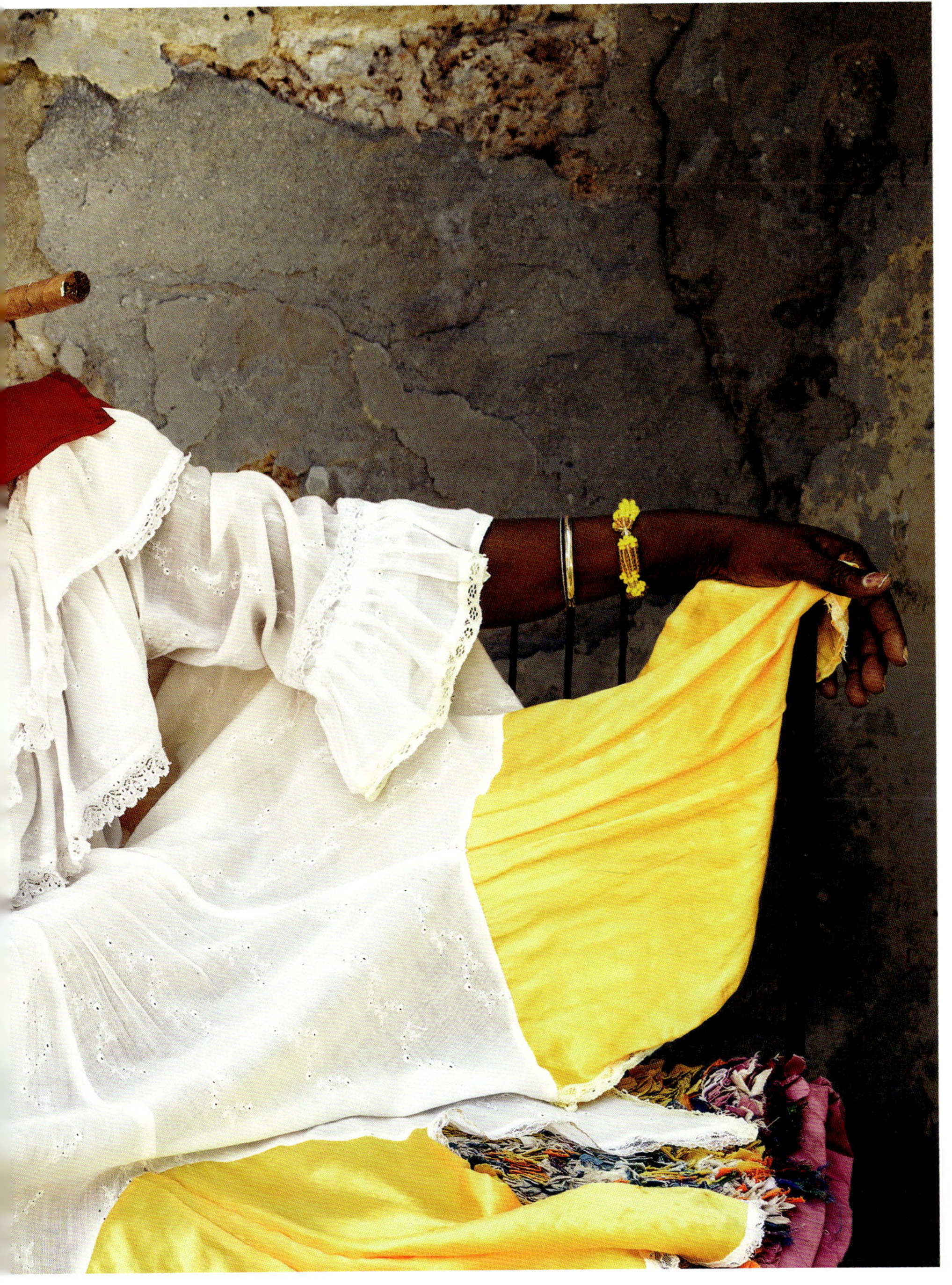

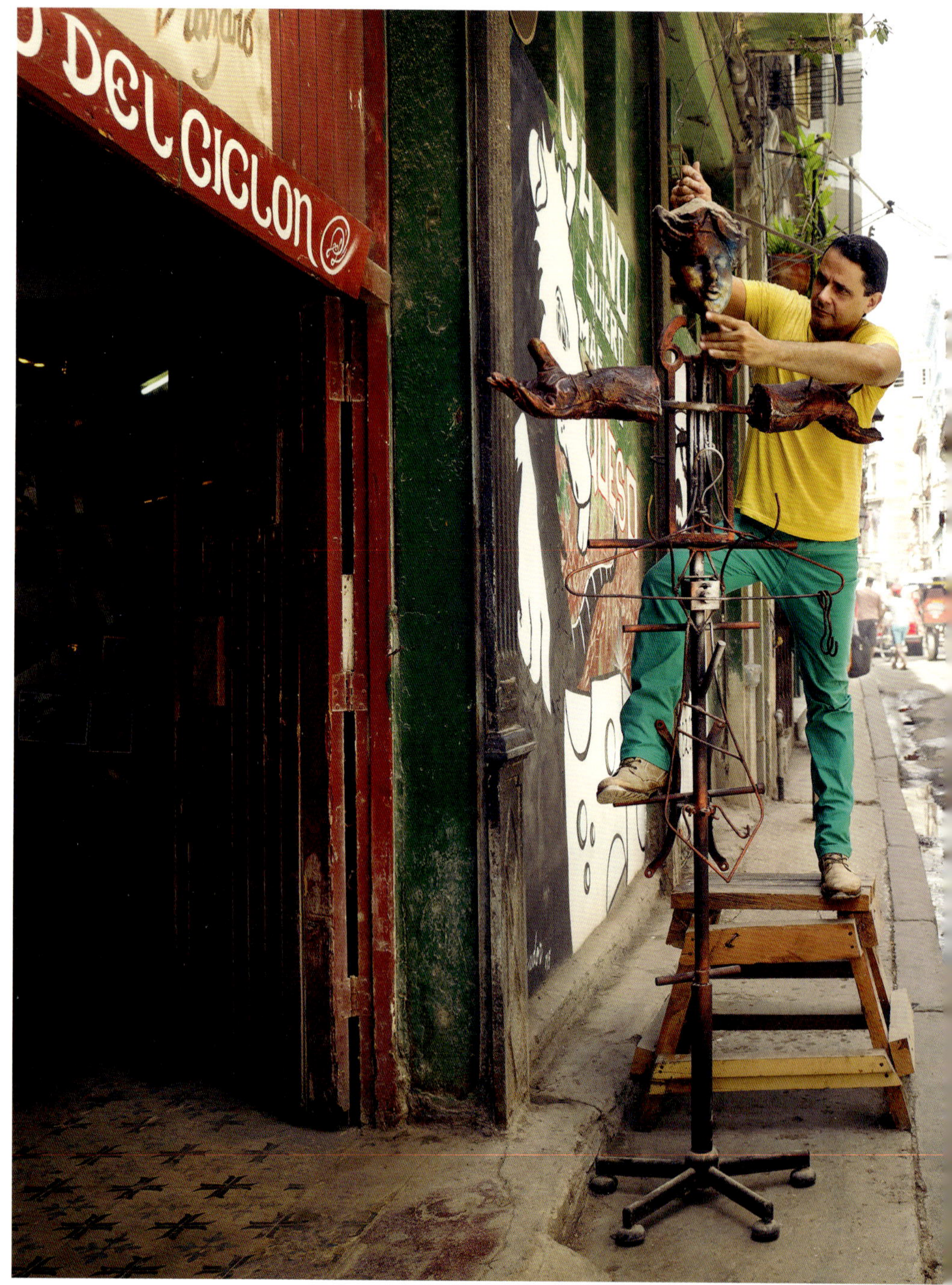

Leo de Lazaro Sculptor, Modern Anthropology > Havana, Cuba

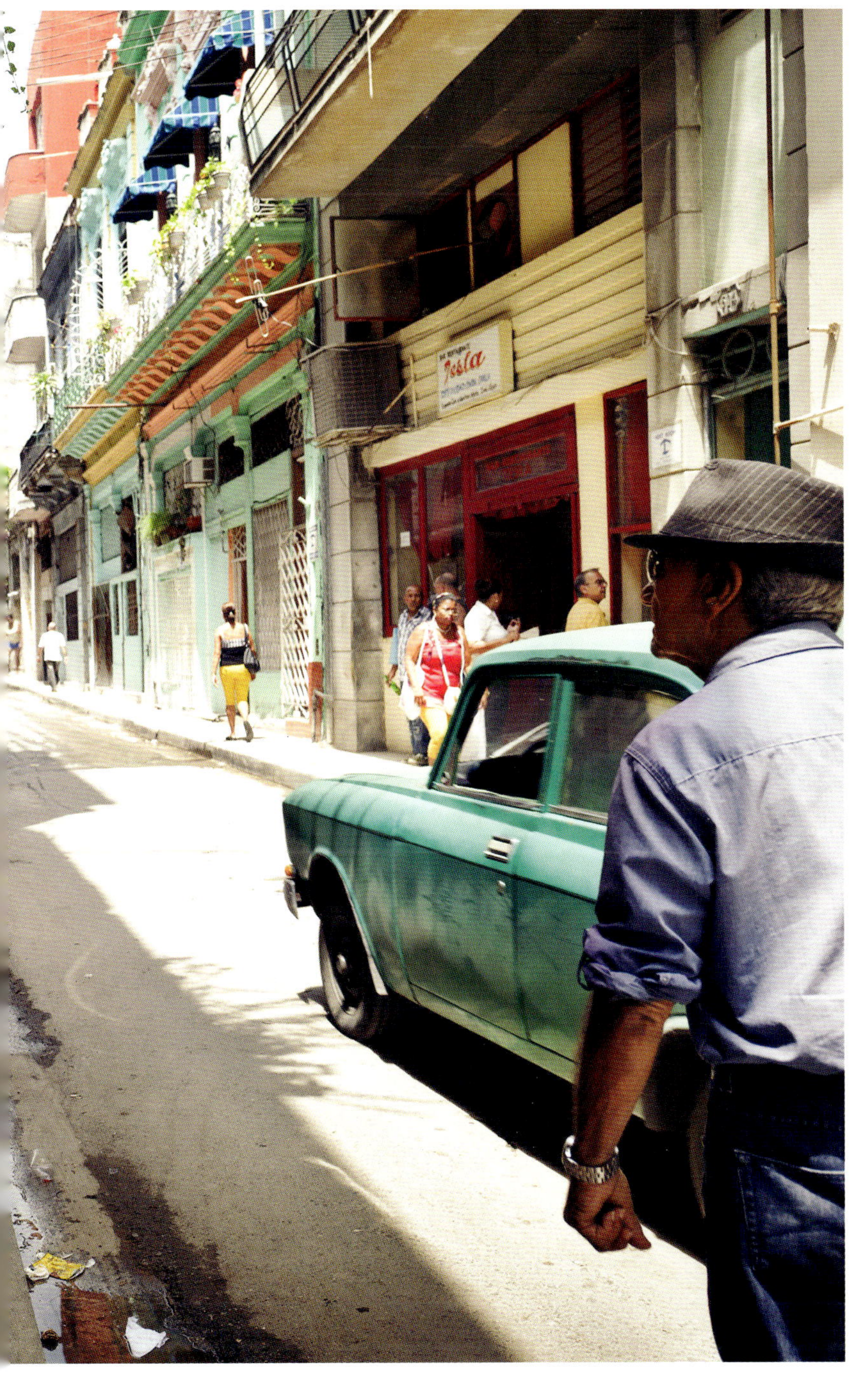

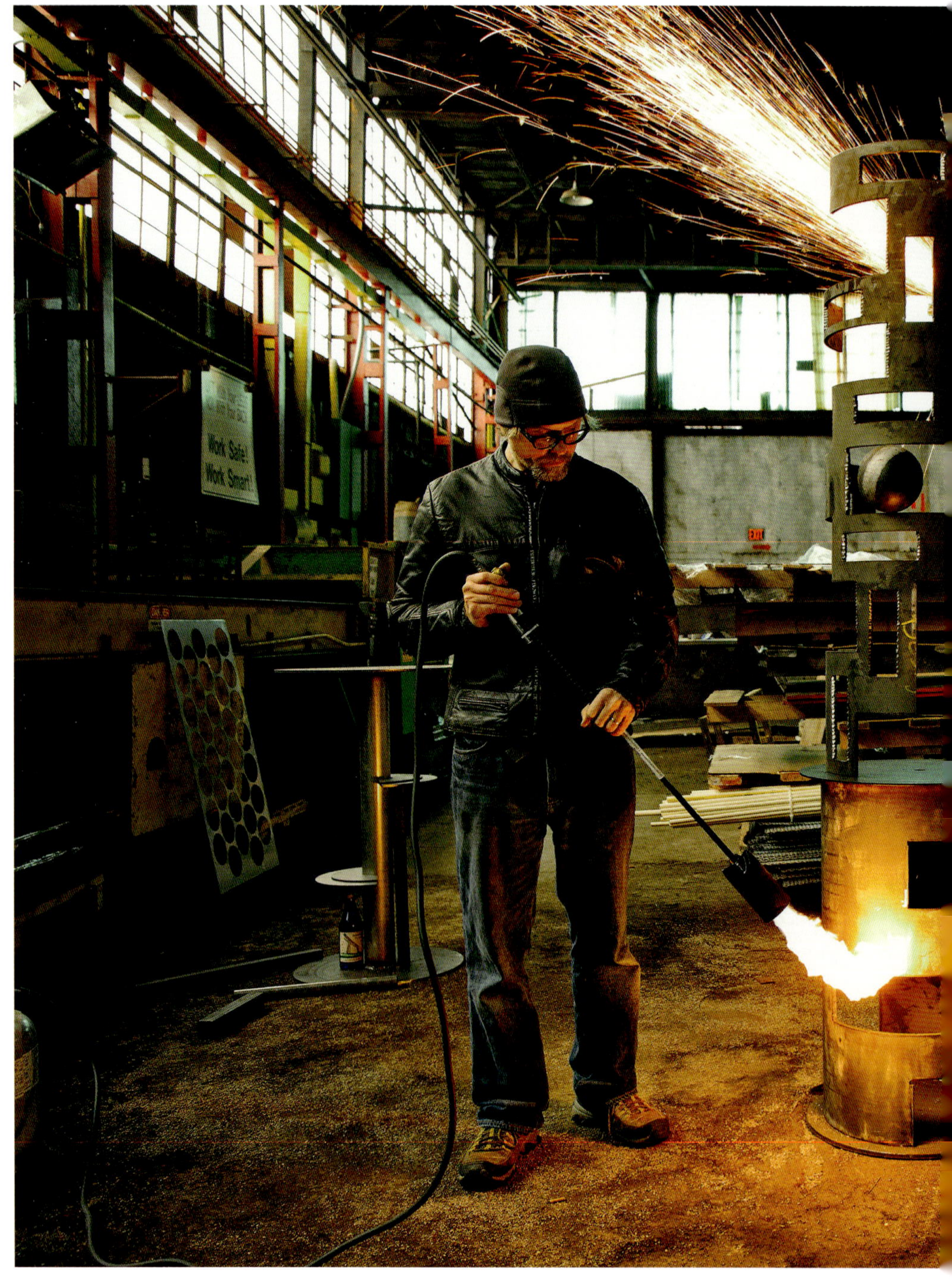

Erik & Israel Nordin Large Scale Glass and Metal Sculptors, Detroit Design Studio > Detroit, Michigan

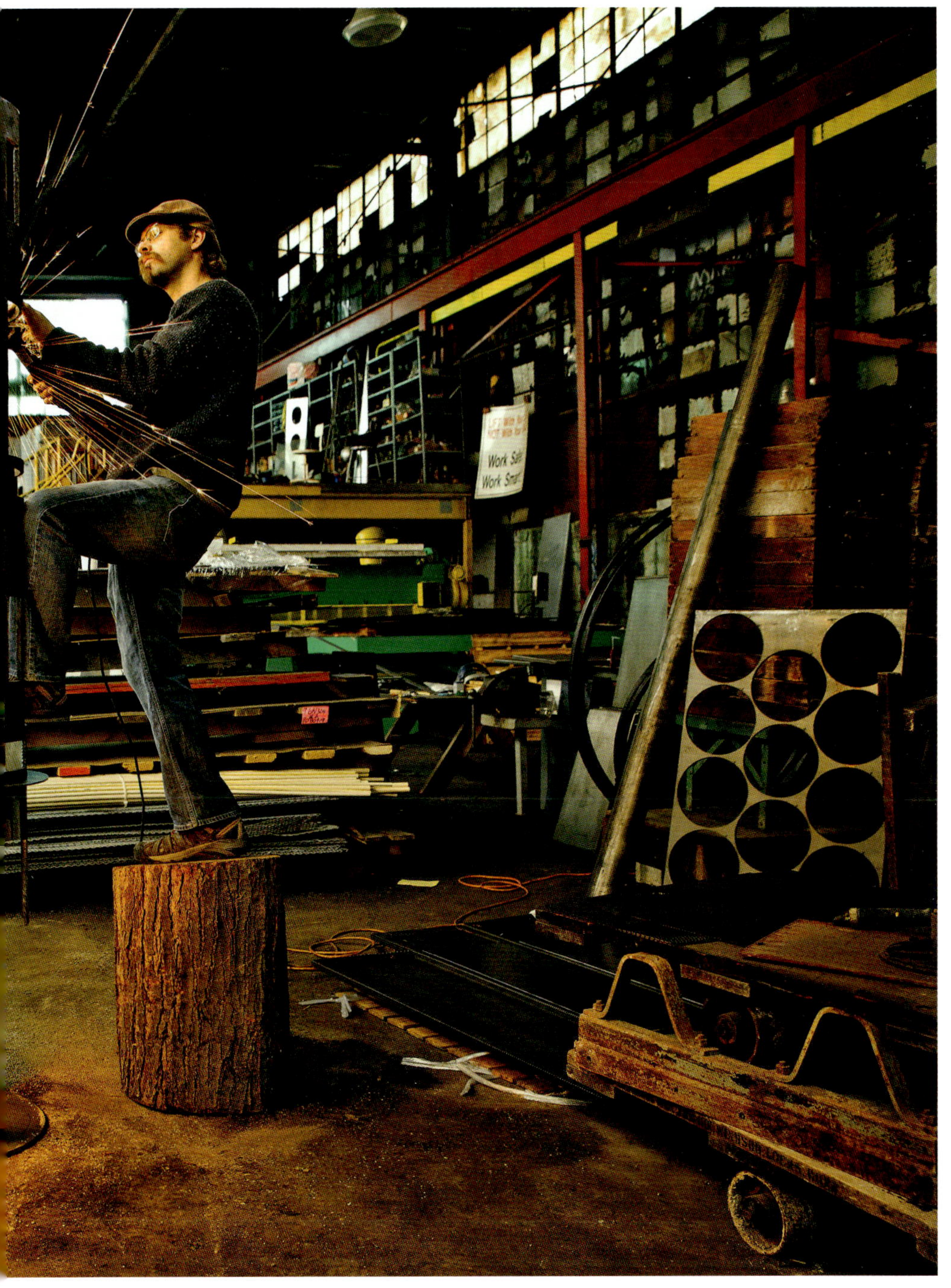

Work Saf
Work Smar

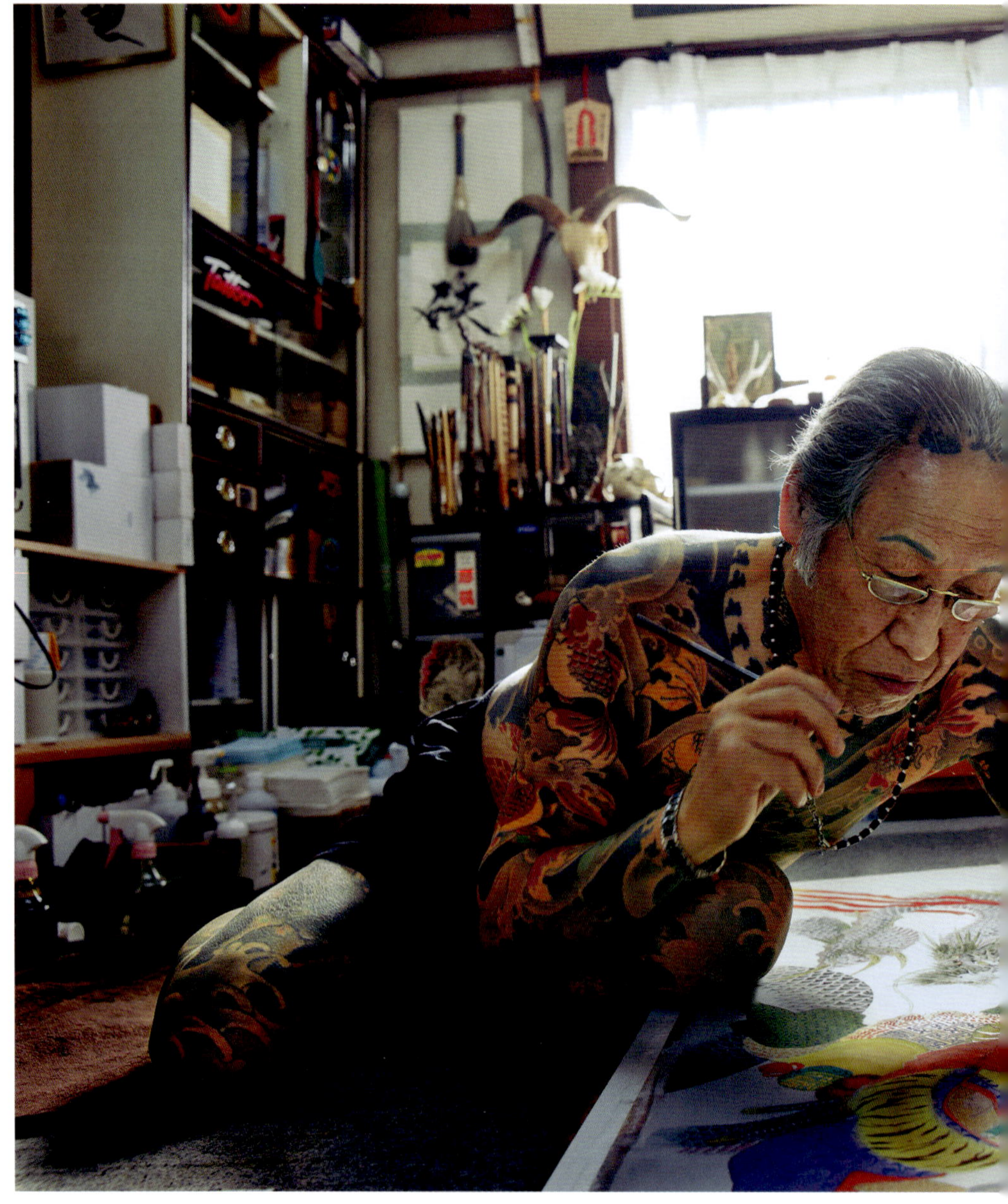

I had my mind set on getting a phoenix tattooed on my chest while I was in Japan.

Getting to Horiyohi was a little tricky. Tattooing is taboo in Japan. And Horiyohi, though a sought-after artist, is also known for tattooing members of the yakuza. I get it. Any kind of association with gangsters, anywhere, would give a person a certain aura.

But he didn't strike me as a tough guy. He was really kind. And like my dad, he had kidney trouble. He wanted me to come after his next dialysis session.

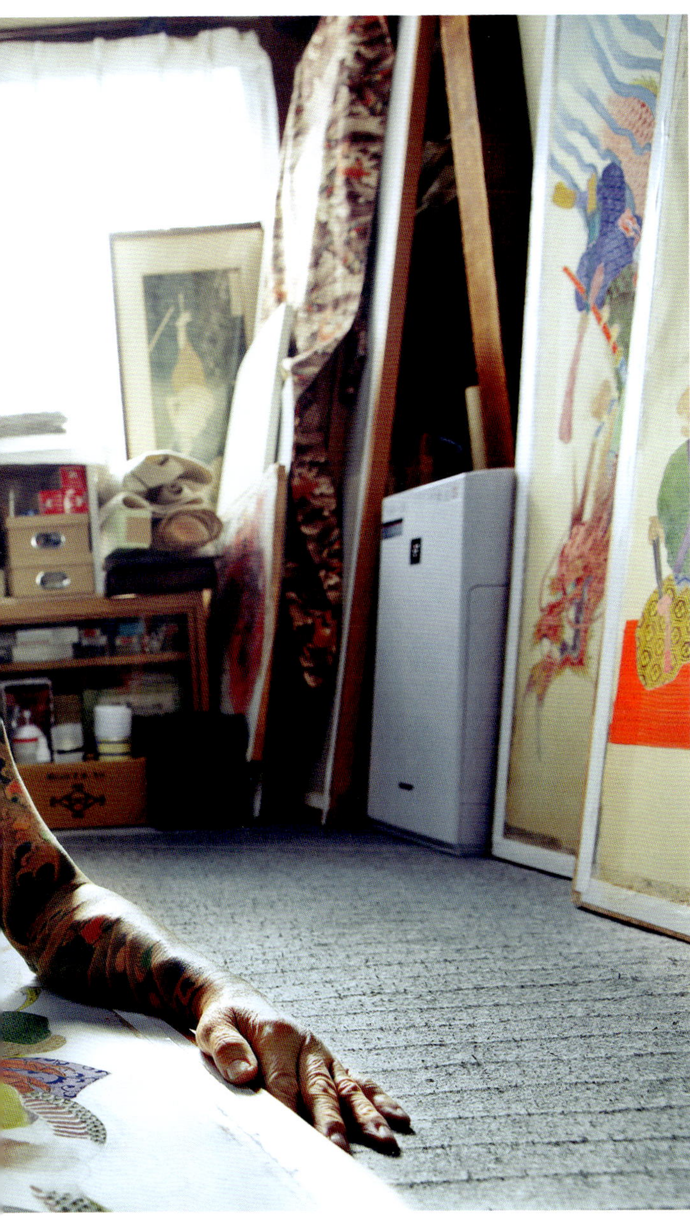

I asked to see a sketch of the tattoo. "I don't do sketches," he said.

When he was done with my tattoo, he gave me a roll of Saran Wrap to bandage my bleeding chest. Then and there, he asked that I photograph him working on a silk screen. As I was leaving, he handed me a piece of paper with a sketch of a phoenix.

Yoshihito Nakano (Horiyohi) Tattoo Artist > Tokyo, Japan

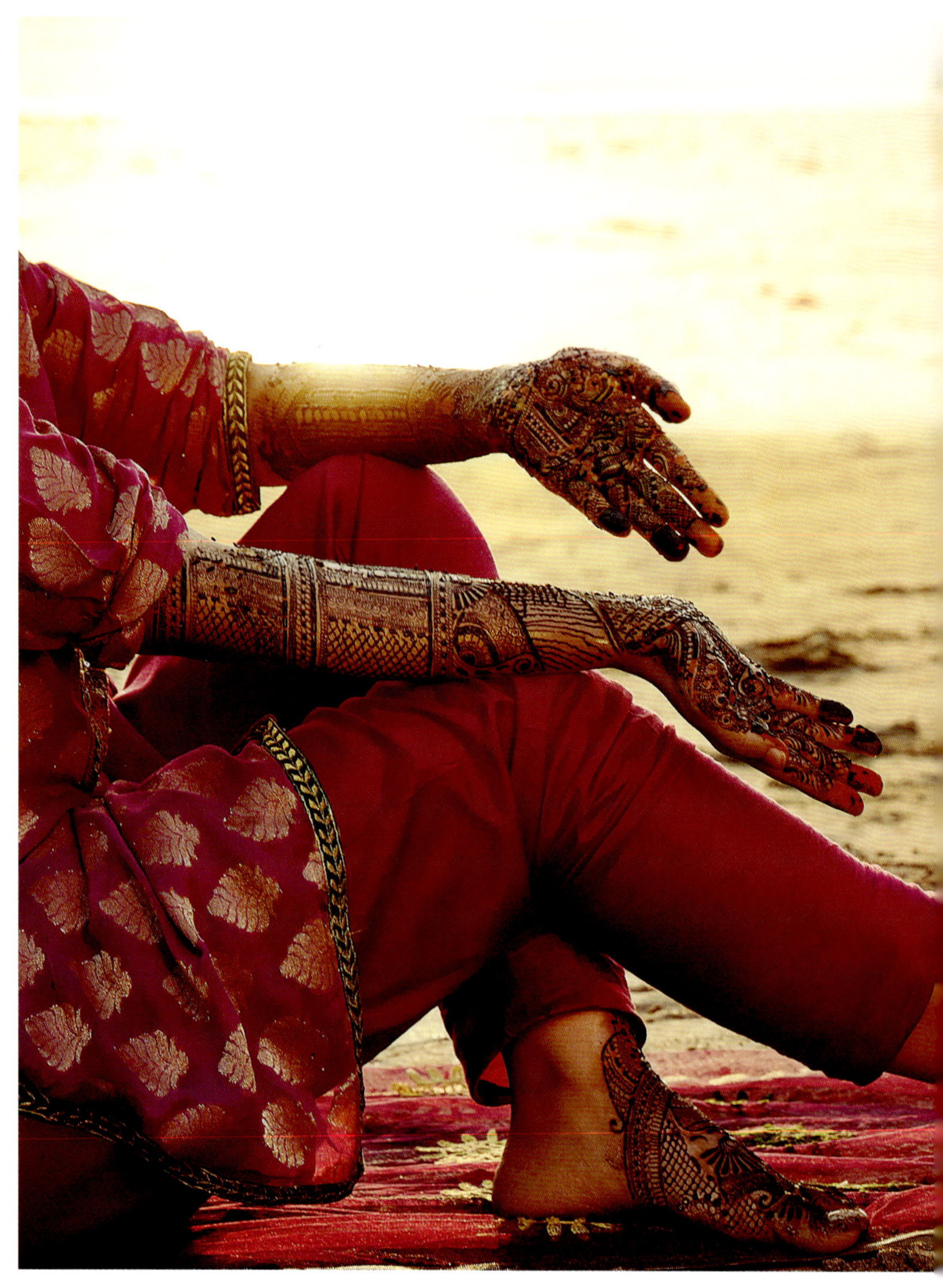

Henna Artist > Mumbai, India

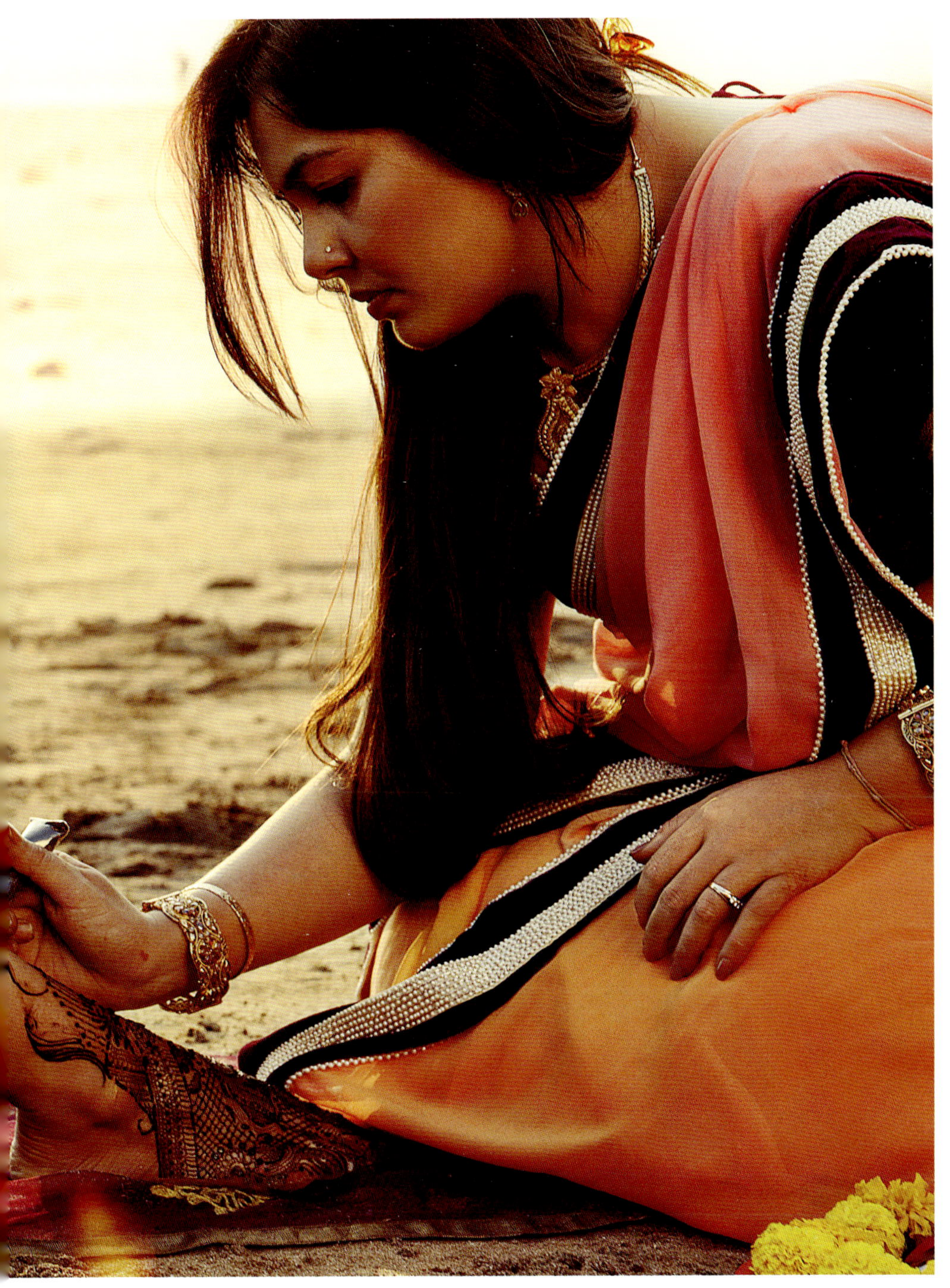

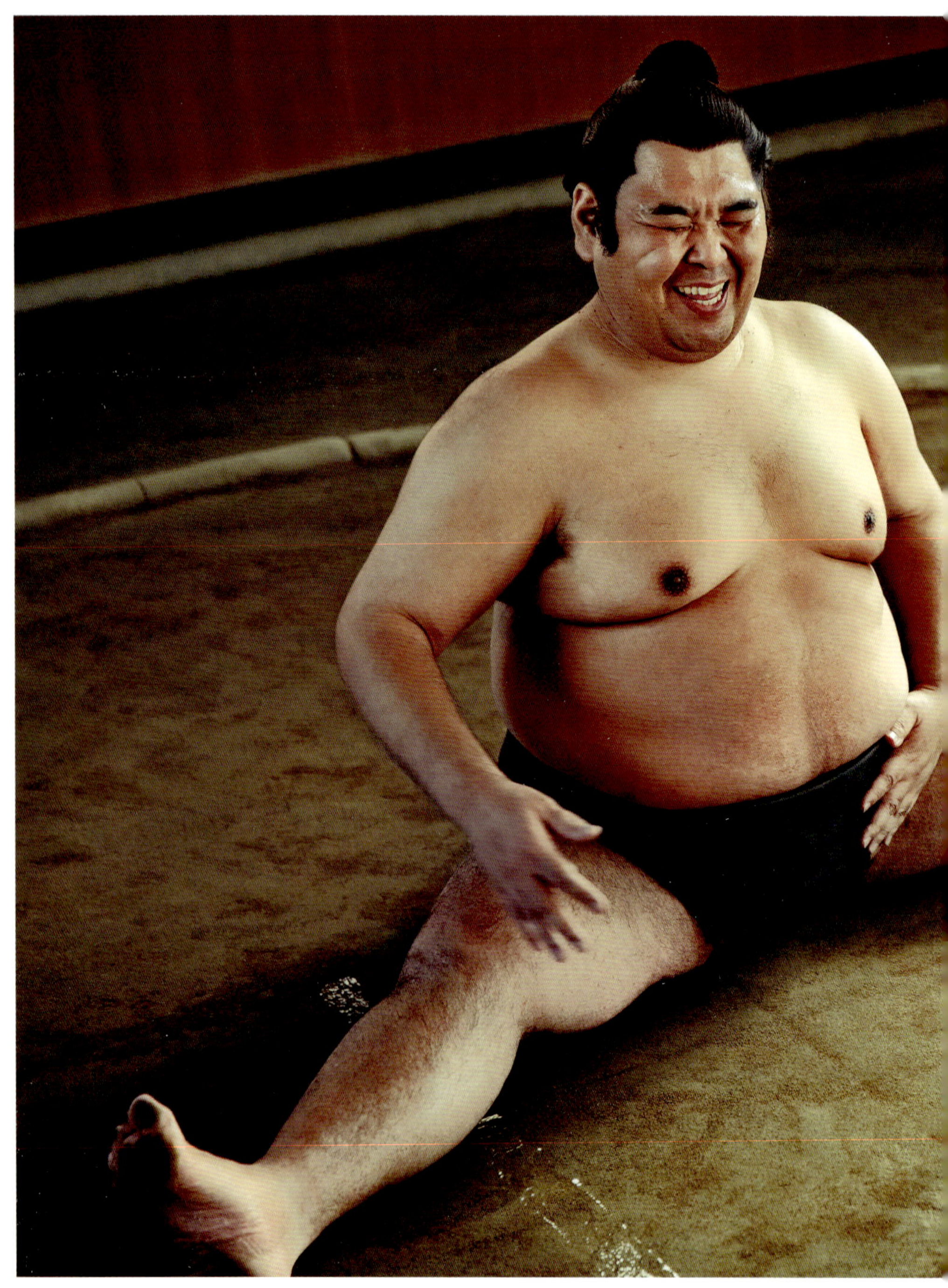

Tunada Masafumi Sumo Wrestler > Tokyo, Japan

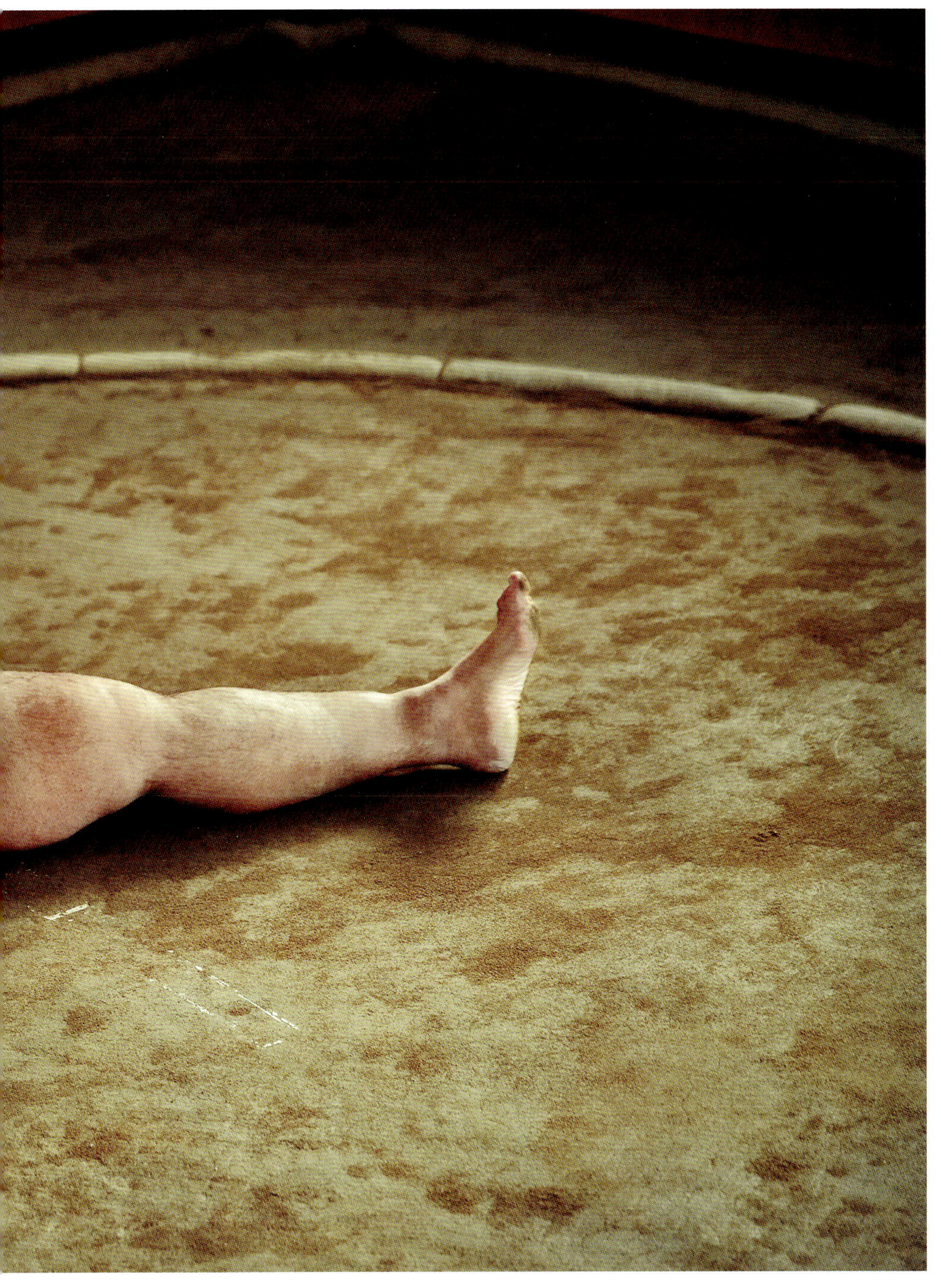

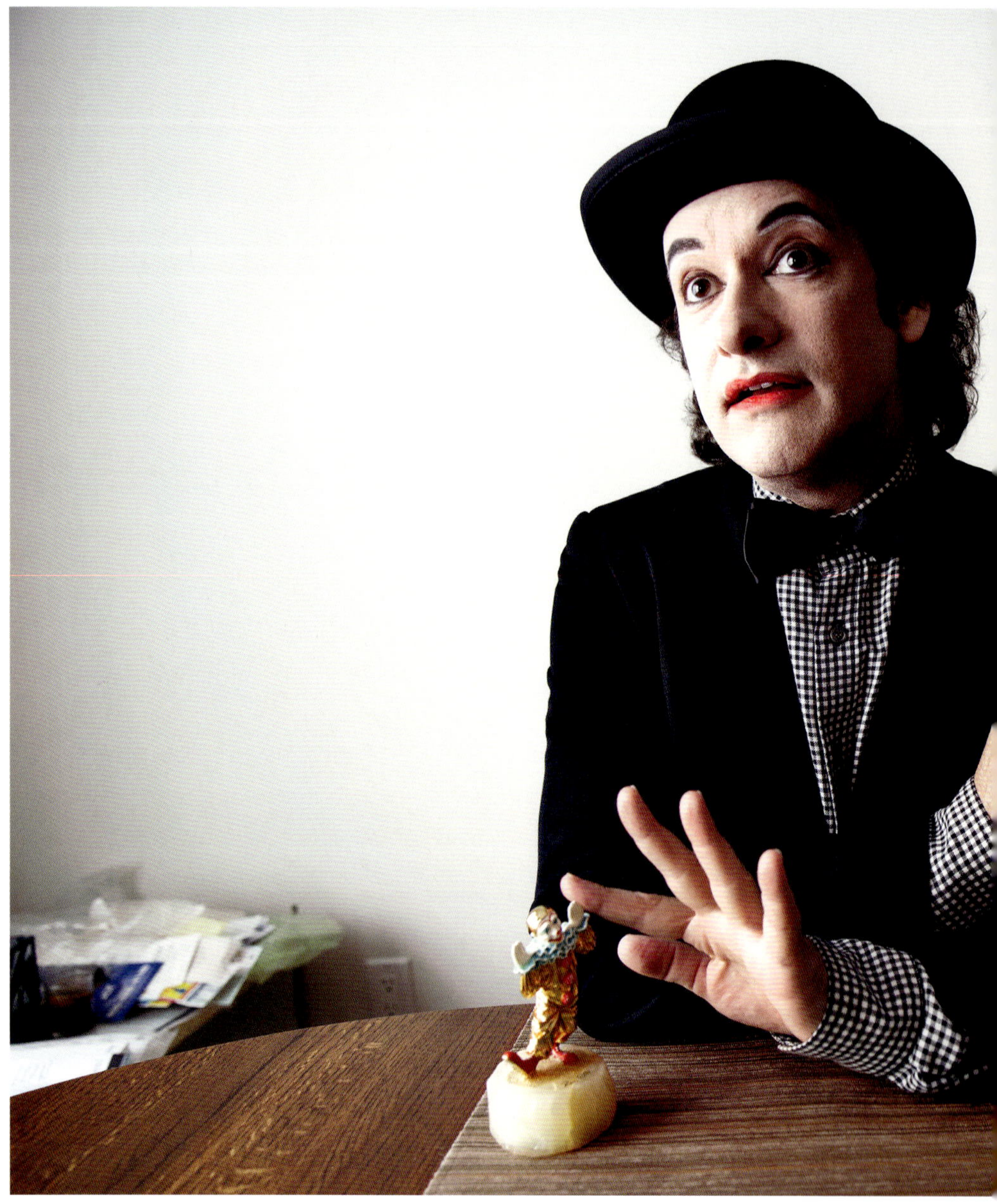

Sometimes, the best moments unfold in silence. I've always valued photographs that invite interpretation, and for me, this is one of those moments.

Lorin Eric Salm Theatrical Mime Artist > Los Angeles, California

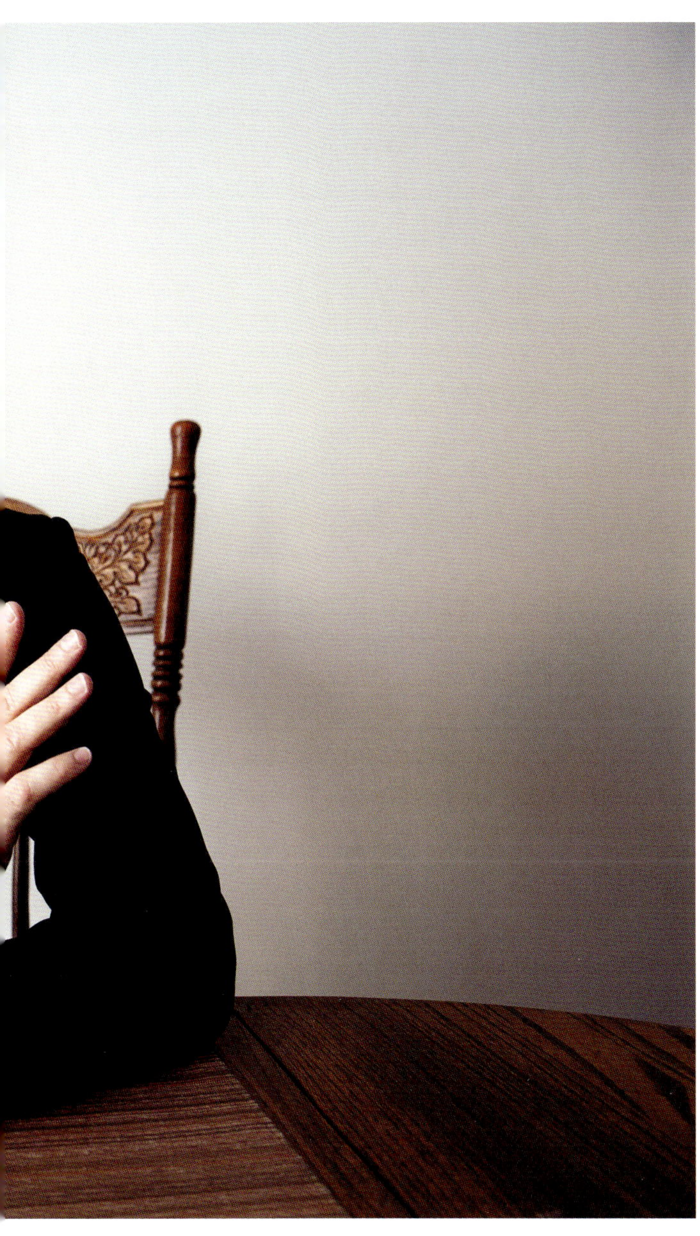

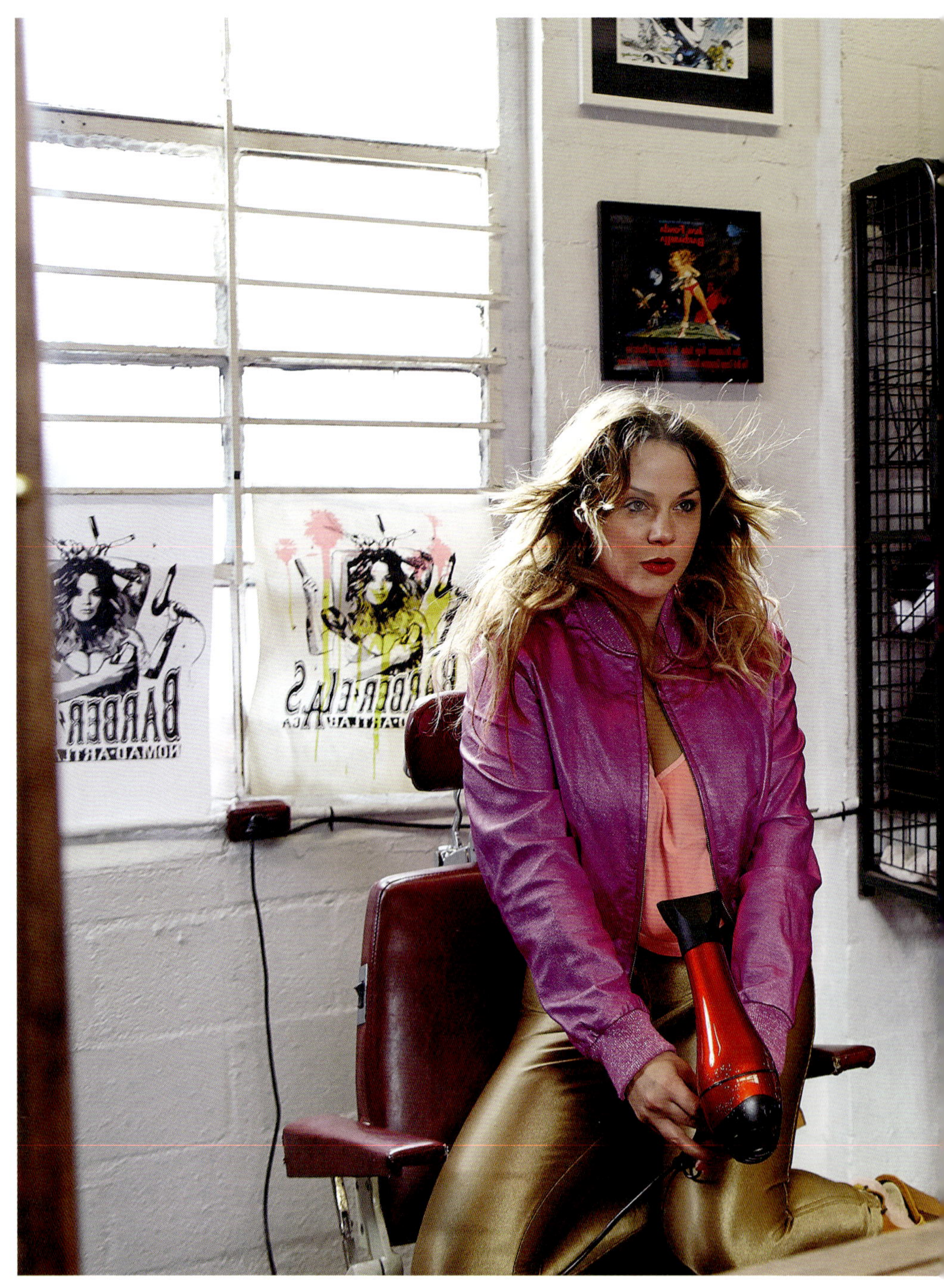

Bethany Brune Hair Stylist, Barber'elas Barber Shop > Los Angeles, California

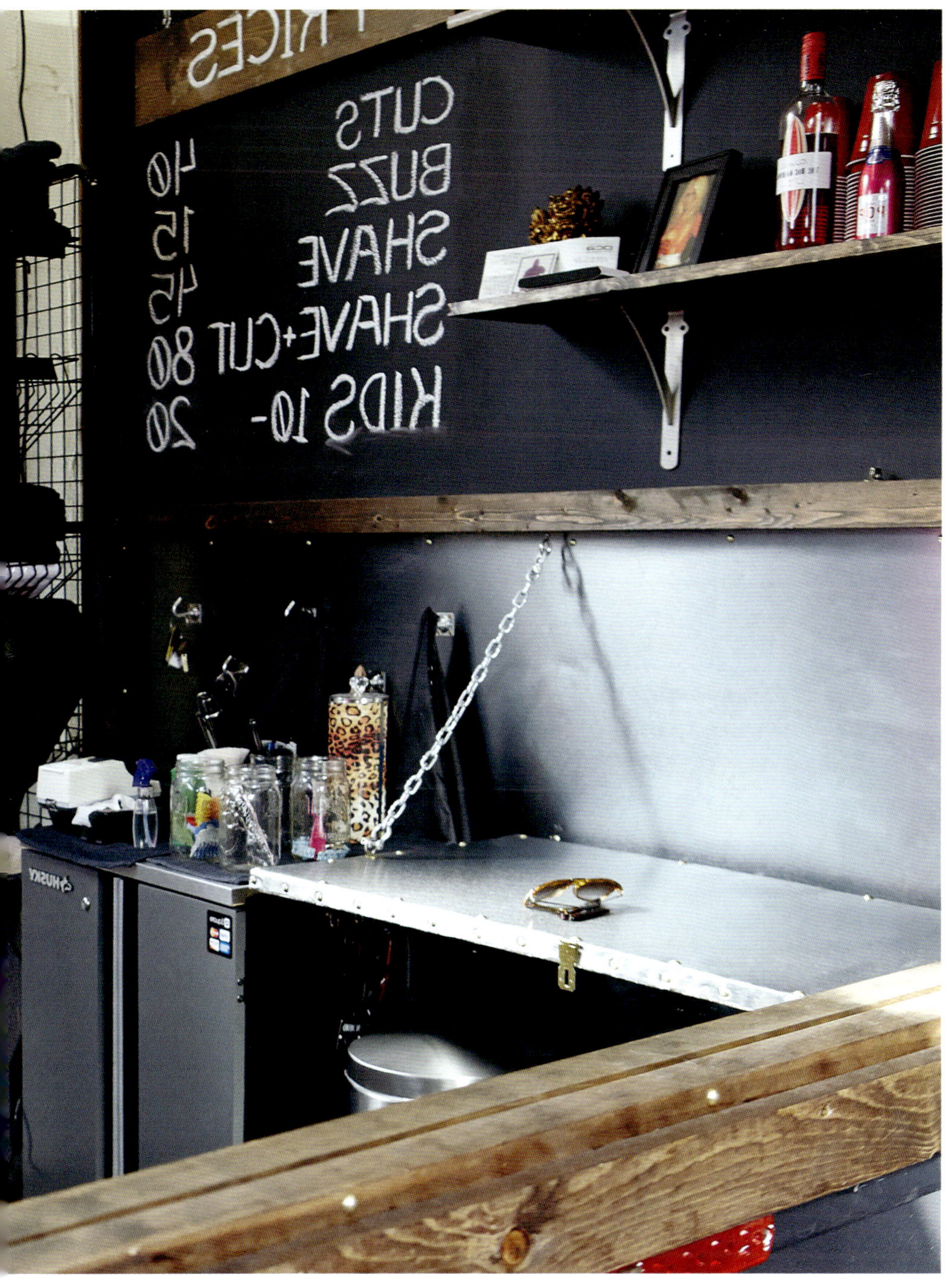

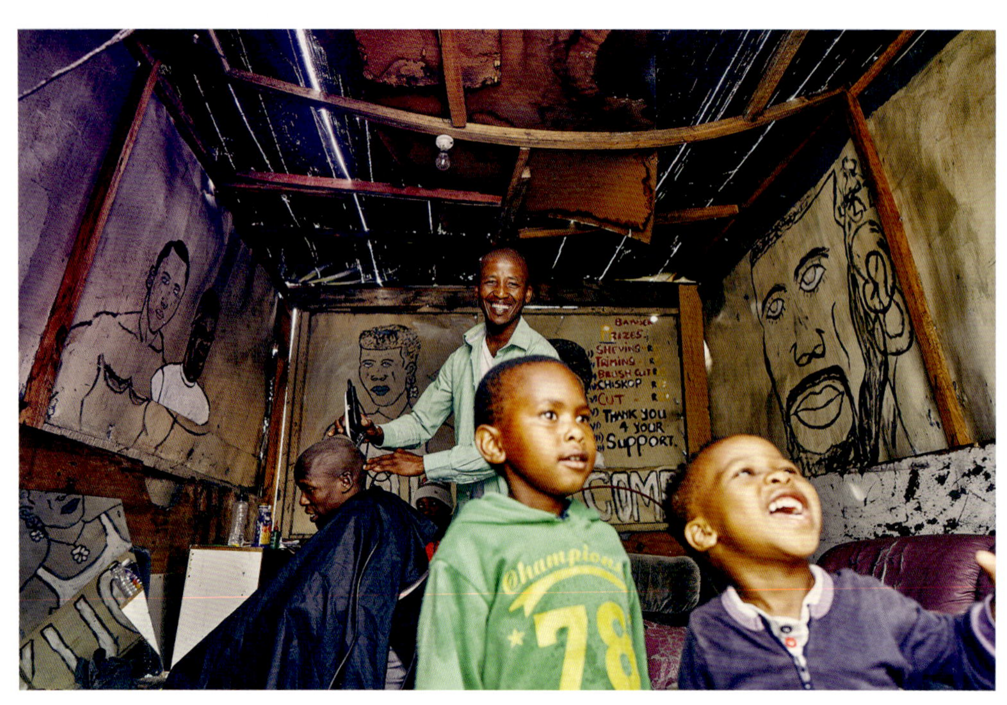

Bule Lani Barber > Langa Township, Cape Town, South Africa

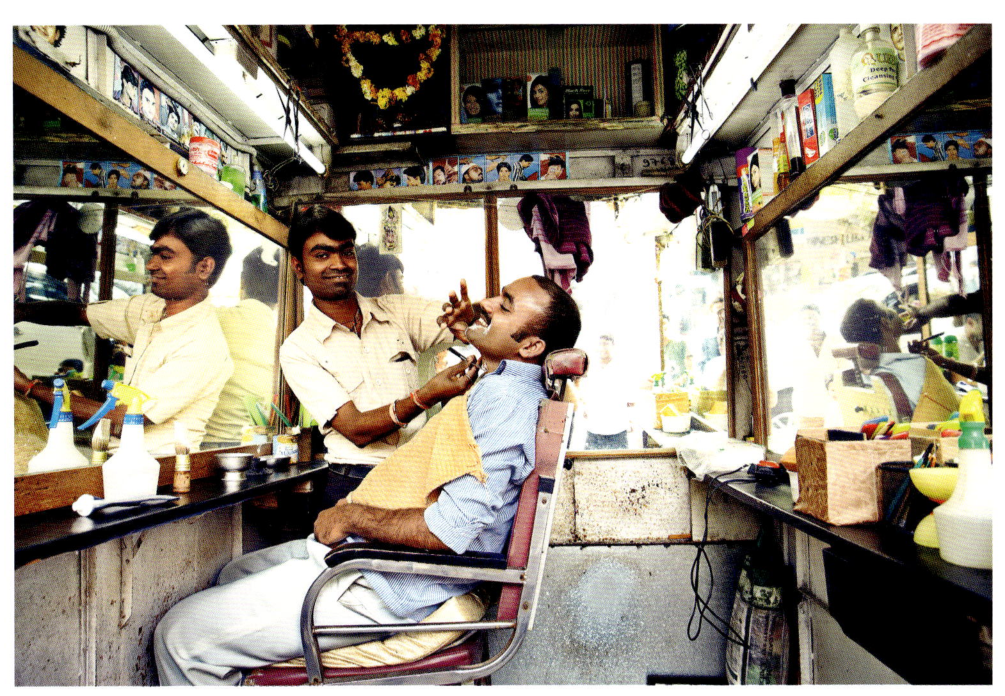

Barber > Mumbai, India

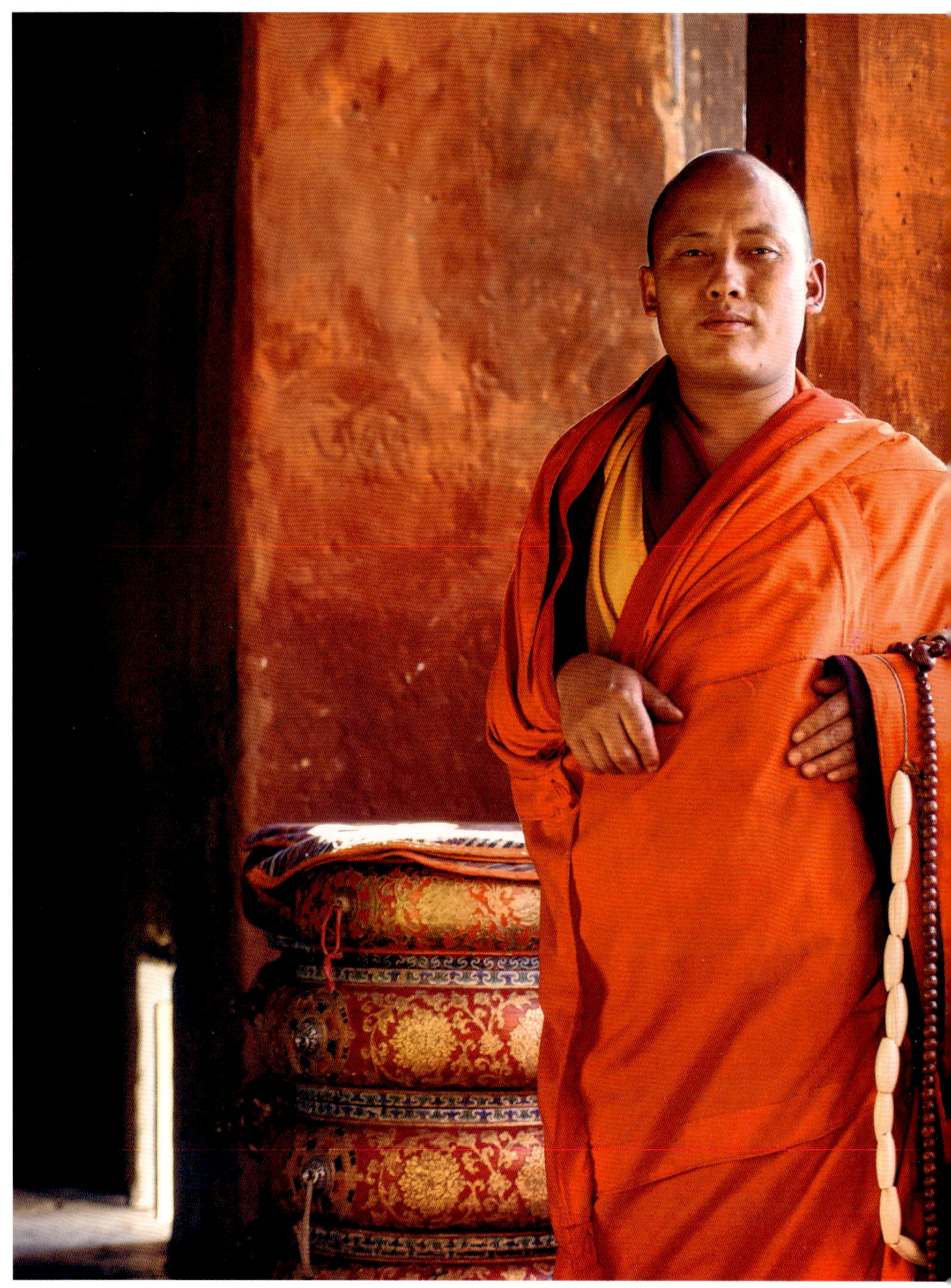

Buddhist Monk > Paro, Bhutan

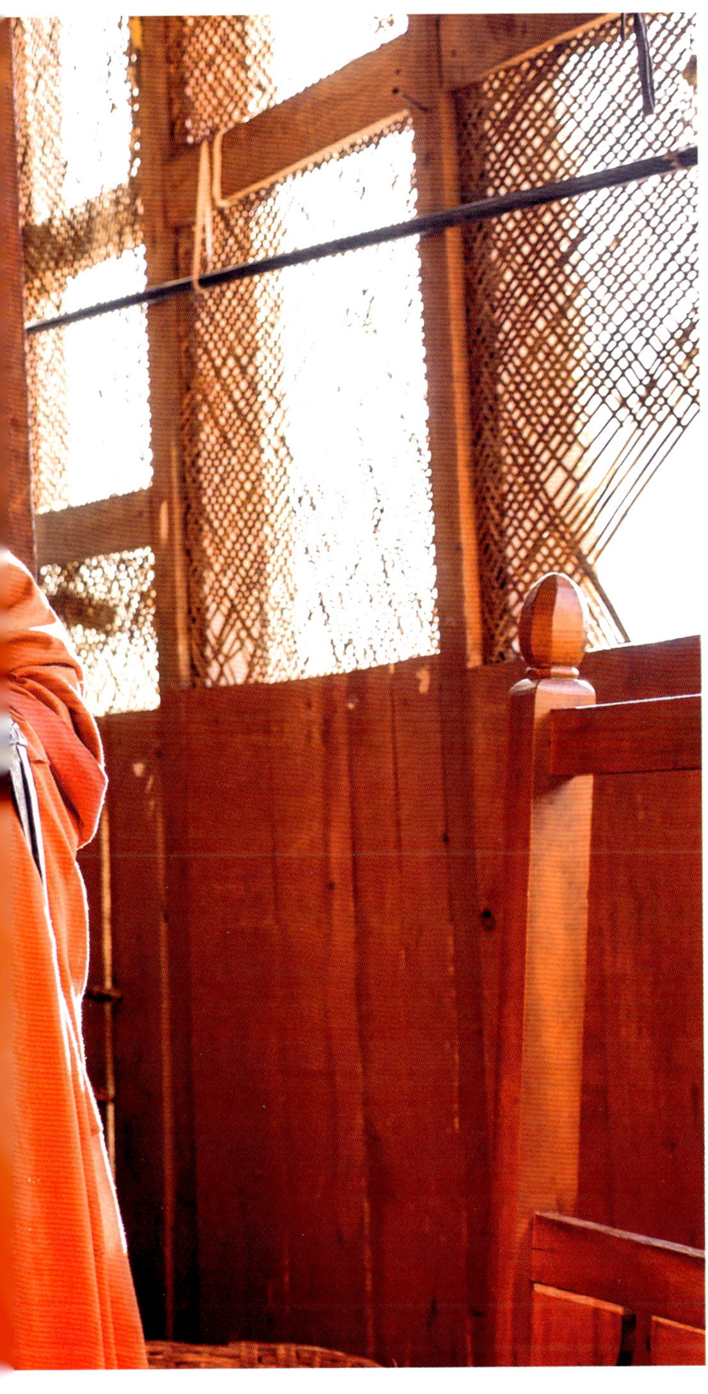

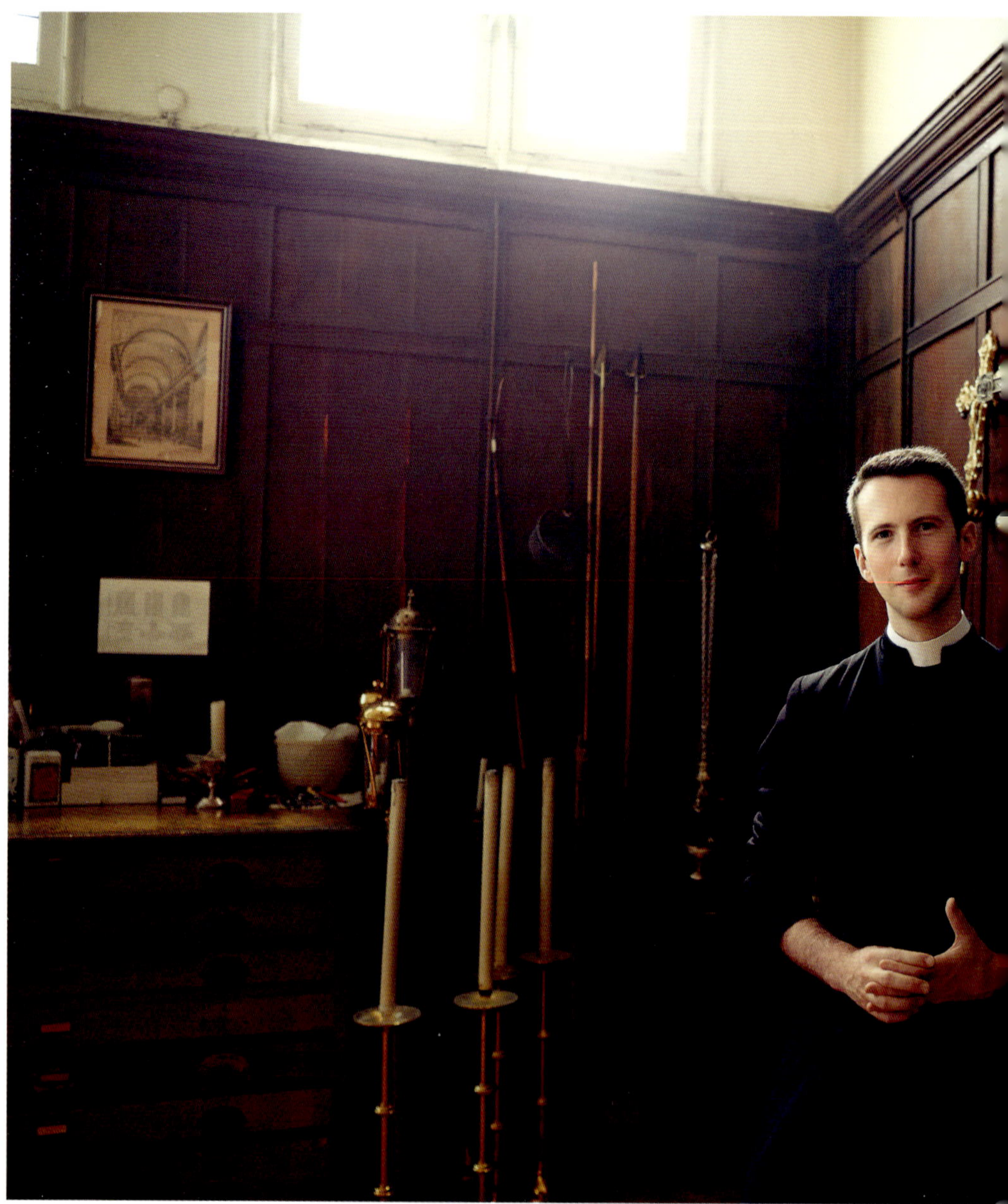

As a military chaplain, Christopher works with soldiers who have returned from war zones. He helps them to process and understand their experiences: to make peace with the past, and their communities.

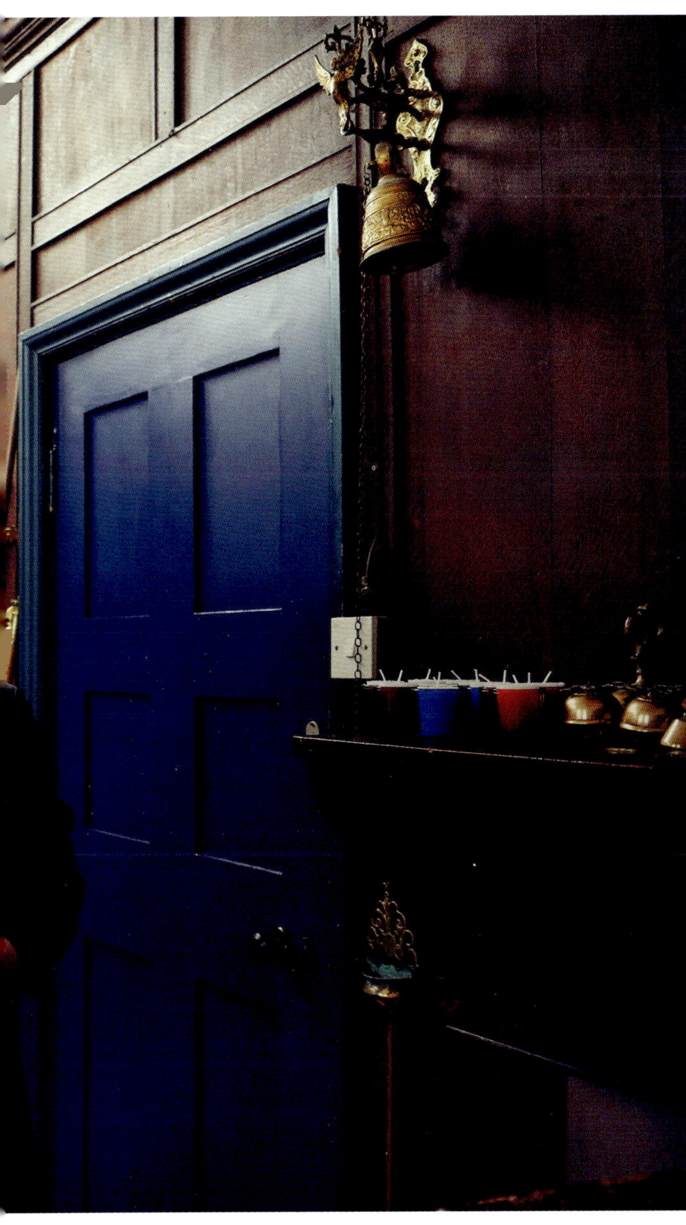

What he said of these veterans is true for all of us, no matter what we've been through: "If you keep sweeping things under the carpet, sooner or later you're going to trip on it."

The Rev. Christopher Trundle Anglican Priest > London, England

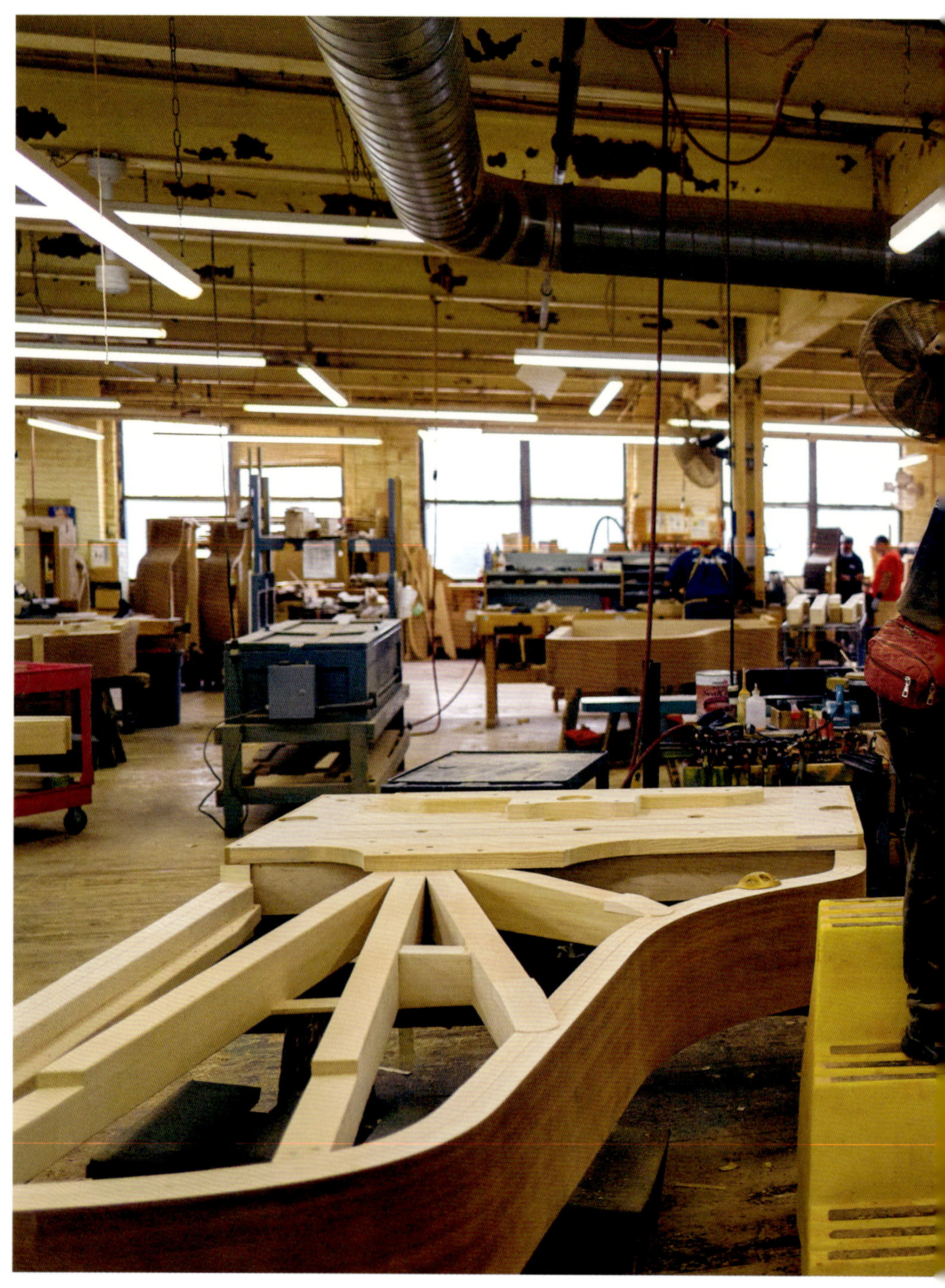

Prenta Liucovic Piano Craftsman, Steinway & Sons > Astoria, New York

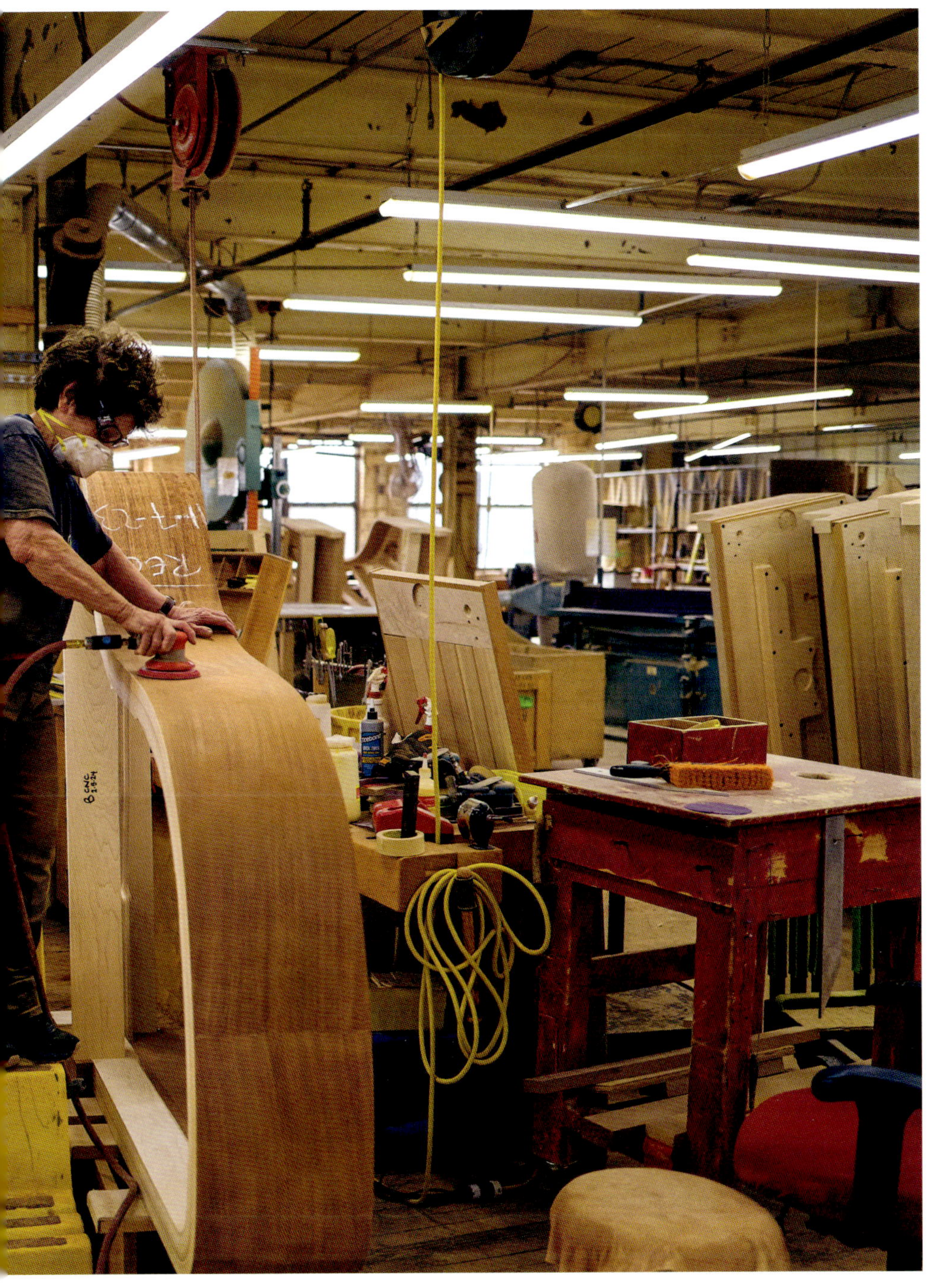

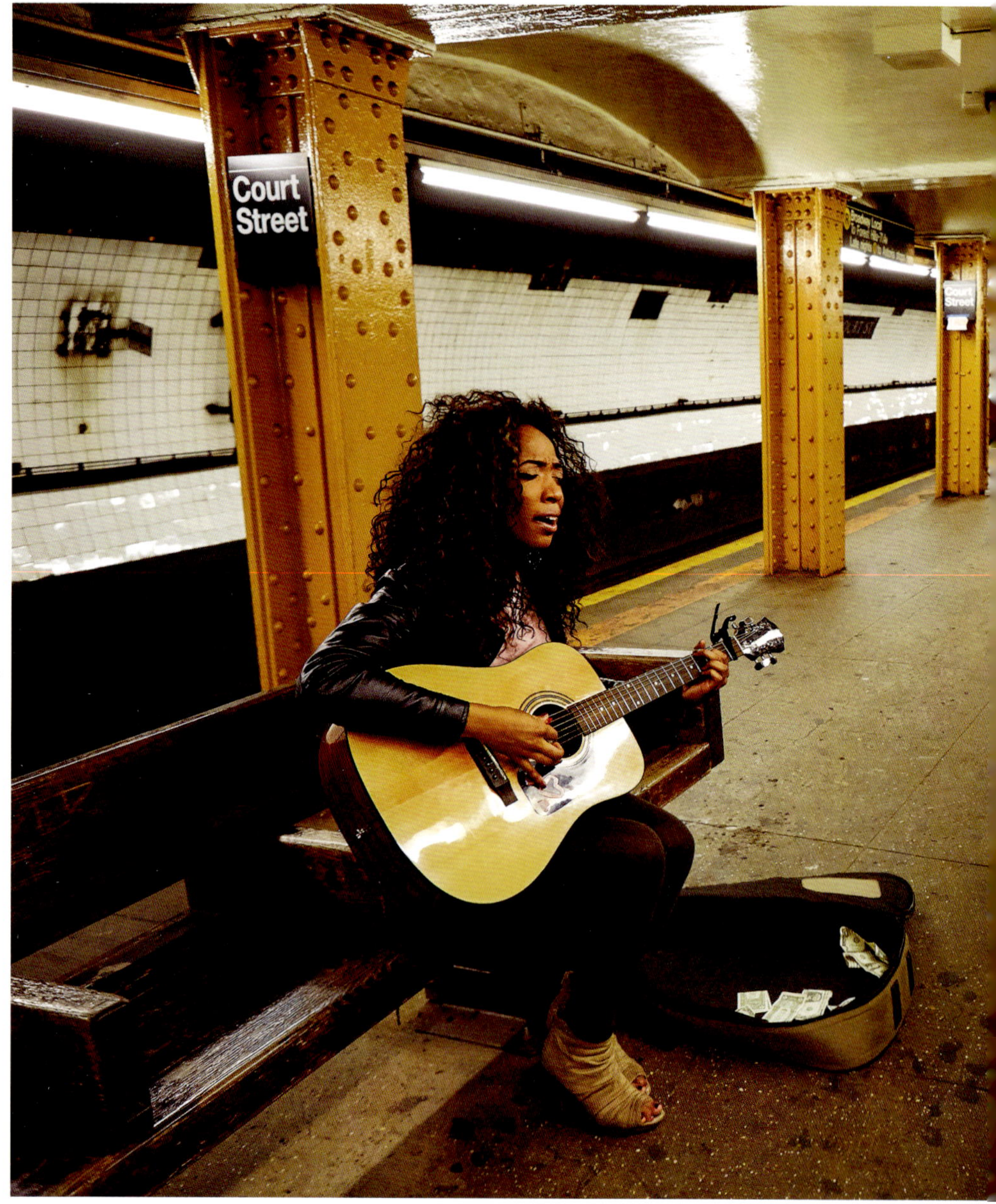

I got off the train at Court Street, and followed the sound of a beautiful voice coming from the other end of the empty platform.

There was Najah. By herself. With just her gift, her guitar, and her dream. Singing a song

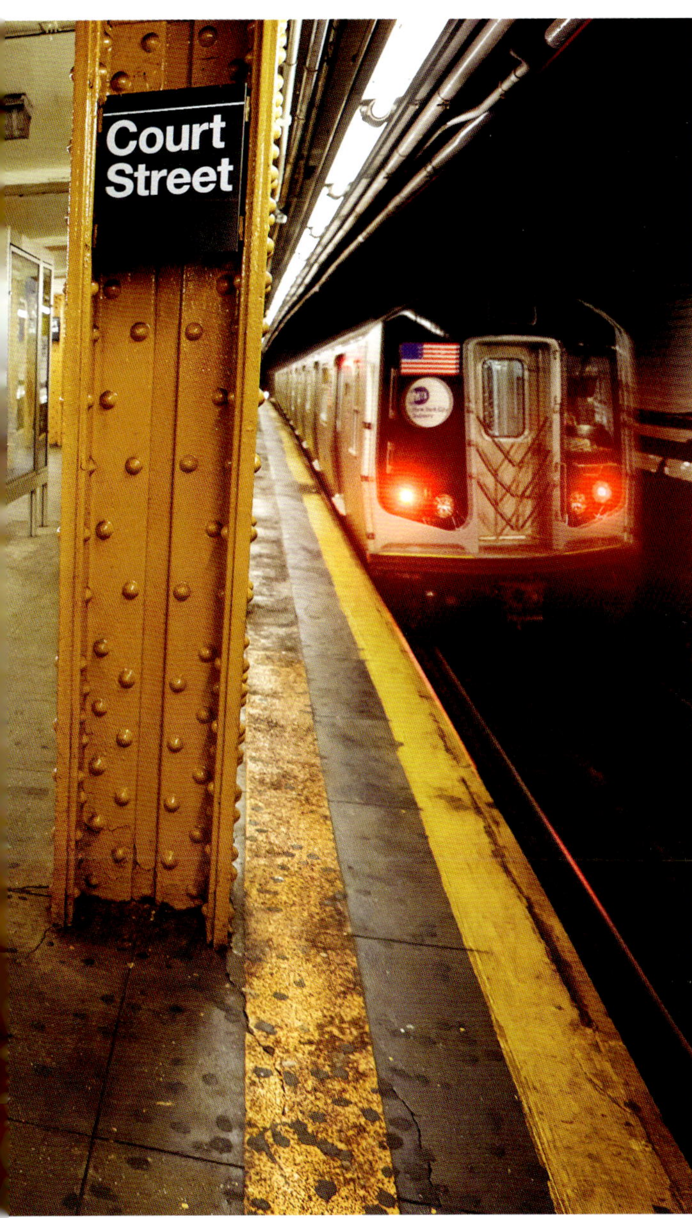

she'd written. I thought of my daughter. A dancer with her own gift, and her own dream.
   "Don't worry about the audience," I tell her. "You just stay true to yourself."
I created this image, and this whole book, to remind her of that.

Najah Lewis Singer > New York, New York

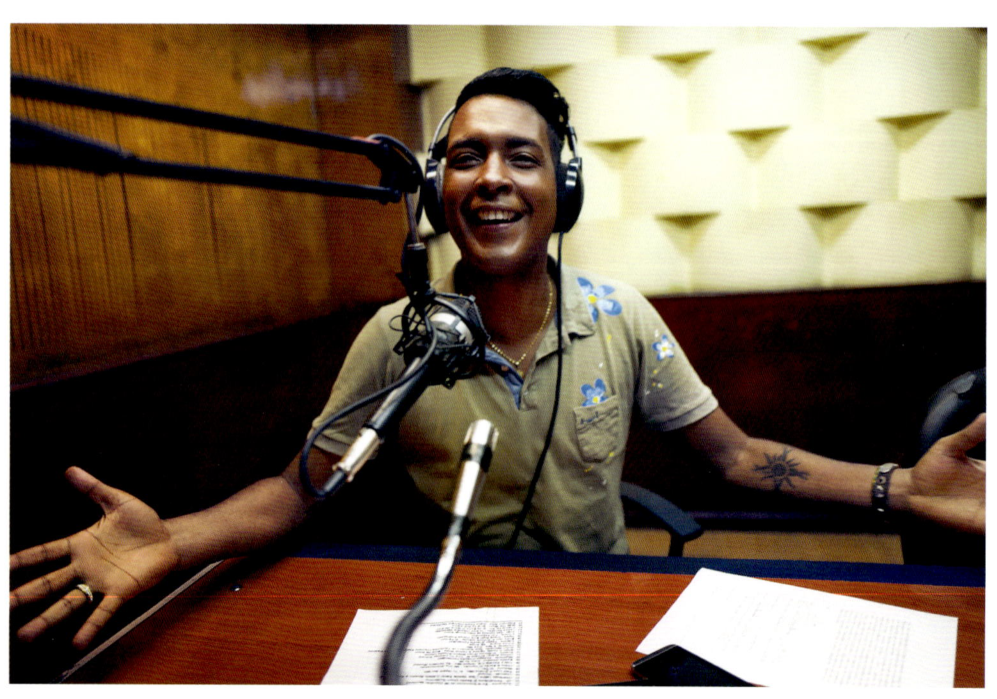

Francisco Abel Radio DJ > Havana, Cuba

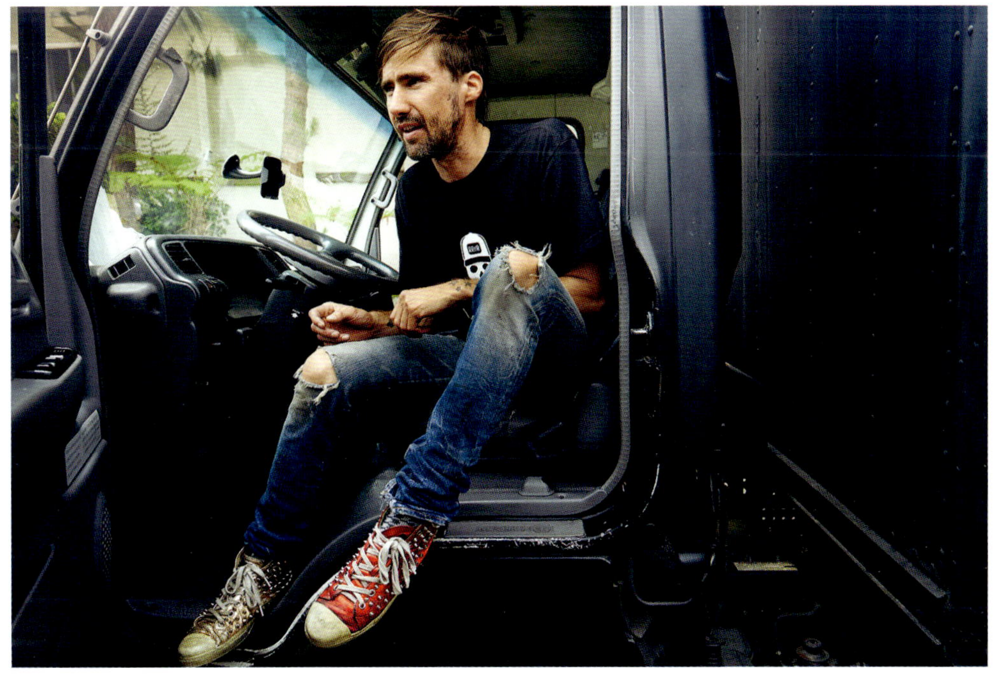

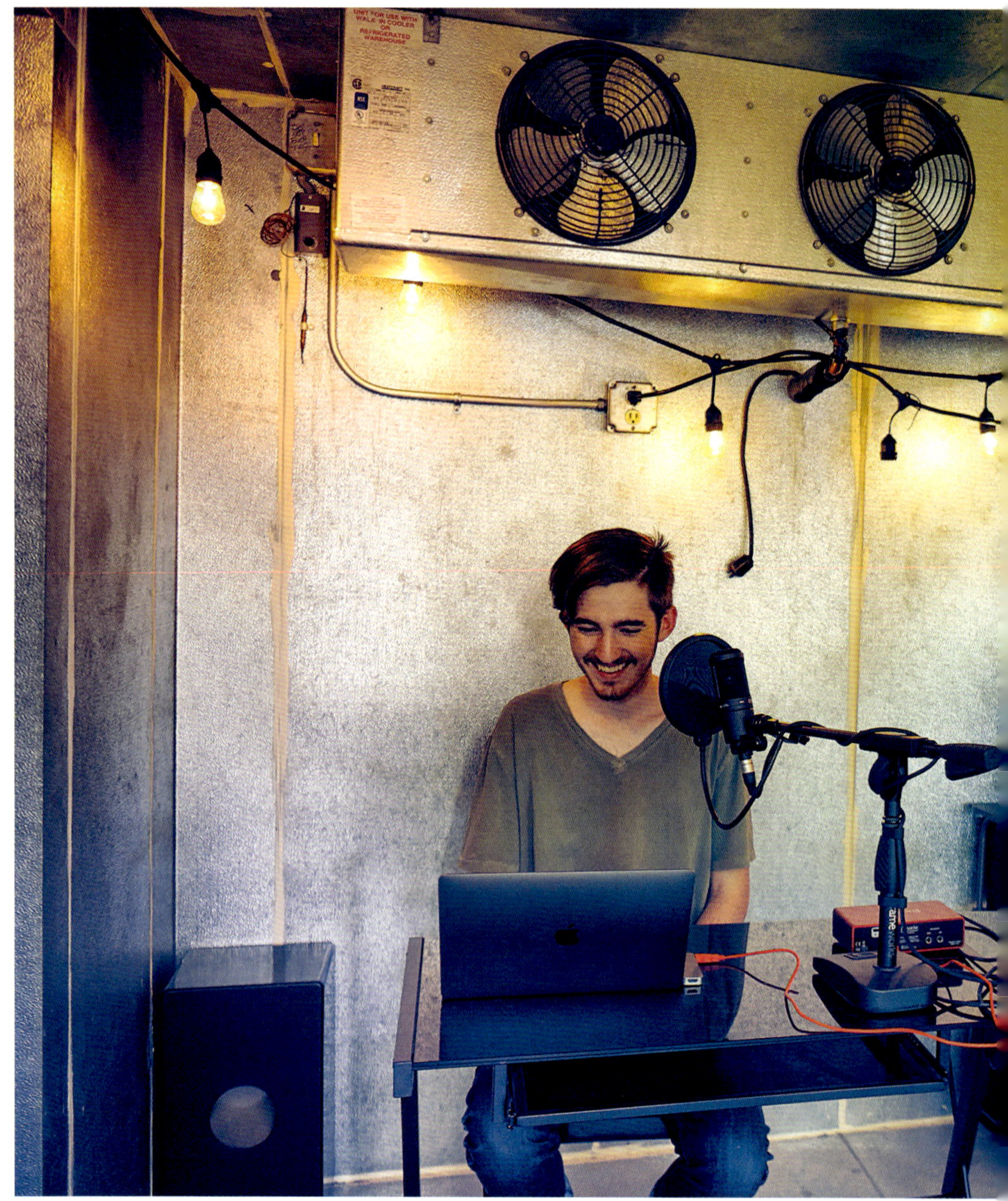

Driving through Nebraska, I craved coffee. A web search led me to a gas station, which initially seemed to have none. But tucked away inside was a charming coffee shop. The coffee was excellent.

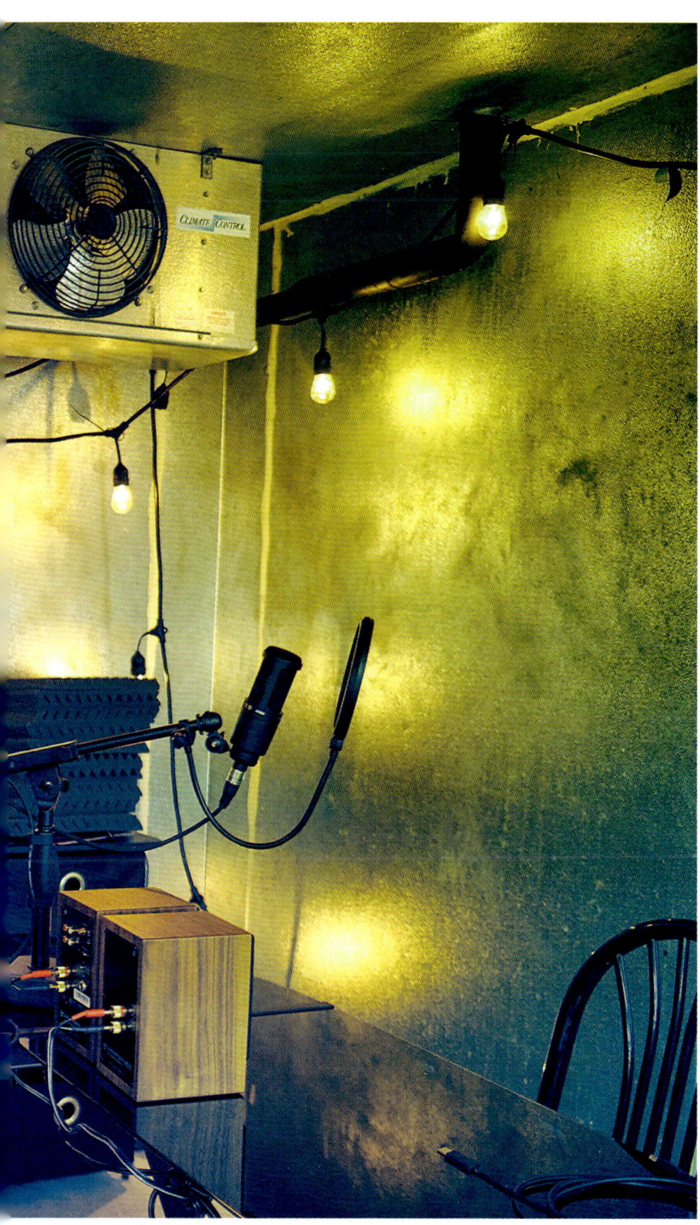

Dawson explained it was his family's gas station. He'd started the coffee shop, wanting to create an alternative to the big chains. Hearing about my *At Work* project, he led me to some coolers. Now transformed into a podcast studio.

Sometimes you just have to keep digging.

Dawson Schrader Owner, Vena Amoris > Lincoln, Nebraska

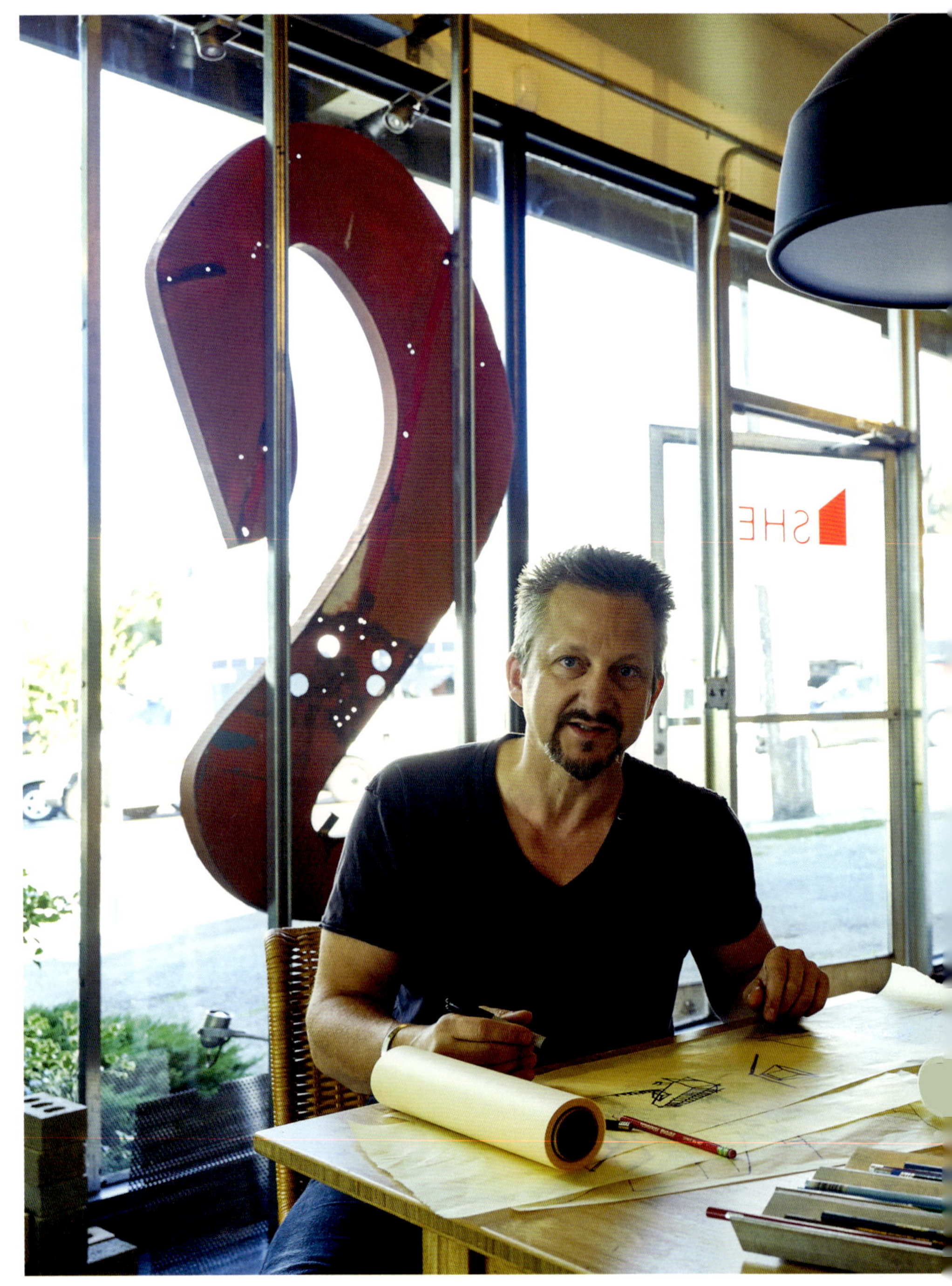

Prentis Hale & Thomas Schaer Architects, Shed Built > Seattle, Washington

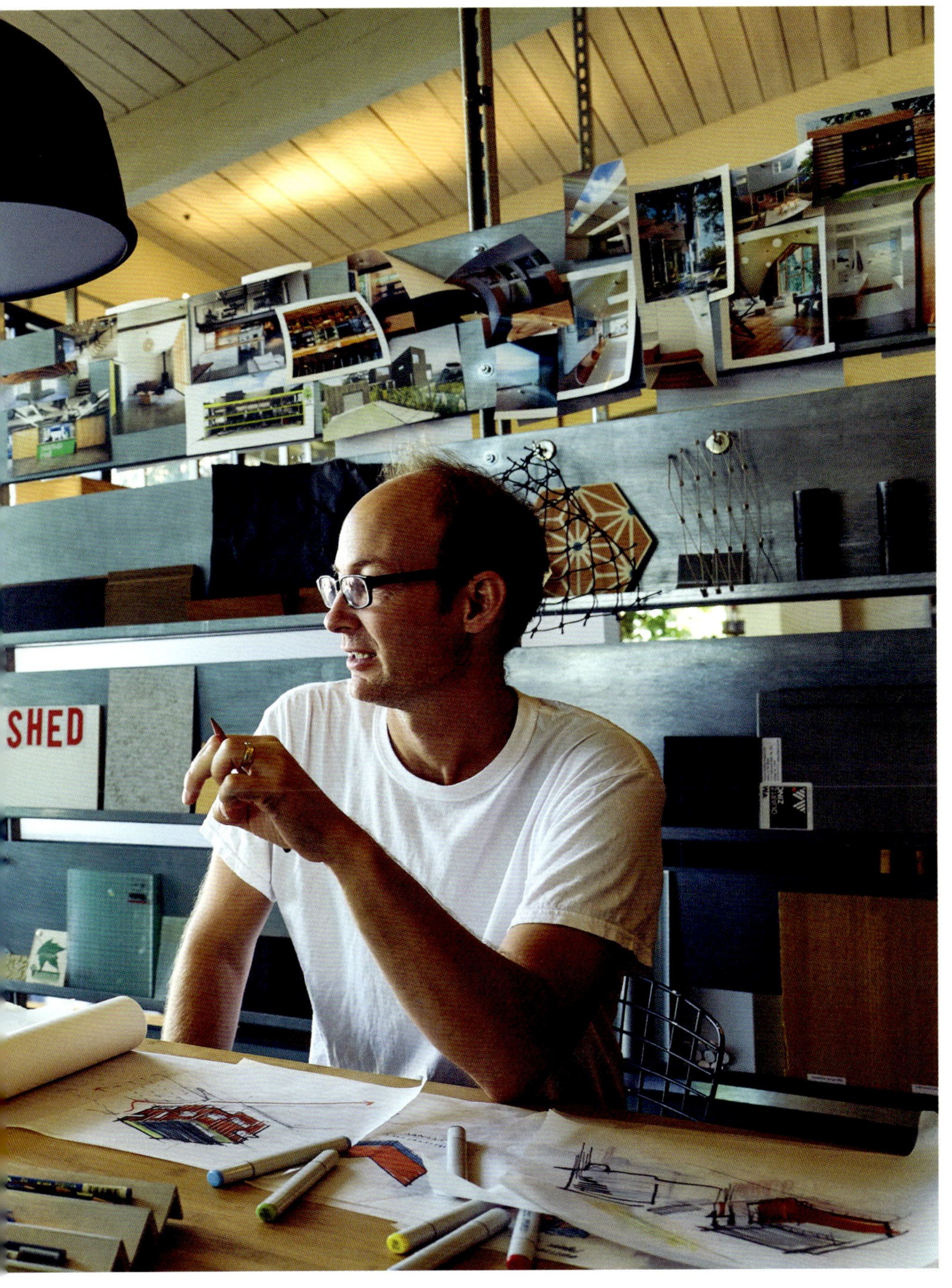

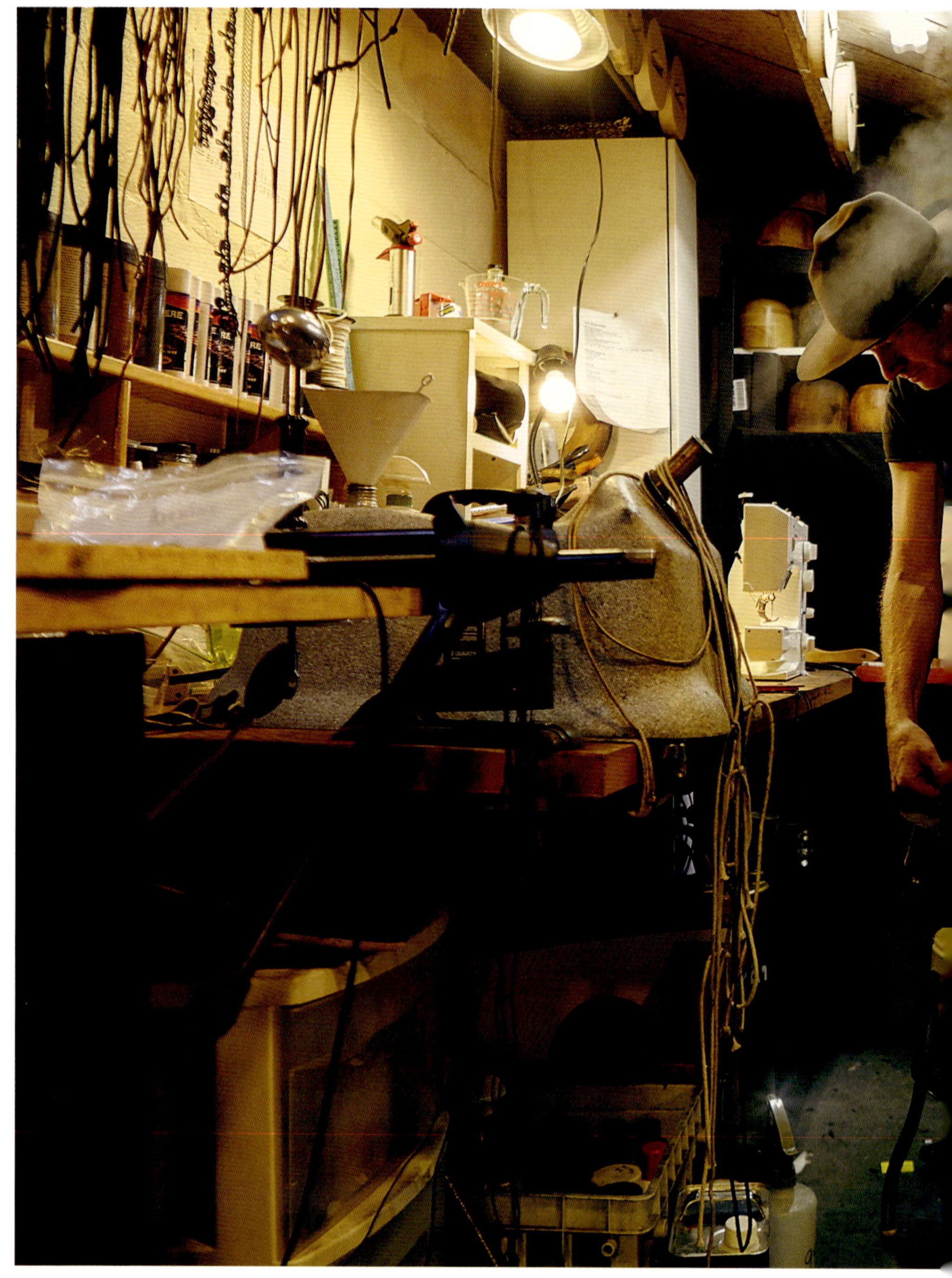
Todd Fink Hat Maker, Recapitate > Omaha, Nebraska

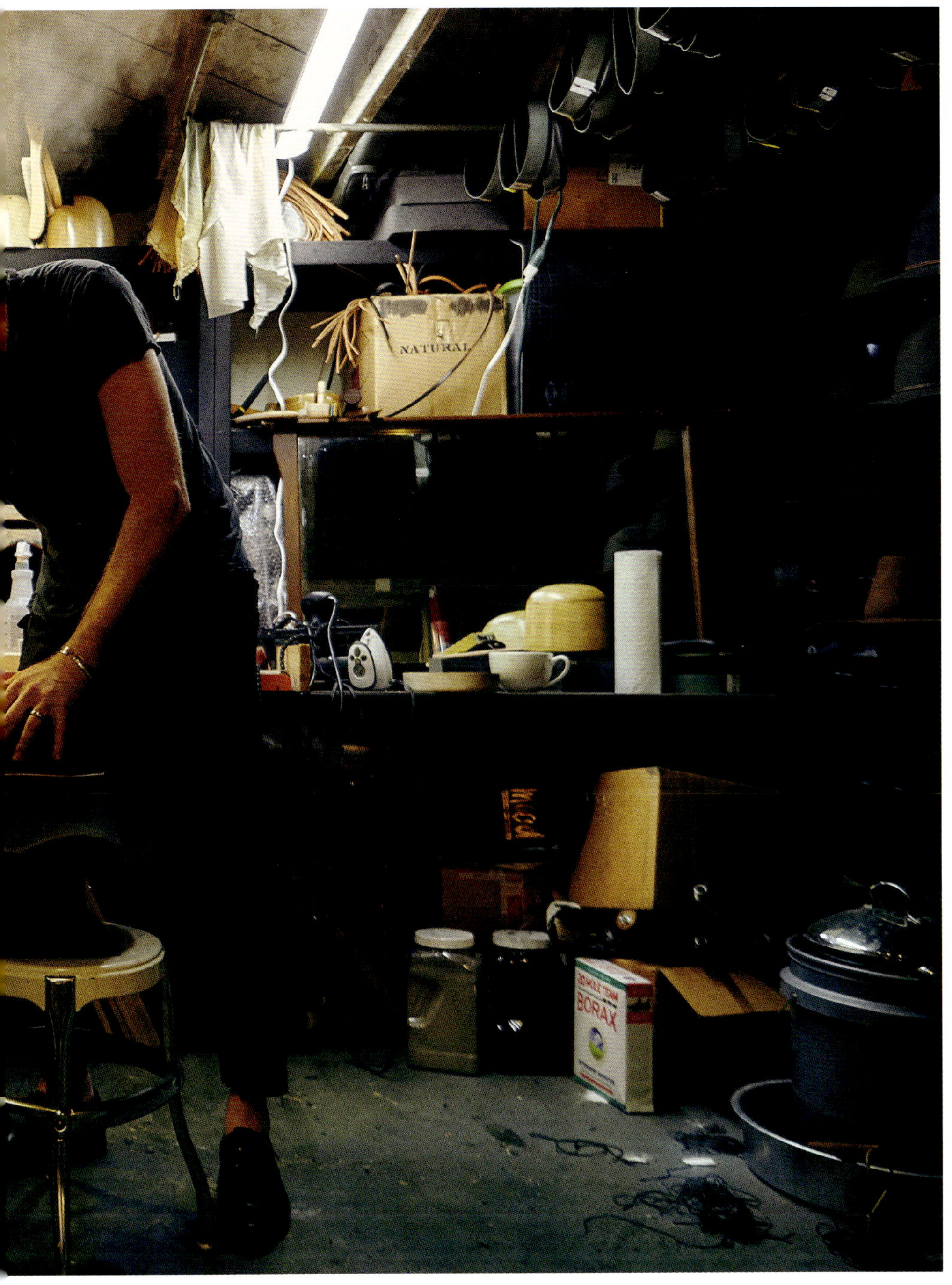

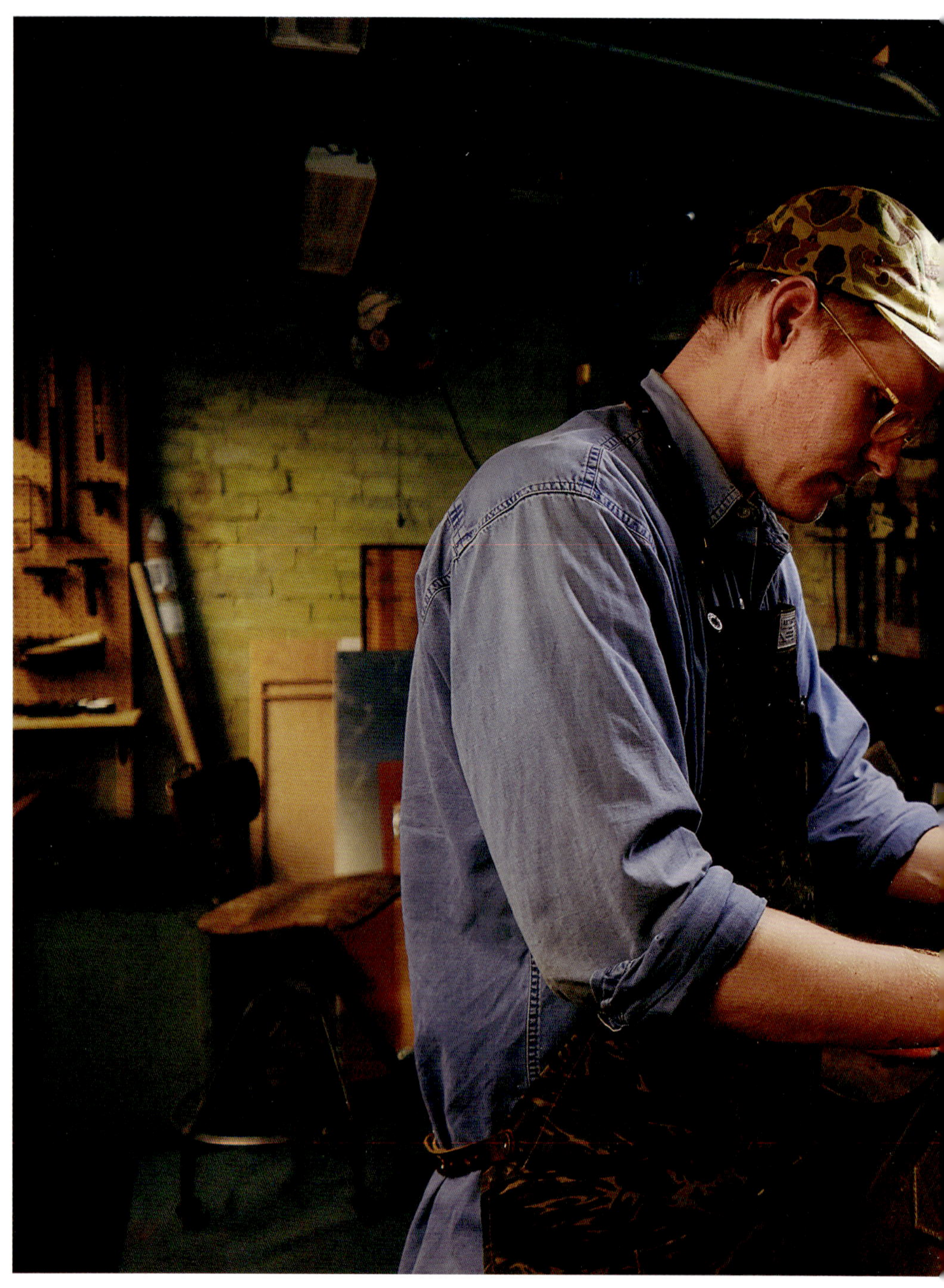

Chris Hughes Designer, Artifact Bags > Omaha, Nebraska

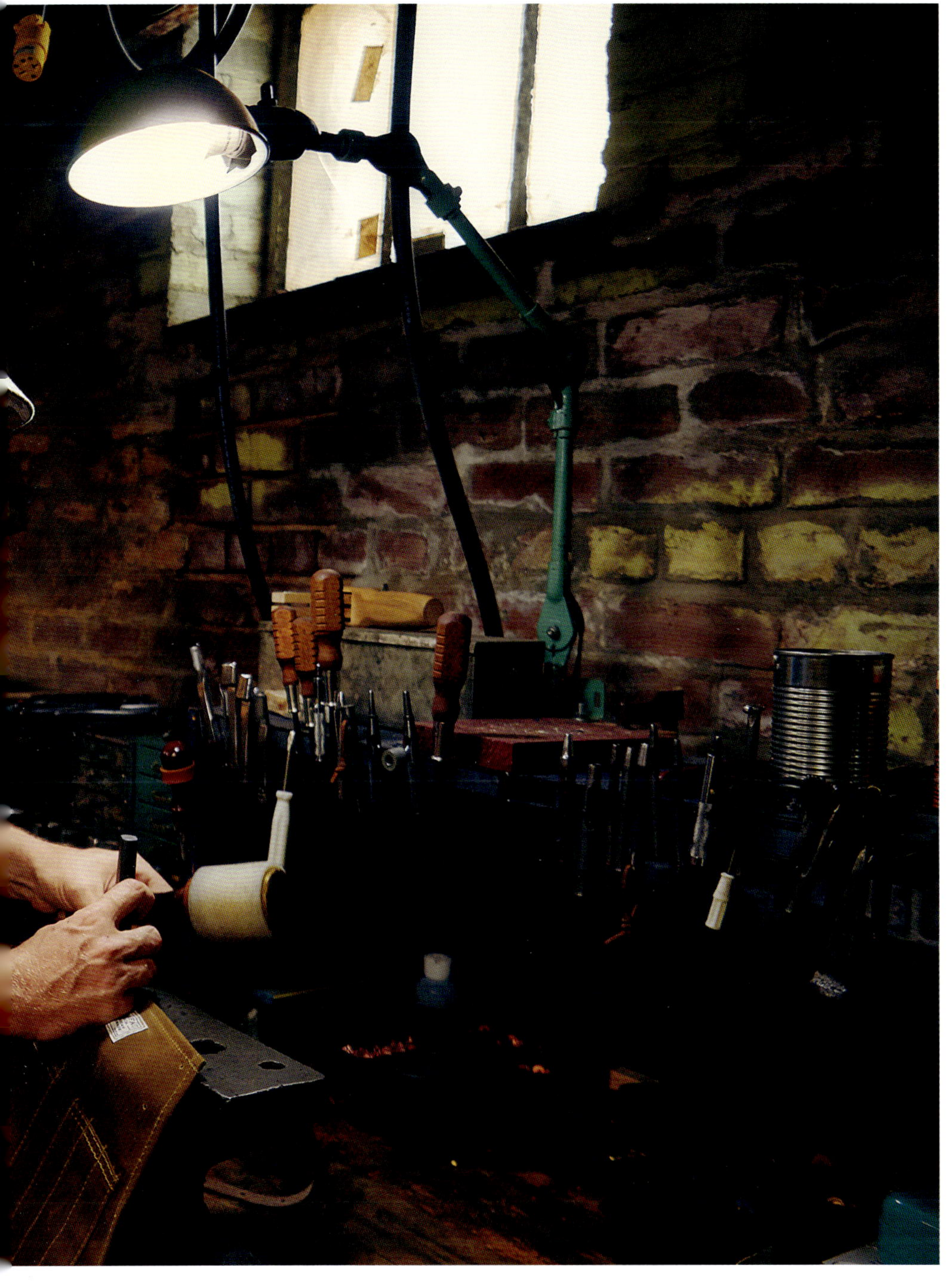

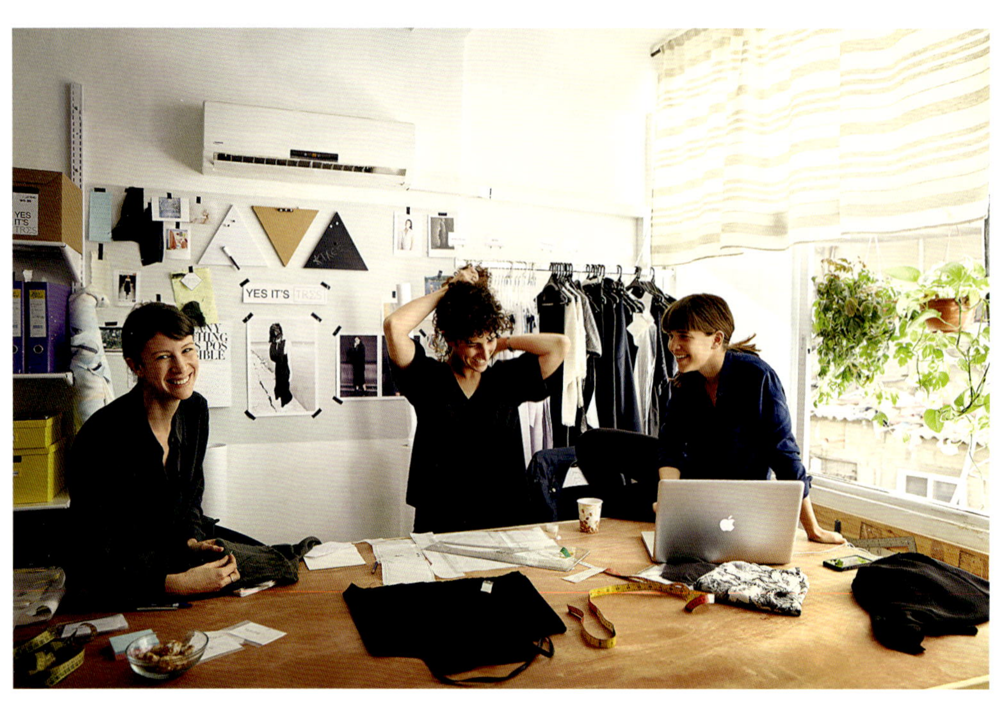

Noa Gur, Dafna Rubin & Noy Goz Tres Fashion Designers > Tel Aviv, Israel

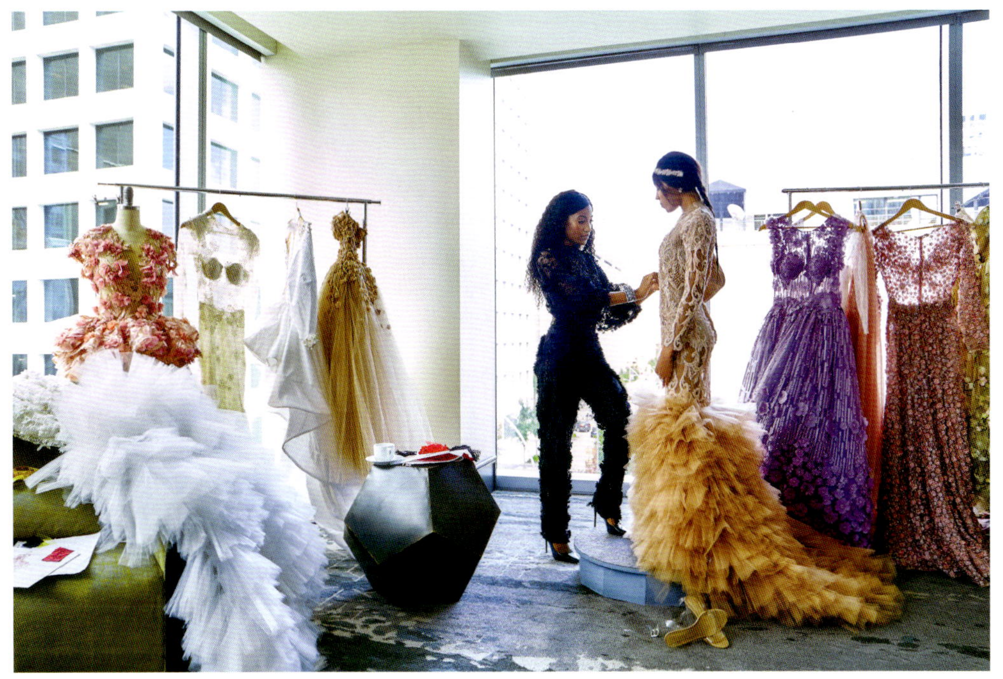

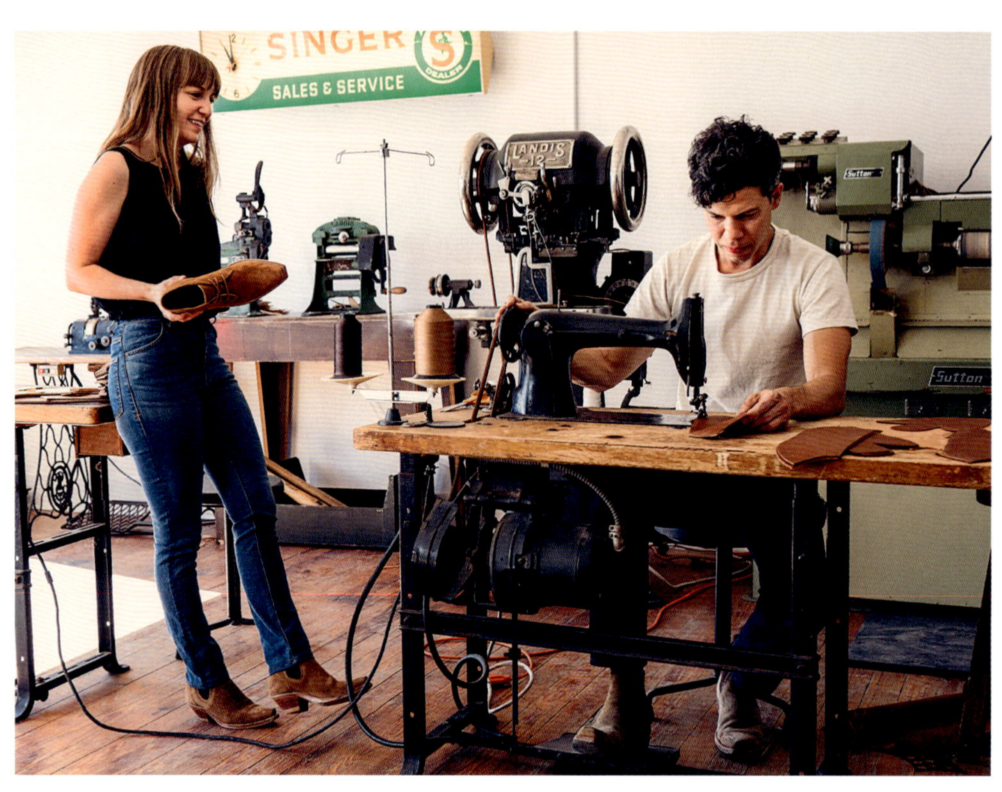

Colt Miller & Logan Caldbeck Shoe and Boot Designers, Cobra Boot > Marfa, Texas

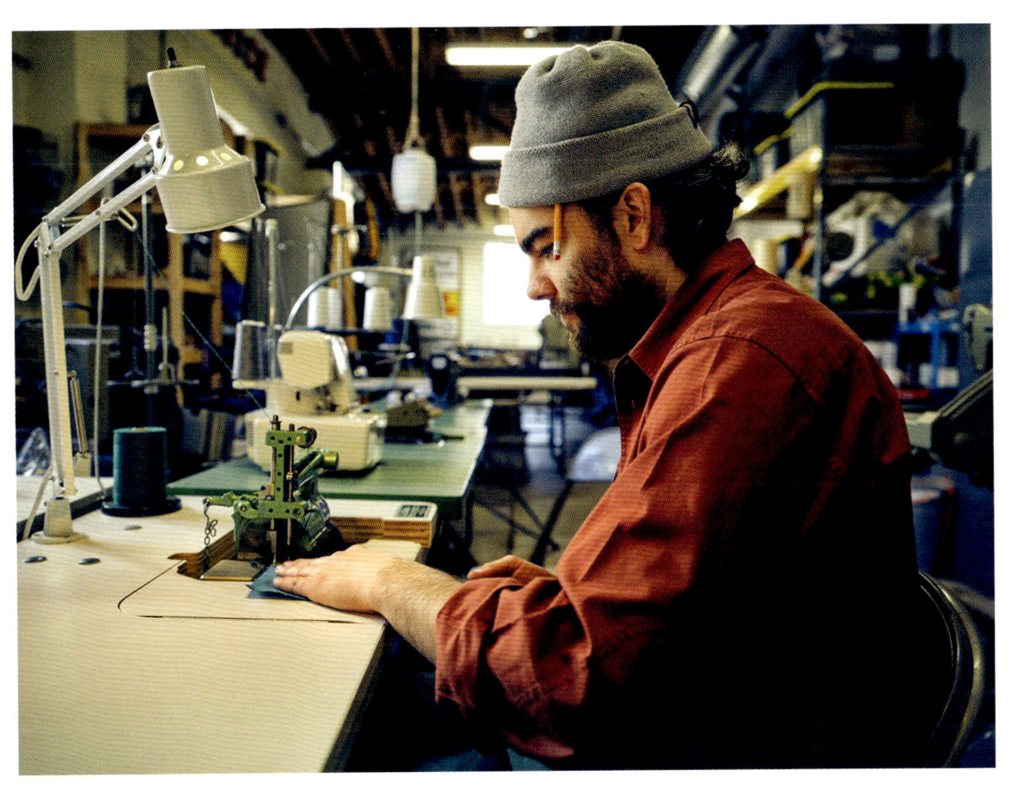

Benjamin Kelly Owner and Designer, Dinosaur Hampton Clothing Store > Minneapolis, Minnesota

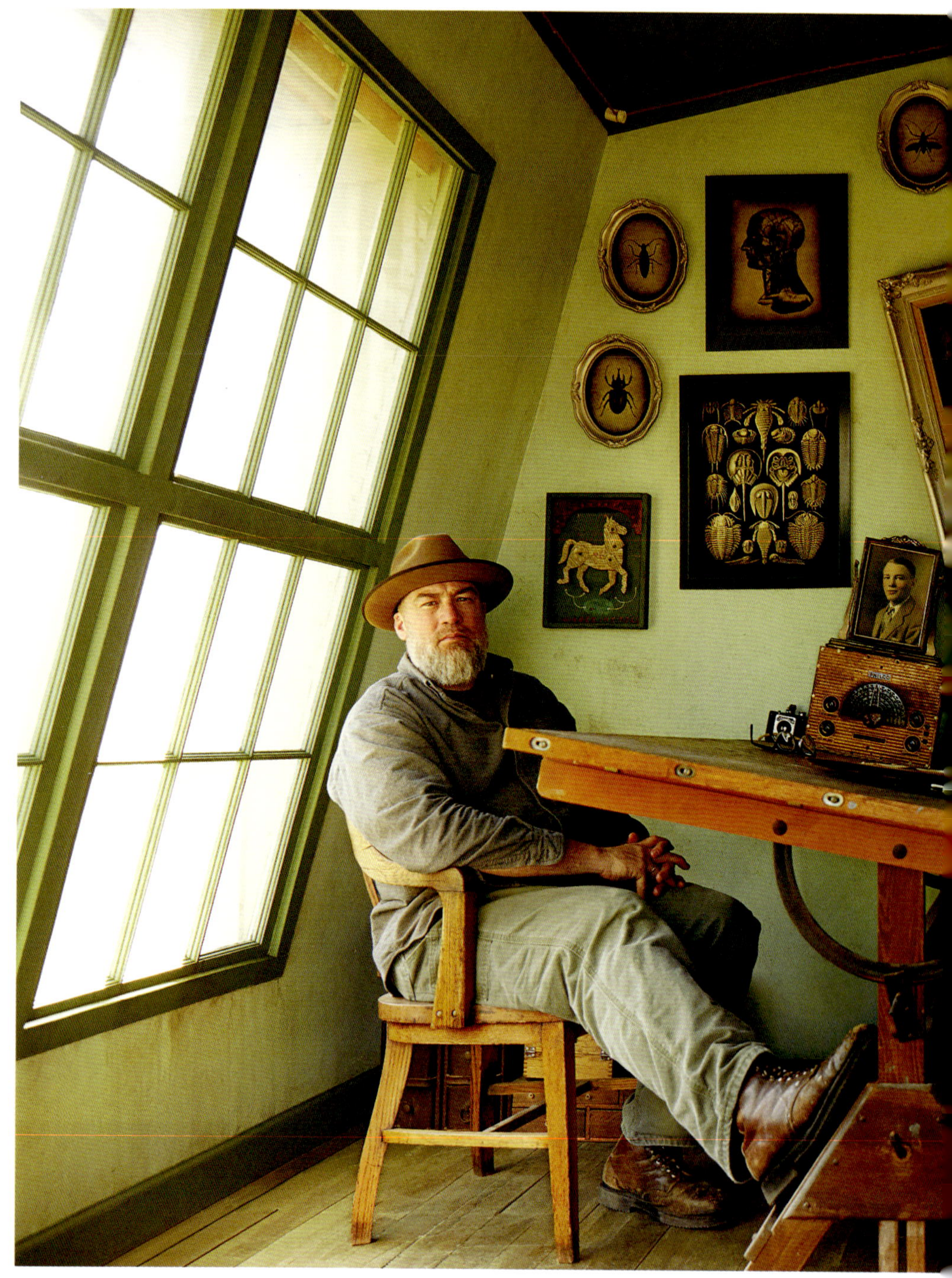

Dan Winters Photographer, Illustrator, Filmmaker, and Writer > Denton County, Texas

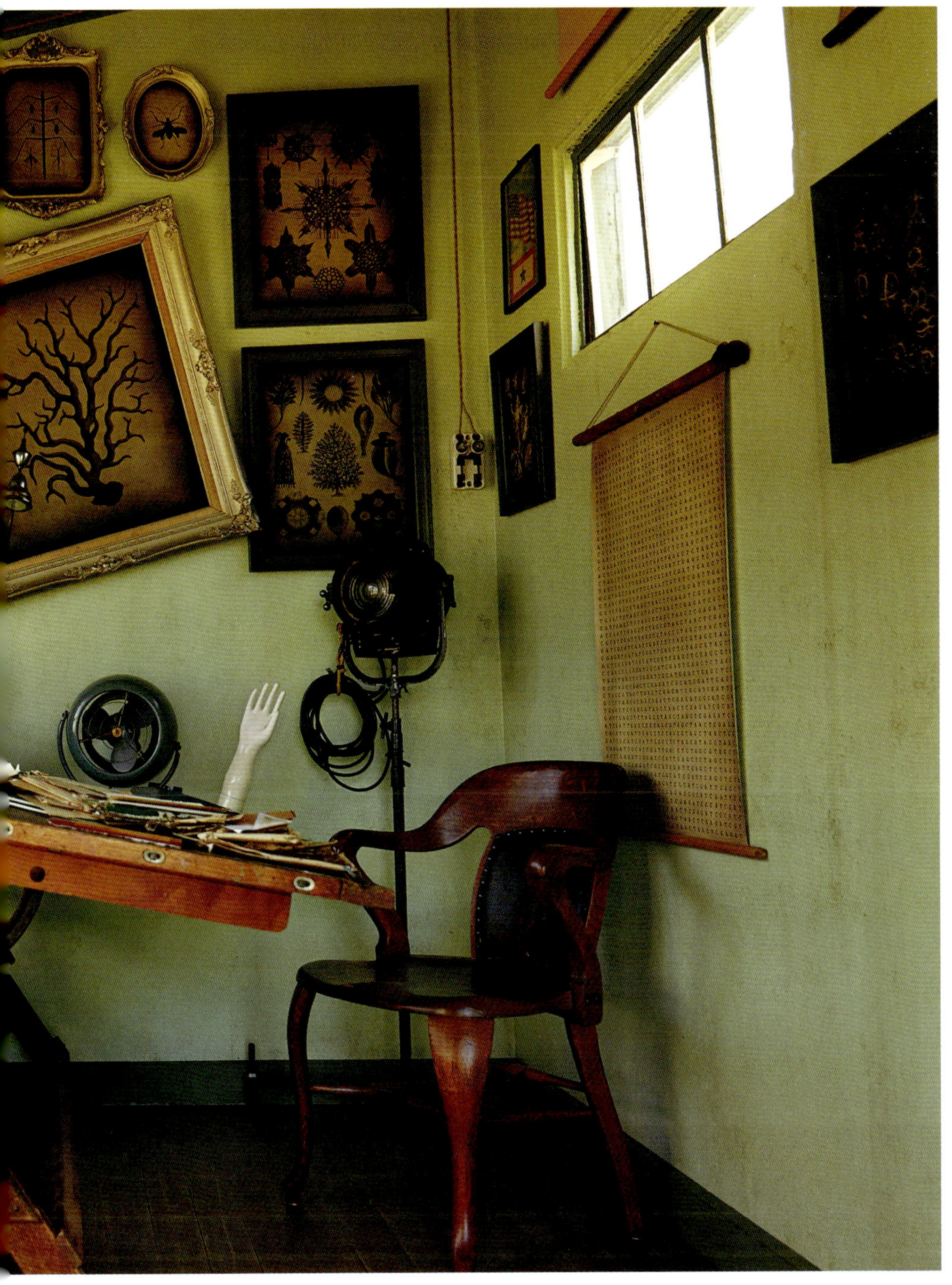

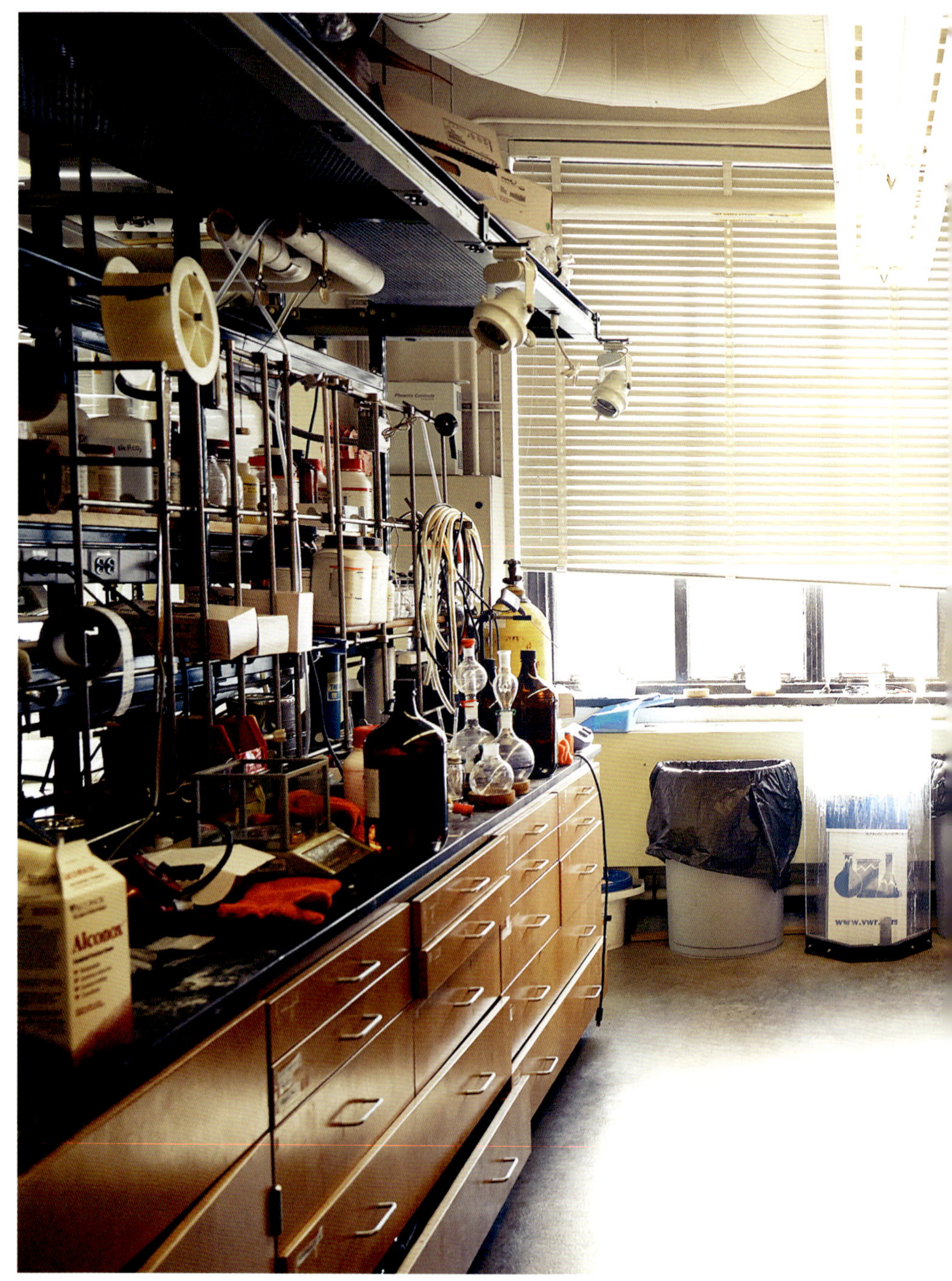

Matthew Cain Post Doc Research Fellow, MIT > Cambridge, Massachusetts

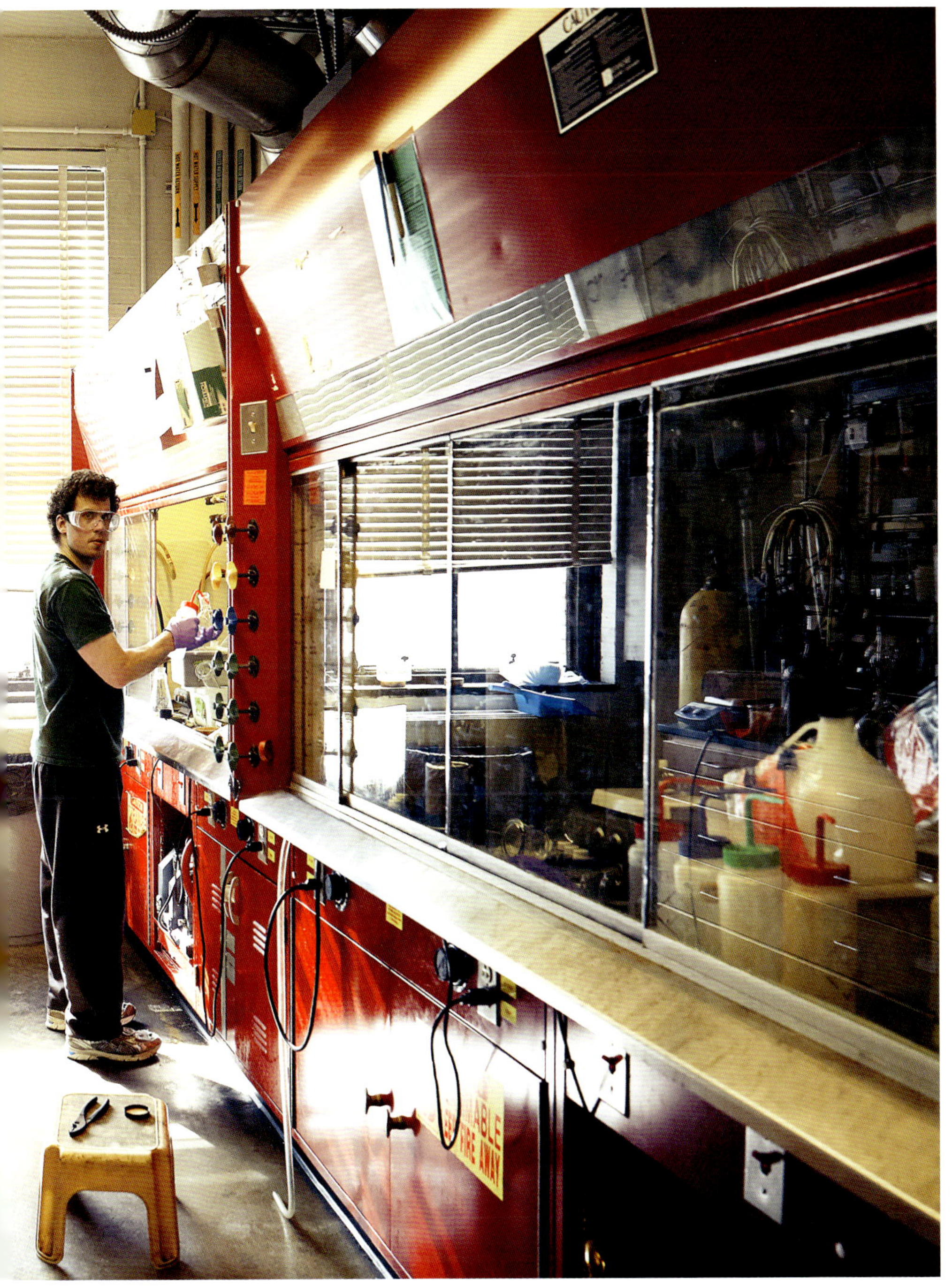

FLAMMABLE
FIRE AWAY

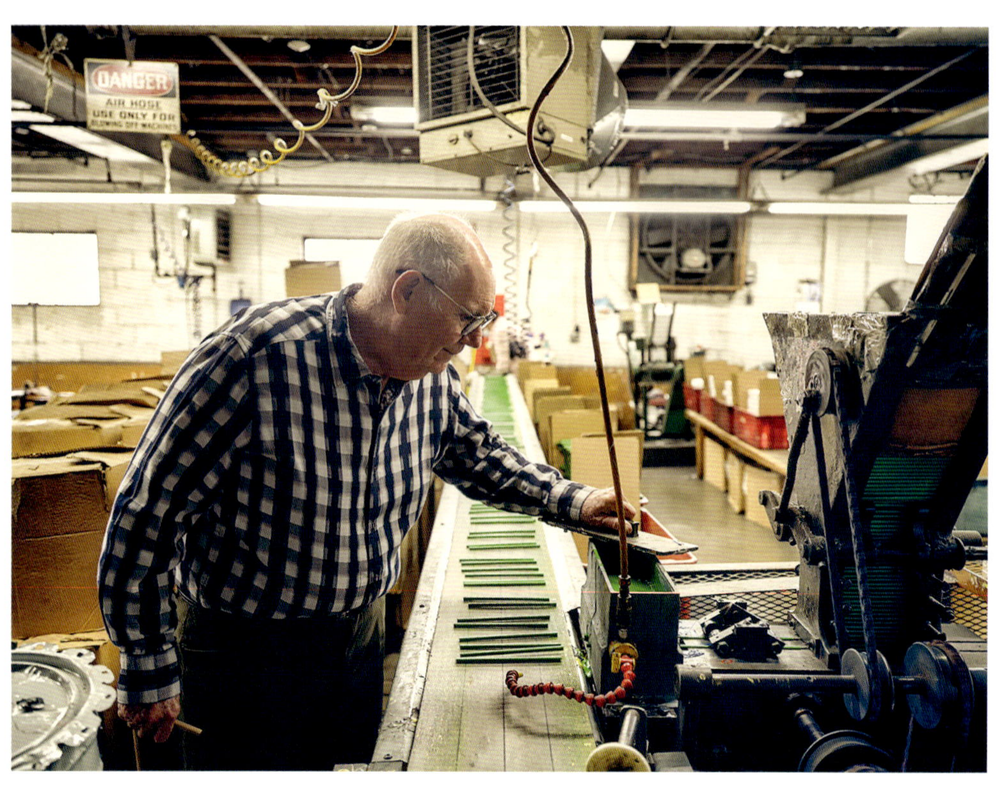

Henry Hulan Musgrave Pencil Company > Shelbyville, Tennessee

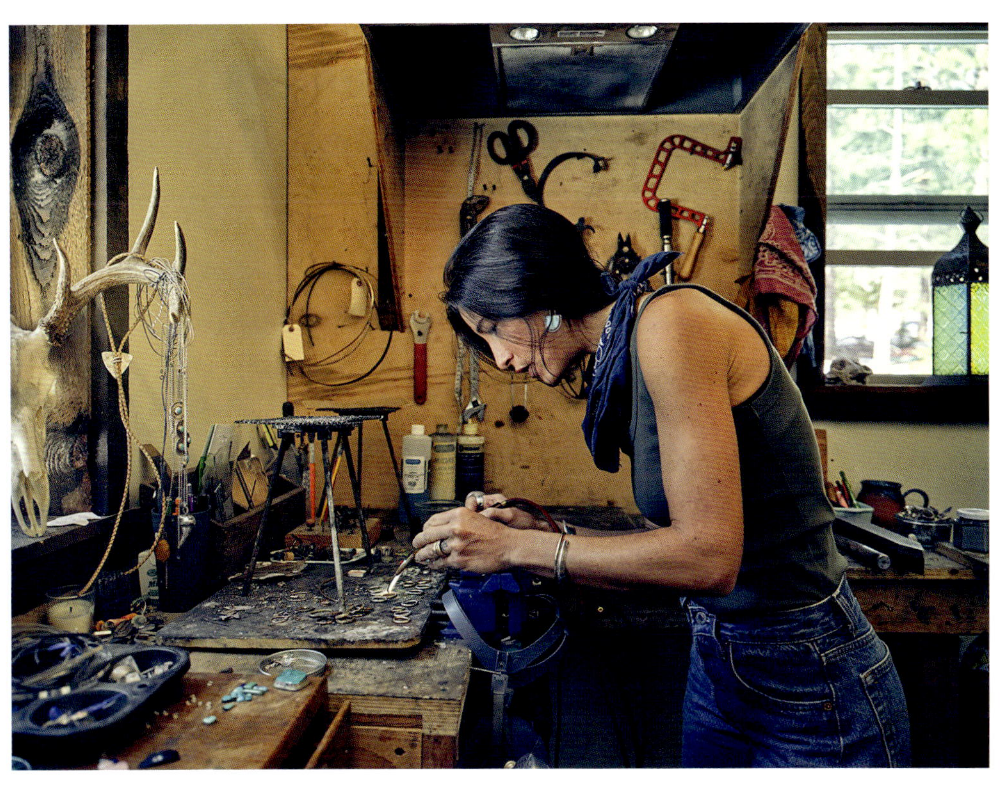

Jessica Lewis Jewelry Designer, Ruby & Revolver > Missoula, Montana

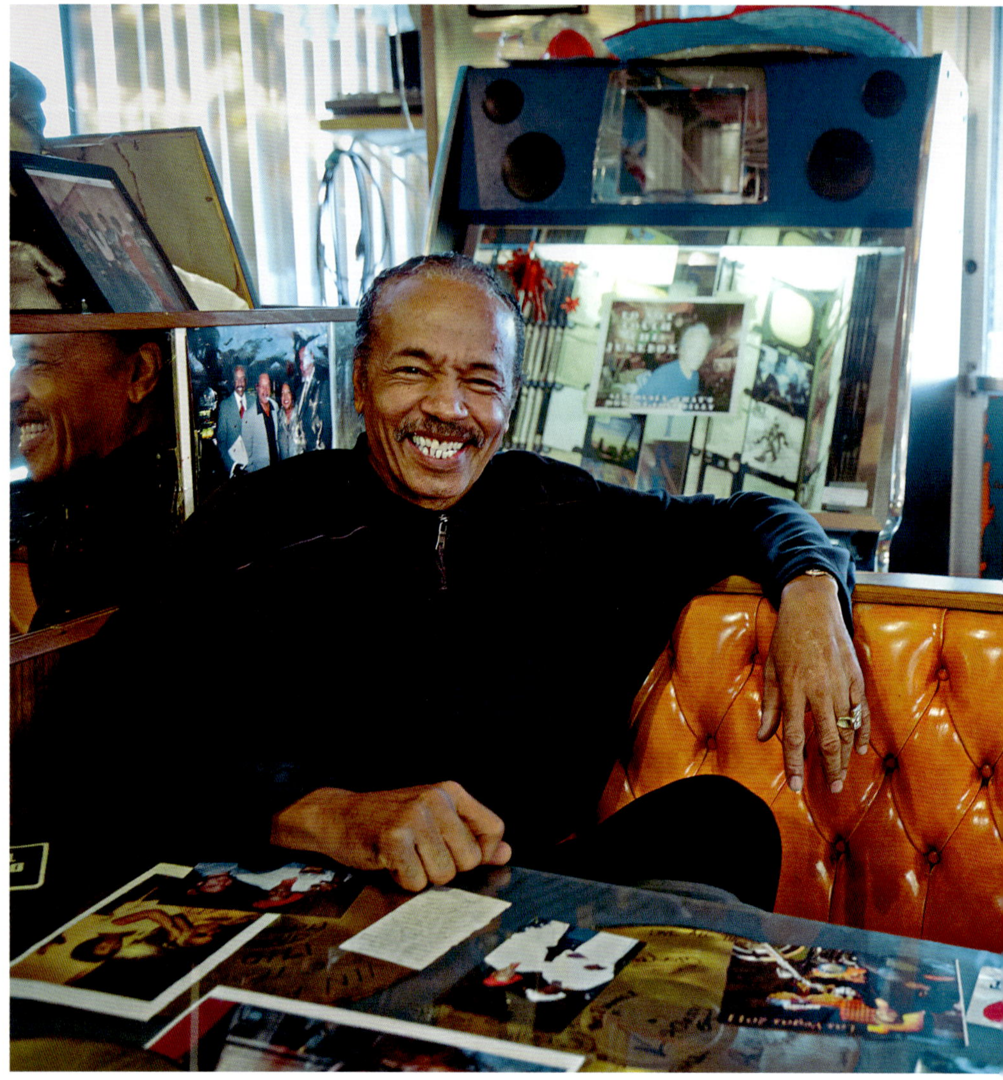

Larry's pretty famous in Detroit. D'Mongo's Speakeasy is an institution that attracts people from all over. Folks come in for a drink, but more importantly, to talk.
To connect with each other.

I could tell that for Larry, I was yet another photographer there to take a picture of him for a magazine.

We sat at a table across from each other, getting acquainted. I mentioned something about being from Brooklyn.

"You're Jewish?" he asked.

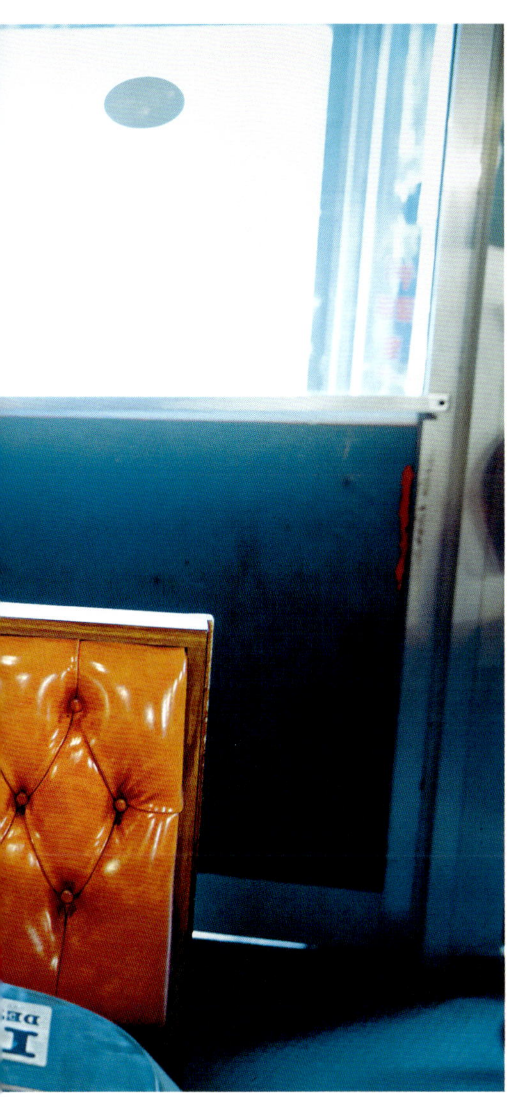

And with that, we went from just chatting to talking. He told me that growing up,
he had learned something important from his Jewish neighbors: Holocaust survivors,
as were my own family. They turned out to be kindred spirits — like him, persecuted for
something that they couldn't control.

He gravitated towards them, he said, because of their resilience. They showed him
that he didn't have to be a victim.

Given all that, it made a kind of sense that he was able to create a place that made
people feel welcome, no matter who they were.

Larry Mongo Owner, D'Mongo's Speakeasy > Detroit, Michigan

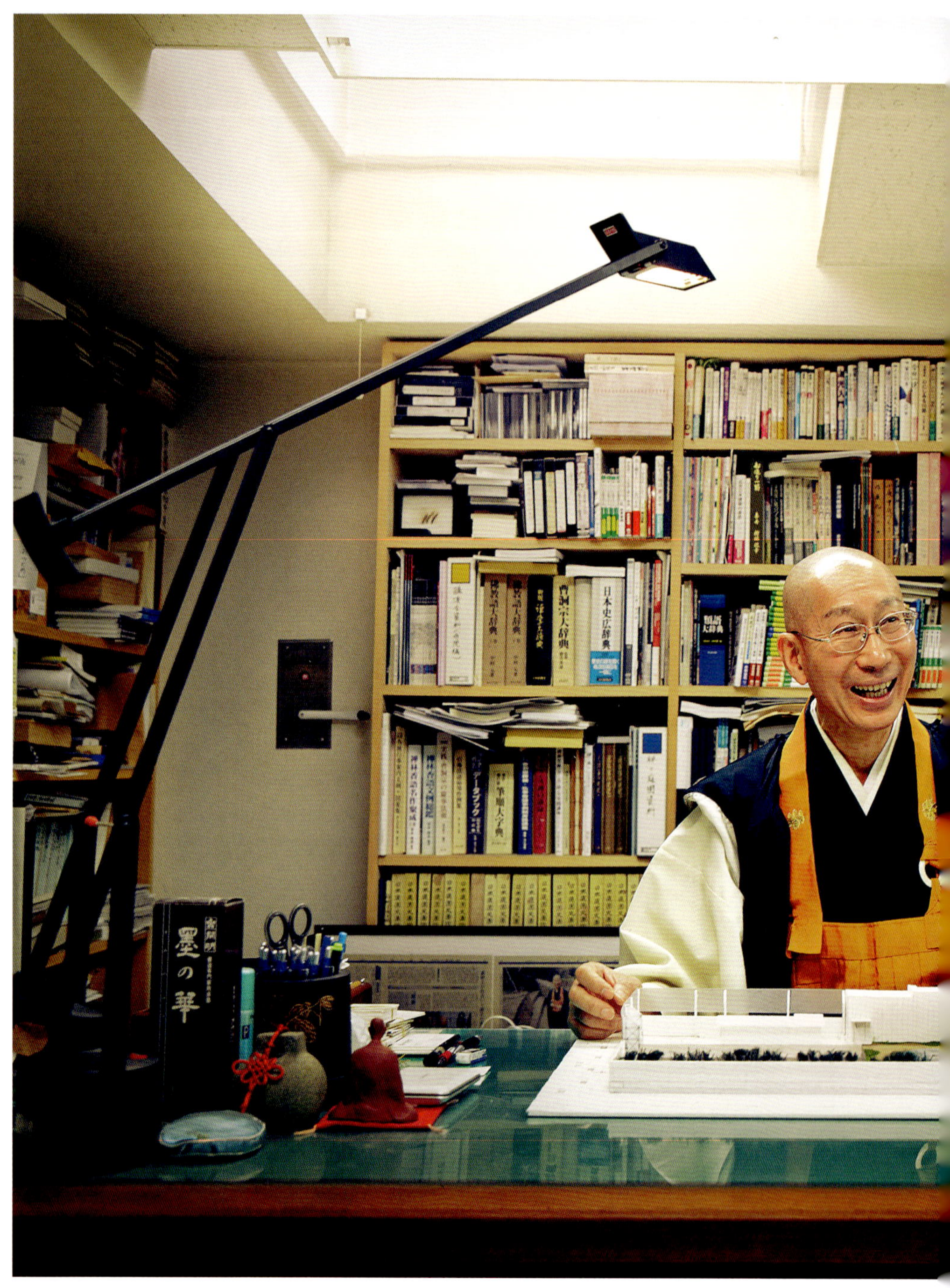

Monk Shunmyo Masuno Zen Priest > Tokyo, Japan

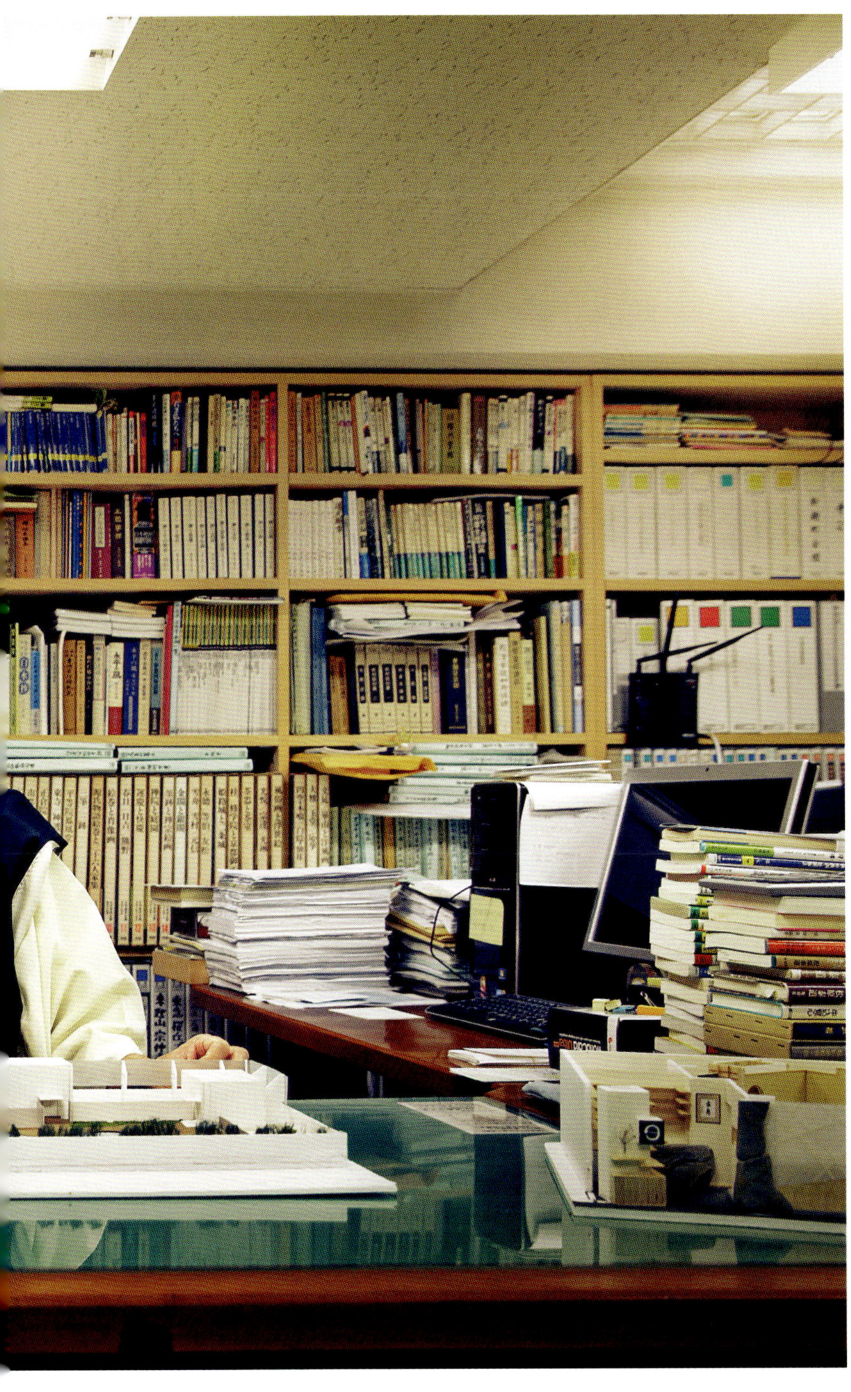

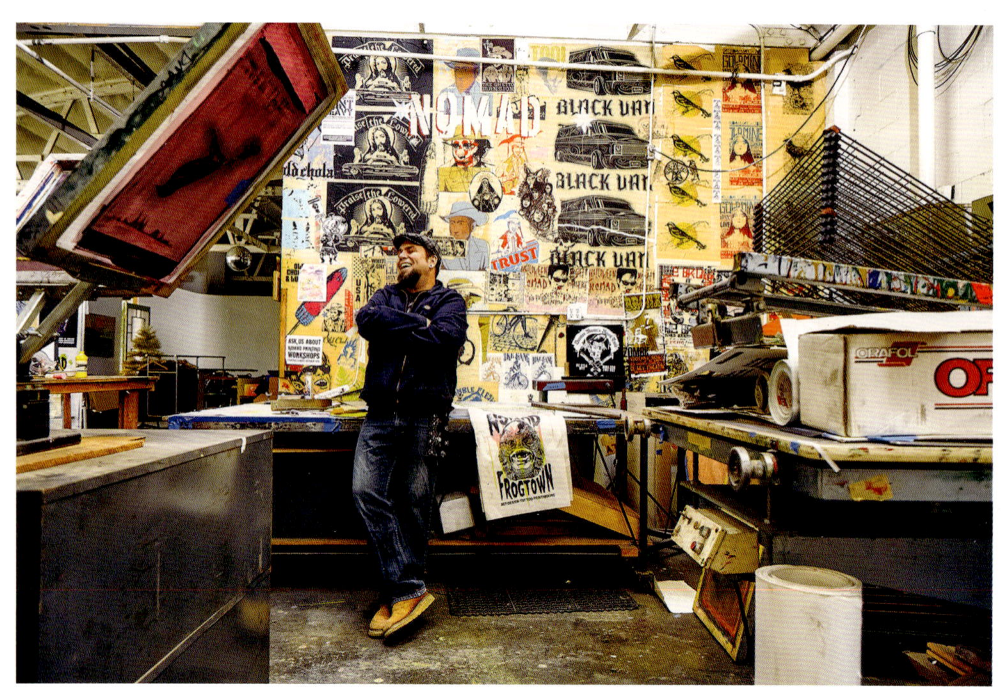

Damon Robinson Printmaker and Founder, NOMAD Art Compound > Los Angeles, California

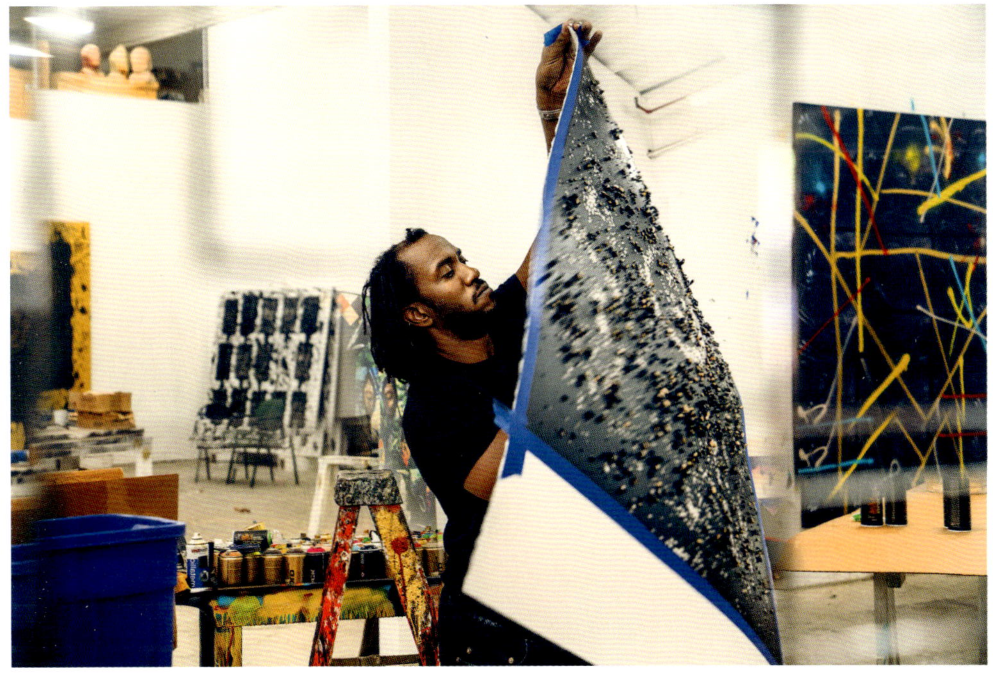

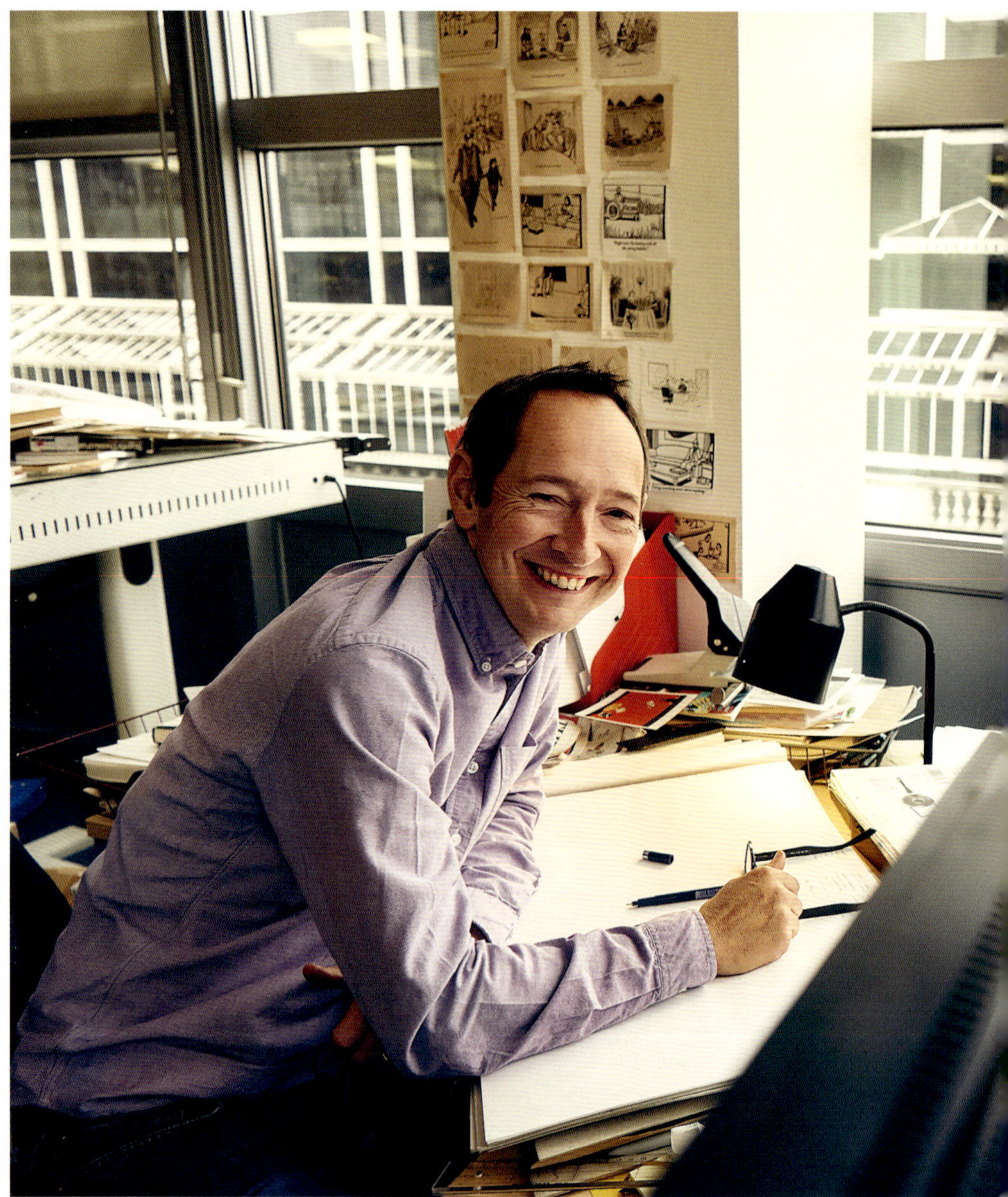

When Matt had his first cartoon published in *The Telegraph*, the man in charge of that page had been away from the office. When he came back the following Monday, he blew up the cartoon onto an enormous piece of paper. He hung it over Matt's desk, writing on it,

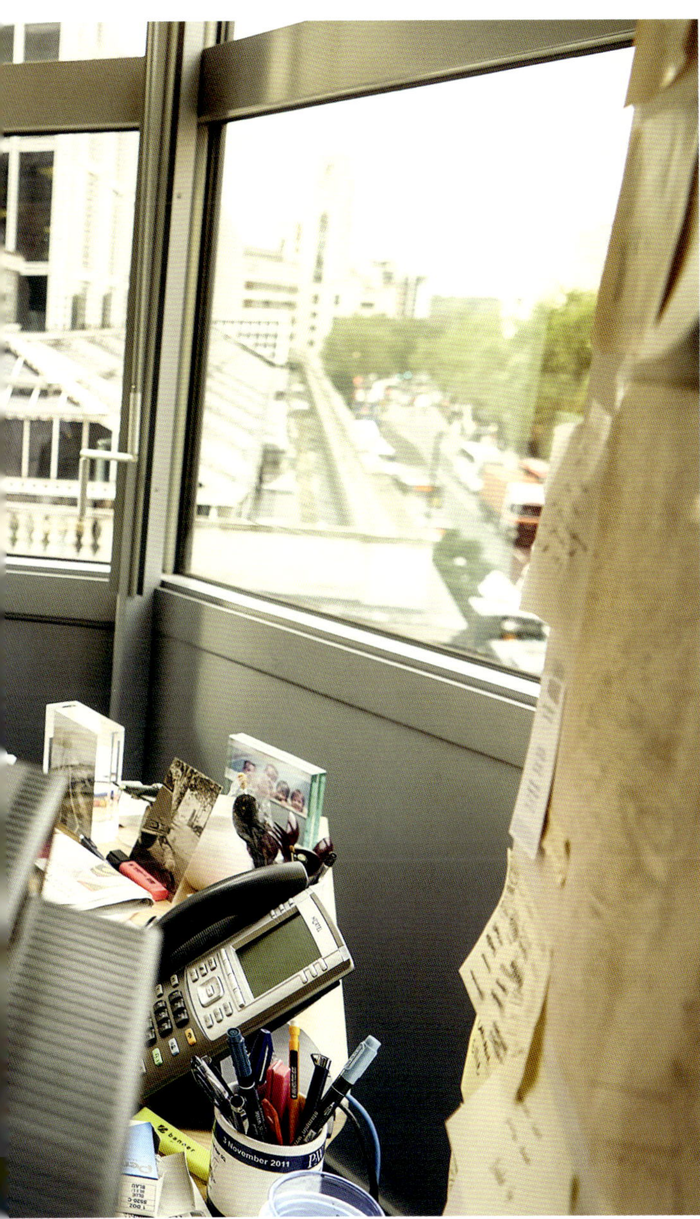

"This is the worst fucking cartoon that has ever appeared in any publication anywhere."
Matt said to himself, "Well, I'll do another one and it will be better."

Thirty years later, he's still at *The Telegraph*. And every morning he thinks to himself,
"Today could be the day I'll do the joke I'm most proud of."

Matthew Pritchett Cartoonist, *The Telegraph* > London, England

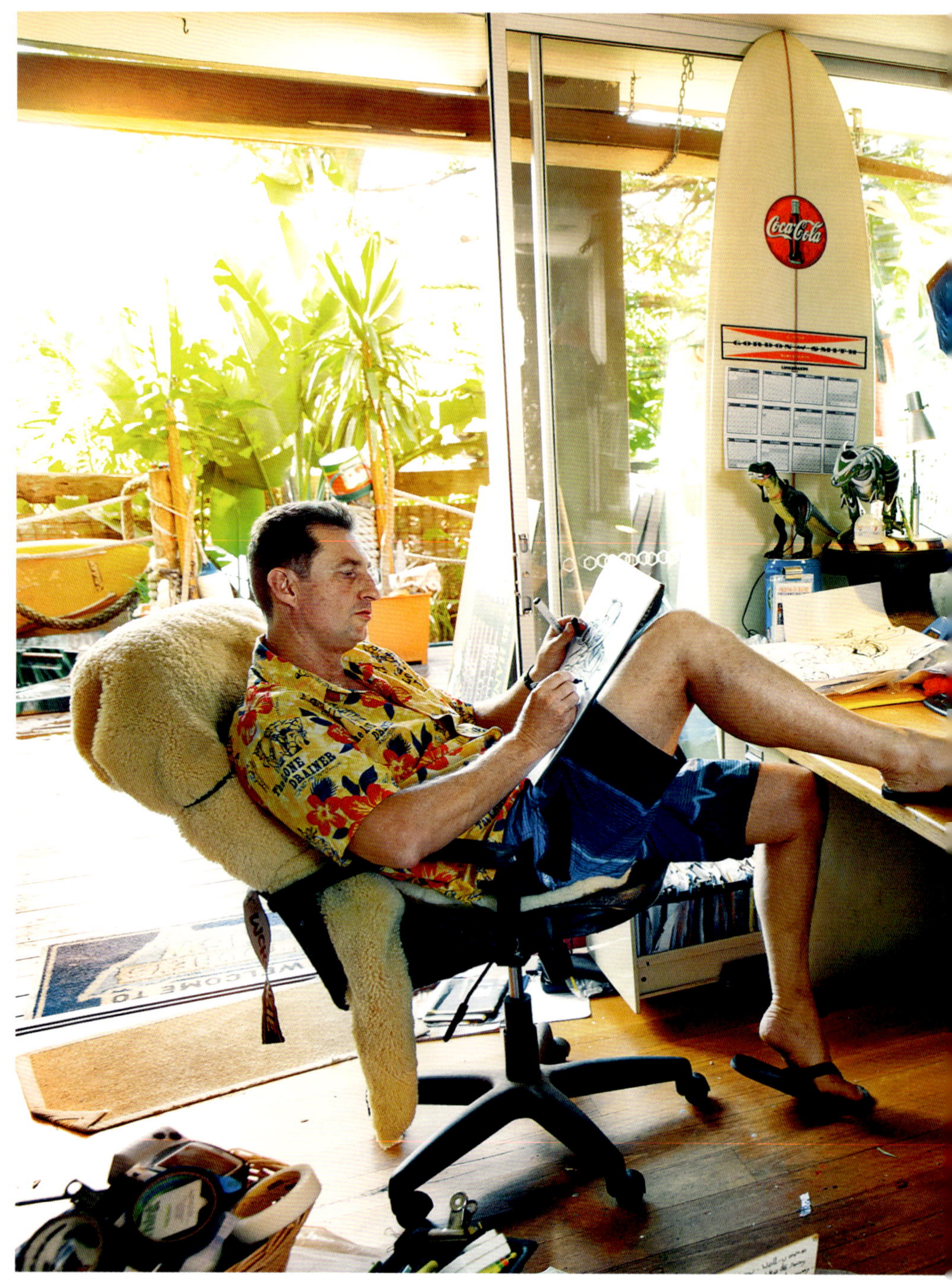

Peter Byrne Cartoonist > Sydney, Australia

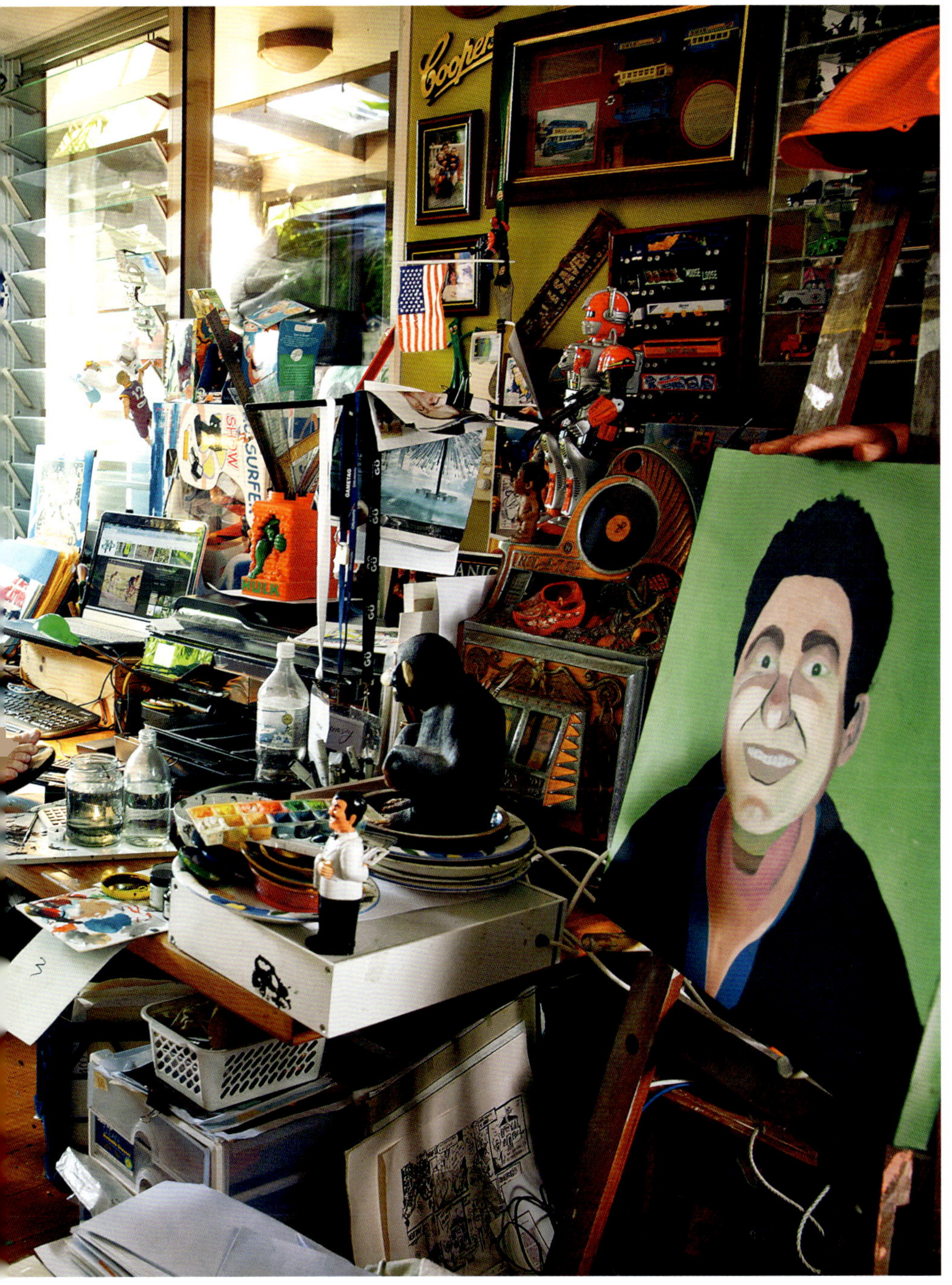

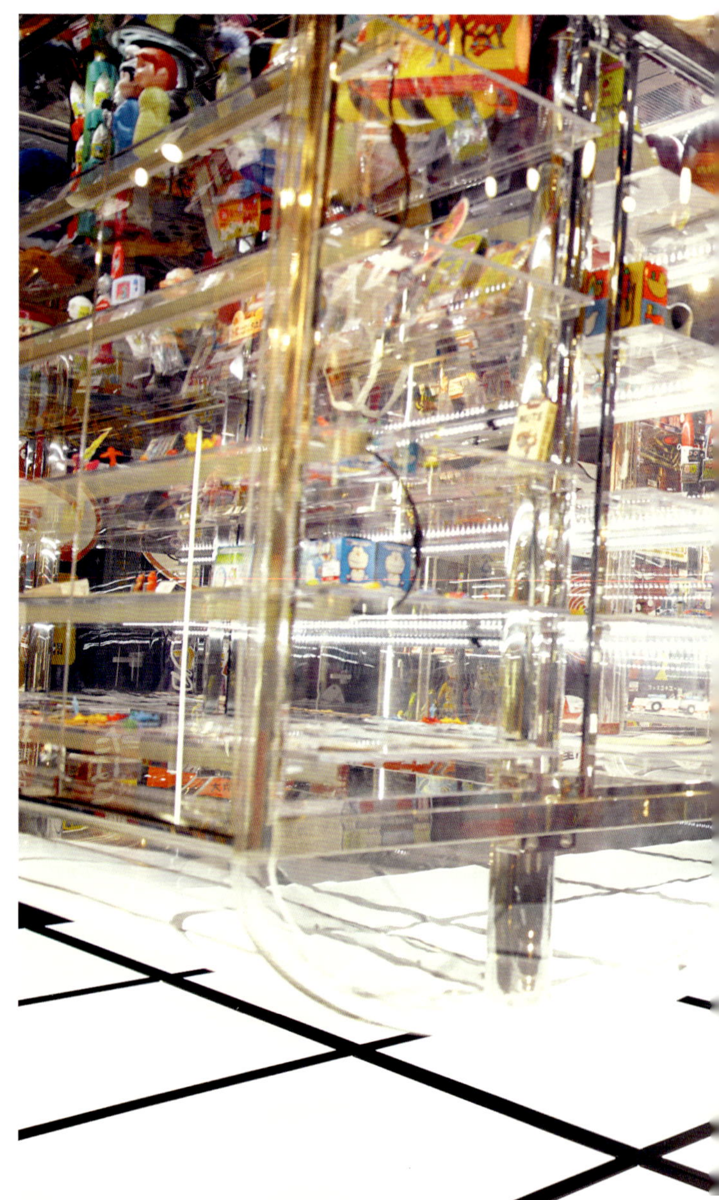

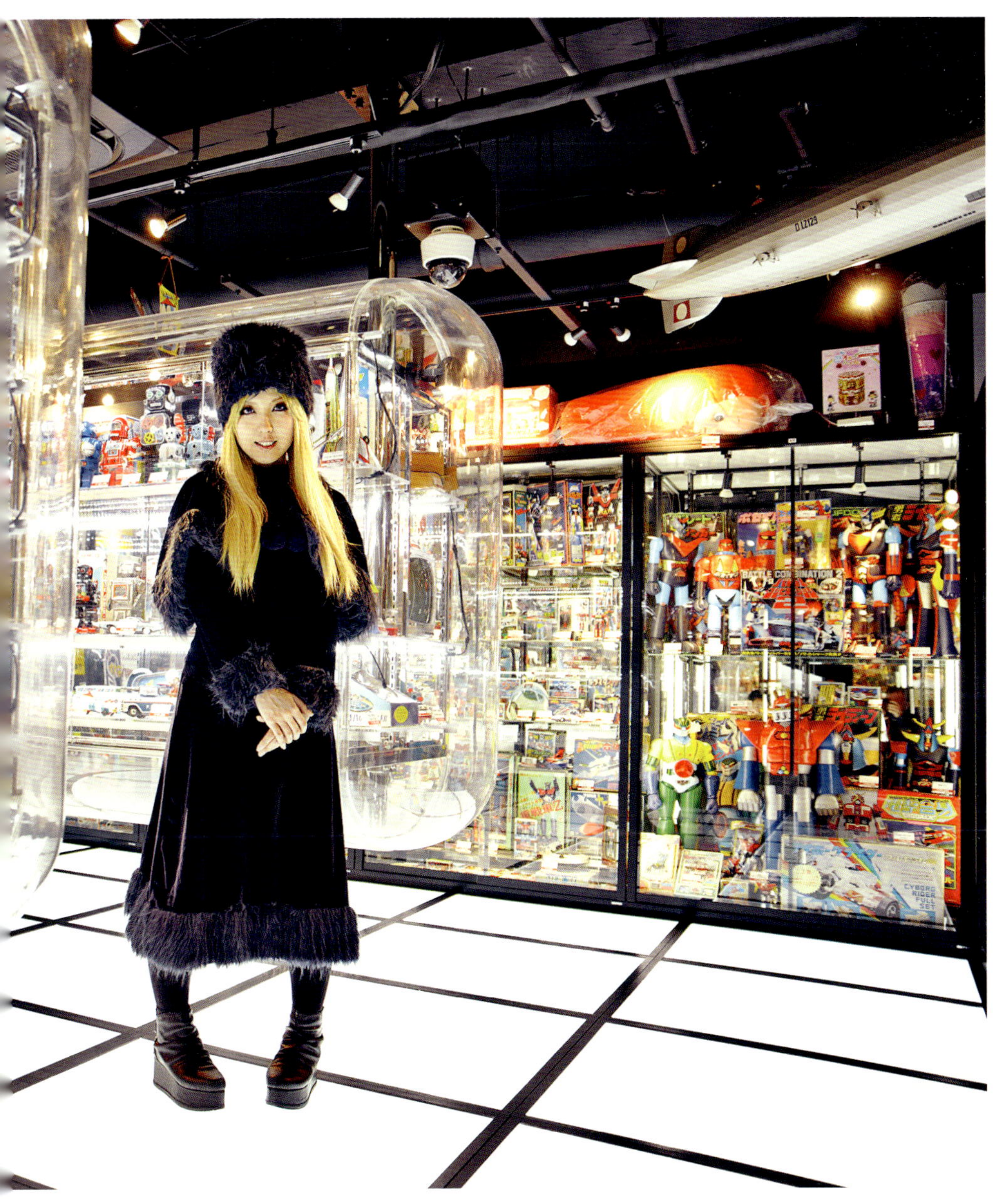

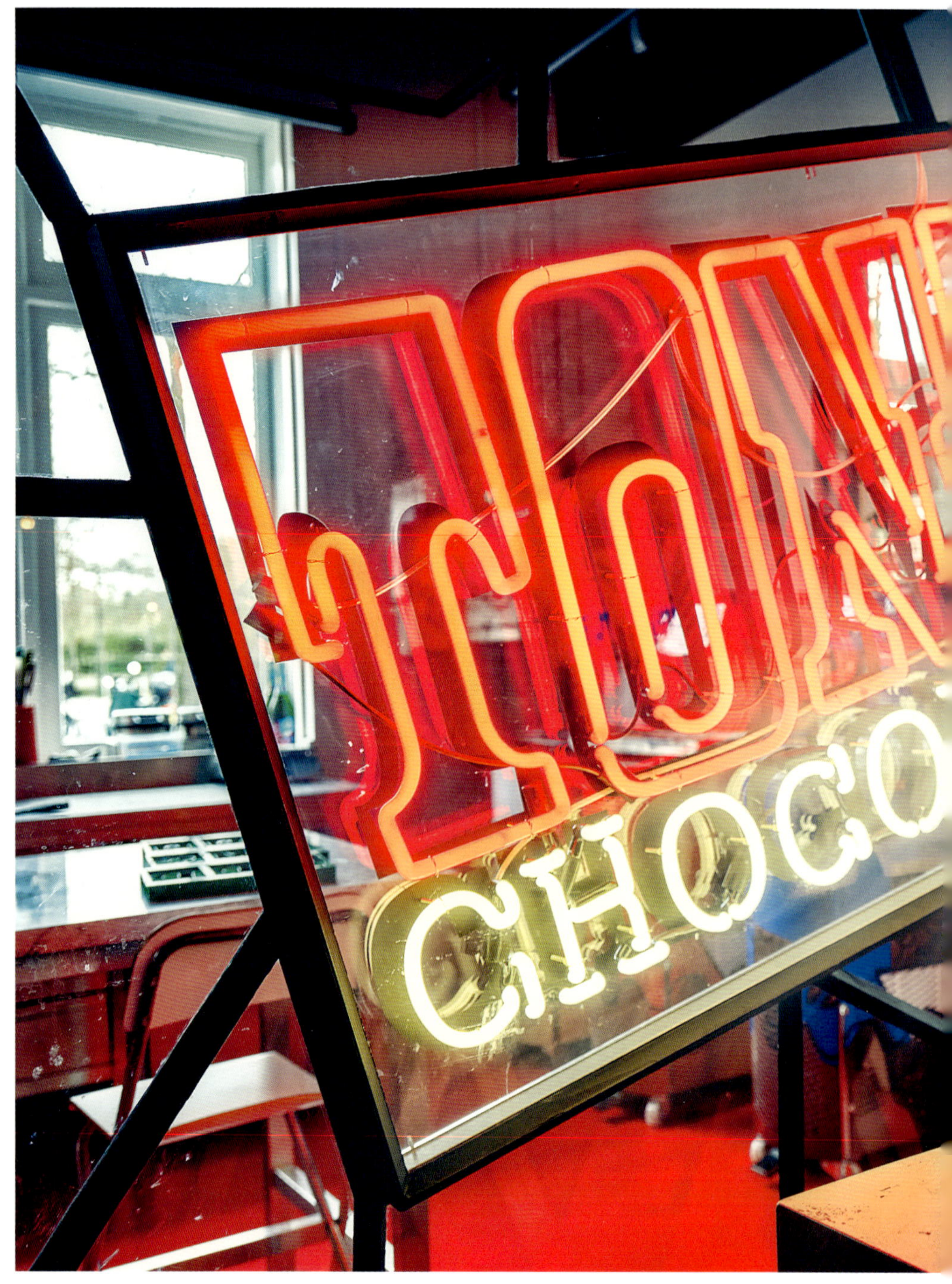

B.L.A. Klarenbeek Chocolate Innovator, Tony's Chocolonely > Amsterdam, Netherlands

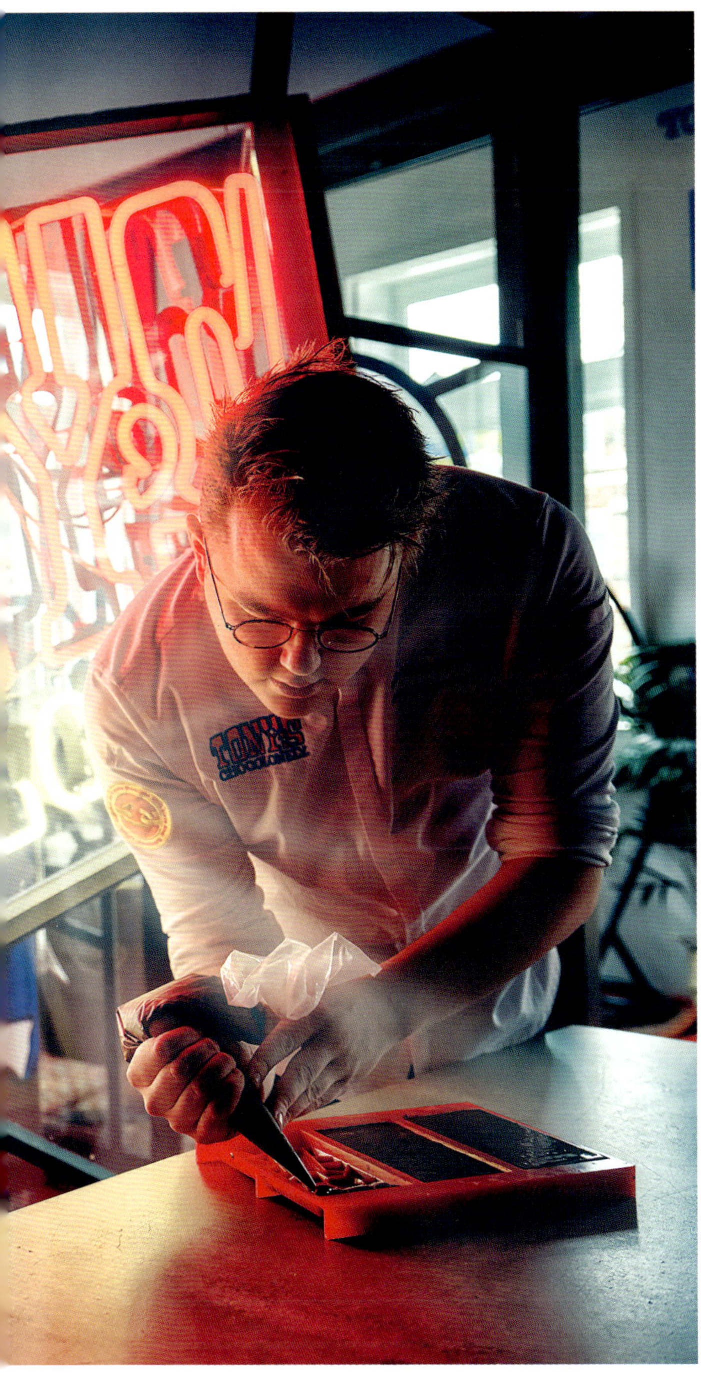

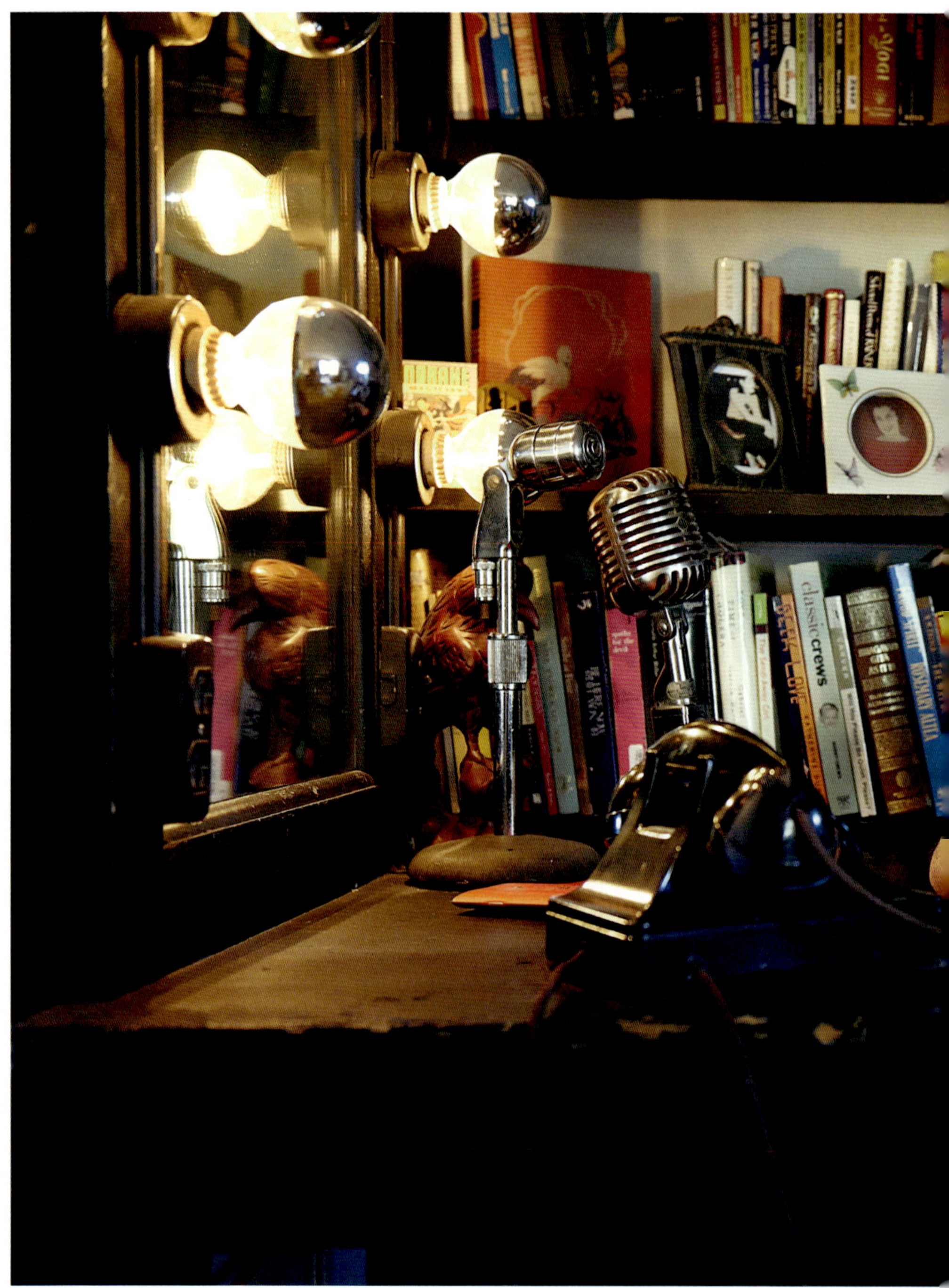

Rob Zabrecky Magician > Los Angeles, California

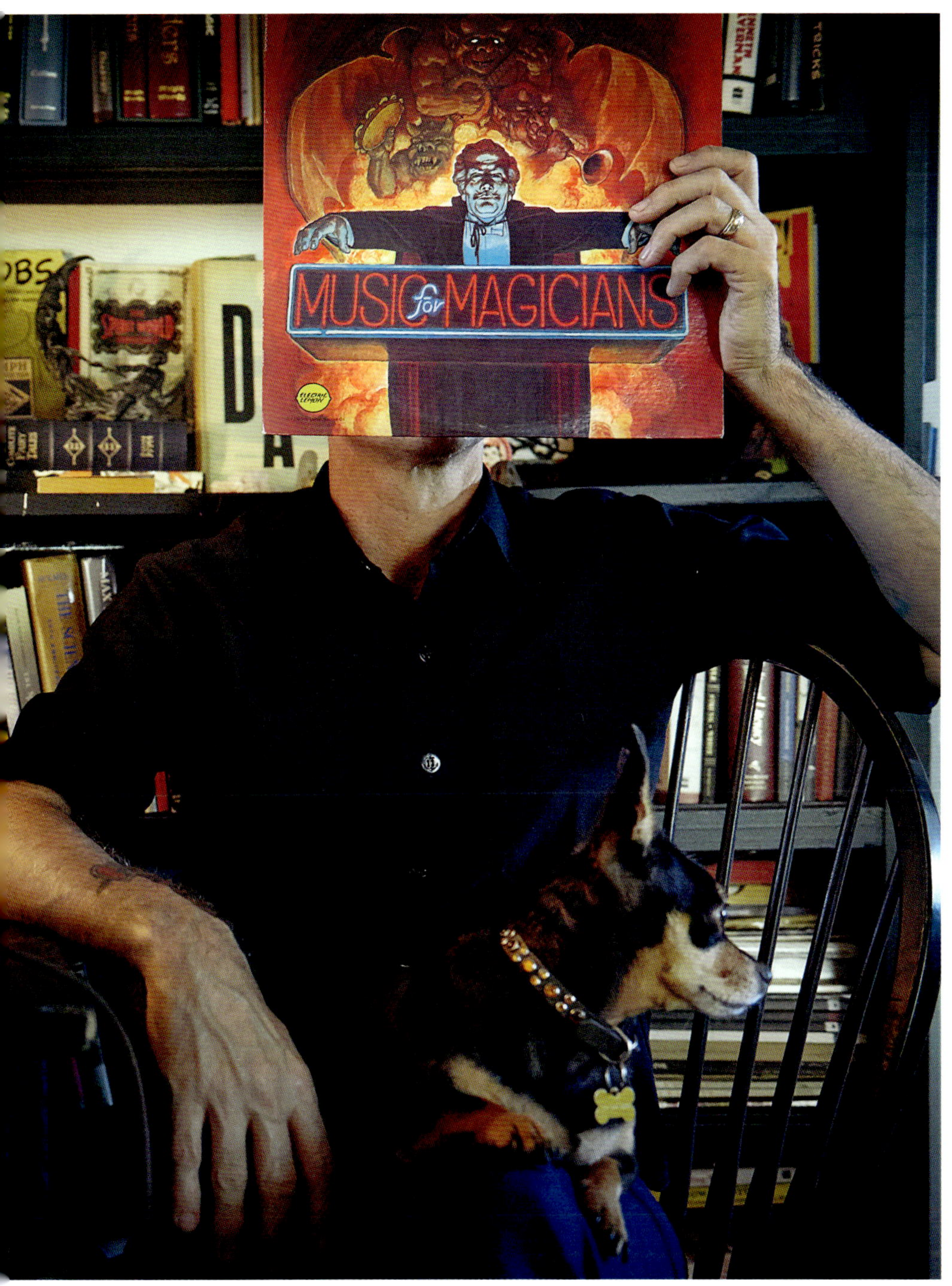
MUSIC for MAGICIANS
ELECTRIC LEMON

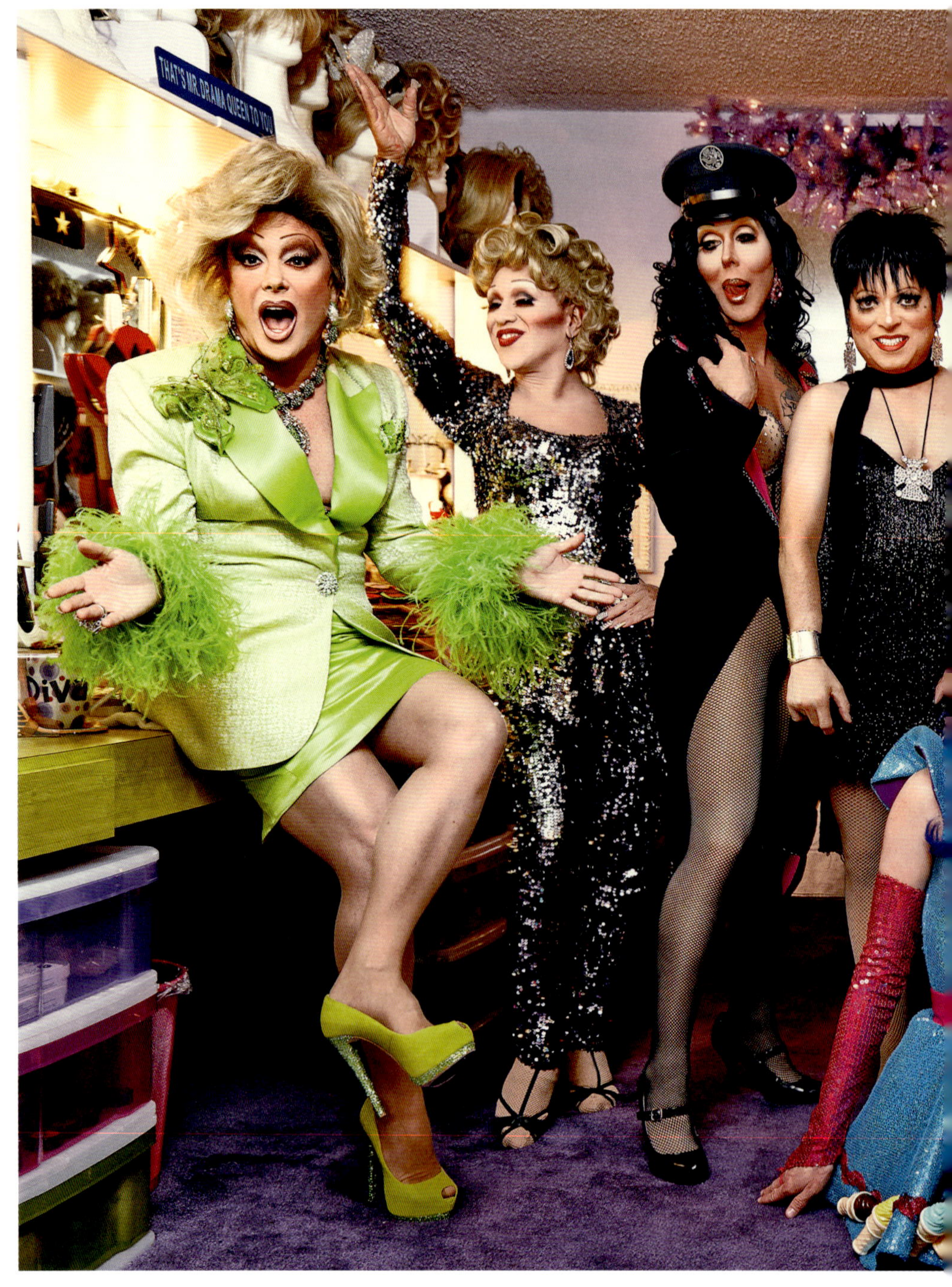

Frank Marino & Divas Female Impersonators > Las Vegas, Nevada

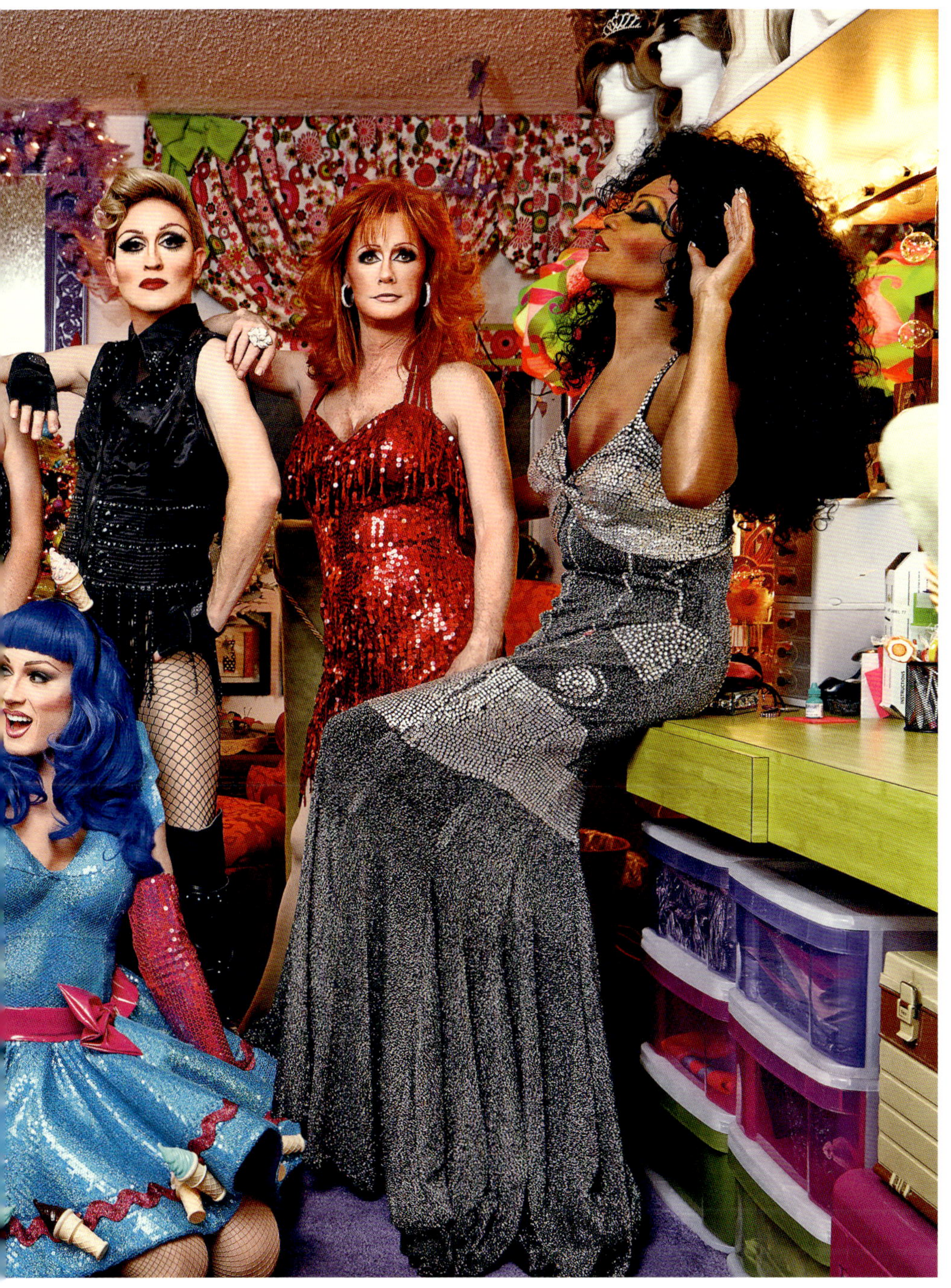

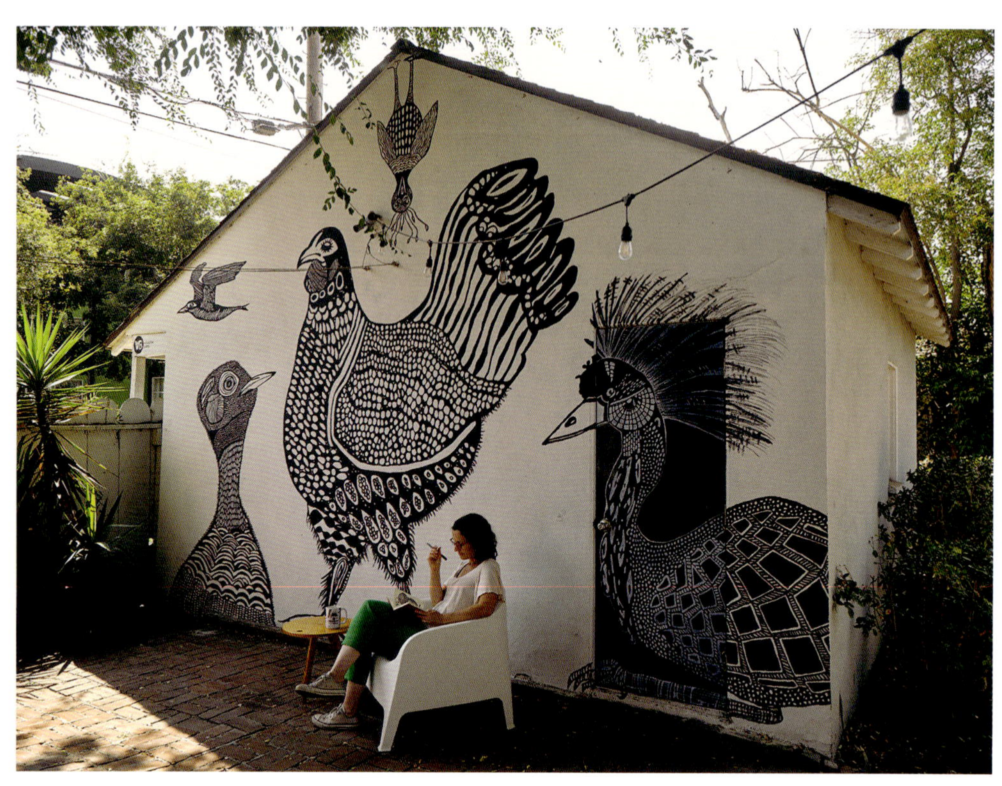

Orit Harpaz Artist, Weirdoh Birds > Los Angeles, California

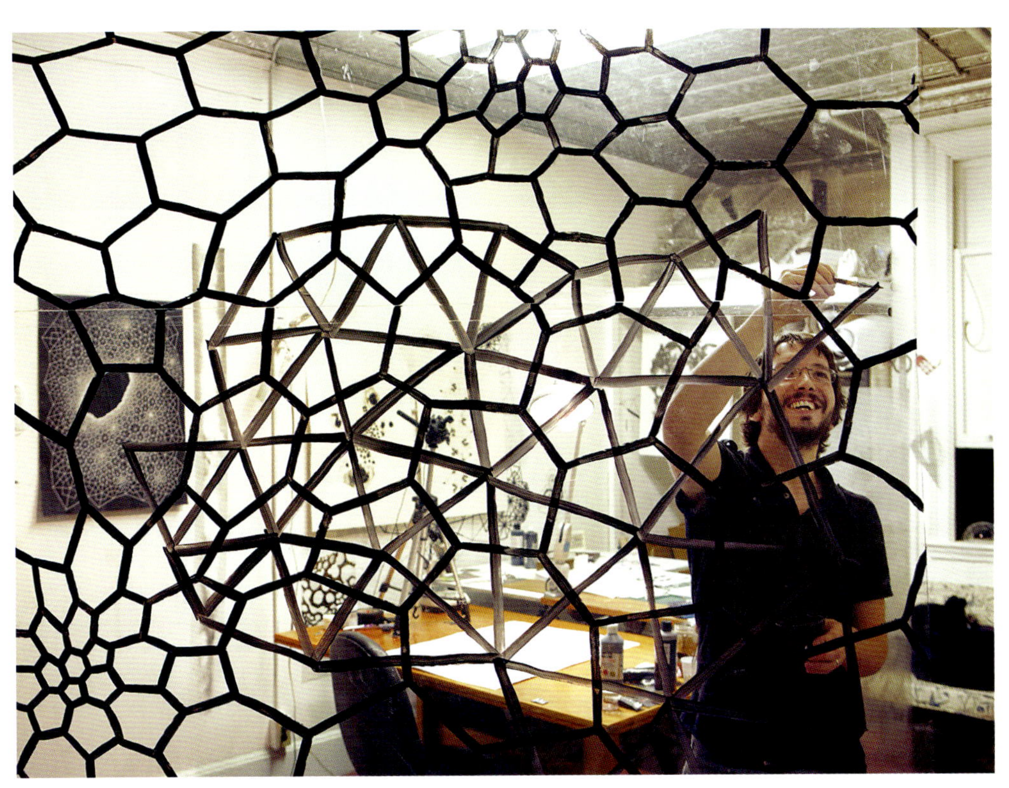

Clint Fulkerson Artist > Portland, Maine

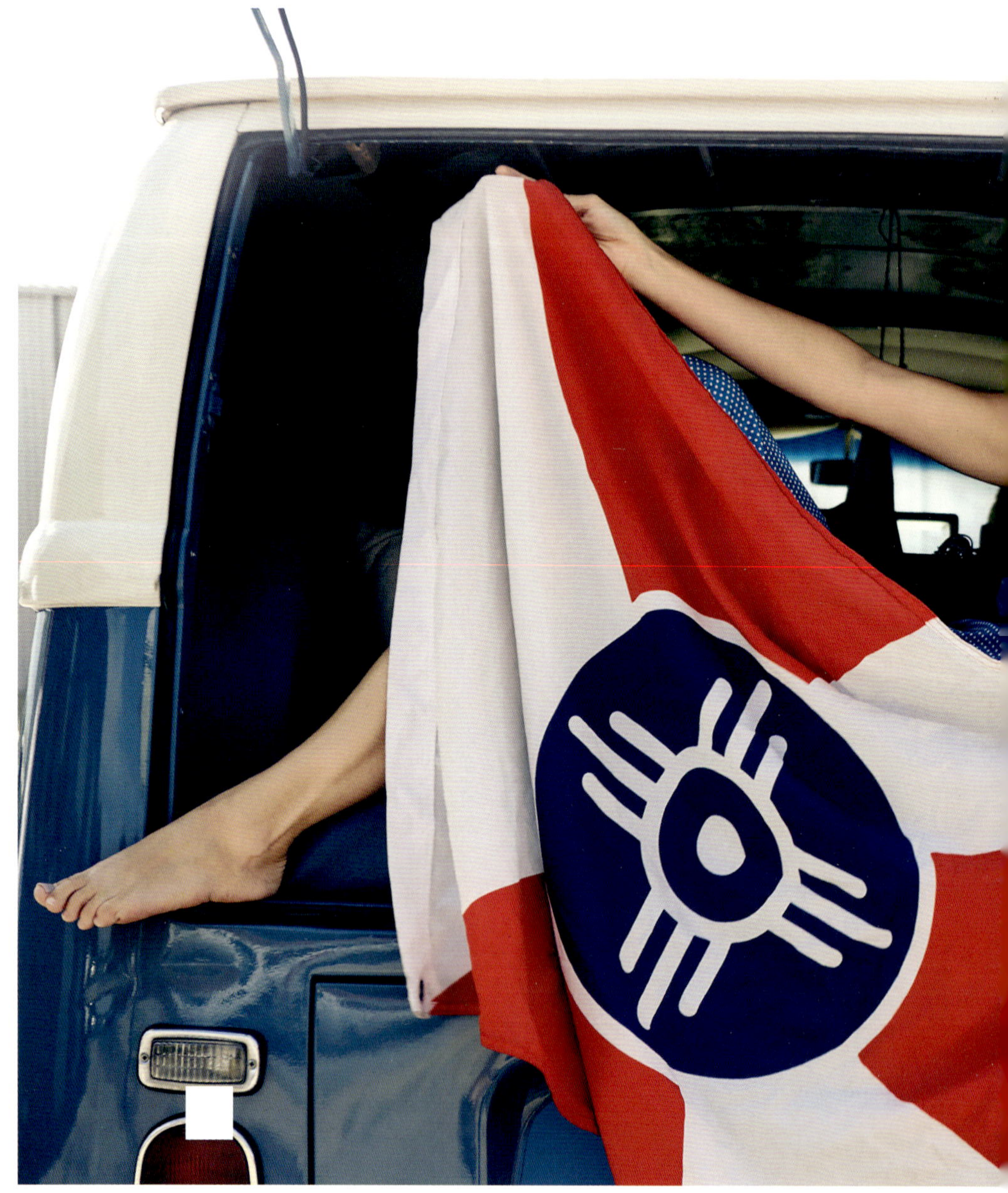

Janelle left her hometown of Wichita, but missed it so much that she just had to come back. She has since become her city's biggest booster and cheerleader. Working tirelessly to share her pride in her community is how she waters her roots.

Janelle King The Workroom Arts Space > Wichita, Kansas

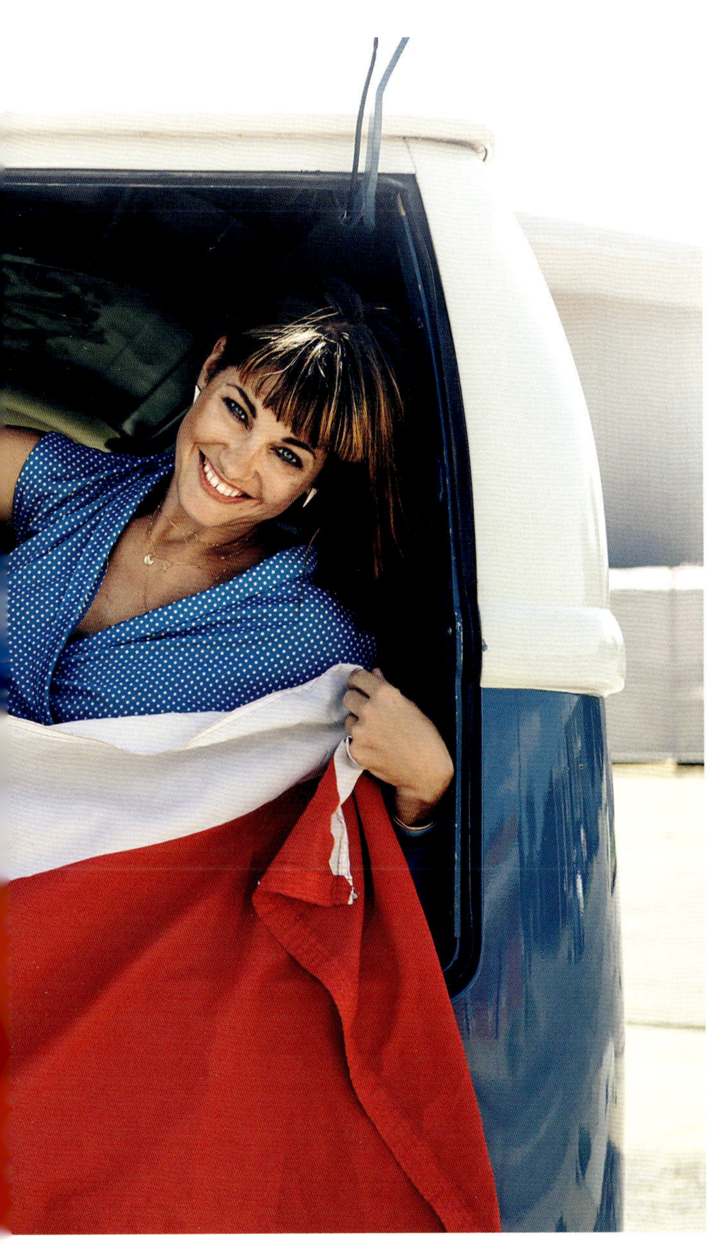

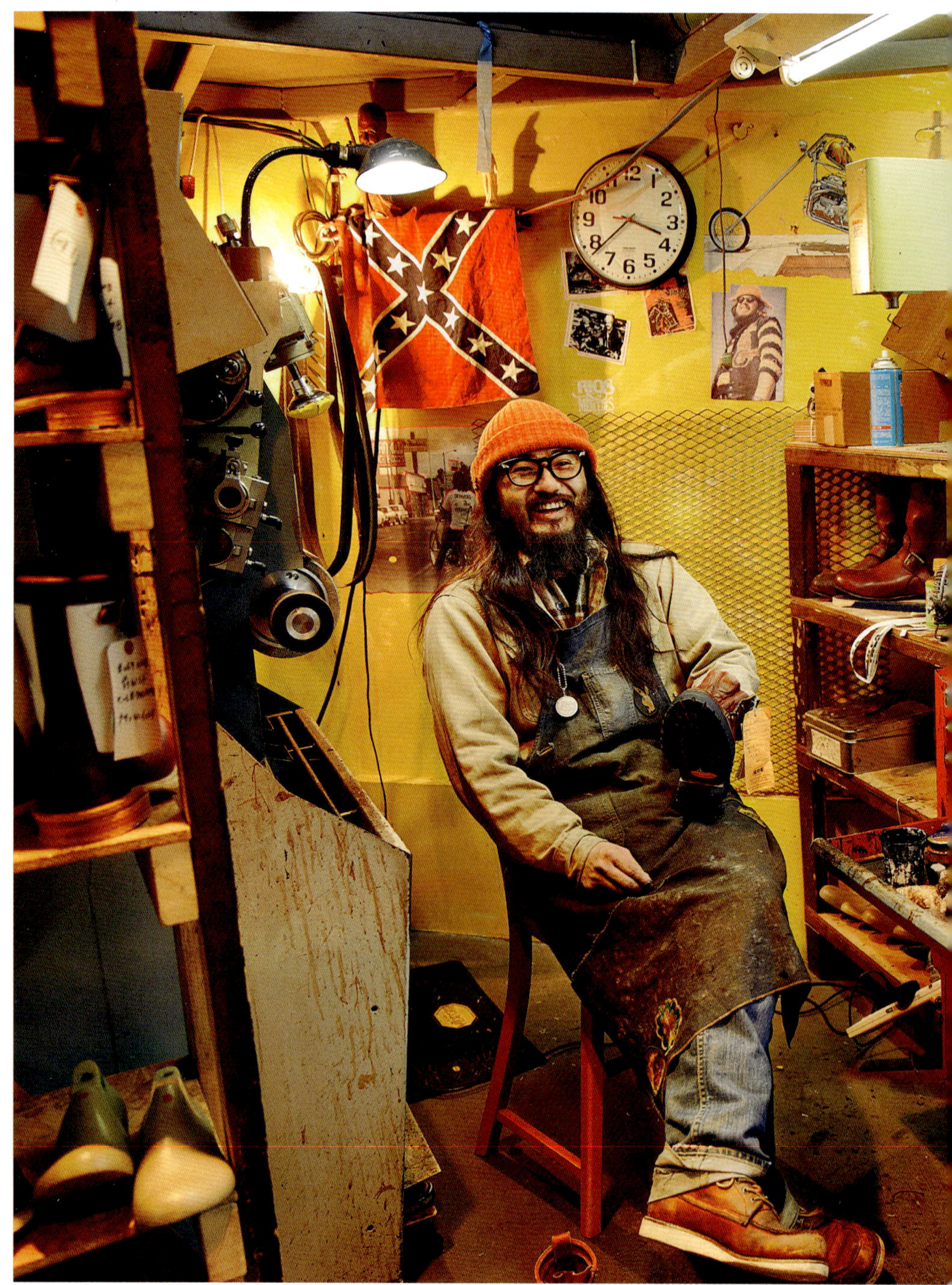

Takeshi Okuyama Fukurokuju Boot Repair > Tokyo, Japan

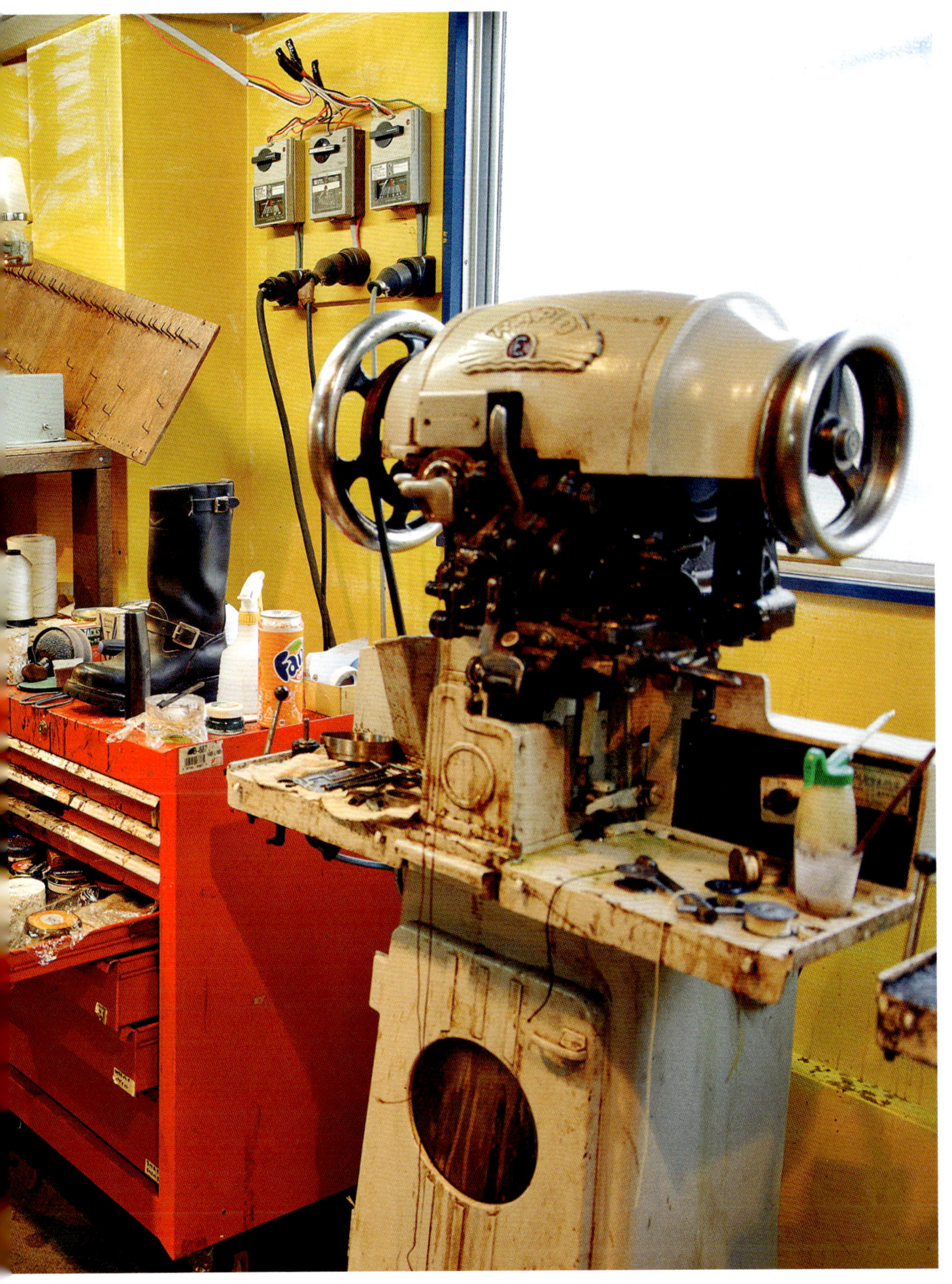

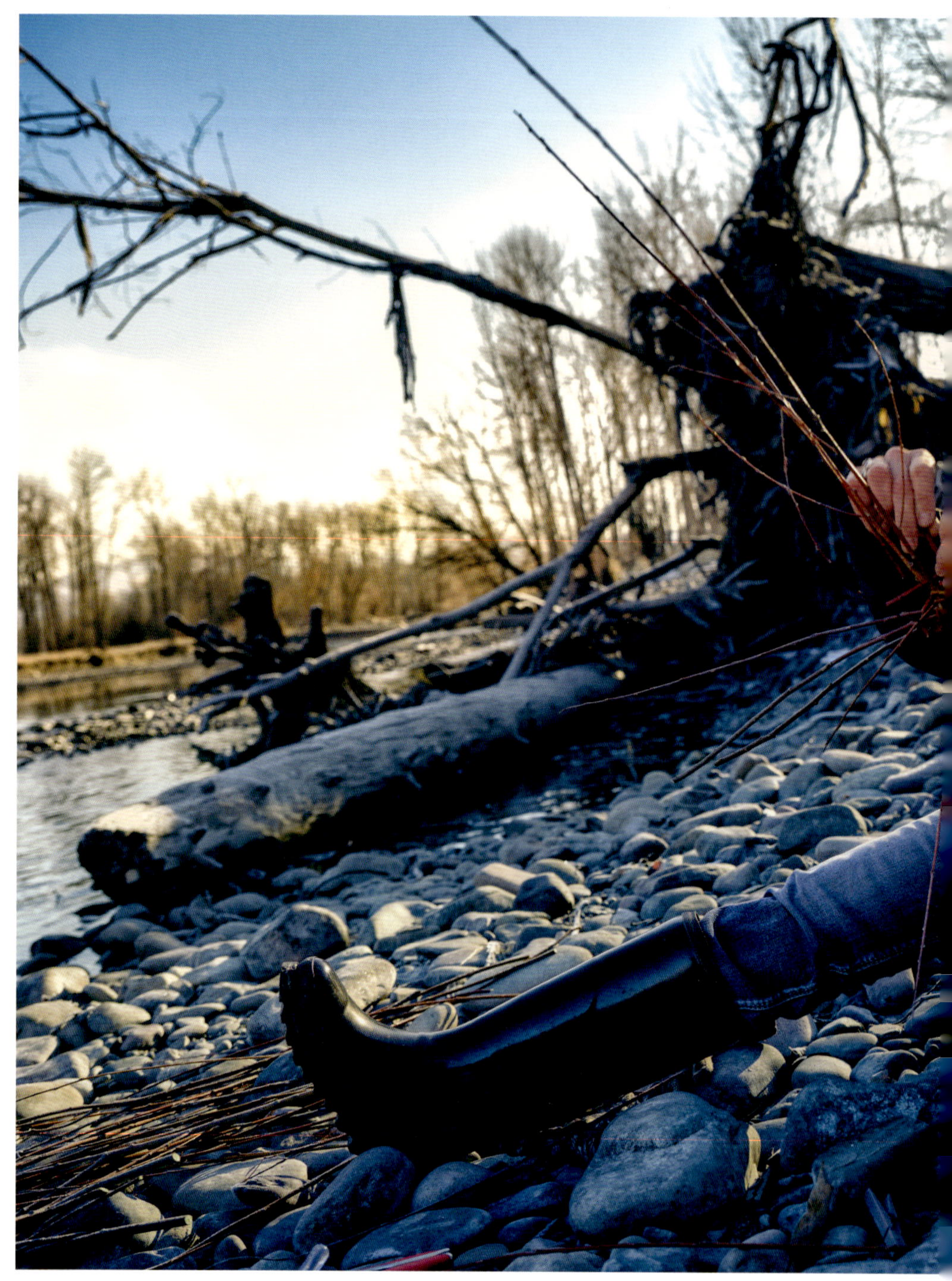

Valerie Veis Basket Weaver > Missoula, Montana

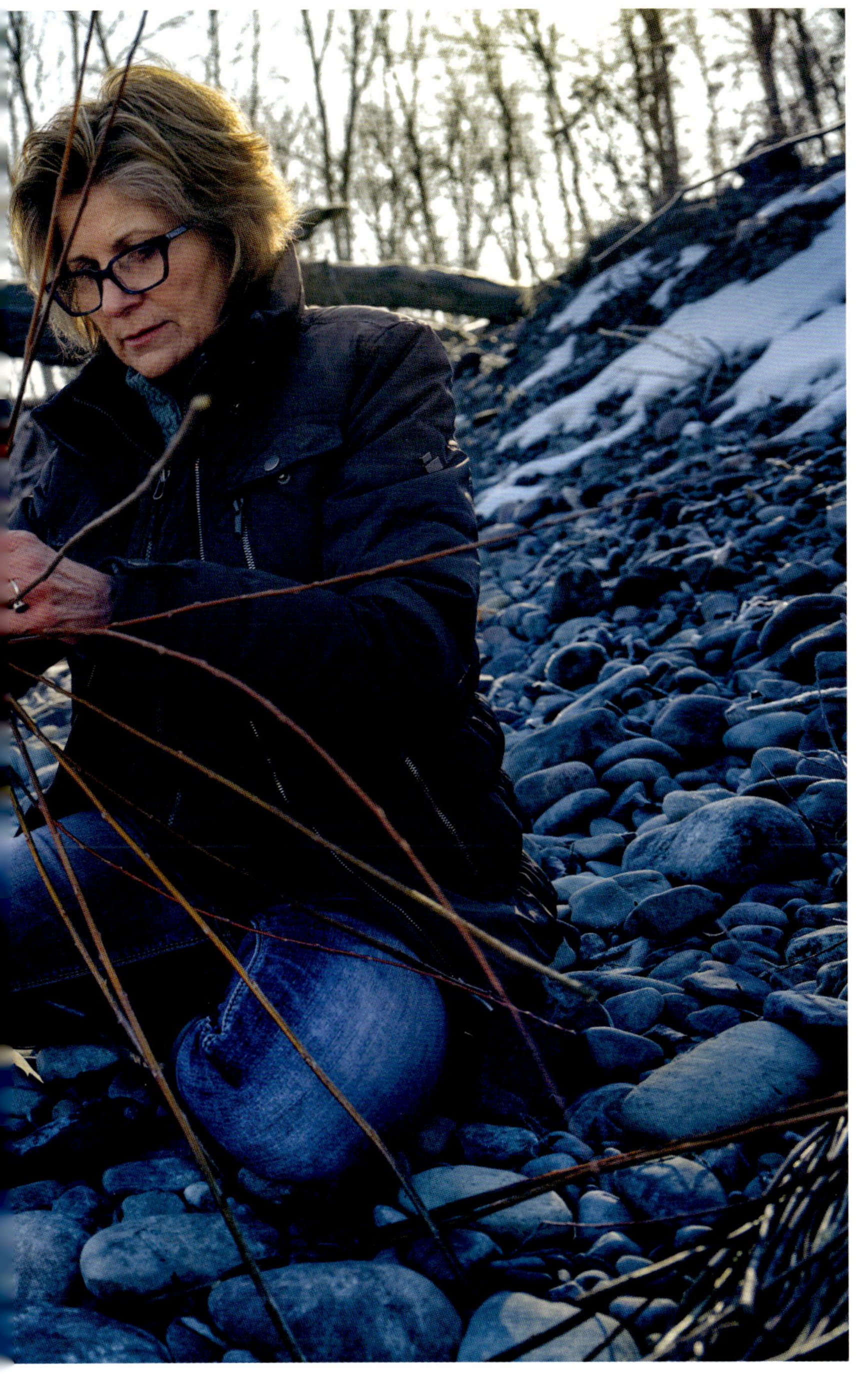

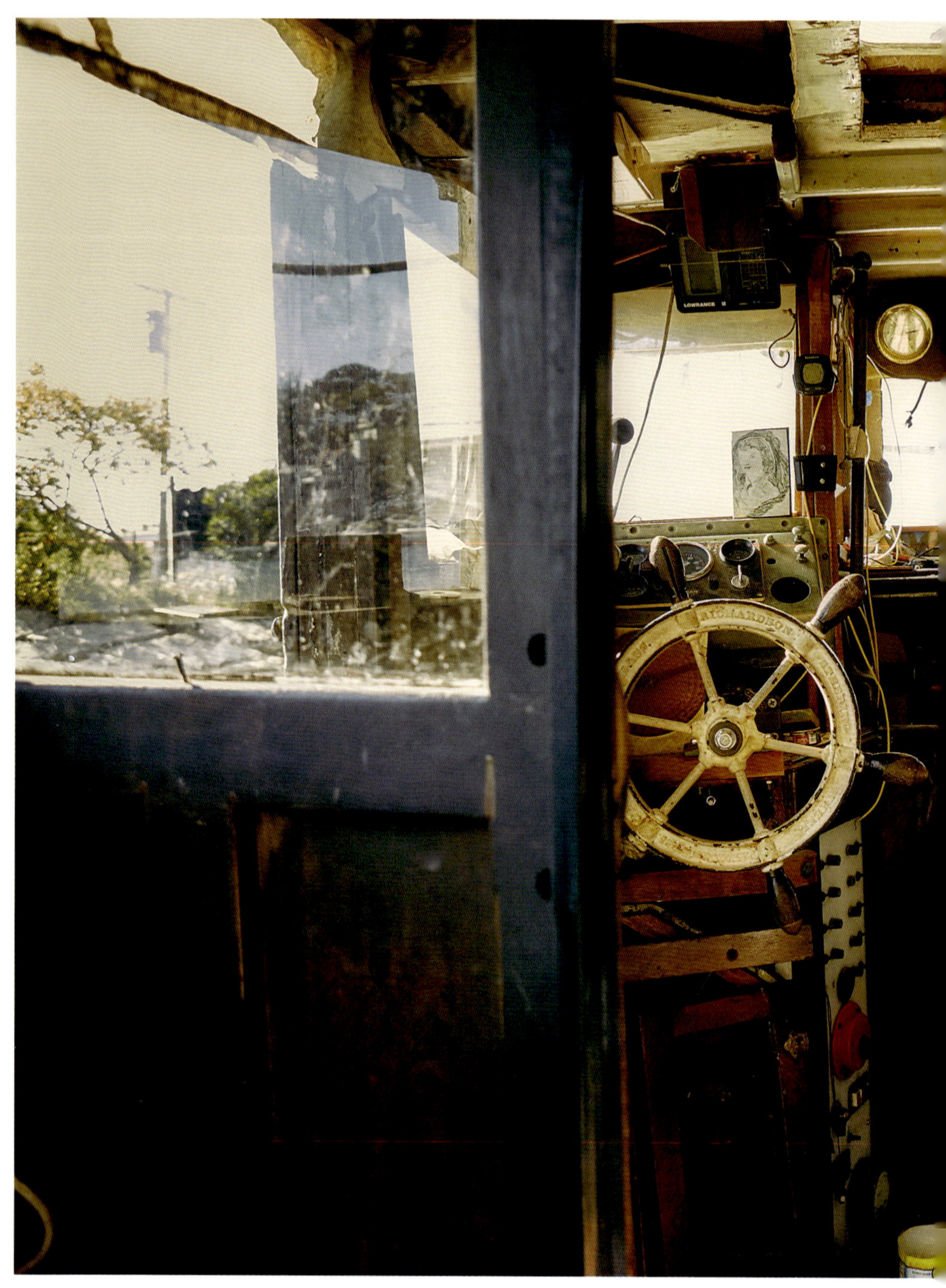

Larry Dahlmer Artist > Gloucester, Massachusetts

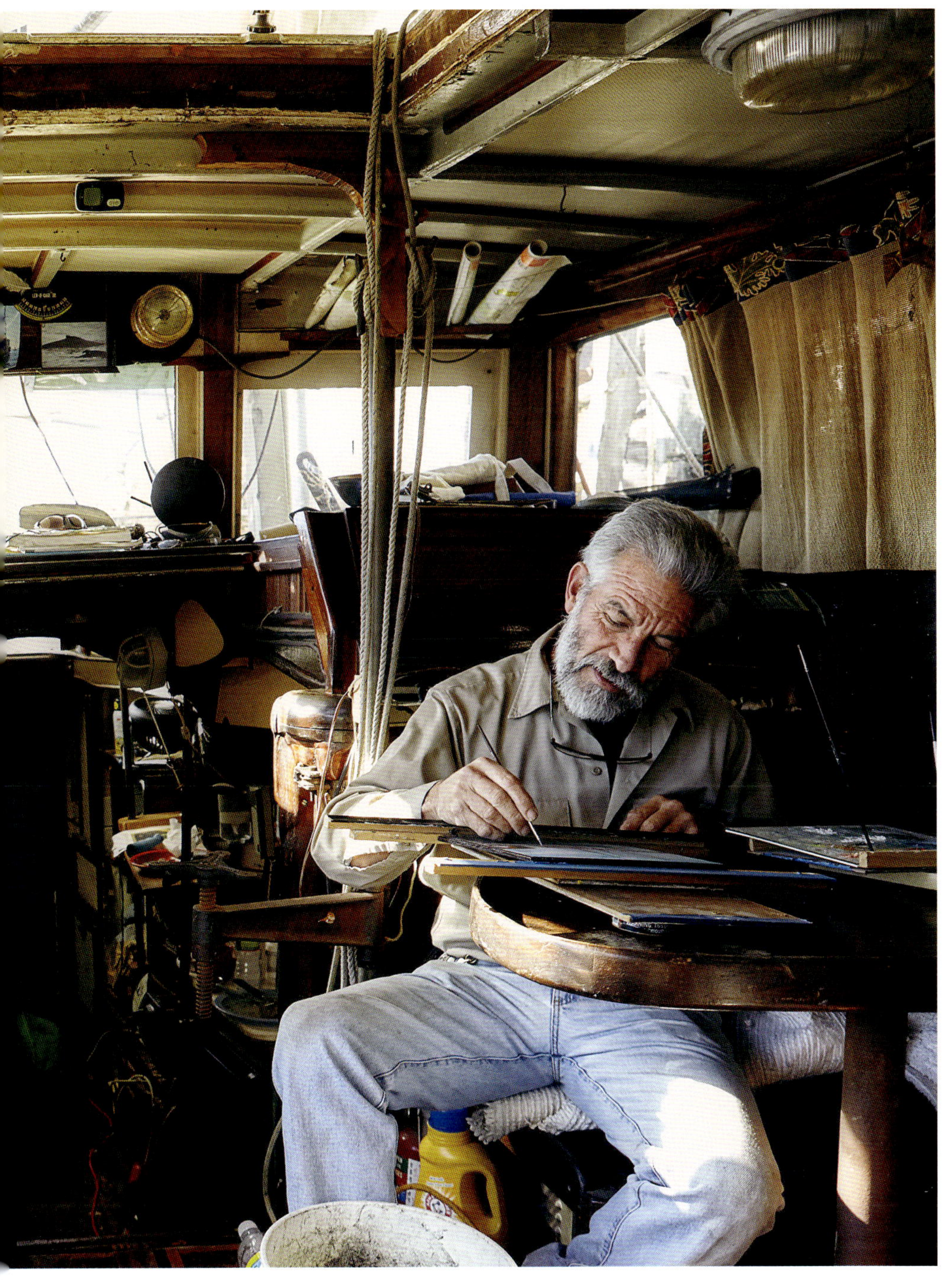

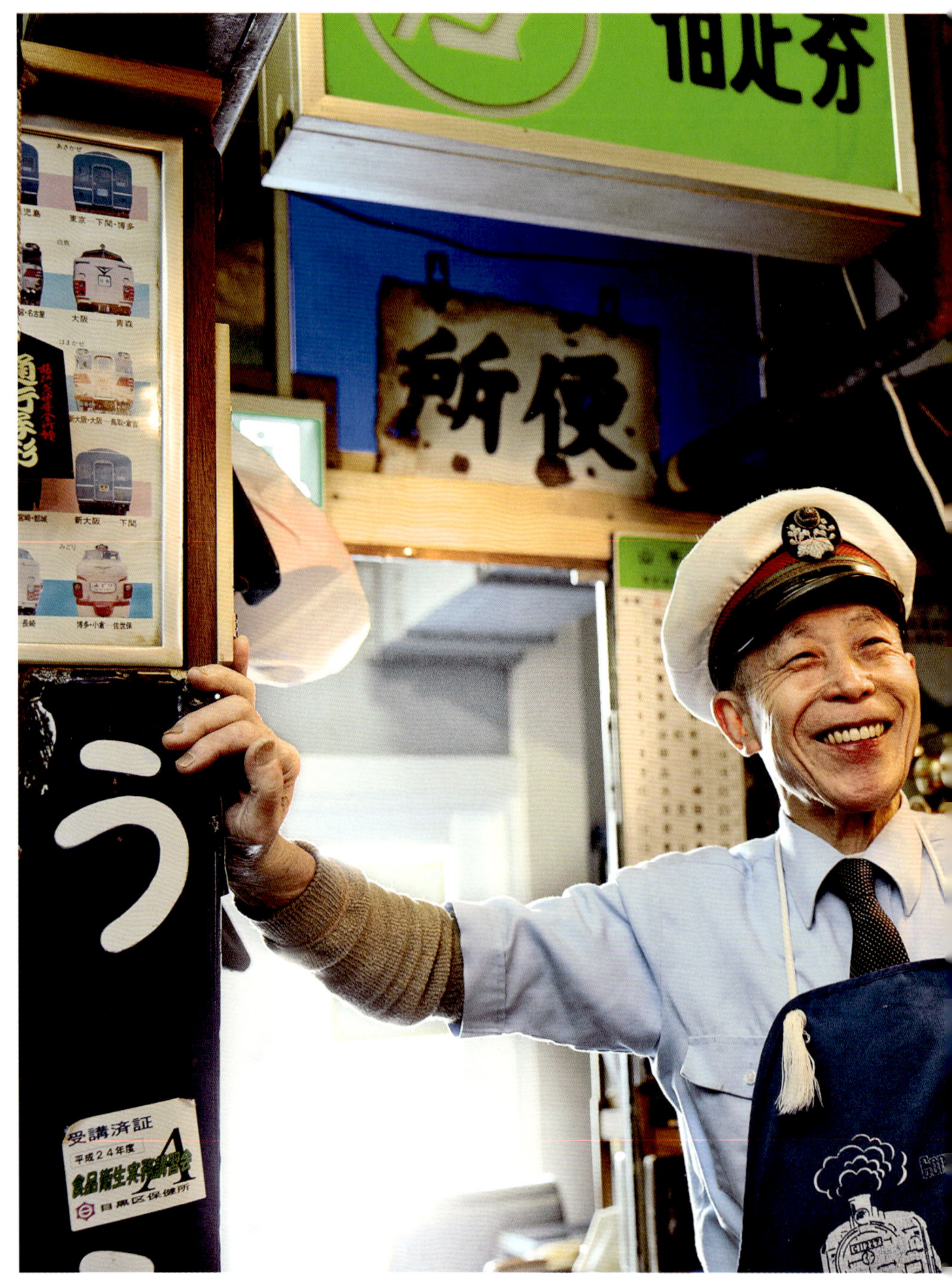

Naito Hirotoshi Tetsudo Mudo No Mise, Train Café > Tokyo, Japan

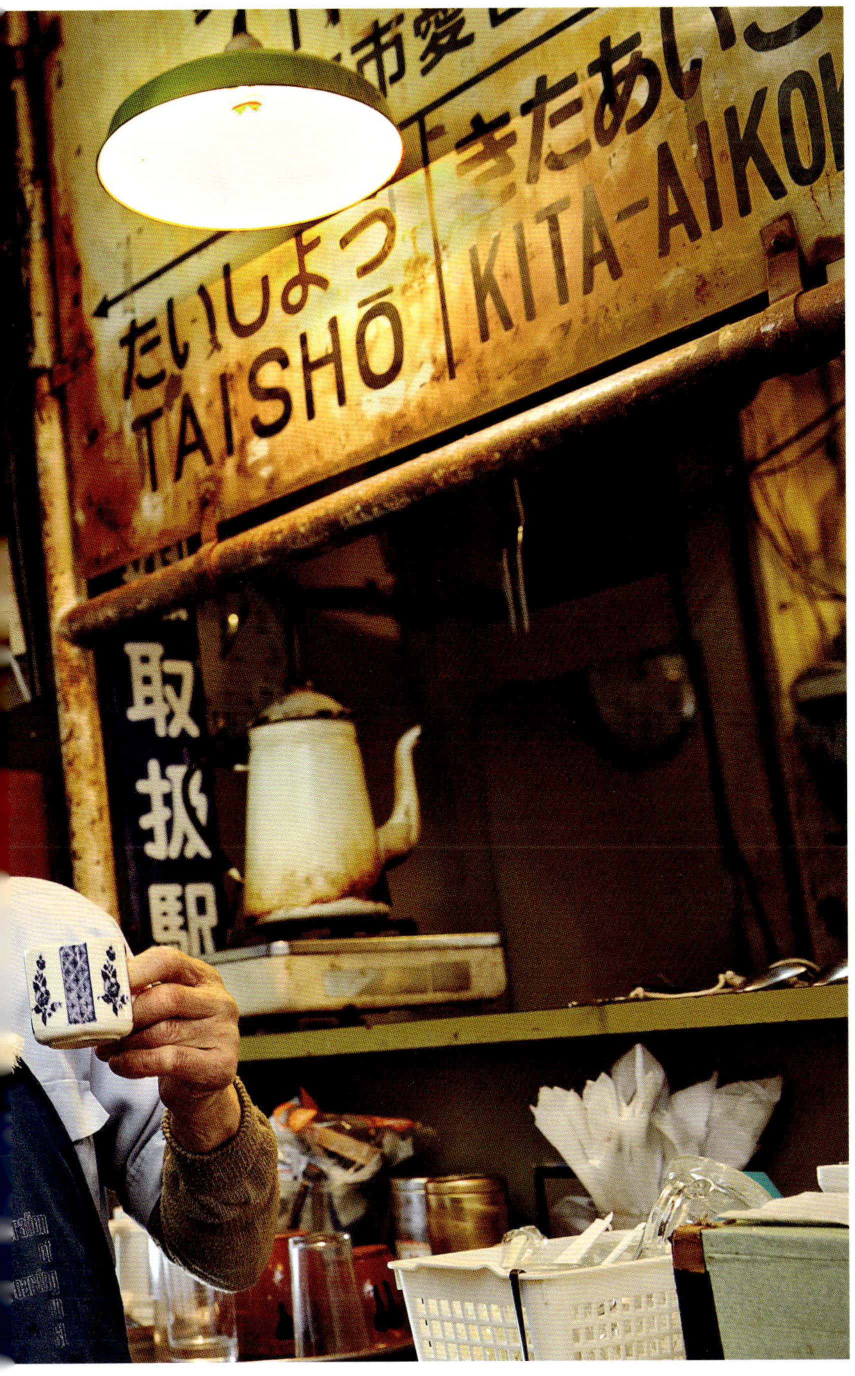
市愛 きたあいこ
KITA-AIKOK
たいしょう
TAISHO
取扱駅

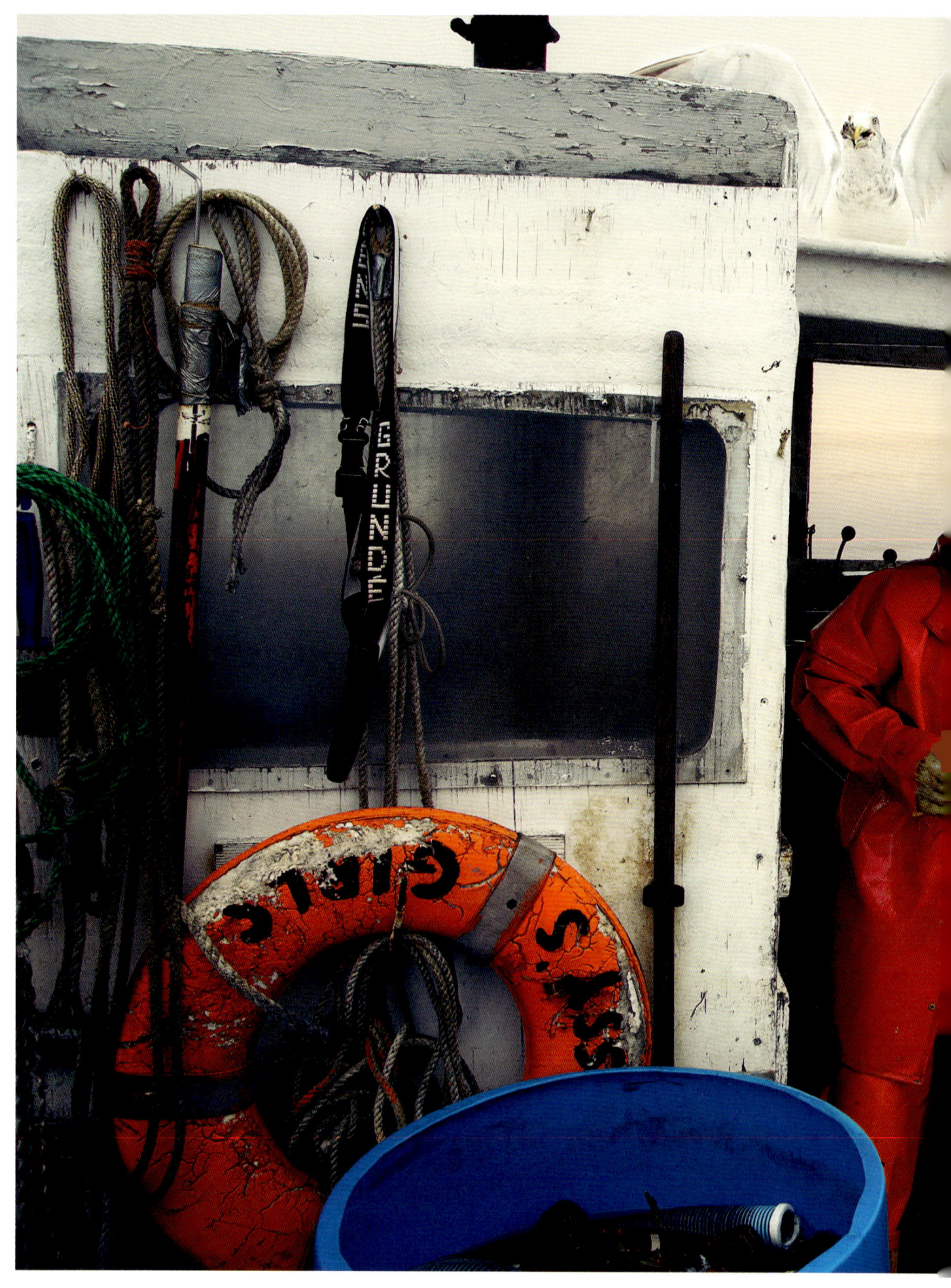

Lobsterman > Rockport, Massachusetts

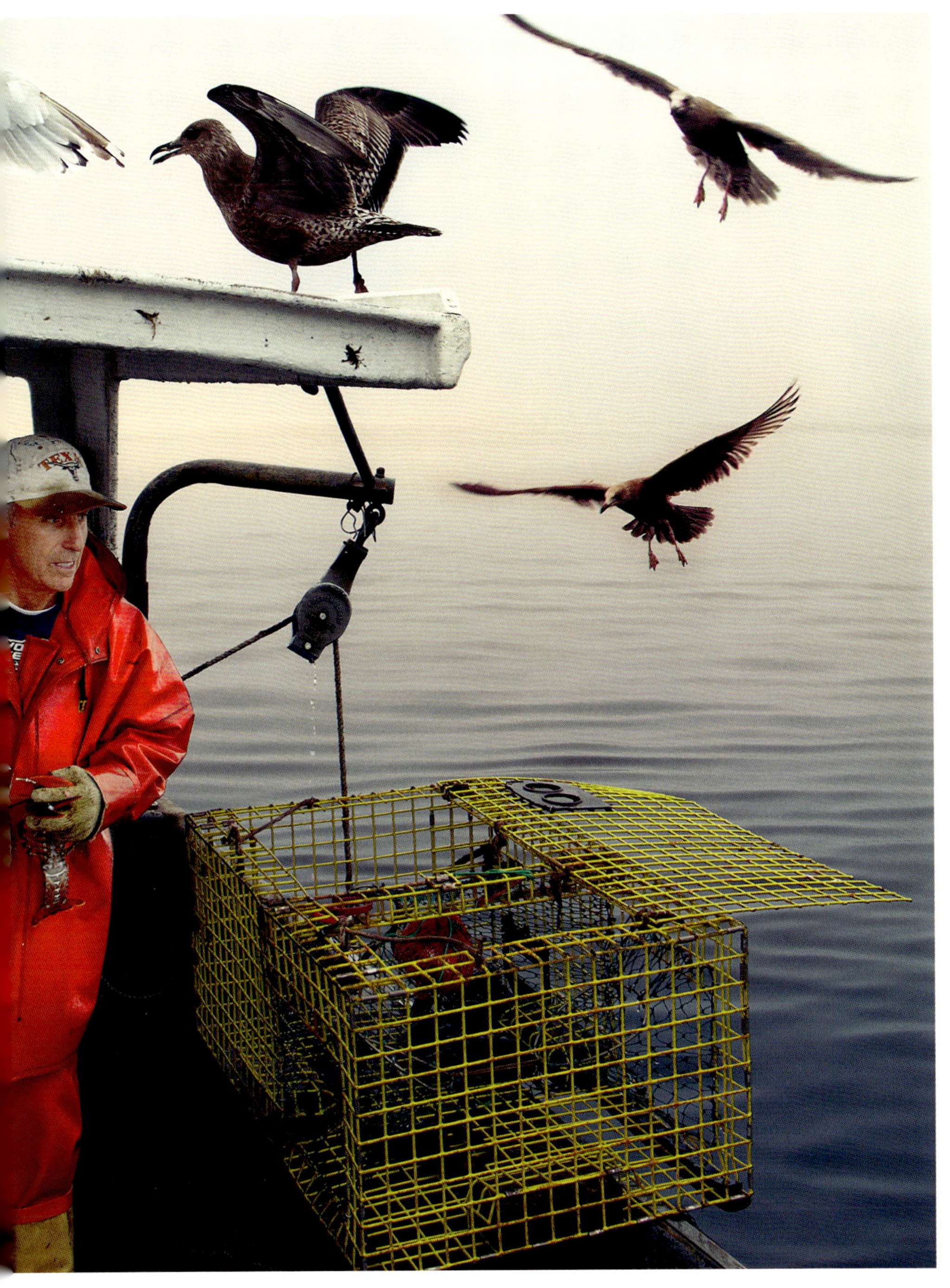

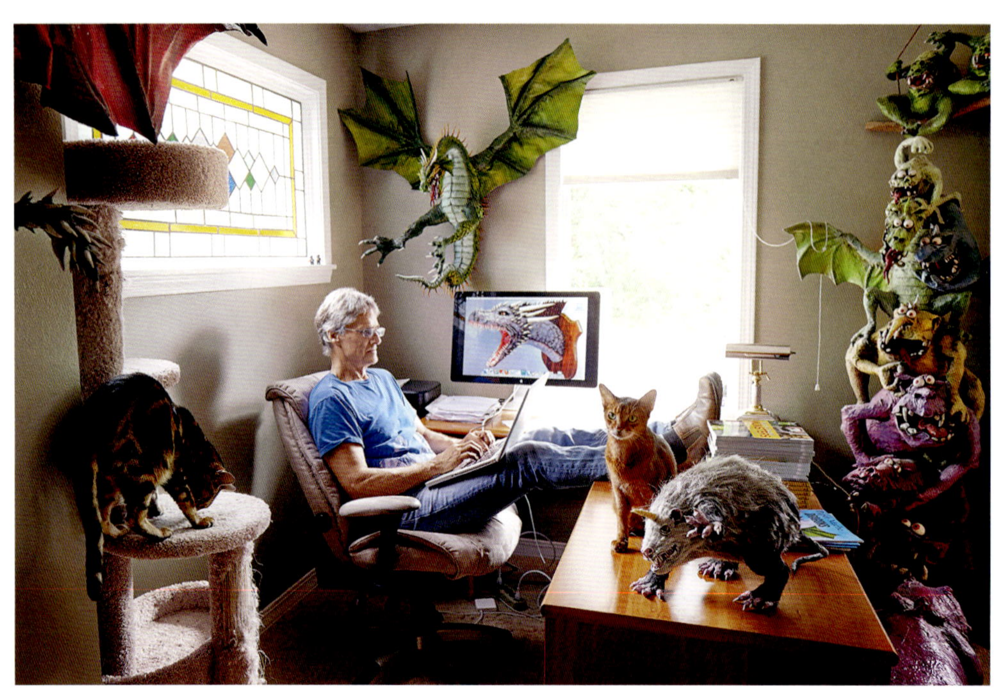

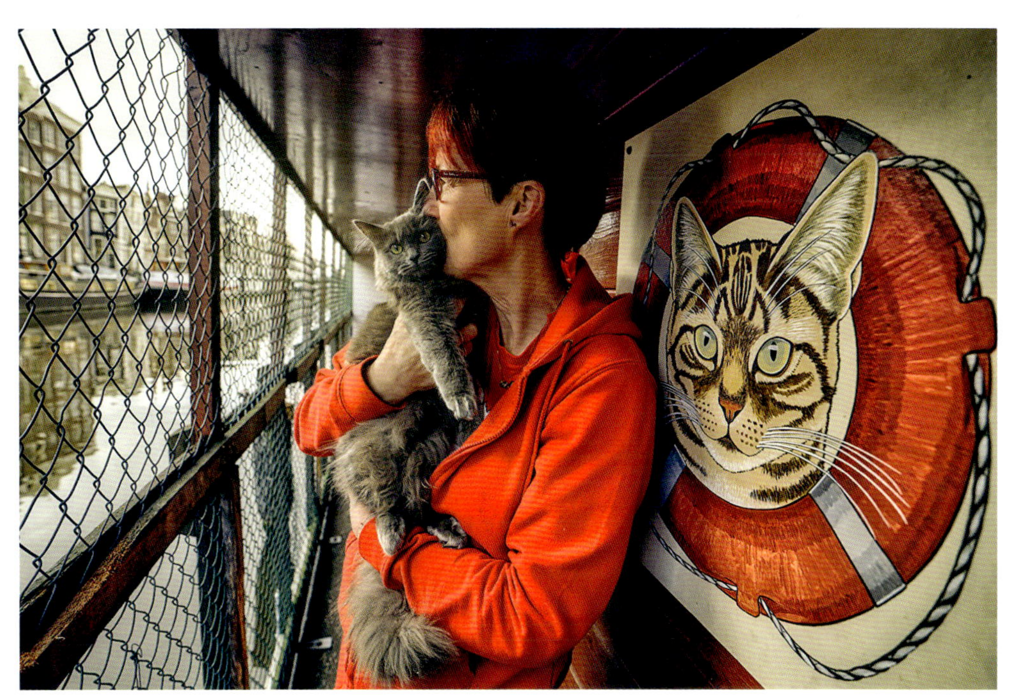

Judith Gobets De Pozenboot Cat Rescue > Amsterdam, Netherlands

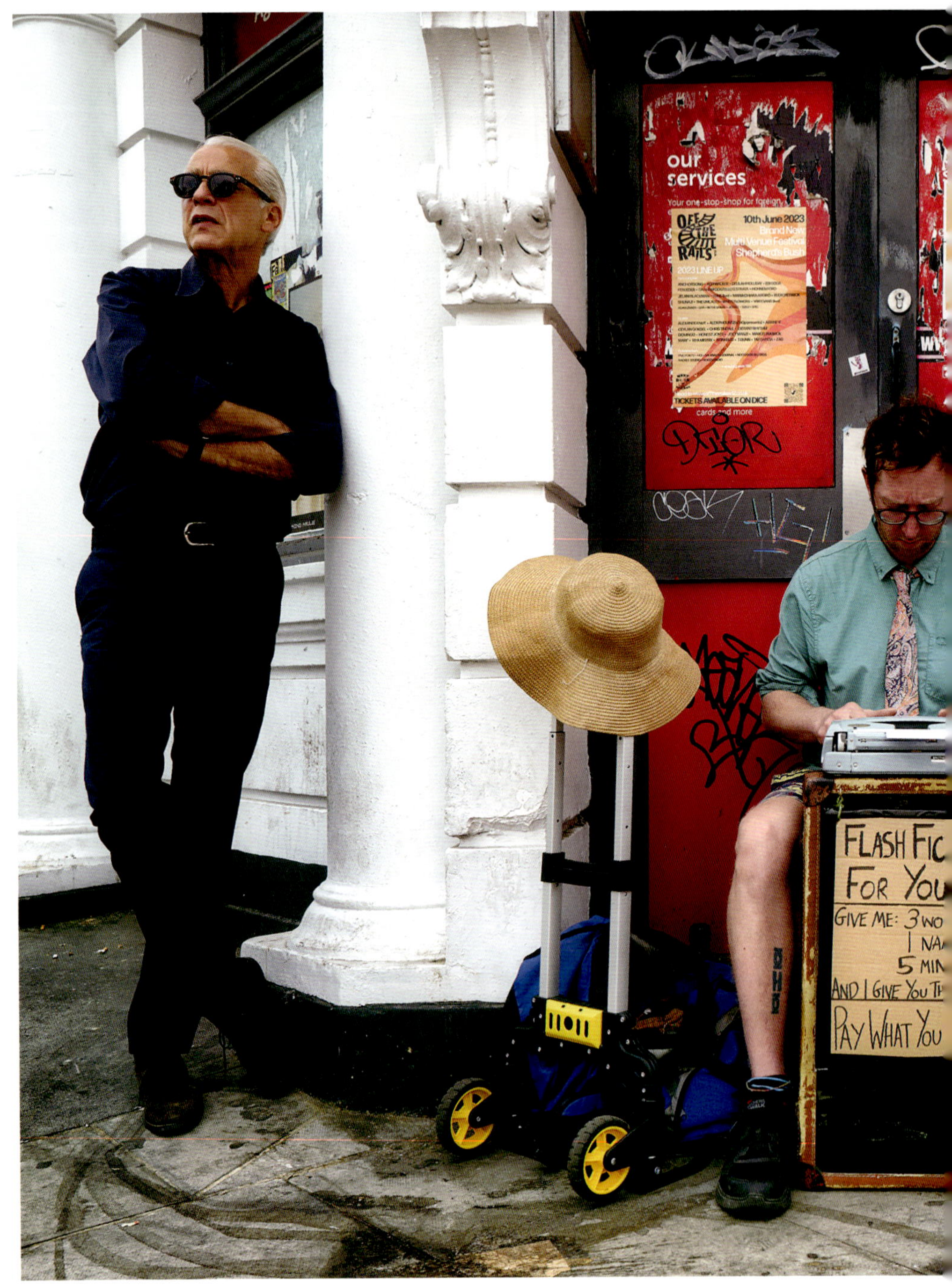

Flash Fiction Writer > London, England

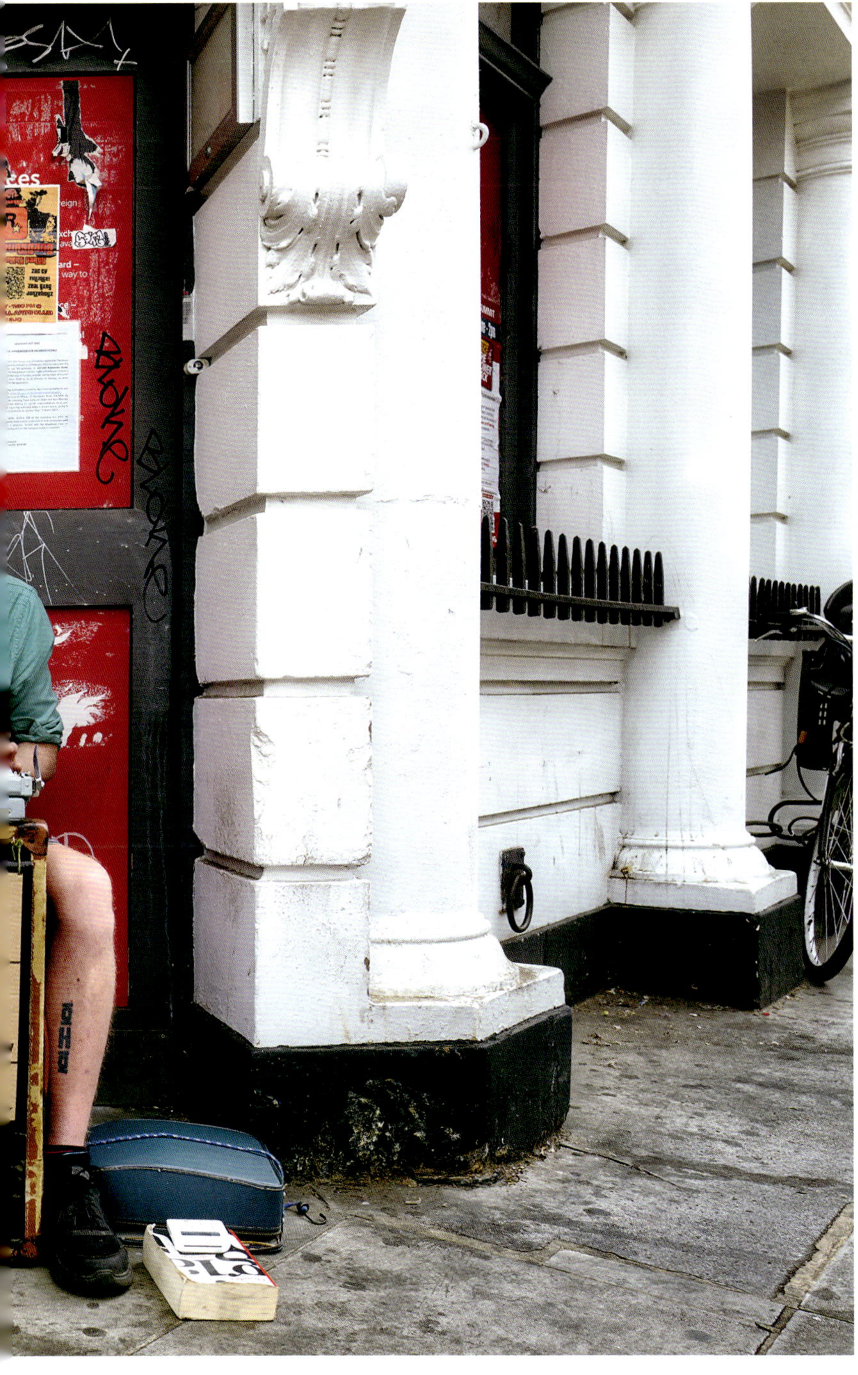

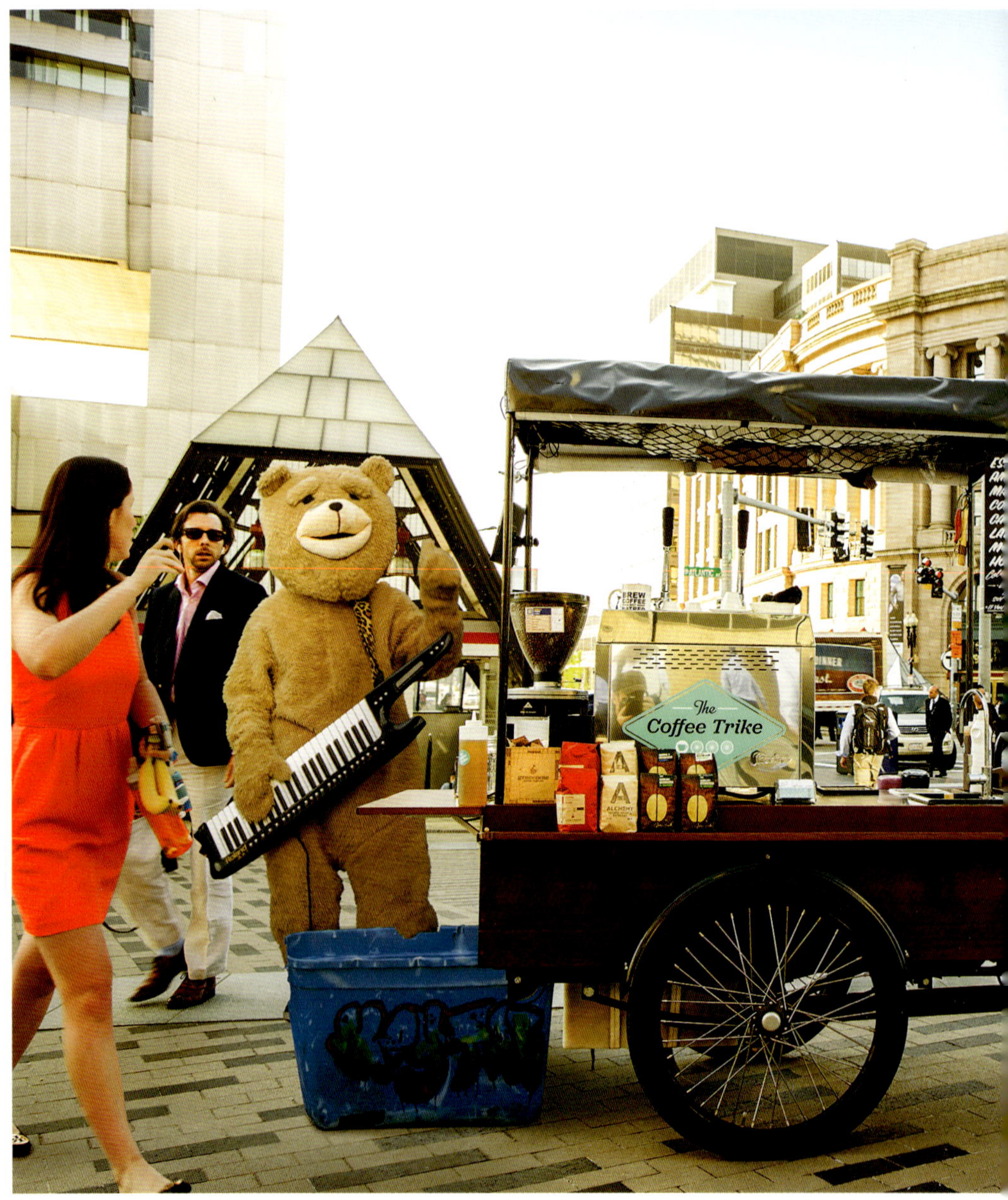

I don't know what impressed me more: that this image coalesced all at once in front of me, or that for perhaps the first time in the history of caffeine, there was no line for coffee.

Alessandra Bellino Coffee Trike Vendor > Boston, Massachusetts

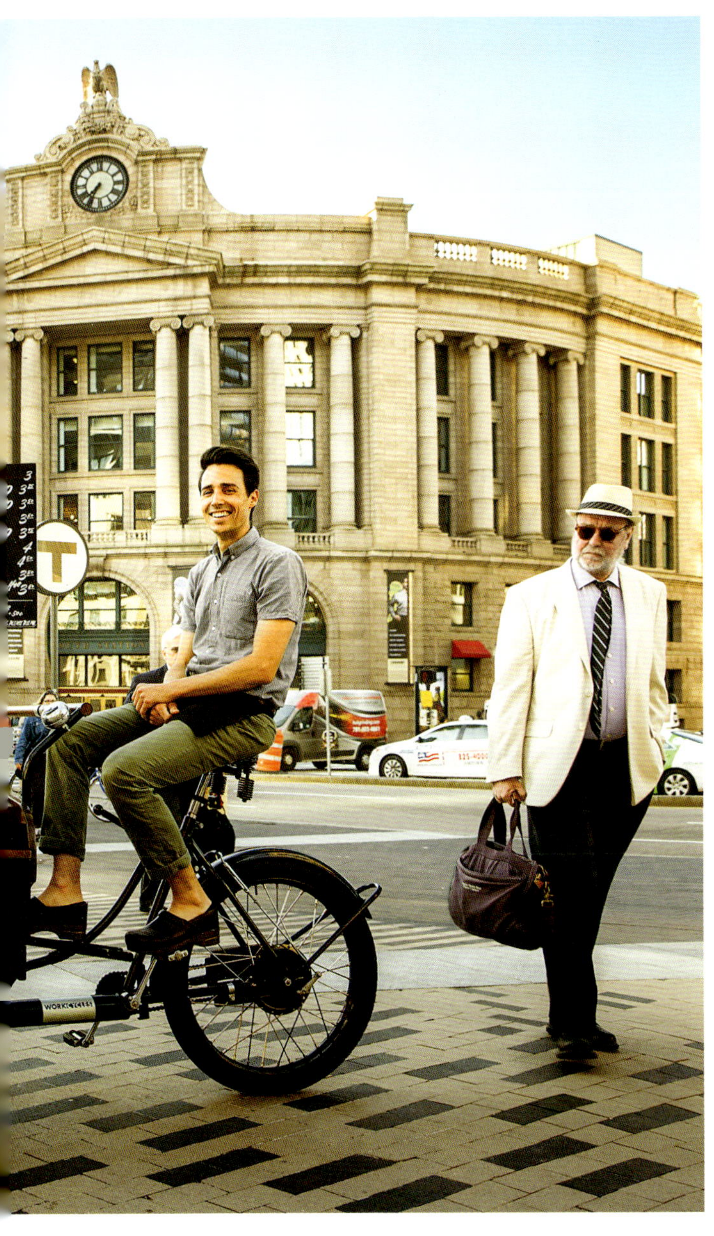

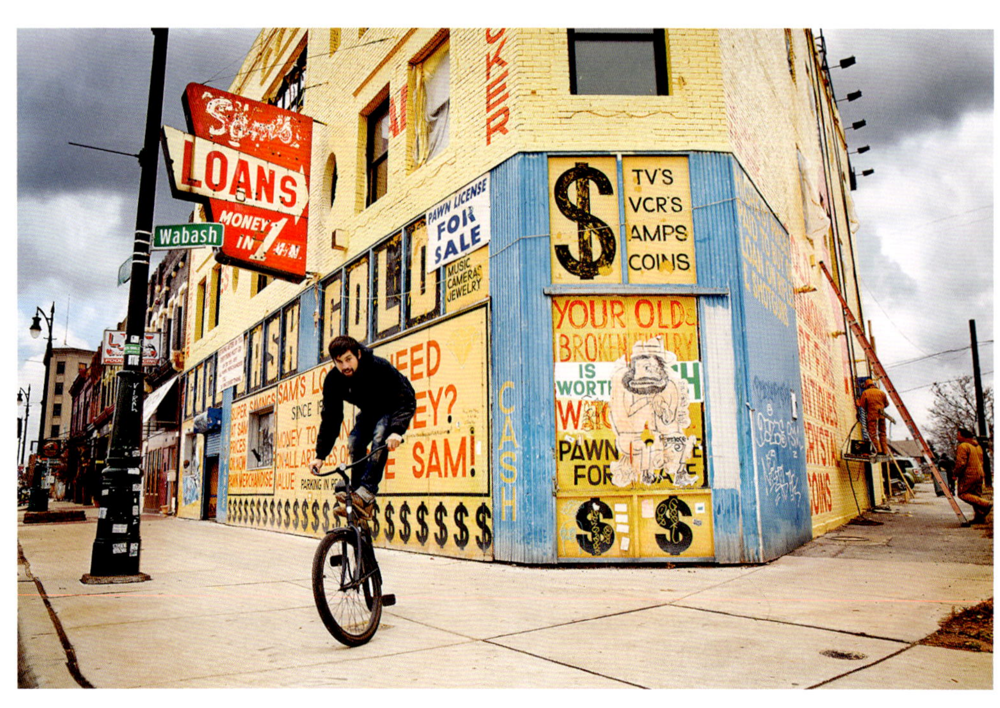

Phillip Cooley Entrepreneur > Detroit, Michigan

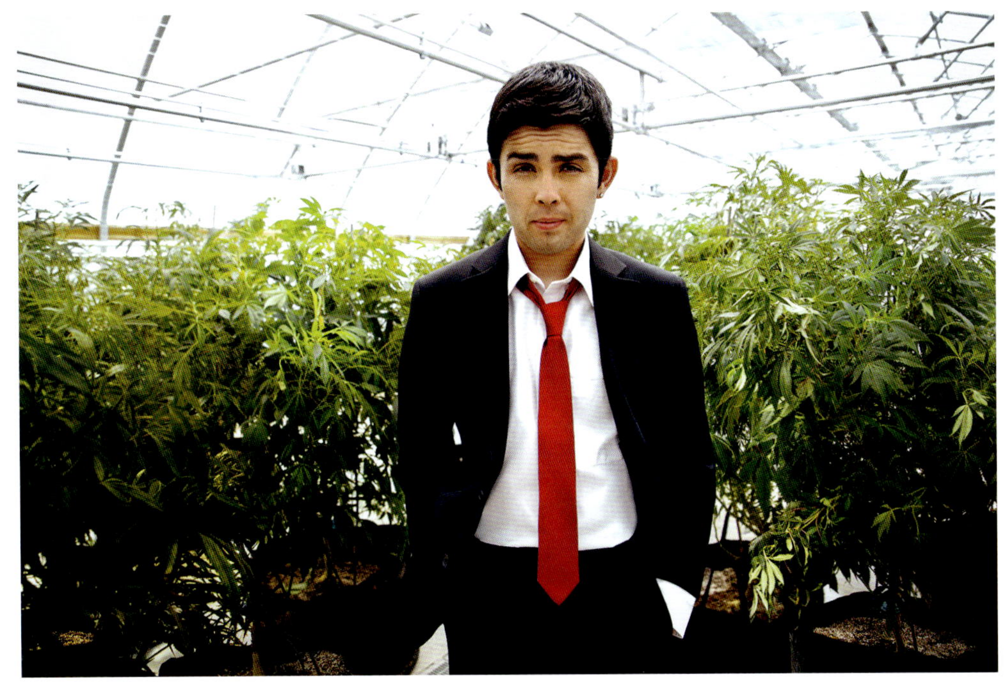

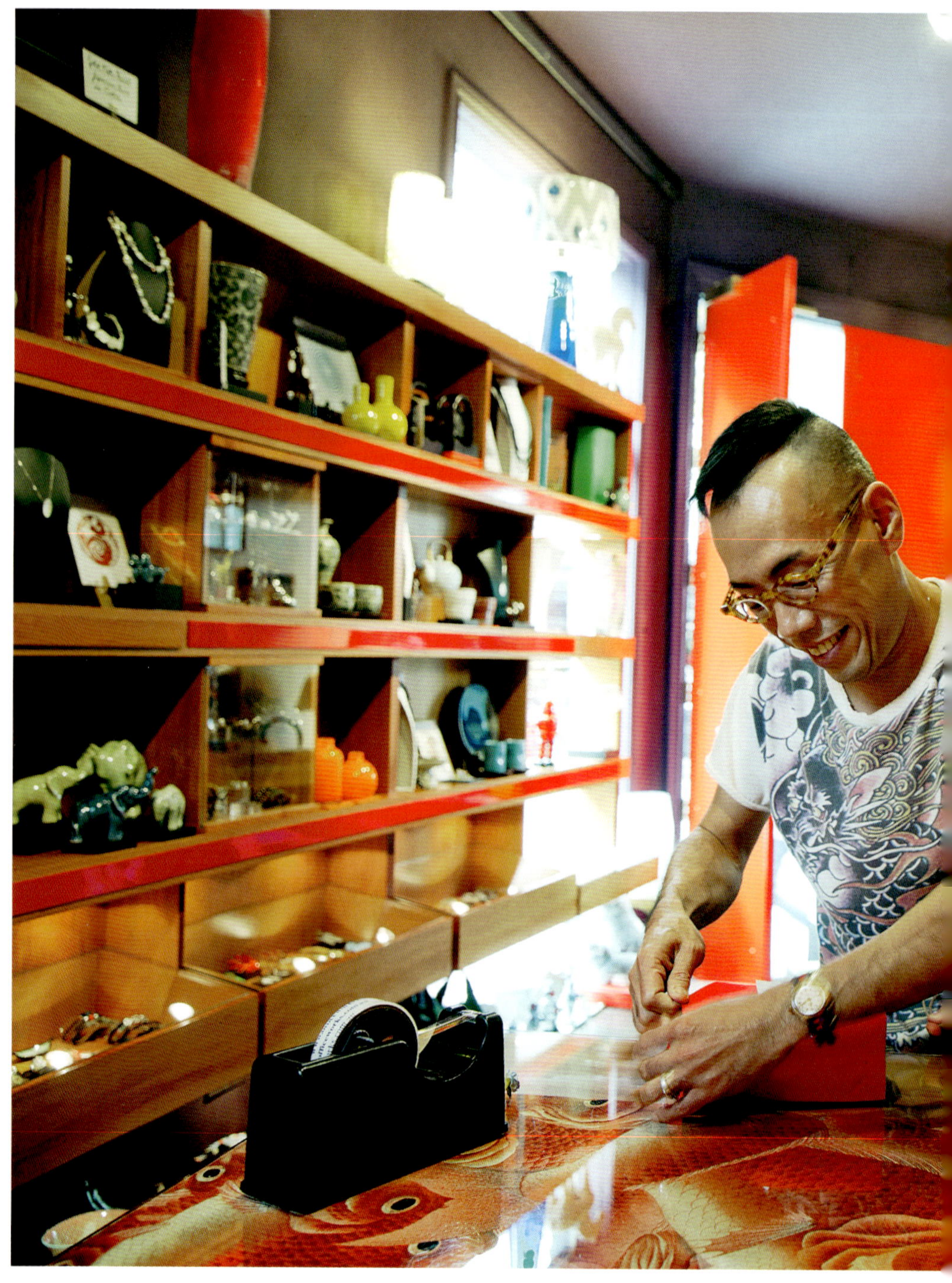

Amorn Thangbanchirtsuk & Wasan Panjamawat Mrs. Red & Sons Gift Shop > Surrey Hills, Australia

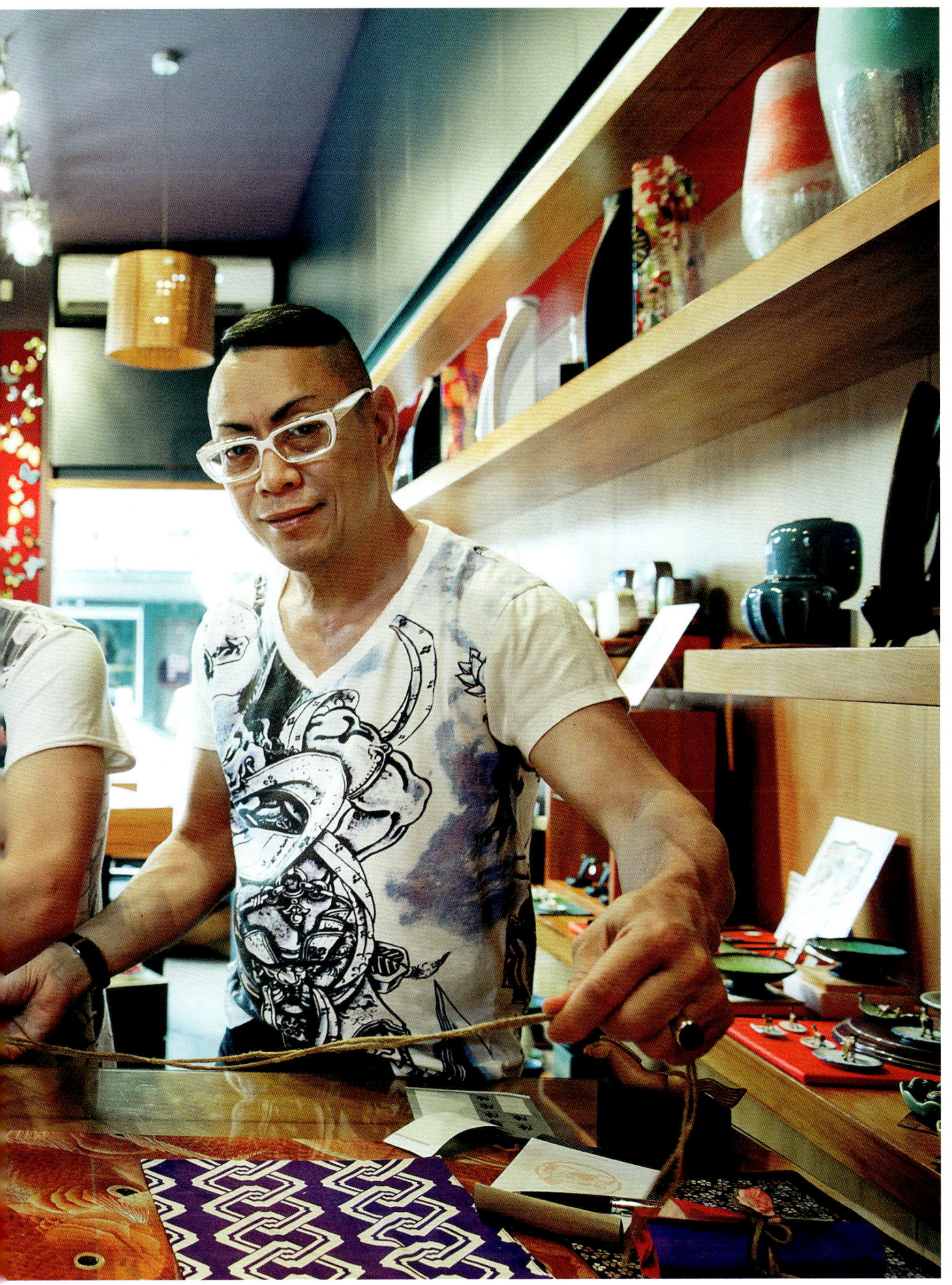

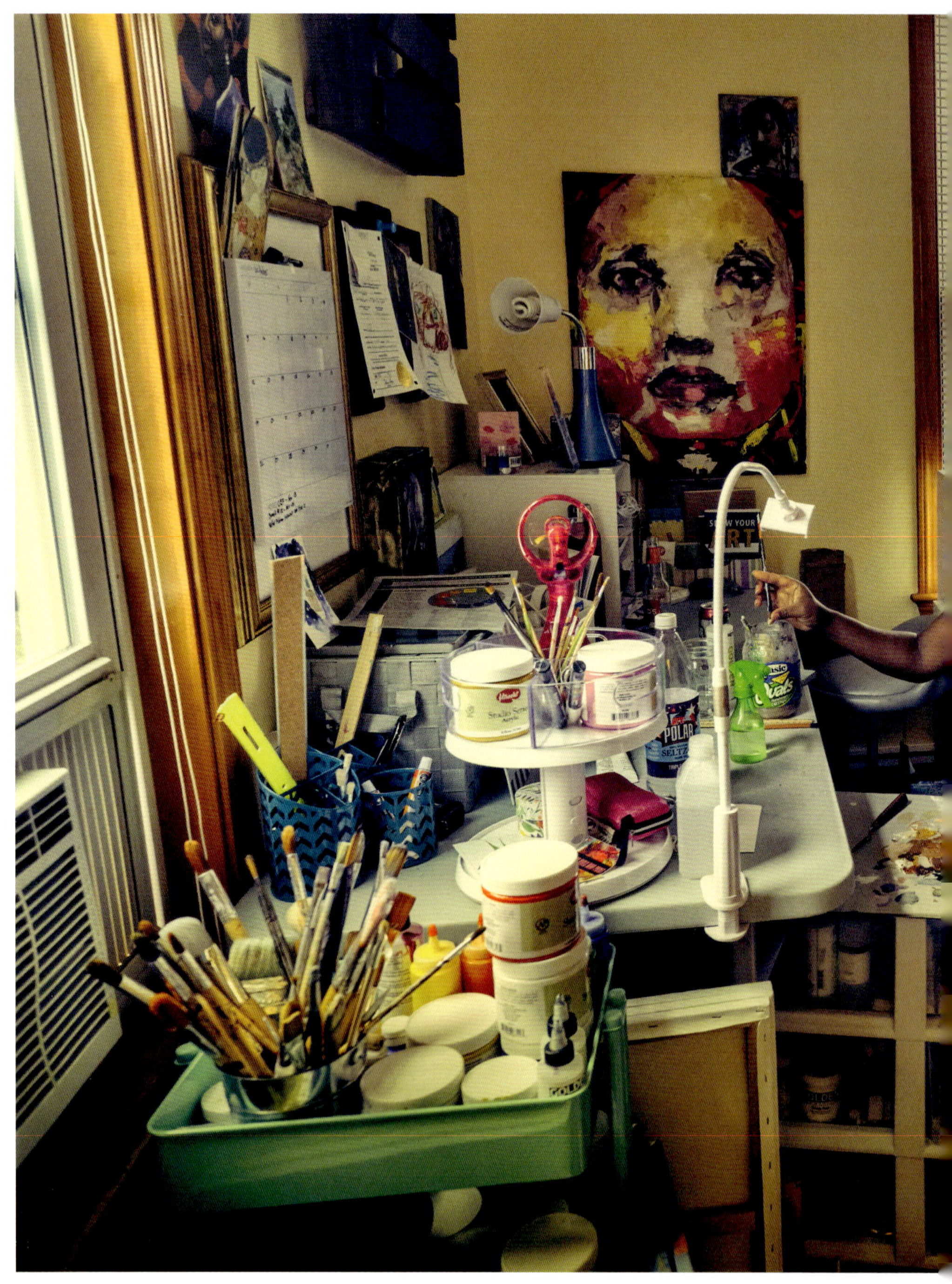

Robyn Thompson-Duong Artist > Boston, Massachusetts

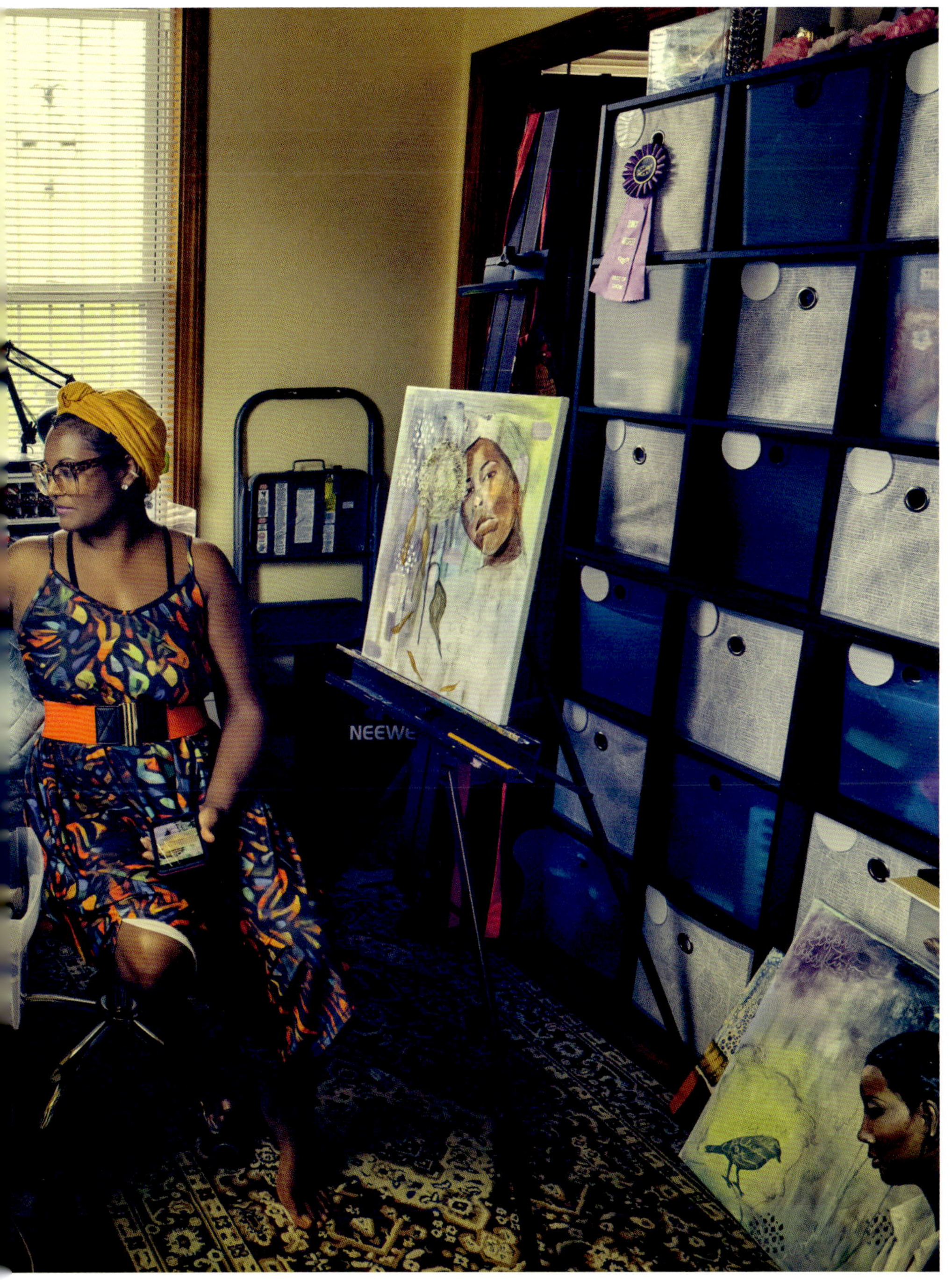

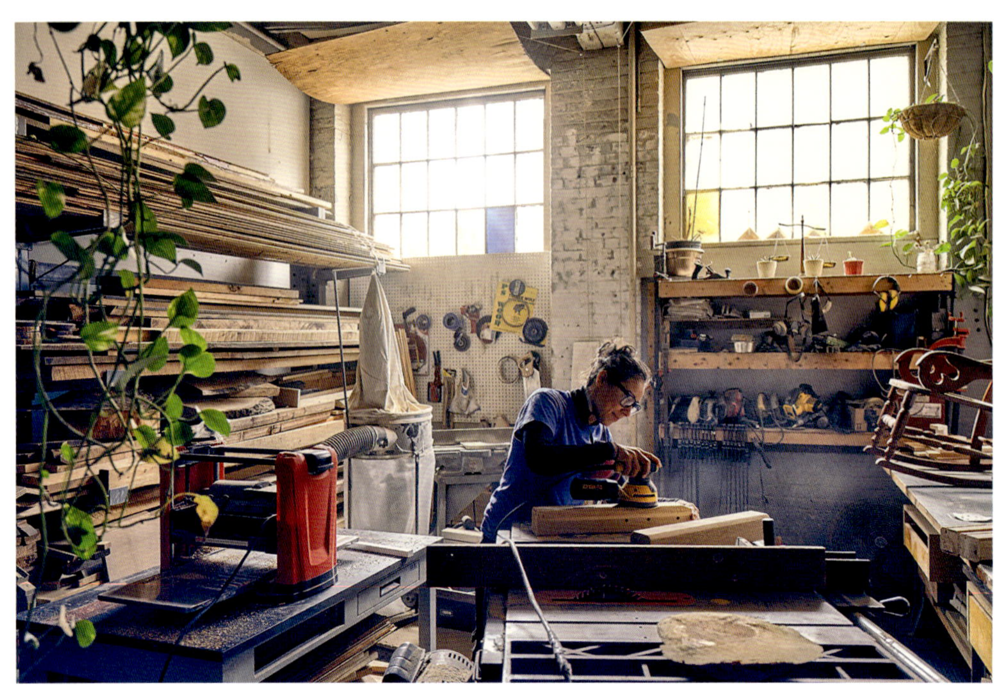

Ana Torres Woodworker, ACT Designs > Boston, Massachusetts

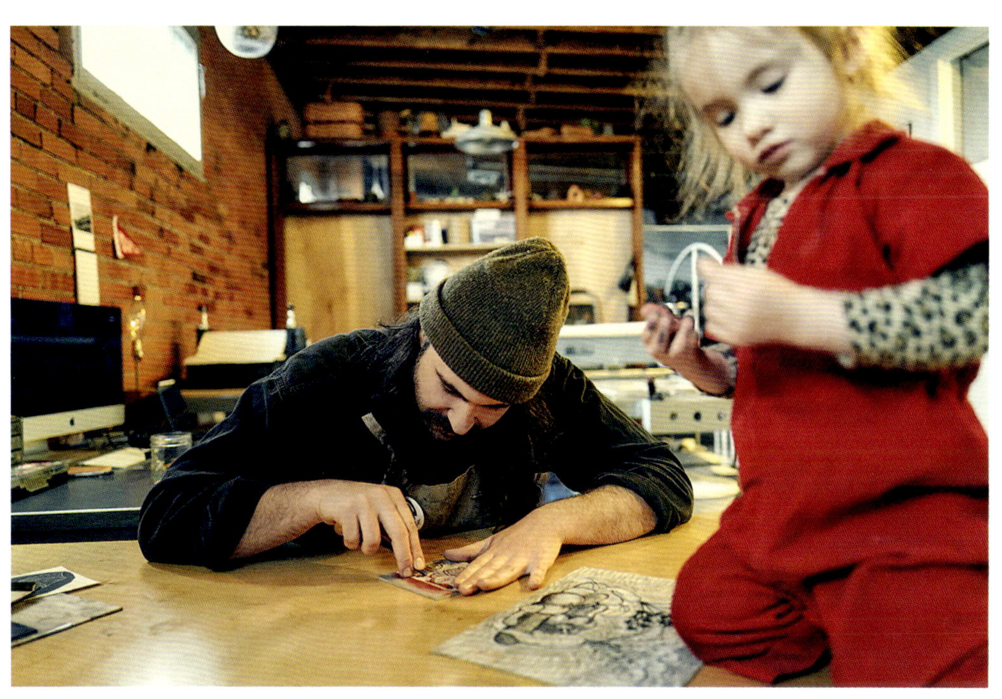

David & Blue Lusk Printmaker, Anomal Press > Missoula, Montana

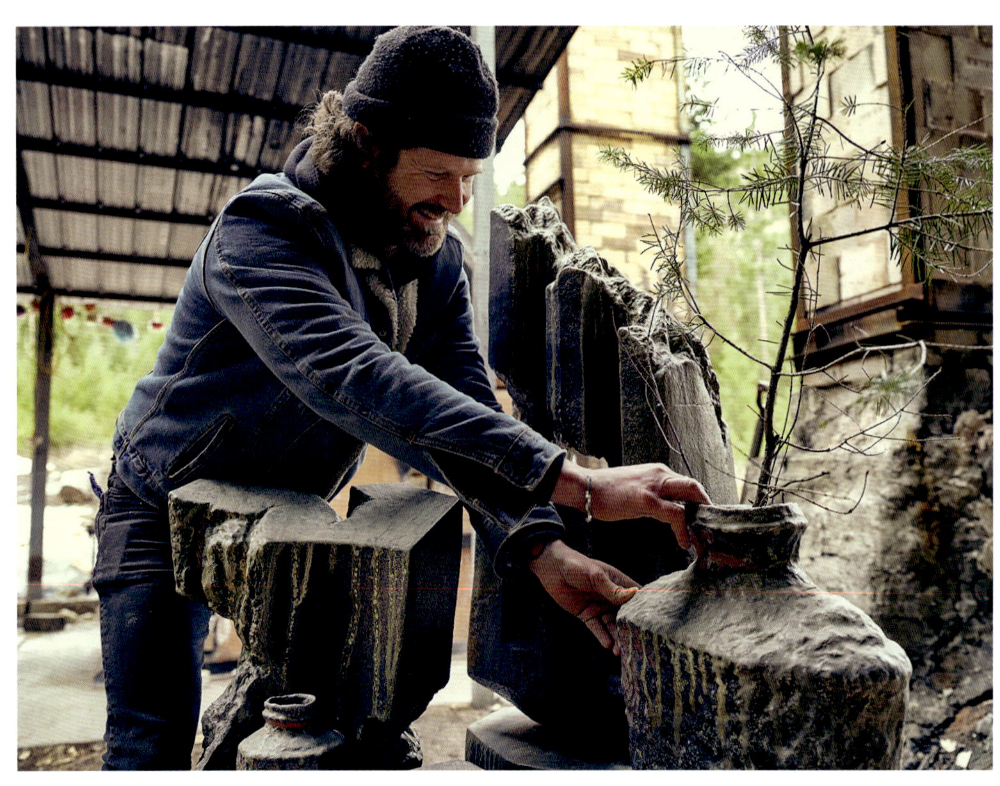

Casey Zablocki Clay Sculptor > Missoula, Montana

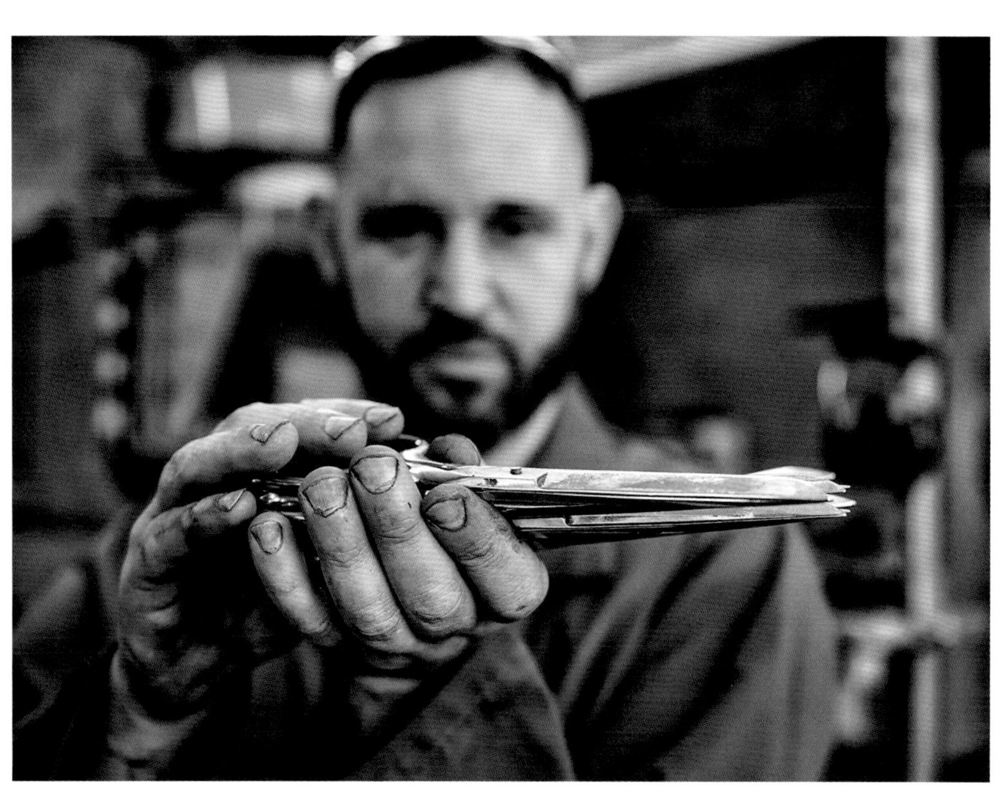

Neil Wilson Scissor Maker, Ernest Wright > Sheffield, England

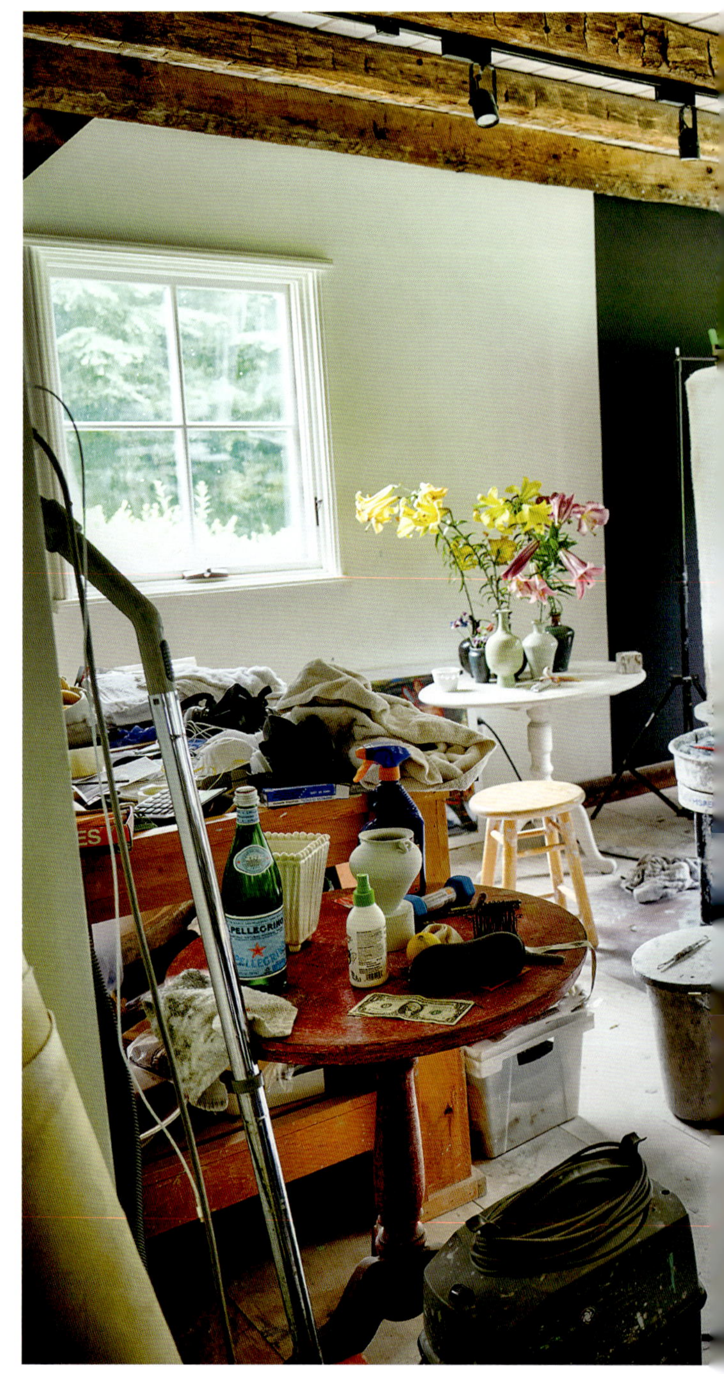

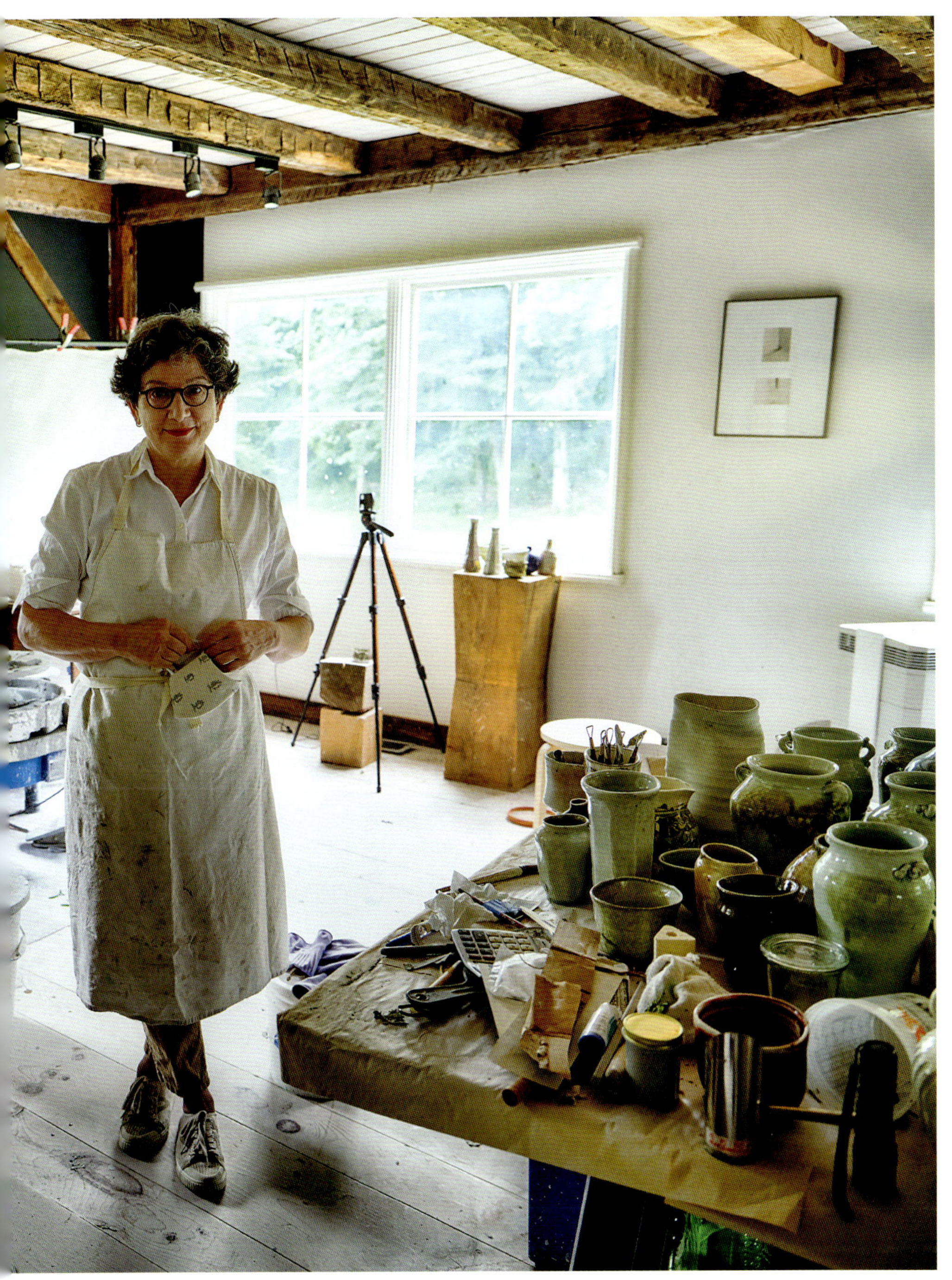

Frances Palmer Ceramic Artist > Weston, Connecticut

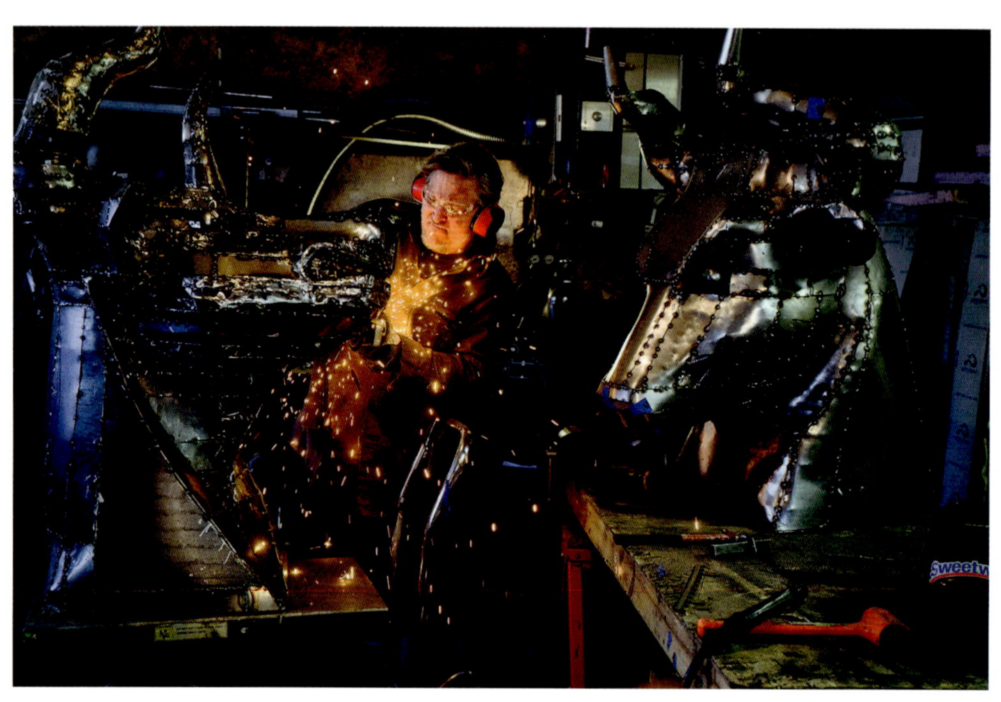

Kyle Fokken Sculptor > Minneapolis, Minnesota

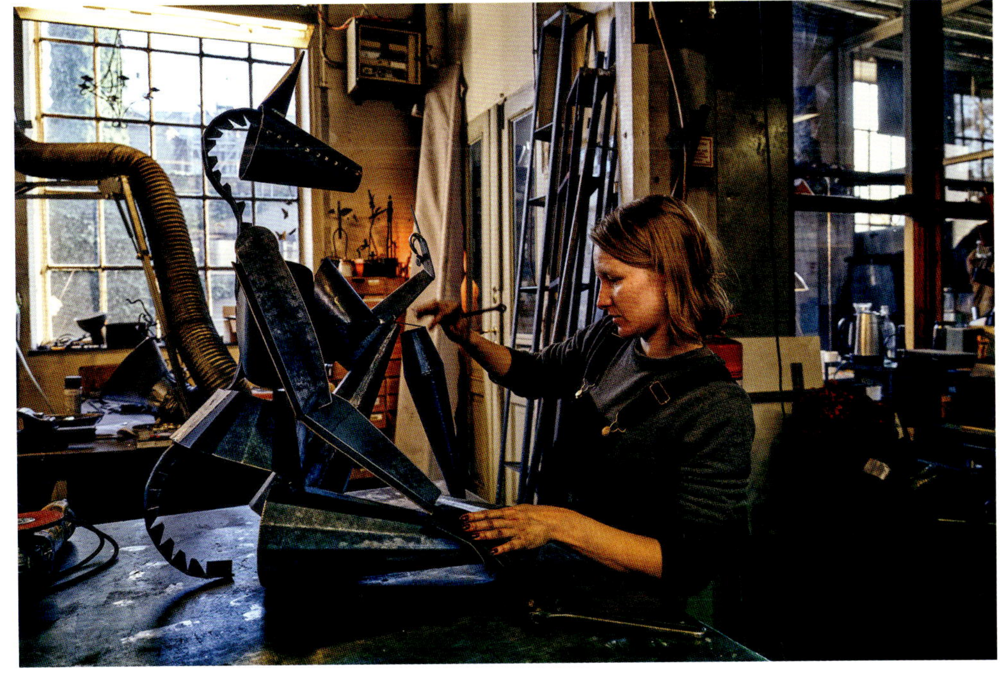

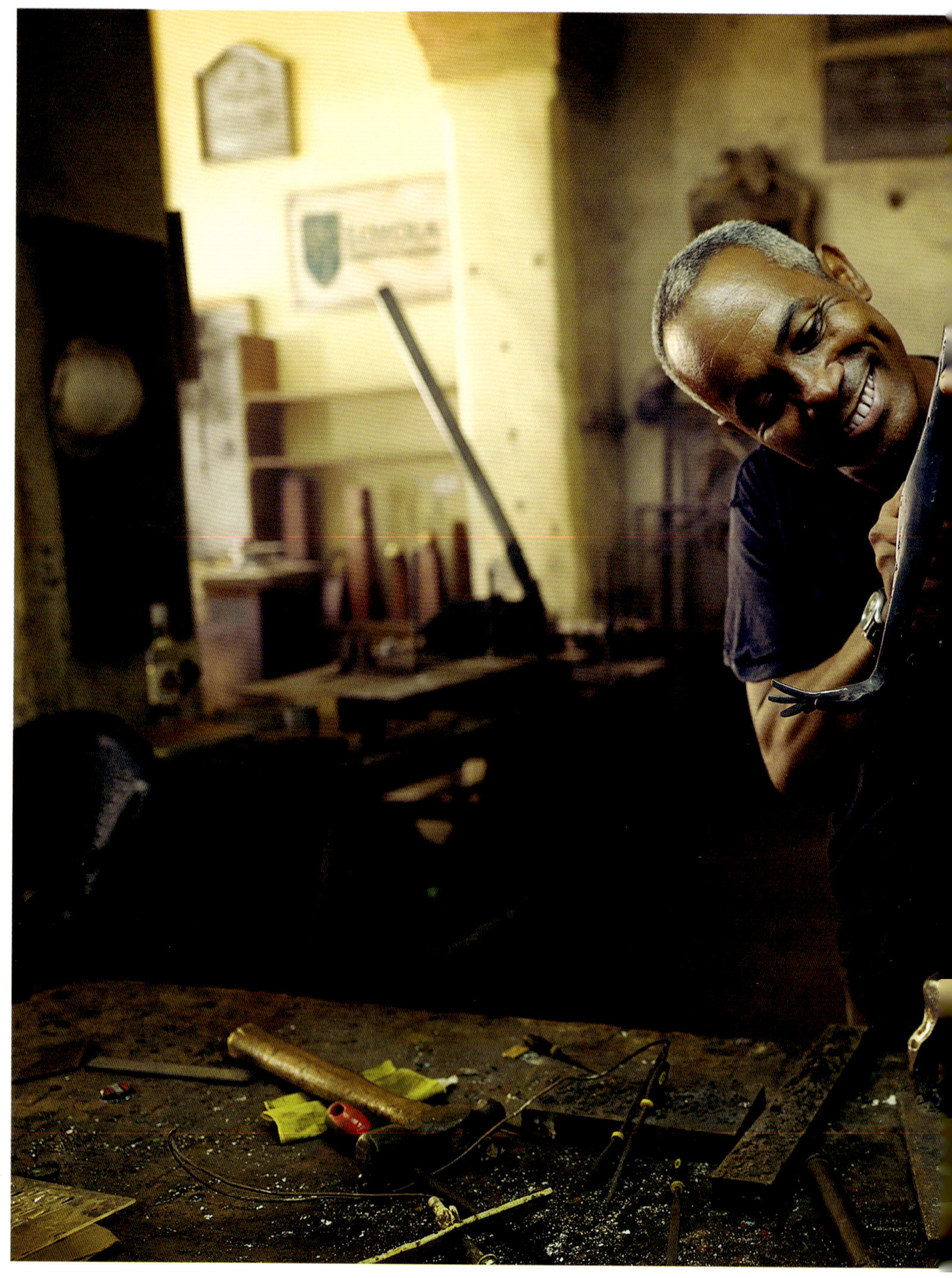

José Durerger Sculptor > Havana, Cuba

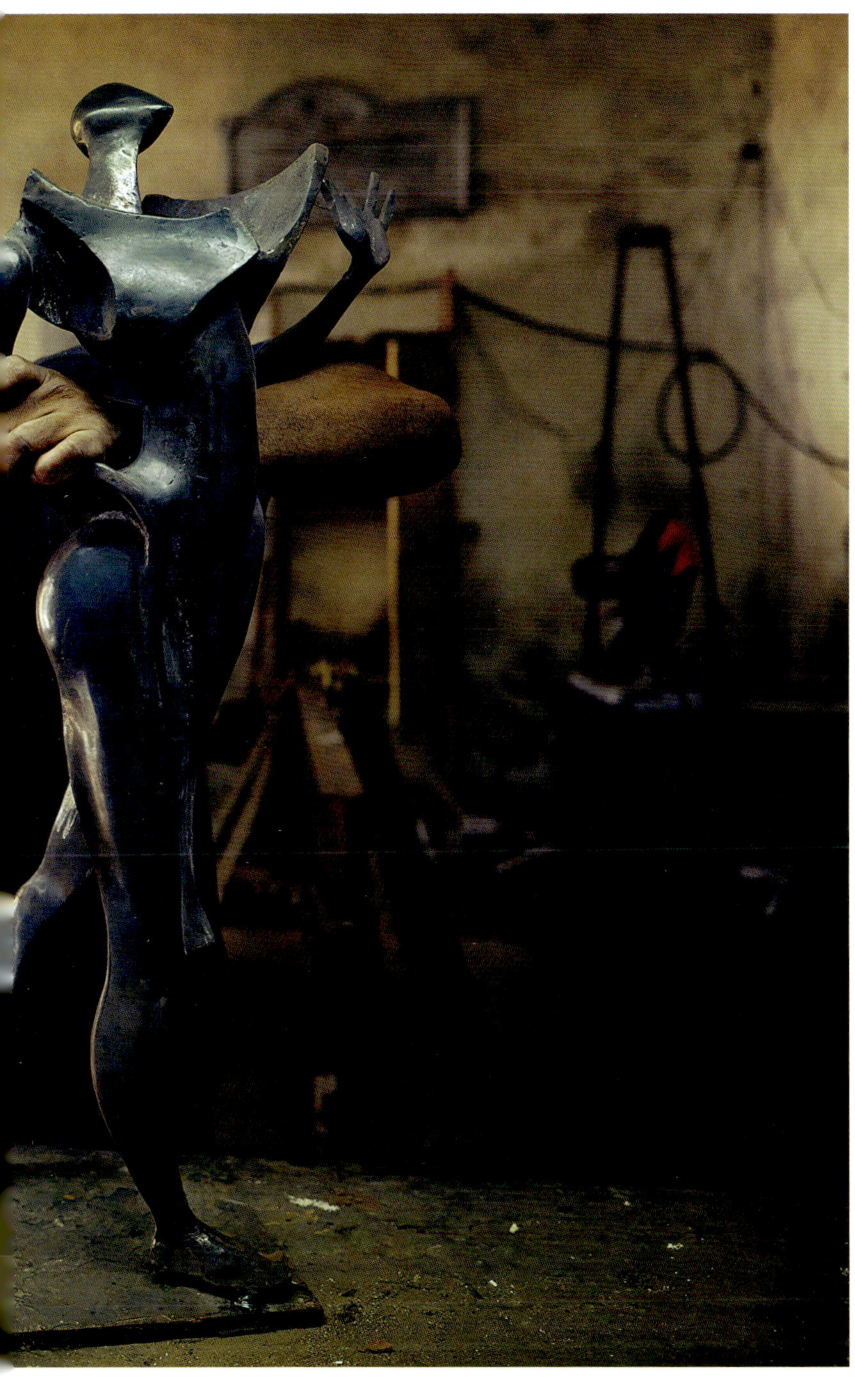

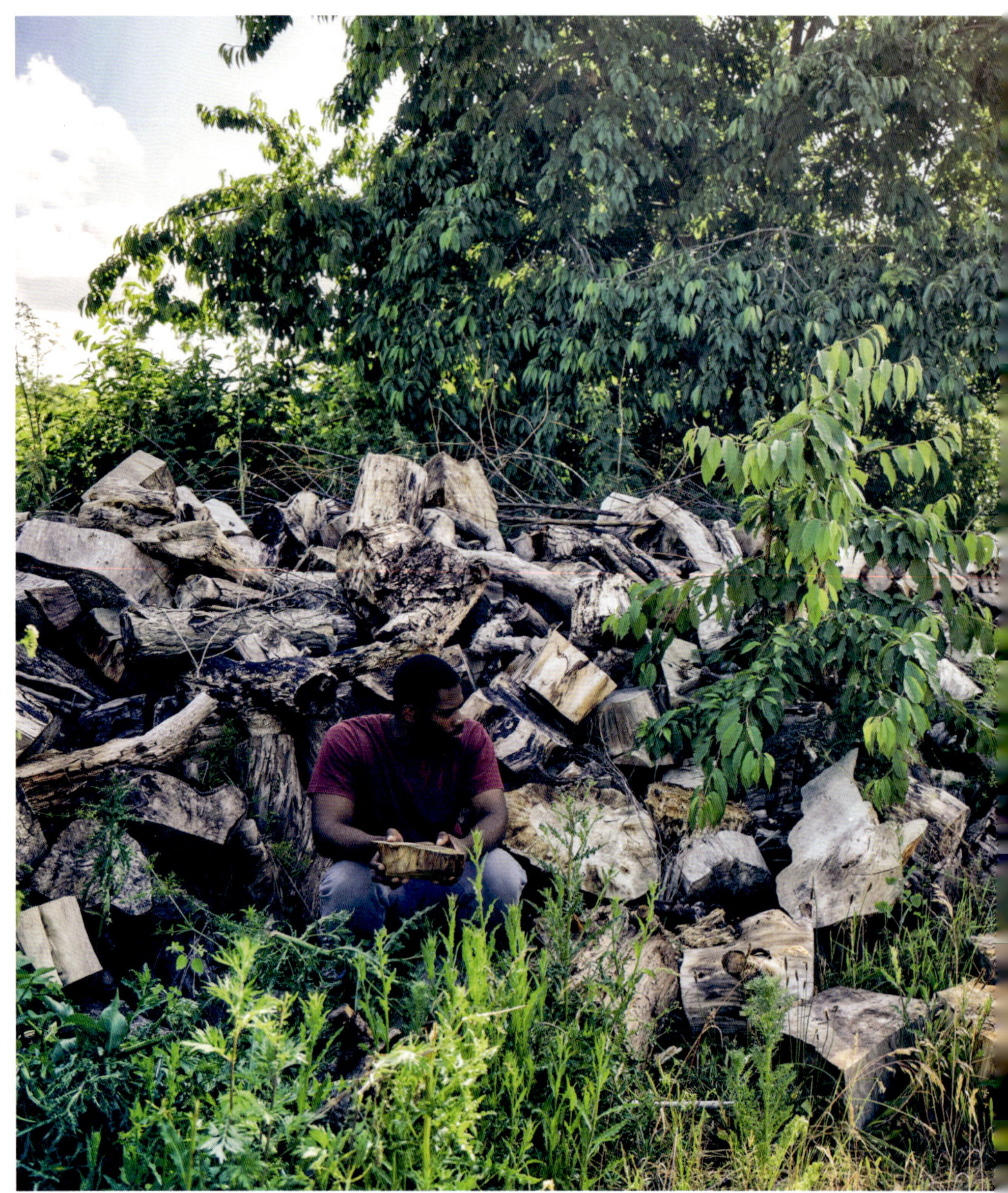

Darren and I met in the studio where he transforms discarded wood into art. Seeing the finished product, I needed to know more about how the work actually began.

We set off on foot to the place where Darren sources wood reclaimed from construction sites. Along the way, we compared notes on our childhoods: his in England; mine in Brooklyn.

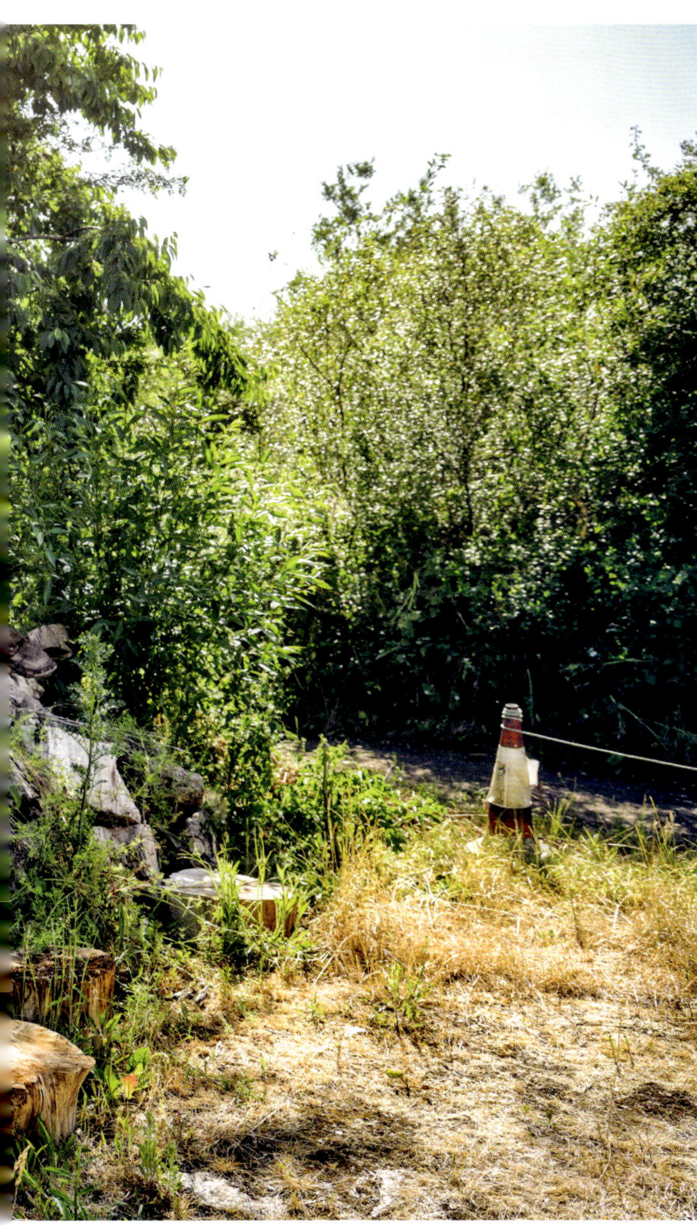

He explained that he was looking for pieces that spoke to him. It struck me that his experiences as a boy were at the heart of his creative drive. He sought to reveal the beauty and possibility in things that would otherwise go overlooked and disregarded.

Darren Appiagyei Wood Artist > London, England

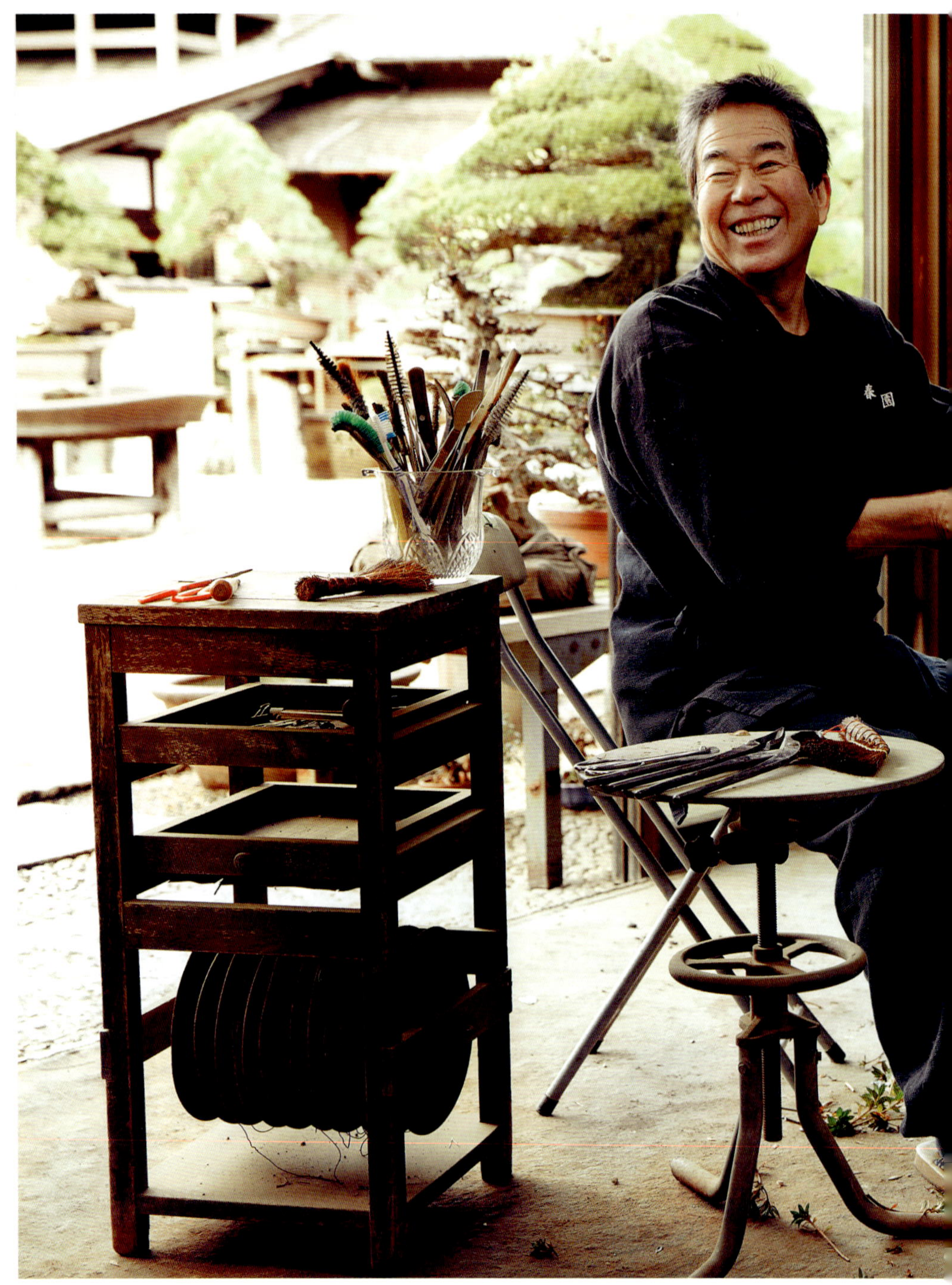

Kunio Kobayashi Bonsai Master > Tokyo, Japan

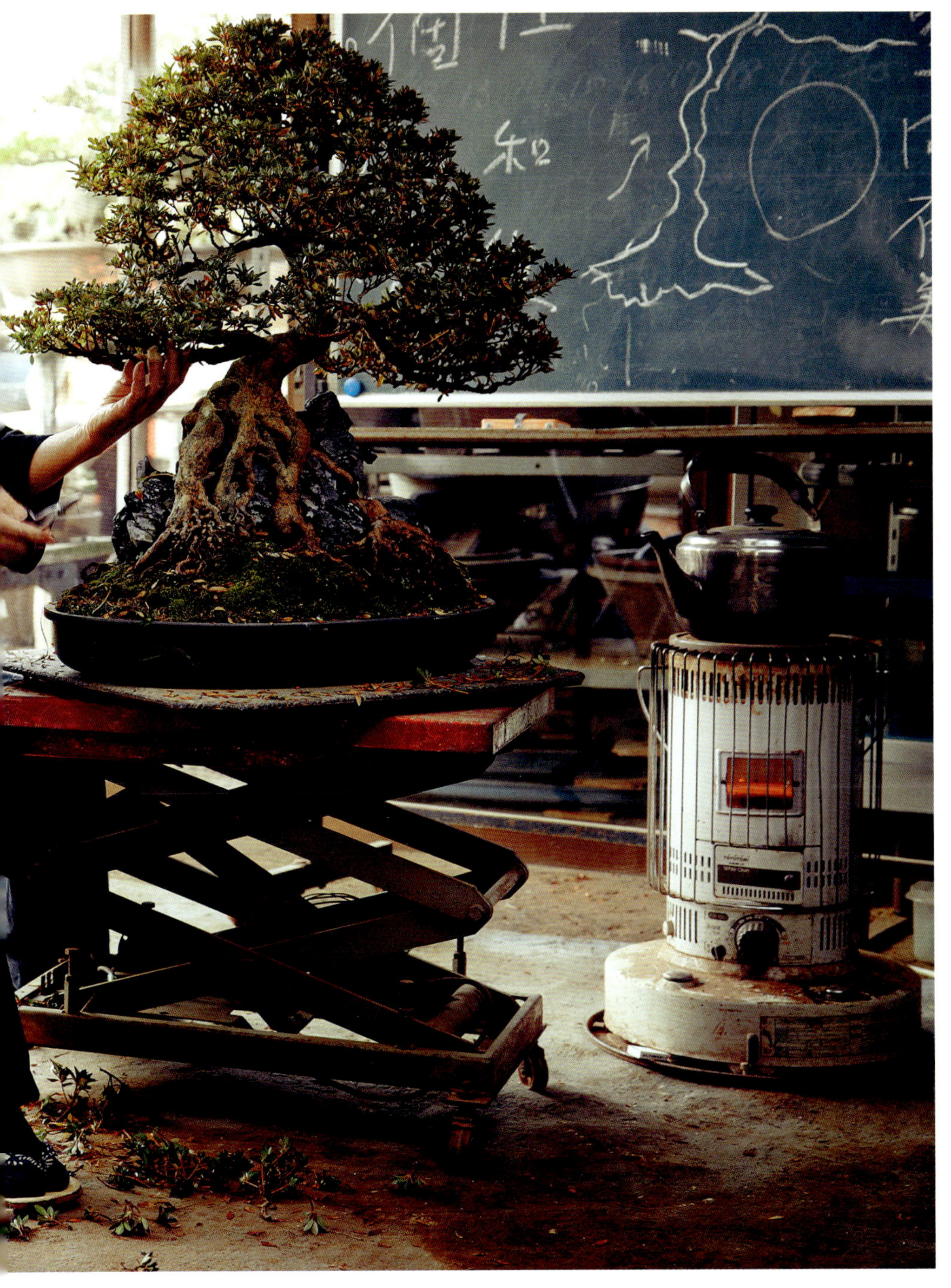

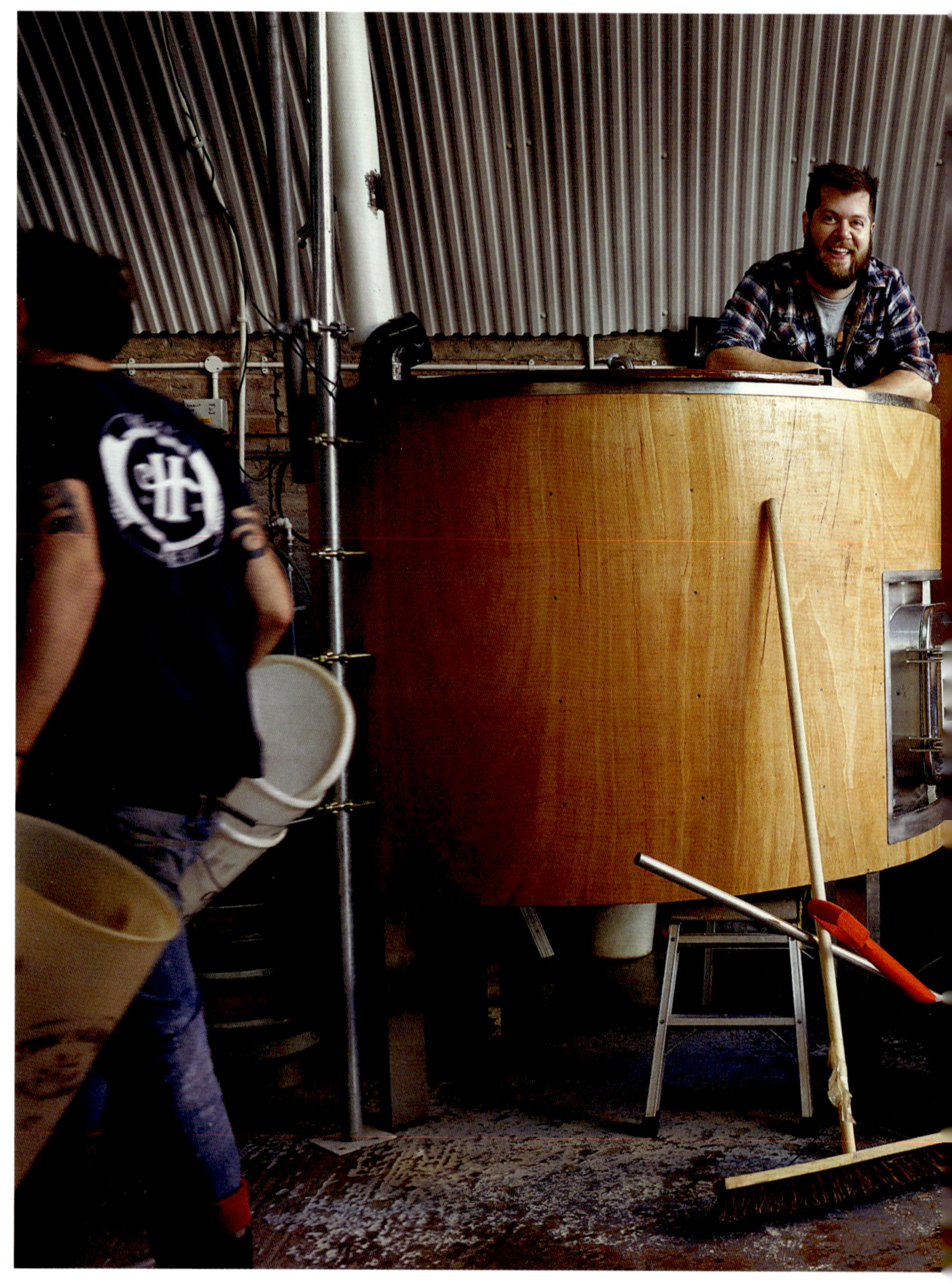

Jon Swain & Peter Hills Hackney Brewery > London, England

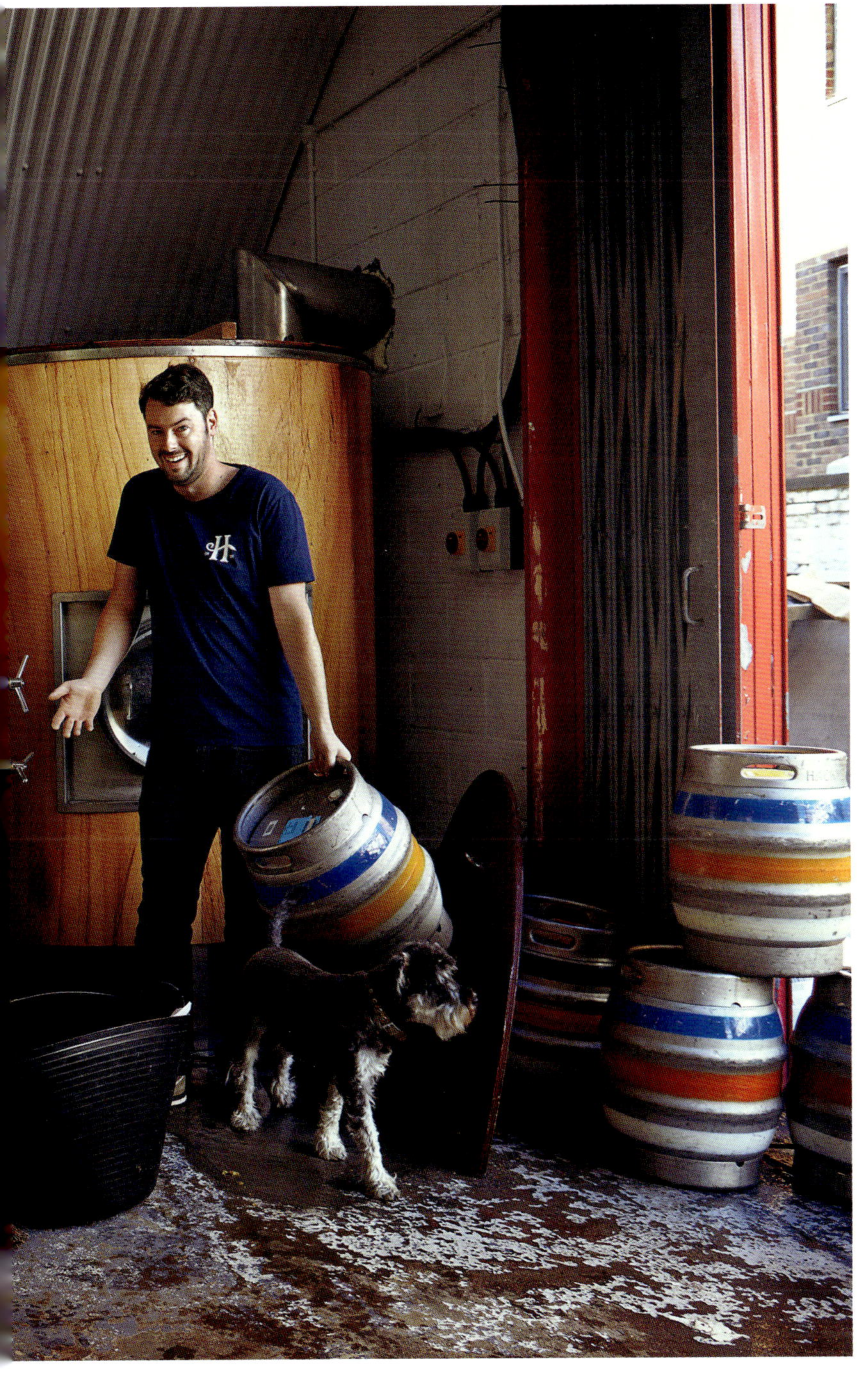

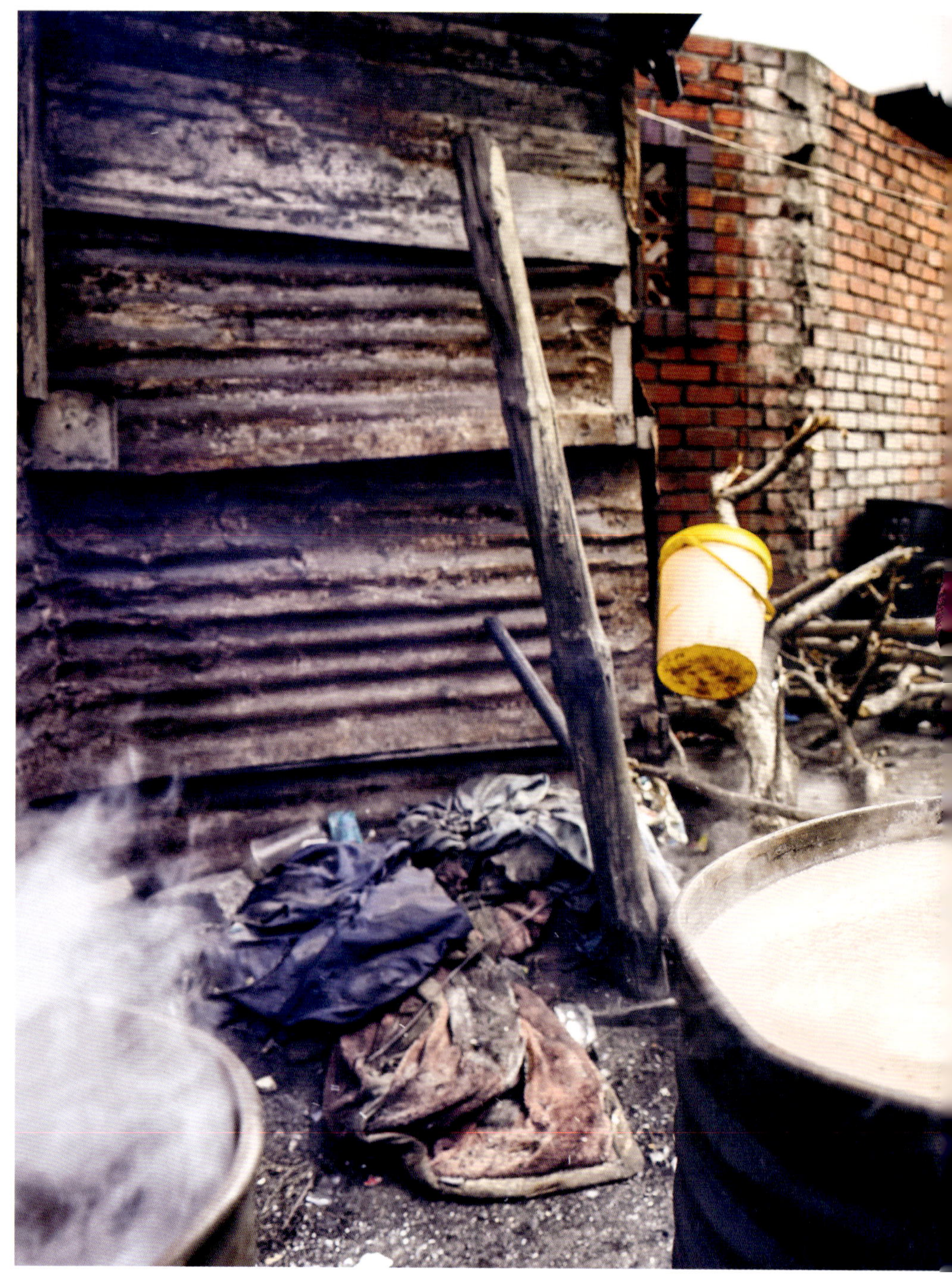

Mangxabane Beer Maker > South Africa

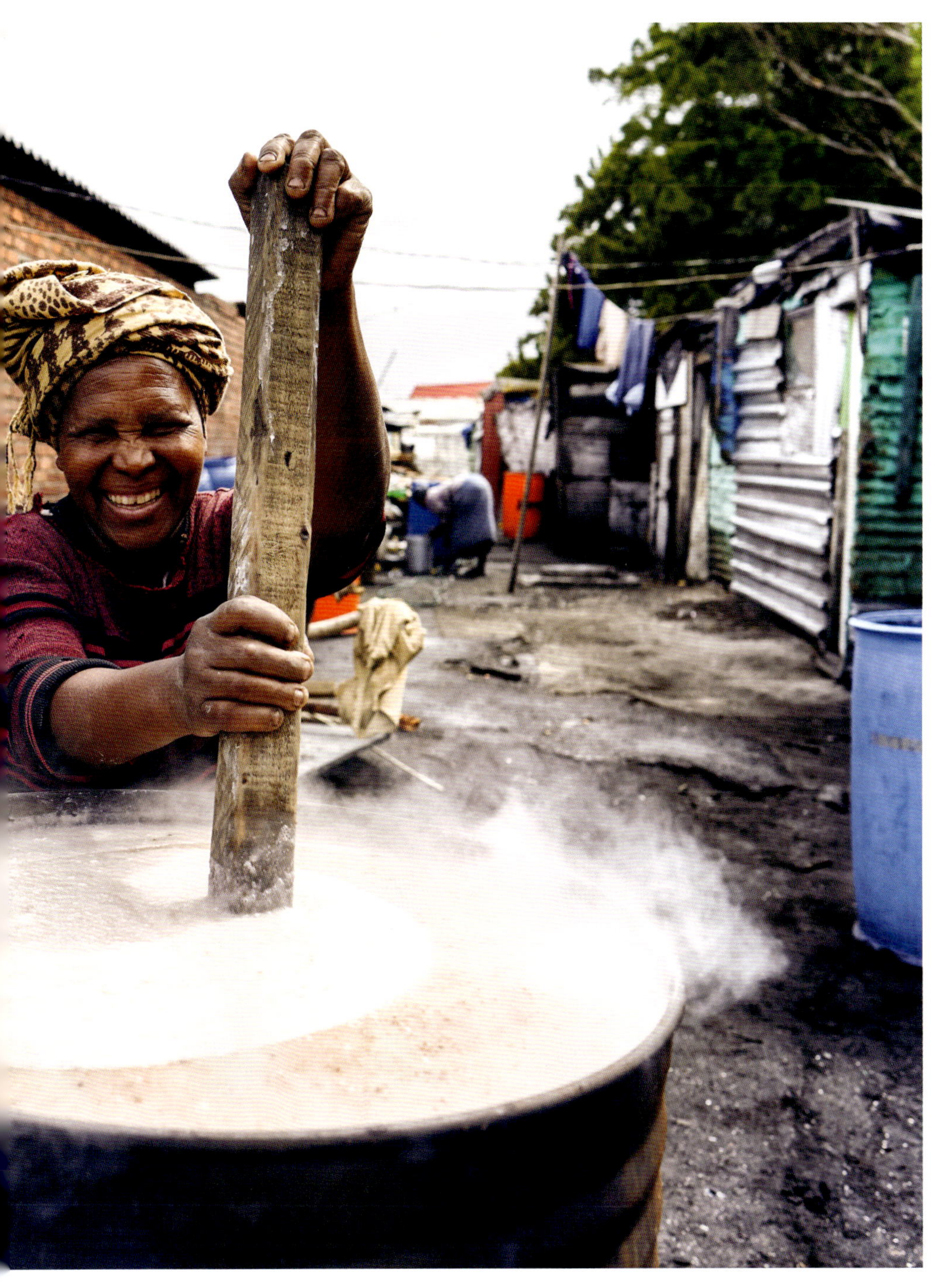

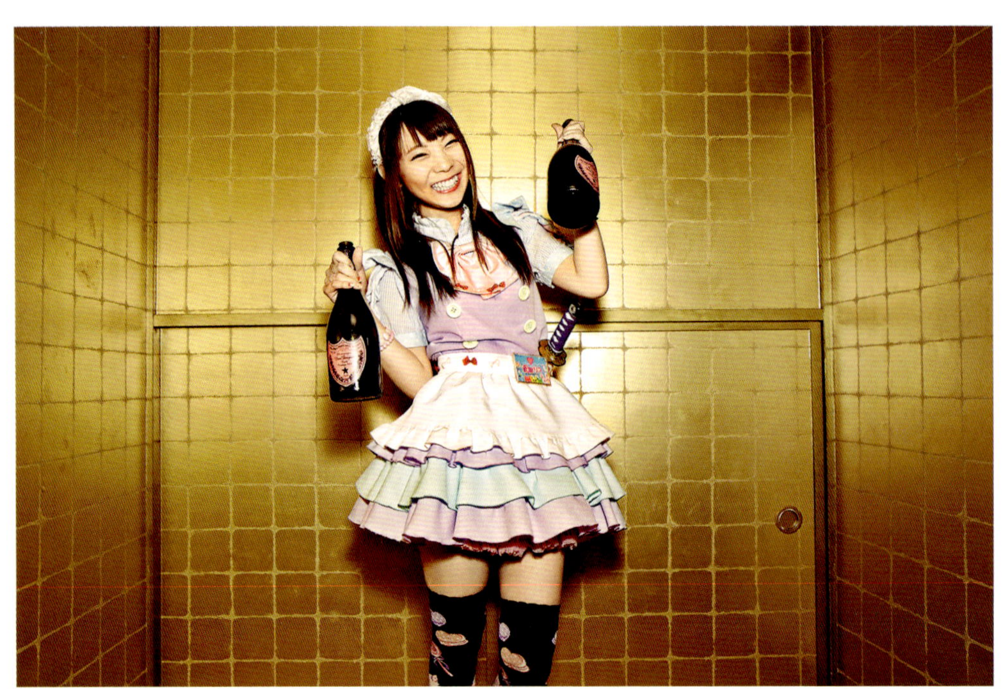

Momoko Nomura Waitress, Maid Café > Tokyo, Japan

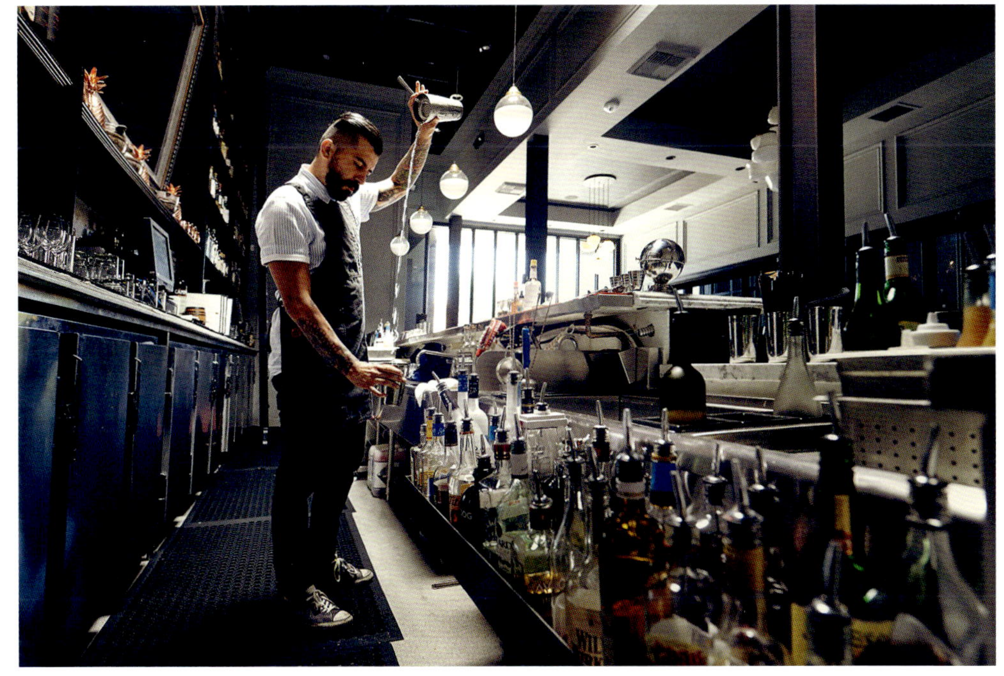

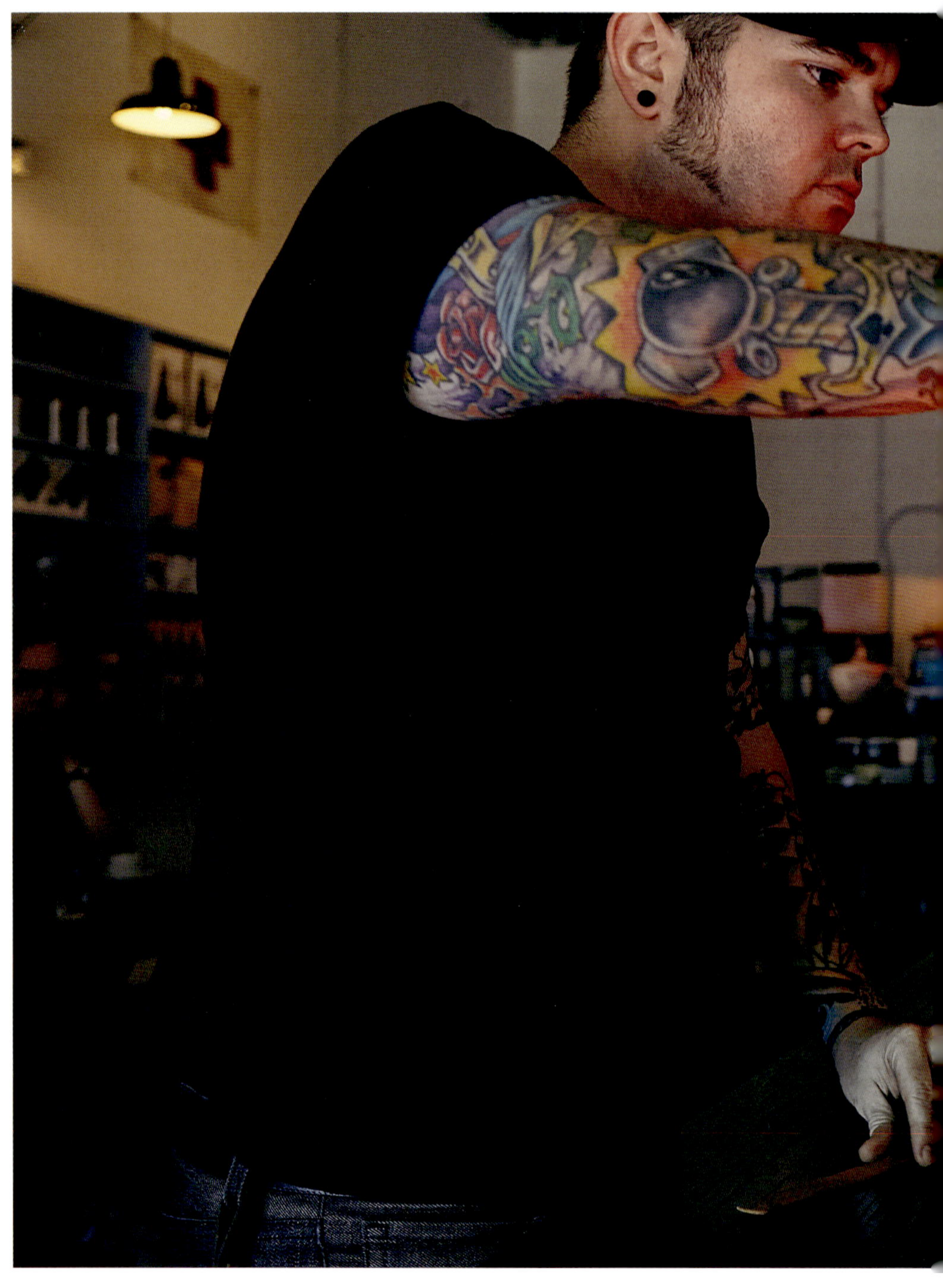

Andy Mumma Barista, Parlor > Nashville, Tennessee

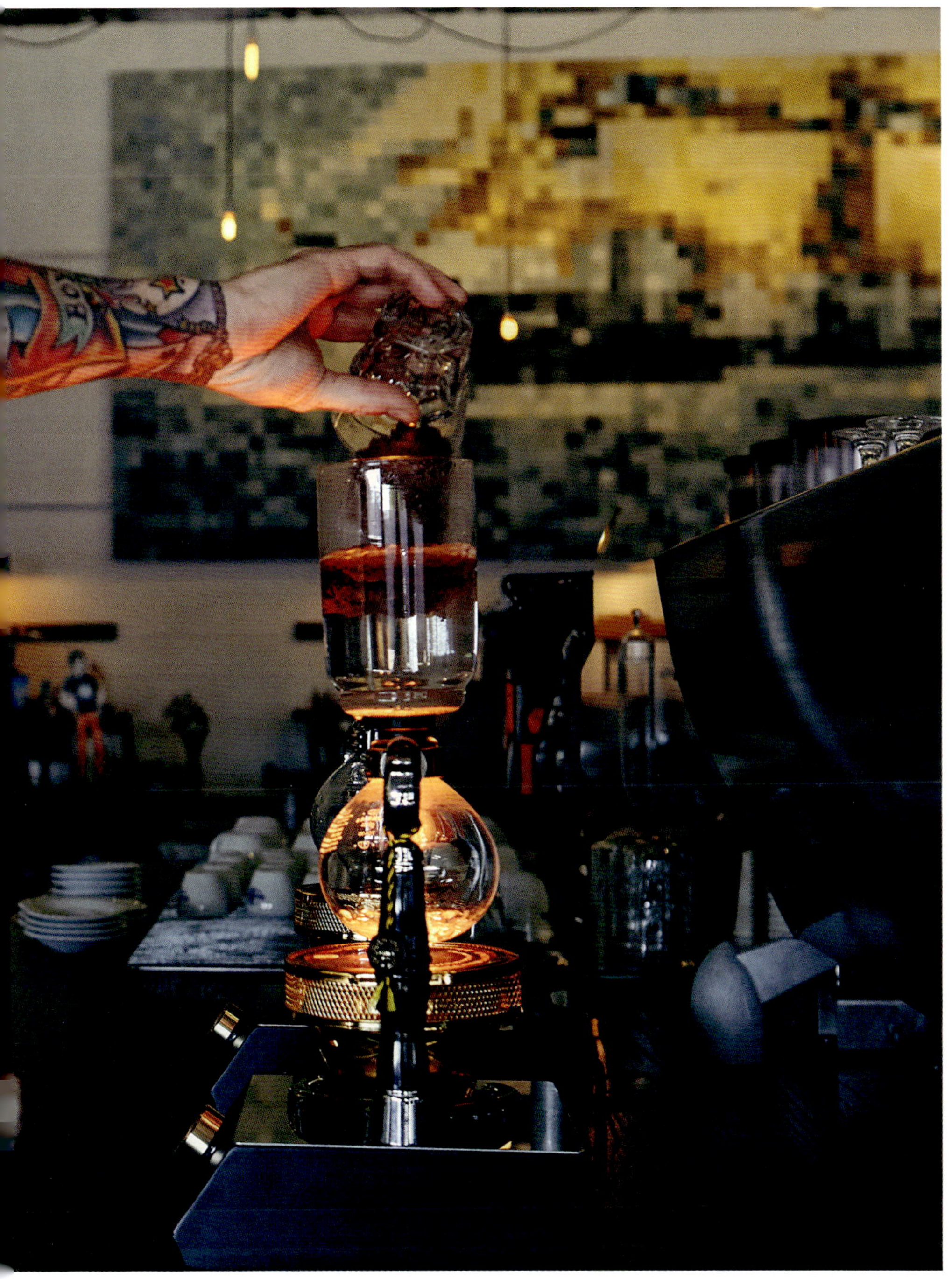

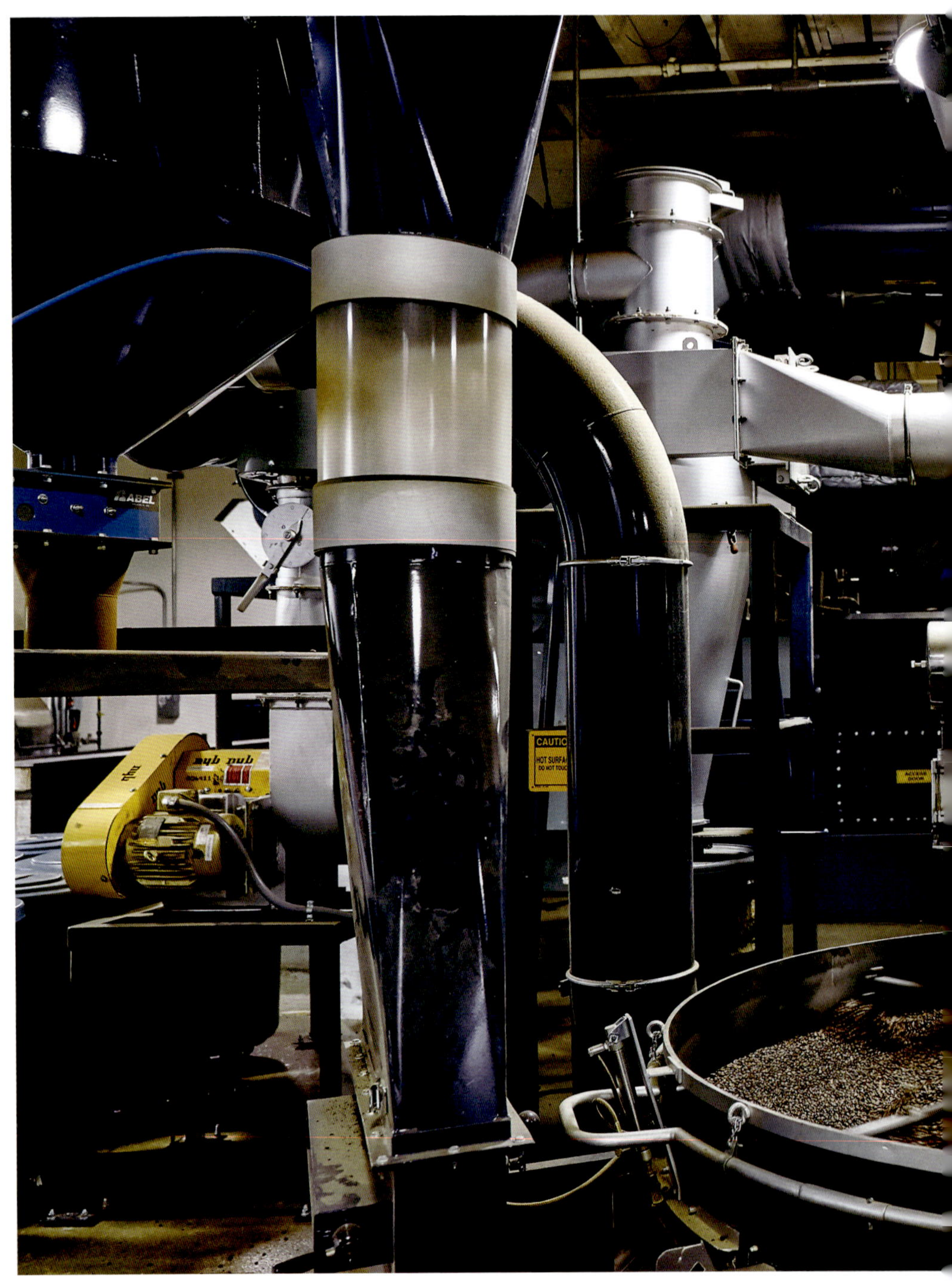

Steve Kirbach Director, Stumptown Coffee > Portland, Oregon

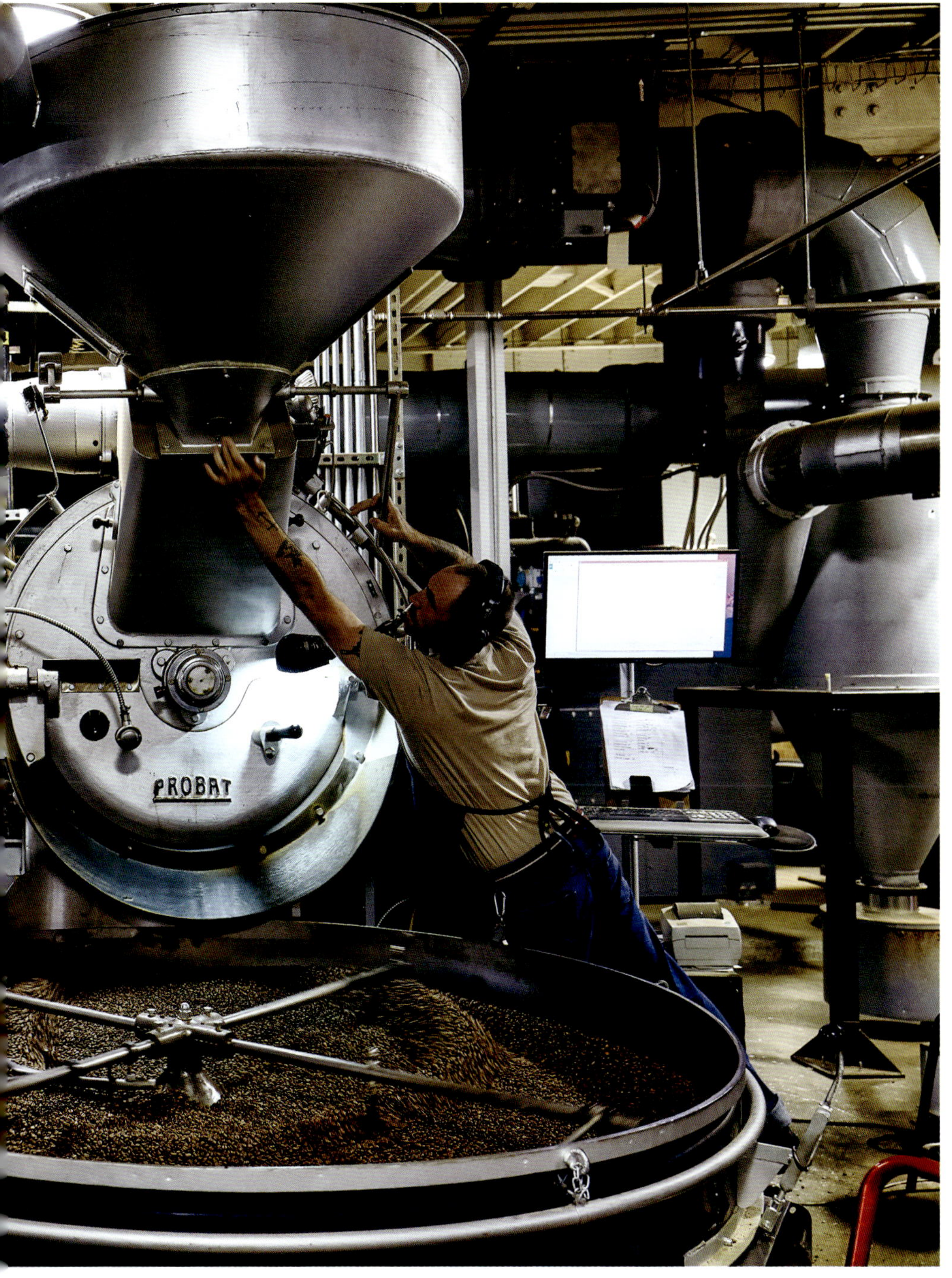
PROBAT

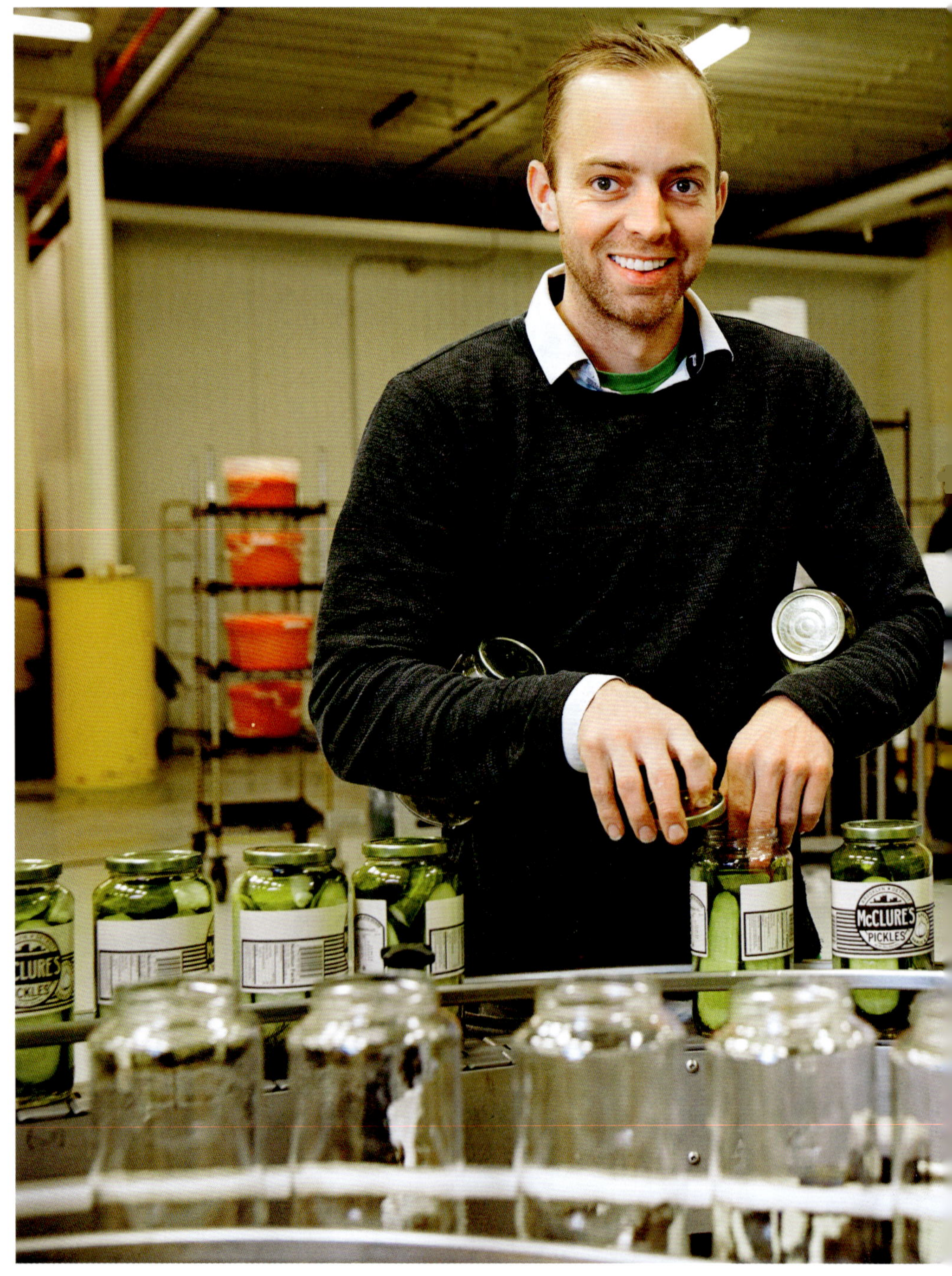

Robert & Joseph McClure Owners and Pickle Makers, McClure's Pickles > Detroit, Michigan

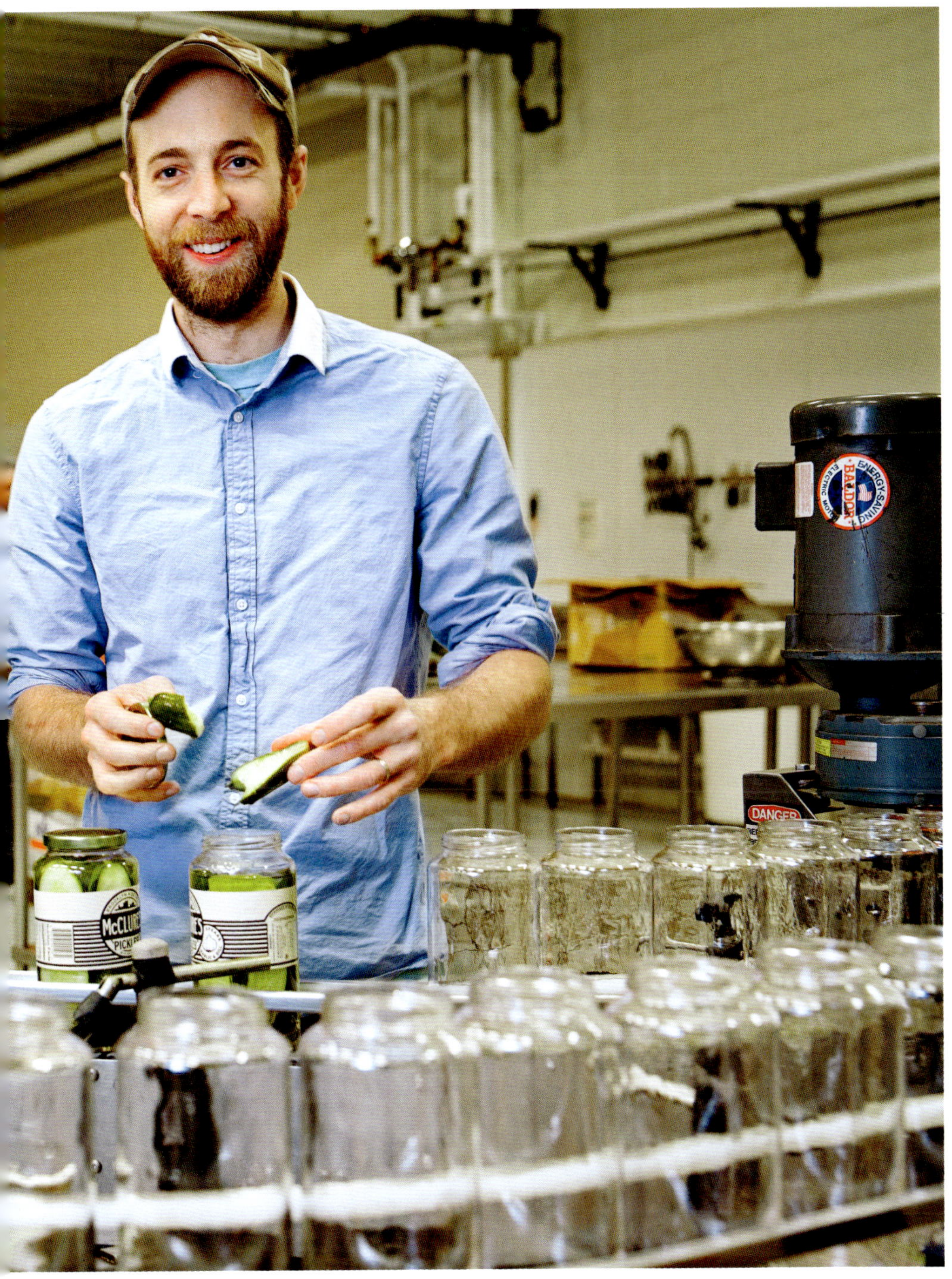

McCLURE'S
PICKLES

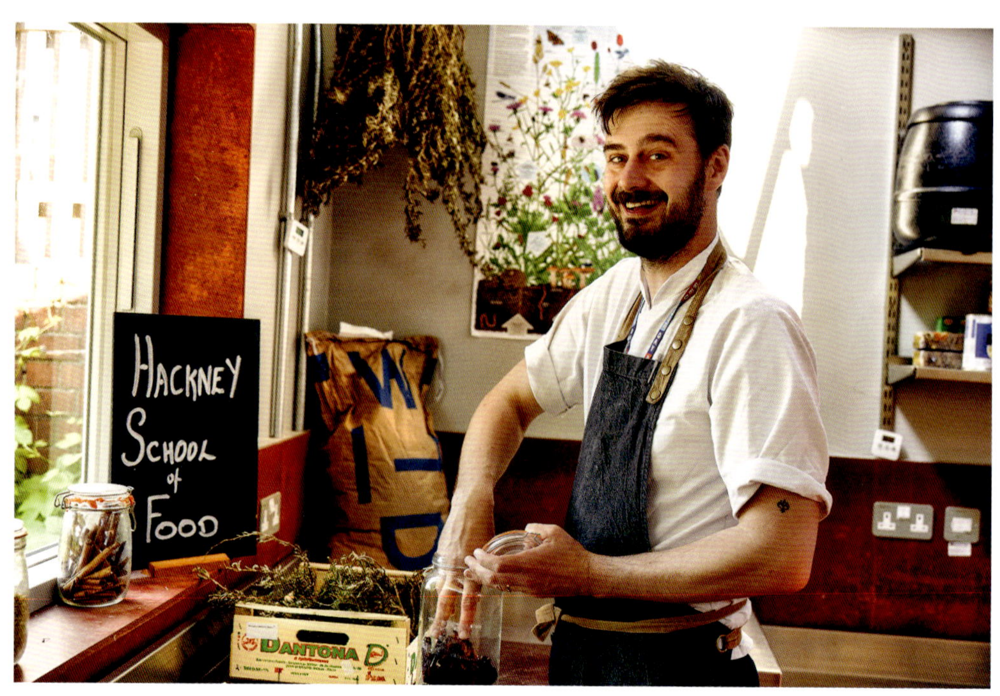

Thomas Walker Chef, Hackney School of Food > Hackney, England

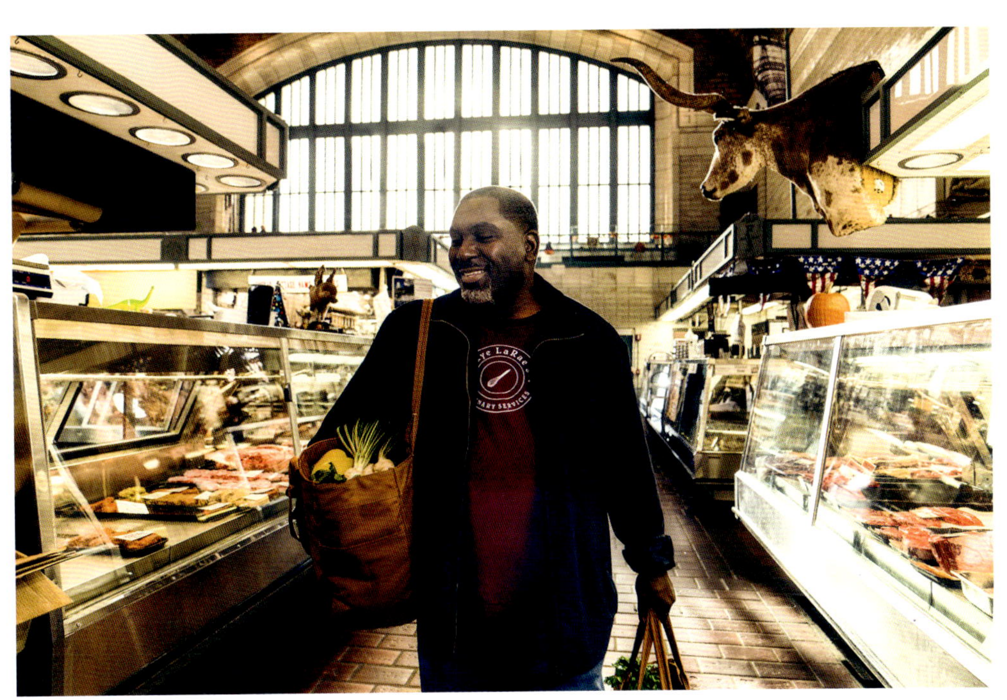

Eric Wells Private Chef, Skye LaRae's Culinary Services > Cleveland, Ohio

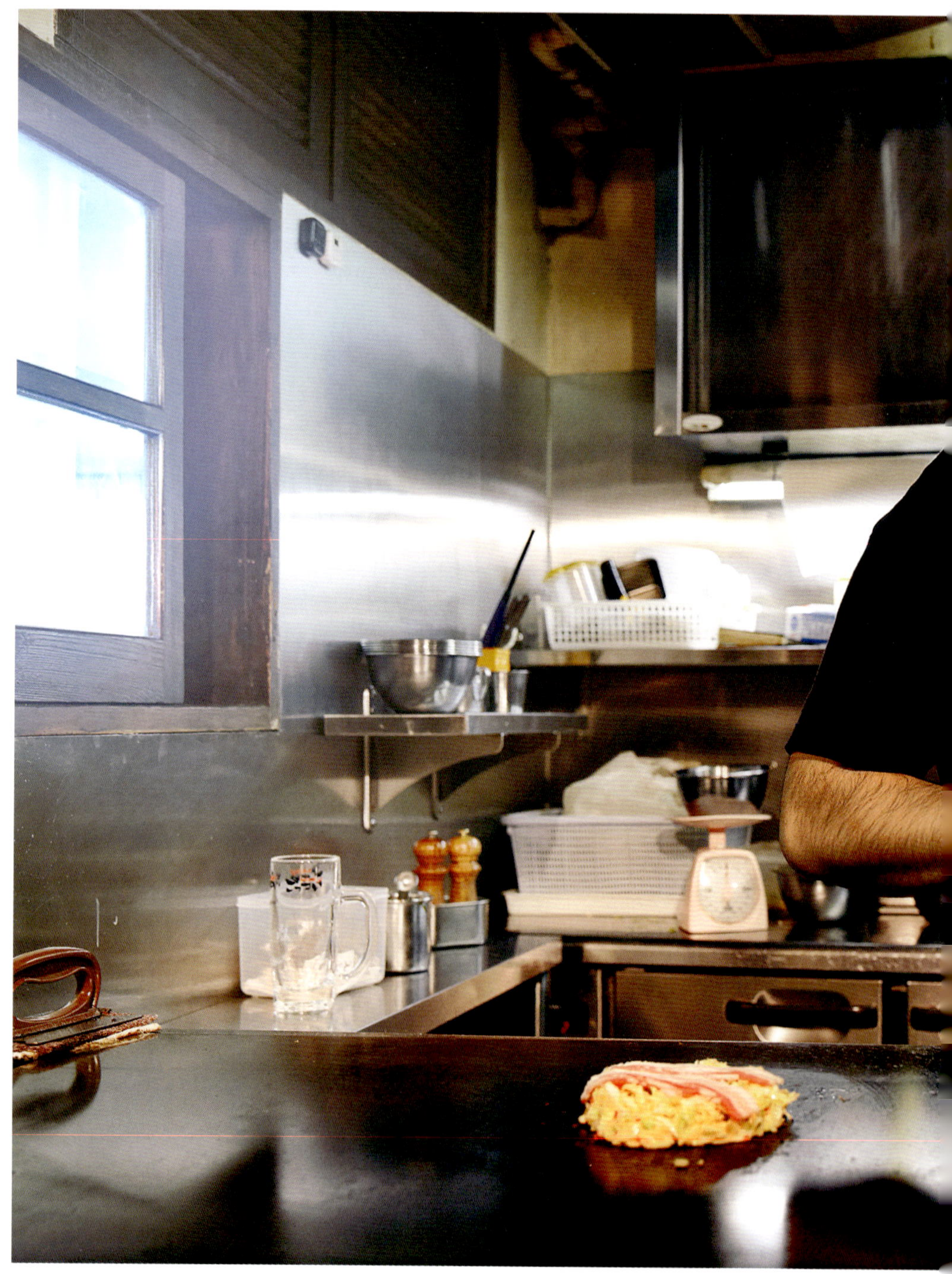

Jun Tokuyama Chef, Gottsui > Tokyo, Japan

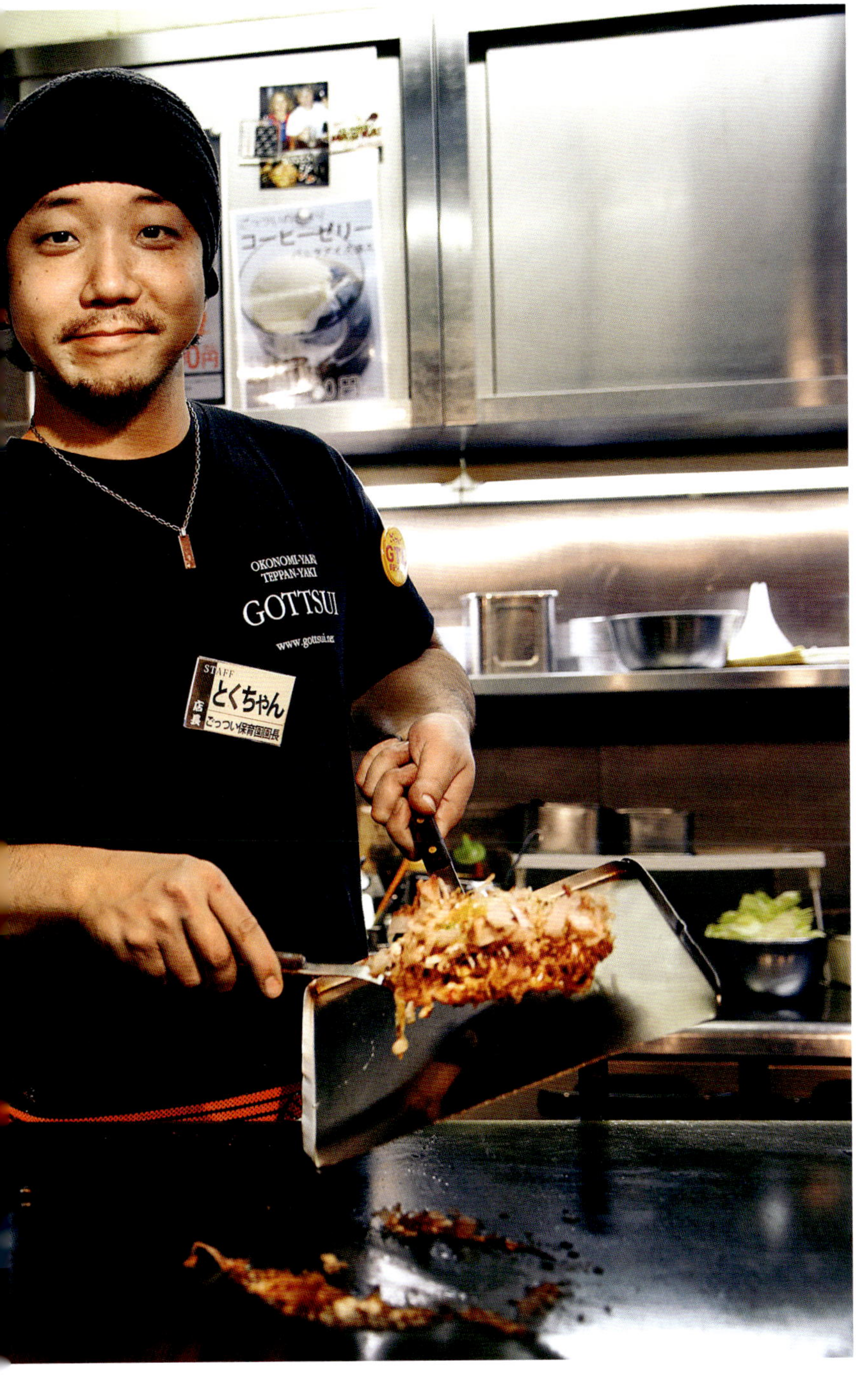
OKONOMI-YAKI
TEPPAN-YAKI
GOTTSUI
www.gottsui.te
STAFF
店長 とくちゃん
ごっつい保育園園長
コーヒーゼリー

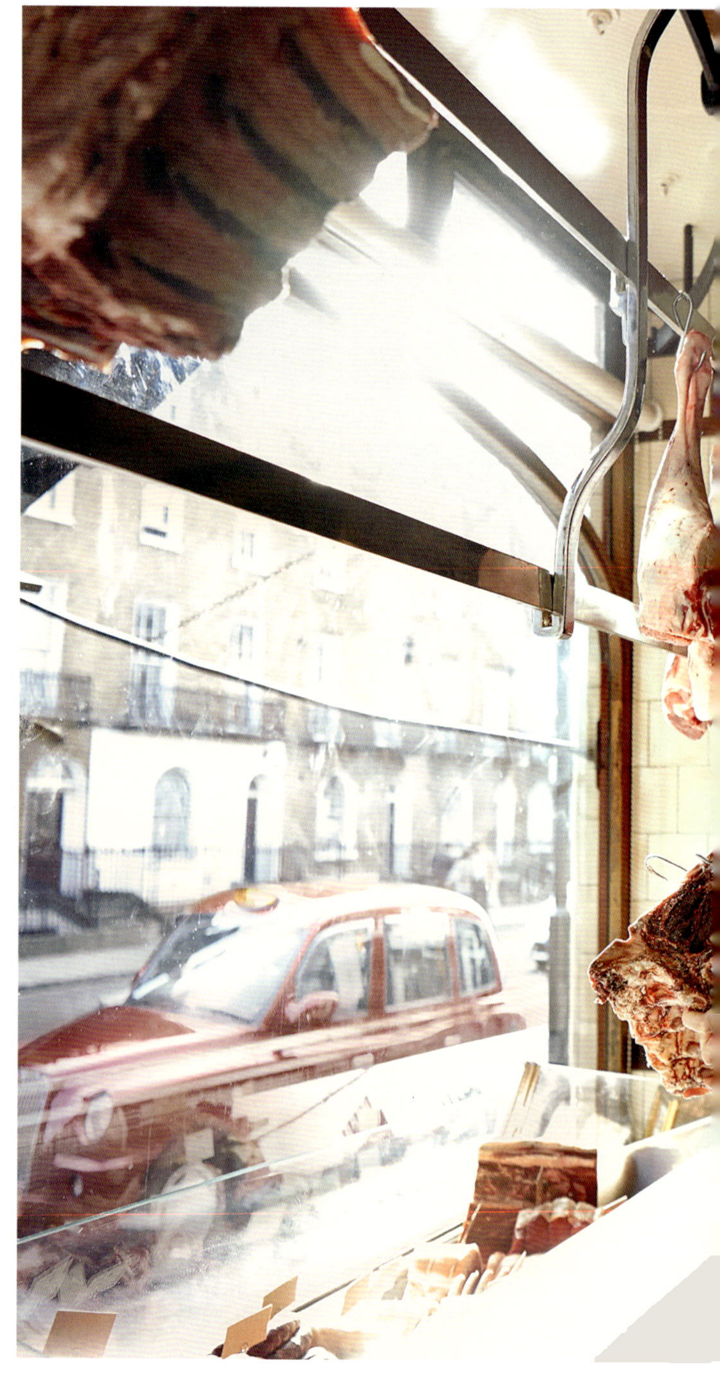

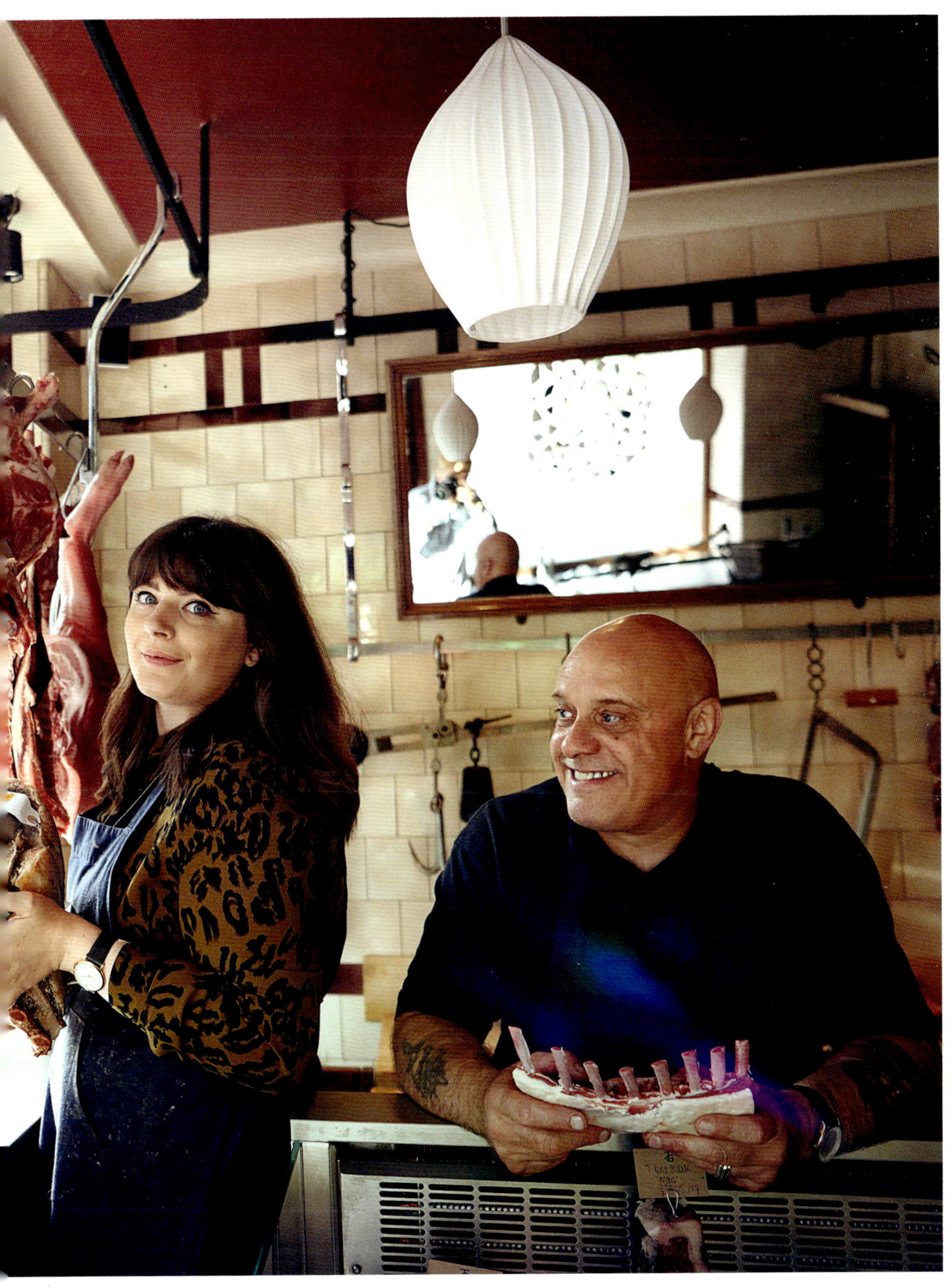

Jessica Wragg & Rob Thaine Butchers, Turner & George Butcher Shop > London, England

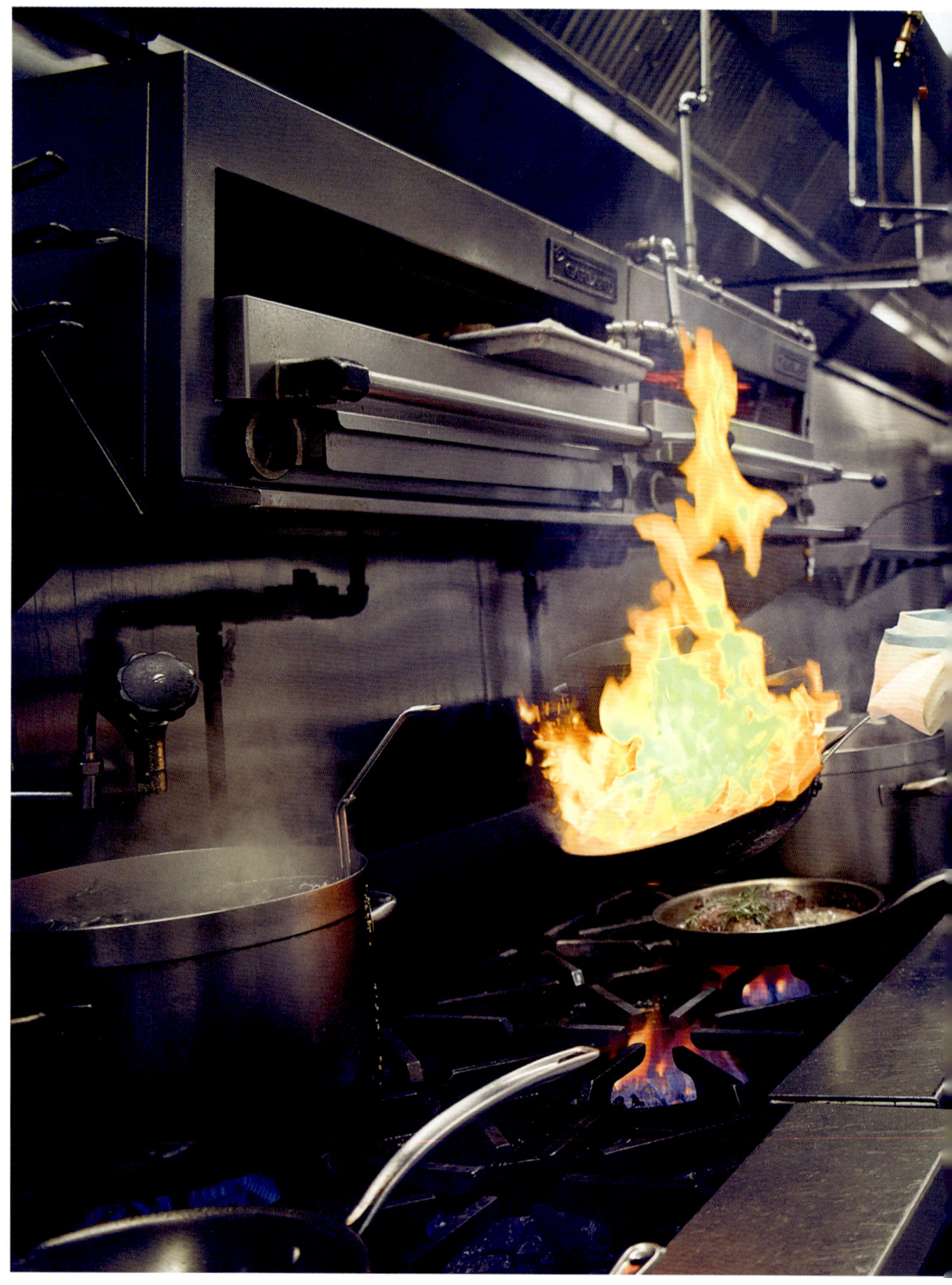

Kristen Kish Chef > Boston, Massachusetts

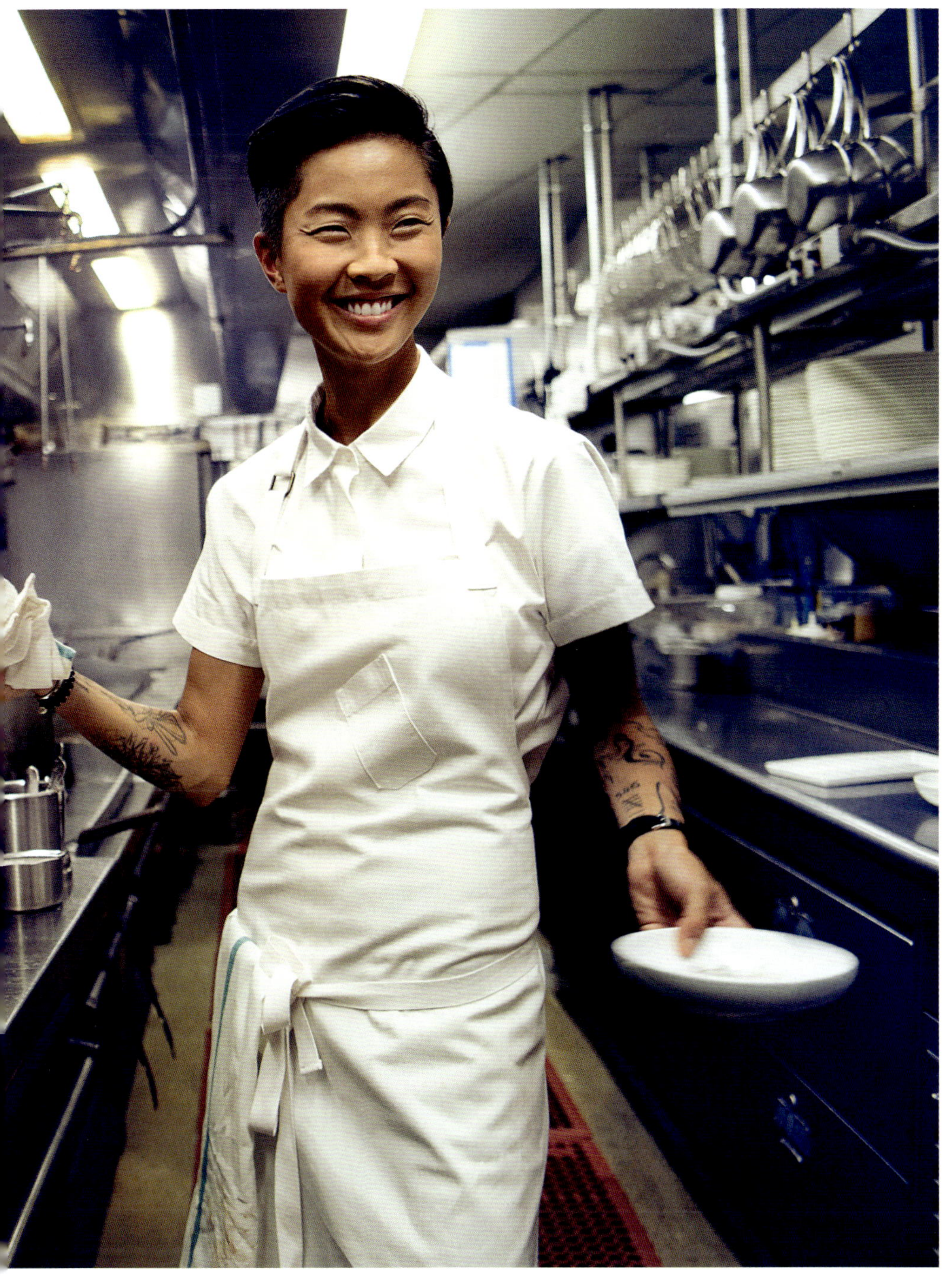

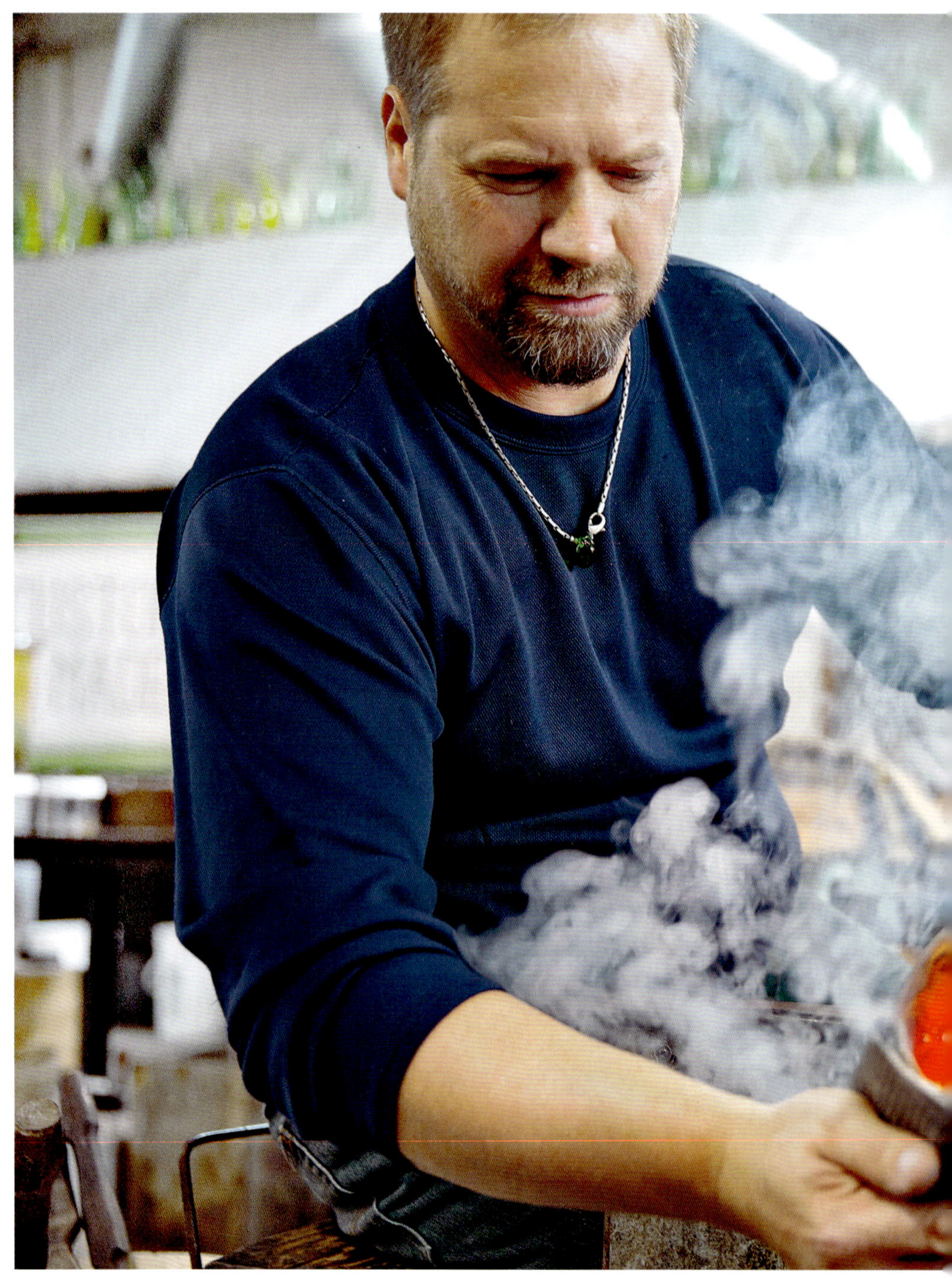

Chris Nordin Glassblower, Glass Academy Detroit > Detroit, Michigan

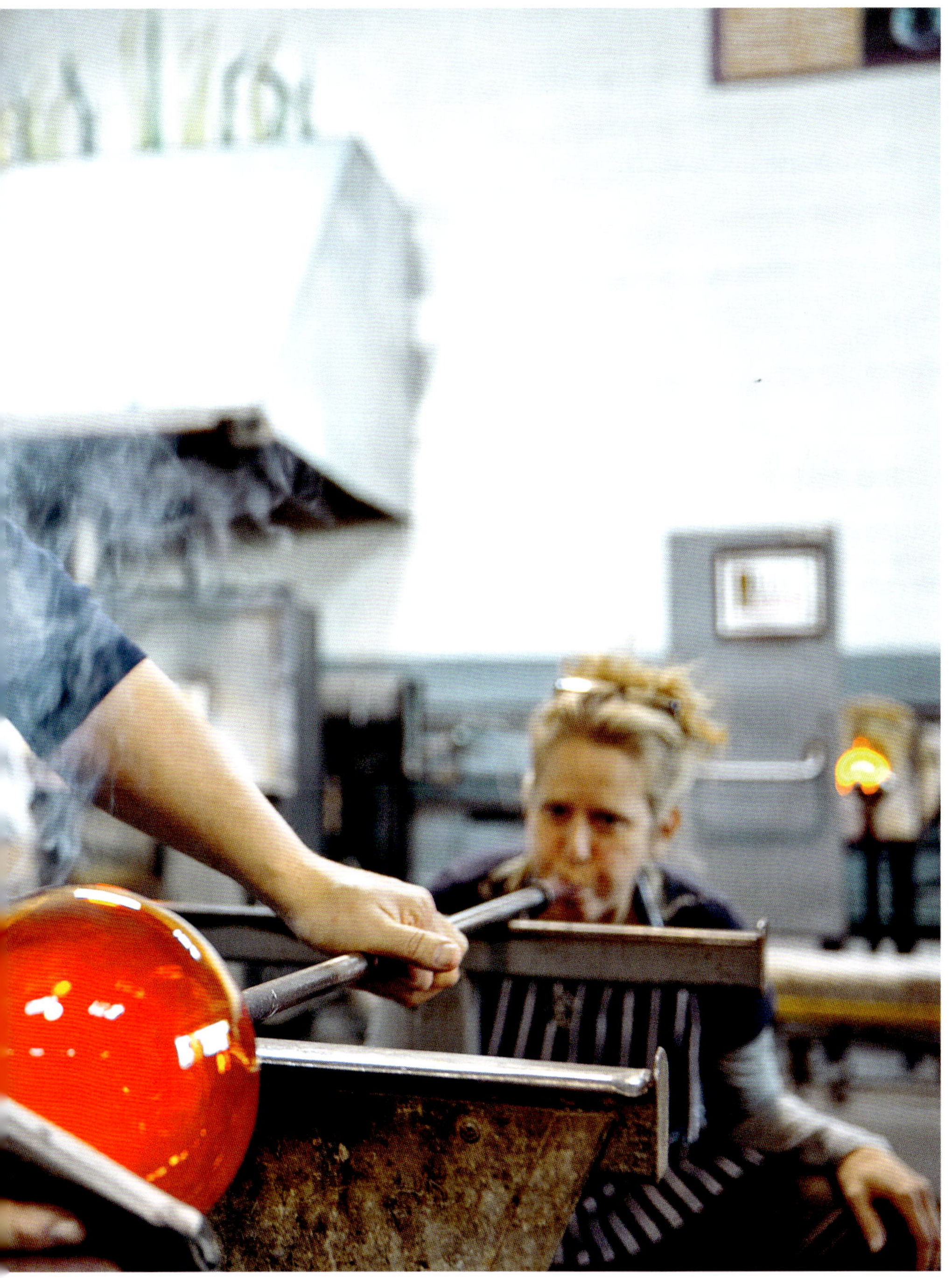

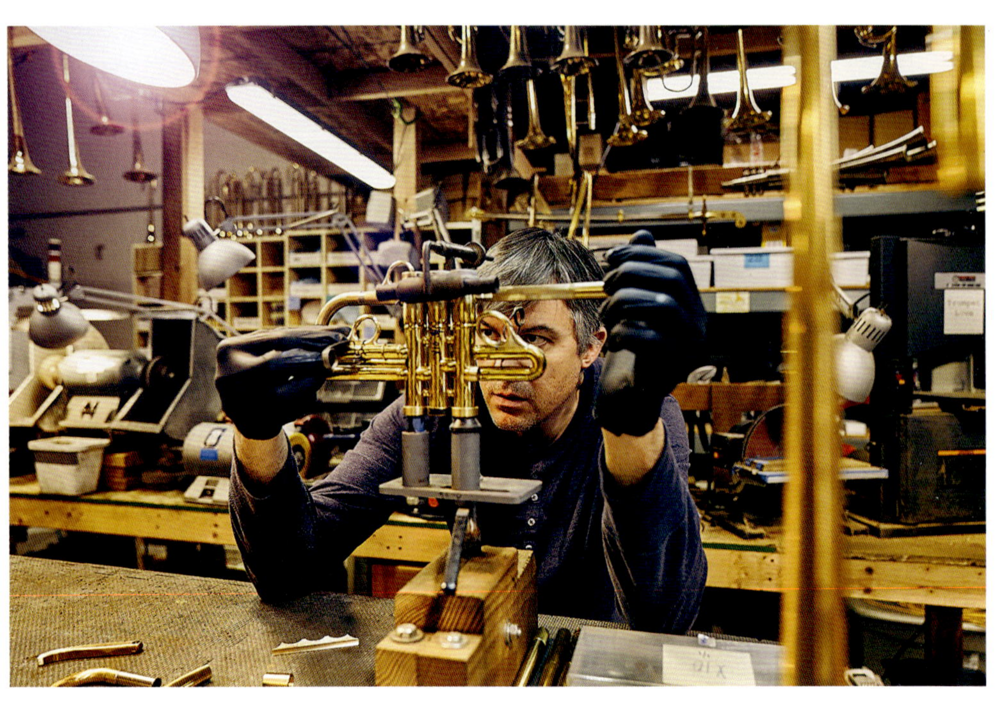

Jason Harrelson Trumpet Maker, Harrelson Trumpets > Denver, Colorado

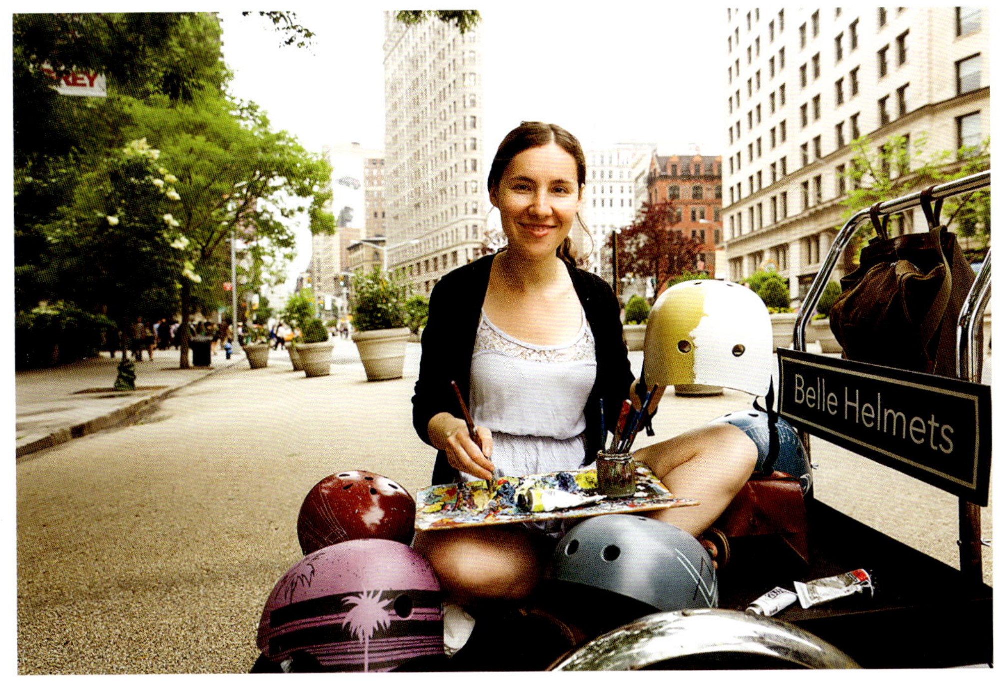
Belle Helmets

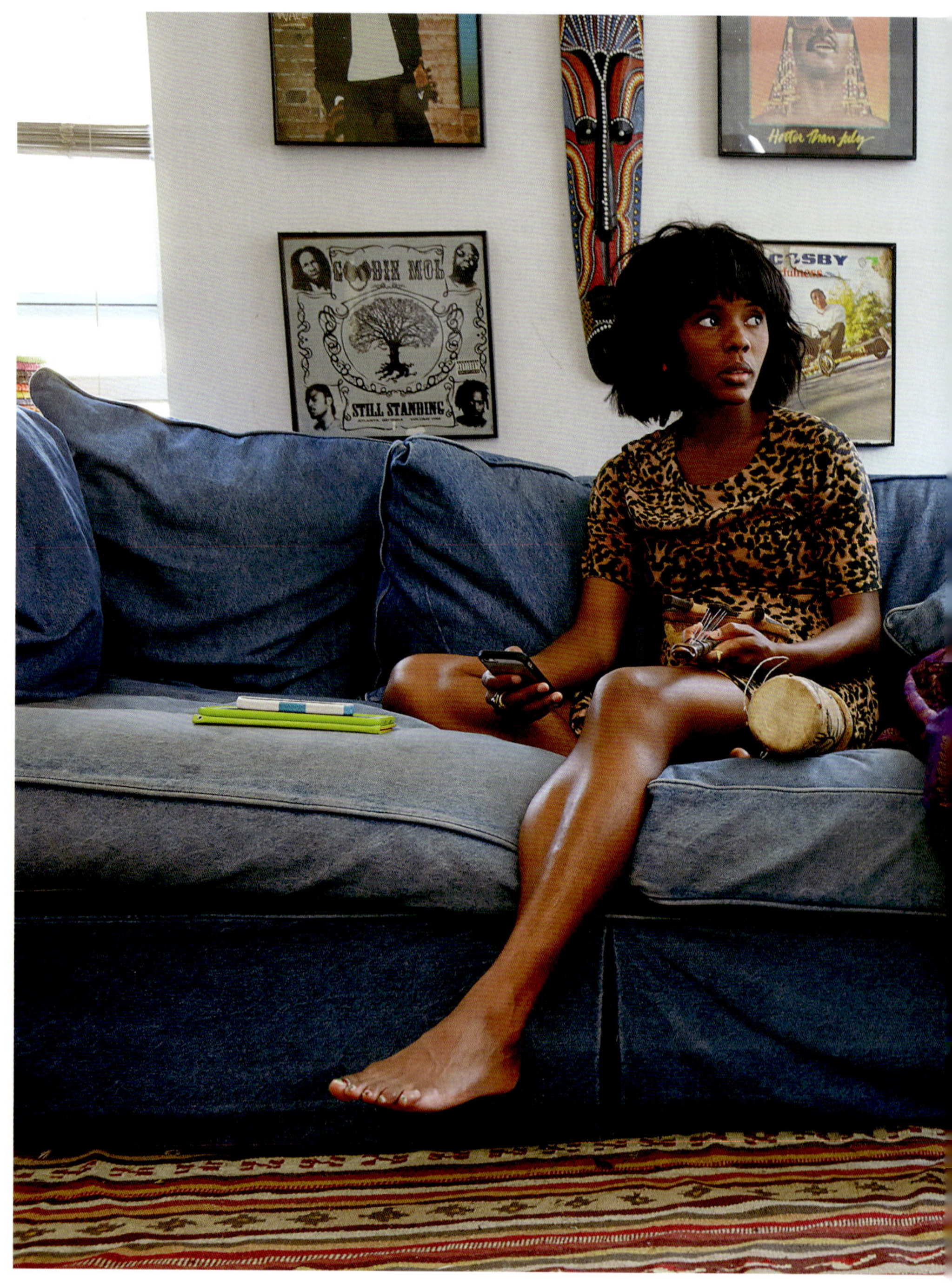

Lizzy & Darlene Okpo Fashion Designers, William Okpo > New York, New York

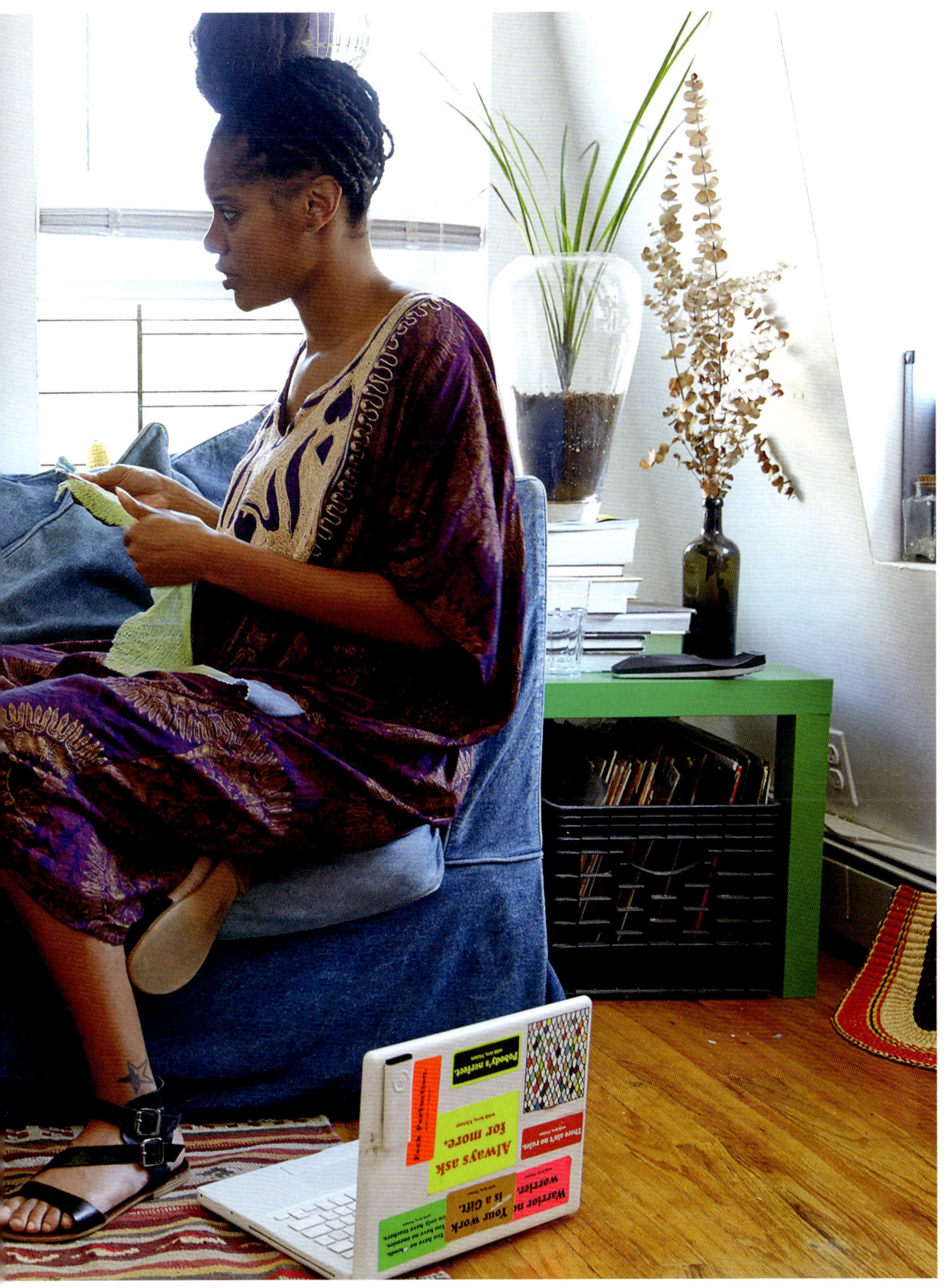

Warrior not worrier.
Your work is a Gift.
You have no friends. You have no enemies. You only have teachers.
There ain't no rules.
Always ask for more.
Peck Perfection
Pobody's nerfect.

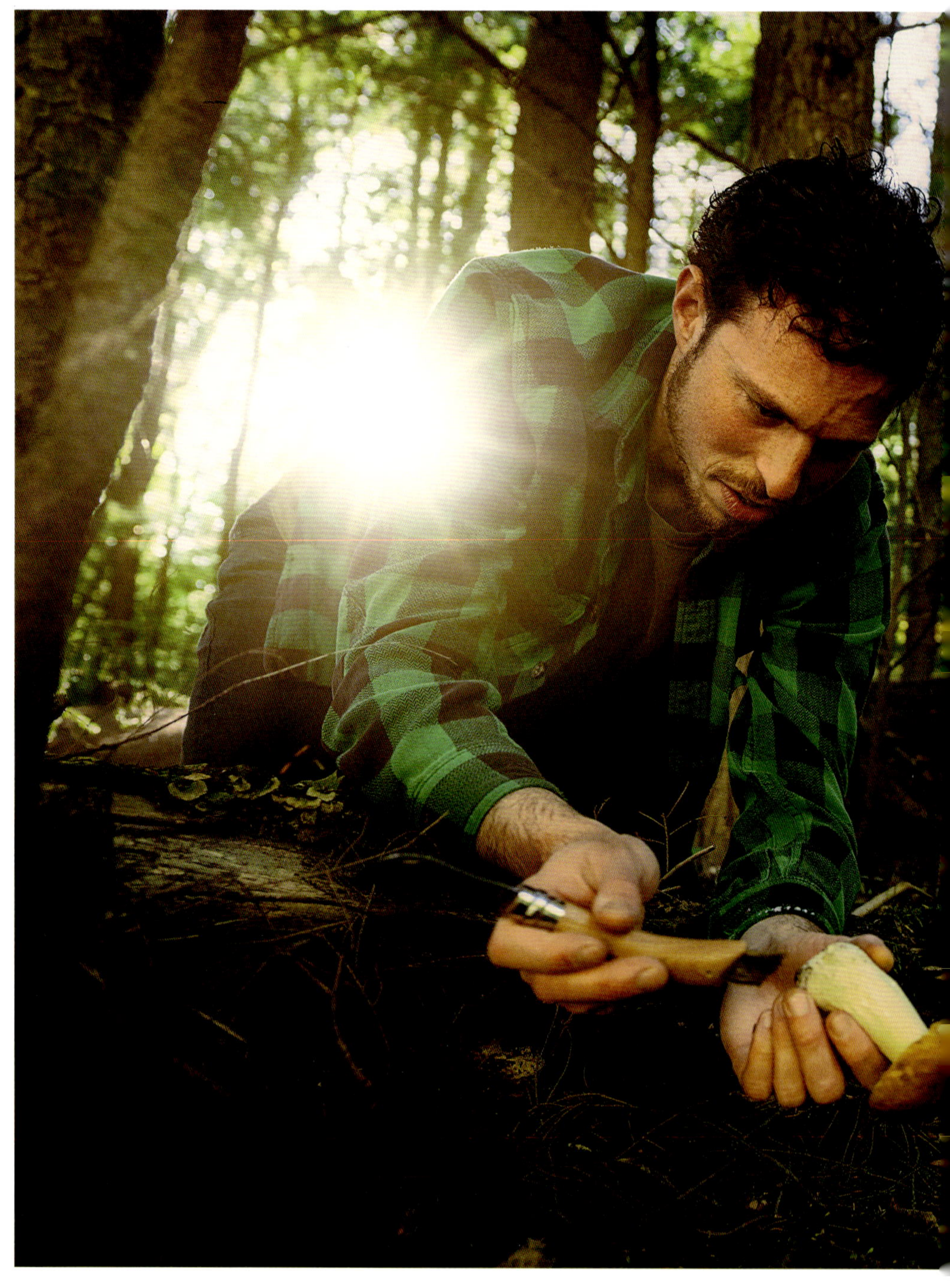

Ari Rockland-Miller Founder, The Mushroom Forager > Richmond, Vermont

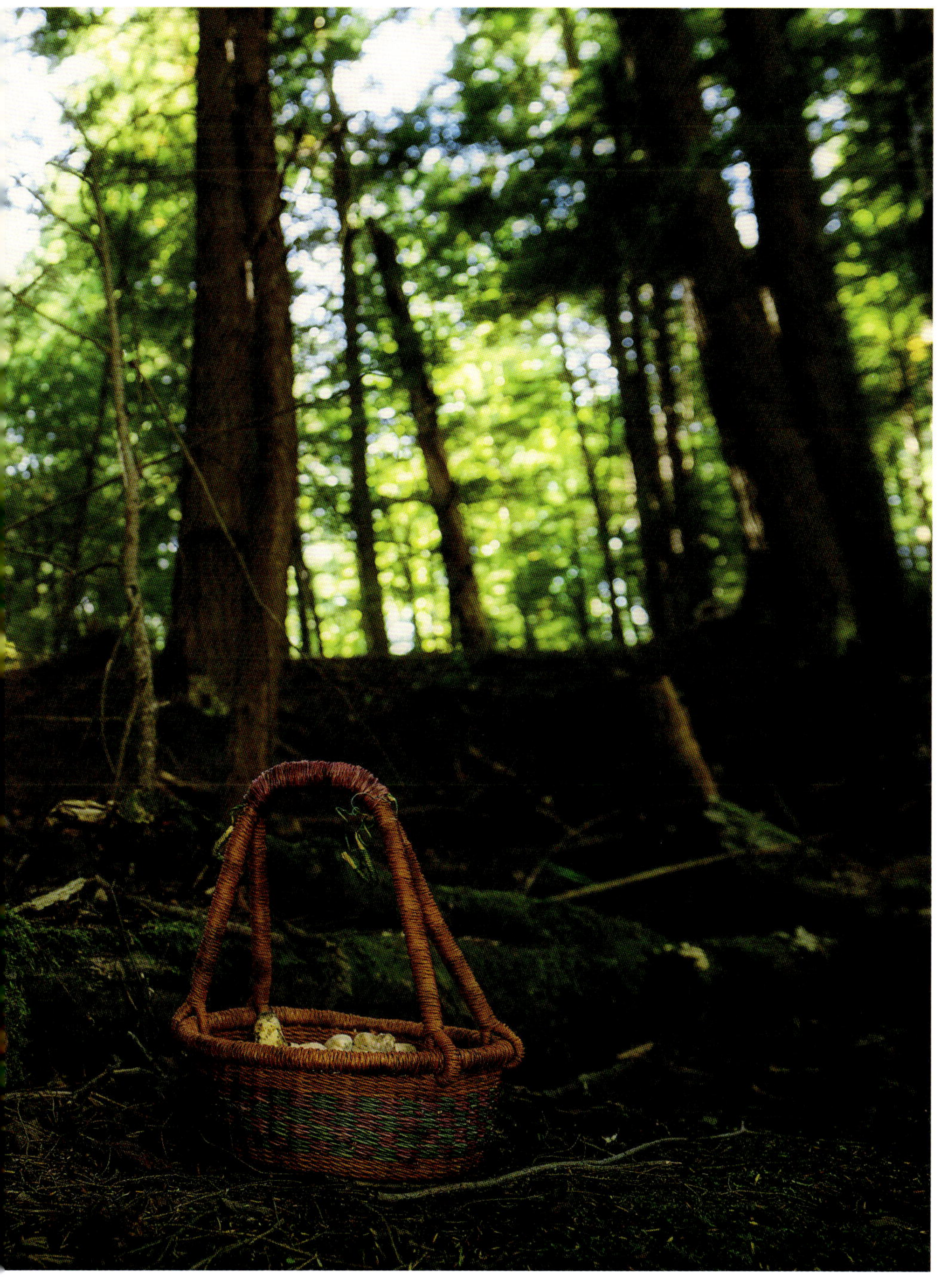

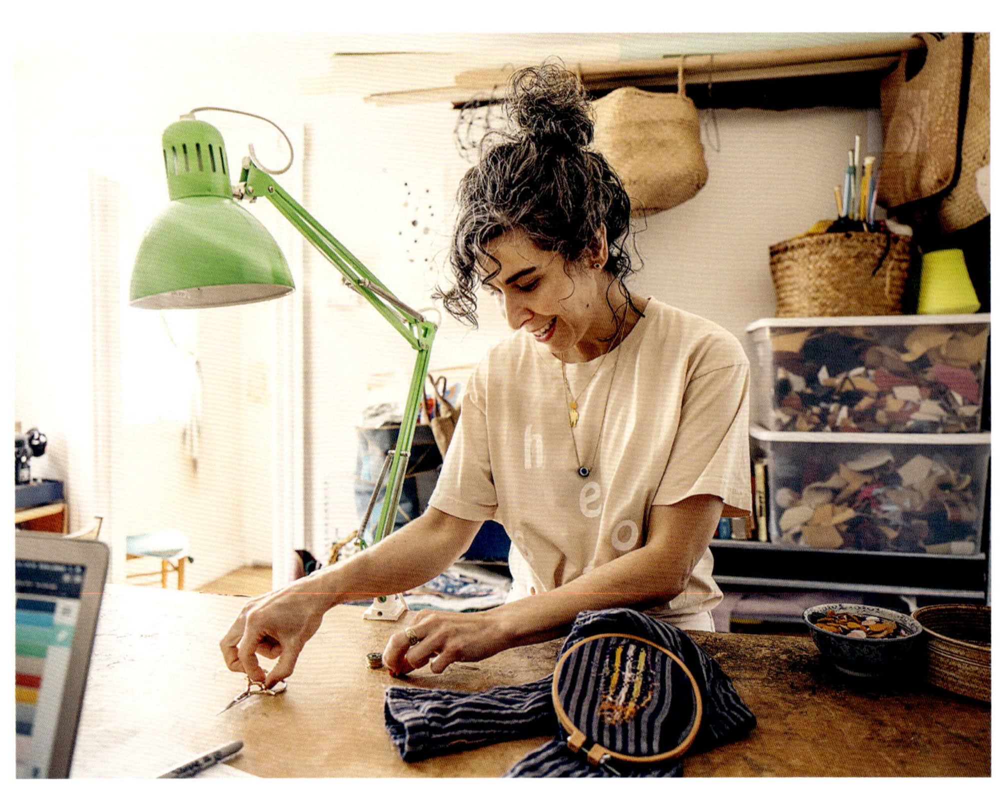

Kristen Lombardi Leather and Denim Designer, Manimals > Roslingdale, Massachusetts

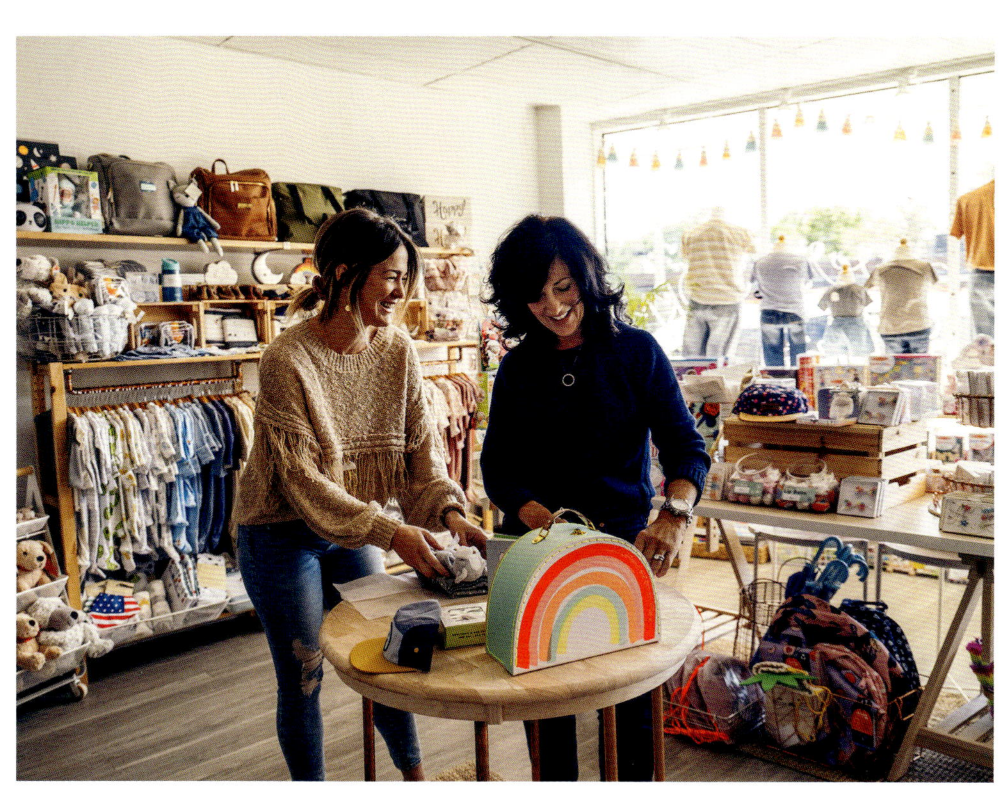

Lauren Noonan & Diane Moran Shopkeepers, The Merry Lion > Wakefield, Massachusetts

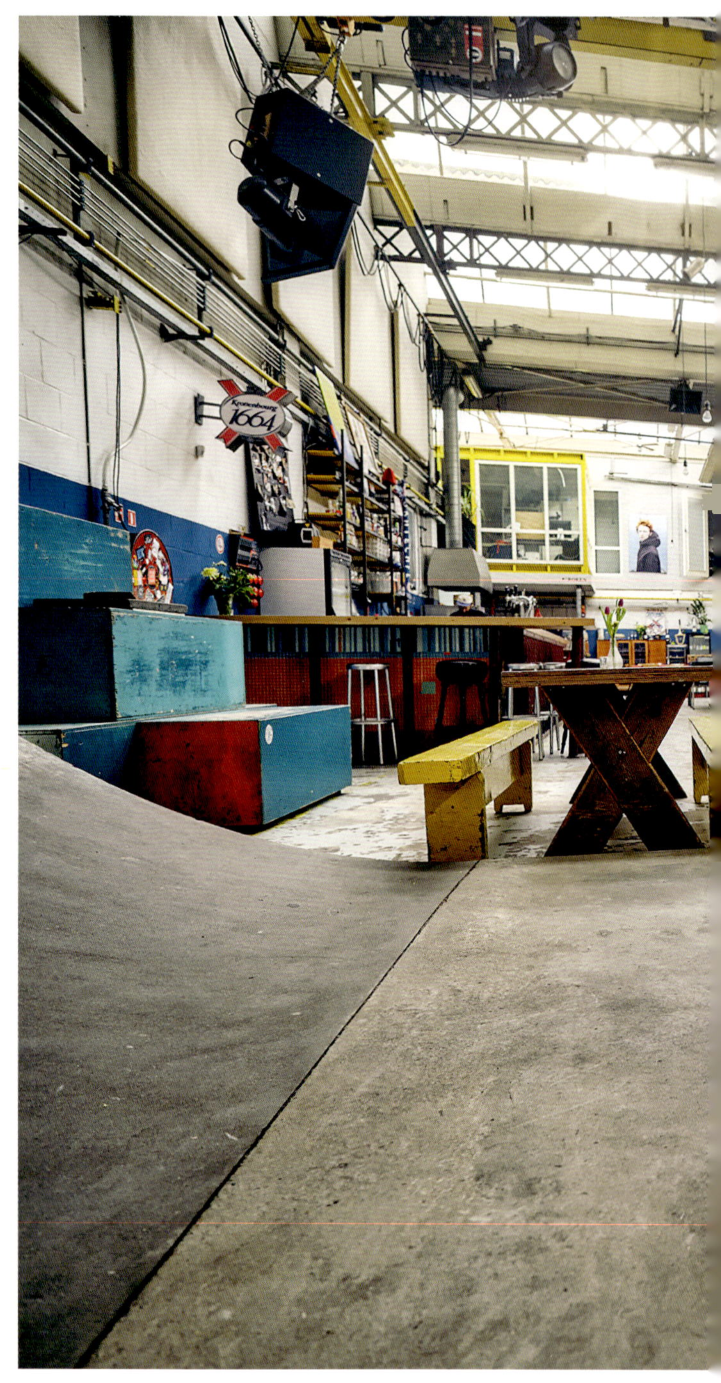

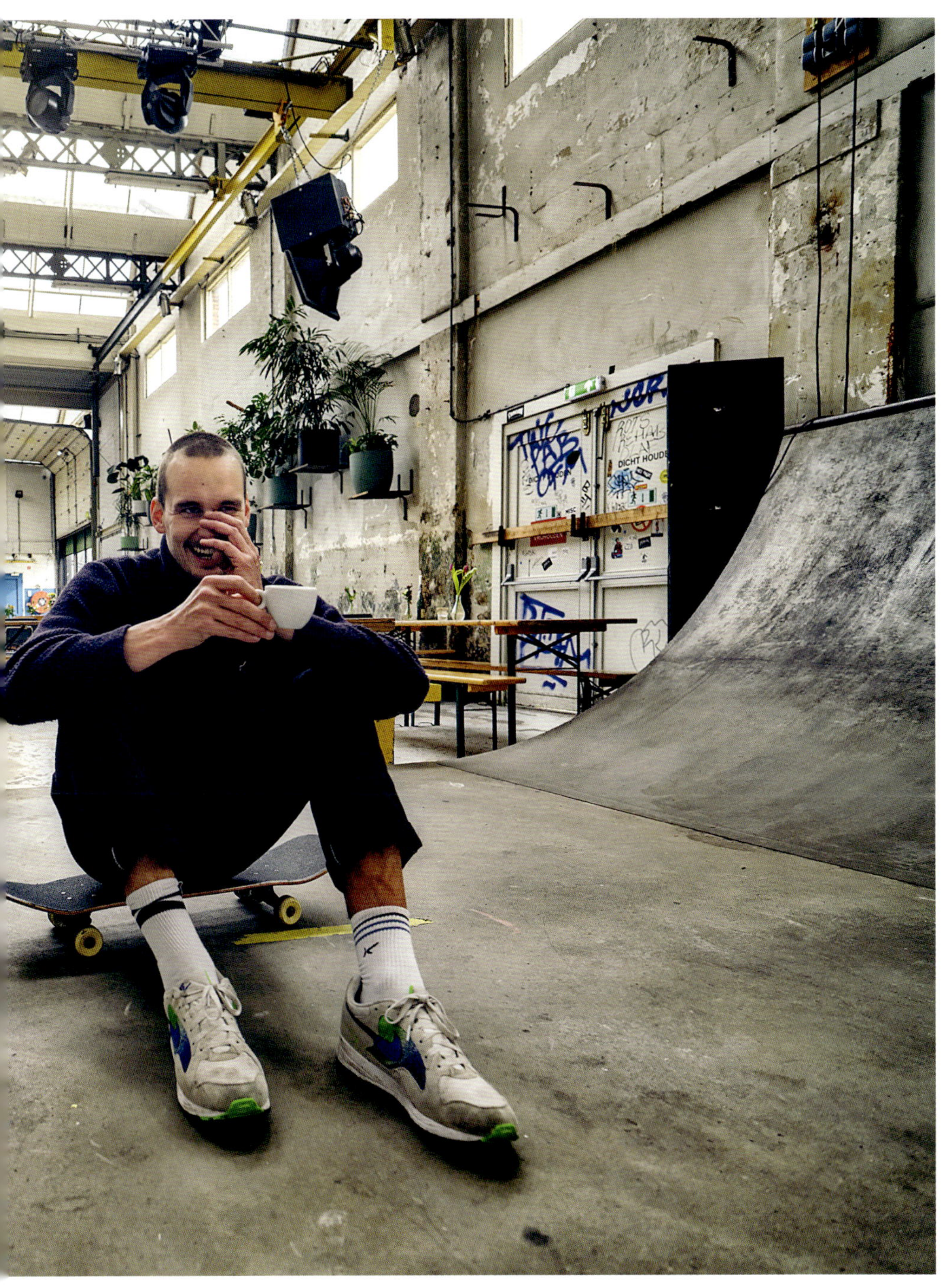

Colin Vlaar Facilitator of Dreams, Skate Café > Amsterdam, Netherlands

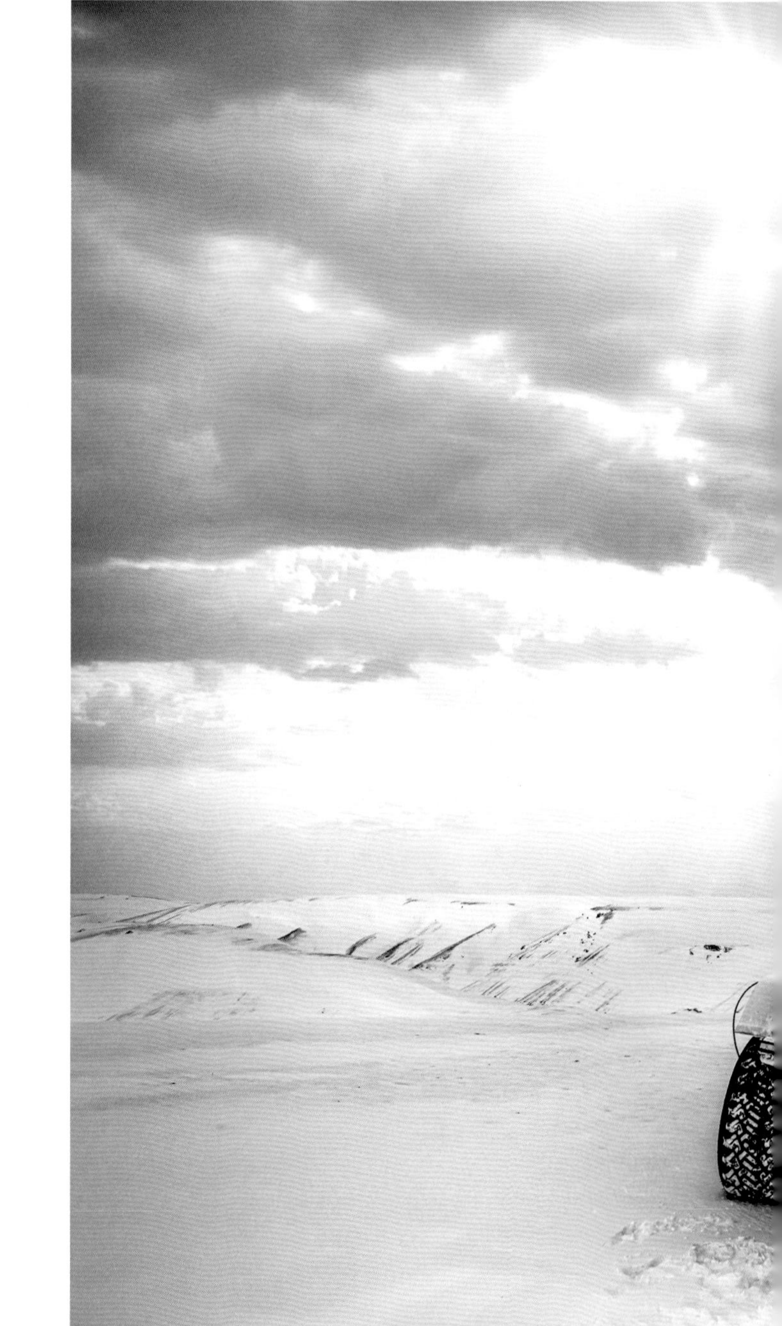

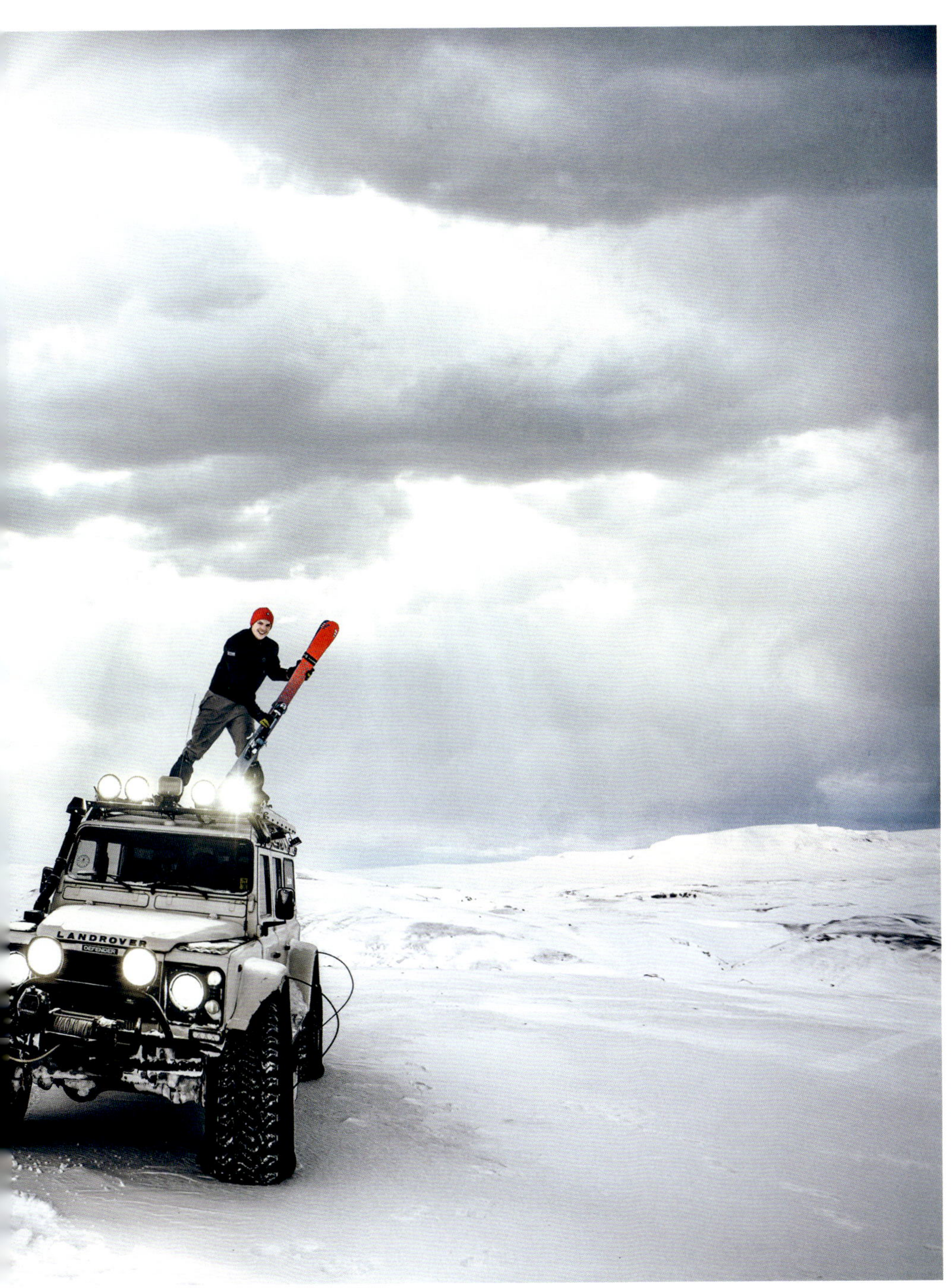

Davíd Thór Sigurdsson Icebike Expeditions > Hrunamannahreppur, Iceland

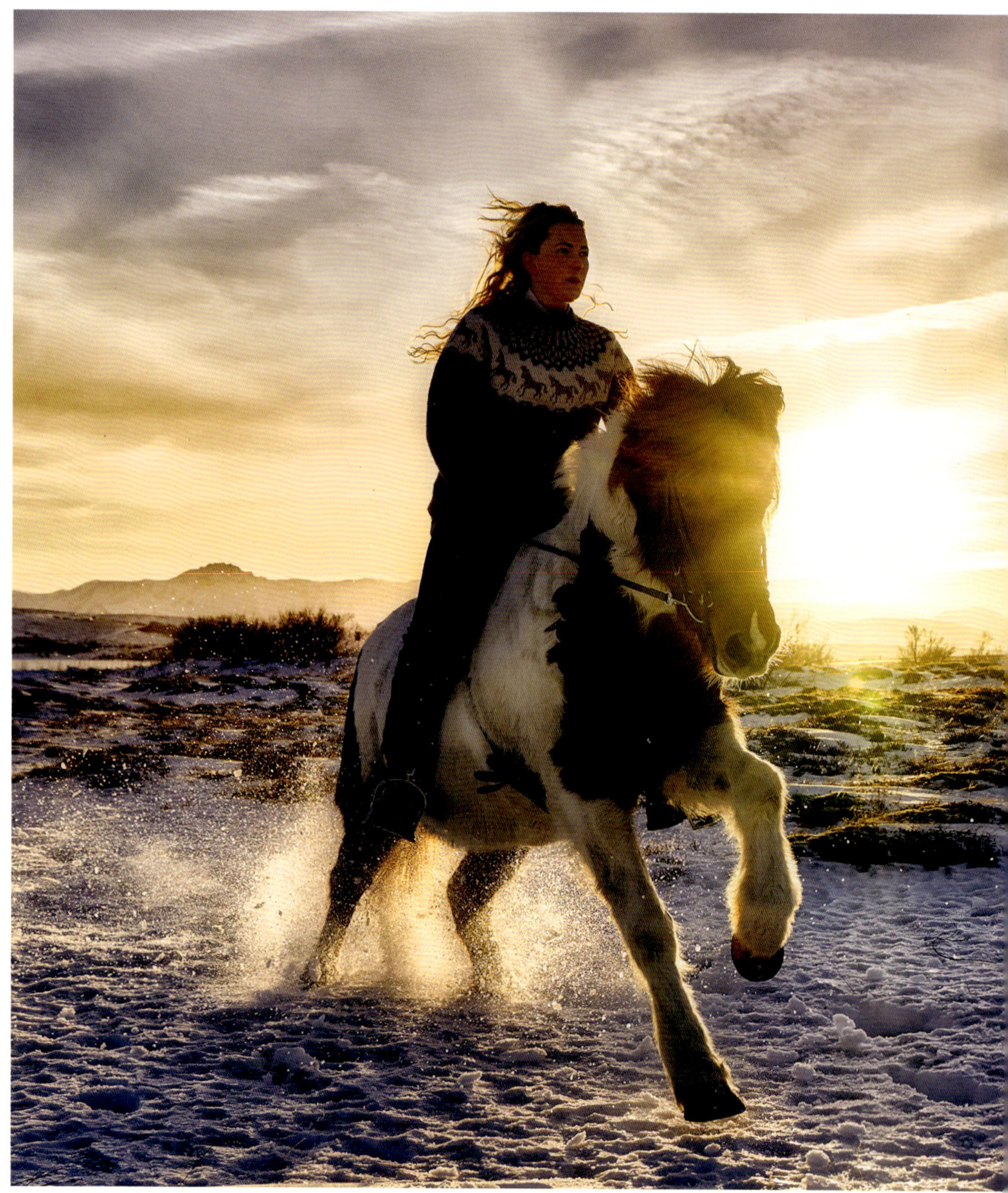

Jonina had worked for years as an office assistant. And though she enjoyed working with her colleagues, something was missing. She had a deep love of horses. She dreamed of having a life centered around them. But where to begin? She didn't have enough money to buy a horse.

When life presented her with a horse in need of rescuing and rehabilitation, she

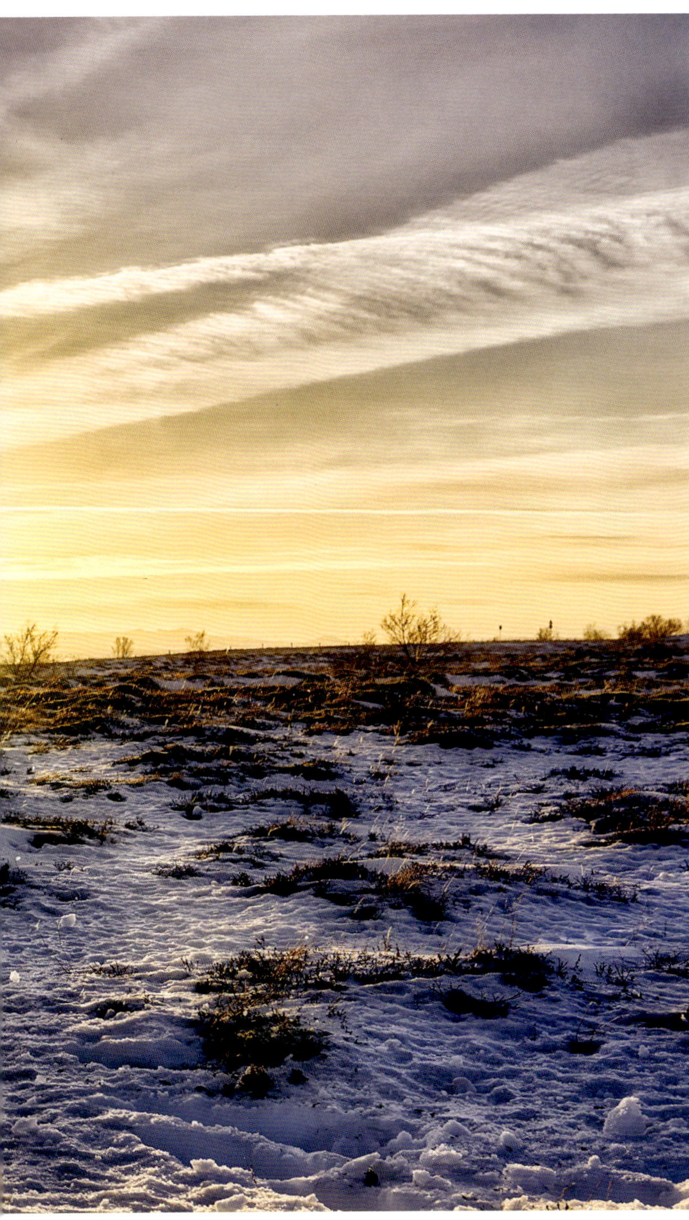

didn't hesitate. And over time, she has built a business leading private horseback tours, introducing visitors to Iceland's breathtaking landscapes, and to the Icelandic horses she so loves.

This image reminds me that not-knowing is not a reason to give up.

Jonina Sif Eyþórsdóttir Horseback Tours > Mosfellsbær, Iceland

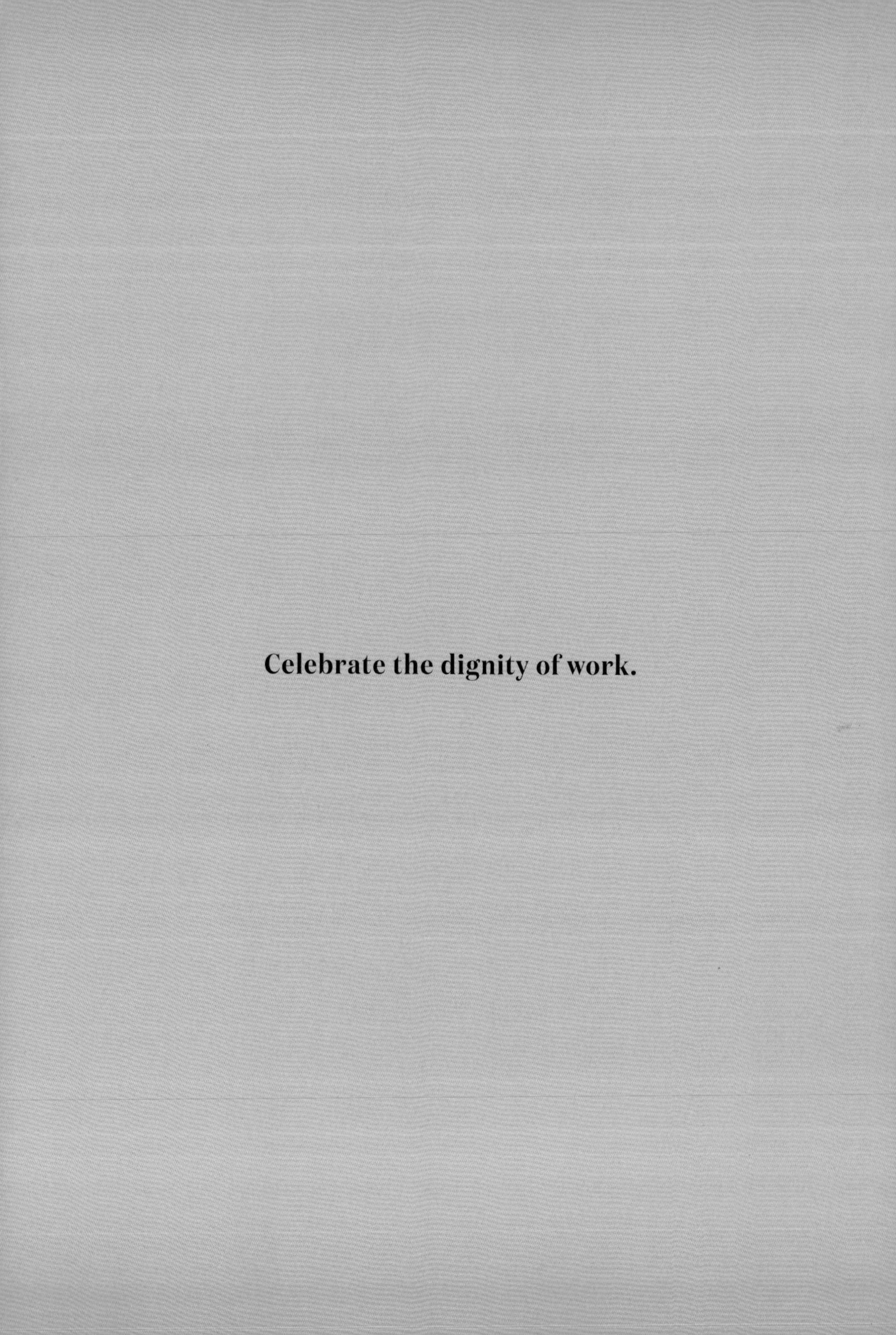

Celebrate the dignity of work.

Afterword

Passion for a vocation, the ardor of deep engagement in an ambition, that drive toward a long-held dream coming true—this is the substance of Brian Doben's *At Work*.

Work, to some, is simply toil, another day with nose-down, doing what needs to be done. For others, work means merging with their métier, perhaps even connecting to what feels like destiny calling. The subjects photographed for *At Work* are all in that illustrious latter category.

So, one might wonder, what differentiates the toilers from the mergers: the nature of the work itself, or the individual's inherent nature? More likely it is neither one nor the other, but some mysterious combination of the two, a way of personality blending with profession, which, in the best-case scenario, becomes the foundation for a passion, persistent and resistant to obstacles in its path. But without clear action, passion exists in a vacuum, yielding no real results. Passion demands action; it will not rest or surrender. It is an intense emotion which, when combined with intimacy and commitment, becomes love.

In a psychological context, work—whether perceived as a job, a career, or a calling—is fundamental to human life, a central source of meaning and self-identity. Whether we love, like or hate what we do for a living, we are indelibly impacted, and imprinted upon by it, for better or for worse. The fortunate ones, fueled by passion for their occupation, are bound to experience life as overflowing with meaning and purpose.

Meaning and purpose, amongst the most researched topics in the social sciences, are associated with *eudaimonia*, a term used by Ancient Greek philosopher Aristotle to describe the greatest human good and the steady reach toward individual potential. In modern terms, eudaimonia means, essentially, living authentically. Eudaimonia, the cultivation of which connects to human flourishing and fulfillment, is distinct from hedonia— from which we get the word hedonism—commonly known as gratification, the satisfaction that comes from indulging desires and experiencing pleasure.

Happiness, the theory goes, is inclusive of these two sources: passing pleasure (hedonia) and lasting joy (eudaimonia), the former in small doses and the latter as the lion's share. Too much pleasure will impede upon the achievement of our potential. The dedicated hedonist, going from thrill to buzz, is unlikely to flourish over the lifespan: consume little but passing pleasures and you've sacrificed lasting joy.

Pleasure certainly has its place. It is the vibrant burst of excitement that shoots through you, the instant pick-me-up, like an afternoon espresso. When we love what we do, we surely get pleasure from it. Pleasure elevates the moment. However, the moment, like the proverbial center, cannot hold. Eating and drinking are common sources of pleasure and certain kinds of shopping—"add to cart" culture has created a host of new distractions and addictions. Passing pleasure diverts our eyes off the prize of greater goals, and so, away from our greater good: it is lust with an unparalleled power to undermine our passion. From reading their stories, we know that the subjects of *At Work* are invested in their personal potential, conscious of the lasting joy that arises from meeting the demands of passionate pursuits, the fulfillment that follows from answering their destiny calling: they are remarkable illustrations of eudaimonia.

Though every portrait in *At Work* is distinct—the diversity of livelihoods and locations is stunning—there is a palpable and powerful sense of calm running throughout the images. Every subject seems wonderfully at ease, and yet entirely enlivened. We, the viewer, expect a photographer's visual gifts to be on display, which they clearly are here, and perhaps we take for granted that photographer and subject will have made an emotional connection.

But in *At Work* we feel the burgeoning bonds being forged, we sense the depth of human communication. Instinctively, we trust in the relationship between observer and observed, photographer and subject. We trust, too, that we are granted our own access to the subjects, and to their joyful pursuits. We are welcome into their worlds. Inspired, one may even feel compelled to put aside distractions and reach for a long-held dream. Brian Doben, having found the courage to overcome personal challenges and press on with his own passionate profession, gives us, in *At Work*, a work of art that also serves as an object lesson in loving what you do, and letting it love you back.

Lynne F. Corbett
Research Psychologist, MSc, MA
London, England

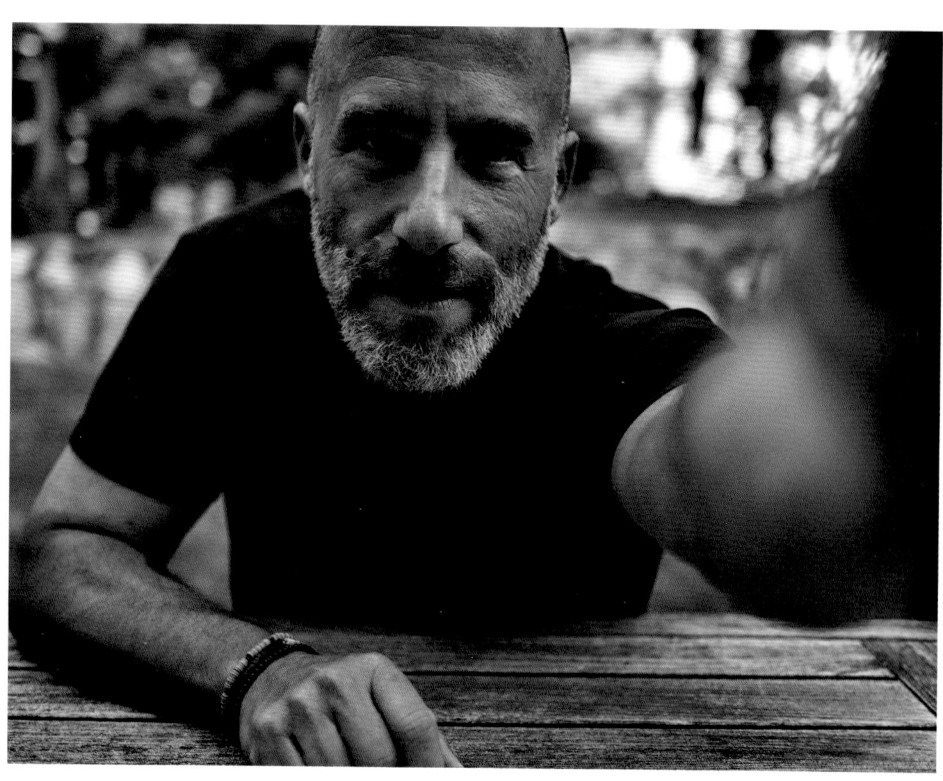

About Brian Doben

Brian Doben, a native of Brooklyn, New York, discovered his passion for photography in college when his mother bought him his first camera. After graduating from the Rochester Institute of Technology, Brian's love for photography took him on incredible adventures across the globe, capturing moments for renowned publications like *GQ, National Geographic Travel, Vanity Fair, Travel & Leisure,* and *Town & Country.* His global adventures in photography have spanned over 50 magazine covers, encompassing celebrity, travel, and fashion. From the Arctic to the Antarctic, Bhutan to Paris, Europe's cities to Madagascar and Argentina's wild terrains, his lens has embraced diverse cultures, infusing his work with captivating human narratives.

In the advertising domain, Doben is highly esteemed for his skill in crafting visuals that seamlessly blend complexity with genuineness. A diverse array of clients, spanning from renowned brands like AT&T, NBC and Walmart to significant players such as American Express, Apple, Ford, Google, Lexus, UPS, YouTube, and Sony, have reaped the rewards of his talent. His ability extends beyond orchestrated scenes, delving into capturing unscripted, authentic moments that add depth to every image.

His talent hasn't gone unnoticed. Brian's work has been honored by prestigious institutions like the Society of Publication Designers, American Photography, and Photo District News. Awards like PDN's 30 Under 30 and the coveted Kodak Photographer of the Year have cemented his reputation. Notably, his impactful photography is showcased in the Museum of the City of New York, especially his moving photographs in the book *Brotherhood,* which beautifully depicts the resilience and spirit of New York City firefighters following September 11.

Brian now resides in New England with his family, continuing to weave compelling visual stories. Through his photographs, he invites readers on an enchanting journey that transcends boundaries, revealing the rich tapestry of human stories through his captivating imagery.

Acknowledgements

The saying "it takes a village" certainly applies here. I have so many people to thank for helping me every step along the way. I am grateful to all the people who allowed me to capture their stories, and to share their truth. I am forever changed by your generosity, time, and goodwill. You didn't just give me material for a book: you gave me back my creative life. My purpose. You are my inspiration.

Thank you to *Jamie Koval* for all your advice, and the guidance that enabled this book to go from theoretical to actual.

FAMILY

Nancy Doben, without you I would not be me.
Genevieve Doben, you are the air in my lungs.
Mom, what can I say except "thank you" for giving me the belief that I can fly.
Dad, I wish you were here to see this book.
Jeannette Corbett, thank you for always being interested. Perhaps 30% fewer questions...
Steven Doben, ah, big brother, no words here. Love ya.
Special thank you to my studio manager, *Judy Putman-Sette*. You are always up for the challenge, even when I give just one week's notice that I want to go to Alaska in the middle of the winter! Thank you for being such an instrumental part of the project.

AGENTS

Howard Bernstein, thank you for taking a chance on me early in my career.
Carol Alda, thank you for all your guidance.
Sam Summerskill, thank you for all your enthusiasm!
Ehrin Feeley, you are my "ride or die."

ASSISTANTS

I have always been fortunate to have the finest people on set with me. Grateful beyond words to my assistants who always have my back and make travel an adventure. Thank you for being people I am proud to call friends. A few special shout outs to... *Andy Bray, Carlos Ruiz, Gal Harpaz, Jesper Justesen, Joel Micah Dennis*, and *Roberto Kozek*.

Derin Thorpe, thank you for coming out to Montana to help tell my story.

There are many people who have helped me find my subjects all over the world, I am forever thankful for your help. *Pascale Smets, Marielle Dieghan, Jessie Cowan, Elle Sullivan Wilson, Lisa Wagenbach, Yoshiko Tanaka, Ymke & Sophie, Sheila Bridges, Lynne Corbett, Raquel Isabel Diaz, Nancy Doben*, and *Judy Putman-Sette*.

The Team at *Trope Publishing* in Chicago.

Jean Mandel, who walked the last miles with me.

Cherry Gonzalez, your passing put a fire under my ass to appreciate today, to live in the moment, and to see the beauty life offers.